THE ESSENTIAL
PLANT GUIDE

THE ESSENTIAL
PLANT GUIDE

every plant you need for your garden

GLOBAL BOOK
PUBLISHING

First published in 2013 by
Global Book Publishing
201 (Suite 9) Lakeside Corporate Centre
29–31 Solent Circuit, Baulkham Hills
NSW 2153, Australia
Tel: +61 2 9634 6220
Email: rightsmanager@globalpub.com.au
www.globalbookpublishing.com.au

ISBN 978-1-74048-035-2

Publisher	James Mills-Hicks
Managing Editor	Barbara McClenahan
Project Manager	Helen Bateman
Cover and Internal Design	Vivien Valk
Picture Researcher	Jo Collard
Consultants	Tony Rodd, Kate Bryant
Indexer	Puddingburn Publishing Services
Production Coordinator	Chrysoula Aiello
Editorial Coordinators	Kristen Donath, Chrysoula Aiello
Color separation	Pica Digital Pte Ltd, Singapore

Printed in China by 1010 Printing International Limited

This publication and arrangement
© Global Book Publishing Pty Ltd 2013

Photographs from the Global Book Publishing Photo Library
(except where credited otherwise on page 831)
Text © Global Book Publishing Pty Ltd 2013
Maps © Global Book Publishing Pty Ltd 2013

CONTENTS

THE
REWARDING
GARDEN

GROWING PLANTS

As our daily existence becomes busier and more complex, plants play an increasingly important role in our lives. Especially for city dwellers, gardening, whether tending a few house plants or maintaining a large vegetable patch, provides a connection to the earth and the seasons that no other activity can offer. Gardening also provides a rewarding creative outlet, from choosing what plants will go where to deciding what mood or feeling the garden should have.

There are many factors to consider, whether renovating a garden or creating a new one from scratch. How much time do you have to devote to maintenance? What kinds of plants are a priority, given the available space and local climate? These questions should be kept in mind as you contemplate the many different plants that are available and the ways in which they can be used in the garden.

Structure and Screening

The "bones" of a garden are the defining structures upon which everything else is built. This can consist of fixed structures such as outbuildings as well as patios, walls, fences, arbours and paths. It also includes trees and larger shrubs whose consistent year-round presence serves as a solid structure against which smaller shrubs and perennials can

shine. These foundation plants also protect understorey plants from excessive heat, cold and wind, and serve as a screen for unwanted views.

All areas of Australia have species best suited as "backbone" trees for their particular climate, from the slow-growing cold-tolerant southern beeches (*Nothofagus* species) to the stately palms of warmer climates. For smaller gardens, large shrubs may be better suited, and range from relatively cold-tolerant camellias and rhododendrons to those more at home in the tropics and subtropics, such as hibiscus. If winter light is desired, deciduous backbone trees and shrubs provide welcome shade during the summer months and permit the warmth of the sun to reach the house and garden in winter.

Using Height and Layers

Many of the best gardens are multi-layered and the plants occupy various niches, taking advantage of vertical space by growing through one another. This reflects the natural arrangement found in

RIGHT *The Mexican native* Salvia darcyi *begins flowering in summer, and can still be blooming in late autumn in warmer areas.*

LEFT *An appealing and well-designed garden inspires outdoor entertaining, particularly during the summer months.*

woodland and rainforest environments, where the canopy protects and supports herbaceous plants, shrubs and climbers and creepers.

Of course, plants in more open environments with few trees grow in layers as well. Small perennials often grow in the shade of taller ones, and in seasonally dry climates tender plants can be found growing through tough evergreens whose leaves offer protection from sun and wind. Even desert plants grow in layers, with small, less heat-tolerant succulents nestled in the shade of bulkier cacti.

ABOVE *Ideal for cooler climates, the fragrant white flowers of* Jasminum polyanthum *open from pink buds in winter.* **LEFT** *The outstanding feature of* Acer griseum *is the texture and colour of the bark on its slender trunk. It also offers orange, scarlet and crimson leaves in autumn.*

Colour

Gardeners often create schemes that involve contrasting or harmonious colours, or revolve around single colours. And clever gardeners know that colour can be found in more than just flowers. Green leaves can range from chartreuse to almost black-green, and may be variegated with cream, white, red, pink, orange or yellow. Where the seasons are marked, the autumn foliage colour of plants like sweet gums (*Liquidambar* species) and oaks (*Quercus* species) can often rival the most vividly hued spring flowers.

Fruit, stems and bark can contribute striking colour to the garden landscape. *Cornus alba* 'Sibirica' offers vivid red branches in winter, and the coppery red peeling bark of *Acer griseum* brings out the red tones in the garden during any season.

Plant Shapes

The use of variously shaped plants can provide contrast and visual interest when juxtaposed in the garden. *Taxus baccata* 'Fastigiata' offers a sense of vertical movement, while horizontal effects are supplied by the flattish flowerheads of yarrow (*Achillea* species) and *Sedum* species.

Ornamental grasses, particularly when in flower, create some of the most dramatically beautiful weeping shapes, as do some flowering shrubs such as fuchsias whose drooping flowers accentuate the plants' somewhat weeping habit. Rounded plants include many lavender cultivars and hydrangeas, particularly those with spherical flowerheads that mimic the rounded shape of the shrub itself.

Year-round Interest

Except for the possibility of summer drought, in the temperate zones spring through early autumn is the easy season, with many plants providing enough colours, textures, shapes, forms and fragrance to fill plant catalogues to the brim. But maintaining continuity through the cooler months of late autumn and winter presents a challenge. And the colder the winter, the greater the challenge—although the options are surprisingly plentiful.

Few areas of Australia experience genuinely cold winters, and for many of us the autumn show of asters, sedums, salvias, Japanese anemone *(Anemone × hybrida)*, toad lily (*Tricyrtis* species) and the like can extend into early winter. In mild frost-free areas, cymbidium orchids, *Citrus* species and jasmines (*Jasminum* species) continue to bloom through winter. And even in our colder areas the first *Forsythia*, witch hazel (*Hamamelis* species) and cherry (*Prunus* species) buds often open in mid-winter.

CARING FOR YOUR GARDEN

It is not difficult to create a beautiful and rewarding garden that requires less care over time. Choosing appropriate plants for the climate is critical—but equally important is the initial preparation that goes into the site, particularly soil improvement.

Soil Preparation

The most important factor in healthy plant growth lies in the soil. Local councils, government agencies and universities frequently offer information about local soils as well as testing services that evaluate soil structure, pH and available nutrients.

Since the composition of soil varies widely, the amendments needed to build healthy soil vary— and most soils can use some improvement. Most garden plants grow best in well-drained, nutrient-rich, moisture-retentive soil. Compost increases the ability of sandy or gravelly soils to hold moisture and nutrients. It also improves the aeration and drainage of heavy clay. If soil composition indicates the need for improvement, then good soil-building composts such as animal manure or aged leaf mould, mushroom compost, kitchen waste compost or aged bark or sawdust should be used. The selected compost should be liberally incorporated to a depth of around 60 cm (24 in).

Watering

Good water practices begin with careful initial design and planning. One technique is to group plants requiring a lot of water in one area, accessible to a hose or a sprinkler system. Mulch is needed to retain moisture in the soil while plants settle in.

Watering in the morning or evening reduces evaporation. Choosing watering methods that reduce the amount of spray released into the atmosphere is recommended. Hand watering remains the best way to water the soil immediately around plants, but carefully situated drip systems can also be useful.

Fertilising

While the best fertilising practices should focus on building healthy soil that contains readily available nutrients for plants, there are situations where commercial fertiliser is useful. Vegetables, annual flowers and container plants that need to produce rapid growth respond well to a quick boost. Otherwise, slow-release fertilisers are best, particularly if applied early in the growing season.

If necessary, a test will confirm any deficiencies specific to your soil, and local agencies often have information on nutrient deficiencies in your area and their solutions.

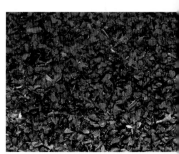

LEFT *Like many vegetables,* Capsicum annuum, *Conioides Group, 'Shishito' needs an application of fertiliser early in the growing season to bulk up the plant.*
BELOW *Straw (left) and coconut hulls (right) are two types of mulch with different uses. Straw breaks down quickly, while the harder coconut hulls last longer.*

 ABOVE *Successful pruning depends on both the timing and the method of cutting back the plant. Always use secateurs that are sharp and clean.*
RIGHT *Plants in similarly sized containers tend to dry out at the same rate, so group them together in an interesting display for ease of watering.*

Mulching

Defined as a material that provides a protective layer over the ground, mulch retains moisture in the soil, keeps roots cool and suppresses weeds.

Mulch can be non-degradable such as thick gravel, which is sometimes used around Mediter-ranean plants and alpines for its durability and drainage-promoting qualities, or it can consist of organic material, such as pine needles, wood chips, shredded bark, chopped leaves, grass clippings, nutshells and coconut husks. Degradable organic materials improve the nutrition of the soil as they decompose, as well as encouraging earthworms and beneficial microbes that, in turn, improve the soil's tilth and aeration. However, it is best to use mat-erials that are well rotted, shredded or chopped.

Weeding

While mulching is perhaps the most important tool for the suppression of annual weeds, it can help only where perennial weeds have already been well eradicated from the area.

Where formidable perennial weed problems exist, serious tactics must be adopted, beginning with regular aggressive hand pulling and digging. Many of the most noxious weeds will respond to little else. Other methods include the use of weed matting, solarising (a method in which the heat of the summer sun is harnessed by thick, clear plastic to essentially cook weed seeds on the soil's surface), and—as a last resort—herbicide.

Once an area has been cleared of roots, the application of a thick layer of mulch will often suppress any seeds from emerging, as long as the soil's surface is not disturbed. In frequently cultivated soils, applying a layer of mushroom compost over the surface will usually suppress weed seed germination, though its relatively high pH limits its use to vegetable crops.

Pruning

Pruning can be performed to improve a plant's health, to enhance flowering and fruiting or for aesthetic reasons. While some shrubs tolerate severe shearing for hedges, screens and topiary, it is generally best for plants' health to accentuate their natural growth habit.

Minor trimming can be done at almost any time of the year but serious pruning of deciduous shrubs and trees is best saved for winter dormancy or in very early spring for evergreens, including conifers. While making correct pruning cuts is not very difficult, it is best to consult a manual, as trees in particular need to be pruned in the correct place if they are to heal properly.

Herbaceous perennials are usually kept down to size by winter division, while evergreen perennials and subshrubs, such as *Pelargonium* plants, are best trimmed in spring, not long after growth resumes.

HARDINESS ZONES

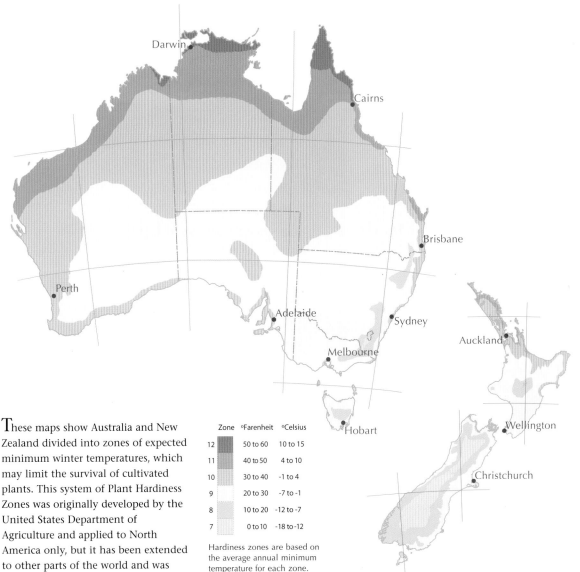

Zone	ºFarenheit	ºCelsius
12	50 to 60	10 to 15
11	40 to 50	4 to 10
10	30 to 40	-1 to 4
9	20 to 30	-7 to -1
8	10 to 20	-12 to -7
7	0 to 10	-18 to -12

Hardiness zones are based on the average annual minimum temperature for each zone. Zones 1 to 6 do not occur in Australia or New Zealand.

These maps show Australia and New Zealand divided into zones of expected minimum winter temperatures, which may limit the survival of cultivated plants. This system of Plant Hardiness Zones was originally developed by the United States Department of Agriculture and applied to North America only, but it has been extended to other parts of the world and was updated in 2012. The coldest zone is Zone 1, corresponding to a subarctic climate such as central Canada or Siberia; the warmest zone is Zone 12, which covers the warmest areas around the equator.

Each zone covers a range of 5.5 degrees Celsius (10 degrees Fahrenheit), as shown in the accompanying table (the Celsius rounded to the nearest degree). The lowest zone that is mostly frost free is Zone 10.

For each plant listed in this book, both a minimum and maximum zone are indicated, for example 8–10 for

Acacia dealbata. This means that the tree will survive the average winter frosts expected in at least the warmer parts of Zone 8, in which temperatures fall below –7°C (20°F); but that it will also grow reasonably well in zones up to at least the cooler parts of Zone 10, where winter minimums are above –1°C (30°F). The indicating of a maximum zone goes beyond the original intent of the Plant Hardiness Zones, but we believe it serves a useful purpose here, in that most non-tropical plants have definite limits as to how

warm a climate they will tolerate—in many cases they will survive in warmer zones but may fail to flower or fruit, or may prove very short lived.

These zones indicate only one part of a plant's climatic requirements. There are many plants, for example, that are extremely frost hardy but will grow well only in climates with hot humid summers; other plants require climates with cool wet winters and bone-dry summers. These and other requirements are indicated in the text wherever possible.

CHOOSING THE RIGHT PLANT

A worthy goal in planning a garden is to grow plants that are so well suited to the climate and site that they require a minimum of extra care and resources to maintain. Although young gardens often require extra attention while they grow in, the workload will lessen over time if suitable plants are chosen and good design principles are used. Experienced (and determined) gardeners with a collector's habit know that almost anything can be grown, as long as it is given special care. The idea is to keep the number of plants requiring special care at a manageable level.

USDA Climate Zones

Where frosts occur, cold hardiness is the major factor determining what can be grown. The United States Department of Agriculture (USDA) has produced a graded scale of climate zones that—while originally intended only for the United States—has become something of a de-facto international standard. The Plant Hardiness Zones map on page 14 offers general guidelines for conditions throughout Australia, which has a climate that falls mainly into the Zones 7–11 range.

Although the zonal system provides a general guide for selecting plants, low temperatures within a zone can still vary. Plants can be situated in slightly warmer or cooler parts of a given zone, and other factors—such as a plant's size and age, the moisture level of the soil and temperatures during the previous summer—can also affect whether a plant will survive the following winter's cold.

Most nurseries offer climatically appropriate plants, as well as plants of borderline hardiness that are suitable as house plants and for adventurous gardeners to try outdoors. A good understanding of a plant's natural range is your best guide to its suitability for your garden.

ABOVE *Waterfalls and ponds can affect the temperature and humidity in nearby areas of the garden.*
LEFT Cymbidium *hybrids like 'James Toya Royale' will need to be kept in a greenhouse in colder climate zones.*

Topography, Site and Microclimates

Having developed a general sense of your climate zone, the next step is to look at regional climatic challenges. Some are difficult: frequent droughts, repeated frosts or exposure to constant winds. Others can be viewed as opportunities in disguise: moist coastal breezes may leave salty deposits but they also mitigate the summer heat and lessen the risk of frost. Even snow, which causes so much damage when it makes its rare appearance in coastal gardens, can be a blessing in the mountains, where it provides insulation from severe frosts. These, and many other seemingly difficult conditions, can be exploited if the appropriate plants are used.

Regional topographical variations also affect local gardening conditions. These include hills and plateaus, which are more exposed to rain and wind but, on a cold night, might remain a few degrees warmer than a nearby valley where cold air collects. A forest canopy might provide cover for understorey plants, whereas a nearby open field is scoured by frigid wind. Built-up areas with expanses of concrete often remain several degrees warmer at night than outlying regions, and large bodies of water can also moderate surrounding areas.

Small variations within a garden, sometimes known as microclimates, can also be exploited. The quality of the soil can vary from one side of a house to another, as can the sun and wind exposure, which is affected by the house and trees. Stormwater run-off and the proximity of roads can also affect soil quality.

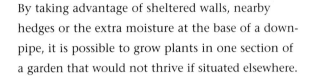

By taking advantage of sheltered walls, nearby hedges or the extra moisture at the base of a down-pipe, it is possible to grow plants in one section of a garden that would not thrive if situated elsewhere.

The Right Plant for the Right Place

In addition to the more obvious aesthetic concerns, a plant's specific features should be considered. For example, its ultimate height and width, shape, growth rate and type of root system are all part of the picture. Mistakes are less important with herbaceous plants that can be readily moved if they outgrow their space. But these features should be carefully considered prior to planting trees and large shrubs so that they can survive and flourish. Planting a tree near sewerage pipes is looking for trouble.

Additionally, any relevant environmental tolerances a plant possesses can be considered, including how it survives winter cold, summer heat, late frosts, humidity, drought, wind, salt spray, insects and diseases. Plants' varied genetic adaptations have given them different levels of suitability under various conditions, and these adaptations can be used to the gardener's advantage.

Observing neighbouring gardens and nearby natural areas can provide clues as to what kinds of plants will grow well in your garden. Ideas can be gleaned from the wild, from public gardens and parks and from neighbours who seem to have the knack for putting the right plant in just the right place to make it thrive.

ABOVE Aster alpinus *will flourish in a sunny spot in well-drained soil that stays moist but not too wet during the growing season.*
LEFT *Light-coloured walls reflect heat towards plants growing close by—particularly in summer—drying them out more quickly.*

Illustrated Guide to
FRUIT TYPES

Fruits are the seed-carrying organs (ovaries) of any of the flowering plants, and may be fleshy or dry, hard or soft, large or tiny. They protect the seed until it has developed and is ready to be dispersed by the wind, animals, birds or insects, depending on the genus.

Drupe

Berry

Capsule

Follicle

Schizocarp

Pod

Achene

Nut

Samara

Illustrated Guide to

FLOWER TYPES

STRUCTURE

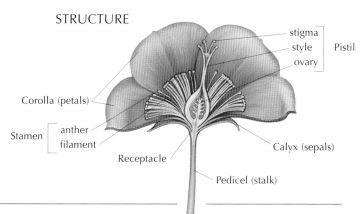

Flowers are the plant's reproductive centre, producing seed in a protected chamber, the ovary, which develops into the fruit. To ensure this, flowers have evolved into a wide range of colours, sizes and shapes. With cultivation, this diversity has only increased.

SHAPES

Star-shaped   Saucer-shaped   Cup-shaped   Bell-shaped   Tubular

Pitcher-shaped   Funnel-shaped   Trumpet-shaped   Salverform   Two-lipped

ORIENTATION

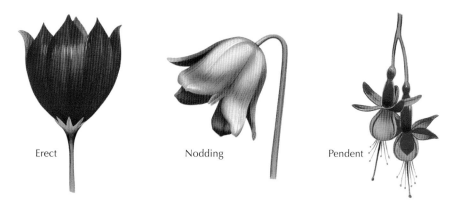

Erect   Nodding   Pendent

INFLORESCENCES

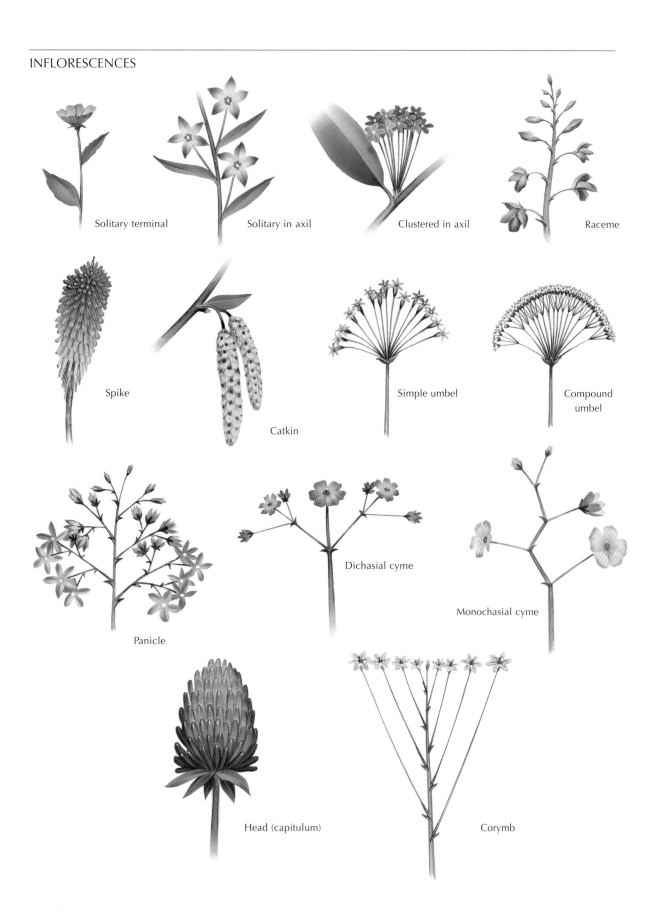

Solitary terminal

Solitary in axil

Clustered in axil

Raceme

Spike

Catkin

Simple umbel

Compound umbel

Panicle

Dichasial cyme

Monochasial cyme

Head (capitulum)

Corymb

Illustrated Guide to
LEAF TYPES

Leaves have adapted to a multitude of environments in order to successfully capture the Sun's vital energy, and to allow the passage of water out of the plant through their cells. The result is a wonderful variety in the shape, size and arrangement of leaves.

STRUCTURE

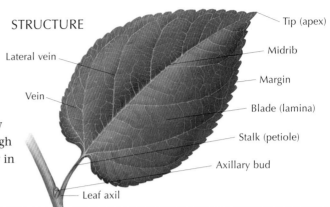

Lateral vein
Vein
Leaf axil
Tip (apex)
Midrib
Margin
Blade (lamina)
Stalk (petiole)
Axillary bud

SHAPES

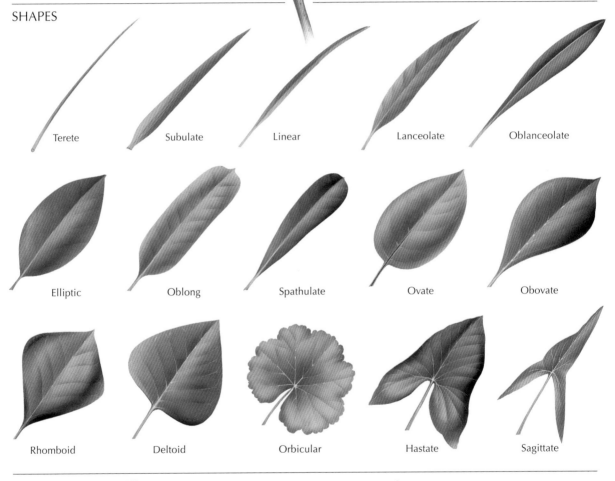

Terete

Subulate

Linear

Lanceolate

Oblanceolate

Elliptic

Oblong

Spathulate

Ovate

Obovate

Rhomboid

Deltoid

Orbicular

Hastate

Sagittate

COMPOUND LEAVES

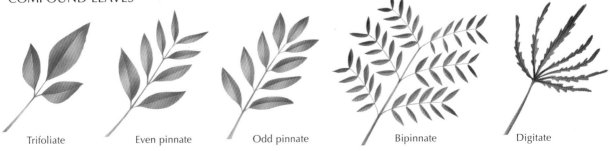

Trifoliate

Even pinnate

Odd pinnate

Bipinnate

Digitate

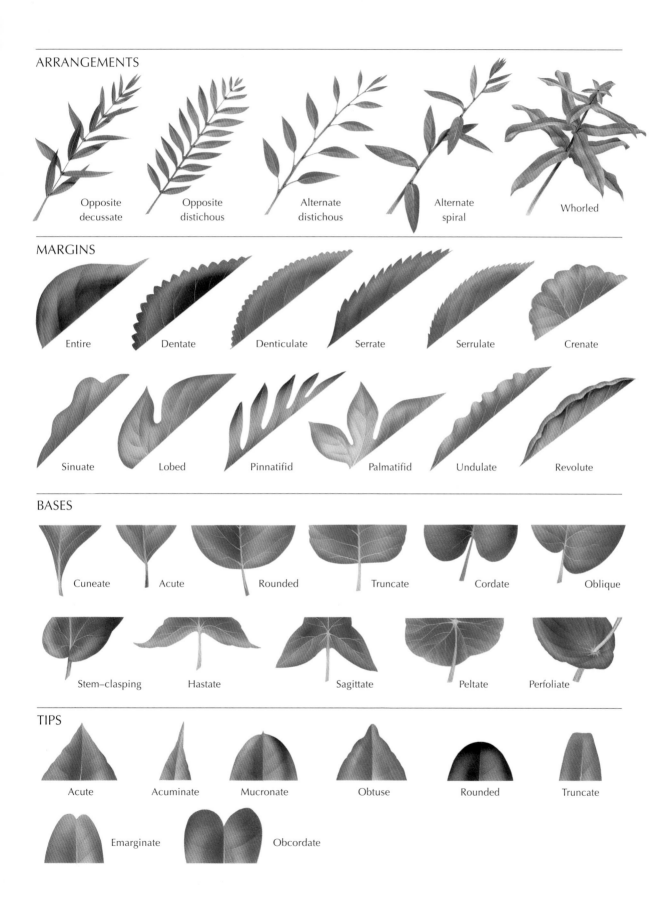

ARRANGEMENTS

Opposite decussate

Opposite distichous

Alternate distichous

Alternate spiral

Whorled

MARGINS

Entire

Dentate

Denticulate

Serrate

Serrulate

Crenate

Sinuate

Lobed

Pinnatifid

Palmatifid

Undulate

Revolute

BASES

Cuneate

Acute

Rounded

Truncate

Cordate

Oblique

Stem–clasping

Hastate

Sagittate

Peltate

Perfoliate

TIPS

Acute

Acuminate

Mucronate

Obtuse

Rounded

Truncate

Emarginate

Obcordate

TREES

Trees are more than just the aesthetic backbone of a landscape, although undoubtedly that is an important contribution. Trees also lend dignity to places where they grow, provide shelter for a variety of creatures and play an essential role in the life of the planet. On a global level, they are major producers of oxygen, without which life on Earth would not exist. Forest ecosystems nurture populations of plants, animals, fungi and microscopic organisms. Regionally, trees help define local character and are used as landmarks to guide us in our travels. And on a more personal level, trees invariably resonate with some of our earliest memories.

ABOVE *The autumn leaves of trees such as* Acer rubrum *bring burnished golds and reds to the garden, and act as markers for the passing of the seasons.*
LEFT *Some trees, like* Magnolia grandiflora, *bear exquisitely beautiful flowers, while others are valued for their attractive foliage or bark, or their interesting shape.*

THE BACKBONE OF THE GARDEN

Defined as woody perennial plants possessing a dominant trunk, or a few trunks, and a crown of foliage, trees are broadly distinguished from shrubs by exceeding 3–4.5 m (10–15 ft) in height. Most trees are quite long lived: the Earth's oldest recorded living entity, at some 4,800 years old, is a bristlecone pine *(Pinus aristata)* growing in California's Sierra Nevada, in the USA. And trees constitute some of the tallest living entities: redwoods *(Sequoia sempervirens)*, also native to California, can exceed 110 m (360 ft) in height.

While most garden trees will never attain such an age or height, it is nevertheless important to consider long-term issues when selecting which tree to plant—and where to plant it.

Trees are typically chosen for their ornamental characteristics: showy or fragrant flowers, unique leaf colour and texture, colourful bark, autumn foliage or attractive fruit. These qualities should guide us but not completely drive our decisions. For it is the practical considerations that determine whether the tree will survive in a given position in 5, 10, 20, 40 or 100 years.

Practical issues to consider include the tree's cultivation requirements: its cold or heat tolerance, and moisture and sunlight needs. The tree's characteristics should also be examined, including growth rate, eventual height and width and pest and disease resistance. Features such as canopy density and texture, and whether the tree is deciduous or evergreen are also relevant.

Ultimately, if the right tree is planted where it can mature without interfering with buildings, paving, utilities and other obstacles, its chances of survival are better and it will only grow increasingly handsome with age. A little planning at the selection stage (and at planting) makes the difference between a tree that creates more problems than it solves and one that becomes an asset and a beloved fixture in the landscape over time.

And there are many beautiful and adaptable trees from which to choose. Trees can be selected for their blossoms—flowering crabapples *(Malus* species), flowering dogwoods *(Cornus* species) and magnolias are perennially popular in cooler climates for their lovely and often fragrant blooms. Others include the Japanese snowbell *(Styrax japonicus)*, with fragrant, pendent, white flowers in late spring, or the paperbark maple *(Acer griseum)*, with peeling mahogany bark and blazing red autumn foliage. Other trees renowned for their fiery autumn foliage include the sweet gum *(Liquidambar styraciflua)*, tulip trees *(Liriodendron* species) and birches *(Betula* species).

ABOVE LEFT *Some trees with decorative bark display a texture that appeals, such as this paperbark maple* (Acer griseum), *while others offer variegated colour or intricate patterns.*
LEFT *Flowering deciduous trees bring variety to the garden with every season. This dogwood* (Cornus macrophylla) *is covered with flowers in summer, but in winter it looks very different.*

ABOVE *Apple trees such as* Malus pumila *'Tuscan' are valued for both their wonderful spring blossoms and their delicious fruit.*
RIGHT *Before deciduous trees like this sweet gum* (Liquidambar styraciflua) *lose their leaves, the foliage changes colour. The richness of colour can be affected by climatic conditions.*

For those seeking trees of stature and presence that can provide shade, there are beeches (*Fagus* species), oaks (*Quercus* species), maples (*Acer* species) and a range of conifers such as firs (*Abies* species), spruces (*Picea* species) and pine trees (*Pinus* species). Also, in warmer areas can be found jacarandas, crepe myrtles (*Lagerstroemia* species), larger magnolias like the southern magnolia (*Magnolia grandiflora*) and strawberry trees (*Arbutus* species).

Trees with large or heavy evergreen leaves provide deep shade, such as the European beech *(Fagus sylvatica)*, while others—with smaller and thinner leaves—cast only a light shade, such as the Japanese snowbell *(Styrax japonicus)*.

Trees can also be planted to attract wildlife, as they can offer fruit for them to eat and nesting space for them to live. Mountain ashes (*Sorbus* species), fruit trees such as apple trees (*Malus* species) and nut trees attract birds and other wildlife to the garden. In warm areas, flowers of wattles (*Acacia* species) and eucalyptus trees attract a variety of different hummingbirds, honeyeaters and other birds.

And if an accent or screen is desired, there are extremely narrow trees such as the fastigiate maple (*Acer rubrum* 'Columnare'). The range in shape, size, density and colour among trees is astounding.

The joys and pleasures associated with trees are significant, but the civic and cultural values associated with them are considerable as well. Trees buffer noise, help mitigate air pollution and stormwater run-off, shelter wildlife and lend an ineffable sense of calm and security to urban and rural landscapes alike. But trees are also capable of outliving us. In their growth rings, they capture the history of the Earth and put our own existence in perspective.

LEFT Abies koreana *is native to the mountains of South Korea and has striking purple cones. This cultivar, 'Compact Dwarf', is a popular bonsai subject.*

BELOW Abies concolor *grows in western USA down to northern Mexico. 'Masonic Broom' is a dwarf cultivar and grows no more than 75 cm (30 in) in height.*

ABIES

Around 50 species of evergreen conifer trees make up this genus in the pine (Pinaceae) family, which is widely distributed across the northern temperate zones. They usually have an erect conical habit with tiered branches and short, narrow, blunt leaves, often with pale undersides, rather than needles. The cones are very distinctive. The male cones are often brightly coloured, usually in purple-pink shades, and the female cones stand erect on top of the branches and may turn a bright purple-blue as they mature. All parts of the trees are very resinous and the cones often exude resin. The Pacific fir *(Abies amabilis)* yields Canada balsam, which is a clear resin widely used as a cement in optics before modern synthetics.

CULTIVATION

Most species are very hardy and grow better in cool conditions. They do not like hot summers. Plant in full sun or part-shade with moist, humus-rich, well-drained soil, and water well during the growing season. These trees are naturally symmetrical and are best left to develop naturally, untrimmed. Propagation is by grafting or from stratified seed.

Favourites	Cone Colour	Cone Shape	Cone Length
Abies alba	red-brown	cylindrical	4–6 in (10–15 cm)
Abies concolor	mid-green to brown	cylindrical	3–5 in (8–12 cm)
Abies koreana	purple	cylindrical	6 in (15 cm)
Abies nordmanniana	green to purple-brown	cylindrical	6 in (15 cm)
Abies nordmanniana **'Golden Spreader'**	green to purple-brown	cylindrical	6 in (15 cm)
Abies religiosa	green or purple to brown	cylindrical	6 in (15 cm)

Top Tip

Honey fungus mushrooms can destroy *Abies* trees. Once identified, remove all dead and dying stumps and root systems before the pest spreads further.

ABOVE Abies alba, *European silver fir, produces Europe's tallest tree. Its timber is used for telegraph poles and was used for ship masts in ancient Greece and Rome.*

BELOW *Stands of* Abies religiosa, *known as Mexican fir, provide a winter habitat for the Monarch butterfly. This fir is not as hardy as most others in this genus.*

Plant Height	Plant Width	Hardiness Zone	Frost Tolerance
200 ft (60 m)	20 ft (6 m)	6–9	yes
120 ft (36 m)	25 ft (8 m)	5–9	yes
50 ft (15 m)	5 ft (1.5 m)	5–8	yes
180 ft (55 m)	20 ft (6 m)	4–8	yes
50 ft (15 m)	30 ft (9 m)	4–8	yes
100 ft (30 m)	20 ft (6 m)	8–10	yes

ACACIA

Widespread in the southern tropics and subtropics, most of the 1,200 species in this mimosa subfamily of the legume (Fabaceae) family are found in Australia and Africa. Commonly known as wattle or mimosa, they range from small shrubs to large trees and include a few climbers. The African species frequently bear fierce spines. The foliage, often blue-green or silver-grey, is ferny when young and in many species remains that way, but often the leaves change to narrow phyllodes as the plants mature. The flowers are yellow, cream or white and are densely clustered in rounded heads or short spikes. The flowering season varies with the species, though many bloom from late winter into spring. Acacias yield a resinous gum that has many uses, from medicinal and culinary to use as a cement.

ABOVE *Most often found in eastern Australia,* Acacia crassa *is a tall shrub or small tree up to 12 m (40 ft) high. The golden yellow flower spikes are borne in pairs.*

CULTIVATION

Plant in full sun with light free-draining soil. Although drought tolerant, once established most grow better with reliable summer moisture. Many species are short-lived and some may self-sow too freely, becoming weeds. Propagate from well-soaked seeds.

RIGHT Acacia spectabilis *or Mudgee wattle has ferny, grey-green leaves that disappear under the abundance of golden yellow flowers produced in early spring. Prune every year to just beyond where the flowers were.*

Favourites	Flower Colour	Blooming Season	Flower Fragrance	Plant Height	Plant Width	Hardiness Zone	Frost Tolerance
Acacia crassa	golden yellow	late winter to early spring	yes	40 ft (12 m)	35 ft (10.5 m)	9–11	yes
Acacia dealbata	pale to bright yellow	late winter to spring	yes	80 ft (24 m)	20–35 ft (6–10.5 m)	8–10	yes
Acacia pravissima	golden yellow	spring	yes	10–25 ft (3–8 m)	10–20 ft (3–6 m)	8–11	yes
Acacia retinoides	lemon yellow	late spring to summer	yes	10–25 ft (3–8 m)	10 ft (3 m)	8–10	yes
Acacia spectabilis	golden yellow	early spring	yes	10–20 ft (3–6 m)	14–20 ft (4.3–6 m)	8–9	yes
Acacia stenophylla	creamy yellow	autumn to winter	yes	15–50 ft (4.5–15 m)	10–20 ft (3–6 m)	8–10	yes

Top Tip

When growing acacias from seed, place them in a cup of boiling water first. Then soak them in cold water for a day before planting.

ABOVE *In mild climates, acacias are among the most easily grown trees and shrubs. The leaves of* Acacia pravissima *are olive green on drooping branches.*

BELOW *Known in Europe as mimosa,* Acacia dealbata *can grow as tall as 24 m (80 ft) high in the wild. Generally, it will reach only 18 m (60 ft) in cultivation.*

RIGHT *Acer palmatum 'Shishigashira' is known as the lion's head maple. In autumn the foliage turns from deep green to rich red-brown or yellow. It grows well on the coast.*

ACER

Distributed through the northern temperate zone, this largely deciduous genus of 120 species of tree is the type form for the maple (Aceraceae) family. Most are graceful and round-headed trees with broad, often lobed leaves that frequently colour brilliantly in autumn. Variegated or coloured foliage is common among garden forms. In spring, usually before the foliage develops, they produce small flowers in clusters, upright spikes or drooping tassels. After flowering, maple trees produce winged fruit also known as samara or sycamores. Well known as timber trees and for producing maple syrup, these plants can be put to many other practical uses.

Top Tip

The maple tree is very versatile. Use it to add bright autumn colour to a garden, or as a shade tree. Some species are popular bonsai specimens.

CULTIVATION

Although a few maples are found in subtropical regions, most generally prefer climates with clearly defined seasons. They grow best in sun or part-shade with a humus-rich well-drained soil that remains moist through the growing season. The species are usually raised from seed, hybrids and cultivars by grafting.

BELOW *Known as fernleaf maple, Acer japonicum 'Aconitifolium' is native to the dry mountains of Japan. A small tree, the foliage colours crimson in autumn.*

Favourites	Flower Colour	Blooming Season	Flower Fragrance	Plant Height	Plant Width	Hardiness Zone	Frost Tolerance
Acer campestre	yellowish green	spring	no	30 ft (9 m)	12 ft (3.5 m)	3–8	yes
Acer griseum	green	spring	no	40 ft (12 m)	35 ft (10 m)	4–8	yes
Acer japonicum	purplish red	spring	no	30 ft (9 m)	30 ft (9 m)	6–8	yes
Acer palmatum	purplish red	spring to summer	no	20 ft (6 m)	25 ft (8 m)	6–9	yes
Acer palmatum 'Sango-kaku'	purplish red	spring to summer	no	20 ft (6 m)	25 ft (8 m)	6–9	yes
Acer saccharum	yellowish green	spring	no	100 ft (30 m)	40 ft (12 m)	4–8	yes

LEFT Acer griseum *is a very attractive tree. It features beautifully textured and coloured bark which peels to reveal smooth cinnamon red branches.*

BELOW Acer saccharum *produces the best sap of all the species from which to make maple syrup.*

AESCULUS

The type genus for the horse chestnut (Hippocastanaceae) family, this group of around 15 species of deciduous trees is found in North America—where they are commonly known as buckeye—and Eurasia. They are usually round-headed or pyramidal, with a sturdy trunk and large palmate leaves composed of 5 to 11 smooth-edged to slightly toothed leaflets. In spring, shortly after the leaves have expanded, upright panicles of white to red or yellow flowers develop near the branch tips. A horse chestnut in full flower is among the most colourful of the hardy deciduous trees. Large, sometimes spiny, seed capsules follow the flowers and contain paired nuts. Horse chestnuts are so-called because the fruit is inedible—fit only for horses—unlike that of the edible chestnut (*Castanea sativa*).

CULTIVATION

These hardy deciduous trees are most at home in climates with clearly defined seasons and relatively moist summers. Plant in sun with moist humus-rich soil and water well until established. The species are raised from seed, the cultivars by grafting.

LEFT *The crimson flowers of* Aesculus pavia *have earned it the common name of red buckeye. The cultivar 'Atrosanguinea', left, has pretty flowers of an even deeper red than the species.*
BELOW *Known as the red horse chestnut,* Aesculus × carnea *is a magnificent sight when in bloom, with masses of deep reddish pink flowers covering the tree.*

Top Tip

Many *Aesculus* species grow to an impressive size. Choose smaller species for the garden and limit pruning to the removal of dead wood.

RIGHT *The dense foliage of* Aesculus × carnea *'Briottii' offers wonderful shade. At blooming time spectacular deep red-pink blossoms smother the tree.*

Favourites	Flower Colour	Blooming Season	Flower Fragrance	Plant Height	Plant Width	Hardiness Zone	Frost Tolerance
Aesculus × *carnea*	reddish pink; yellow blotches	spring	no	30 ft (9 m)	15 ft (4.5 m)	6–9	yes
Aesculus flava	yellow	summer	no	90 ft (27 m)	35 ft (10 m)	4–9	yes
Aesculus hippocastanum	white; yellow to red blotches	late spring	no	100 ft (30 m)	70 ft (21 m)	6–9	yes
Aesculus indica	white	early to mid-summer	no	100 ft (30 m)	70 ft (21 m)	6–9	yes
Aesculus × *neglecta*	yellow	summer	no	50 ft (15 m)	30 ft (9 m)	5–9	yes
Aesculus pavia	crimson	early summer	no	15 ft (4.5 m)	10 ft (3 m)	6–10	yes

RIGHT *Native to central and eastern USA, Aesculus flava bears yellow flowers during summer. The flowers are followed by the rounded horse chestnuts.*

ABOVE *The brilliant flowers of* Alloxylon flammeum *blaze like beacons. The colour advertises the plants' presence to nectar-feeding birds that pollinate the flowers.*

ALLOXYLON

There are only 4 species in this genus of tropical and subtropical rainforest trees. Three are found only in Australia's tropical and subtropical rainforests, with the fourth being native to New Guinea. Despite these warm-climate origins, *Alloxylon* are adaptable and will tolerate the odd light frost in cooler areas and do well in temperate areas that are frost-free. All are evergreen, upright trees in the protea family (Proteaceae), which makes them related to banksias and grevilleas. They are a good size for gardens when grown out in the open but rather taller if grown among other trees. As in other plants in the family, the flowers are big and nectar-rich so as well as being showy, they're attractive to nectar-feeding birds.

CULTIVATION

Grow in full sun wherever possible as this not only maximises flower production, it keeps the tree to a better size. Average garden soil will do as long as it drains freely. The trees have little tolerance for extended dry spells and should be watered deeply if the rain stays away for more than a month in summer. Feed once in spring with controlled-release fertiliser.

LEFT *Although known as the Dorrigo waratah,* Alloxylon pinnatum *is found through northern NSW and into Queensland. Crimson flowers on long stalks appear in spring and summer.* **BELOW** Alloxylon flammeum, *from Queensland's Atherton Tableland, produces a magnificent floral display from late winter to spring. It grows and blooms well out of the tropics.*

Top Tip

Prune back newly planted trees to encourage bushiness. Repeat annually after bloom until you can no longer reach. Branches can be cut back by up to a third their length.

Favourites	Flower Colour	Blooming Season	Flower Fragrance	Plant Height	Plant Width	Hardiness Zone	Frost Tolerance
Alloxylon flammeum	scarlet	spring	no	50–100 ft (15–30 m)	30–50 ft (9–15 m)	9–11	yes
Alloxylon pinnatum	red	spring to summer	no	40–50 ft (12–15 m)	30–40 ft (9–12 m)	9–10	yes

ARBUTUS

A genus of around 8 to 10 species of small evergreen trees, it has a scattered distribution in the warmer parts of the northern temperate zone. Members of the heath (Ericaceae) family, they are known as strawberry trees because of their large, fleshy, orange-red to red fruit, which develop from sprays of small, bell-shaped, pink or white flowers. The colourful fruit is edible but not always pleasant tasting. The leaves are usually simple, dark green, leathery ovals, sometimes pointed or toothed. Most species have warm brown bark that flakes or peels to reveal a brighter underbark. Native Americans found medicinal uses for the fruit, bark and foliage of their local species.

CULTIVATION

While not extremely hardy to frost, most of these trees withstand prolonged cold conditions and are easily cultivated in sun or part-shade with cool, moist, humus-rich soil. Like most plants in the heath family, they resent lime. Trim lightly to shape, and propagate from half-hardened cuttings taken in autumn or winter, grafts or seed.

LEFT Arbutus menziesii, *from the North American Pacific coast, is commonly known as madrone. It sheds its outer brick red bark to reveal green underbark.*
BELOW *The white flowers of* Arbutus unedo *are followed by the red fruit that have earned it the common name of strawberry tree.*

RIGHT *An eastern Mediterranean native known as the Grecian strawberry tree,* Arbutus andrachne *sheds its warm brown bark to reveal a greenish cream underbark.*

Favourites	Flower Colour	Blooming Season	Flower Fragrance	Plant Height	Plant Width	Hardiness Zone	Frost Tolerance
Arbutus andrachne	white	spring	no	20 ft (6 m)	20 ft (6 m)	6–9	yes
Arbutus × *andrachnoides*	white	late winter	no	25 ft (8 m)	25 ft (8 m)	8–10	yes
Arbutus glandulosa	dull pink	winter	no	20 ft (6 m)	40 ft (12 m)	9–10	yes
Arbutus 'Marina'	pink	year-round	no	25–50 ft (8–15 m)	20–40 ft (6–12 m)	8–10	yes
Arbutus menziesii	white	late spring	yes	30 ft (9 m)	30 ft (9 m)	7–9	yes
Arbutus unedo	white	autumn to winter	yes	25 ft (8 m)	20 ft (6 m)	7–10	yes

Top Tip

Arbutus species are low-maintenance trees once established, requiring little in the way of pruning apart from minor trimming to thin out and keep a tidy appearance.

BELOW *Bearing similar characteristics to the species,* Arbutus unedo *'Compacta' is a smaller form, with a maximum height of around 3 m (10 ft).*

Top Tip

Prune birches only when essential. Vulnerable to several serious pests and diseases, any open cuts can provide opportunities for attack.

BETULA

A genus of some 60 species of deciduous shrubs and trees that are widespread in the cool temperate Northern Hemisphere and the subarctic, *Betula* is the type genus for the birch (Betulaceae) family. While the smaller species can be dense and twiggy, the trees tend to have an open airy growth habit with light branches and fine twigs. Many species have pale, sometimes white, bark that peels in small strips or sheets. The pointed oval leaves have small teeth and often develop vivid yellow autumn tones. Buff catkins appear in spring and shed many tiny seeds. Birch sap can be used as a maple syrup substitute, and the bark was a popular canoe-skinning material among Native Americans.

CULTIVATION

Very hardy and easily grown in normal garden soils, many birches are natural riverside plants that can tolerate quite damp conditions. Trim lightly to shape but otherwise allow the natural form to develop. Propagate from softwood or half-hardened cuttings, or from seed.

ABOVE *Characterised by grey to red-brown peeling bark and purple-red new growth,* Betula alnoides, *a native of the Himalayas, can reach an immense size.*
LEFT *The long, drooping, yellow, male catkins of* Betula albosinensis *appear in spring as the glossy green leaves unfurl.*

Favourites	Flower Colour	Blooming Season	Flower Fragrance	Plant Height	Plant Width	Hardiness Zone	Frost Tolerance
Betula albosinensis	yellow (male) yellow-brown (female)	spring	no	80 ft (24 m)	30 ft (9 m)	6–9	yes
Betula alleghaniensis	chartreuse (male) green (female)	early spring	no	80 ft (24 m)	30 ft (9 m)	4–9	yes
Betula alnoides	yellow-brown	early spring	no	100 ft (30 m)	20 ft (6 m)	8–10	yes
Betula mandschurica	yellow-brown	early spring	no	70 ft (21 m)	30 ft (9 m)	2–9	yes
Betula nigra	yellow	early spring	no	30 ft (9 m)	15 ft (4.5 m)	4–9	yes
Betula pendula	yellow (male) chartreuse (female)	early spring	no	80 ft (24 m)	35 ft (10 m)	2–8	yes

RIGHT *Native to riversides of eastern USA, the river birch (Betula nigra) has smooth white bark initially, which turns to shades of cream, pink and brown.*

BRACHYCHITON

A mostly Australian genus of over 30 species in the family Sterculiaceae. The bulk are found in the tropics though the most spectacular member, the flame tree, occurs along the high rainfall east coast well into a cooler, temperate region. Other species inhabit drier, tropical and subtropical inland areas, the remarkable bottle tree being a good example. No *Brachychiton* suits a cold climate, but many will grow in temperate areas and near-coastal locations made mild by proximity to the sea. Coolness has the advantage of slowing growth and reducing ultimate size. Once established, these trees are able to withstand long dry spells but they are not well adapted to boggy conditions, demanding fast soil drainage wherever they are grown.

CULTIVATION

Plant in full sun in an open position. In wet areas, plant on higher ground or on a slope to prevent water from accumulating around the roots. No regular pruning is needed although you can use selective pruning to shape trees as needed. Average garden soil suits *Brachychiton* as they are well adapted to poorish soils. In general, don't feed.

ABOVE *Lacebark kurrajong or* Brachychiton discolor *is found in scrubby bush along the coastal plain of central eastern Australia. Its flowers are spectacular when the tree loses all its leaves before the pink flowers appear in masses in early summer.*

Top Tip

Spectacular though it is in bloom, the flame tree drops considerable litter. Don't plant where it will overhang a pool or where fallen flowers and seed pods will cause unwanted labour.

ABOVE Brachychiton popul-neus *can withstand long dry spells and its foliage can be cut to feed stock. Creamy-pink flowers appear in spring, usually after leaves have fully or partially fallen.*

ABOVE *Not reliably wonder-ful, but when* Brachychiton acerifolius *does come into full bloom with all its leaves fallen, it's magnificent—a tower of scarlet in late spring.*

Favourites	Flower Colour	Blooming Season	Flower Fragrance	Plant Height	Plant Width	Hardiness Zone	Frost Tolerance
Brachychiton acerifolius	scarlet	late spring to summer	no	33–100 ft (10–30 m)	30–50 ft (9–15 m)	8–11	yes
Brachychiton discolor	pinkish red	summer	no	30–100 ft (9–30 m)	15–30 ft (4.5–9 m)	9	yes
Brachychiton populneus	pink or white	summer	no	20–65 ft (6–20 m)	10–20 ft (3–6 m)	8–9	yes
Brachychiton rupestris	yellow	summer	no	20–50 ft (6–15 m)	15–30 ft (4.5–9 m)	8–9	yes

CASSIA

This is a big genus containing hundreds of species but only about 30 are trees that all come from tropical and subtropical regions including those in Australia. Several are extremely showy in bloom, usually flowering in shades of yellow or pink. The *Cassia* genus is in the pea family, Fabaceae, and while many of the tree types are deciduous over the winter dry season, they often don't lose their leaves in tropical areas that are reasonably rainy year-round. *Cassia* have compound leaves and the flowers are produced in pendulous or upright clusters. Flowering often occurs when trees are bare or nearly so and even if they have leaves, the sheer density of flowers obscures the foliage. The native *Cassia tomentella* is one of the loveliest of all.

CULTIVATION

Grow in full sun or with only a little light shade in free-draining soil of at least average fertility. In higher rainfall areas, the trees tend to be moderately fast growing but they can be slow in inland tropical areas unless irrigated periodically. Pruning isn't necessary although trees can be shaped if desired. They are suscep- tible to borers but trees that are grown in good conditions can resist the insects.

RIGHT *The fast growing Leichhardt bean (Cassia brewsteri) occurs along much of the Queensland coast where it makes a spectacular sight during autumn flowering season.* **BELOW** *Cassias have concave, five-petalled flowers with prominent, curving stamens. These are those of the magnificent Cassia fistula.*

Favourites	Flower Colour	Blooming Season	Flower Fragrance	Plant Height	Plant Width	Hardiness Zone	Frost Tolerance
Cassia brewsteri	orange	autumn	no	26–33 ft (8–10 m)	15–20 ft (4.5–6 m)	9–11	no
Cassia fistula	golden yellow	spring or summer	no	40–65 ft (12–20 m)	30–50 ft (9–15 m)	9–11	no
Cassia javanica	pink	spring	no	80–130 ft (25–40 m)	60–100 ft (18–30 m)	10–11	no
Cassia 'Paluma Range'	golden yellow	spring	no	23–33 ft (7–10 m)	20–40 ft (6–12 m)	10–11	no

Top Tip

Seedlings often don't replicate the parent tree in flower colour or abundance. If a particular form is wanted, propagate by air layering as growth begins, or grafting onto a seedling.

BELOW *The golden shower tree or* Cassia fistula *comes from tropical Asia. It is briefly deciduous before or at flowering.*

ABOVE *Called the apple blossom cassia because of its delicate pink flowers,* Cassia javanica *comes from Indonesia but is worth trying in a warm, sunny spot in a frost-free garden.*

CERATOPETALUM

Found only in Australia and New Guinea, *Ceratopetalum* is a genus of just 5 species in the family Cunoniaceae. All types are evergreen rainforest trees or smaller, bushy trees or large shrubs. They occur naturally only in high rainfall, coastal forests in Queensland and NSW, generally on free-draining, often sand-based soils that contain rotted organic matter derived from the surrounding forest. The flowers themselves are tiny, usually cream or white and nothing much to look at. But after they fall, the sepals left behind grow larger and change colour. In the showiest species, the NSW Christmas bush, they turn a remarkable bright red in a display that lasts for weeks. So effective are these that bunches of this plant are widely sold for Christmas flower arrangements.

CULTIVATION

Plant in full sun or with periods of dappled shade. Soil must drain freely yet be moisture retentive—a sloping site can be ideal. Never allow the plants to go dry for extended periods though they will tolerate more dryness in the cooler months than in the summer. Pruning bunches of the colourful sepals keeps the NSW Christmas bush more compact and shrubby.

RIGHT *Found in rainforests of eastern Australia, the coachwood (Ceratopetalum apetalum) yields a fine timber prized by cabinet-makers.*

Favourites	Flower Colour	Blooming Season	Flower Fragrance	Plant Height	Plant Width	Hardiness Zone	Frost Tolerance
Ceratopetalum apetalum	pink or red	summer	no	30–65 ft (9–20 m)	15–30 ft (4.5–10 m)	8–9	yes
Ceratopetalum gummiferum	red	summer	no	10–40 ft (3–12 m)	10–30 ft (3–9 m)	8–9	yes
Ceratopetalum gummiferum 'Albery's Red'	deep red	summer	no	10–40 ft (3–12 m)	10–30 ft (3–9 m)	8–9	yes

LEFT *For the most abundant display of the deepest red colour, grow the NSW Christmas bush in plenty of sun preferably in a sandy loam. It likes consistent moisture but not wetness around its roots, especially during the warmer months. The selection 'Albery's Red' is one of the deepest reds.*

Top Tip

Another Australian plant, *Babingtonia virgata*, becomes a mass of tiny white flowers at the same time as Christmas bush colours red. The two together make a lovely arrangement for the festive season.

CERCIS

ABOVE *The stark stems of Cercis canadensis 'Forest Pansy' are adorned with rosy-red buds opening to reveal pink-red flowers. The burgundy leaves appear throughout the season.*

This small genus of 6 or 7 deciduous trees and shrubs is found in the temperate zone from North America to South-East Asia and is grown for the showy spring flowers. The leaves are alternate and mostly broadly egg-shaped. The flowers are pea-shaped, with 5 petals in a squat calyx, usually borne on bare stems before or with the early leaves. The fruit is a flat legume with a shallow wing along the edge. In North America, this genus is commonly known as the redbud, but in some parts of the world it is known as the Judas tree. Tradition holds that it was a *Cercis* tree from which Judas hanged himself after betraying Christ.

Top Tip

As *Cercis* species do not transplant well, consideration should be given to their suitability and long-term needs when choosing a site to plant.

CULTIVATION
Cercis species prefer a moderately fertile soil that drains well, and exposure to sun for most of the day. All species are frost hardy. Some early shaping is needed to select a main leader, but little regular pruning is needed after that. They do not respond well to transplanting. Propagation is usually from freshly harvested seeds, which need pre-soaking in hot water to soften the hard coat. Half-hardened cuttings may be taken in summer or early autumn.

ABOVE *Red, pink or purple flowers cover the bare stems* of Cercis canadensis *before the attractive heart-shaped leaves appear.*
RIGHT *The flowers of* Cercis siliquastrum *are followed by bean-like pods that contain up to 12 seeds. The decorative pods persist on the stems until winter.*

Favourites	Flower Colour	Blooming Season	Flower Fragrance	Plant Height	Plant Width	Hardiness Zone	Frost Tolerance
Cercis canadensis	lilac-pink to crimson	spring to early summer	no	15–30 ft (4.5–9 m)	20 ft (6 m)	5–9	yes
Cercis canadensis **'Forest Pansy'**	lilac-pink to crimson	spring to early summer	no	15–30 ft (4.5–9 m)	20 ft (6 m)	5–9	yes
Cercis chinensis	lavender to red-purple	spring to early summer	no	12–15 ft (3.5–4.5 m)	15 ft (4.5 m)	6–9	yes
Cercis griffithii	mauve to purple	spring to early summer	no	15–20 ft (4.5–6 m)	15 ft (4.5 m)	7–9	yes
Cercis occidentalis	pink to magenta	spring	no	15 ft (4.5 m)	12 ft (3.5 m)	7–9	yes
Cercis siliquastrum	pinkish magenta	spring	no	20–30 ft (6–9 m)	15–20 ft (4.5–6 m)	7–9	yes

BELOW *The slender maroon seed pods of* Cercis griffithii *are similar in shape to those of* C. siliquastrum, *but are smaller and contain fewer seeds.*

CHAMAECYPARIS

A North American and temperate East Asian genus, it features 8 species of evergreen coniferous trees in the cypress (Cupressaceae) family. They have small scale-like leaves that are tightly pressed to the stems and borne in fan-shaped sprays. The cones are rounded, small and often very hard. A great number of cultivars have been developed, covering a huge range of foliage colours and growth forms, and these are far more widely grown than the true species. The foliage can cause a type of contact dermatitis in some people. The rapid-growing nature of these trees, particularly the Lawson cypress *(Chamaecyparis lawsoniana)*, has made them popular for shelter belts.

CULTIVATION

These hardy adaptable trees are tolerant of a wide range of soil and climatic conditions but generally do best with moist, slightly acidic soil and fairly cool, moist summers. Trim to shape when young and thin later. Propagation is usually from half-hardened summer cuttings under mist, or by grafting.

Top Tip

The smaller *Chamaecyparis* species and cultivars can be used for hedging—using types with different coloured foliage will add interest.

ABOVE *The golden yellow foliage of* Chamaecyparis lawsoniana *'Minima Aurea', an award-winning tree, will provide interest in the garden throughout the year.*
LEFT *Cultivars of* Chamaecyparis lawsoniana, *such as 'Handcross Park', offer a range of growth habits and foliage colour.*

LEFT *The unusual spiralling growth habit of* Chamaecyparis obtusa *'Spiralis' gives a somewhat sculptured look, enhanced by the bright green foliage.*
BELOW Chamaecyparis pisifera *is most often represented in gardens by cultivars such as 'Plumosa', which has mid-green leaves and red-brown bark.*

Favourites	Cone Colour	Cone Shape	Cone Length	Plant Height	Plant Width	Hardiness Zone	Frost Tolerance
Chamaecyparis lawsoniana	grey to rusty brown	round	$\frac{1}{2}$ in (12 mm)	100 ft (30 m)	10–15 ft (3–4.5 m)	4–9	yes
Chamaecyparis lawsoniana 'Ellwoodii'	grey to rusty brown	round	$\frac{1}{2}$ in (12 mm)	6–8 ft (1.8–2.4 m)	3–4 ft (0.9–1.2 m)	4–9	yes
Chamaecyparis nootkatensis	brown	round	$\frac{1}{2}$ in (12 mm)	100 ft (30 m)	25 ft (8 m)	4–9	yes
Chamaecyparis obtusa	orange-brown	round	$\frac{1}{2}$ in (12 mm)	60 ft (18 m)	20 ft (6 m)	5–10	yes
Chamaecyparis pisifera	black-brown	round	$\frac{1}{2}$ in (12 mm)	75 ft (23 m)	15 ft (4.5 m)	5–10	yes
Chamaecyparis thyoides	purplish black	round to oval	$\frac{1}{4}$ in (6 mm)	50 ft (15 m)	12 ft (3.5 m)	4–9	yes

CHIONANTHUS

Belonging to the olive (Oleaceae) family, this principally temperate and subtropical East Asian genus comprises around 100 species of mostly deciduous trees. One well-known and widely grown species, the fringe tree *(Chionanthus virginicus)*, occurs in eastern North America. The leaves are simple, smooth-edged or toothed and colour only slightly in autumn. The main attraction is the fragrant, 4-petalled, white flowers, which are borne in billowing panicles. Single-seeded purple-blue fruit follows. Extracts from the bark of the roots have extensive medicinal uses, and the fruit is sometimes preserved or pickled in the same manner as olives.

CULTIVATION

Although the cultivated species are generally hardy, they are prone to damage from late frosts and flower best after a long hot summer. Plant in full sun with moist, humus-rich, well-drained soil. Propagate by sowing fresh seed as soon as it is ripe. Germination is slow, and can take up to 18 months.

BELOW *Native to China and Taiwan, and known as the Chinese fringe tree,* Chionanthus retusus *has fissured, sometimes peeling bark and bright green leaves.*
BOTTOM *In full bloom,* Chionanthus virginicus *is a glorious sight, its branches laden with panicles of fragrant, fringed, white blossoms.*

Top Tip

Keep soil type in mind when selecting *Chionanthus* species, as soil preferences vary. Some species tolerate alkaline soils, while others prefer neutral or acid soil.

Favourites	Flower Colour	Blooming Season	Flower Fragrance	Plant Height	Plant Width	Hardiness Zone	Frost Tolerance
Chionanthus retusus	white	summer	yes	10 ft (3 m)	10 ft (3 m)	6–10	yes
Chionanthus virginicus	white	summer	yes	10 ft (3 m)	10 ft (3 m)	4–9	yes
Chionanthus virginicus 'Angustifolius'	white	summer	yes	10 ft (3 m)	10 ft (3 m)	4–9	yes

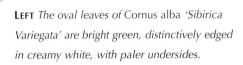

CORNUS

This North American and Eurasian genus of around 40 species of mainly deciduous, spring-flowering shrubs and trees is the type form for the dogwood (Cornaceae) family. The leaves are usually broadly lance-shaped and many of the cultivated plants have variegated leaves that colour well in autumn. A few have brightly coloured stems that are attractive in winter. The true flowers are tiny but are surrounded by 4 large, decorative, white, cream or pale green bracts that may become flushed red or pink. Several of the species produce soft edible fruit, the seeds contain a flammable oil and the young twigs can be used in basketry.

CULTIVATION

Dogwoods are hardy adaptable trees, though most need winter cold to flower well and are at home in a climate with distinct seasons. Plant in sun or part-shade with fertile, humus-rich, well-drained soil and water well during the warmer months. Clumping forms may be raised from suckers, otherwise try stratified seed, hardwood cuttings or grafting.

LEFT *The oval leaves of* Cornus alba *'Sibirica Variegata' are bright green, distinctively edged in creamy white, with paler undersides.*

RIGHT *The flowers of* Cornus nuttallii *are small, and are easily hidden by the large white, cream or pale green bracts that surround them.*

RIGHT *The dense foliage of* Cornus alternifolia *'Argentea' features mid-green leaves marked with white variegations.*

ABOVE Cornus alba *'Argenteo-Marginata' has attractive green leaves edged in creamy white, and features a rounded form. It does well when situated in either sun or shade.*

RIGHT *Gorgeous rosy pink bracts distinguish* Cornus florida f. rubra *from the species. Persistent red berries follow, providing a winter food source for birds.*

Favourites	Flower Colour	Blooming Season	Flower Fragrance	Plant Height	Plant Width	Hardiness Zone	Frost Tolerance
Cornus alba	white to creamy white	late spring to early summer	yes	6–10 ft (1.8–3 m)	10 ft (3 m)	4–9	yes
Cornus alternifolia	white to lemon yellow	early summer	no	20–25 ft (6–8 m)	20 ft (6 m)	3–9	yes
Cornus florida	green; white to pinkish bracts	late spring to early summer	no	20–30 ft (6–9 m)	25 ft (8 m)	5–9	yes
Cornus kousa	green; cream bracts	early summer	no	20–25 ft (6–8 m)	15 ft (4.5 m)	5–9	yes
Cornus nuttallii	green; pink-flushed white bracts	late spring and early autumn	no	60 ft (18 m)	40 ft (12 m)	7–8	yes

BELOW Cornus florida—*known as the flowering dogwood—is a magnificent ornamental tree. The white to pinkish bracts put on a spectacular show from late spring to early summer, then in autumn the fiery foliage colour dominates.*

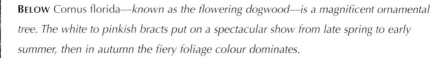

LEFT Cornus kousa *comes from Japan and Korea. It is a deciduous tree that prefers a position in full sun. The tiny green flowers are surrounded by cream bracts.*

Top Tip

The young growth of red-stemmed *Cornus* species is the most vibrant. To encourage colourful new growth, cut back—almost to the ground—in early spring.

LEFT *From the SW of Western Australia the red flowering gum (Corymbia ficifolia) has the most spectacular flowering display of any species. It does very well across far southern Australia but often disappoints when grown along the east coast.*

CORYMBIA

Most gardeners will know these as gum trees and, until genetic research uncovered differences, all *Corymbia* were included in the big genus *Eucalyptus*. Now over 100 former eucalypts make up the genus *Corymbia*, which includes trees popular in gardens such as the spectacular red flowering gum (*C. ficifolia*) and its hybrids such as 'Summer Red', the lemon-scented gum (*C. citriodora*) and the swamp bloodwood (*C. ptychocarpa*). In general, a gum tree might be a *Corymbia* if the bark is either dark brown, rough and fissured and not confined to just the lower trunk; or if it is smooth and pale as in the lemon-scented gum; or smooth but flaking and spotted as in the spotted gum (*C. maculata*). Like *Eucalyptus*, *Corymbia* is included in the Myrtaceae.

CULTIVATION

Corymbias are native to a wide range of different climates in their homeland, Australia. The red flowering gum, for example, likes rainy winters and dry summers. However, its hybrid 'Summer Red' was crossed with a tropical species making it suitable for summer-rainfall areas. All demand full sun and develop their best form when planted in the open, not crowded by other trees.

ABOVE *The lemon-scented gum (Corymbia citriodora) has a beautiful straight, smooth, almost white trunk and strongly lemon-scented leaves most noticeable in hot weather.*

Favourites	Flower Colour	Blooming Season	Flower Fragrance	Plant Height	Plant Width	Hardiness Zone	Frost Tolerance
Corymbia calophylla	white, pink	summer to autumn	yes	45–80 ft (13.5–25 m)	33–45 ft (10–13.5 m)	8–9	yes
Corymbia citriodora	white	winter	yes	50–100 ft (15–30 m)	33–80 ft (10–25 m)	8–10	yes
Corymbia ficifolia	red, orange, pink, white	summer	yes	20–50 ft (6–15 m)	20–65 ft (6–20 m)	8–9	yes
Corymbia maculata	white	autumn to winter	no	65–100 ft (20–30 m)	33–65 ft (10–20 m)	8–9	yes
Corymbia ptychocarpa	red, pink, white	summer to winter	yes	20–50 ft (6–15 m)	10–30 ft (3–9 m)	9–11	no

LEFT *Mostly white or cream in colour, the blooms of the marri* (Corymbia calophylla) *are abundantly produced, showy and very attractive to nectar-feeding birds.*

BELOW *'Summer Red' is one of the new hybrid gum trees with bigger, showier flowers that can grow and bloom well in areas with high summer rainfall.*

Top Tip

Research the *Corymbia* species you are considering to ensure that both its ultimate size and spread and climatic needs are suitable. They vary widely, depending on where they come from.

EUCALYPTUS

Although they fuel fierce bushfires and are responsible for increasing soil salinity, eucalypts are the quintessential Australian trees. The genus contains around 800 species of evergreen trees of the myrtle (Myrtaceae) family and is predominantly Australian, with a few stragglers in New Guinea, Indonesia and the southern Philippines. Usually graceful and open in habit, they are known for their peeling, often multi-coloured bark and volatile aromatic oils. When young, many species have circular leaves that encircle the stems, but mature trees generally have sickle-shaped leaves. The filamentous flowers appear at varying times and while often insignificant, those of some species are large and colourful.

The botanical name is derived from the Greek *eu-kalypto*, meaning "to cover", and refers to the cap of the flower bud.

CULTIVATION

Hardiness varies with the species, though none will tolerate repeated severe frosts or prolonged winters. Plant in light well-drained soil and keep moist when young. They are drought tolerant once established. Propagate from seed.

Favourites	Flower Colour	Blooming Season	Flower Fragrance
Eucalyptus cinerea	creamy white	summer	no
Eucalyptus erythrocorys	bright yellow	summer to autumn	no
Eucalyptus gunnii	creamy white	summer	no
Eucalyptus scoparia	creamy white	spring to summer	no
Eucalyptus tetraptera	red	spring	no
Eucalyptus torquata	pink, red	spring to summer	no

Top Tip

Fast growing and drought tolerant, eucalypts place few demands on gardeners. Pruning is necessary only to enhance shape or to remove old or dead wood.

LEFT *An ornamental species, Eucalyptus scoparia is rare in the wild. It is valued for its graceful weeping habit, peeling bark and glossy green pendulous leaves.*
BELOW *Eucalyptus torquata puts on a floral display of pink and red in spring and summer—year-round in favourable climates. The long leaves are sickle-shaped.*

Plant Height	Plant Width	Hardiness Zone	Frost Tolerance
30–50 ft (9–15 m)	20–30 ft (6–9 m)	8–11	yes
25 ft (8 m)	10 ft (3 m)	9–11	yes
30–80 ft (9–24 m)	20–30 ft (6–9 m)	7–9	yes
40 ft (12 m)	20 ft (6 m)	9–11	yes
10 ft (3 m)	8 ft (2.4 m)	9–11	yes
40 ft (12 m)	15–30 ft (4.5–9 m)	9–11	yes

Top Tip

Take care when siting beech trees. The surface roots will take over the area beneath them, and the dense foliage will plunge underlying plants into deep shade.

FAGUS

The deciduous beech trees, of which there are 10 species spread over the northern temperate zone, make up the type genus for the beech (Fagaceae) family. They are sturdy trees with solid smooth-barked trunks and broad rounded crowns of toothed or wavy-edged, pointed oval leaves. Although the small spring flower clusters are interesting, beeches are grown for their statuesque form and their foliage. Their fresh, translucent green or purple-bronze, spring foliage positively glows at sunset, and their autumn colours should not be underestimated. Beech flowers develop into small bristly seed pods, which when shed form a layer of litter known as beech mast. The oil-rich seeds have some culinary uses, including being roasted to produce a coffee substitute. The wood is also oily and yields creosote.

CULTIVATION

Beeches grow best in deep, fertile, moist, well-drained soil and prefer climates with distinct seasons. Trim lightly to allow the natural shape to develop. Propagate the species from seed, cultivars by grafting.

ABOVE LEFT *The coppery seed pods of* Fagus sylvatica *'Quercina' have a prickly outer coating. They make a striking contrast with the glossy leathery foliage.*

BELOW *The oriental beech,* Fagus orientalis *is a fast-growing tree. It reaches up to 30 m (100 ft) tall in its native habitat, but is much smaller in cultivation.*

LEFT *The American beech,* Fagus grandifolia, *hails from eastern North America. This tall deciduous tree resembles its European relative,* F. sylvatica, *but has larger leaves.*

BELOW *Twisted branches distinguish* Fagus sylvatica f. tortuosa. *These branches carry the glossy green, strongly veined leaves. Prickly greenish seed pods follow the flowers.*

Favourites	Flower Colour	Blooming Season	Flower Fragrance	Plant Height	Plant Width	Hardiness Zone	Frost Tolerance
Fagus crenata	yellow-green	spring	no	30 ft (9 m)	20 ft (6 m)	6–8	yes
Fagus grandifolia	yellow-green	spring	no	80 ft (24 m)	35 ft (10 m)	4–8	yes
Fagus orientalis	yellow-green	spring	no	100 ft (30 m)	40 ft (12 m)	6–8	yes
Fagus sylvatica	yellow (male) green (female)	spring	no	100 ft (30 m)	50 ft (15 m)	5–8	yes
Fagus sylvatica 'Purpurea'	yellow-green	spring	no	50–60 ft (15–18 m)	35–50 ft (10–15 m)	5–8	yes
Fagus sylvatica 'Riversii'	yellow-green	spring	no	100 ft (30 m)	50 ft (15 m)	5–8	yes

GINKGO

There is but one species in this genus, which is the sole member of its family, the Ginkgoaceae. Now unknown in the wild, *Ginkgo biloba* has long been cultivated in China. It is a deciduous, broad-based, conical tree more closely allied to the conifers than the flowering trees. The bark is light and deeply fissured, and the foliage, bright green when young and brilliant yellow in autumn, resembles that of the maidenhair fern. Catkins appear in spring and those of female trees develop into soft, pungent, single-seeded, yellow fruit. Ginkgo extracts are used medicinally and the edible seeds are nutritious, but should be cooked to destroy a mild toxin they contain.

LEFT *The bright green fan-shaped leaves of* Ginkgo biloba *have earned it the common name of maidenhair tree. This deciduous tree eventually becomes quite large and is an impressive sight year-round.*

Top Tip

Ginkgo biloba needs little maintenance once established. However, regular watering and pruning when young will encourage a pleasing tree shape.

BELOW *The unique* Ginkgo biloba *is an ancient tree that has adapted well to modern times, undeterred by environmental pollutants and extreme conditions.*

CULTIVATION
The ginkgo is a tough adaptable tree that is planted extensively in parks, but can be too large for small gardens. The fruit is very messy, so avenue specimens should be cutting-grown male trees. Propagate from seed or half-hardened cuttings under mist.

Favourites	Flower Colour	Blooming Season	Flower Fragrance	Plant Height	Plant Width	Hardiness Zone	Frost Tolerance
Ginkgo biloba	yellow	spring	no	100 ft (30 m)	25 ft (8 m)	3–10	yes
Ginkgo biloba 'Autumn Gold'	green	spring	no	50 ft (15 m)	30 ft (9 m)	3–10	yes
Ginkgo biloba 'Tremonia'	yellow	spring	no	35 ft (10 m)	10–20 ft (3–6 m)	3–10	yes

GLEDITSIA

This genus of 14 species of deciduous trees belongs to the cassia subfamily of the legume (Fabaceae) family. Commonly known as locusts, they are found in the Americas, central Asia and parts of Africa. Spreading when young, they eventually develop an open crown of slightly pendulous branches clothed in large pinnate or bipinnate leaves. The foliage may colour well in autumn and several coloured foliage cultivars are available. The branches are often thorny, sometimes fiercely so. The late spring to early summer sprays of largely insignificant flowers are followed by long bean-like pods that contain edible seeds. In some drought-prone areas locusts are cultivated for these pods, which are a nutritious stock food.

ABOVE Gleditsia japonica *var.* koraiensis *is a native of eastern China. The long leaves—up to 30 cm (12 in) in length—consist of pairs of glossy yellow-green leaflets.*

CULTIVATION

Gleditsia species thrive in areas with hot summers and short, sharp, clearly defined winters. Late frosts can cause damage. Plant in a sunny position with well-drained fertile soil. Young trees need irrigation but are drought tolerant once established. Propagate the species from seed, the cultivars by budding or grafting.

LEFT *A recent introduction from the USA,* Gleditsia triacanthos 'Trueshade' *makes an attractive shade tree with its large domed crown and spreading branches.*
BELOW *Commonly known as the Japanese locust,* Gleditsia japonica *is heavily armed with sharp thorns on its trunk and branches.*

Top Tip

Gleditsia trees are robust, and are ideally suited to street planting or open spaces. For pain-free gardening, choose from the many thornless cultivars available.

ABOVE *An immensely popular cultivar,* Gleditsia triacanthos *f. inermis 'Sunburst' (syn. 'Aurea') is fast growing. The attractive new foliage emerges bright yellow in spring, gradually maturing to a fresh lime green colour.*

RIGHT *Earning its common name of Caspian locust from its native habitat—the Caspian Sea region of northern Iran—*Gleditsia caspica *is heavily armed with thorns.*

Favourites	Flower Colour	Blooming Season	Flower Fragrance	Plant Height	Plant Width	Hardiness Zone	Frost Tolerance
Gleditsia caspica	green	late spring to early summer	no	40 ft (12 m)	30 ft (9 m)	6–10	yes
Gleditsia japonica	whitish green	late spring to early summer	no	70 ft (21 m)	35 ft (10 m)	6–10	yes
Gleditsia triacanthos	whitish green	late spring to early summer	yes	150 ft (45 m)	70 ft (21 m)	3–10	yes
Gleditsia triacanthos **f.** *inermis*	whitish green	late spring to early summer	yes	50–60 ft (15–18 m)	40–50 ft (12–15 m)	3–10	yes
Gleditsia triacanthos **f.** *inermis* **'Rubylace'**	whitish green	late spring to early summer	yes	50–60 ft (15–18 m)	40–50 ft (12–15 m)	3–10	yes
Gleditsia triacanthos **f.** *inermis* **'Sunburst'**	whitish green	late spring to early summer	yes	30–60 ft (9–18 m)	40–50 ft (12–15 m)	3–10	yes

BELOW *Casting off its bare winter outline, the spring foliage of* Gleditsia triacanthos *f. inermis 'Sunburst' (syn. 'Aurea') fills the branches with colour. It makes an excellent specimen tree.*

RIGHT *Somewhat heavily armed with thorns,* Gleditsia triacanthos *features bright green ferny foliage that develops glorious colour in autumn. Since their introduction, the thornless cultivars are more often seen in cultivation.*

BELOW Gleditsia triacanthos *f. inermis 'Moraine' is a tall, elegant, thornless cultivar. Fern-like leaves emerge in spring, densely covering the wide-spreading branches.*

JACARANDA

A member of the trumpet-vine (Bignoniaceae) family, this genus comprises approximately 50 species of evergreen or deciduous trees found in drier areas of central and subtropical South America. The shape and foliage vary but many species develop a broad spreading crown of ferny bipinnate leaves. Deciduous species may develop some foliage colour before leaf fall, which is usually brief. Large, brilliantly showy panicles of mauve-blue, rarely pink or white flowers appear from spring to summer, depending on the species. Conspicuous seed pods follow but are not a feature. *Jacaranda* is a Portuguese corruption of the original Brazilian Indian name.

CULTIVATION

Though most *Jacaranda* trees will tolerate some frost once established, both warm summers and mild winters are necessary to ensure that the plants flower heavily. Young trees often appear more luxuriant in light shade, and they should be sheltered from wind or staked firmly. Only light trimming is necessary. Propagate from seed in late winter or early spring or from half-hardened cuttings taken during the summer months.

Top Tip

Once established, jacarandas are generally fuss-free, although they will appreciate a regular watering routine throughout the growing season.

Favourites	Flower Colour	Blooming Season	Flower Fragrance
Jacaranda caerulea	purple, blue, white	late spring	no
Jacaranda cuspidifolia	bright blue-violet	late spring	no
Jacaranda jasminoides	dark purple	late spring	no
Jacaranda mimosifolia	mauve-blue	late spring to early summer	no
Jacaranda mimosifolia 'Variegata'	mauve-blue	late spring to early summer	no
Jacaranda mimosifolia 'White Christmas'	white	late spring to early summer	no

LEFT *Nature puts on an impressive show when the branches of* Jacaranda mimosifolia *are laden with beautiful mauve-blue blooms.*
BELOW Jacaranda caerulea, *an evergreen tree, is native to the West Indies. In late spring the attractive bell-shaped flowers appear, in shades of purple, blue or white.*
BOTTOM *With a spreading canopy, branching habit, and bright green fern-like foliage,* Jacaranda cuspidifolia *makes a fine specimen tree or shade tree.*

Plant Height	Plant Width	Hardiness Zone	Frost Tolerance
40–70 ft (12–21 m)	10 ft (3 m)	10–11	yes
15–40 ft (4.5–12 m)	30 ft (9 m)	10–11	yes
12–15 ft (3.5–4.5 m)	4–8 ft (1.2–2.4 m)	10–11	yes
25–50 ft (8–15 m)	20–35 ft (6–10 m)	10–11	yes
25–50 ft (8–15 m)	20–35 ft (6–10 m)	10–11	yes
25–50 ft (8–15 m)	20–35 ft (6–10 m)	10–11	yes

JUNIPERUS

This genus of around 60 species of evergreen coniferous shrubs and trees, widespread in the Northern Hemisphere, is a member of the cypress (Cupressaceae) family. The juvenile foliage is usually very dense, composed of short sharp needles, often with a blue-green tint, while the foliage of mature trees is usually scale-like in the typical cypress fashion. Some species produce fleshy berry-like cones, others have small scaly cones. All parts are very resinous and aromatic. The timber is used to make small objects and is an important fuel source in many remote areas. Juniper berries are edible and perhaps best known for their use in gin distillation.

CULTIVATION

Hardiness varies; all will tolerate repeated frosts but the toughest species can survive subarctic winters and may also prefer correspondingly cool summers. Plant in an open, airy, sunny situation with light but humus-rich well-drained soil. Most junipers are drought tolerant but they respond well to reliable summer moisture. Propagate the species from seed, cultivars from hardwood cuttings, layers or grafting.

ABOVE *A Himalayan native,* Juniperus recurva *var.* coxii *has a graceful weeping style. Slow growing, it can reach an ultimate height of 15 m (50 ft) in the wild.*

ABOVE *The common juniper,* Juniperus communis *is an extremely variable species. So too are its cultivars, which offer a range of shapes, foliage and colours, such as 'Pendula', with a classic weeping habit.*

Top Tip

Lightly prune junipers to maintain appearance and enhance shape. Do not prune bare wood as it is unlikely to produce any new growth.

RIGHT *Juniperus* chinensis *'Pyramidalis' is a perfect plant for borders, rockeries and containers—its pyramidal form and blue-green foliage provide interest and colour.*

Favourites	Cone Colour	Cone Shape	Cone Length	Plant Height	Plant Width	Hardiness Zone	Frost Tolerance
Juniperus chinensis	blue-green	round	¹/₄–¹/₂ in (6–12 mm)	30 ft (9 m)	15 ft (4.5 m)	4–9	yes
Juniperus communis	green to black	round	¹/₃ in (9 mm)	20 ft (6 m)	3–15 ft (0.9–4.5 m)	2–8	yes
Juniperus communis 'Depressa Aurea'	green to black	round	¹/₃ in (9 mm)	2–4 ft (0.6–1.2 m)	3 ft (0.9 m)	2–8	yes
Juniperus recurva	blue-black	round	¹/₄–¹/₂ in (6–12 mm)	30 ft (9 m)	15 ft (4.5 m)	7–9	yes
Juniperus virginiana	purple	round	¹/₄ in (6 mm)	40 ft (12 m)	12–20 ft (3.5–6 m)	2–8	yes
Juniperus virginiana 'Burkii'	purple	round	¹/₄ in (6 mm)	10 ft (3 m)	6–8 ft (1.8–2.4 m)	2–8	yes

LAGERSTROEMIA

Though commonly known as crepe myrtles, *Lagerstroemia* species are not really myrtles, but members of the loosestrife (Lythraceae) family. The 53 species of deciduous and evergreen trees in this genus are found from temperate East Asia through the tropics to northern Australia. They are renowned for their showy summer display of vivid flower panicles. The deciduous species are often also colourful in autumn, when their foliage develops rich red, orange and bronze tones. The leaves are most often simple, pointed ovals in opposite pairs and can be thick and leathery. Their dark green colour contrasts well with the attractive, peeling, mostly red-brown bark. The large species are the source of a very hard and dense timber.

CULTIVATION

The commonly cultivated crepe myrtle (*Lagerstroemia indica*) is frost hardy but needs a hot summer to flower well. Most other species are far more tender and require a subtropical to tropical climate. Plant in a warm sunny position with fertile well-drained soil. Propagate the species from seed and take half-hardened or hardwood cuttings of the cultivars.

ABOVE *The shiny green leaves of* Lagerstroemia speciosa *are arranged in opposite pairs. Throughout autumn, they delight with a spectacular display of coppery tones.*

Favourites	Flower Colour	Blooming Season	Flower Fragrance
Lagerstroemia fauriei	white	summer	no
Lagerstroemia floribunda	lavender-pink	spring to summer	no
Lagerstroemia indica	white, pink to dark red, purple	mid-summer to autumn	no
Lagerstroemia limii	lavender-pink	spring to summer	no
Lagerstroemia speciosa	white, pink, purple	summer to autumn	no
Lagerstroemia 'Tuscarora'	dark coral pink	summer	no

Top Tip

Crepe myrtles are known for being adaptable, reliable, easy-to-grow plants. To maximise their flowering potential, prune in winter or early spring.

ABOVE Lagerstroemia floribunda *is native to Myanmar, the Malay Peninsula and southern Thailand. Its glossy leaves and vibrant spring flowers add a tropical touch to the garden.* **LEFT** *Native to China and Japan,* Lagerstroemia indica *has been embraced by gardeners around the world for its rich foliage, attractive peeling bark and papery-textured flowers.* **BELOW** *Known as the pride of India or the queen crepe myrtle,* Lagerstroema speciosa *features grey-yellow peeling bark, lustrous green leaves and showy flowers.*

Plant Height	Plant Width	Hardiness Zone	Frost Tolerance
25 ft (8 m)	15–25 ft (4.5–8 m)	6–10	yes
15–40 ft (4.5–12 m)	15–25 ft (4.5–8 m)	10–12	no
20–25 ft (6–8 m)	20–25 ft (6–8 m)	7–11	yes
17–25 ft (5–8 m)	15–17 ft (4.5–5 m)	7–9	yes
25–50 ft (8–15 m)	15–30 ft (4.5–9 m)	10–12	no
25 ft (8 m)	8–25 ft (2.4–8 m)	7–11	yes

LEFT Magnolia × loebneri *is a prolifically flowering deciduous small tree or large shrub, adaptable to a wide range of soils.*
BELOW *The magnificent blooms of* Magnolia grandiflora *are large, creamy white, saucer-shaped, fragrant and appear in early summer.*

MAGNOLIA

A member of the Magnoliaeceae family, this large and varied genus consists of around 100 species of deciduous and evergreen trees as well as countless cultivars, and occurs naturally throughout Asia and North America. The leaves are usually large, oval and smooth edged. The handsome flowers are generally large, fragrant and solitary and vary in shape from almost flat and saucer-like to a narrow goblet shape. They occur in shades of white, yellow, pink or purple. The flowers are primitive, pollinated largely by beetles, and their simplicity, often seen to advantage on bare limbs before the foliage appears, contributes to their appeal. The fruit that follows the flowers is often pink or red, cone-like, in showy clusters, with colourful seeds. *Magnolia* takes its name from the French botanist Pierre Magnol.

BELOW *This developing seed pod of* Magnolia virginiana *emerges from the cream or white, lemon-scented, cup-shaped flowers. Glossy leaves are silvery beneath. This tree is from coastal swampy areas in the USA.*

CULTIVATION
Generally fast growing, magnolias prefer light shade and sheltered spots in the garden away from the wind and late frosts. Although some species are lime tolerant, most prefer well-drained acid soils that are rich in humus. Propagate from cuttings in summer, by sowing seed in autumn or by grafting in winter.

ABOVE *Magnolia stellata 'Royal Star' is a large deciduous shrub valued for its abundant clusters of double snow white flowers that appear in late winter.*

LEFT *Deep maroon to burgundy flowers fading to white at the tips of the petals are the prime reason for growing Magnolia × soulangeana 'Picture'.*

Favourites	Flower Colour	Blooming Season	Flower Fragrance	Plant Height	Plant Width	Hardiness Zone	Frost Tolerance
Magnolia 'Apollo'	deep rose to violet	early to mid-spring	yes	35 ft (10 m)	20 ft (6 m)	5–9	yes
Magnolia 'Elizabeth'	soft yellow	mid- to late spring	yes	30 ft (9 m)	20 ft (6 m)	6–9	yes
Magnolia grandiflora	white to creamy white	summer to autumn	yes	30–80 ft (9–24 m)	20–60 ft (6–18 m)	6–11	yes
Magnolia 'Iolanthe'	soft pink	early to mid-spring	yes	25 ft (8 m)	25 ft (8 m)	6–9	yes
Magnolia kobus	white	early to mid-spring	yes	15–40 ft (4.5–12 m)	20 ft (6 m)	5–9	yes
Magnolia × *loebneri*	white to pink	mid-spring	yes	20–30 ft (6–9 m)	25 ft (8 m)	5–9	yes
Magnolia × *soulangeana*	white, pink to purple-pink	late winter to mid-spring	yes	25 ft (8 m)	15 ft (4.5 m)	5–10	yes
Magnolia stellata	white, sometimes flushed pink	late winter to early spring	yes	10 ft (3 m)	10 ft (3 m)	5–9	yes
Magnolia virginiana	creamy white	summer	yes	30 ft (9 m)	20 ft (6 m)	5–10	yes
Magnolia wilsonii	white	late spring to early summer	yes	20 ft (6 m)	20 ft (6 m)	7–10	yes

Top Tip

Wind and late frosts can damage the large magnolia flowers, so a sheltered spot is best for these plants.

RIGHT *This decorative, many-petalled, white-flowered cultivar is the award-winning fragrant 'Merrill'. It is derived from* Magnolia × loebneri, *itself the result of crossing between* M. kobus *and* M. stellata.

ABOVE *Magnolia 'Elizabeth' is very popular for its fragrant primrose yellow flowers in late spring.*
RIGHT *The cultivar* Magnolia × loebneri *'Leonard Messel' is especially valued for its abundant winter deep rose-lilac buds and pink narrow-petalled flowers, which are white on the inside.*

ABOVE Magnolia *'Iolanthe'*
is an award-winning large-
flowered hybrid. Its goblet-
shaped blooms are
rose-purple outside, and the
palest of shell pinks inside.

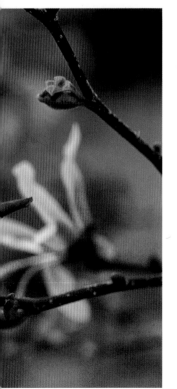

ABOVE Magnolia stellata *'Pink Star' is*
a hardy tree that produces delicately
coloured pale pink to white flowers in
spring. It is shorter than the species,
reaching just 3 m (10 ft) high.
RIGHT *The flowers of* Magnolia ×
soulangeana *appear before the foliage,*
even on young trees.

MALUS

The apples and crabapples comprise a large genus of 35 species of deciduous flowering and fruiting trees. They belong to the rose family and are widely cultivated throughout the temperate regions of the world. The leaves are soft "apple" green and are generally simple and tooth-edged. The flowers grow in clusters that vary in colour from white to deep rose pink and bold reddish purple. The cultivated apple is one of the most widely grown of all edible fruits and historical evidence shows that the Egyptians grew them as early as 1300 BC. While not all crabapples are edible—some being too bitter—the species and cultivars are greatly appreciated as ornamental trees.

CULTIVATION

Very frost hardy, *Malus* trees prefer a cool moist climate and full sun, protection from strong winds and fertile, well-drained, loamy soil. Cultivated apples need pruning in winter and regular spraying to protect against a variety of pests and diseases. Propagation is by budding in summer or grafting in winter.

Favourites	Flower Colour	Blooming Season	Flower Fragrance
Malus floribunda	pale pink	mid- to late spring	yes
Malus hupehensis	white	mid- to late spring	yes
Malus ioensis	white, pink on the outside	late spring	yes
Malus × 'Gorgeous'	rose-pink buds open white	mid-spring	yes

BELOW LEFT *One of the oldest cultivated crabapples,* Malus floribunda *is a spreading tree with dark pink buds, light pink blooms and red and yellow fruit.*

BELOW *The edible apple,* Malus × domestica *features a range of forms, flowers and fruit. 'Shakespeare', below, bears pink-flushed blooms that are paler inside.*

Plant Height	Plant Width	Hardiness Zone	Frost Tolerance
25 ft (8 m)	30 ft (9 m)	4–9	yes
15–20 ft (4.5–6 m)	25 ft (8 m)	4–10	yes
20 ft (6 m)	25 ft (8 m)	2–9	yes
10–14 ft (3–4.3 m)	14–17 ft (4.3–5 m)	7–8	yes

ABOVE *One of the most beautiful crabapples,* Malus ioensis *is native to Midwest USA, occurring in woodlands and thickets. In late spring it is covered with pale pink flowers that gradually fade to white.*

ABOVE LEFT Malus hupehensis, *a spreading tree, has deep green leaves and pink buds opening to white fragrant flowers. Fruit is green-yellow, with a red cheek.*

Top Tip

Apples and crab-apples flower in spring, and the fruit follows in clusters of 3 to 5. Some thinning may be necessary for a maximum crop.

METROSIDEROS

A mostly Southern Hemisphere genus, *Metrosideros* is centred on New Zealand and the Pacific Islands and extending north to Hawaii. It includes about 60 species of ever-green trees, shrubs and climbers, 3 of which are found in Australia. The genus does not occur in South America. All *Metrosideros* have leathery, somewhat aromatic, leaves and have the typical staminate or puff-ball flowers of their family, the Myrtaceae, which includes *Eucalyptus*, *Melaleuca* and *Callistemon* or bottle-brush. These are highly attractive to honey-eating birds. The New Zealand species are among the most spectacular and are widely planted in temperate areas in coastal and near-coastal parts where they do best. Flowers in most species are red but pink, yellow and white flowered species are known.

CULTIVATION

Grow in full sun in fertile, moisture-retentive yet free-draining soil. *Metrosideros* do well at the coast but can also be grown further inland provided they can be kept evenly moist. The New Zealand species prefer the cooler condi-tions of temperate coasts, but there are tropi-cal species including Hawaii's *M. polymorpha*. As it is an island native, it, too, likes a sea-influenced climate.

ABOVE *Found on the Kermadec Islands to the northeast of New Zealand,* Metrosideros kermadecensis *is almost identi-cal to New Zealand's famous pohutukawa except that its leaves are smaller and it flowers in flushes through the year.*

Favourites	Flower Colour	Blooming Season	Flower Fragrance	Plant Height	Plant Width	Hardiness Zone	Frost Tolerance
Metrosideros excelsa	red	late spring or summer	no	17–65 ft (5–20 m)	20–80 ft (6–24 m)	8–9	yes
Metrosideros kermadecensis 'Variegata'	red	summer	no	17–30 ft (5–9 m)	13–17 ft (4–5 m)	8–9	yes
Metrosideros robusta	red	late spring to summer	no	50–80 ft (15–24 m)	30–80 ft (9–24 m)	8–9	yes

LEFT *The magnificent pohutukawa or New Zealand Christmas tree* (Metrosideros excelsa) *occurs on dunes, sea cliffs and headlands producing its foliage-hiding, bird-attracting floral display in December. It grows slowly into a large tree.*

BELOW *The rata* (Metrosideros robusta) *is a strangling vine that eventually encases its host tree, taking its trunk for its own. In summer, the vine produces a showy display of brilliant red flowers. A spectacular plant for a big garden.*

Top Tip

Long droughts often weaken *Metrosideros* leading to attack by pests and diseases. Extended dryness kills them. In dry times, apply 2 watering cans over each 1 m² (3 ft²) beneath the foliage canopy once a fortnight.

NYSSA

Top Tip

Once the roots of *Nyssa* species have gained a foothold on their position, they are very difficult to transplant. Plant where they are to remain.

The 5 deciduous trees of this North American and South-East Asian genus are renowned for their autumn foliage colour, which develops best after a hot summer with a long warm autumn. Members of the dogwood (Cornaceae) family, they are erect, often rather open trees that in the wild tend to occur in the damp margins of streams, lakes and swamps. The simple oval leaves can become quite large on mature trees and in the right conditions will develop strong gold and orange tones before falling. Tiny inconspicuous flowers open in spring and are followed by small purple-blue fruit that is edible, though tart. While not particularly strong, the wood has an interesting grain and is occasionally used in veneers.

CULTIVATION

Plant in sun or part-shade with deep, fertile, well-drained soil that remains moist. A sheltered position will help prolong the autumn display. Trim to shape when young, otherwise leave to develop naturally. Propagate from fresh seed or half-hardened cuttings.

ABOVE *Hailing from North America,* Nyssa sylvatica—*known as the black gum—is a rather stately tree with an upright form and horizontal branches.*

LEFT Nyssa sinensis *is known as the Chinese tupelo. It has a spreading habit and in autumn the foliage develops wonderful russet and yellow tones.*

Favourites	Flower Colour	Blooming Season	Flower Fragrance	Plant Height	Plant Width	Hardiness Zone	Frost Tolerance
Nyssa sinensis	green	spring	no	40 ft (12 m)	30 ft (9 m)	7–10	yes
Nyssa sylvatica	green	spring	no	50 ft (15 m)	30 ft (9 m)	3–10	yes
Nyssa sylvatica 'Wisley Bonfire'	green	spring	no	50 ft (15 m)	30 ft (9 m)	3–10	yes

PICEA

This genus, a member of the pine (Pinaceae) family, contains about 45 species of evergreen coniferous trees, better known to most as spruces. They are found in the temperate to subarctic regions of the Northern Hemisphere, often in mountainous areas. Mainly conical in shape and superficially similar to the firs (*Abies* species), with rather broad needles, they differ most noticeably in that spruce cones are pendulous, not erect. The foliage often has a strong blue tint that in some of the best forms is an almost metallic silver-blue. Spruces are commercially important trees that are often grown in large plantations. The wood of most species is often weak but the timber is ideal for producing pulp.

CULTIVATION

Hardiness varies, though most tolerate severe frosts and prefer cool summers. Plant in sun with deep, cool, moist, humus-rich, acidic soil. They are best left untrimmed. Propagate species from seed, cultivars from cuttings or by grafting.

LEFT Picea orientalis, *the Caucasian spruce, has given rise to a number of cultivars, such as the shorter-growing 'Connecticut Turnpike' with dense, glossy green foliage.*

ABOVE *Known as the Black Hills spruce, Picea glauca 'Densata' grows to around 8 m (25 ft) high and features fine, needle-like, green to blue-green foliage.*

LEFT *The spreading branches of Picea abies 'Nidiformis' form a bowl shape at the apex—hence the common name of bird's nest spruce.*

Favourites	Cone Colour	Cone Shape	Cone Length	Plant Height	Plant Width	Hardiness Zone	Frost Tolerance
Picea abies	light brown	cylindrical	8 in (20 cm)	200 ft (60 m)	20 ft (6 m)	2–9	yes
Picea breweriana	light brown	cylindrical	4 in (10 cm)	120 ft (36 m)	15 ft (4.5 m)	2–8	yes
Picea glauca	green to light brown	narrowly cylindrical	2 in (5 cm)	80 ft (24 m)	12–20 ft (3.5–6 m)	1–8	yes
Picea omorika	purple to dark brown	spindle	3 in (8 cm)	100 ft (30 m)	20 ft (6 m)	4–8	yes
Picea orientalis	purple	cylindrical	4 in (10 cm)	100 ft (30 m)	20 ft (6 m)	3–8	yes
Picea pungens	light brown	cylindrical	5 in (12 cm)	100 ft (30 m)	20 ft (6 m)	2–8	yes

RIGHT *Initially purple, and maturing to a rich brown colour, the spindle-shaped cones of* Picea omorika *sit among the bright green needle-like foliage.*
BELOW *The long, cylindrical, light brown cones of* Picea abies *'Cranstonii' initially sit erect on the branches, then gradually hang downwards.*

RIGHT *A slow-growing form,* Picea abies *'Procumbens' has a spreading habit. The densely layered branches are clothed in bright green needle-like foliage.*

ABOVE *Clad with bright green needles, the graceful drooping branches of* Picea omorika *curve upwards at the ends, giving the tree an elegant and graceful form.*

RIGHT *The stunning silvery blue foliage of* Picea pungens *'Glauca Compacta' can be used to good effect for creating contrast when planted in conifer gardens.*

Top Tip

Though most *Picea* species are too large for suburban gardens, many dwarf cultivars have been raised that are ideal for use as rockery or container plants.

PINUS

RIGHT Pinus sylvestris, *the Scotch pine, is valuable for timber and Christmas trees. The variety here is* P. s. var. lapponica, *which has smaller leaves and cones.*

robably the best known of the large conifers, the genus *Pinus* is the type form for the pine (Pinaceae) family. It is made up of over 100 species that are widely distributed in the Northern Hemisphere, from the near-arctic to the mountains of the tropics. Their long needle-like foliage is instantly recognisable and that of the warm climate species can be particularly luxuriant. Pine bark is thick, deeply furrowed and often flakes to reveal brighter bark underneath. The cones are often an attractive feature and some yield edible seeds. Pines are extremely resinous and in addition to their commercially important timber, they are sources of turpentine, pine tar and pine oil.

ABOVE Pinus mugo *is one of the few pine species that will tolerate a shaded position. It will grow well in a container or a rock garden and its size and density can be controlled by pruning.*

CULTIVATION

Hardiness varies considerably, so choose species suitable for the climate. Many are too large or too untidy for domestic gardens, shedding needles and cones. Plant in full sun with well-drained soil that can be kept moist until the trees are well established. Trim to shape when young. Propagate the species from seed, cultivars by grafting.

Top Tip

It is usually not necessary to prune pine trees, except to remove dead or broken branches or to cut to achieve a triangular Christmas tree effect.

Favourites	Cone Colour	Cone Shape	Cone Length
Pinus densiflora	dull brown	egg-shaped	2 in (5 cm)
Pinus mugo	greyish brown	egg-shaped	1–2 in (2.5–5 cm)
Pinus nigra	light brown	egg-shaped	2–3 in (5–8 cm)
Pinus radiata	yellowish brown	egg-shaped	5 in (12 cm)
Pinus strobus	green to brown	cylindrical	4–7 in (10–18 cm)
Pinus sylvestris	grey-green	conical	2–3 in (5–8 cm)

ABOVE *Generally* Pinus strobus *is a very tall tree that may reach 50 m (165 ft). This cultivar is 'Prostrata' and has a low spreading habit.*
BELOW Pinus strobus *is more commonly known as the eastern white pine. This cultivar, 'Pendula', has weeping branches.*

Plant Height	Plant Width	Hardiness Zone	Frost Tolerance
70 ft (21 m)	20 ft (6 m)	4–9	yes
25 ft (8 m)	12 ft (3.5 m)	2–8	yes
120 ft (36 m)	25 ft (8 m)	4–9	yes
100 ft (30 m)	25 ft (8 m)	8–10	yes
165 ft (50 m)	20 ft (6 m)	3–9	yes
100 ft (30 m)	20 ft (6 m)	2–9	yes

PLUMERIA

O ne of the most popular small flowering trees in warmer, frost-free regions, the *Plumeria*, or frangipani as it is most commonly known, is mainly represented by the species *P. rubra*. Of the other 16 species only a few are ever seen and then mostly in the subtropics and tropics. Most are deciduous, succulent trees that produce clusters of often sweetly fragrant flowers during the warmer months. These, combined with their relatively low height and wide spread, make them one of the best, most attractive shade trees for suburban gardens. The milky sap of all species is toxic but as a large amount of the bitter sap must be taken to cause poisoning, the tree is not considered dangerous. It is included in the Apocynaceae.

CULTIVATION

Frangipanis love sun and heat. They cast good shade but won't grow well in it. They like regular rain during the warmer months but can take total dryness from autumn until spring. In areas where winters are rainy, plant them on a slope or mound of sandy, gravelly soil to ensure speedy drainage. Where summers are rainy and winters dry, you'll never need to water a frangipani.

Top Tip

Frangipanis grow quickly from seed harvested by splitting open the ripe, brown seed pods. Pods are rarely produced but easily seen at branch ends. Sow seed in mid-spring.

RIGHT *The common frangipani (*Plumeria rubra*) comes in a huge range of colours apart from the typical yellow-throated, white form. It is a beautiful and practical choice of shade tree for a smaller garden.*

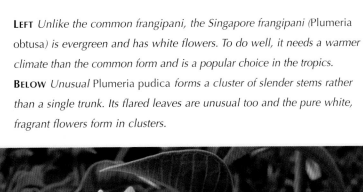

LEFT *Unlike the common frangipani, the Singapore frangipani (Plumeria* obtusa) *is evergreen and has white flowers. To do well, it needs a warmer climate than the common form and is a popular choice in the tropics.*
BELOW *Unusual* Plumeria pudica *forms a cluster of slender stems rather than a single trunk. Its flared leaves are unusual too and the pure white, fragrant flowers form in clusters.*

Favourites	Flower Colour	Blooming Season	Flower Fragrance	Plant Height	Plant Width	Hardiness Zone	Frost Tolerance
Plumeria rubra	white, pink, yellow, orange, red	spring to winter	yes	10–20 ft (3–6 m)	14–25 ft (4.3–8 m)	9–11	no
Plumeria obtusa	white	spring to winter	yes	20–25 ft (6–8 m)	20–25 ft (6–8 m)	10–11	no
Plumeria pudica	white	summer, autumn	yes	17–20 ft (5–6 m)	10–14 ft (3–4.3 m)	10–11	no

BELOW Quercus rubra *is also known as the northern red oak. Its leaves turn bright red before falling in autumn.*

BELOW Quercus robur *f. fastigiata has a more columnar habit than other forms of this species. This tree is native to Europe, West Asia and North Africa.*

QUERCUS

The broad crown of the common or English oak is instantly recognisable in any season, but it is just one of some 600 deciduous and evergreen trees that make up this genus of the beech (Fagaceae) family. While many have the characteristic lobed leaves, others have simpler, toothed foliage. In spring, sprays of tiny green or pale yellow flowers open, followed by the cupped fruit, called acorns, that are such a defining feature of the genus. Oaks have been used for so many things over the years, from providing timber for furniture and corks to supplying feed for pigs. They are clearly a most useful tree whose main task is perhaps making our world more beautiful.

CULTIVATION

Hardiness varies, with the evergreen species generally less hardy than the deciduous species. Most oaks are too large and ground robbing for small gardens but are magnificent specimen trees for large gardens, arboretums and parks. Young oaks tolerate shade and prefer deep humus-rich soil that remains moist. Propagation is most often from seed; cultivars are grafted.

Top Tip

When attempting to grow oaks from seed, place the acorn in a bucket of water. Those that sink to the bottom of the bucket are best for planting.

Favourites

	Flower Colour	Blooming Season	Flower Fragrance
Quercus glauca	brown	spring	no
Quercus phillyreoides	greenish brown	spring	no
Quercus robur	yellow-green	spring	no
Quercus rubra	yellow-green	spring	no
Quercus texana	yellow-green	spring	no
Quercus virginiana	yellowish green	spring	no

Plant Height	Plant Width	Hardiness Zone	Frost Tolerance
50 ft (15 m)	15 ft (4.5 m)	7–9	yes
15 ft (4.5 m)	40 ft (12 m)	6–10	yes
100 ft (30 m)	70 ft (21 m)	3–10	yes
100 ft (30 m)	70 ft (21 m)	3–9	yes
50–70 ft (15–21 m)	50–70 ft (15–21 m)	7–10	yes
70 ft (21 m)	35 ft (10 m)	7–11	yes

ABOVE *This acorn is the fruit of the* Quercus texana *species, which is found naturally in Texas and Oklahoma. The acorns ripen in the second year.*

TOP Quercus virginiana *is an evergreen species. It is the only American species that produces valuable timber, which is used for shipbuilding and posts.*

LEFT *Native to mountainous regions of Taiwan,* Sorbus randaiensis *produces small clusters of white to cream flowers, followed by showy tiny red fruit in autumn.*

Top Tip

Grow in a humus-rich, moderately fertile, deep soil with ample summer moisture for best results. Plant in sun or partial shade and prune to shape in autumn or winter.

SORBUS

Spread throughout the northern temperate zones, this genus in the rose (Rosaceae) family is composed of around 100 species of deciduous trees and shrubs. Most have pinnate foliage, though a few species have simple oval leaves with serrated edges. During spring they produce an abundance of flat-topped clusters (corymbs) of small white to cream flowers that can be somewhat unpleasantly scented. These flowers develop into showy clusters of fruit in colours ranging from gold, orange and red to white, pink or mauve-purple, depending on the species. In good years bright red autumn foliage tones may develop. In the past, *Sorbus* species were planted beside doors and gates, as they were thought to protect houses and ward off unwelcome visitations.

BELOW *From western China,* Sorbus sargentiana, *also called Sargent's rowan, is known for stunning autumn foliage. Red berries, loved by birds, follow the flowers.*

CULTIVATION

Mostly *Sorbus* species are very hardy and prefer a cool climate, suffering in high summer temperatures. Propagation is from stratified seed or by grafting and sometimes from hardwood cuttings. Prune as necessary after fruiting and be wary of fireblight, which can cause damage.

LEFT *The lobed leaves of* Sorbus hupehensis *turn a strong pink tone, redden then fall in autumn. Small white berries turn blush pink as they ripen.* **BELOW** Sorbus alnifolia *has serrated leaves that turn orange and red in autumn. Masses of showy white flowers are followed by red or yellow fruit.*

Favourites	Flower Colour	Blooming Season	Flower Fragrance	Plant Height	Plant Width	Hardiness Zone	Frost Tolerance
Sorbus alnifolia	white	spring	yes	50 ft (15 m)	25 ft (8 m)	6–9	yes
Sorbus americana	white	spring	yes	20–30 ft (6–9 m)	20 ft (6 m)	2–9	yes
Sorbus aria	white	spring	yes	20–40 ft (6–12 m)	25 ft (8 m)	5–9	yes
Sorbus hupehensis	white	spring	yes	30 ft (9 m)	20 ft (6 m)	6–9	yes
Sorbus randaiensis	white to cream	spring	yes	20 ft (6 m)	10 ft (3 m)	7–10	yes
Sorbus sargentiana	white	summer	yes	20–30 ft (6–9 m)	20 ft (6 m)	6–9	yes

STYRAX

A genus of around 100 species of deciduous and evergreen trees and shrubs in the storax (Styraceae) family, it occurs in the northern temperate and tropical zones. Though slow to establish, their size, seldom exceeding 8 m (25 ft) tall, makes them a good option for smaller gardens. The leaves are usually simple, dark green and have serrated edges, though some species have larger leaves with felted undersides. In spring, showy clusters of small, scented, white to pale pink flowers are borne beneath the branches. Small fleshy fruit then follows. The storax tree *(Styrax officinalis)* is a source of the fragrant resin storax, which is used in perfumery, cosmetics and sometimes in food. The hard seeds are often made into beads.

Top Tip

The fragrant bell-shaped flowers are best viewed from below, and so site selection needs some thought. A terrace planting is very effective.

ABOVE *Commonly known as the Japanese snowbell, Styrax japonicus is native to Korea as well as Japan. Short pendulous clusters of white blooms are borne from late spring to early summer.*
BELOW *The vigorous Styrax japonicus 'Fargesii' has bigger leaves than the species, and elegant scented blooms.*

CULTIVATION

Styrax prefer deep, fertile, humus-rich soil, and a sheltered position in sun or part-shade. They like regular but not overly abundant watering, and hardy deciduous types grow best in areas with cool moist summers and mild winters. Propagation is from half-hardened cuttings or seed, which may need stratification.

Favourites	Flower Colour	Blooming Season	Flower Fragrance	Plant Height	Plant Width	Hardiness Zone	Frost Tolerance
Styrax japonicus	white	spring to summer	yes	20–30 ft (6–9 m)	15 ft (4.5 m)	5–9	yes
Styrax obassia	white	spring to summer	yes	35 ft (10 m)	20 ft (6 m)	6–10	yes
Styrax officinalis	white	summer	yes	20 ft (6 m)	15 ft (4.5 m)	8–10	yes

TABEBUIA

Remarkably showy tropical trees from the Caribbean and Central and South America, a few of the 100 species are now grown in subtropical and tropical regions. Habitat of the different species varies from dry, near-barren islands to savannah and rainforest resulting in species that are either evergreen or deciduous. The *Tabebuia* favoured by gardeners are mostly deciduous, the flowers occurring on bare branches in spectacular fashion. Flowering occurs in mid-winter or early spring, the big clusters of trumpet-shaped blooms being similar in size and shape to those of other members of the family (Bignoniaceae) such as *Jacaranda*. After bloom, trees produce a crop of seed pods, which may result in unwanted seedlings.

CULTIVATION
Plant in full sun. Trees are adaptable to different soils as long as they are free draining. Where summers are usually rainy and winters dry and mild, these trees can get by on rain alone, and in many parts of the tropical world you'll see them flowering brilliantly as street trees. They are tolerant of coastal conditions and can be confined to a large pot.

ABOVE *In late winter or early spring the ipe (*Tabebuia impetiginosa*) produces masses of pink blossom on bare branches. It also flowers in flushes at other times of the year.*
RIGHT *The golden trumpet tree (*Tabebuia chrysantha*) grows as a narrowly upright tree. In early spring it produces an impressive display of golden flowers on bare branches.*

Top Tip

All *Tabebuia* are fast growing. When young, cut back branches by a third straight after bloom to encourage a dense, more rounded and less tall crown. Don't be generous with the fertiliser.

ABOVE *A good choice of a small tree, the silver trumpet tree (*Tabebuia caraiba *syn.* T. argentea*) grows to only 9 m (30 ft). Golden flowers are produced in late winter and in flushes at other times. This is a very pretty tree for a warm climate garden.*
RIGHT *Anytime from midwinter to early spring (depending on climate),* Tabebuia rosea *bursts into bloom on bare branches.*

Favourites	Flower Colour	Blooming Season	Flower Fragrance	Plant Height	Plant Width	Hardiness Zone	Frost Tolerance
Tabebuia chrysantha	golden yellow	spring	no	50–100 ft (15–30 m)	40–80 ft (12–25 m)	9–11	no
Tabebuia impetiginosa syn. **T. palmeri**	pink	winter to spring	no	30–50 ft (9–15 m)	25–45 ft (8–13.5 m)	9–11	no
Tabebuia rosea	pink	spring	no	60–85 ft (18–26 m)	45–70 ft (13.5–21 m)	9–11	no

TILIA

LEFT Tilia platyphyllos is a dome-shaped tree found in various forms from western Europe to South-West Asia. It bears clusters of pale yellow flowers in summer.

BELOW LEFT Fragrant and a valuable honey producer, Europe's linden (Tilia × europaea) grows into a large deciduous shade tree.

The linden (Tiliaceae) family is based around this genus of 45 species of North American and Eurasian deciduous trees, which are widely cultivated in parks and avenues. Lindens have deep green, heart-shaped to deltoid leaves that often have pale undersides and which often develop attractive yellow tones in autumn. In summer the trees are smothered in fragrant, small, cream flowers backed by pale bracts. To walk under flowering linden trees is to know the hum of bees, which find them irresistible. The flowers are followed by tiny, hard, round seed capsules. This genus is the source of basswood, a soft but easily worked wood that is widely used for interior linings and cheap furniture, as well as for paper pulp.

CULTIVATION

Lindens are hardy adaptable trees that tolerate most soils provided they are deep and moist. They grow best in areas with clearly defined seasons. Trim when young in order to encourage a high-branched even crown. Propagate from stratified seed, cuttings, layers or by grafting.

RIGHT The extremely popular Tilia americana 'Redmond' is one of the most attractive street or lawn trees as it has pleasantly scented flowers.

Top Tip

Tilia (linden) trees tend to become drought stressed if left without enough water for too long. Give them a deep watering once a week in areas of inadequate rainfall.

Favourites	Flower Colour	Blooming Season	Flower Fragrance	Plant Height	Plant Width	Hardiness Zone	Frost Tolerance
Tilia americana	pale yellow	summer	yes	100 ft (30 m)	40 ft (12 m)	3–9	yes
Tilia cordata	cream	summer	yes	80–100 ft (24–30 m)	40 ft (12 m)	3–9	yes
Tilia × europaea	cream	summer	yes	100 ft (30 m)	40 ft (12 m)	5–9	yes
Tilia platyphyllos	pale yellow	summer	yes	100 ft (30 m)	50 ft (15 m)	5–9	yes

ULMUS

Some 45 species of deciduous trees and shrubs make up *Ulmus*, the type genus for the elm (Ulmaceae) family. Elms occur naturally in the northern temperate zones and at higher altitudes in the subtropics where at least one rather tender semi-evergreen species can be found. Elms have heavily veined, coarsely serrated, pointed oval leaves of variable size, depending on the species. Clusters of flowers open in spring, usually before the foliage develops. These are largely insignificant but are soon followed by conspicuous, usually pale green, winged fruit (samara). Elm timber is very water-resistant and was extensively used for the keels of large wooden sailing ships.

CULTIVATION

Elms are tough, adaptable trees that succeed in most well-drained soils. Most species prefer a distinctly seasonal climate. Dutch elm disease, spread by beetle larvae, has in many areas devastated these stately trees. Cultivars are propagated by grafting, which regretfully may help to spread Dutch elm disease. The species may be raised from seed.

ABOVE *A disease-resistant tree from Japan, China and Korea,* Ulmus parvifolia *will keep its small glossy leaves almost all year in mild climates.*

RIGHT *The fruit (samara) of* Ulmus × hollandica *'Modolina' consists of a seed surrounded by a thin wing. The fruit ripens in spring as the leaves appear.*

Favourites	Flower Colour	Blooming Season	Flower Fragrance	Plant Height	Plant Width	Hardiness Zone	Frost Tolerance
Ulmus glabra	red	spring	no	100 ft (30 m)	70 ft (21 m)	5–9	yes
Ulmus glabra 'Camperdownii'	red	spring	no	25 ft (8 m)	30 ft (9 m)	5–9	yes
Ulmus × hollandica	red	spring	no	100 ft (30 m)	80 ft (24 m)	5–9	yes
Ulmus parvifolia	red	summer	no	70 ft (21 m)	30 ft (9 m)	5–10	yes
Ulmus procera	red	spring	no	70–100 ft (21–30 m)	50 ft (15 m)	4–9	yes
Ulmus 'Sapporo Autumn Gold'	red	spring	no	50 ft (15 m)	35 ft (10 m)	4–9	yes

BELOW Ulmus *'Sapporo Autumn Gold'* is a cultivar developed with resistance to Dutch elm disease. It requires pruning to achieve the classic elm vase shape.

BELOW *Commonly known as the tabletop Scotch elm, due to its horizontal spreading branches, Ulmus glabra 'Pendula' is an excellent shade tree for the garden.*

Top Tip

Elms make good outdoor bonsai subjects, but need protection from frost at temperatures below -5°C (23°F) to avoid damage to roots.

SHRUBS

With a reputation for being reliable yet somehow dull and old-fashioned, shrubs are too often seen as dense green plants that just grow alongside houses. Many of us remember the traditional clipped boxwood or privet hedges of yesteryear, which—while functional—did little to add to the beauty of the garden. Yet shrubs are a genuinely diverse group of plants, spanning many different genera from virtually all parts of the planet, and they possess a vast array of aesthetic attributes and uses in the garden. Some burst into flower, adding fragrance to the air and encouraging wildlife to the garden; others are simply striking in form.

ABOVE *The rose of Sharon* (Hibiscus syriacus) *has been cultivated in parts of Asia for many centuries. Now there are more than 200 cultivars, such as 'Blue Bird' seen here.*
LEFT *Many shrubs bear colourful flowers, and rhododendrons are among the most spectacular.* Rhododendron *'Madame van Hecke' is an evergreen Indica Azalea Hybrid.*

ADDING DIMENSION TO THE GARDEN

LEFT *Shrubs carry flowers in many different arrangements.* Buddleja davidii *'Dart's Ornamental White' has large eye-catching panicles of fragrant flowers.* **BELOW** *Camellias are popular in gardens for their ornamental qualities.* Camellia reticulata *'Change of Day' is one of the pretty Yunnan camellias.*

Defined simply as woody perennials, often with multiple stems arising from a single point, shrubs can range from less than 30 cm (12 in) to 3–4.5 m (10–15 ft) in height, and their variation in height can add a pleasing visual dimension to the garden. While the distinctions between shrubs and trees can be rather loose, shrubs rarely grow with a solitary trunk unless so pruned. Some, such as the rose of Sharon *(Hibiscus syriacus),* lead double lives, depending on how they are shaped. Likewise, some vigorous trees such as catalpa can be pruned to the ground each spring, thus stimulating some 3 m (10 ft) of lush multi-stemmed growth each summer that very much resembles a shrub in form.

Those who live in warm- and cool-temperate climates will be familiar with the hardier shrubs: forsythias, hydrangeas, lilacs (*Syringa* species), spiraeas and viburnums. Most of these bloom in spring or early summer, but many also provide a show of colour in autumn before their leaves drop. Warmer climate gardeners have a still greater range of possibilities, with evergreen shrubs such as camellias, azaleas (*Rhododendron* species), daphnes, gardenias and rock roses (*Cistus* species). Those who garden in the subtropics and tropics enjoy a still different, but often very colourful and sometimes striking palette of shrubs including tropical *Hibiscus* species.

Part of the reason for the diversity of shrub form relates to their habitat of origin. Many shrubs, such as California lilac (*Ceanothus* species), come from fire-prone regions. These plants can survive a fire and resprout from their tough bases. Yews (*Taxus* species) tolerate severe pruning because they have adapted to the damage caused by browsing animals. Still other shrubs, like rock roses (*Cistus* species) and lavender (*Lavandula* species), have very aromatic, sticky or hairy leaves that repel browsing beasts—but attract humans who enjoy the delicious scent of the volatile oil on the leaves.

The chief reason for the delivery of shrubs from their formerly unexciting reputation is the relatively recent introduction into the West of so many beautiful plants from Asia during the latter part of the twentieth century. Expeditions into China and other previously off-limits regions have expanded Western gardeners' horticultural options with a wealth of new and exciting plant discoveries.

As the options expand, we discover the many creative roles shrubs can play in our gardens. Although they make useful hedges and screens and make great backdrops for other elements in the garden, many are themselves worthy of a featured place in mixed borders and beds.

In terms of flower, fruit and leaf colour, there are shrubs of interest for virtually every season in all but the very coldest regions. Roses (*Rosa* species and hybrid cultivars) feature flowers in every colour except blue, while *Deutzia* and *Spiraea* shrubs both become smothered in white to pink flowers during the summer months. Bright red, purple or orange fruit is a feature of the winterberry *(Ilex verticillata)* and tea viburnum *(Viburnum setigerum)*. *Aucuba* species are grown for the appealing gold speckling on the leathery dark green leaves, while *Nandina* species develop fiery red foliage in winter.

Fragrance is easy to bring into the garden, with a plethora of shrubby choices: *Daphne odora*, a mid-winter bloomer, and the sweet pepper bush *(Clethra alnifolia)*, a summer-bloomer, planted near the entrance of a building or alongside a path, provide pleasure to anyone passing by. The delectably scented flowers of mock orange *(Philadelphus* species) may last for only a few weeks in summer, but there is little to match the fragrance.

A whole range of reasonably hardy shrubs flower in late winter or earliest spring, reminding us that the plant world is still active, even as we bundle up in our cold-weather boots and jackets. Winter- and early spring-blooming shrubs include winter heaths *(Erica* species), the tea camellia *(Camellia sinensis),* and witch hazels *(Hamamelis* species).

Autumn-bloomers such as silverberry *(Elaeagnus pungens)* and the pretty late-blooming *Camellia sasanqua* extend the garden enjoyment still further.

In short, shrubs are coming into their own as plants of beauty as well as mere backdrops, frames and accents. There is a shrub for virtually every imaginable garden situation, whether the soil is wet, damp or dry and rocky; acid or alkaline; and whether the position is shady or bright. The difficult part is choosing the best possible shrub from among the seemingly endless options.

ABOVE *Roses are among the most widely grown shrubs.* David Austin's English Rose, *'Sophy's Rose' adds fragrance and colour to the garden.*
RIGHT *The fragrant deep purple flower spikes of Lavandula angustifolia 'Lodden Blue' appear in early summer. This shrub makes a good low hedge.*

ABELIA

A northern temperate to subtropical genus of around 30 species of evergreen and deciduous shrubs, *Abelia* belongs to the woodbine (Caprifoliaceae) family. Most have a densely bushy habit, often with slightly arching branches and small glossy leaves tapering to a fine point. The young foliage has bronze to golden tints that in some cultivars persist to maturity. From late summer, small white to pink flowers smother the bushes. These have darker sepals that continue to provide colour after petal-fall. The deciduous species may develop attractive yellow and orange autumn foliage tones. The genus name honours Dr Clarke Abel (1780–1826), who corresponded with English botanist Sir Joseph Banks and served with the British embassy in China, where he wrote a book of naturalist observations.

CULTIVATION

Although hardiness varies considerably, most are not suitable in areas with severe winters. Plant in sun or part-shade with moist, humus-rich, well-drained soil. Trim to shape in late winter or spring; *Abelia* shrubs may be used for hedging. Propagate from half-hardened or soft-wood cuttings.

RIGHT *Award-winning* Abelia schumannii, *also known as Schumann's abelia, is a native of China. Its lightly scented flowers are borne in clusters.*

Favourites	Flower Colour	Blooming Season	Flower Fragrance
Abelia biflora	white to pale pink	summer	no
Abelia chinensis	white to pink	late summer to autumn	yes
Abelia engleriana	rose pink	summer	no
Abelia floribunda	pale rose to deep red	summer to autumn	no
Abelia × grandiflora	white to mauve-pink	summer	yes
Abelia schumannii	rosy mauve	summer to autumn	yes

Top Tip

When pruning abelias, cut back some of the older growth to ground level after flowering to maintain an open form and encourage good flower display.

Plant Height	Plant Width	Hardiness Zone	Frost Tolerance
7–10 ft (2–3 m)	3–7 ft (0.9–2 m)	7–8	yes
6 ft (1.8 m)	8 ft (2.4 m)	8–10	yes
4–6 ft (1.2–1.8 m)	4–6 ft (1.2–1.8 m)	3–9	yes
6 ft (1.8 m)	6 ft (1.8 m)	9–11	no
6 ft (1.8 m)	6 ft (1.8 m)	7–10	yes
4 ft (1.2 m)	8 ft (2.4 m)	7–10	yes

BELOW *The striking flowers of* Abelia engleriana *will be produced over a longer period if this evergreen shrub is grown in a sheltered position.*

LEFT Abelia chinensis *is a native of China, as its name implies. Very free flowering, it loses its glossy green leaves in winter.*

BELOW *Flowering profusely over the summer months,* Abelia × grandiflora *is one of the most popular abelias. It has numerous attractive cultivars.*

ABUTILON

Found in the warm temperate to subtropical regions of Central and South America, Australia and Africa, this genus in the mallow (Malvaceae) family is made up of around 150 species of perennials, shrubs and trees. They are often short-lived but grow quickly to become densely foliaged bushes with maple-like palmate leaves and very attractive, pendulous, 5-petalled, bell-shaped flowers that may be borne through most of the year. Because of their quick growth, they are sometimes used as short-term bedding plants. The flowers are edible and quite sweet, as they are nectar-rich. The flower shape is the reason for their common name of Chinese lantern.

CULTIVATION

These are most suited to areas with mild winters, because while they are tolerant of moderate frosts, the bark and thin stems will split with repeated freezing. Plant in fertile moist soil in sun or part-shade and water well until established. Trim and thin in late winter, and propagate from half-hardened cuttings.

ABOVE *The mottled leaves of* Abutilon × hybridum *'Cannington Skies', distinctive red flowers and dwarf habit make this an ideal plant for containers.*

LEFT Abutilon megapotamicum *has several forms, from an erect shrub with arching branches to an almost prostrate form. All carry the same brightly coloured flowers.*

Top Tip

The pendent bell-shaped flowers of *Abutilon* can be appreciated best when seen from below. Use in hanging baskets or train on pillars or over archways.

RIGHT Abutilon ochsenii *is a shrubby Chilean species. Weak-branched and deciduous, it has maple-like leaves, and the inside of the flowers is spotted with dark purple.*

Favourites	Flower Colour	Blooming Season	Flower Fragrance	Plant Height	Plant Width	Hardiness Zone	Frost Tolerance
Abutilon × *hybridum*	red, orange, yellow	spring to autumn	no	6–15 ft (1.8–4.5 m)	5–10 ft (1.5–3 m)	8–11	yes
Abutilon megapotamicum	red and yellow	spring to autumn	no	2–8 ft (0.6–2.4 m)	5–8 ft (1.5–2.4 m)	8–10	yes
Abutilon megapotamicum 'Variegatum'	red and yellow	spring to autumn	no	18 in (45 cm)	5 ft (1.5 m)	8–10	yes
Abutilon ochsenii	mauve	summer	no	12 ft (3.5 m)	10 ft (3 m)	8–10	yes
Abutilon × *suntense*	purple, mauve	spring to autumn	no	12–15 ft (3.5–4.5 m)	8 ft (2.4 m)	8–9	yes
Abutilon vitifolium	pink, mauve	spring to summer	no	15 ft (4.5 m)	8 ft (2.4 m)	8–9	yes

ARGYRANTHEMUM

O ften treated as perennials, the 24 or so members of this genus from the Canary Islands and Madeira are evergreen shrubs, part of the huge daisy family. Most species are low spreading, though some are erect, and have rather crowded leaves clustered at the tips of brittle stems; the leaves vary from coarsely toothed to deeply dissected, and have a slightly aromatic or bitter smell when bruised. Flowers rise above the foliage, borne on long stems. Of the numerous cultivars, the majority have double or semi-double flowerheads in shades varying from white through pink to rose-purple. In the original 'single' forms, each head consists of a ring of ray florets around an eye of tiny yellow disc florets. Flowers appear over a long season.

RIGHT Argyranthemum 'Butterfly', with its cheerful yellow and white blooms, makes a welcome sight in spring. The long-stemmed flowers are excellent for bedding or borders, and appear over a long season. They are also favourites as cut flowers.

CULTIVATION

Argyranthemum plants are marginally frost hardy and in cold climates need to be brought under shelter over winter. For permanent out-door use they prefer a temperate climate. Soil should be very well drained and not too rich, and a sunny position is essential. Propagate from tip cuttings in autumn for a spring and summer display.

ABOVE Argyranthemum gracile *is appreciated for the simplicity of its white flowerheads and golden central disc floret.*
LEFT *Recent interest in the genus has produced various new cultivars designed for garden use.* Argyranthemum 'Donnington Hero' *is one such example.*

BELOW *As its name suggests,* Argyranthemum *'Petite Pink' is a neat subshrub. Pale pink flowers with yellow disc florets appear on slender stems above grey-green leaves. This is a good container plant.*

Top Tip

Young plants can be shaped by gently pinching out growing tips; pruning lanky old plants should be done with caution as they often die if cut back hard.

Favourites

	Flower Colour	Blooming Season	Flower Fragrance	Plant Height	Plant Width	Hardiness Zone	Frost Tolerance
Argyranthemum 'Butterfly'	yellow and white	spring to autumn	no	18 in (45 cm)	24 in (60 cm)	8–11	yes
Argyranthemum 'Donnington Hero'	white	spring to summer	no	24 in (60 cm)	24 in (60 cm)	8–11	yes
Argyranthemum frutescens	white	late spring to early summer	no	27 in (70 cm)	27 in (70 cm)	8–11	yes
Argyranthemum gracile	white	late spring to early summer	no	36 in (90 cm)	24 in (60 cm)	9–11	yes
Argyranthemum maderense	pale yellow	late spring to early summer	no	36 in (90 cm)	20 in (50 cm)	9–11	yes
Argyranthemum 'Petite Pink'	pale pink	late spring to early summer	no	12 in (30 cm)	12 in (30 cm)	8–11	yes

ARTEMISIA

This genus of about 300 species of evergreen herbs and shrubs is spread throughout northern temperate regions with some also found in southern Africa and South America. It is a member of the large daisy family, but most species bear small white or yellow flowers. The beauty of these plants lies in their attractive foliage, which is well dissected and of palest grey to silver. The overall appearance is often soft and silky, and various species can be used to good effect in a border or clipped and used as a low hedge. The plants are often aromatic. Tarragon, the popular culinary herb, is a member of this genus.

CULTIVATION

These shrubs are perfect for hot dry climates as most can withstand considerable drought. They should be grown in full sun in light well-drained soil. Prune back quite hard in spring to prevent legginess and lightly clip at flowering time if the flowers are not wanted. Propagation is usually from softwood or half-hardened cuttings in summer.

Top Tip

The foliage of some *Artemisia* species is not only decorative but also quite aromatic; plant those species in the garden for a natural way to ward off leaf-eating insects.

FAR RIGHT *Commonly known as white mugwort, Artemisia lactiflora is native to China. It is tall growing and has dark green foliage. The cultivar 'Guizhou' has purple stems and creamy white flowerheads.*

ABOVE *Artemisia vulgaris was thought by ancient herbalists to have magical properties. This bushy cultivar, 'Oriental Limelight', has yellow and green leaves.*
LEFT *Artemisia 'Powis Castle' has a delightfully sprawling habit. It occurs naturally in southwestern regions of the USA.*

BELOW *The yellow-brown flowers of* Artemisia alba *'Canescens' are insignificant; the attraction of this plant lies mainly in its distinctive, fluffy, silver leaves.*

Favourites	Flower Colour	Blooming Season	Flower Fragrance	Plant Height	Plant Width	Hardiness Zone	Frost Tolerance
Artemisia alba	yellowish	late spring to early summer	no	36 in (90 cm)	36 in (90 cm)	8–10	yes
Artemisia dranunculus	creamy white to yellow	late summer	no	36 in (90 cm)	12 in (30 cm)	6–9	yes
Artemisia lactiflora	white	summer	no	4–5 ft (1.2–1.5 m)	18 in (45 cm)	5–9	yes
Artemisia ludoviciana	brownish grey	summer	no	4 ft (1.2 m)	24 in (60 cm)	4–10	yes
Artemisia 'Powis Castle'	silvery	late summer	no	24–36 in (60–90 cm)	3–6 ft (0.9–1.8 m)	6–10	yes
Artemisia vulgaris	red-brown	summer to autumn	no	4–8 ft (1.2–2.4 m)	36 in (90 cm)	4–10	yes

Top Tip

Because they prefer at least part-shade, aucubas are useful plants for under the canopy of trees. They also grow well in containers on shady balconies.

AUCUBA

A temperate East Asian genus, this has 3 or 4 species of lushly foliaged evergreen shrubs of the dogwood (Cornaceae) family. Their large, leathery, dark green leaves have coarsely toothed edges and the glossy foliage of the garden cultivars is often flecked and splashed with gold variegations. Sprays of inconspicuous purple or green flowers appear in spring and are followed by slow-ripening red or orange fruit that contain a single nut-like seed. There are separate male and female plants and both are required for fruit to develop. *Aucuba* is a corruption of the Japanese name.

CULTIVATION

Very hardy for such large-leafed evergreens, *Aucuba* adds a semi-tropical touch to the temperate garden. Plant in deep, cool, fertile, humus-enriched soil that remains moist. Plants will fruit more heavily with sun, but the foliage is better in light shade. Propagate from half-hardened summer cuttings. The seed germinates freely, but most seedlings have plain green leaves.

ABOVE *Slow-growing* Aucuba japonica *'Variegata' is the most popular of the aucubas. The gold-coloured speckling on the leaves is quite uneven in size and distribution, and can vary considerably between plants.*

ABOVE Aucuba japonica *'Gold Dust' is an excellent choice for a spot in deep shade. The strongly speckled leaves are 15 cm (6 in) long.*

Favourites	Flower Colour	Blooming Season	Flower Fragrance	Plant Height	Plant Width	Hardiness Zone	Frost Tolerance
Aucuba japonica	purple	late spring	no	6 ft (1.8 m)	6 ft (1.8 m)	7–9	yes
Aucuba japonica 'Crotonifolia'	purple	late spring	no	6 ft ft (1.8 m)	6 ft (1.8 m)	7–9	yes
Aucuba japonica 'Gold Dust'	purple	late spring	no	6 ft (1.8 m)	6 ft (1.8 m)	7–9	yes
Aucuba japonica 'Golden King'	purple	late spring	no	6 ft (1.8 m)	6 ft (1.8 m)	7–9	yes
Aucuba japonica 'Rozannie'	purple	late spring	no	3–4 ft (0.9–1.2 m)	4 ft (1.2 m)	7–9	yes
Aucuba japonica 'Variegata'	purple	late spring	no	6 ft (1.8 m)	6 ft (1.8 m)	7–9	yes

ABOVE *The yellow-spotted leaves of* Aucuba japonica *'Marmorata' will look especially striking when set against plants with darker coloured leaves.*
LEFT Aucuba japonica *'Salicifolia' (syn. 'Longifolia') is a very fruitful cultivar that copes well with shady positions. The fruit is borne throughout winter.*

BANKSIA

Banksia belongs to the protea (Proteaceae) family and is a genus of around 50 species of evergreen shrubs and trees confined to Australia. Sturdy plants, often with a stout trunk, their leaves tend to be leathery, long and coarsely toothed, though a few species have finer or more needle-like foliage. Their nectar-rich thread-like flowers are densely packed in cylindrical or globular spikes and are followed by woody long-lasting fruiting cones. Flowering time varies with the species. The name of the genus celebrates Sir Joseph Banks (1743–1820), botanist on James Cook's first expedition to Australia in 1770 and founder of the Royal Horticultural Society.

CULTIVATION

Southwestern Australia is home to the most interesting species, though these can be difficult to cultivate. The eastern species are more adaptable, though they will not withstand hard frosts. The soil should be acidic, very free draining and preferably be free of phosphorus. Plant in full sun. Propagate from seed, which often germinates better if heated or smoked. Some easy-to-cultivate species will also grow from half-hardened cuttings.

RIGHT *The complex flower spikes of* Banksia ericifolia *are made up of several hundred individual flowers. The plant is commonly known as the heath banksia.*
BELOW *The showy banksia,* Banksia speciosa, *makes a rounded dense shrub that can be used as a feature plant. The flowers are used in floral arrangements.*

Favourites	Flower Colour	Blooming Season	Flower Fragrance	Plant Height	Plant Width	Hardiness Zone	Frost Tolerance
Banksia coccinea	scarlet	winter to summer	no	25 ft (8 m)	8 ft (2.4 m)	9–10	no
Banksia ericifolia	yellow to orange-red	autumn to late winter	no	10–20 ft (3–6 m)	6–15 ft (1.8–4.5 m)	9–10	no
Banksia 'Giant Candles'	orange	autumn to winter	no	15 ft (4.5 m)	12 ft (3.5 m)	9–11	no
Banksia prionotes	orange	autumn to winter	no	15–30 ft (4.5–9 m)	10 ft (3 m)	10–11	no
Banksia serrata	cream to yellow-green	summer to winter	no	10–70 ft (3–21 m)	6–25 ft (1.8–8 m)	9–11	no
Banksia speciosa	pale green to light yellow	summer to autumn	no	10–15 ft (3–4.5 m)	10–25 ft (3–8 m)	9–10	no

Top Tip

Usually banksias do not need feeding, as their root system is very efficient, but if fertilising is required, use only slow-release products low in phosphorus.

ABOVE RIGHT *The soft, woolly, white buds of* Banksia prionotes *open from the bottom of the flowerhead into orange flowers. This ornamental shrub makes a good container plant.*
RIGHT Banksia *'Giant Candles' is grown for its extremely large flower spikes, which reach 38 cm (15 in). Low branching, it can be used as a windbreak or hedge.*

BERBERIS

Widespread in the Northern Hemisphere and also quite common in temperate South America, this group of around 450 species of deciduous and evergreen shrubs is the type genus for the barberry (Berberidaceae) family. They usually form dense thickets of thin whippy branches armed with fierce thorns. The leaves may be thin and dull or thick, glossy and leathery, and those of the evergreens often have spine-tipped lobes. Clusters of small yellow or orange flowers appear in spring and are followed by showy, variably coloured, edible berries. The common name for the genus is barberry. *Berberis* flowers yield a yellow dye and the roots contain berberine, which has antibacterial properties and is used in the treatment of dysentery.

ABOVE Berberis × stenophylla *'Corallina Compacta' is a very ornamental plant. An award-winner, its size makes it suitable for the smaller garden.*

RIGHT *Award-winning* Berberis julianae *is native to China. Very dense and spiny, with bright flower clusters, it can make a decorative and effective barrier.*

BELOW LEFT Berberis darwinii *is a vigorous and free-flowering plant, with the flowers emerging from attractive orange to red buds. It is one of the most popular species.*

CULTIVATION

Mostly very hardy and easily cultivated in sun or part-shade, these like moist well-drained soil. Trim as required; they may be used for hedging. Some species can be invasive, so ensure that barberry is not a weed in your area. Propagation is from seed or soft to half-hardened cuttings.

Favourites	Flower Colour	Blooming Season	Flower Fragrance
Berberis* × *bristolensis	yellow	late spring	no
Berberis darwinii	deep yellow, orange	late spring to early summer	no
Berberis* × *gladwynensis	yellow	spring	no
Berberis julianae	yellow-red, yellow	early spring	no
Berberis* × *stenophylla	deep yellow	late spring	no
Berberis thunbergii	pale yellow, yellow-red	mid-spring	no

Top Tip

Some species of *Berberis* have sharp-pointed spines. It is best to place these away from paths so that contact can be avoided. Wear protective gloves when pruning them.

BELOW *In winter some of the leaves of* Berberis × bristolensis *turn bright red, providing a vivid contrast with the white-bloom-covered black fruit.*

Plant Height	Plant Width	Hardiness Zone	Frost Tolerance
5 ft (1.5 m)	6 ft (1.8 m)	6–9	yes
10 ft (3 m)	10 ft (3 m)	7–10	yes
3–6 ft (0.9–1.8 m)	4 ft (1.2 m)	6–9	yes
10 ft (3 m)	10 ft (3 m)	5–9	yes
10 ft (3 m)	15 ft (4.5 m)	6–9	yes
3 ft (0.9 m)	8 ft (2.4 m)	4–9	yes

BRUGMANSIA

Belonging to the South American potato family (Solanaceae), this genus contains just 5 species of large evergreen shrubs or small trees. Extensive hybridisation, however, has produced a wide range of garden forms. The large downy leaves shield impressively long, hanging, trumpet-like flowers with flared lobes that curve delicately back towards the base of the flower. Colours range from white, cream and yellow to pink and red. *Brugmansia* species generally flower in spring and autumn and can look quite spectacular when flowering en masse. Most plants bear fragrant flowers, with their scent being more noticeable in the evening. The common name of angel's trumpet comes from the shape of the flower but belies the dangerous effect of the narcotic substances found in all parts of the plant.

CULTIVATION

Frost tender and best suited to mild climates, these plants prefer full or half sun and deep, moist, humus-rich, well-drained soil. During the summer growing season they need to be watered and fed well. Regular trimming will help keep the plant in a dense rounded shape. Propagate from half-hardened cuttings.

Top Tip

Prune brugmansias in early spring, removing old, dead or surplus stems, to encourage an abundant display of flowers throughout the blooming season.

RIGHT *The boldly coloured, trumpet-shaped flowers of the red angel's trumpet,* Brugmansia sanguinea, *make a spectacular impact in the garden.*

BELOW LEFT *In soft colours of cream, yellow or apricot, the elegant, trumpet-shaped flowers of* Brugmansia aurea *exude a sweet fragrance in the evening.*

Favourites	Flower Colour	Blooming Season	Flower Fragrance
Brugmansia aurea	cream to yellow or pale apricot	late summer	yes
Brugmansia × candida	white	summer to autumn	yes
Brugmansia 'Charles Grimaldi'	orange-yellow	autumn to spring	yes
Brugmansia 'Inca Queen'	orange-red	spring to autumn	no
Brugmansia sanguinea	orange, red, yellow or bicoloured	spring to autumn	no
Brugmansia suaveolens	white to cream	early summer to autumn	yes

ABOVE *The attractive, bell-shaped, fragrant flowers of*
Brugmansia suaveolens *are usually white, though there
are also pink and yellow forms. With regular pruning,
this species can make an attractive garden shrub.*
BELOW Brugmansia × candida *is a fast-growing species
with slender trumpets of cream to white, delicately veined
in green. The scented flowers appear in profusion from
summer to autumn and occasionally bloom at other times.*

Plant Height	Plant Width	Hardiness Zone	Frost Tolerance
12–20 ft (3.5–6 m)	10–15 ft (3–4.5 m)	10–12	no
10–20 ft (3–6 m)	6–10 ft (1.8–3 m)	10–12	no
6–12 ft (1.8–3.5 m)	5–8 ft (1.5–2.4 m)	10–12	no
12–15 ft (3.5–4.5 m)	10–12 ft (3–3.5 m)	9–11	no
12–15 ft (3.5–4.5 m)	12 ft (3.5 m)	9–11	no
12–20 ft (3.5–6 m)	8–12 ft (2.4–3.5 m)	10–12	no

BUDDLEJA

This genus consists of about 100 species of deciduous, semi-deciduous and evergreen shrubs and small trees from America, Asia and South Africa, and includes many tropical and subtropical species. The attractive leaves are large, pointed, often crepe-textured and usually grow in opposite pairs on the stem. Most species are grown for their flowers, however, and there are many decorative cultivars to choose from. Small, usually fragrant, flowers form loose branching clusters, and occur in shades of pink, mauve, reddish purple, orange and yellow. The genus can be spelt *Buddleja* or *Buddleia* and is named after the seventeenth-century English botanist Adam Buddle.

CULTIVATION

These plants are hardy, quick growing, salt tolerant, and will thrive in any soil type. They prefer full sun and good drainage. Pruning in early spring will keep the plant tidy. Propagate from half-hardened cuttings in summer.

ABOVE *The name of the South African species* Buddleja salviifolia *derives from the plant's similarity in appearance to members of the sage* (Salvia) *genus.*
BELOW *A native of Argentina and Chile,* Buddleja globosa *features tight bobble-like clusters of orange-yellow flowers.*

Top Tip

The nectar-rich flowers of *Buddleja davidii* varieties often attract feeding butterflies to the garden in summer.

ABOVE Buddleja × weyeriana *is a cross between* B. davidii *and* B. globosa. *The petals of its orange-yellow flowers can sometimes be flushed soft purple.*

Favourites	Flower Colour	Blooming Season	Flower Fragrance	Plant Height	Plant Width	Hardiness Zone	Frost Tolerance
Buddleja alternifolia	mauve-pink	late spring to early summer	yes	15 ft (4.5 m)	12 ft (3.5 m)	5–9	yes
Buddleja davidii	purple, pink, white, red	summer	yes	10–20 ft (3–6 m)	10–20 ft (3–6 m)	4–10	yes
Buddleja fallowiana	pale lavender	summer and early autumn	yes	10 ft (3 m)	10 ft (3 m)	8–9	yes
Buddleja globosa	orange-yellow	late spring and early summer	yes	10–20 ft (3–6 m)	10–20 ft (3–6 m)	7–9	yes
Buddleja salviifolia	mauve	late autumn and winter	yes	10–25 ft (3–8 m)	10–15 ft (3–4.5 m)	8–10	yes
Buddleja × weyeriana	orange-yellow	summer to autumn	yes	15 ft (4.5 m)	10 ft (3 m)	6–9	yes

LEFT Buddleja davidii *'Nanho Blue' has bluish purple flowers clustered on 15-cm (6-in) long panicles. The tiny flowers are highly aromatic, and the flower spikes may be cut and placed in a vase to add both colour and fragrance to the home.*

CALLISTEMON

Commonly known as bottlebrush, this Australian genus of about 30 species of highly ornamental evergreen shrubs and small trees includes a large range of hybrids and cultivars. They have leathery linear or lance-shaped leaves arranged spirally around the stem, and new growth is often richly coloured, usually pink or bronze. Callistemons are famed for their showy flowers, which when massed together in terminal spikes form cylindrical bottlebrush-like shapes. The flowers usually open in spring and summer, and sometimes again in autumn, and are followed by long-lasting, round, woody seed capsules crowded into a cylindrical group along the stem. The main flower colours are generally in shades of pink, red, cream or green, although many cultivars have extended this range even further. The flowers are highly attractive to small nectar-feeding birds. Callistemons offer a colourful display over long periods and will fit into most landscape situations. Many of the larger species are suitable for use as street plantings in mild climates.

Top Tip

The colourful, sun-loving and adaptable bottlebrush looks particularly attractive in a shrub border or along the wall of a house. Monthly fertilising is advised.

ABOVE RIGHT *The bright red flowers of* Callistemon polandii *are a welcome sight in a mild-climate winter garden.*

Favourites	Flower Colour	Blooming Season	Flower Fragrance	Plant Height	Plant Width	Hardiness Zone	Frost Tolerance
Callistemon citrinus	bright red to crimson	late spring to autumn	no	10 ft (3 m)	8 ft (2.4 m)	8–11	no
Callistemon citrinus 'Splendens'	carmine red	late spring to autumn	no	8 ft (2.4 m)	8 ft (2.4 m)	8–11	no
Callistemon 'Mauve Mist'	mauve-pink	summer	no	6–12 ft (1.8–3.5 m)	6–12 ft (1.8–3.5 m)	8–11	no
Callistemon polandii	red	winter and early spring	no	15 ft (4.5 m)	8 ft (2.4 m)	9–12	no
Callistemon rigidus	deep red	summer	no	4–12 in (10–30 cm)	8 in (20 cm)	9–10	no
Callistemon viridiflorus	greenish yellow	late spring and summer	no	8 ft (2.4 m)	8 ft (2.4 m)	8–10	no

CULTIVATION

Most bottlebrushes prefer moist, well-drained, slightly acid soil in a sunny position and are only marginally frost tolerant. All species respond well to pruning in the final days of flowering, which prevents the seed capsules from forming and stimulates bushier growth and a greater number of flowers next season. The lower branches of the larger species can be removed, leaving the top to branch out. Most species are propagated from the fine seed, though selected forms and cultivars are grown from half-hardened tip cuttings.

ABOVE RIGHT Callistemon *'Mauve Mist' is a dense, rounded shrub that bears mauve-pink flowers in summer.*
RIGHT *'Burgundy' is a cultivar of* Callistemon citrinus. *It has dense foliage and a profusion of wine red flowers in spikes up to 10 cm (4 in) long.*
LEFT *Native to Tasmania,* Callistemon viridiflorus *is somewhat frost tolerant. Its flowers are greenish yellow and appear in late spring and summer.*
BELOW Callistemon citrinus *provides a mass of red flower spikes in spring and occasionally in autumn. Several forms and cultivars are available.*

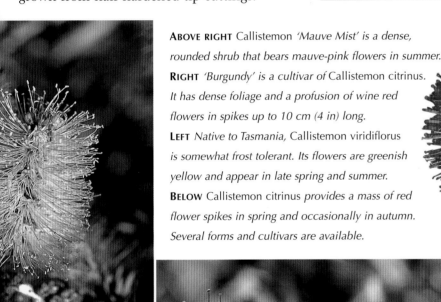

LEFT *Calluna vulgaris 'Rica' makes a broad spreading shrub that produces its pretty little pink flowers in great abundance.*
BELOW *Like most heather cultivars, Calluna vulgaris 'Robert Chapman' has foliage that changes colour over the seasons. Golden in summer, it turns red in winter.*

RIGHT *The tiny buds of* Calluna vulgaris *'Con Brio' open to crimson-red flowers. The yellow-green summer foliage will turn to bronze-red in the winter months.*

CALLUNA

Although there are hundreds of Scotch heather (or ling) cultivars, there is but one species: a small, spreading, mounding, evergreen shrub belonging to the heath (Ericaceae) family. Found in open moorlands through much of the temperate and subarctic Northern Hemisphere, wild Scotch heather has wiry stems, tiny closely overlapping leaves and produces a haze of small mauve-pink flowers from late summer. Cultivars have been developed in a wide range of sizes and foliage colours, with white, pink, mauve or purple-red flowers. Scotch heather has a long history of local medicinal use, and extracts of its flowering stems have antiseptic properties.

CULTIVATION

Scotch heather is very cold hardy but has a tendency to be short-lived in areas with hot summers. Plant in a sunny position with cool, moist, humus-rich, acidic soil. Add plenty of peat or leaf mould at planting time to give the bushes a good start. The best time to trim is after flowering or in late winter. Propagation is usually from half-hardened cuttings, though established plants often self-layer.

Favourites	Flower Colour	Blooming Season	Flower Fragrance	Plant Height	Plant Width	Hardiness Zone	Frost Tolerance
Calluna vulgaris	mauve-pink	mid-summer to late autumn	no	24 in (60 cm)	30 in (75 cm)	4–9	yes
Calluna vulgaris 'Blazeaway'	lilac	mid-summer to mid-autumn	no	12–18 in (30–45 cm)	18–24 in (45–60 cm)	4–9	yes
Calluna vulgaris 'Gold Haze'	white	mid-summer to mid-autumn	no	10–12 in (25–30 cm)	12–18 in (30–45 cm)	4–9	yes
Calluna vulgaris 'Kinlochruel'	white	mid-summer to mid-autumn	no	8–10 in (20–25 cm)	12–18 in (30–45 cm)	4–9	yes
Calluna vulgaris 'Robert Chapman'	purple	mid-summer to mid-autumn	no	8–10 in (20–25 cm)	24–30 in (60–75 cm)	4–9	yes
Calluna vulgaris 'Silver Queen'	lavender	mid-summer to mid-autumn	no	12–18 in (30–45 cm)	18–24 in (45–60 cm)	4–9	yes

Top Tip

Calluna plants must be grown in well-drained soil, as their roots are highly susceptible to disease in very damp conditions. The soil must also be lime-free.

RIGHT *The double white flowers of* Calluna vulgaris *'Alba Plena' look clean and crisp against the mid-green foliage. The plant makes a dense compact bush.*

CAMELLIA

Well-loved throughout the world for their undoubted beauty, this genus contains nearly 300 evergreen shrubs or small trees, as well as innumerable cultivars. They are native to the mountainous regions of eastern Asia, which may yet produce new species. Camellias have glossy, mid- to dark green, toothed leaves and bear short-stalked flowers that bloom during the colder months, many in mid-winter when the plants are semi-dormant. Of the many cultivars, most adopt a formal, upright, shrubby stance, though smaller, bushy, less formal cultivars are becoming increasingly popular. There are camellias for all situations, be it a formal garden or a woodland setting.

ABOVE *Glossy dark foliage provides a wonderful backdrop for the large, pure white, semi-double flowers of* Camellia japonica *'Silver Waves'.*
LEFT *Upright in habit,* Camellia *'Night Rider' bears small semi-double blooms in darkest black-red.*
BELOW Camellia japonica *'Drama Girl' bears large semi-double flowers shaded deep salmon pink to rose pink.*

CULTIVATION

Plant camellias in late autumn and winter, withholding nutrition and additional water during this time. Shaded or semi-shaded positions, acid to neutral soils, dry winters and wet summers suit the majority. A freely draining site and purpose-designed potting mixes are essential for all species. Propagate by grafting, or from cuttings in late summer to winter.

LEFT Camellia sasanqua *'Jennifer Susan'* has lovely semi-double blooms. The pale pink petals are somewhat curled, giving a soft delicate appearance to this stunning cultivar.

Favourites	Flower Colour	Blooming Season	Flower Fragrance	Plant Height	Plant Width	Hardiness Zone	Frost Tolerance
Camellia hiemalis	white or pale pink	winter and early spring	no	10 ft (3 m)	8 ft (2.4 m)	7–10	yes
Camellia hiemalis 'Chansonette'	pink-lavender	winter and early spring	no	10 ft (3 m)	8 ft (2.4 m)	8–10	yes
Camellia japonica	red	late autumn to early spring	no	15 ft (4.5 m)	8 ft (2.4 m)	7–10	yes
Camellia japonica 'Nuccio's Gem'	white	late autumn to early spring	no	15 ft (4.5 m)	8 ft (2.4 m)	7–10	yes
Camellia lutchuensis	white	winter	yes	8 ft (2.4 m)	6–12 ft (1.8–3.5 m)	8–10	no
Camellia 'Night Rider'	blackish red	mid-winter to late spring	yes	6–12 ft (1.8–3.5 m)	4–8 ft (1.2–2.4 m)	7–10	yes
Camellia nitidissima	pale gold	winter	yes	10 ft (3 m)	10 ft (3 m)	10–11	no
Camellia pitardii	pink, white	winter to early spring	no	10–20 ft (3–6 m)	8–12 ft (2.4–3.5 m)	8–10	yes
Camellia reticulata	pinkish red	mid-winter to early spring	no	12–20 ft (3.5–6 m)	10 ft (3 m)	8–10	yes
Camellia reticulata 'Captain Rawes'	carmine	mid- to late spring	no	12–20 ft (3.5–6 m)	10 ft (3 m)	8–10	yes
Camellia saluensis	white, pink, red	late winter to early spring	no	10–15 ft (3–4.5 m)	8–15 ft (2.4–4.5 m)	7–10	yes
Camellia sasanqua	pink to carmine	early autumn to early winter	yes	15 ft (4.5 m)	10 ft (3 m)	8–11	yes
Camellia sasanqua 'Shishigashira'	pinkish red	autumn to winter	no	6–10 ft (1.8–3 m)	10 ft (3 m)	8–10	yes
Camellia sinensis	white	winter	no	8–20 ft (2.4–6 m)	8 ft (2.4 m)	9–12	no
Camellia tsaii	white	winter	yes	10–20 ft (3–6 m)	15 ft (4.5 m)	10–11	no
Camellia × williamsii	white to pink	late winter to spring	no	10–15 ft (3–4.5 m)	8 ft (2.4 m)	7–10	yes
Camellia × williamsii 'Bow Bells'	rose pink	winter to spring	no	10 ft (3 m)	8 ft (2.4 m)	7–10	yes
Camellia × williamsii 'Donation'	pink	late winter to early spring	no	10–15 ft (3–4.5 m)	8 ft (2.4 m)	7–10	yes

FLOWER FORM, SIZE AND COLOUR

Due to extensive hybridisation, camellia flowers are wonderfully diverse. To make them easier to identify, gardeners have recognised a number of flower forms, sizes and petal markings. Flower forms are divided into single, semi-double, formal double and informal double—the latter categories also include peony-form and anemone-form types—and petal colours range between shades of white, pink, rose red, puce, scarlet, dark red and purple-red. On some varieties, the stamens can be pronounced or almost invisible, with their colours ranging between yellow, white and a rarely seen but spectacular bright red. As well, some bear attractively bronzed limpid new growth, while a few are sweetly scented. It is worth remembering that some cultivars bear flowers that discolour in rough weather, particularly the whites and paler shades, while a few others retain disfiguring spent blooms. For the amateur gardener, however, camellias remain a great choice for their abundance of blooms and bold foliage.

RIGHT *The rich deep pink petals of* Camellia sasanqua *'Paradise Belinda' are highlighted by the central mass of gold stamens, some of which bear tiny pink and white petaloids.*
BELOW *Superb, glossy, dark green leaves and gorgeous, shell pink, double blooms are the trademark characteristics of* Camellia sasanqua *'Jean May'.*

LEFT Camellia sasanqua 'Shishigashira' bears deep rosy pink-red semi-double flowers among lush glossy foliage. This cultivar is a particularly good ground cover or espalier plant.

ABOVE RIGHT *The often very large semi-double flowers of* Camellia reticulata *'Pink Sparkle' feature ruffled pink petals around the dull gold stamens.*

RIGHT Camellia × williamsii *'Buttons 'n' Bows' has beautiful formal double flowers in shades of pink. The inner petals are palest pink; the colour gradually deepens to a rich pink at the outermost petals.*

BELOW *Autumn-flowering* Camellia sasanqua *'Yuletide' is a lovely cultivar with single red flowers and golden yellow stamens.*

ABOVE Camellia pitardii *is a slow-growing species that can reach a height of 6 m (20 ft) and is equally useful as a bonsai specimen. Seen above is the cultivar 'Sprite', a small, pink, double form.*

Top Tip

As the sun and wind can damage camellia petals, causing unsightly brown marks, these plants do best if sited in a spot with some protection from the elements.

ABOVE *Spring-flowering* Camellia × williamsii *'Francis Hanger' is an extremely hardy cultivar with single snow white flowers and glossy crinkled leaves.*
RIGHT Camellia nitidissima *'Golden Camellia' has soft yellow petals surrounding a central mass of gold stamens.*

LEFT *The simple elegance of* Camellia lutchuensis *is seen in its single white flowers. It has a wonderful fragrance.*
BELOW Camellia japonica *'William Honey' bears attractive, medium-sized, carmine-streaked white flowers.*

ABOVE Camellia japonica *'Virginia Franco Rosea'* is a particularly striking example of the formal double camellia. Layers of overlapping pink petals are perfectly complemented by the lustrous deep green leaves.

ABOVE With its crisp, white, formal double flowers and glossy dark green leaves, Camellia japonica *'Nuccio's Gem'* is a hardy award-winning cultivar.

LEFT Camellia hiemalis *'Chansonette'*, a formal double type, has lovely pink petals, sometimes with lilac overtones.

ABOVE *Award-winning* Camellia × williamsii *'Donation' bears a profusion of pink semi-double flowers during spring. This evergreen shrub is a particularly hardy cultivar.*

ABOVE *A delicate edging of rich rose pink adorns the milky white semi-double blooms of* Camellia sasanqua *'Wahroongah'.*

LEFT *Carmine-flowered* Camellia reticulata *'Captain Rawes' is named in honour of the man who, in 1820, brought the first* C. reticulata *to England from China.*

CEANOTHUS

Native to North America, and commonly known as the Californian lilac, this genus of around 50 species of evergreen and deciduous shrubs and small trees belongs to the buckthorn (Rhamnaceae) family. Plants are characterised by deep green foliage and vivid blue flowers. Size and shape of the leaves vary, but they are usually small, with noticeable veining and shallow-toothed edges. The individual flowers are tiny but are borne in rounded heads or conical branching clusters. As well as shades of blue they may be white, cream or occasionally pink. In common with *Monarda,* the leaves of some species were used as a tea substitute during the American Revolution.

CULTIVATION

Hardiness varies, with the common western USA natives being more tender than the few eastern species in cultivation. Plant in full sun with moist, well-drained soil. They are drought tolerant but need regular watering when in flower. Propagate from cuttings, by layering or raise from seed.

Top Tip

Ceanothus plants are undemanding and are tolerant of coastal conditions. Low-growing varieties are suited to rock-garden planting or for use as a ground cover.

TOP *During the flowering season, the lustrous mid-green leaves of* Ceanothus thyrsiflorus *are highlighted with flowers in shades of blue, earning it the common name of blueblossom.*
LEFT *From mid- to late spring* Ceanothus incanus *bears lightly fragranced, fluffy, white blossoms. This thorny evergreen shrub has dull grey-green leaves with paler undersides.*

Favourites	Flower Colour	Blooming Season	Flower Fragrance	Plant Height	Plant Width	Hardiness Zone	Frost Tolerance
Ceanothus americanus	white	summer	no	24–36 in (60–90 cm)	3–5 ft (0.9–1.5 m)	4–9	yes
Ceanothus 'Dark Star'	purple-blue	late spring	yes	6 ft (1.8 m)	10 ft (3 m)	7–9	yes
Ceanothus × delileanus 'Gloire de Versailles'	pale blue	mid-summer to autumn	yes	12 ft (3.5 m)	5 ft (1.5 m)	7–9	yes
Ceanothus griseus	violet-blue	spring	no	10 ft (3 m)	10 ft (3 m)	8–10	yes
Ceanothus incanus	creamy white	spring	yes	10 ft (3 m)	12 ft (3.5 m)	8–10	yes
Ceanothus thyrsiflorus	pale to dark blue	spring to early summer	no	6–20 ft (1.8–6 m)	20 ft (6 m)	7–9	yes

LEFT *The oval leaves of* Ceanothus griseus *var.* horizontalis *'Hurricane Point' are extremely glossy, and are interspersed with clusters of pale blue blooms during spring.*

BELOW *From summer to autumn, the dark green leaves of* Ceanothus × delileanus *'Gloire de Versailles' are accompanied by delicately scented pale blue flowers.*

CHAENOMELES

This genus belonging to the Rosaceae family, and commonly known as flowering quince, has 3 species of spiny, deciduous shrubs that are native to the high-altitude woodlands of Japan and China. Some species grow into small trees up to 6 m (20 ft) tall. Their early pink, red or white flowers appear before the leaves on last year's wood and are highly valued. The leaves are alternate, serrated, oval and deep green. The flowers, usually with 5 petals, unless double, are cup-shaped and appear from late winter to late spring, singly or in small clusters. The roughly apple-shaped, rounded, green fruit turns yellow when ripe and is used in jams and preserves.

CULTIVATION

Chaenomeles species will grow in most soils, except for very alkaline types. In too rich a soil they will produce more foliage and less flowers. Generally, a well-drained moderately fertile soil, in sun or part-shade, will give best results. In colder climates, they will carry more flowers if grown against a south wall. They can also be used for hedging and as ornamental shrubs. Half-hardened cuttings can be taken in summer or autumn. Seed can be sown in autumn in containers with protection from winter frosts or in a seedbed in the open ground.

ABOVE *From early spring, lovely saucer-shaped blossoms, in shades of pink to light red, cover the dark stems of* Chaenomeles × californica.

LEFT *Select* Chaenomeles × superba *'Rowallane' for situations requiring a low-growing plant. This cultivar will add vibrant colour to the garden, producing clusters of bright red flowers.*

Favourites	Flower Colour	Blooming Season	Flower Fragrance	Plant Height	Plant Width	Hardiness Zone	Frost Tolerance
Chaenomeles × californica	pink to red	spring	no	6 ft (1.8 m)	8 ft (2.4 m)	5–10	yes
Chaenomeles cathayensis	pink-flushed white	early to mid-spring	no	8–15 ft (2.4–4.5 m)	10 ft (3 m)	5–10	yes
Chaenomeles japonica	orange-red	late winter to early spring	no	36 in (90 cm)	6 ft (1.8 m)	6–9	yes
Chaenomeles speciosa	pink to red	winter to summer	no	6–10 ft (1.8–3 m)	10–15 ft (3–4.5 m)	6–9	yes
Chaenomeles × superba	white, pink to orange-scarlet	spring	no	3–6 ft (0.9–1.8 m)	8 ft (2.4 m)	6–10	yes
Chaenomeles × superba 'Rowallane'	bright red	spring	no	36 in (90 cm)	6 ft (1.8 m)	6–10	yes

LEFT *A quirky cultivar,* Chaenomeles speciosa *'Toyo Nishiki' produces clusters of pink, red and white flowers on the same branch and sometimes in the same cluster.*

BELOW *Appearing in clusters along the bare stems of the previous year's growth, the flowers of* Chaenomeles × superba *are produced in a range of colours including red, pink and orange.*

Top Tip

Easy to grow, this adaptable genus is ideal for cutting. From early spring cut stems can be brought indoors to add long-lasting vibrant colour to the home.

CISTUS

This genus is made up of around 20 species of resinous evergreen shrubs from the Mediterranean region and nearby Atlantic islands. Commonly known as rock roses, they have simple, grey-green to bright green elliptical leaves, sometimes shallowly toothed. The foliage and young stems are often sticky to the touch and covered with fine downy hairs. Reminiscent of single roses, the flowers have 5 crepe-like petals and a central boss of golden stamens. They come in white or pink shades, sometimes with contrasting central blotches. The aromatic resin, known as gum labdanum, has a history dating back to ancient Greek and Roman times and is still used as a fragrant binding agent by perfumers.

CULTIVATION

Although they are frost tolerant, these temperate-climate plants are not suitable for harsh winter conditions. Situate in full sun with light, gritty, free-draining soil. While they are drought and heat resistant, rock roses flower better if well watered and fed. Propagate from cuttings or seed.

ABOVE *The 5-cm (2-in) wide flowers of* Cistus × pulverulentus *have bright pink to purple-pink papery petals around a centre of golden yellow stamens.*

ABOVE LEFT *With lovely flowers in pink to magenta,* Cistus × purpureus *is a resilient species, well suited to coastal conditions.*

Top Tip

Tip prune young plants to encourage thicker growth. Established plants will remain tidy if they are given a light trim and old stems are removed.

Plant Height	Plant Width	Hardiness Zone	Frost Tolerance
4 ft (1.2 m)	4 ft (1.2 m)	8–10	yes
3 ft (0.9 m)	3 ft (0.9 m)	7–9	yes
5 ft (1.5 m)	5 ft (1.5 m)	8–10	yes
24 in (60 cm)	36 in (90 cm)	8–10	yes
4 ft (1.2 m)	4 ft (1.2 m)	7–10	yes
30 in (75 cm)	36 in (90 cm)	7–9	yes

BELOW Cistus ladanifer *has crisp white-petalled flowers, often marked with a dark red basal spot, and fragrant dark green leaves.*

RIGHT Cistus aguilarii *bears large, snow white, showy flowers, with the papery petals surrounding bright gold stamens.*

CORYLOPSIS

This is a genus of 10 species of deciduous shrubs and trees in the witch hazel (Hamamelidaceae) family, naturally occurring in temperate areas from the Himalayas to Japan. They have rounded, toothed, dull, mid-green leaves that sometimes taper to a point. The autumn foliage often colours well, but the main feature of the plant is the flowers: masses of small cream to butter yellow blooms in short pendulous racemes. These appear when the plants are leafless, in winter and spring, enhancing their graceful airy effect. Insignificant woody seed capsules follow. The name *Corylopsis* refers to the resemblance between its foliage and that of the hazels *(Corylus)*.

Top Tip

As each plant completes its blooming cycle, prune it back to improve its shape and to keep it compact. Feed it at the same time with a fertiliser that is well balanced.

CULTIVATION

Mostly very hardy, they are easily grown in any moist, well-drained, slightly acidic soil. They are best planted in a position shaded from the hottest summer sunlight. Propagate from freshly ripened seed in autumn or half-hardened early summer cuttings.

ABOVE RIGHT *When in flower, Corylopsis sinensis var.* clavescens *f.* veitchiana *bears broad pale lemon flowers with red anthers.*
RIGHT Corylopsis pauciflora *is known as buttercup winter-hazel and is native to Taiwan and Japan. Its foliage is bronze in spring and matures to bright green.*

ABOVE Corylopsis spicata, *spike winter-hazel, eventually grows wider than it is tall. It needs some shelter, especially from winter winds.*

LEFT *The yellow spring flowers of* Corylopsis glabrescens *are not as showy as other species in this genus, but they have an elegant beauty. This species is reported to be the hardiest within the genus and does well in a woodland garden.*

Favourites	Flower Colour	Blooming Season	Flower Fragrance	Plant Height	Plant Width	Hardiness Zone	Frost Tolerance
Corylopsis glabrescens	light yellow	spring	yes	15 ft (4.5 m)	15 ft (4.5 m)	6–9	yes
Corylopsis pauciflora	yellow	early spring	yes	8 ft (2.4 m)	8 ft (2.4 m)	7–9	yes
Corylopsis sinensis	yellow	mid-spring to early summer	yes	15 ft (4.5 m)	15 ft (4.5 m)	6–9	yes
Corylopsis sinensis var. *clavescens* f. *veitchiana*	pale lemon	mid-spring to early summer	yes	15 ft (4.5 m)	15 ft (4.5 m)	6–9	yes
Corylopsis sinensis **'Spring Purple'**	yellow	mid-spring to early summer	yes	15 ft (4.5 m)	15 ft (4.5 m)	6–9	yes
Corylopsis spicata	bright yellow	spring	yes	6 ft (1.8 m)	10 ft (3 m)	6–9	yes

Top Tip

It is absolutely essential to keep daphnes damp. One of the easiest ways to kill these shrubs is to plant them in soil that dries out too rapidly.

BELOW *This is the fruit of* Daphne bholua. *It ripens to black. This species is known as paper daphne as paper and ropes were once made from its bark.*

DAPHNE

The principal genus of the daphne (Thymelaeaceae) family is made up of around 50 species of evergreen and deciduous shrubs found from Europe to East Asia. They are famed for the scent of their flowers, though not all are fragrant. Most species are evergreen, forming neat compact bushes with leathery lance-shaped leaves. The deciduous plants have less heavy-textured foliage. Their flowers open from mid-winter to late spring, depending on the species, and are usually pale to deep pink or lavender. Small fruit follows and may be brightly coloured. Daphnes have been used in herbal medicines and their fragrance is widely used in the cosmetics industry.

CULTIVATION

Hardiness varies with the species, though all will tolerate light frosts. Plant in moist, humus-rich, well-drained, slightly acidic soil in half-sun or dappled shade. Trim lightly to shape. Beware of yellowing associated with iron and magnesium deficiencies. Propagation is usually from cuttings or layers, though species may be raised from seed.

LEFT Daphne laureola *is a tough adaptable plant that tolerates shade. Its fragrant flowers are pale green, and blooms are seen in late winter and early spring.*

RIGHT Spring brings fragrant pink flowers to Daphne × burkwoodii. *This cultivar, 'Carol Mackie', is a variegated foliage form that is perhaps more interesting when not in flower.*

BELOW Daphne cneorum *'Ruby Glow' will grow well in a rockery or alpine trough, or even in a mixed border alongside plants such as rhododendrons.*

Favourites	Flower Colour	Blooming Season	Flower Fragrance	Plant Height	Plant Width	Hardiness Zone	Frost Tolerance
Daphne bholua	white tinged with pink	winter to spring	yes	10 ft (3 m)	4 ft (1.2 m)	7–10	yes
Daphne × burkwoodii	light pink	mid- to late spring	yes	5 ft (1.5 m)	5 ft (1.5 m)	5–9	yes
Daphne cneorum	pale to deep pink	spring	yes	8 in (20 cm)	2–7 ft (0.6–2 m)	4–9	yes
Daphne cneorum 'Eximia'	pink to crimson	spring	yes	8 in (20 cm)	2–7 ft (0.6–2 m)	4–9	yes
Daphne laureola	pale green	late winter to spring	yes	5 ft (1.5 m)	5 ft (1.5 m)	7–10	yes
Daphne × odora	pale pink	mid-winter	yes	5 ft (1.5 m)	5 ft (1.5 m)	8–10	yes

DEUTZIA

A mainly temperate Asian genus of 60 or so species, *Deutzia* belongs to the hydrangea (Hydrangeaceae) family. Only a few species are evergreen, the rest being fully deciduous and often looking particularly lifeless in winter. Come spring, however, they quickly leaf up with small lance-shaped leaves and then become a mass of blooms, completely smothering themselves in small, starry, white or pink flowers. Regretfully, despite looking as though they should be fragrant, many species are scentless. The name was originated by Peter Thunberg in honour of his patron Johann van der Deutz (1743–1788).

CULTIVATION

Mainly very hardy and easily grown in sun or part-shade in any temperate garden, they prefer moist well-drained soil. Any trimming and thinning should be done immediately after flowering to avoid lessening the next season's show. Remove the thin twigs to promote a sturdy framework of main branches. Propagate the hybrids and cultivars from half-hardened cuttings, the species from seed.

BELOW *The white star-shaped flowers of* Deutzia setchuenensis *are carried in loose clusters. This profusely flowering deciduous shrub is from China.*

RIGHT *A deciduous native of western China,* Deutzia longifolia *is very free flowering. The buds are deep pink.*

Top Tip

Strong winds can damage the thin leaves of *Deutzia* plants and strip the flowers from the branches, so it is wise to choose a sheltered position for them.

ABOVE *The pink-flushed white flowers of* Deutzia × kalmiiflora *are borne on arching branches. The leaves may turn purple in autumn, before they fall.*
RIGHT Deutzia compacta *is a deciduous species from the Himalayan region. The cascading branches bear an abundance of flowers in small heads.*

Favourites	Flower Colour	Blooming Season	Flower Fragrance	Plant Height	Plant Width	Hardiness Zone	Frost Tolerance
Deutzia compacta	white	early to mid-summer	no	6 ft (1.8 m)	7–8 ft (2–2.4 m)	6–9	yes
Deutzia × elegantissima	pink	early summer	no	5 ft (1.5 m)	5 ft (1.5 m)	5–9	yes
Deutzia × elegantissima 'Rosealind'	white and pink	early summer	no	3–5 ft (0.9–1.5 m)	5 ft (1.5 m)	5–9	yes
Deutzia × kalmiiflora	white and pink	early to mid-summer	no	5 ft (1.5 m)	5 ft (1.5 m)	6–9	yes
Deutzia longifolia	pale pink	early summer	no	7 ft (2 m)	6 ft (1.8 m)	6–9	yes
Deutzia setchuenensis	white	summer	no	5–7 ft (1.5–2 m)	6 ft (1.8 m)	6–9	yes

ELAEAGNUS

A diverse genus of up to 40 species of deciduous and evergreen shrubs and trees, this is allied to the olives but placed in a separate family, the oleasters (Elaeagnaceae). They are principally Eurasian, with one North American species, and because of their hardiness and acceptance of trimming, they are mainly used as utility plants for hedging, screens and shelters. The leaves range from near linear to broad, are silver-grey to deep green, and variegated foliage is common among the cultivars. The leaves are covered in small glands that make them sticky and sometimes aromatic. Clusters of insignificant white to cream or yellow flowers are followed by olive-like green to near-black fruit. The fruit and seeds are edible when fully ripe.

CULTIVATION

Mostly very hardy, these are easily grown in any sunny position with well-drained soil that is not excessively alkaline. Trim to shape as required but do not cut too severely. Propagate the species from seed, and cultivars from softwood or half-hardened cuttings.

LEFT Elaeagnus umbellata *is a strong-growing shrub with small bell-shaped flowers. It is commonly known as the autumn olive because that is when the olive-shaped fruit is ripe.*

Favourites	Flower Colour	Blooming Season	Flower Fragrance	Plant Height	Plant Width	Hardiness Zone	Frost Tolerance
Elaeagnus angustifolia	yellow	mid-summer	yes	25 ft (8 m)	20 ft (6 m)	2–9	yes
Elaeagnus commutata	silver and yellow	late spring to early summer	yes	15 ft (4.5 m)	8 ft (2.4 m)	2–9	yes
Elaeagnus × *ebbingei*	creamy white	autumn	yes	10 ft (3 m)	7–10 ft (2–3 m)	8–11	yes
Elaeagnus pungens	creamy white	autumn	yes	15 ft (4.5 m)	20 ft (6 m)	7–10	yes
Elaeagnus 'Quicksilver'	yellow	summer	yes	15 ft (4.5 m)	15 ft (4.5 m)	3–8	yes
Elaeagnus umbellata	yellow to white	late spring to early summer	yes	30 ft (9 m)	30 ft (9 m)	3–9	yes

LEFT *Smaller than the species,* Elaeagnus pungens *'Aurea' has variegated leaves scattered with brown scales underneath. The fruit is attractive to birds.*

RIGHT *Award-winning* Elaeagnus × ebbingei *'Gilt Edge' has strikingly variegated leaves growing to about 10 cm (4 in) long on a dense, fast-growing shrub.*

Top Tip

These fast-growing shrubs with sweet-smelling flowers are easy to care for, and are especially useful in coastal gardens, as they cope well with salt-laden winds.

RIGHT *The showy foliage of* Elaeagnus pungens *'Maculata' has made it one of this evergreen species' most popular cultivars.*

ERICA

The type genus for the heath (Ericaceae) family is made up of around 750 species of evergreen shrubs, the majority of which are native to southern Africa. A few species occur in East Africa, Madagascar and the Atlantic Islands, but the most widely cultivated species are those from Europe and the Mediterranean, because of their greater hardiness. Most species have very narrow needle-like foliage in whorls around fine whippy stems. The flowers are usually clustered at the stem tips. Southern African species tend to have tubular flowers, often in bright colours, while the Europeans have small bell-shaped flowers in muted pink and lavender tones or white. Commonly known as heath or heather, these plants have few practical uses except as fuel and as the source of a yellow dye.

CULTIVATION

Plant in full sun in moist, humus-rich, well-drained soil. Heaths have abundant surface roots, so do not cultivate but use mulch to suppress weeds. Trim lightly after flowering. Propagation is usually from small half-hardened cuttings or seed.

Top Tip

Winter-flowering heathers are lime tolerant and will grow in neutral or alkaline soil, while those that flower in summer prefer either neutral or acid soil.

LEFT Erica carnea *is a low, spreading, eastern European species. 'Pirbright Rose', seen here, grows into a dense mound covered with masses of rose pink flowers.*

LEFT *A low-growing compact shrub that spreads vigorously, Erica cinerea 'Alice Ann Davies' is one of many cultivars of this western European species.*

ABOVE *Erica lusitanica has pink buds that open to white tubular flowers. This species has naturalised in southern England, New Zealand and Australia.*

RIGHT *From South Africa's Western Cape region, Erica ventricosa bears its clusters of flowers at the branch tips. As the buds open the base swells, making an urn shape.*

Favourites	Flower Colour	Blooming Season	Flower Fragrance	Plant Height	Plant Width	Hardiness Zone	Frost Tolerance
Erica bauera	white, pink	all year	no	4 ft (1.2 m)	5 ft (1.5 m)	9–10	no
Erica carnea	purple-pink	winter to spring	no	12 in (30 cm)	22 in (55 cm)	5–9	yes
Erica cinerea	white, purple, pink	summer to early autumn	no	24 in (60 cm)	30 in (75 cm)	5–9	yes
Erica erigena	lilac-pink	winter to spring	yes	8 ft (2.4 m)	3 ft (0.9 m)	7–9	yes
Erica lusitanica	white	winter to spring	yes	5–10 ft (1.5–3 m)	3 ft (0.9 m)	8–10	yes
Erica ventricosa	pinkish red	spring	no	20 in (50 cm)	20 in (50 cm)	9–10	no

FORSYTHIA

This small genus of deciduous shrubs in the olive (Oleaceae) family is made up of just 7 species, 6 from temperate Asia and 1 from southeastern Europe, but it has given rise to many garden hybrids and cultivars. The plants develop into small thickets of upright cane-like stems with bright to deep green, toothed, lance-shaped leaves that sometimes colour well in autumn. From late winter into spring, in most cases while still leafless, they become smothered in 4-petalled golden-yellow flowers. *Forsythia suspensa,* known as lian qiao, has a 4,000-year history of primarily antibacterial use in Chinese medicine and is included in the 50 fundamental herbs.

Favourites	Flower Colour	Blooming Season	Flower Fragrance
Forsythia 'Arnold Dwarf'	yellow-green	early spring	no
Forsythia 'Happy Centennial'	yellow	early spring	no
Forsythia × *intermedia*	lemon yellow	spring	no
Forsythia Maree d'Or/'Courtasol'	yellow-gold	early spring	no
Forsythia 'New Hampshire Gold'	yellow	early spring	no
Forsythia suspensa	golden yellow	spring	no

RIGHT *The brilliant yellow flowers of* Forsythia × intermedia *'Goldzauber' appear before the leaves. This is one of the most cold-hardy forsythias.*

CULTIVATION

These hardy and adaptable shrubs thrive in any reasonably bright position with moist well-drained soil. They do, however, need a period of cold to flower well and are best grown in cool-temperate gardens. Thin out unproductive wood after flowering. Propagation is from half-hardened or hardwood cuttings, layers or seed.

RIGHT *The arching branches of* Forsythia *'New Hampshire Gold' bear masses of deep yellow flowers. The leaves of this fast-growing hybrid cultivar change colour in autumn.*

Plant Height	Plant Width	Hardiness Zone	Frost Tolerance
18–36 in (45–90 cm)	6 ft (1.8 m)	4–9	yes
12–24 in (30–60 cm)	60 in (150 cm)	3–9	yes
10–15 ft (3–4.5 m)	7–10 ft (2–3 m)	5–9	yes
30 in (75 cm)	60 in (150 cm)	4–9	yes
4–6 ft (1.2–1.8 m)	4–6 ft (1.2–1.8 m)	4–9	yes
10–12 ft (3–3.5 m)	8–10 ft (2.4–3 m)	4–9	yes

ABOVE Forsythia *Maree d'Or/'Courtasol'* is a dwarf cultivar that makes an excellent ground cover. Its yellow-gold flowers appear in profusion very early in the season.

Top Tip

Some *Forsythia* species rapidly grow into a mound the size of a small room. Check the growing information carefully before planting.

ABOVE *An erect spreading bush,* Forsythia × intermedia *'Arnold Giant' has large, nodding, rich yellow flowers and oval-shaped sharply toothed leaves.*

FREMONTODENDRON

There are 3 species of evergreen shrubs in this genus from southwestern North America and Mexico. The lobed leaves vary in shape from almost rounded to a pointed oval, while colour varies from dull to dark green. The eye-catching flowers are large, bowl-shaped and have 5 petal-like sepals, usually a bright golden colour, though one extremely rare species has copper-coloured flowers. Flowers are borne in flushes from spring onwards, sometimes appearing for many months. The genus gets its unusual common name, flannel bush, from the dense covering of fine bronze bristles on the stems, undersides of the leaves, flower buds and seed capsules. These may irritate the skin if brushed.

CULTIVATION

These shrubs require a sunny sheltered site and in cool climates they need the protection of a wall. Poor dry soils suit them best as rich soils produce an excess of foliage rather than flowers. Once established, they should not be moved. Avoid over-watering. Propagate from seed and softwood or half-hardened cuttings.

BELOW Fremontodendron decumbens *is a rare and endangered species from the Sierra Nevada range. It forms a low spreading shrub whose copper flowers last for 9 months of the year.*

LEFT *Another endangered species,* Fremontodendron mexicanum *is found in San Diego and Baja California. Its sunny yellow flowers are almost star-like in appearance. They can grow up to 8 cm (3 in) wide.*

Top Tip

A little care is needed with these plants. Rich soils can reduce the plant's life span, as can too much moisture and root disturbance. Key factors are sunshine, shelter and protection from frost.

ABOVE Fremontodendron californicum *is at home both in the wild and in cultivation, and has produced numerous cultivars such as the woody ornamental 'Margo' (seen above). All are fast growers and flower young.*

RIGHT Fremontodendron *'California Glory' is a hybrid between* F. californicum *and* F. mexicanum. *It has proved superior to either parent, being hardier, more vigorous and capable of producing a heavier crop of characteristically cheerful, large, yellow flowers.*

Favourites	Flower Colour	Blooming Season	Flower Fragrance	Plant Height	Plant Width	Hardiness Zone	Frost Tolerance
Fremontodendron 'California Glory'	yellow	late spring to mid-autumn	no	20 ft (6 m)	12 ft (3.5 m)	8–10	yes
Fremontodendron californicum	yellow	spring to summer	no	20 ft (6 m)	12 ft (3.5 m)	8–10	yes
Fremontodendron decumbens	coppery yellow	spring to autumn	no	24 in (60 cm)	10 ft (3 m)	8–10	yes
Fremontodendron 'Ken Taylor'	orange-yellow	spring to autumn	no	4–6 ft (1.2–1.8 m)	10 ft (3 m)	8–10	yes
Fremontodendron mexicanum	golden yellow	spring to mid-autumn	no	20 ft (6 m)	12 ft (3.5 m)	9–11	yes
Fremontodendron 'Pacific Sunset'	bright yellow	spring to summer	no	20 ft (6 m)	12–15 ft (3.5–4.5 m)	8–10	yes

FUCHSIA

There are about 100 species of evergreen or deciduous spreading or climbing shrubs and small to medium-sized trees in this genus, almost all of which come from South and Central America, with a few from New Zealand. They have long mid- to deep green leaves growing in whorls on stems but it is their arresting flowerheads that have attracted the interest of gardeners and have given rise to many thousands of hybrids and cultivars. The hanging flowers are mostly tubular, growing singly or in clusters along the stem and come in shades of red, white, pink and purple, as well as bicoloured. Fuchsias are ideal in hedges, hanging baskets or trained on espaliers.

CULTIVATION

Moderately frost hardy to frost tender, these plants require moist but well-drained fertile soil in sun or partial shade, and some shelter from wind. Propagate the species from seeds and cuttings. Cultivars are propagated from softwood cuttings in spring or half-hardened cuttings in late summer.

ABOVE *The hybrid* Fuchsia *'Mrs Popple' is a popular choice for its frost tolerance and brightly coloured single flowers. A vigorous grower, plant this shrub in a border.*

Favourites	Flower Colour	Blooming Season	Flower Fragrance	Plant Height	Plant Width	Hardiness Zone	Frost Tolerance
Fuchsia arborescens	rose purple	mid-autumn to spring	no	8–20 ft (2.4–6 m)	6 ft (1.8 m)	9–11	no
Fuchsia boliviana	pale pink to scarlet	all year long	no	12 ft (3.5 m)	3–4 ft (0.9–1.2 m)	10–11	no
Fuchsia denticulata	orange-red, red	summer to autumn	no	4–8 ft (1.2–2.4 m)	4 ft (1.2 m)	9–11	no
Fuchsia 'Eva Boerg'	white, pink, purple-pink	late spring to summer	no	24 in (60 cm)	3 ft (0.9 m)	9–11	no
Fuchsia magellanica	red, purple	late spring to early winter	no	10 ft (3 m)	6–10 ft (1.8–3 m)	7–10	yes
Fuchsia 'Mrs Popple'	bright red and purple	late spring to autumn	no	3 ft (0.9 m)	3 ft (0.9 m)	8–11	yes
Fuchsia 'Orange Flare'	light orange to orange-red	late spring to autumn	no	4 ft (1.2 m)	3 ft (0.9 m)	9–11	no
Fuchsia paniculata	lavender-pink	mid autumn to spring	no	12–15 ft (3.5–4.5 m)	8 ft (2.4 m)	9–11	yes
Fuchsia procumbens	orange, green, purple	summer	no	2 in (5 cm)	3–4 ft (0.9–1.2 cm)	9–10	yes
Fuchsia 'Swingtime'	red and white	late spring to autumn	no	24 in (60 cm)	18–30 in (45–75 cm)	9–11	no
Fuchsia thymifolia	white to pink	late spring to autumn	no	3–10 ft (0.9–3 m)	3–10 ft (0.9–3 m)	8–11	yes
Fuchsia triphylla	orange to coral red	summer to early autumn	no	30 in (75 cm)	2–4 ft (0.6–1.2 m)	9–11	no

RIGHT *A large erect shrub native to Central America,* Fuchsia arborescens *bears striking panicles of pinkish purple tubular flowers. The round fruit is purple and wrinkled when ripe.*
BELOW Fuchsia magellanica *var.* molinae *is a pale pink-flowered cultivated variant of* F. magellanica. *It can make an attractive hedge.*

ABOVE Fuchsia procumbens *is a prostrate, spreading, evergreen subshrub. Small heart-shaped leaves offset the upward-facing flowers, which have greenish to pale orange tubes and purple-tipped green sepals; there are no petals. This is a good plant for a rock garden.*

Top Tip

Most fuchsias are frost tender and benefit from being potted up and sheltered over winter. Hardy types can stay in the ground but need generous mulching to protect their root systems.

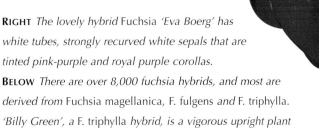

RIGHT *The lovely hybrid* Fuchsia *'Eva Boerg' has white tubes, strongly recurved white sepals that are tinted pink-purple and royal purple corollas.*
BELOW *There are over 8,000 fuchsia hybrids, and most are derived from* Fuchsia magellanica, F. fulgens *and* F. triphylla. *'Billy Green', a* F. triphylla *hybrid, is a vigorous upright plant with olive green leaves and pink flowers.*

GARDENIA

A mainly African and Asian genus, it has around 250 species of evergreen shrubs or small trees in the madder (Rubiaceae) family. They have luxuriant, often glossy, deep green leaves and fragrant white to creamy yellow flowers. Cultivated forms often have double rose-like flowers, which open from large buds with a distinctive whorl of petals. Fleshy berries then follow. The genus name was given by Linnaeus in honour of Dr Alexander Garden (1730–1791), a Scottish physician who emigrated to South Carolina and corresponded with the Swedish botanist about American plants.

CULTIVATION

Many gardenias will tolerate light frosts, but they need warm summers, in particular warm evenings, to promote flowering. Plant in sun or part-shade in fertile, moist, humus-rich, acidic soil. Water and feed well to promote lush foliage and heavy flowering. Mulch to control weeds, and avoid surface cultivation or the roots may be damaged. Propagate from half-hardened cuttings in late spring and summer, though the species may also be raised from seed.

LEFT *Native to the humid forests of South Africa,* Gardenia thunbergia *is an upright shrub or small tree that has glossy dark green leaves with wavy margins.*

Favourites	Flower Colour	Blooming Season	Flower Fragrance	Plant Height	Plant Width	Hardiness Zone	Frost Tolerance
Gardenia augusta	white, creamy white	summer to autumn	yes	4–7 ft (1.2–2 m)	3–6 ft (0.9–1.8 m)	10–11	no
Gardenia augusta **'Chuck Hayes'**	white	summer to autumn	yes	4–7 ft (1.2–2 m)	3–6 ft (0.9–1.8 m)	10–11	no
Gardenia augusta **'Florida'**	white	summer to autumn	yes	4–7 ft (1.2–2 m)	3–6 ft (0.9–1.8 m)	10–11	no
Gardenia augusta **'Kleim's Hardy'**	white	summer to autumn	yes	24–36 in (60–90 cm)	24–36 in (60–90 cm)	9–11	no
Gardenia augusta **'Radicans'**	white	summer to autumn	yes	6–12 in (15–30 cm)	24–36 in (60–90 cm)	10–11	no
Gardenia thunbergia	white, cream	mid-spring to summer	yes	8–15 ft (2.4–4.5 m)	8 ft (2.4 m)	9–11	no

Top Tip

Plant gardenias in spots frequented by people—around decking or patios, paths, windows or doors—which will allow their sweet fragrance to be best enjoyed by all.

LEFT Gardenia augusta *is a native of southeastern China and Japan with a bushy form and white, wheel-shaped, summer-borne flowers that are strongly fragrant.*

RIGHT Gardenia augusta *'Magnifica' has semi-double creamy white flowers that age to yellow. Also known as Cape jasmine, it needs a protected spot to thrive.*

LEFT Gardenia thunbergia *has fragrant, white or cream, solitary flowers with spoke-like petals at the end of a long tube. The blooms are borne in summer.*

Favourites	Flower Colour	Blooming Season	Flower Fragrance
Grevillea alpina	cream, yellow, pink, red, green	spring to autumn	no
Grevillea juncifolia	golden orange	winter to spring	no
Grevillea juniperina	red, yellow, apricot, orange	winter to spring	no
Grevillea lanigera	pink, red, orange, yellow	winter to spring	no
Grevillea 'Robyn Gordon'	pinkish red	all year long	no
Grevillea victoriae	pink, red, orange, yellow	spring to summer	no

ABOVE *Called the honeysuckle grevillea because of the volume of bird-attracting nectar in the flowers, Grevillea juncifolia grows into a biggish shrub. Best in drier, inland gardens.*

GREVILLEA

Mostly confined to Australia except for a few Melanesian natives, the 340-odd species of this genus in the protea (Proteaceae) family range from small shrubs to large trees. They are evergreen, with needle-like to narrow leaves or ferny pinnate foliage, usually in whorls around the stems. Their flowerheads, which open at varying times, are composed of many small flowers, usually in shades of yellow, orange or red, with long filamentous styles. Some have flowers in rounded heads, others are more spread out, and sometimes they are densely packed and one-sided in the manner of a toothbrush head. The genus is named after Charles Francis Greville (1749–1809), a founder of the Royal Horticultural Society and friend of botanist Sir Joseph Banks.

CULTIVATION

Plant in full sun with light, gritty, free-draining soil low in phosphates. Although drought tolerant once established, they flower more freely and the foliage is healthier for occasional deep watering. Propagation is from half-hardened cuttings; a few cultivars are grafted, and the species may be raised from seed.

Plant Height	Plant Width	Hardiness Zone	Frost Tolerance
2–7 ft (0.6–2 m)	3 ft (0.9 m)	9–11	no
20 ft (6 m)	7 ft (2 m)	8–11	no
8 ft (2.4 m)	7 ft (2 m)	8–10	yes
5 ft (1.5 m)	4 ft (1.2 m)	7–10	yes
3–6 ft (0.9–1.8 m)	5–7 ft (1.5–2 m)	9–11	yes
6 ft (1.8 m)	6 ft (1.8 m)	8–10	yes

Top Tip

Many species of *Grevillea* will encourage birds to visit a garden as the flowers are rich in nectar. The dense and prickly shrubs also give shelter and protection.

ABOVE Grevillea juniperina *flowers make an attractive show against the soft needle-like leaves once all the buds have opened. It is native to southeast Australia.*

BELOW *The fleshy leaves of* Grevillea lanigera *have a soft felting that gives them a silvery appearance in some lights. The flowers are borne in semi-erect clusters.*

ABOVE Grevillea *'Robyn Gordon' shows the bottlebrush-like type of grevillea flower. Compact in shape and very free flowering, it is one of the most popular hybrid cultivars.*

HAMAMELIS

A genus of 5 or 6 species of mainly winter-flowering deciduous shrubs, *Hamamelis* belongs to the witch hazel (Hamamelidaceae) family, and is native to temperate East Asia and eastern North America. They have an upright twiggy growth habit and during the colder months, while leafless, the branches are studded with spidery strappy-petalled flowers in cream, yellow or orange-bronze that on a still day can scent the garden with their spicy fragrance. Rounded, heavily veined, serrated leaves follow later and often develop gold and orange tones in autumn. The plants are also known as witch hazel; extracts of *Hamamelis virginiana* bark and leaves are used in herbal remedies.

CULTIVATION

Witch hazels grow best in a cool temperate climate with clearly defined seasons and should be planted in sun or light shade with moist well-drained soil. They are naturally rangy plants that cannot really be shaped. Species may be raised from stratified seed; cultivars are usually layered.

RIGHT Hamamelis × intermedia *'Pallida' is an award-winning cultivar with the mop-like flowers that are typical of the genus.*
BELOW LEFT *The 4-petalled yellow flowers with red-brown sepals of* Hamamelis mollis *are borne in clusters, giving the appearance of a much bigger flower.*

Favourites	Flower Colour	Blooming Season	Flower Fragrance	Plant Height	Plant Width	Hardiness Zone	Frost Tolerance
Hamamelis 'Brevipetala'	yellow	winter	yes	10–17 ft (3–5 m)	10–15 ft (3–4.5 m)	6–9	yes
Hamamelis × *intermedia*	cream, red, apricot	winter	yes	12 ft (3.5 m)	12 ft (3.5 m)	4–9	yes
Hamamelis × *intermedia* 'Arnold Promise'	dark yellow	winter	yes	12 ft (3.5 m)	12 ft (3.5 m)	4–9	yes
Hamamelis japonica	yellow	winter	yes	15 ft (4.5 m)	12 ft (3.5 m)	4–9	yes
Hamamelis mollis	golden yellow	autumn	yes	15 ft (4.5 m)	12 ft (3.5 m)	4–9	yes
Hamamelis virginiana	yellow	autumn	yes	12–15 ft (3.5–4.5 m)	8–12 ft (2.4–3.5 m)	7–9	yes

LEFT Hamamelis japonica *bears its small to medium flowers from mid- to late winter. They withstand quite severe weather conditions without difficulty.*
BELOW *Award-winning 'Jelena', another of the many cultivars of* Hamamelis × intermedia, *bears flowers suffused with copper red on a large spreading bush.*

Top Tip

The stunning display of autumn foliage is one of the main reasons for growing these shrubs. Shades of purple, orange, red and yellow vary with the species.

LEFT Hebe macrocarpa *var.* brevifolia *has a stiff upright habit, thick fleshy leaves and rich pink flowers. This attractive shrub adapts well to coastal conditions.*

RIGHT Hebe × andersonii *'Variegata' bears spikes of purple flowers and attractive leaves in varying shades of green, boldly edged in rich creamy white.*

BELOW *Produced in long spikes, the small tubular flowers of* Hebe *'Margret' put on an interesting show throughout the flowering season. Emerging sky blue, they gradually age to white.*

HEBE

Members of the foxglove (Scrophulariaceae) family, most of the 100 species of ever-green shrubs in this genus are native to New Zealand, with a few from Australia and South America. There are two distinct foliage types: the whipcords, which have scale-like leaves reminiscent of cypress foliage; and the broad-leafed type with fleshy elliptical leaves. The small tubular flowers, in pink, mauve and purple-red shades or white, are borne in short spikes that develop in the leaf axils. In mild areas flowers may occur year-round, reaching a peak in late spring. The genus is named after Hebe, the Greek goddess of youth, possibly for their ease of propagation.

CULTIVATION

The whipcord types are far hardier than those with large broad leaves. They also prefer to grow in full sun with a cool climate, while broad-leafed hebes will do just as well in part-shade and mild conditions, including coastal environments. Hebes are not fussy about the soil type, provided it is well-drained. Propagate from half-hardened cuttings or seed.

RIGHT *Thick, fleshy, oval leaves of dark green provide a backdrop for the rich imperial purple flowers of* Hebe macrocarpa *var.* latisepala.

Top Tip

Prune hebes after flowering to maintain shape. To achieve this it may be necessary to cut them back quite drastically, but they will respond with strong growth.

Favourites	Flower Colour	Blooming Season	Flower Fragrance	Plant Height	Plant Width	Hardiness Zone	Frost Tolerance
Hebe albicans	white	spring to summer	no	18–24 in (45–60 cm)	27 in (70 cm)	8–10	yes
Hebe × andersonii	violet	summer to autumn	no	3–7 ft (0.9–2 m)	4 ft (1.2 m)	9–11	yes
Hebe macrocarpa	white	autumn to spring	no	7 ft (2 m)	3 ft (0.9 m)	9–11	no
Hebe 'Margret'	sky blue	spring to early summer	no	16 in (40 cm)	12–24 in (30–60 cm)	8–11	yes
Hebe 'Midsummer Beauty'	lilac-purple	summer	no	6 ft (1.8 m)	4 ft (1.2 m)	8–11	yes
Hebe odora	white	spring to late summer	no	3 ft (0.9 m)	4 ft (1.2 m)	7–10	yes

HIBISCUS

This genus of over 200 annual or perennial herbs, shrubs or trees is found throughout warm-temperate, subtropical and tropical regions of the world. The species are mostly grown for their large, open, bell-shaped flowers, which grow as single flowers or in clusters. They are made up of 5 overlapping petals with a central column of fused stamens surrounded by a darker colouring in the centre of the flower. Colours include white, yellow and orange as well as dramatic pinks, purples and reds. The beautiful flowers are followed by a fruit capsule. The light to dark green simple leaves grow alternately on the stem and take the shape of an outspread hand.

ABOVE *The cultivar* Hibiscus rosa-sinensis *'Eileen McMullen' is grown for its stunning blooms of orange-red, attractively edged with yellow and featuring golden stamens.*

CULTIVATION

Most species of hibiscus are susceptible to drought and are frost tender, needing a position in full sun with a rich and moist soil. The annuals are best grown from seed, while perennial varieties of hibiscus are propagated from seed or by division.

Top Tip

Hibiscus species are usually easy to grow, but they do need a warm position, and regular watering and feeding during the growing season. To keep the plant shape, trim after flowering.

LEFT Hibiscus rosa-sinensis *'Persephone' bears its single, red-centred, pink flowers throughout summer. The glossy dark green leaves have toothed edges.*

ABOVE *Another favourite cultivar is* Hibiscus rosa-sinensis *'Jason Blue', with its bright yellow blooms and pale pink centre. It needs lots of sunshine.*

RIGHT Hibiscus syriacus *'Boule de Feu' responds well to pruning in the first 2 years of growth, and rewards this treatment with dusky pink flowers.*

Favourites	Flower Colour	Blooming Season	Flower Fragrance	Plant Height	Plant Width	Hardiness Zone	Frost Tolerance
Hibiscus brackenridgei	yellow	spring and early summer	no	10 ft (3 m)	5 ft (1.5 m)	10–12	no
Hibiscus moscheutos	white, pink, red	summer to early autumn	no	3–8 ft (0.9–2.4 m)	3 ft (0.9 m)	5–9	yes
Hibiscus mutabilis	whitish pink to deep pink	summer to autumn	no	6–15 ft (1.8–4.5 m)	5–12 ft (1.5–3.5 m)	8–12	yes
Hibiscus rosa-sinensis	red to dark red	mid-summer to early winter	no	5–15 ft (1.5–4.5 m)	4–8 ft (1.2–2.4 m)	9–12	no
Hibiscus schizopetalus	pink, red	summer to autumn	no	10–12 ft (3–3.5 m)	3–5 ft (0.9–1.5 m)	10–12	no
Hibiscus syriacus	white, pink, purple; red base	summer to autumn	no	10 ft (3 m)	6 ft (1.8 m)	5–10	yes

RIGHT *The aptly named* Hibiscus syriacus *'Red Heart' bears its white flowers over a long period in the warmer months. The leaves are coarsely toothed.*

BELOW Hibiscus mutabilis, *or cotton rose, is a large spreading shrub with attractive 5-petalled flowers that open white and age to pink or red.*

BOTTOM *Long arching branches and pendulous reddish pink flowers with an extra long stamen make* Hibiscus schizopetalus *one of the more unusual species.*

RIGHT Hibiscus rosa-sinensis *'Rosalind' bears semi-double flowers with ruffled petals in the most dazzling shades of orange and yellow. The vibrant colouring of this cultivar adds a tropical atmosphere to the garden.*

LEFT *The rich ruby red blooms of* Hibiscus moscheutos *'Lord Baltimore' make a striking contrast with the large mid-green leaves. Grow this plant in a sheltered spot.* **BELOW** *The pale pink, almost white, double flowers of* Hibiscus mutabilis *'Plena' account for the popularity of this freely branching large shrub.*

HYDRANGEA

There are about 100 species of deciduous and evergreen shrubs, trees and climbers in this genus. They are native to eastern Asia and North and South America, where they grow in moist woodland areas. Though famed for their profusion of cheerful blooms, the foliage, with large oval leaves, often with serrated edges, makes a pleasant backdrop. Flowerheads are made up of very small fertile flowers surrounded by larger, eye-catching, 4-petalled, sterile florets. They may be conical, flat-topped (lacecap) or rounded (mophead), and usually emerge in spring and summer. Colours range from white through to red, purple and blue and, in *Hydrangea macrophylla*, these can vary depending on the soil—acid soils produce blue flowers and alkaline soils produce reds and pinks.

CULTIVATION

This is an adaptable genus suitable for a range of situations. Position in sun or dappled shade with good composted soil, and feed lightly. Propagate from seed or tip cuttings in spring, or hardwood cuttings in winter.

ABOVE *Hydrangea arborescens* subsp. radiata *produces an interesting creamy white flowerhead, where the majority of the flowers in the cluster are sterile.*

Favourites	Flower Colour	Blooming Season	Flower Fragrance	Plant Height	Plant Width	Hardiness Zone	Frost Tolerance
Hydrangea arborescens	creamy white	late spring and summer	no	8 ft (2.4 m)	8 ft (2.4 m)	6–9	yes
Hydrangea involucrata	white and mauve	late summer	no	18–36 in (45–90 cm)	3–6 ft (0.9–1.8 m)	7–10	yes
Hydrangea macrophylla	pink and blue	summer	no	3–6 ft (0.9–1.8 m)	8 ft (2.4 m)	6–10	yes
Hydrangea paniculata	creamy white to pinkish white	late summer to early autumn	no	10–20 ft (3–6 m)	8 ft (2.4 m)	5–10	yes
Hydrangea quercifolia	white fading to pink	mid-summer to mid-autumn	no	4–8 ft (1.2–2.4 m)	8 ft (2.4 m)	5–10	yes
Hydrangea serrata	white, pink, blue	summer to autumn	no	4 ft (1.2 m)	4 ft (1.2 m)	6–10	yes

RIGHT Hydrangea macrophylla 'Parzifal' is one of the many mophead hydrangeas in cultivation. Easily grown, it does best in an alkaline soil.
BELOW Blue hydrangeas, such as Hydrangea macrophylla 'Blue Sky', need an acid soil to produce their richly coloured flowerheads. Application of an acidic fertiliser can also help.

ABOVE *A classic lacecap variety,* Hydrangea macrophylla *'Buchfink' has a central circle of tiny fertile flowers surrounded by crimson sterile florets.*
RIGHT *The pale pink, almost white, flowers of* Hydrangea involucrata *'Hortensis' appear in late summer, ringed by dark green leaves.*

Top Tip

Hydrangeas are equally at home in borders, in group plantings or in containers, but they do need some protection from cold winds.

BELOW *Hydrangea quercifolia 'Snow Queen' has larger sterile florets than the species, and boasts exceptional autumn foliage colour. The white flowers eventually develop pinkish tones.*

ABOVE Hydrangea macrophylla *'Hatfield Rose' is a popular choice in gardens because of its delicate lilac-pink flowerheads and its neat rounded shape.*

RIGHT *A large, vigorous, upright shrub,* Hydrangea paniculata *produces small, cream, fertile flowers and large, pinkish white, sterile florets that usually darken as they age. Prune the stems in late winter or early spring.*

RIGHT *With unusual, cup-shaped, pale lilac flowers, Hydrangea macrophylla 'Ayesha' is valued both in garden settings and as a potted indoor specimen.*
BELOW *Hydrangea arborescens 'Annabelle' bears rounded heads of small, mostly sterile, white flowers. The dark green leaves are equally attractive.*

ABOVE *Small, mauve-purple, fertile flowers with pinked edges, and white sterile florets turning pink as they age are produced in broad heads on* Hydrangea serrata *'Grayswood'.*
RIGHT *Coming into bloom a little later than most other hydrangeas,* Hydrangea paniculata *'Tardiva' is valued for its elegant spikes of white flowers and large dark green leaves.*
FAR RIGHT *Hydrangea macrophylla 'Mariesii Perfecta' shows off its gorgeous, purple, sterile florets and central, yellow and purple, fertile flowers during summer. Remove dead flowerheads.*

BELOW *A distinctive garden variety, crimson-flowered* Hydrangea macrophylla *'Konigin Wilhelmina' gets its beautiful colour from the alkaline soil.*

HYPERICUM

This genus, composed of more than 400 species of evergreen and deciduous annuals, perennials, shrubs and trees, belongs to the St John's wort (Clusiaceae) family and has a near-world-wide distribution. The shrubby species often develop into a congested mass of fine twigs and arching branches, usually with opposite pairs of simple dull green leaves. The flowers are very similar throughout the genus. Except for a few pale pink-flowered forms, all have 5-petalled bright yellow flowers with a prominent central cluster of stamens. Other than the widely used perennial St John's wort *(Hypericum perforatum)*, several species have local medicinal uses and many yield a golden-orange dye.

CULTIVATION

Hypericum species are hardy and are easily grown in any free-draining soil in sun or shade. Evergreen species are best sheltered from drying winds. Some species produce runners that can become a nuisance. Propagation is mainly from softwood or half-hardened cuttings.

RIGHT *In dry shade,* Hypericum calycinum *makes a good ground-cover plant. It takes root along its prostrate branches and is a useful plant for stabilising steep ground.*

Top Tip

Most *Hypericum* species are suited to shrub borders, and make useful container plants. To prevent growth becoming too congested, trim and thin as necessary.

ABOVE *Hypericum 'Hidcote' is an evergreen or semi-evergreen shrub. The dark green foliage is a perfect foil for the large, 5-petalled, cup-shaped, yellow flowers.*

ABOVE *A cluster of filamentous stamens protrudes from the centre of the starry bright yellow flowers of* Hypericum androsaemum *'Dart's Golden Penny'. Red and black fruit follows the flowers.* **LEFT** Hypericum olympicum *makes an excellent rock-garden plant, but to perform well it needs sharply drained soil. It will reward with a summer display of starry golden yellow flowers.*

Favourites	Flower Colour	Blooming Season	Flower Fragrance	Plant Height	Plant Width	Hardiness Zone	Frost Tolerance
Hypericum androsaemum	yellow	mid-summer to autumn	no	36 in (90 cm)	30 in (75 cm)	6–9	yes
Hypericum calycinum	bright yellow	mid-summer to autumn	no	8–24 in (20–60 cm)	60 in (150 cm)	6–9	yes
Hypericum frondosum	golden yellow	summer to autumn	no	2–4 ft (0.6–1.2 m)	2–4 ft (0.6–1.2 m)	5–10	yes
Hypericum 'Hidcote'	deep yellow	summer to autumn	no	4 ft (1.2 m)	4 ft (1.2 m)	7–10	yes
Hypericum olympicum	golden yellow	summer	no	15 in (38 cm)	10 in (25 cm)	6–10	yes
Hypericum 'Rowallane'	golden yellow	late summer to autumn	no	4 ft (1.2 m)	5 ft (1.5 m)	8–10	yes

IXORA

Considering we only ever see 2 or 3 types it comes as a surprise to learn there are more than 400 species of *Ixora* in the madder family (Rubiaceae). All are evergreen shrubs or trees that are found from tropical Africa through India and South-East Asia to the Pacific Islands. Six are native to Australia but they're not exciting enough to interest gardeners. The most popular ones in Australia are bushy, evergreen shrubs that have both regular and dwarf forms. The regular types can reach 4 m (15 ft) in the tropics though in cooler areas, a metre or so (3–5 ft) is about their maximum size. Flowers come in orange, pink, scarlet or yellow shades and are produced through spring, summer and autumn.

CULTIVATION

Full sun or at least plenty of sun gives the best flowering display but these will grow and bloom reasonably well in bright shade with some sun. *Ixora* are not very dryness tolerant and do best in better quality, moisture-retentive soils that drain well. The dwarf forms have smaller leaves and can be grown as a hedge but if so, will need frequent pruning to keep their shape.

RIGHT Ixora chinensis *is popular as a hedge in tropical and subtropical climates. Bright orange-red flowers are produced in rounded heads at branch tips.*

Top Tip

Pinch out the growing tips of all stems on young plants in order to develop a dense, bushy habit from an early stage. Larger plants can be cut back or sheared all over.

LEFT Ixora chinensis 'Prince of Orange' sports globular clusters of scarlet blossom all summer. It's virtually ever-blooming in warm climates.

RIGHT 'Super King' grows into a dense, rounded shrub liberally dotted with orange-scarlet flowerheads from mid-spring until autumn at least. It takes sun or part shade.

Favourites	Flower Colour	Blooming Season	Flower Fragrance	Plant Height	Plant Width	Hardiness Zone	Frost Tolerance
Ixora 'Prince of Orange'	orange	spring to autumn	no	6–12 ft (1.8–3.5 m)	4–10 ft (1.2–3 m)	9–11	no
Ixora 'Super King'	scarlet	spring to autumn	no	6–12 ft (1.8–3.5 m)	4–10 ft (1.2–3 m)	9–11	no
Ixora chinensis	orange, yellow, white, pink	spring to autumn	no	4–10 ft (1.2–3 m)	3–8 ft (0.9–2.4 m)	9–11	no

KALMIA

BELOW *The attractive, fluted, crimson buds of* Kalmia latifolia *'Pink Charm' open to reveal flowers of rich pink, often with darker markings on the interior.*

Found mainly in northeastern USA, this genus contains 7 species of evergreen shrubs, some of which are among the most frost-hardy broad-leafed evergreens. They form neat rounded bushes with lance-shaped leaves. In spring they produce small white, pink or red flowers that open from buds resembling cake decoration rosebuds. Hard seed capsules follow. *Kalmia* is named for Pehr Kalm (1716–1779), an early student of Linnaeus who spent a number of years in North America studying the native flora.

CULTIVATION

As with most heath (Ericaceae) family plants, *Kalmia* resents lime and prefers to grow in moist, humus-rich, well-drained, slightly acid soil. A lightly shaded position is best, or at least one protected from the hottest sun. If necessary, trim lightly after flowering. Because cuttings are slow to strike and seedlings slow to develop, layering is the easiest propagation method.

BELOW Kalmia latifolia *'Myrtifolia' is a dwarf cultivar. In spring, the attractive dark green leaves are accompanied by abundant flowers of palest pink.*

Favourites	Flower Colour	Blooming Season	Flower Fragrance
Kalmia angustifolia	reddish pink	early to mid-summer	no
Kalmia latifolia	pale to dark pink	late spring to summer	no
Kalmia latifolia 'Olympic Fire'	pink	late spring	no
Kalmia latifolia 'Ostbo Red'	pink	late spring	no
Kalmia 'Pink Charm'	deep pink	late spring	no
Kalmia polifolia	pinkish purple	spring	no

Top Tip

Most *Kalmia* species are relatively undemanding. However, they do not tolerate heat well, and during dry periods they should receive ample water.

LEFT *In spring, the beautifully crafted red buds of Kalmia latifolia 'Ostbo Red' open to reveal dainty pink flowers. The flower colour intensifies with age.*
BELOW *Kalmia latifolia 'Minuet' is a dwarf cultivar. It features pink buds that open to white flowers distinctively marked with bands of maroon within.*

Plant Height	Plant Width	Hardiness Zone	Frost Tolerance
3 ft (0.9 m)	4–5 ft (1.2–1.5 m)	2–9	yes
5–10 ft (1.5–3 m)	6–10 ft (1.8–3 m)	3–9	yes
5–8 ft (1.5–2.4 m)	6 ft (1.8 m)	3–9	yes
6 ft (1.8 m)	6 ft (1.8 m)	3–9	yes
5–8 ft (1.5–2.4 m)	6 ft (1.8 m)	3–9	yes
2 ft (0.6 m)	3 ft (0.9 m)	3–9	yes

LAVANDULA

The 28 species of evergreen aromatic shrubs that belong to this genus are distributed from northern Africa and the Mediterranean to western Asia, India and the Canary and Cape Verde Islands. Although their natural habitat is dry, sunny and exposed rocky areas, lavender plants are at home in the garden, and their distinctive spikes of fragrant purple flowers and grey-green foliage can provide colour for much of the year. Cultivated species belong to 3 groups: the hardy Spica (English lavender) Group, which produces the best oil; the slightly tender Stoechas Group, with fatter flower spikes topped by petal-like bracts and the tender Pterostoechas Group, with flowers that lack the true lavender fragrance. *Lavandula* is part of the large mint family, which includes herbs such as sage and rosemary.

CULTIVATION

Lavender plants are excellent for containers, hedges and positions where they can be brushed against to release their aroma. They grow in a wide range of soils that must be well-drained, particularly in winter. Hardy species should be pruned after flowering. Lavenders are usually propagated from tip cuttings in spring or half-hardened cuttings in autumn.

Favourites	Flower Colour	Blooming Season	Flower Fragrance	Plant Height	Plant Width	Hardiness Zone	Frost Tolerance
Lavandula angustifolia	purple	summer to early autumn	yes	3 ft (0.9 m)	30 in (75 cm)	6–10	yes
Lavandula dentata	mauve-blue	spring to summer	yes	3–4 ft (0.9–1.2 m)	5 ft (1.5 m)	8–10	yes
Lavandula ×intermedia	purple	summer	yes	3 ft (0.9 m)	12–20 in (30–50 cm)	6–10	yes
Lavandula lanata	purple	mid- to late summer	yes	30 in (75 cm)	36 in (90 cm)	8–9	yes
Lavandula 'Sawyers'	purple	summer	yes	18 in (45 m)	30 in (75 cm)	6–10	yes
Lavandula stoechas	purple	summer to early autumn	yes	18–30 in (45–75 cm)	18–30 in (45–75 cm)	7–10	yes

LEFT Lavandula angustifolia 'Folgate' is an evergreen cultivar with a broad habit. It has violet flowers that are strongly scented, and grey-green foliage.

BELOW CENTRE *The scented* Lavandula stoechas 'Kew Red' *makes a perfect small hedge or container plant. Its deep pink-purple flowers are topped with pale pink bracts.*

BELOW Lavandula angustifolia 'Royal Purple' *is admired for its elegantly shaped flowers, which are bright violet-blue fading to dark lavender-blue.*

ABOVE *A low-growing shrub,* Lavandula 'Sawyers' *has silvery leaves and bears purple flowers on tall slender stems. This is an attractive summer flowerer.*

Top Tip

Not only is the aroma of lavender known to relieve stress and nausea, it is also a natural insect repellant. Use the fragrant flower buds in place of mothballs.

RIGHT *A popular perennial, Lavandula angustifolia 'Lodden Blue' is an excellent ornamental lavender. It is also common in potpourri.* **BELOW** *Lavandula stoechas is a variable species that is lower growing than many others. It bears many plump flowering spikes of deep purple topped by eye-catching petal-like bracts.*

ABOVE *A member of the hardy Spica Group, Lavandula angustifolia is a good shrub for the garden. 'Hidcote', above, produces densely packed spikes of purple flowers.*

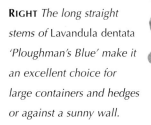

RIGHT *The long straight stems of Lavandula dentata 'Ploughman's Blue' make it an excellent choice for large containers and hedges or against a sunny wall.*

BELOW *A robust dwarf cultivar that flowers profusely in spring,* Lavandula angustifolia *'Munstead' is a popular choice for edging. Prune heavily after flowering.*

LEPTOSPERMUM

This genus is made up of around 80 species of evergreen shrubs or small trees that have narrow leaves that are often aromatic, or occasionally lemon-scented, when crushed. All are Australian, apart from 1 species widespread in New Zealand and 2 found in South-East Asia. They are collectively known as tea-trees because the leaves of some species were used as a tea substitute by Captain James Cook's crew and early settlers to Australia. The small open flowers with 5 petals are mostly white and pink or occasionally red, and are usually produced in profusion during the flowering season. The small woody capsules often persist for a long period. As a group, they are very popular in cultivation, and many are in great demand as cut flowers.

CULTIVATION

Good growers, most plants will tolerate an occasional light frost. They are best suited to well-drained soil in full sun, but some species can cope with wet conditions and nearly full shade. Regular pruning from an early age and each year after flowering is recommended to retain bushiness. Cultivars must be propagated from cuttings to maintain their characteristics.

Top Tip

These graceful screening plants will adapt to a variety of soil types and conditions; a light feeding with slow-release fertiliser in spring is beneficial.

RIGHT Leptospermum poly-galifolium *may vary in size from shrub to bushy tree. It has narrow aromatic leaves and bears masses of white flowers along the branches.*
BELOW Leptospermum lanigerum *forms an erect bushy shrub. The new growth is covered in woolly hairs and leaves are silvery grey to dark green. Flowers are white, occasionally pink-tinged.*

Favourites	Flower Colour	Blooming Season	Flower Fragrance
Leptospermum javanicum	white	spring to autumn	no
Leptospermum lanigerum	white	late spring to summer	no
Leptospermum polygalifolium	white, cream	late spring to summer	no
Leptospermum rupestre	white	late spring to summer	no
Leptospermum scoparium	white, pink, red	late spring to summer	no
Leptospermum scoparium 'Kiwi'	deep pink	late spring to summer	no

ABOVE AND BELOW *The erect shrub* Leptospermum scoparium *has produced many wonderful cultivars, displaying a large range of flower colour and size. 'Big Red', above, lives up to its name with its covering of red flowers, and the deep pink blooms of 'Helene Strybing', below, make it a popular choice.*

Plant Height	Plant Width	Hardiness Zone	Frost Tolerance
10–25 ft (3–8 m)	8–12 ft (2.4–3.5 m)	10–11	no
8–15 ft (2.4–4.5 m)	5–10 ft (1.5–3 m)	8–10	yes
6–20 ft (1.8–6 m)	3–10 ft (0.9–3 m)	9–12	no
3–5 ft (0.9–1.5 m)	3–6 ft (0.9–1.8 m)	7–10	yes
5–10 ft (1.5–3 m)	3–6 ft (0.9–1.8 m)	8–10	yes
3 ft (0.9 m)	3 ft (0.9 m)	8–10	yes

LEUCOSPERMUM

Mostly shrubs, the 46 or so species of *Leucospermum* are all found in southern Africa. They are in the protea family (Proteaceae) and closely related to Australia's banksias, grevilleas and waratahs. The bulk of *Leucospermum* come from the winter rainfall parts of South Africa but a few extend into the summer rainfall eastern parts of the country. All are evergreen shrubs with leathery leaves and often extraordinarily showy flowers, usually produced in spring for 6–8 weeks. The flowers are highly attractive to nectar-feeding birds and last well when cut. *Leucospermum* come in a range of sizes from knee high or less to about 2 m (6 ft). They have been extensively hybridised and most sold today are named varieties rather than natural species.

Top Tip

Water *Leucospermum* around the base of the plant rather than over it. This minimises wetness in the interior of the plant and therefore reduces the chance of foliage and stem diseases.

CULTIVATION

Full sun and gravelly, sandy or other fast-draining soil give the best results. Like many Australian natives, *Leucospermum* are adapted to poor soils and do not need much in the way of fertiliser. They like to receive most of their rain or water between late autumn and early spring, with spring and summer becoming increasingly dry. Prune by cutting faded flowers on long stems.

RIGHT *Hybrids of* Leucospermum cordifolium *are among the showiest of all and they come in a range of warm flower colours. This variety is the golden 'Aurora'.*

ABOVE *Known as the nodding pincushion,* Leucospermum cordifolium *can grow into a dense, bun-shaped shrub 2 m (7 ft) high and wide, though half that size is more usual.*
RIGHT Leucospermum *are related to Australia's banksias and waratahs and the family resemblance to waratahs is clearly seen in this example, the hybrid 'Firedance'.*

Favourites	Flower Colour	Blooming Season	Flower Fragrance	Plant Height	Plant Width	Hardiness Zone	Frost Tolerance
Leucospermum cordifolium	orange	spring	no	6–7 ft (1.8–2 m)	6–7 ft (1.8–2 m)	8–9	yes
Leucospermum cuneiforme 'Mardi Gras Petite'	yellow/ orange	spring	no	6–7 ft (1.8–2 m)	6–7 ft (1.8–2 m)	8–9	yes
Leucospermum heterophyllum 'Hullabaloo'	white	spring	no	low ground cover	6–7 ft (1.8–2 m)	8–9	yes
Leucospermum lineare 'So Sincere'	red	spring	no	6–7 ft (1.8–2 m)	6–7 ft (1.8–2 m)	8–9	yes
Leucospermum reflexum 'So Exquisite'	orange	spring	no	6–7 ft (1.8–2 m)	6–7 ft (1.8–2 m)	8–9	yes

LONICERA

K nown mainly for strongly twining climbers, this Northern Hemisphere genus, which defines the woodbine (Caprifoliaceae) family, also includes several shrubs among its 180 species. Most develop into dense twiggy bushes with somewhat arching stems. The foliage consists of pairs of simple stemless leaves that often partly encircle the stems, and except for the box honeysuckle *(Lonicera nitida)* most of the shrubby species are deciduous. While the vines have long tubular flowers, those of the shrubs are shorter, though often just as fragrant. Small, sometimes colourful berries follow. The genus name honours Adam Lonitzer (1528–1586), a German physician, who like many of his day also wrote about plants.

Top Tip

Plant *Lonicera* species to attract birdlife. The flowers are sought out by nectar-eating birds, while many types of birds will feed on the berries.

CULTIVATION
Honeysuckles are hardy and easily grown in sun or part-shade, provided the soil remains moist. They respond well to trimming and may be trained as hedges. The seed germinates freely if stratified but it is usually simpler to take half-hardened cuttings, or alternatively, they can be grown from layers. Cultivars and hybrids must be propagated from cuttings.

RIGHT *Each panicle on Lonicera etrusca 'Superba' bears many fragrant flowers that are cream on opening, ageing to yellow-orange.*

LEFT *A summer-flowering shrub, Lonicera korolkowii 'Floribunda' features small white flowers and ovate leaves. Red berries follow the flowers.*

ABOVE Lonicera maackii *is a tall deciduous shrub from East Asia. It has a dense bushy habit, purple-stemmed leaves and small, fragrant, white flowers.*

RIGHT *Dainty, tubular, cream to yellow flowers appear on* Lonicera chaetocarpa *during summer. They are followed by attractive red berries.*

Favourites	Flower Colour	Blooming Season	Flower Fragrance	Plant Height	Plant Width	Hardiness Zone	Frost Tolerance
Lonicera chaetocarpa	creamy yellow	summer	no	6 ft (1.8 m)	6 ft (1.8 m)	5–9	yes
Lonicera etrusca	cream with red tints	summer to early autumn	yes	12 ft (3.5 m)	10 ft (3 m)	7–10	yes
Lonicera japonica	white to pale yellow	early summer to late autumn	yes	25–30 ft (8–9 m)	25 ft (8 m)	4–11	yes
Lonicera korolkowii	light pink	summer	yes	10 ft (3 m)	12 ft (3.5 m)	5–9	yes
Lonicera maackii	white	spring to summer	yes	15 ft (4.5 m)	15 ft (4.5 m)	2–9	yes
Lonicera xylosteum	cream with red tints	summer	no	6–10 ft (1.8–3 m)	10 ft (3 m)	3–9	yes

ABOVE *Mahonia aquifolium 'Compacta' is a dwarf form, with spiny-edged leaves and yellow flowers followed by edible berries.*
BELOW *The widely cultivated Mahonia lomariifolia develops into a clump of strongly upright stems with bronze, later green, leaves and soft yellow flowers.*

MAHONIA

This genus of some 70 species of evergreen shrubs is found in Asia and North America with a few species extending into Central America. The leaves grow alternately on the stems or in whorls at the top of the stem, and are often very spiny. The foliage frequently passes through several colour changes as it matures: light green or red-tinted in spring when new, deep green in summer, and red- or orange-tinted in winter. Sprays of small yellow flowers, sometimes scented, are clustered at the branch tips and appear in spring, summer or autumn to early winter depending on the species. *Mahonia* is also known as holly grapes, which the berries resemble.

CULTIVATION

Most *Mahonia* species are temperate-zone plants that tolerate moderate to hard frosts. For lush foliage, plant in moist well-drained soil that is fertile and humus-rich and protect from the hottest summer sun. Propagate from cuttings or from the rooted suckers that grow at the base of established plants.

Favourites	Flower Colour	Blooming Season	Flower Fragrance	Plant Height	Plant Width	Hardiness Zone	Frost Tolerance
Mahonia aquifolium	yellow	spring	no	6 ft (1.8 m)	5–8 ft (1.5–2.4 m)	5–10	yes
Mahonia fremontii	yellow	late spring to summer	no	12 ft (3.5 m)	6 ft (1.8 m)	8–11	yes
Mahonia lomariifolia	yellow	spring	no	10–12 ft (3–3.5 m)	6–10 ft (1.8–3 m)	7–10	yes
Mahonia × media	yellow	autumn to winter	yes	15 ft (4.5 m)	12 ft (3.5 m)	6–10	yes
Mahonia nevinii	yellow	spring	no	6 ft (1.8 m)	6 ft (1.8 m)	8–11	yes
Mahonia repens	deep yellow	spring	yes	12 in (30 cm)	36 in (90 cm)	6–9	yes

RIGHT Mahonia × media *was originally bred to combine lush foliage with hardiness. The cultivar 'Arthur Menzies', right, is notable for its long flowering spikes and blue-black berries.*

BELOW *Native to California,* Mahonia nevinii *is a tall shrub with greyish blue-green leaves. Small open racemes of light yellow flowers are borne in spring, followed by tiny red berries.*

MUSSAENDA

For a long blooming, highly ornamental plant for a warm-climate garden, it's hard to go past a *Mussaenda*. The 200 or so species of mostly shrubs come from the tropics of Africa, Asia and the Pacific but are not found in nearby Australia. They are part of the madder family, the Rubiaceae. The apparent flowers, which are large and obvious, are actually coloured expanded sepals that together make up the calyx from which the tiny, starry flowers emerge. They can be white, pink, yellow or red. All *Mussaenda* love it hot and humid and though they will grow in warm, frost-free areas south of the subtropics, they usually look scrappy for months over winter and sometimes die. In the right climate however, they are easy to grow and attractive.

CULTIVATION

Grow in bright dappled shade with a few hours direct sun. The plants demand moisture (but not wetness) around them always and do best in a soil that is well enriched with rotted organic matter. When the first lot of flowers finishes, prune the shrub all over to encourage another flush of growth and more blooms. Apply controlled-release fertiliser at the same time.

Favourites	Flower Colour	Blooming Season	Flower Fragrance
Mussaenda erythrophylla	red	spring to autumn	no
Mussaenda 'Queen Sirikit'	whitish pink	spring to autumn	no
Mussaenda philippica	white	spring to autumn	no

LEFT *From the Philippines,* Mussaenda philippica *is a rounded spreading shrub 3–4 m (10–15 ft) across. The white sepals bloom all summer in a warm garden.*

Plant Height	Plant Width	Hardiness Zone	Frost Tolerance
12–15 ft (3.5–4.5 m)	15–20 ft (4.5–6 m)	9–11	no
6–10 ft (1.8–3 m)	6–10 ft (1.8–3 m)	9–11	no
12–15 ft (3.5–4.5 m)	15–20 ft (4.5–6 m)	9–11	no

BELOW *'Queen Sirikit' is a cross between the white* Mussaenda philippica *and the red* M. erythrophylla. *The cross has created a pretty and floriferous pink bush.*

Top Tip

Mussaenda make attractive container plants but do need to be pruned regularly to maintain a compact, dense habit. The hybrid 'Queen Sirikit' is one of the best for pots.

RIGHT *Known as Ashanti blood,* Mussaenda erythrophylla *comes from tropical West Africa. It grows as a large, sprawling shrub and produces a long display in hot climates.*

RIGHT *Nandina domestica 'Nana Purpurea' shares many of the characteristics of the species, but has a more compact habit and shorter leaves made up of wider leaflets.*

NANDINA

The sole species in this genus is an evergreen cane-stemmed shrub found from Himalayan India to Japan. Although commonly known as heavenly or sacred bamboo, it is not a bamboo but a member of the barberry (Berberidaceae) family. It has pinnate foliage that develops intense red tones, especially in winter. Conical heads of mildly scented creamy white flowers open in spring to summer and are followed by showy clusters of red berries that last through winter. The genus name is derived from Nanten, the Japanese name for the plant.

CULTIVATION

Nandina will grow in sun or part-shade with moist well-drained soil. The foliage is often more luxuriant with a little shade but colours better in sun. Planting several together will ensure a better fruit crop. Cut out any old unproductive stems in summer. Propagation is usually from half-hardened cuttings.

Favourites	Flower Colour	Blooming Season	Flower Fragrance	Plant Height	Plant Width	Hardiness Zone	Frost Tolerance
Nandina domestica	creamy white	summer	no	7 ft (2 m)	4 ft (1.2 m)	7–10	yes
Nandina domestica 'Firepower'	non-flowering	—	—	2 ft (0.6 m)	2 ft (0.6 m)	7–10	yes
Nandina domestica 'Harbor Dwarf'	white	summer	no	2–3 ft (0.6–0.9 m)	2 ft (0.6 m)	7–10	yes
Nandina domestica 'Richmond'	white	summer	no	4 ft (1.2 m)	2–3 ft (0.6–0.9 m)	7–10	yes
Nandina Plum Passion/'Monum'	white	summer	no	4–5 ft (1.2–1.5 m)	3 ft (0.9 m)	7–10	yes
Nandina 'San Gabriel'	white	summer	no	7 ft (2 m)	4 ft (1.2 m)	7–10	yes

BELOW *Ever-changing, the leaves of* Nandina domestica *transform from their red spring colouring to become green and lustrous before developing beautiful russet tones in autumn.*

ABOVE *Upon the arrival of cooler weather, the blue-green colouring of the summer foliage of* Nandina domestica *'Gulf Stream' is superseded by stunning red hues.*

BELOW *In autumn and winter, the dense foliage of* Nandina domestica *'Wood's Dwarf' develops spectacular crimson hues. This cultivar does not produce flowers.*

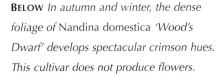

Top Tip

Generally compact and easy to keep under control, *Nandina* plants are ideal for use in shrub borders and containers, and are effective for hedging and screening.

NERIUM

This small genus belongs to the dogbane family and consists of only 2 species of long-flowering evergreen shrubs native to the area from southwestern Asia across to China. The leaves are simple, smooth-edged, narrow and lance-shaped, providing a background for the attractive flowers that range in colour from white and pale pink to red. The numerous cultivars further broaden the colour spectrum. Appearing in clusters, the flowers are made up of 5 broad petals that are fused into a narrow tube at one end and flare open at the other into a disc or a shallow cup. *Nerium* plants are very beautiful garden subjects but are also extremely poisonous; care is needed when working with them in the garden.

CULTIVATION

Plant in almost any type of soil, except wet, in full sun. They will tolerate light frosts if grown in a sheltered position. Well-established plants may be pruned quite severely in winter, about once every 3 years, to maintain their shape. Propagate from half-hardened cuttings taken in autumn or from seed in spring.

ABOVE LEFT *Nerium oleander 'Petite Salmon', as its name suggests, bears blooms of a delicate salmon pink shade on an attractive dwarf bush. It is suitable as a hedging plant.*
ABOVE *Bearing single pink blooms,* Nerium oleander *'Docteur Golfin' is a popular landscaping plant in warm climates. Once established, it needs very little watering.*
RIGHT Nerium oleander *comes in a variety of colours and sizes. It is a long-lived plant and is often grown as an informal hedge, in a shrub border or in a large container.*

Favourites	Flower Colour	Blooming Season	Flower Fragrance
Nerium oleander	white, yellow, pink, red	spring to early autumn	no
Nerium oleander 'Album'	white; creamy white at centre	spring to early autumn	no
Nerium oleander 'Docteur Golfin'	bright pink	spring to early autumn	no
Nerium oleander 'Petite Salmon'	salmon pink	spring to early autumn	no
Nerium oleander 'Splendens'	rosy pink	spring to early autumn	no
Nerium oleander 'Splendens Variegatum'	rosy pink	spring to early autumn	no

Top Tip

Although they are extremely hardy plants in mild climates, in cooler areas *Nerium oleander* and its cultivars need to be overwintered indoors as they are not cold hardy.

BELOW *The attractive foliage is the first thing that catches the eye on* Nerium oleander *'Splendens Variegatum'. The leaves contrast with the stunning double pink flowers.*

Plant Height	Plant Width	Hardiness Zone	Frost Tolerance
8–15 ft (2.4–4.5 m)	6–12 ft (1.8–3.5 m)	8–11	yes
8–15 ft (2.4–4.5 m)	6–12 ft (1.8–3.5 m)	8–11	yes
8–15 ft (2.4–4.5 m)	6–12 ft (1.8–3.5 m)	8–11	yes
2–4 ft (0.6–1.2 m)	2–4 ft (0.6–1.2 m)	8–11	yes
6–15 ft (1.8–4.5 m)	6–12 ft (1.8–3.5 m)	8–11	yes
6–15 ft (1.8–4.5 m)	6–12 ft (1.8–3.5 m)	8–11	yes

PAEONIA

There are 30 or so species in this genus of beautiful herbaceous perennials and deciduous shrubs, all native to temperate parts of the Northern Hemisphere. They have long-lived, rather woody rootstocks and stems, and bold foliage. Leaves are dark green to blue-green, usually toothed or lobed and are sometimes maroon or red-tinged. The large flowers are usually erect and solitary, cup- or saucer-shaped and have brightly coloured petals surrounding a mass of short stamens. Petals may be white, yellow or shades of pink, sometimes flushed red at the centre, and stamens are mostly white or yellow. The genus name goes back to ancient Greek times and refers to the supposed medicinal properties of the species.

CULTIVATION

Paeonia species can survive in cold climates as long as they have protection from early spring frosts, strong winds and hot sun. They prefer full or slightly filtered sunlight with cool moist soil. Propagate from seed or by division.

ABOVE LEFT *The gorgeous, bright yellow, cup-shaped flowers of* Paeonia lutea *have a dramatic centre of orange-yellow stamens, wonderfully set off by the green foliage.*
BELOW Paeonia anomala *var.* intermedia, *with its blood red blooms, is an excellent cut flower. Keep the flowers in a cool part of the home and change the water each day.*

LEFT *Perfect for a mixed or shrub border,* Paeonia tenuifolia *bears large, single, cup-shaped, deep red blooms complemented by a cluster of yellow stamens.*

ABOVE *Valued for its yellow flowers with a deep orange centre,* Paeonia × lemoinei *'Roman Child' is an upright deciduous shrub with dark green divided leaves.*

Favourites	Flower Colour	Blooming Season	Flower Fragrance	Plant Height	Plant Width	Hardiness Zone	Frost Tolerance
Paeonia anomala	bright red	early summer	no	20–24 in (50–60 cm)	24 in (60 cm)	5–8	yes
Paeonia cambessedesii	deep pink	late spring	no	18 in (45 cm)	18–24 in (45–60 cm)	8–10	yes
Paeonia delavayi	dark red	summer	no	6 ft (1.8 m)	4 ft (1.2 m)	6–9	yes
Paeonia lactiflora	white, pink to deep red	late spring to mid-summer	yes	24 in (60 cm)	24 in (60 cm)	6–9	yes
Paeonia × lemoinei	yellow with red or orange marks	spring to early summer	no	6 ft (1.8 m)	5 ft (1.5 m)	6–9	yes
Paeonia lutea	bright yellow	spring to early summer	no	5 ft (1.5 m)	5 ft (1.5 m)	6–9	yes
Paeonia mascula	deep pink to red, sometimes white	summer	no	24–36 in (60–90 cm)	24–36 in (60–90 cm)	8–10	yes
Paeonia mlokosewitschii	pale to bright yellow	spring	no	30–36 in (75–90 cm)	30–36 in (75–90 cm)	6–9	yes
Paeonia officinalis	rose pink to purple, red	spring to mid-summer	no	24 in (60 cm)	24 in (60 cm)	8–10	yes
Paeonia suffruticosa	white, yellow, pink, red	spring	no	3–6 ft (0.9–1.8 m)	3–6 ft (0.9–1.8 m)	4–9	yes
Paeonia tenuifolia	deep red	late spring to early summer	no	20–27 in (50–70 cm)	20–27 in (50–70 cm)	5–8	yes
Paeonia veitchii	pale to bright magenta, white	late spring to early summer	no	20–24 in (50–60 cm)	20–24 in (50–60 cm)	6–8	yes

ABOVE *The maroon-veined dark green leaves of* Paeonia cambessedesii *are reddish purple underneath: the perfect foil for the deep pink flowers and showy yellow stamens.*

BELOW *All peonies benefit from the applicaton of a general fertiliser in spring and* Paeonia mascula *subsp.* arietina *is no exception, rewarding this effort with longer-lasting blooms.*

Top Tip

Paeonia plants are susceptible to grey mould, which rots leaf bases, stems and buds. Spray affected plants with a fungicide and make sure the soil is well drained.

BELOW Paeonia veitchii *has deep green leaves and solitary, single, bowl-shaped blooms that are either white or a shade of pink.*

ABOVE *The glorious double white blooms of Paeonia suffruticosa 'Mountain Treasure' have deep red markings at the centre and a mass of golden stamens, making this plant a delight in any garden.*

LEFT Paeonia lactiflora *'Bowl of Beauty' is just one of numerous lovely cultivars, enjoyed by gardeners for their delicious scent and beautiful summer blooms.*

PHILADELPHUS

This genus of 60 species is a member of the Hydrangeaceae/Philadelphaceae family and is made up of deciduous shrubs from the temperate regions of East Asia, the Himalayas, the Caucasus and Central and North America. The plants generally have peeling bark and light green roughly elliptical leaves that are smooth; in some species, the leaves are slightly hairy on the undersides. They flower in spring and summer, mostly bearing 4-petalled white or cream flowers that grow in loose clusters at the end of the leaf stem. Blooms can be single, semi-double or double. The scent of the flower is very similar to that of orange blossom, hence the common name of mock orange.

CULTIVATION

Philadelphus plants are easily grown in full sun, partial shade or in deciduous open woodland in moist well-drained soil. Planting in full sun will increase the number of flowers. Propagate from softwood cuttings taken in summer or hardwood cuttings in autumn and winter.

ABOVE Philadelphus *'Manteau d'Hermine' is a popular dwarf variety of the mock orange. It bears superb clusters of double, vanilla-scented, creamy white flowers. This hardy deciduous plant makes an excellent ground cover.* **RIGHT** *The single white blooms of* Philadelphus *'Rosace' often open in late spring, and can be useful for providing some simple elegance to shrub borders.*

Favourites	Flower Colour	Blooming Season	Flower Fragrance
Philadelphus **'Belle Etoile'**	white; small red blotch	late spring to early summer	yes
Philadelphus **coronarius**	white	early summer	yes
Philadelphus **'Manteau d'Hermine'**	creamy white	summer	yes
Philadelphus **mexicanus**	creamy white	summer	yes
Philadelphus **'Rosace'**	white	late spring to early summer	yes
Philadelphus **subcanus**	white	early summer	yes

RIGHT *Golden yellow foliage turning yellow-green in summer is the hallmark of Philadelphus coronarius 'Aureus', which is an old garden favourite valued for its creamy blooms.*

Top Tip

The delicious fragrance of *Philadelphus* flowers can be enjoyed indoors. Simply float fresh-cut flowerheads in a shallow bowl filled with water.

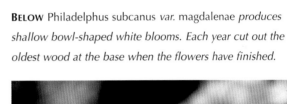

BELOW *Philadelphus subcanus var. magdalenae produces shallow bowl-shaped white blooms. Each year cut out the oldest wood at the base when the flowers have finished.*

Plant Height	Plant Width	Hardiness Zone	Frost Tolerance
6 ft (1.8 m)	8 ft (2.4 m)	5–9	yes
10 ft (3 m)	5 ft (1.5 m)	2–9	yes
30 in (75 cm)	5 ft (1.5 m)	5–9	yes
10–20 ft (3–6 m)	6 ft (1.8 m)	9–10	no
5 ft (1.5 m)	4 ft (1.2 m)	5–9	yes
20 ft (6 m)	6–10 ft (1.8–3 m)	6–9	no

PIERIS

This Erica family genus consists of 7 species, mainly evergreen shrubs from the subtropical and temperate regions of the Himalayas and eastern Asia, as well as a vine and some shrubby species from eastern America and the West Indies. The species have been widely cultivated and extensively hybridised, and the best known are extremely popular evergreen shrubs for temperate gardens. Typically, the glossy green leaves are simple, pointed and elliptical-shaped, often with serrated edges, and the flowers are bell-shaped, downward-facing and are borne in panicles of white to pale pink clusters. The flowers usually open in spring and are sometimes scented.

CULTIVATION

Pieris plants will perform best in cool, moist, humus-rich, well-drained soil. A position in full sun yields more flowers, whereas light shade produces foliage that is more lush. They are naturally tidy plants, but a light trimming will help keep them that way. Propagate from half-hardened cuttings or by layering.

ABOVE Pieris japonica *'Mountain Fire'* is grown for the bright red colour of the new leaves and its pretty, red, bell-shaped blooms that appear in spring.
BELOW LEFT The white blooms of Pieris japonica *open from pinkish brown buds, and hang in drooping clusters early in spring. It needs protection from strong winds.*

Favourites	Flower Colour	Blooming Season	Flower Fragrance	Plant Height	Plant Width	Hardiness Zone	Frost Tolerance
Pieris 'Flaming Silver'	white	early spring	no	4–10 ft (1.2–3 m)	4–8 ft (1.2–2.4 m)	6–9	yes
Pieris 'Forest Flame'	white	mid-spring	no	12 ft (3.5 m)	8 ft (2.4 m)	6–9	yes
Pieris *formosa*	white; sometimes pink-tinged	mid-spring	no	10 ft (3 m)	12 ft (3.5 m)	6–9	yes
Pieris *japonica*	white	early spring	no	6–12 ft (1.8–3.5 m)	6–12 ft (1.8–3.5 m)	4–10	yes
Pieris japonica 'Scarlett O'Hara'	creamy white; scarlet markings	early spring	no	6–12 ft (1.8–3.5 m)	6–12 ft (1.8–3.5 m)	4–10	yes
Pieris japonica 'Valley Valentine'	pink to deep red	early spring	no	5–7 ft (1.5–2 m)	5–7 ft (1.5–2 m)	4–10	yes

BELOW *Dense clusters of creamy white flowers make Pieris japonica 'Scarlett O'Hara' a charming garden plant. As the flowers fade they should be removed.*

Top Tip

Pieris species make good companion plants for heath (*Erica* species), azaleas and rhododendrons as they all enjoy an acid soil and warm, but not hot, summers.

ABOVE *The flowers of* Pieris japonica *'Valley Valentine' start pink and turn a rich deep red as they age. Like other* P. japonica *varieties, the new leaves are red.*

PIMELEA

This genus contains more than 100 species of mostly shrubs, the vast majority of which occur only in Australia. The rest are native to New Zealand. Of the Australian species, one or another is found in every state and in virtually every type of habitat there is. Of the total number of species, only relatively few are commonly available to gardeners, these being among the most showy of the genus. Flowers are clustered in hemispherical heads and while the individual blooms may be small, the heads are abundantly produced, creating an impressive floral display, usually in spring and summer. Flowers may be white, pink or rose. *Pimelea* is a member of the daphne family, Thymelaeaceae and, like that fragrant favourite, some species of *Pimelea* have fragrant flowers.

CULTIVATION

Plant in fast-draining but humus-rich soil. Full sun is the default aspect for these plants but most are adaptable and will take to life in bright dappled shade or part-shade. In the hottest of areas, however, afternoon shade is welcomed. A single, none-too-generous dose of controlled-release fertiliser applied once in early spring is all the fertilising these plants need.

TOP *Found through eastern Australia,* Pimelea linifolia *is an attractive small shrub for sun or part-shade. Prune moderately after flowering to promote bushy growth and longer life.*
ABOVE *A short but showy life should be the epitaph of* Pimelea spectabilis. *But plants are easily replaced from cuttings in late spring which you should do after the third year.*

Top Tip

Young small plants are the best buys and most easy to establish. On planting, pinch out the growing tip of each stem to create a bushy framework of branches.

Favourites	Flower Colour	Blooming Season	Flower Fragrance	Plant Height	Plant Width	Hardiness Zone	Frost Tolerance
Pimelea ciliata	white	late winter and spring	no	to 3 ft (0.9 m)	30–48 in (75–130 cm)	8–9	yes
Pimelea ferruginea	pink, rose	spring and summer	no	2–5 ft (0.6–1.5 m)	3–8 ft (0.9–2.4 m)	8–9	yes
Pimelea linifolia	white or pink	winter and spring	no	3–5 ft (0.9–1.5 m)	3–5 ft (0.9–1.5 m)	9–10	yes
Pimelea spectabilis	white, pink or lemon	spring	no	30–72 in (75–200 cm)	30–72 in (75–200 cm)	8	yes

ABOVE Pimelea ferruginea *is one of the most popular and easily grown species. It comes from the coast and has a dense habit.*

RIGHT *Profusely produced, the flowerheads of* Pimelea spectabilis *are about 8 cm (3 in) across and very attractive to butterflies and bees.*

PROTEA

This is the plant after which the entire family, Proteaceae, was named. When the Dutch originally colonised the Cape, the first plant they collected and described for science was *Protea neriifolia*, still one of the most garden-worthy species and a parent of many of today's hybrids. There are nearly 120 species of *Protea*, all native to southern Africa. However, the great majority of them are restricted to South Africa itself, most clustered around the winter-rainfall Cape region. *Protea* are now grown all over the world and, in Australia, they are frequently thought to be native plants. All are evergreen and most are shrubs, but within that classification they are highly variable in size and form and colour of flower.

CULTIVATION

Fast-draining soil, full sun and regular rain or water between late autumn and early spring is a good rule of thumb for gardening success with *Protea*. Most will tolerate long dry spells in summer if winter rain is adequate but if summer rain is heavy and persistent, grow them only on sloping ground or a mound of gravelly soil so excess water can drain away.

ABOVE At 20 cm (8 in) across the flowers of Protea magnifica *live up to their specific name. It is one of the most cold hardy of the proteas.*

ABOVE So rich in sugary nectar, the flowers of the sugarbush, Protea repens, were once harvested as a source of sweetener.

FAR RIGHT Good for pots or small gardens, Protea nana has pendulous red flowers in spring. Fast draining, sandy soil is essential.

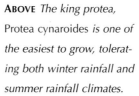

Top Tip

Proteas make long-lasting cut flowers. Cut blooms on long stems to keep the plants bushy and compact. If you don't want to cut the blooms, wait until they're finished then cut on long stems.

ABOVE *The king protea,* Protea cynaroides *is one of the easiest to grow, tolerating both winter rainfall and summer rainfall climates.*

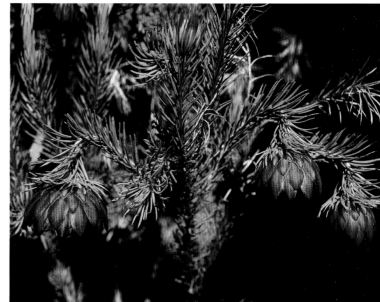

Favourites	Flower Colour	Blooming Season	Flower Fragrance	Plant Height	Plant Width	Hardiness Zone	Frost Tolerance
Protea cynaroides 'King Pink'	pink	autumn, winter	no	3 ft (0.9 m)	3–4 ft (0.9–1.2 m)	8–9	yes
Protea 'Juliet'	pinkish red	autumn to spring	no	3 ft (0.9 m)	3 ft (0.9 m)	8–9	yes
Protea nana	red and cream	winter to spring	no	3 ft (0.9 m)	3–4 ft (0.9–1.2 m)	8–9	yes
Protea 'Pink Ice'	silvery pink	late summer to spring	no	6–12 ft (1.8–3.5 m)	8–15 ft (2.4–4.5 m)	8–9	yes
Protea repens 'Honeyglow'	yellow	autumn	no	6–10 ft (1.8–3 m)	6–10 ft (1.8–3 m)	8–9	yes

RHODODENDRON

This very diverse genus of 800 or more species is widely distributed across the Northern Hemisphere, with the majority growing in temperate to cool regions. They range from tiny ground-hugging plants to small trees and even epiphytes, which grow in the branches of trees or on rock faces. Foliage comes in great diversity of form, and most rhododendrons bear "trusses" of up to 24 spectacular blooms, in colours ranging from white to pink, red, yellow and mauve. Flowers are often multicoloured, with spots, stripes, edging or a single blotch of a different colour in the throat of the flower. With the exception of some Vireya species and hybrids, fragrant rhododendrons are always white or very pale pink. Blooms vary in size and shape but are generally bell-shaped, appearing from early spring to early summer. The fruit is a many-seeded capsule, normally woody, and sometimes bearing wings or tail-like appendages to aid transportation.

CULTIVATION

All rhododendrons prefer acidic soils, high in organic matter and freely draining. While most prefer some protection from wind, sun and frost, many others tolerate these conditions. Evergreen rhododendrons may be propagated by taking tip cuttings of the new growth in spring; deciduous azaleas are best grown from hardwood cuttings taken in winter.

BELOW With a spreading habit, Rhododendron 'Elsie Watson' is a Hardy Medium Hybrid. The lavender-pink, funnel-shaped flowers are marked and edged in a rich pink-red.

BELOW The Vireya Hybrids, such as 'Pink Veitch', bear trumpet-shaped or bell-shaped flowers in heads of between 5 and 9 blooms.

RIGHT *Medium-sized Rho-dodendron,* Tender Hybrid, *'Countess of Haddington' has hair-edged leaves and white blooms tinged pink.*

LEFT *Growing to around 0.9 m (3 ft) in height,* Rhododendron *'Patricia's Day', a Yak Hybrid, produces its dainty pinkish white blooms in mid-season.*

Favourites	Flower Colour	Blooming Season	Flower Fragrance	Plant Height	Plant Width	Hardiness Zone	Frost Tolerance
Rhododendron, **Azaleodendron Hybrids**	mauve, pink, yellow, cream	late spring to early summer	yes	3–8 ft (0.9–2.4 m)	4–8 ft (1.2–2.4 m)	5–9	yes
Rhododendron, **Ghent Hybrids**	white, pink, red, orange, yellow	early summer	yes	6 ft (1.8 m)	4 ft (1.2 m)	5–9	yes
Rhododendron, **Hardy Medium Hybrids**	various	spring	varied	3–6 ft (0.9–1.8 m)	3–8 ft (0.9–2.4 m)	3–9	yes
Rhododendron, **Hardy Small Hybrids**	various	spring	varied	1–4 ft (0.3–1.2 m)	2–5 ft (0.6–1.5 m)	4–9	yes
Rhododendron, **Hardy Tall Hybrids**	various	spring	varied	7–20 ft (2–6 m)	7–15 ft (2–4.5 m)	4–9	yes
Rhododendron, **Indica Hybrids**	various	winter	no	3–6 ft (0.9–1.8 m)	3–8 ft (0.9–2.4 m)	8–11	yes
Rhododendron, **Knap Hill and Exbury Hybrids**	various	mid- to late spring	no	6–10 ft (1.8–3 m)	6 ft (1.8 m)	5–9	yes
Rhododendron, **Kurume Hybrids**	various	spring	no	3–5 ft (0.9–1.5 m)	3–5 ft (0.9–1.5 m)	7–10	yes
Rhododendron macrophyllum	purple-pink to white	late spring to early summer	no	15 ft (4.5 m)	15 ft (4.5 m)	6–9	yes
Rhododendron maximum	white to dark pink; green spots	summer	no	3–15 ft (0.9–4.5 m)	4–10 ft (1.2–3 m)	3–9	yes
Rhododendron, **Mollis Azalea Hybrids**	orange, red, yellow, cream	spring	no	6–8 ft (1.8–2.4 m)	3–6 ft (0.9–1.8 m)	5–9	yes
Rhododendron, **Occidentale Azalea Hybrids**	pink, white	summer	yes	8 ft (2.4 m)	7 ft (2 m)	6–9	yes
Rhododendron, **Rustica Azalea Hybrids**	yellow to red	late spring to early summer	yes	10 ft (3 m)	15 ft (4.5 m)	5–9	yes
Rhododendron, **Satsuki Azalea Hybrids**	white, pink, purple, red	late spring to early summer	no	20–36 in (50–90 cm)	36 in (90 cm)	7–11	yes
Rhododendron, **Tender Hybrids**	various	spring	varied	3–12 ft (0.9–3.5 m)	3–12 ft (0.9–3.5 m)	9–10	no
Rhododendron, **Vireya Hybrids**	various	throughout the year	varied	2–7 ft (0.6–2 m)	2–5 ft (0.6–1.5 m)	9–12	no
Rhododendron, **Viscosum Hybrids**	orange, red, yellow	late spring to early summer	yes	8 ft (2.4 m)	8 ft (2.4 m)	4–8	yes
Rhododendron, **Yak Hybrids**	white, pink	mid-spring	no	3–4 ft (0.9–1.2 m)	3–6 ft (0.9–1.8 m)	4–9	yes

CLASSIFICATION

Rhododendrons can be broadly divided into 5 groups: rhododendron species; rhododendron cultivars (including the 'hardy' hybrids and the Vireya rhododendrons); deciduous azaleas; evergreen azaleas; and the azaleodendrons. Azaleas, which had originally been classified as a separate genus, are now regarded as botanically part of this genus and have contributed numerous cultivars and hybrids. In evergreen rhododendrons, the new leaf shoots often form attractive perpendicular "candle-sticks", while the foliage of deciduous azaleas progresses from bright green shoots in spring to bronze in summer, followed by rich reds to yellows in autumn. The epiphytic Vireya rhododendrons can flower at various times, often in winter, and vary greatly in shape and colour. Deciduous azaleas flower in spring on bare branches just before or at the same time as new leaf growth. Azaleodendrons are mostly semi-evergreen shrubs with yellow, pink or mauve flowers. Rhododendrons make excellent ornamental plants with their masses of colourful flowers. Many also have year-round foliage, attractively textured bark, and a rich fragrance.

ABOVE *Because it is a fast-growing and vigorous plant, Rhododendron,* Hardy Tall Hybrid, *'Alice' needs plenty of room. The pink trusses appear after a few seasons.*
BELOW *Rhododendron 'Fastuosum Flore Pleno' is a free-flowering Hardy Tall Hybrid that tolerates both wind and sun, making it a desirable addition to a temperate garden.*

ABOVE *'Elizabeth' is considered one of the best Hardy Small rhododendrons. Its pinkish red flowers are funnel shaped and appear in early to mid-spring, and again randomly in autumn.*

Top Tip

Mulching is important for successful rhododendrons. In warm areas, mulch keeps soil cool; in cold areas, mulch helps the soil retain some warmth.

BELOW *The Rutherford Indica Hybrids are larger than the Belgian Indica Hybrids and are bred for their excellent flower quality.* Rhododendron 'Purity' (pictured) *has large snow white flowers.*

LEFT Rhododendron 'Arpège' *is a Viscosum Hybrid that, like the French perfume for which it is named, has a gorgeous scent. The flowers are a delightful shade of yellow.*

RIGHT Rhododendron *'Snow Prince', a Southern Indica Hybrid, becomes smothered in an abundance of pink-tinted white flowers quite early in the season. It is a vigorous and sun-tolerant shrub.*

BELOW *When in bloom, the masses of pink-red flowers of* Rhododendron *'Favourite', one of the Kurume Azalea Hybrids, almost obscure the mid- to dark green foliage.*

LEFT *Growing up to 1.5 m (5 ft) high,* Rhododendron *'Florence Mann' is a Hardy Medium Hybrid. It is a classic example of the "blue" rhododendrons.*

ABOVE Rhododendron, *Ghent Hybrid, 'Pucella' has lovely pink flowers with a bright orange blotch. The Ghent hybrids bear large trusses of relatively small flowers.*

LEFT Rhododendron *'Leopold Astrid'* is a Belgian Indica Hybrid with large, frilled, double, white flowers edged in red. The Indicas are widely grown in temperate climates. **BELOW** Occidentale Hybrids, such as Rhododendron *'Coccinto Speciosa'* seen here, are the most drought, heat and humidity tolerant of all deciduous azaleas.

Top Tip

Providing their cultural requirements are met, rhododendrons require little maintenance or pruning. Simply removing spent flowers will maintain their beauty.

RIGHT Densely packed clusters of yellow flowers bring sunny colour to Rhododendron *'Sun Chariot'*, one of the Knap Hill and Exbury Azalea Hybrids.

ROSA

The genus Rosa is one of the most widely grown and best loved of all plant genera around the world. Since ancient times roses have been valued for their beauty and fragrance as well as for their medicinal, culinary and cosmetic properties. There are between 100 and 150 species of rose, which range in habit from erect and arching shrubs to scramblers and climbers. The majority of species are deciduous and most have prickles or bristles. They are found in temperate and subtropical zones of the Northern Hemisphere. The leaves are usually composed of 5 to 9 serrated-edged leaflets. Flowers, borne singly or in clusters, range from single, usually 5-petalled blooms to those with many closely packed petals. Many are intensely fragrant. Most species and old garden roses flower only once a year but many of the modern cultivars are repeat blooming. Rose fruit (hips or heps) are usually orangey red, but can be dark.

ABOVE Rosa, *Large-flowered (Hybrid Tea), 'New Zealand' (syn. 'Aotearoa-New Zealand') has soft pink fragrant flowers that open from long pointed buds.*

BELOW Rosa, *Large-flowered (Hybrid Tea), 'Pristine' keeps its colours even in a range of climatic conditions, which would ordinarily result in colour variations.*

CULTIVATION

Roses can be grown in formal and informal settings, in separate beds or mixed borders, as ground covers, climbing up arches and pergolas, as hedging and in containers. Most roses require a sunny site and well-drained medium-loamy soil. Roses should be pruned to maintain strong healthy growth and a good shape. Except for the old Tea roses, most roses are very hardy. Propagation is from hardwood cuttings in autumn or softwood cuttings in summer.

LEFT *Grown for its rich red blooms and delightful fragrance, 'Crimson Glory', a Large-flowered (Hybrid Tea) rose, is a reliable repeat-flowering plant.*
RIGHT *A very hardy Cluster-flowered (Floribunda) rose, 'Betty Prior' has an upright habit and bears masses of 5-petalled pink blooms that are paler at the centre.*

Favourites	Flower Colour	Blooming Season	Flower Fragrance	Plant Height	Plant Width	Hardiness Zone	Frost Tolerance
Rosa, Alba	white, pale pink	mid-summer	yes	6–8 ft (1.8–2.4 m)	4–6 ft (1.2–1.8 m)	4–10	yes
Rosa blanda	pink	spring	no	5 ft (1.5 m)	5 ft (1.5 m)	3–9	yes
Rosa, Bourbon	white, pink, red	summer to early autumn	yes	4–7 ft (1.2–2 m)	3–6 ft (0.9–1.8 m)	6–10	yes
Rosa, China	pink, red	summer to autumn	yes	3–6 ft (0.9–1.8 m)	3–6 ft (0.9–1.8 m)	7–11	yes
Rosa, Cluster-flowered (Floribunda)	various	summer to autumn	yes	3–5 ft (0.9–1.5 m)	2–4 ft (0.6–1.2 m)	5–11	yes
Rosa, Damask	white, pale pink	spring or summer	yes	3–7 ft (0.9–2 m)	3–5 ft (0.9–1.5 m)	5–10	yes
Rosa, Gallica	pink, red, pinkish purple	spring or summer	yes	4–6 ft (1.2–1.8 m)	3–5 ft (0.9–1.5 m)	5–10	yes
Rosa, Hybrid Perpetual	white, pink, red	spring to autumn	yes	4–7 ft (1.2–2 m)	3–5 ft (0.9–1.5 m)	5–10	yes
Rosa, Hybrid Rugosa	white, pink, yellow, red	summer to autumn	yes	3–7 ft (0.9–2 m)	3–7 ft (0.9–2 m)	3–10	yes
Rosa laevigata	white	late spring to summer	yes	15 ft (4.5 m)	5 ft (1.5 m)	4–11	yes
Rosa, Large-flowered (Hybrid Tea)	various	summer to autumn	yes	4–7 ft (1.2–2 m)	3–5 ft (0.9–1.5 m)	4–11	yes
Rosa, Miniature	various	summer to autumn	yes	8–30 in (20–75 cm)	8–18 in (20–45 cm)	5–11	yes
Rosa, Moss	white, pink, red	summer	yes	4–6 ft (1.2–1.8 m)	4–6 ft (1.2–1.8 m)	5–10	yes
Rosa, Patio (Dwarf Cluster-flowered)	various	summer to autumn	no	2 ft (0.6 m)	6 ft (1.8 m)	4–11	yes
Rosa, Polyantha	various	summer to autumn	no	2 ft (0.6 m)	18 in (45 cm)	3–10	yes
Rosa setigera	deep pink fading to white	early to late summer	yes	5 ft (1.5 m)	10 ft (3 m)	4–9	yes
Rosa, Shrub	various	summer to autumn	yes	4–10 ft (1.2–3 m)	3–8 ft (0.9–2.4 m)	4–11	yes
Rosa, Tea	cream, yellow, pink, red	summer to autumn	yes	4–7 ft (1.2–2 m)	3–5 ft (0.9–1.5 m)	7–11	yes

ABOVE *'Amber Queen' is an award-winning Cluster-flowered (Floribunda) rose, well suited as a standard or as a bedding rose. A layer of mulch will keep it healthy.*
RIGHT *It's always a treat to see the delicate pink blooms of Rosa, Large-flowered (Hybrid Tea), 'Portrait'. Regular deadheading of roses encourages more flowers.*

ROSE TYPES

Roses have been bred for centuries and are divided into groups. The old garden roses were originally bred from a handful of species and include the groups Gallica, Damask, Moss, Alba, China, Tea, Bourbon and Hybrid Perpetual. In the late eighteenth century the repeat-flowering China rose (*Rosa chinensis*) arrived in Europe. The Tea roses, also repeat-flowering, followed in the nineteenth century, and 50 years later a Frenchman bred the first modern Large-flowered rose. Large-flowered (Hybrid Tea), Polyantha, Cluster-flowered (Floribunda), Shrub, Hybrid Rugosa, Miniature and Patio (Dwarf Cluster-flowered) modern roses proliferated in the twentieth century. While most species and old roses are in shades of pink, red and purple or white, modern rose-breeding programs have seen yellow and orange flowers appear.

BELOW *The popular 'Queen Elizabeth' is a Cluster-flowered (Floribunda) rose named for the mother of Britain's Queen Elizabeth II. It tolerates a hard cutting back every few years.*

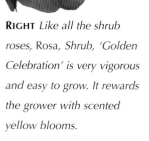

RIGHT *Like all the shrub roses, Rosa, Shrub, 'Golden Celebration' is very vigorous and easy to grow. It rewards the grower with scented yellow blooms.*

LEFT *Most roses, such as Rosa, Large-flowered (Hybrid Tea), 'Double Delight', make perfect hedges because they have minimal water requirements.* **RIGHT** *Rosa, China, 'Old Blush' dates from the mid-1700s. Many advances have been made in repeat-flowering rose cultivation since its introduction.*

ABOVE *Blooming profusely from summer to autumn, Rosa, Polyantha, 'Mevrouw Nathalie Nypels' is a tidy shrub useful in borders or beds. Its compact habit also makes it ideal for containers.* **BELOW** *Rosa, Hybrid Perpetual, 'Ferdinand Pichard', produces red-striped pink blooms that change colour as they age.*

ABOVE *Pure old-style elegance, dark green foliage and large, velvety, crimson-purple blooms make Rosa, Gallica, 'Charles de Mills' one of the finest of the Old roses. The Gallicas flower once in spring or summer.*

LEFT Rosa, *Cluster-flowered (Floribunda),* *'Sexy Rexy'* is an award-winning rose that is covered in large clusters of soft salmon pink camellia-like flowers.

LEFT *Because it is simple and easy to look after,* Rosa, *Cluster-flowered (Floribunda), 'Simplicity' is often used as a landscaping plant. Remove old dead wood when flowering has finished.*

RIGHT *'Happy Child' is a Shrub rose often classified as an English rose. It has a tidy habit and reaches an average height, making it a good border plant.*

Top Tip

To maintain strong healthy growth, a simple "tidying up" of dead wood and pruning for size can be just as effective as stricter pruning regimes.

RIGHT *The yellow-pink blooms of* Rosa, *Hybrid Rugosa, 'Dr Eckener' are usually followed by attractive orange-red hips.*

RIGHT *Also called 'Queen of Denmark',
Rosa, Alba, 'Königin von Dänemark' is an
award-winner, which has smaller double
flowers of a deeper pink than other Albas.*
BELOW *Returning from the Middle East,
Crusaders took the first Damask roses
back to Europe. Rosa, Damask, 'Rose de
Rescht' has deep pink double flowers.*
BOTTOM *Rosa, Large-flowered (Hybrid
Tea), 'Medallion' is widely grown
throughout the USA, chosen for
cottage gardens or formal beds.*

RIGHT Rosa, Tea, 'Mrs Reynolds Hole' has fragrant, rich purple-pink, double flowers. Tea roses grow better in warmer climates.
BELOW Rosa, *China*, 'Mutabilis' has buff red-streaked buds opening to single yellow flowers that change in colour, moving through shades of pink and soft crimson.

ABOVE *The fragrant pink blooms of Rosa, Bourbon, 'Gros Choux d'Hollande' open from red buds. Humid climates see Bourbon roses prone to fungal diseases.*

RIGHT *Moss roses are large, double, fragrant bloomers, usually flowering only once a year. 'James Veitch' is a vigorous example with mauve-pink blooms.*

SPIRAEA

Found mainly in temperate East Asia and North America, this genus from the rose (Rosaceae) family has around 70 species of deciduous to semi-evergreen spring- and summer-flowering shrubs. Most have fine arching stems and simple alternate leaves, often toothed or lobed. Usually as the new foliage develops, they burst into bloom, bearing masses of tiny 5-petalled white to deep pink flowers. The flowers can occur right along the stems or may be clustered in spikes at the tips. While a few species are used in herbal teas, *Spiraea* plants are grown almost exclusively for their ornamental properties.

CULTIVATION

Spiraea are generally hardy and easily grown in any temperate climate garden with moist well-drained soil. They flower best in sun but in areas with hot summers they may need a little shade. Some flower on the old wood and should be pruned immediately after flowering; others flower on the current season's growth and may be trimmed in winter. Propagate from softwood or half-hardened cuttings.

ABOVE Spiraea thunbergii *is a vase-shaped shrub that is generally as wide as it is tall. It mostly branches from the base and has a yellow-orange autumn colour.*
LEFT *The red summer flowers and orange autumn leaves of* Spiraea japonica *'Goldflame' make this cultivar an attractive choice for gardens.*

Top Tip

When positioning a spiraea in your garden, it is best placed in front of green-foliaged plants to provide a backdrop for its beautiful flowers.

ABOVE Spiraea mollifolia *is native to western China. The leaves and young stems of this tall shrub are covered in a silky down. Its branches nod slightly at the tips.*

RIGHT Spiraea japonica *'Dart's Red' has pink-red flowers. Like other* S. japonica *plants, it is an extremely durable shrub and enhances any mass or group planting.*

Favourites	Flower Colour	Blooming Season	Flower Fragrance	Plant Height	Plant Width	Hardiness Zone	Frost Tolerance
Spiraea japonica	rose pink	summer	no	2–6 ft (0.6–1.8 m)	2–6 ft (0.6–1.8 m)	3–10	yes
Spiraea mollifolia	white	summer	no	6–8 ft (1.8–2.4 m)	7 ft (2 m)	6–9	yes
Spiraea nipponica	white	summer	no	3–6 ft (0.9–1.8 m)	3–6 ft (0.9–1.8 m)	5–10	yes
Spiraea thunbergii	white	late spring to summer	no	5 ft (1.5 m)	6 ft (1.8 m)	4–10	yes
Spiraea trichocarpa	white	summer	no	6 ft (1.8 m)	4 ft (1.2 m)	5–9	yes
Spiraea trilobata	white	summer	no	4 ft (1.2 m)	4 ft (1.2 m)	6–9	yes

SYRINGA

Pity the tropical gardener who has never breathed the scent of lilacs in the spring. This olive family (Oleaceae) genus is made up of around only 20 species but was so greatly developed by Lemoine and later hybridisers that the selection is now huge. *Syringa*, or lilac, species are mainly deciduous shrubs and trees, and naturally occur from southeastern Europe to Japan. They have simple, pointed, elliptical or heart-shaped leaves and in spring produce upright panicles of small 4-petalled flowers with an overpowering fragrance. Flowers may be white or shades of pink, red, purple and blue. The genus name comes from the Greek *syrinx* (a pipe), which refers to the hollow stems, and is also the origin of the word syringe.

CULTIVATION
Mostly hardy, *Syringa* plants prefer full or half sun and fertile, moist, humus-rich, well-drained soil. The roots can be invasive, and continually removing suckers can weary even the most ardent lilac lover. Propagate species by seed or cuttings, and cultivars by cuttings or grafting.

ABOVE *'William Robinson' is one of the cultivars of* Syringa vulgaris *and bears light pink to purple double blooms. Spent flowers should be removed immediately after the petals fade.*

Favourites	Flower Colour	Blooming Season	Flower Fragrance	Plant Height	Plant Width	Hardiness Zone	Frost Tolerance
Syringa × *chinensis*	lilac-purple	late spring	yes	12 ft (3.5 m)	12 ft (3.5 m)	5–9	yes
Syringa × *hyacinthiflora*	white, pink blue, lilac, purple	mid- to late spring	yes	15 ft (4.5 m)	10–15 ft (3–4.5 m)	4–9	yes
Syringa × *josiflexa*	lavender-pink	early summer	yes	10 ft (3 m)	6 ft (1.8 m)	5–9	yes
Syringa komarowii	pink	late spring to early summer	yes	10–15 ft (3–4.5 m)	10 ft (3 m)	5–9	yes
Syringa × *laciniata*	lilac	late spring	yes	6 ft (1.8 m)	10 ft (3 m)	5–9	yes
Syringa meyeri	purple-mauve	spring to summer	yes	6 ft (1.8 m)	4 ft (1.2 m)	4–9	yes
Syringa oblata	lilac	spring	yes	8–12 ft (2.4–3.5 m)	8 ft (2.4 m)	5–9	yes
Syringa × *prestoniae*	white, pink, blue, lavender, purple	early summer	yes	12 ft (3.5 m)	12 ft (3.5 m)	4–9	yes
Syringa pubescens	lilac-purple	spring to early summer	yes	12 ft (3.5 m)	12 ft (3.5 m)	5–9	yes
Syringa reticulata	creamy white	summer	yes	15–30 ft (4.5–9 m)	10–20 ft (3–6 m)	3–9	yes
Syringa × *swegiflexa*	pink	late spring to early summer	yes	12 ft (3.5 m)	8 ft (2.5 m)	5–9	yes
Syringa vulgaris	lilac, purple, pink, blue, white	late spring to early summer	yes	8–20 ft (2.4–6 m)	6–10 ft (1.8–3 m)	4–9	yes

LEFT Syringa vulgaris *'Président Grévy' performs best in areas that have cold winters, but it does not like strong winds.*
BELOW Syringa komarowii *grows quickly to 3 m (10 ft) tall, and can eventually exceed 4.5 m (15 ft) in height.*

TAXUS

Agenus of 7 species of evergreen conifers, they are mostly from the Northern Hemisphere temperate zone, with a few found in the mountainous areas of the tropics. They are primarily a foliage plant and their short, pointed, narrow, dark green to deep olive leaves are densely crowded in whorls along the stems for most of the year. However, the small floral cones that may have passed unnoticed in spring develop into fleshy red fruit on female plants and can be a feature from late summer. The famed English longbow weapons popular in the Middle Ages were made from yew. Yew also yields an extract that has been promoted as an anti-cancer drug under the name Taxol.

CULTIVATION

Yews are hardy and undemanding plants that grow well in cool areas with deep, moist, well-drained soil. They withstand severe trimming and are popular hedging and topiary subjects. The seeds germinate well but cultivars are propagated from cuttings or grafts.

LEFT Taxus baccata *'Aurea'* is a hardy and easy-to-grow plant, and is commonly known as golden English yew. Its golden-yellow young growth ages to green.

ABOVE Taxus cuspidata, *the Japanese yew, is suitable for hedging and topiary, and is tolerant of pollution. This variety is* T. c. var. nana *and is a low spreading shrub.*

LEFT Taxus baccata *'Standishii' is a slow-growing, upright, female yew that naturally forms a good growing shape without any clipping or trimming.*

FAR LEFT Taxus × media *is a good shrub for hedging or screening. Do not plant them in windswept sites as some discolouration of the foliage can occur.*

Top Tip

Taxus shrubs are a great background for borders, as their dark green foliage sets off both colourful and pale flowers. They are slow growing but long lived.

Favourites	Fruit Colour	Fruit Shape	Fruit Length	Plant Height	Plant Width	Hardiness Zone	Frost Tolerance
Taxus baccata	red (on female plants only)	ovoid	1/4–1/2 in (6–12 mm)	50 ft (15 m)	25 ft (8 m)	5–10	yes
Taxus baccata 'Aurea'	red (on female plants only)	ovoid	1/4–1/2 in (6–12 mm)	50 ft (15 m)	25 ft (8 m)	5–10	yes
Taxus chinensis	red (on female plants only)	ovoid	1/4–1/2 in (6–12 mm)	20 ft (6 m)	15 ft (4.5 m)	6–10	yes
Taxus cuspidata	red (on female plants only)	ovoid	1/4 in (6 mm)	50 ft (15 m)	20 ft (6 m)	4–9	yes
Taxus × media	red (on female plants only)	ovoid	1/2 in (12 mm)	25 ft (8 m)	20 ft (6 m)	5–9	yes
Taxus × media 'Hicksii'	red (on female plants only)	ovoid	1/4–1/2 in (6–12 mm)	6 ft (1.8 m)	5 ft (1.5 m)	5–9	yes

TELOPEA

There are only 5 species of *Telopea* or waratah, all found only in far eastern Australia from the north coast of NSW down to Tasmania. They are members of the big protea family or Proteaceae and have a striking resemblance to the South African member of the same family, *Leucospermum*. All are multi-stemmed shrubs though the Gippsland waratah, *Telopea oreades*, can reach the size of a small tree. Waratahs occur from coastal woodlands to the highlands of the Great Dividing Range usually in open forest and often on rocky, gravelly or sloping ground. The spectacular NSW waratah has been widely hybridised with the aim of producing plants that are more floriferous and easier to grow in gardens than the natural species.

CULTIVATION

Good soil drainage is the key to success with these plants—they cannot tolerate wetness around them for long though they do like consistent moisture. In general, they will grow in full sun but a position with morning sun then patchy, dappled shade from early afternoon suits them better. If soil is slightly acidic and moderately fertile, no further feeding is needed.

ABOVE *The Latin name,* Telopea, *means "seen from afar"—an apt description of the NSW waratah,* T. speciosissima.

LEFT *A mountain variety,* Telopea mongaensis *has abundant but smaller blooms than the NSW waratah.*

TOP *From the highlands of Tasmania,* Telopea truncata *grows slowly into a small tree or large shrub.*

ABOVE *'Wirrimbirra White' is a rare albino form of the NSW waratah. It is not as vigorous as the natural red form.*

Favourites	Flower Colour	Blooming Season	Flower Fragrance	Plant Height	Plant Width	Hardiness Zone	Frost Tolerance
Telopea aspera	red	spring	no	10–13 ft (3–4.2 m)	6–10 ft (1.8–3 m)	8–9	yes
Telopea mongaensis	red, pink,	late spring	no	6–20 ft (1.8–6 m)	4–15 ft (1–4.2 m)	8–9	yes
Telopea oreades	pink, red	spring	no	15–40 ft (4.5–12 m)	6–26 ft (1.8–8.2 m)	8–9	yes
Telopea speciosissima	red	spring	no	6–16 ft (1.8–5 m)	6–15 ft (1.8–4.2 m)	8–9	yes

TIBOUCHINA

More than 300 species of mostly shrubs, *Tibouchina* belongs to the melastoma family (Melastomataceae). All come from South America and almost all from Brazil. Only a few have ever been available to gardeners, but all of them are showy and garden-worthy subjects for frost-free or near frost-free areas. Flowering time varies with species but is generally in the warmer months from mid-summer to autumn and in subtropical and tropical areas they may flower on and off right through the year. Typical flower colour is deep purple but there are pink and white forms available, too. One of the most popular species, *Tibouchina granulosa*, is always sold as a shrub but, if left unpruned will eventually grow into a small tree up to 12 m (40 ft) tall.

CULTIVATION

Grow in full sun or with periods of broken shade during the day. Plants do best in reasonably good quality, moisture-retentive but free-draining soils and respond to an application of controlled-release fertiliser in spring and again in summer. Prune immediately after flowering or, in cooler areas, in early spring. Over-tall plants can be cut back hard.

ABOVE *Literally covering itself with purple blossom in late summer or early autumn, the named variety 'Alstonville' is one of the showiest of the tibouchinas.*

Top Tip

Though somewhat dryness tolerant, don't allow any *Tibouchina* to endure an extended dry period, especially in summer. Water deeply fortnightly and spray leaves with a commercial seaweed solution.

ABOVE *All tibouchinas have large, 5-petalled flowers with prominent white or golden stamens. Rich, velvety purple is the usual colour.*

Favourites	Flower Colour	Blooming Season	Flower Fragrance	Plant Height	Plant Width	Hardiness Zone	Frost Tolerance
Tibouchina 'Edwardsii'	purple	late summer	no	10–13 ft (3–4.2 m)	10–13 ft (3–4.2 m)	9–10	no
Tibouchina 'Alstonville'	purple	early autumn	no	13–16 ft (4.2–4.9 m)	10–13 ft (3–4.2 m)	9–11	no
Tibouchina 'Jules'	purple	autumn	no	3 ft (0.9 m)	3–5 ft (0.9–1.5 m)	9–11	no

ABOVE *The variety 'Noeline' forms a rounded bush or small tree with flowers that age from purple to pink. It may be a form of* T. mutabilis.
RIGHT *Felty-leaved* Tibouchina urvilleana *flowers in summer on a rounded, spreading shrub. Not as floriferous as 'Alstonville', but its season is longer.*

VIBURNUM

This genus consists of 150 easily grown, cool-climate, deciduous, semi-evergreen or evergreen shrubby plants that are grown for their flowers, autumnal leaf colour and berries. Most have erect branching stems, paired leaves and a spread about two-thirds their height. Small, sometimes fragrant, white flowers are displayed in dense clusters. In certain species the flowers somewhat resemble lacecap hydrangeas; like them, they bear sterile ray florets that surround a centre of small fertile flowers. The buds and petals, particularly in cultivars, may be softly coloured in tints of pink, yellow and green. The berries are vividly coloured, often red, blue or black.

CULTIVATION

Light open positions and light well-drained soils are preferred. Many are drought tender. Prune the evergreens by clipping in late spring and the deciduous species by removing entire old stems after flowering. For a good berry display, grow several shrubs in the same area. Propagation is from cuttings taken in summer, or from seed in autumn.

BELOW *The large, snowball-like, creamy white flower clusters of* Viburnum opulus *'Roseum'—with pale rosy pink markings on some of the petals—usually appear in mid-spring with the leaves. This lovely form is thought to have appeared sometime in the sixteenth century.*

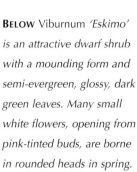

BELOW *Viburnum 'Eskimo' is an attractive dwarf shrub with a mounding form and semi-evergreen, glossy, dark green leaves. Many small white flowers, opening from pink-tinted buds, are borne in rounded heads in spring.*

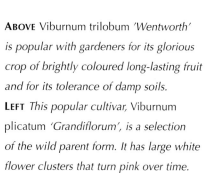

ABOVE Viburnum trilobum 'Wentworth' is popular with gardeners for its glorious crop of brightly coloured long-lasting fruit and for its tolerance of damp soils.
LEFT This popular cultivar, Viburnum plicatum 'Grandiflorum', is a selection of the wild parent form. It has large white flower clusters that turn pink over time.

Favourites	Flower Colour	Blooming Season	Flower Fragrance	Plant Height	Plant Width	Hardiness Zone	Frost Tolerance
Viburnum × *bodnantense*	deep pink to white-pink	autumn to early spring	yes	10 ft (3 m)	6 ft (1.8 m)	5–9	yes
Viburnum *carlesii*	white, sometimes flushed pink	spring	yes	4–8 ft (1.2–2.4 m)	4–8 ft (1.2–2.4 m)	5–9	yes
Viburnum *'Eskimo'*	white	late spring	no	5–7 ft (1.5–2 m)	8–10 ft (2.4–3 m)	5–9	yes
Viburnum *farreri*	white to pink	late autumn to spring	yes	10 ft (3 m)	8 ft (2.4 m)	6–9	yes
Viburnum *lantana*	white	late spring to early summer	no	7–15 ft (2–4.5 m)	6–12 ft (1.8–3.5 m)	3–10	yes
Viburnum *nudum*	white to lemon yellow	summer	no	5–8 ft (1.5–2.4 m)	5–8 ft (1.5–2.4 m)	6–9	yes
Viburnum *opulus*	white	spring	no	8–15 ft (2.4–4.5 m)	6–12 ft (1.8–3.5 m)	3–9	yes
Viburnum *plicatum*	white	late spring to early summer	no	8–10 ft (2.4–3 m)	10–12 ft (3–3.5 m)	4–9	yes
Viburnum *rhytidophyllum*	white, yellowish to pinkish white	spring to early summer	no	15 ft (4.5 m)	12 ft (3.5 m)	6–10	yes
Viburnum *sieboldii*	creamy white	late spring to early summer	no	10–20 ft (3–6 m)	10 ft (3 m)	4–10	yes
Viburnum *tinus*	white to pink	autumn to spring	yes	8–12 ft (2.4–3.5 m)	5–8 ft (1.5–2.4 m)	7–10	yes
Viburnum *trilobum*	white	early summer	no	10–15 ft (3–4.5 m)	6–12 ft (1.8–3.5 m)	2–9	yes

WEIGELA

The 10 or 12 species of this genus within the Caprifoliaceae family are deciduous long-lived shrubs with opposite oblong to elliptic leaves. Their natural habitat is scrubland and the edges of woods in eastern Asia. Cultivated for their bell- or funnel-shaped flowers that are produced in late spring and early summer, they have pink, red, white or sometimes yellow blooms, which grow on the previous year's wood. The leaves make a subtle background to the colourful flowers; mostly dark green, some hybrids have yellow-green, golden yellow or variegated leaves.

CULTIVATION

Weigela shrubs need moist but well-drained fertile soil in sun or partial shade. Propagate by sowing seed in autumn in an area protected from winter frosts or from half-hardened cuttings in summer. Seed may not come true, as they hybridise freely.

Top Tip

These neat shrubs make excellent border plants and ornamentals. There are a great many hybrids, offering a choice of plant size and flower colour.

LEFT Weigela 'Newport Red' is a widely grown hybrid, appreciated for its height, very hardy nature and dark red flowers.

ABOVE *The vivid green leaves of* Weigela middendorfiana *surround pretty, pale yellow, bell-shaped flowers, marked at the throat with orange or red.*

ABOVE *Pink to nearly white flowers appear among the dark green leaves of* Weigela florida. **RIGHT** *A rather beautiful hybrid cultivar,* Weigela *'Looymansii Aurea' is distinguished by its light gold-green leaves and pale pink flowers.*

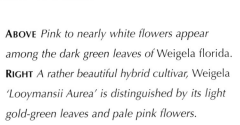

Favourites	Flower Colour	Blooming Season	Flower Fragrance	Plant Height	Plant Width	Hardiness Zone	Frost Tolerance
Weigela 'Bristol Ruby'	dark red	late spring to early summer	no	6 ft (1.8 m)	6 ft (1.8 m)	5–10	yes
Weigela florida	pink	late spring to early summer	no	8 ft (2.4 m)	8 ft (2.4 m)	5–10	yes
Weigela 'Looymansii Aurea'	pink	late spring to early summer	no	5 ft (1.5 m)	5 ft (1.5 m)	5–10	yes
Weigela middendorfiana	yellow, with red or orange throat	mid-spring to mid-summer	no	6 ft (1.8 m)	6 ft (1.8 m)	4–10	yes
Weigela 'Newport Red'	red	spring	no	6 ft (1.8 m)	6 ft (1.8 m)	5–10	yes
Weigela praecox	pink	late spring to early summer	no	8 ft (2.4 m)	6 ft (1.8 m)	5–10	yes

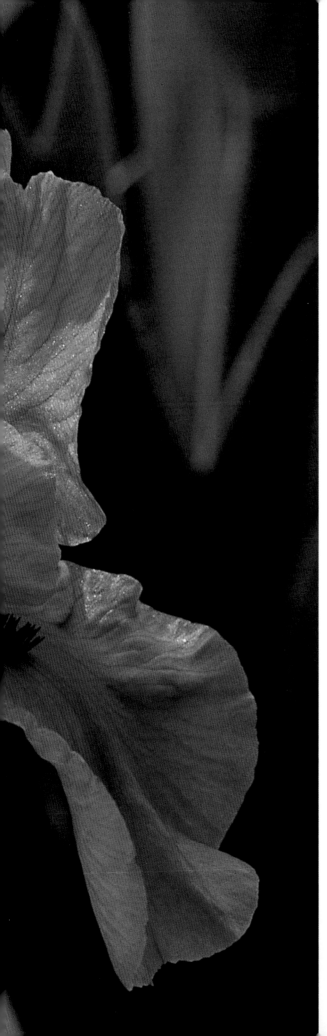

ANNUALS AND PERENNIALS

Annuals, biennials and perennials are some of the most beloved and popular garden plants, offering diversity in flower and form and some of the most nuanced colours and textures. They range from diminutive, tiny-leafed, creeping phlox to brash towering daisies, and lend colour and beauty to a variety of gardens, from tidy urban planters to voluptuous mixed borders. While often used interchangeably by gardeners, there are significant distinctions between the life cycles of annuals, biennials and perennials—distinctions that can guide the savvy gardener in creating a satisfying tapestry of texture and colour in the garden year after year.

ABOVE Viola *hybrid cultivars like 'Crystal Bowl Orange' are treated as annuals or short-lived garden perennials. Plants like these are valued for their prolific colourful flowers.*
LEFT Iris, *Tall Bearded, 'Codicil' is a perennial grown from rhizomes. This plant needs to be divided every 5 to 7 years to achieve the best flower production.*

A BURST OF COLOUR

Some of the most colourful and brightest flowers are annuals—plants whose life cycle (from seed to flowering) is completed within one year of germinating. The life cycle of annuals—rapid growth and flower production followed by (at least in theory) seed—is designed to take advantage of a short or adverse growing season. The abundance of flowers they produce is a means of ensuring their survival before either summer's heat or winter's cold brings their short life to a close. Although the parent plants die, their progeny can continue the species into the following season, if conditions are suitable.

Some of the most charming traditional garden plants are classified among the annuals,

RIGHT *A summer-flowering perennial and a cultivar of common sage,* Salvia officinalis *'Minor' should be divided every 2 or 3 years to maintain vigour.*
BELOW Aquilegia *'Bluebird' is a clump-forming herbaceous perennial that dies down after flowering. One of the Songbird Series, it bears very large flowers.*

such as nasturtiums (*Tropaeolum* species), pansies (*Viola* species), busy lizzies (*Impatiens* species) and zinnias. For gardeners' purposes, plants generally classified as annuals can be divided into 2 main groups: cool-season and warm-season annuals.

Cool-season annuals thrive in moderate temperatures and tolerate light frost, although freezing temperatures will usually fell them. They are also known as half-hardy annuals. In hot summer climates, they are good shoulder-season (spring and autumn) plants and can even grow and flower through the winter in milder climates. In cooler coastal or high-elevation regions, they may flower through the summer too.

Where winters are mild, the seed and young plants of cool-season annuals can be planted in autumn. In cold-winter areas, they should be planted directly in the ground once the soil is workable in spring. Pansies (*Viola* × *wittrockiana*) and sweet peas (*Lathyrus odoratus*) grow vigorously in cooler weather and flower as long as temperatures remain moderate. If or when temperatures rise, they quickly lose vigour and wither away.

At the other end of the spectrum, warm-season or tender annuals require heat to grow and thrive. Plants such as marigolds (*Tagetes* species) and petunias are best planted indoors in spring or outdoors only after the soil has warmed sufficiently. (Seed packets usually include the soil temperature required for germination.) Originating in tropical or subtropical regions, warm-season annuals flourish in summer's heat but perish soon after the first frost.

Unlike their short-lived annual brethren, perennials are plants that live for more than 2 years,

RIGHT Tagetes 'Little Hero Fire' is a very brightly coloured warm-season annual. This dwarf hybrid cultivar is extremely heat tolerant.

BELOW RIGHT The vivid hues of annuals such as Zinnia elegans 'Cherry Ruffles' make them good accent plants against a background of deep green foliage.

taking a couple of seasons to reach flowering size, then flowering each year henceforth. Biennials, often sold as "short-lived perennials" for simplicity's sake, germinate and grow in their first season, flower and set seed in their second and then die. Biennials include the common foxglove *(Digitalis purpurea)*.

The most common perennial plants (excluding woody perennials such as trees and shrubs) are herbaceous. These are plants that disappear below the ground during part of the growing season, typically winter. This protects them from adverse weather conditions. Perennials such as bee balm *(Monarda* species) fall into this group. Other herbaceous perennials die down directly after flowering in spring or summer, emerging again late in the season with a low overwintering rosette of leaves. Such plants include oriental poppies *(Papaver orientale),* columbines *(Aquilegia* species) and cardinal flowers *(Lobelia* species).

Evergreen and semi-evergreen perennials are sometimes classified as shrubs, but many appear on nursery perennial or annual tables (depending on the climate). Generally originating in warmer areas, these plants include sages *(Salvia* species) and Cape fuchsias *(Phygelius* species). Whether a plant is considered an evergreen or semi-evergreen perennial depends, of course, on the climate in which it is growing and even the severity of a given winter in a particular region. The stunning red-flowering pineapple sage *(Salvia elegans)* may be a hardy evergreen shrub in warm-temperate climates, but in

cool-temperate climates, it is a semi-evergreen tender perennial in some areas and an annual in others.

Perennials are among the easiest of plants to grow for beginners. In colder regions, they are best planted out in spring so that their roots can become well established before winter sets in. In milder regions, autumn planting can be beneficial, as it allows time for the plants' roots to become established during a cool moist season.

While earlier gardening trends may have leaned toward the use of showy massed annual bedding plants or the meticulous colour schemes of formal perennial borders, today's gardeners take pride in integrating annuals and perennials, as well as shrubs and trees, thereby gaining the best of all available worlds. Trees and shrubs provide structure for the garden, annuals offer colour and sizzle while the perennials provide ever-changing texture and colour— and the enjoyment of seeing them develop each year.

ACONITUM

Top Tip

The genus name *Aconitum* comes from the Greek and can be translated as "unconquerable poison". This plant is very toxic; use caution when handling it, especially around children.

BELOW *This beautiful plant, Aconitum 'Stainless Steel', is ideal for the front of a border where its pale blue flowers and silver-green foliage can be admired.*

Belonging to the buttercup family, this genus contains about 100 species of mostly tuberous biennials and perennials occurring primarily in the northern temperate zones. Completely dormant over winter, they quickly develop a clump of deeply lobed leaves from which emerge erect flower stems bearing clusters of pendulous, hooded or helmet-shaped flowers, usually white, creamy yellow or mauve-blue to purple in colour. The flowering season may last from summer to autumn. The plant's sap contains several highly toxic alkaloids, principally aconitine, which has a long history of deliberate use as a poison, especially in animal traps, hence the common names of the genus: wolfsbane and badger's bane. Aconitine is used medicinally in controlled doses to slow the heart rate.

CULTIVATION

Species in this genus are mostly very hardy and easily grown in full or half sun. The soil should be moist, humus-rich and well drained. Take care when cutting flowerheads, as the foliage may irritate the skin. Propagate these plants by division when dormant or raise from seed.

ABOVE RIGHT *Aconitum altissimum is native to the European Alps. A handsome robust plant, the tall stems are crowned by clusters of yellow flowers.*
RIGHT *Aconitum napellus var. giganteum is a vigorous grower and a good choice for garden cultivation. It bears purple-blue flowers on tall erect stems.*

BELOW Aconitum carmichaelii *is a highly rewarding garden plant, notable for its long-lasting, large, deep blue flowers.*

Favourites	Flower Colour	Blooming Season	Flower Fragrance	Plant Height	Plant Width	Hardiness Zone	Frost Tolerance
Aconitum altissimum	lemon yellow	summer	no	4 ft (1.2 m)	18 in (45 cm)	4–8	yes
Aconitum carmichaelii	purple, mauve, blue	autumn	no	3–6 ft (0.9–1.8 m)	12–15 in (30–38 cm)	3–9	yes
Aconitum lycoctonum	purple, occasionally yellow	summer	no	3–5 ft (0.9–1.5 m)	12 in (30 cm)	5–8	yes
Aconitum napellus	deep purple-blue	summer	no	4 ft (1.2 m)	12 in (30 cm)	3–9	yes
Aconitum 'Spark's Variety'	deep purple-blue	summer	no	5 ft (1.5 m)	18 in (45 cm)	6–9	yes
Aconitum 'Stainless Steel'	pale lilac-blue	late summer to autumn	no	3 ft (0.9 m)	30 in (75 cm)	4–9	yes

LEFT *At the centre of*
Aechmea fasciata *there is*
a cluster of reddish pink
bracts containing light blue
flowers that age to rose red.
This plant has silvery leaves.
BELOW *The distinctive fea-*
ture of Aechmea weilbachii
is its red stem that bears
purple-blue flowers,
followed by oval fruit.

Top Tip

These plants need
plenty of water
during the growing
season—keep the
central cup filled
with water, and
fertilise monthly
with a mixture that
is low in nitrogen.

AECHMEA

Within this large genus of approximately
240 species and 500 cultivars there is a
wonderful variety of form, size and colour.
The species are mostly epiphytic in their
natural environment—that is, they grow on
another plant for support—and are found
mainly in the humid regions of Central
America down to the cooler areas of southern
Brazil and Argentina. The rosette-forming
foliage ranges in colour from shiny green to
silver, and the edges of the leaves have teeth
that vary from very fine to almost vicious.
Their dramatic spear-like flowerheads can vary
from short to elongated, and many have
bright red bracts beneath the flower branches
that attract hummingbirds as pollinators.

CULTIVATION

An extremely popular genus, plants are mostly
grown in cultivation in pots with some form
of shade. In mild areas they are best grown
indoors; outdoors they need a moist humus-
rich soil. Propagation is mainly by offsets, but
some species can be raised from seed.

ABOVE *Aechmea miniata is a striking Brazilian native, notable for its spiny channelled leaves. As seen above, the popular form* A. miniata *var.* discolor *has red and blue flowers, while its leaves have maroon or rose undersides.* **LEFT** *Also from Brazil,* Aechmea ornata *var.* hoehneana *has strappy green leaves. The erect red bracts are extremely eye-catching, and the flowerhead is a short bristly cylinder bearing many small flowers with blue petals.*

Favourites	Flower Colour	Blooming Season	Flower Fragrance	Plant Height	Plant Width	Hardiness Zone	Frost Tolerance
Aechmea fasciata	light blue; red-pink bracts	summer	no	18 in (45 cm)	20 in (50 cm)	10–12	no
Aechmea fulgens	violet	summer	no	18 in (45 cm)	15 in (38 cm)	11–12	no
Aechmea miniata var. *discolor*	red and blue	summer	no	12–15 in (30–38 cm)	24 in (60 cm)	10–12	no
Aechmea ornata var. *hoehneana*	blue; red bracts	summer	no	24 in (60 cm)	3 ft (0.9 m)	10–12	no
Aechmea recurvata	pale pink, purple; red bracts	summer	no	8 in (20 cm)	20 in (50 cm)	9–12	no
Aechmea weilbachii	blue-purple; red bracts	summer	no	27 in (70 cm)	12 in (30 cm)	10–12	no

Top Tip

Protect *Agapanthus* species from slugs and snails, which can damage young plants. They also need regular watering in spring and summer, as well as loamy soil.

LEFT *There are several* Agapanthus *hybrids and selections available, most of them evergreen. This is an attractive* Agapanthus praecox *cultivar.*

AGAPANTHUS

Commonly known as the lily-of-the-Nile, this is a southern African genus of just 10 species of fleshy-rooted perennials. They have long, strappy, fleshy leaves that form dense clumps of evergreen or deciduous foliage. Tall stems bear blue flowers that are bell-shaped or tubular. In frost-free climates, flowers of evergreens appear over a long season, elsewhere only in summer. This genus makes an ideal border plant due to its narrow upright shape, and dwarf forms are superb in rockeries or containers. In Greek, *Agapanthus* means the flower of love, although the reason for this name is unclear.

CULTIVATION

Agapanthus species are easily grown in full sun or part-shade in any well-drained soil. They are hardy plants and will withstand drought and poor soil, although these situations will affect flower production. Propagate by division in winter or from seed.

LEFT *Also known as the African lily,* Agapanthus *'Lilliput' is a charming dwarf cultivar. The plant bears many deep blue flowers, and the narrow leaves are sparse. 'Lilliput' is useful in containers, mass displays or borders.*

LEFT Agapanthus inapertus *is a many-flowered deciduous species. It has pendent clusters of deep bluish tubular flowers that are unusual in that they do not face the sun. The leaves are bluish green.*

RIGHT *The most popular species in this genus,* Agapanthus praecox *is loved for its starburst flowers that bloom in summer. The evergreen foliage is attractive in its own right and is a year-round asset in the garden.*

Favourites	Flower Colour	Blooming Season	Flower Fragrance	Plant Height	Plant Width	Hardiness Zone	Frost Tolerance
Agapanthus africanus	blue-purple	summer to early autumn	no	18 in (45 cm)	18 in (45 cm)	8–10	yes
Agapanthus campanulatus	pale to deep blue	mid- to late summer	no	36 in (90 cm)	18 in (45 cm)	7–11	yes
Agapanthus inapertus	deep blue-purple	late summer to autumn	no	5 ft (1.5 m)	24 in (60 cm)	8–11	yes
Agapanthus 'Lilliput'	deep blue	mid- to late summer	no	18 in (45 cm)	15 in (38 cm)	8–10	yes
Agapanthus praecox	mauve-blue	summer	no	3 ft (0.9 m)	24 in (60 cm)	9–11	no
Agapanthus 'Rancho White'	white	summer	no	18 in (45 cm)	24 in (60 cm)	9–11	no

AGASTACHE

A member of the mint family (Lamiaceae), this genus of 20 species of aromatic upright or spreading perennials is found in North America, Japan and nearby parts of China. The leaves are usually lance- to heart-shaped with finely lobed or toothed edges. The small flowers are borne in terminal spikes, which vary in length, depending on the species. The flowers appear in summer, and may be white, pink, mauve-blue or purple, though cultivars occur in a wider colour range. Several species have a mint-like flavour and are used in herbal teas or as mint substitutes. Most species have mildly sedating and pain-relieving effects and have been used medicinally wherever they occur.

CULTIVATION

Although intolerant of repeated hard frosts, these plants grow quickly and can be treated as annuals in cold areas. All species can be easily grown in any sunny position with good, moist, well-drained soil. Propagate from basal cuttings of non-flowering stems or seed. Deadhead old flowers so that re-blooming will take place later in the season.

BELOW *From North America,* Agastache foeniculum *bears decorative clusters of light purple flowers with violet bracts. This species tolerates cold and wet more than others in the genus.*

Top Tip

Agastache plants are a welcome addition to mixed borders and herb gardens. They can also be successfully grown as container plants indoors.

LEFT *There are a number of* Agastache *hybrid cultivars available in a wide range of colours. 'Blue Fortune' is a bushy variety with pale blue to lilac flower spikes.*
BELOW *The toothed triangular leaves of* Agastache foeniculum *(also known as anise hyssop) have the aroma and flavour of anise, and are used in herbal teas.*

Favourites	Flower Colour	Blooming Season	Flower Fragrance	Plant Height	Plant Width	Hardiness Zone	Frost Tolerance
Agastache aurantica 'Apricot Sunrise'	deep orange, ageing to apricot	summer to autumn	no	30 in (75 cm)	24 in (60 cm)	7–10	yes
Agastache 'Blue Fortune'	blue	summer to autumn	no	36 in (90 cm)	18–30 in (45–75 cm)	4–10	yes
Agastache cana	red-pink	late summer to autumn	no	24–36 in (60–90 cm)	18 in (45 cm)	5–10	yes
Agastache foeniculum	light purple	mid-summer to early autumn	no	3–5 ft (0.9–1.5 m)	3–4 ft (0.9–1.2 m)	3–10	yes
Agastache rupestris	orange and purple-pink	summer to autumn	no	18–30 in (45–75 cm)	18 in (45 cm)	7–10	yes
Agastache 'Tutti Frutti'	purple-red	summer	no	3–4 ft (0.9–1.2 m)	12–24 in (30–60 cm)	8–10	yes

ALSTROEMERIA

Once classified with the lilies, this South American grouping of around 50 species of fleshy- or tuberous-rooted perennials is now considered the type genus for the Alstroemeriaceae family. Although they have very beautifully marked, long-lasting flowers, their roots can be invasive. Modern hybrids generally have a more restrained habit than the wild species. Most form a clump of upright stems bearing slightly twisted, narrow lance-shaped leaves. The flowers are clustered in heads at the stem tips, opening mainly in summer, and are often used as cut blooms. They are commonly known as Peruvian lilies or lilies of the Incas. Be careful when handling the cut stems as the sap can cause dermatitis.

ABOVE Alstroemeria *'Friendship'* is an award-winning hybrid. In recent years the range of these Alstroemeria *hybrids has increased enormously due to the efforts of plant breeders around the world.*

CULTIVATION

Except where the soil freezes, *Alstroemeria* plants are easily cultivated in any sunny position. The soil should be light, well drained and remain moist through the flowering season. Propagate hybrids and cultivars by division when dormant or raise the species from seed.

RIGHT The Little Miss Series of Alstroemeria *are dwarf plants with large flowers and strong stems.* 'Little Miss Olivia' *has soft cream flowers with a pale yellow throat and red-brown flecks.*

Favourites	Flower Colour	Blooming Season	Flower Fragrance	Plant Height	Plant Width	Hardiness Zone	Frost Tolerance
Alstroemeria **'Friendship'**	soft yellow	summer	no	36 in (90 cm)	24 in (60 cm)	7–10	yes
Alstroemeria **'Fuego'**	red	summer	no	5–6 ft (1.5–1.8 m)	3–4 ft (0.9–1.2 m)	7–10	yes
Alstroemeria psittacina	red-flushed green	summer	no	27–36 in (70–90 cm)	15–20 in (38–50 cm)	8–10	yes
Alstroemeria psittacina **'Royal Star'**	red-flushed green	summer	no	27–36 in (70–90 cm)	15–20 in (38–50 cm)	8–10	yes
Alstroemeria, **Little Miss Series**	various	summer to autumn	no	6–12 in (15–30 cm)	6–12 in (15–30 cm)	7–10	yes
Alstroemeria, **Princess Series**	various	spring to autumn	no	12–18 in (30–45 cm)	12–18 in (30–45 cm)	7–10	yes

BELOW Alstroemeria, *Princess Series, 'Princess Freckles'. The Dutch-raised Princess Series are long flowering and compact, making ideal potted plants.*

BELOW Alstroemeria *'Little Miss Tara' is one of the most colourful in the Little Miss Series. These hybrids have a long flowering period and do not require staking.*

Top Tip

These easily grown plants are known for their very attractive flowers that are excellent for cutting because they last so well in the vase.

AMARANTHUS

There are about 60 species of weedy annuals and short-lived perennials in this exotic-looking genus, which is a member of the Amaranthaceae family. They have a worldwide distribution, often being found in wasteland areas. Species range in form from prostrate to tall, with unusual, long, often drooping tassels of many small blood red or green flowers. Foliage can be just as striking, ranging in colour from red to gold to green. Individual flowers are either male or female, and each sex may be borne on separate plants. Some species are cultivated as leaf or grain crops in tropical areas, while those with dramatic flowers or colourful foliage are ideal for summer bedding displays, in containers and in hanging baskets.

CULTIVATION

Amaranthus are easily grown in well-drained fertile soil in full sun. Protect tall varieties from strong wind. In cooler climates sow seed under glass in early spring and plant out after the danger of frosts has passed. In warmer areas seed can be sown outdoors later in the season.

ABOVE LEFT Amaranthus hypochondriacus 'Pygmy Torch' is a dwarf bushy annual grown for its upright spikes of deep red flowers. **LEFT** Unlike most species in the Amaranthus group, A. tricolor cultivars are valued for their eye-catching leaves, more than their flowers. Colours vary from green and gold to crimson, often in the same plant, as is the case with 'Joseph's Coat'.

Top Tip

Plenty of sun and a sheltered site will ensure healthy and vigorous plants. Prune when young to promote growth, and water regularly during dry periods to prolong the flowering season.

ABOVE *This erect annual,* Amaranthus cruentus, *has dark green to purple leaves that provide a lush backdrop for its long arching branches of red flowers.* **RIGHT** *The pendent tassel-like flowering spikes of* Amaranthus caudatus *'Green Tails', featuring tiny pale green flowers, are indeed like the trailing tail of some strange creature.*

Favourites	Flower Colour	Blooming Season	Flower Fragrance	Plant Height	Plant Width	Hardiness Zone	Frost Tolerance
Amaranthus caudatus	purple-crimson	summer to early autumn	no	3–5 ft (0.9–1.5 m)	18–30 in (45–75 cm)	8–11	no
Amaranthus caudatus **'Green Tails'**	light green	summer to early autumn	no	3–5 ft (0.9–1.5 m)	18–30 in (45–75 cm)	8–11	no
Amaranthus cruentus	dark red	summer to early autumn	no	to 6 ft (to 1.8 m)	18 in (45 cm)	8–11	no
Amaranthus hypochondriacus	crimson	summer to early autumn	no	3–4 ft (0.9–1.2 m)	12–18 in (30–45 cm)	8–11	no
Amaranthus tricolor	green, red	summer	no	3 ft (0.9 m)	18 in (45 cm)	8–11	no
Amaranthus tricolor **'Joseph's Coat'**	green, red	summer	no	3 ft (0.9 m)	18 in (45 cm)	8–11	no

ANIGOZANTHOS

ABOVE RIGHT *The common name for Anigozanthos is kangaroo paw, a reference to the flowers. As seen on A. Bush Gems Series, 'Bush Nugget', the blooms are covered on the outside in woolly hairs, and open at the end into claw-like lobes.*

This genus contains 11 species of evergreen clump-forming perennials, all of which are confined naturally to southwestern Australia. The foliage is usually dark green and varies from grassy to iris-like, with sword-shaped leaves. Tubular-shaped furry blooms (thought to resemble a kangaroo's paw) are borne on slender branching stems, usually during the warmer months. Flowers occur in green and deeper shades of gold, pink, red and russet brown, depending on the species. They make excellent display flowers as they last well when cut, and many new varieties have been developed with the florist trade in mind. A very different use for flowers of *Anigozanthos* plants is the addition of floral extracts to shampoos and conditioners.

CULTIVATION

Plant in a sunny position with good drainage. Most plants perform better if watered well during the growing season but will tolerate drought. Blackened foliage is a sign of ink disease, which can be very damaging, as can slugs and snails. Propagation is most often by division. Species may be raised from seed.

LEFT *Anigozanthos flavidus is one of the hardiest of the kangaroo paws, and can adapt to a variety of climates and soils. In Australia, this species is attractive to native birds.*

Favourites	Flower Colour	Blooming Season	Flower Fragrance	Plant Height	Plant Width	Hardiness Zone	Frost Tolerance
Anigozanthos Bush Gems Series, 'Bush Haze'	bright yellow	spring	no	18 in (45 cm)	18 in (45 cm)	9–11	no
Anigozanthos Bush Gems Series, 'Bush Nugget'	pale orange and green	spring	no	18 in (45 cm)	18 in (45 cm)	9–11	no
Anigozanthos Bush Gems Series, 'Bush Ruby'	deep orange to red	spring	no	18 in (45 cm)	18 in (45 cm)	9–11	no
Anigozanthos flavidus	yellow, green, red	spring	no	3–5 ft (0.9–1.5 m)	3 ft (0.9 m)	9–11	no
Anigozanthos manglesii	yellow-green	mid-spring to early summer	no	1–4 ft (0.3–1.2 m)	15–24 in (38–60 cm)	9–11	no
Anigozanthos 'Pink Joey'	dusky pink	late spring to mid-summer	no	20 in (50 cm)	3 ft (0.9 m)	9–11	no

ABOVE *The bright yellow flowers of the hardy plant* Anigozanthos *Bush Gems Series, 'Bush Haze' appear on the end of tall red stems.*
LEFT *'Bush Ruby' is another plant in the popular Bush Gems Series. As with other cultivars in this series, it has greater resistance to ink disease than most species. A compact plant, its orange-red blooms appear throughout spring.*

ANTHURIUM

This tropical American genus includes some 900 species and is a member of the arum (Araceae) family. Quite often seen as indoor plants, they are also very popular in tropical gardens. They develop into a cluster of upright stems bearing large, deep green, lance- to arrowhead-shaped leaves. The flower stems are topped with a leaf-like heart-shaped bract or spathe that often becomes red, cream or pink as the long flower spike or spadix develops. Anthuriums are also grown as cut flowers. Although some species have been used medicinally where they occur naturally, all parts of the plant are toxic and such use, even externally, is not encouraged.

LEFT *Many cultivars of Anthurium andraeanum have been developed, including this attractive pink version. Like those of the species, these flowers are long-lasting when cut.*

CULTIVATION

These tropical plants require constantly warm humid conditions to flower well. They thrive in moist humus-rich soil with part-shade. They will tolerate brief periods of cool weather but should not be exposed to cold drafts. Feed well to encourage lush foliage and continuous flowering. Propagation is usually by division, though the species may be raised from seed.

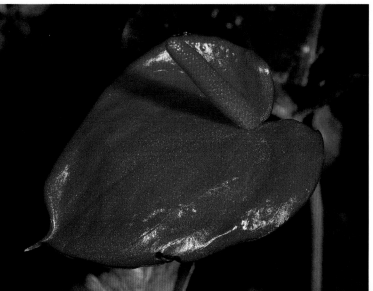

ABOVE *The dark green arrowhead-shaped leaves of Anthurium andraeanum contrast well with the bright red heavily-veined spathes.*
LEFT *Possibly of hybrid origin, Anthurium andraeanum 'Lady Ruth' has brilliant glossy scarlet spathes and similarly coloured spadices.*

Top Tip

As houseplants in non-tropical areas, anthuriums need bright indirect light, moist well-aerated soil and regular feeding to produce flowers.

ABOVE Anthurium andraeanum *'Small Talk Pink'* is a low-growing cultivar with large bright pink spathes and pink-tinted cream spadices.

Favourites	Flower Colour	Blooming Season	Flower Fragrance	Plant Height	Plant Width	Hardiness Zone	Frost Tolerance
Anthurium andraeanum	bright red	all year	no	24 in (60 cm)	8–12 in (20–30 cm)	11–12	no
Anthurium × ferrierense	various	all year	no	24–60 in (60–150 cm)	15–30 in (38–75 cm)	11–12	no
Anthurium scandens	green to purple	all year	no	3–10 ft (0.9–3 m)	1–3 ft (0.3–0.9 m)	11–12	no
Anthurium scherzerianum	bright red	all year	no	15–30 in (38–75 cm)	12–20 in (30–50 cm)	11–12	no
Anthurium upalaense	purple-tinted yellow-green	all year	no	18–30 in (45–75 cm)	36–60 in (90–150 cm)	12	no
Anthurium warocqueanum	green	all year	no	2–5 ft (0.6–1.5 m)	8 ft (2.4 m)	12	no

LEFT AND BELOW LEFT

The common snapdragon, Antirrhinum majus, has produced many cultivars. These can be divided into 3 groups: tall varieties that are valued for their cut flowers; intermediate ones, which are best used in bedding schemes and dwarf forms such as 'Chimes Pink' and the bold 'Chimes Red', at home in pots or borders.

ANTIRRHINUM

N aturally occurring in the temperate Northern Hemisphere, this genus of around 40 species of annuals, perennials and subshrubs belongs in the figwort family (Scrophulariaceae). The best known types are the garden annuals, loved by children for the way the mouth of the flower opens and closes with squeezing, hence they are commonly called snapdragon—although the genus name means nose-like. Most species are compact plants that form a low shrubby mound of simple rounded to lance-shaped leaves, sometimes with a grey-green tint. Flowering

Favourites	Flower Colour	Blooming Season	Flower Fragrance
Antirrhinum grosii	white, purple spots	summer	no
Antirrhinum hispanicum	mauve-pink	all year	no
Antirrhinum majus	white, yellow, pink, red, purple	summer to mid-autumn	no
Antirrhinum majus, Sonnet Series	white, yellow, pink, red, purple	summer to mid-autumn	no
Antirrhinum molle	light pink, white	summer	no
Antirrhinum sempervirens	white, cream	summer	no

stems develop from late spring and carry heads of the familiar 2-lipped tubular blooms from early summer into autumn. Snapdragon seed is rich in oil, which in former times was extracted and used like olive oil.

CULTIVATION
Snapdragons grow best in a fertile, moist, humus-rich soil in full sun. The Mediterranean species are reasonably drought tolerant but still need moisture to flower well. Deadhead to extend the flowering season. Tall plants may need staking. Rust diseases can cause problems in humid conditions. Propagation is usually by seed, though perennials will grow from cuttings of non-flowering stems.

Top Tip

Although they are short-lived perennials, *Antirrhinum majus* cultivars are best treated as annuals. Older plants are at greater risk of disease, and flower quality fades after the first year.

RIGHT *Antirrhinum 'Sonnet White' makes a spectacular display over summer and into autumn. Its bushy habit, clear white blooms and ability to tolerate wet weather makes it ideal for informal garden layouts.*

Plant Height	Plant Width	Hardiness Zone	Frost Tolerance
8 in (20 cm)	12 in (30 cm)	7–10	yes
10 in (25 cm)	12 in (30 cm)	7–10	yes
10–30 in (25–75 cm)	12–18 in (30–45 cm)	6–10	yes
24 in (60 cm)	18 in (45 cm)	6–10	yes
6–8 in (15–20 cm)	8–12 in (20–30 cm)	8–10	yes
6–8 in (15–20 cm)	8–12 in (20–30 cm)	8–10	yes

LEFT *Antirrhinum 'Sonnet Pink' produces 2-lipped pink-purple flowers; other cultivars in this series have bronze, crimson, red, white or yellow blooms.*

AQUILEGIA

This genus belongs to the buttercup family (Ranunculaceae). It contains about 70 species found over much of the temperate and subarctic Northern Hemisphere. These clump-forming perennials have fine-stemmed, often blue-green foliage that emerges from a woody rootstock. The flowering stems usually reach above the foliage and carry attractive, spurred, bell-shaped often pendulous flowers in shades of blue and purple, as well as red, yellow and white. The flowering period can vary among the species; some bloom through much of late spring and summer, others are short-flowering. In contrast to its common name, granny's bonnet, *Aquilegia* is derived from the Latin *aquila* (eagle) and *lego* (to gather), suggesting that the spurs situated at the base of the flower resemble the closing talons of an eagle.

CULTIVATION

This is an adaptable genus, with species and varieties suitable for a range of situations including woodlands, rockeries and perennial borders. Generally, a cool-winter climate and a position in partial shade with cool, moist, humus-rich, well-drained soil is best. Certain species can be very attractive to aphids. Propagation is usually by seed, though some species can be divided when dormant.

LEFT Aquilegia vulgaris, *with its gently nodding flowers, is the eponymous granny's bonnet. Hybrids occur in shades of red, white or green, as well as bicolours like 'Rougham Star'.*

RIGHT *The Songbird Series is well loved for its large upright blooms in a wide range of colours.*

Left Aquilegia caerulea *occurs naturally from New Mexico to Montana, USA. It bears bicoloured white and lilac-blue flowers with slender spurs on erect stems.*

Below *The hybrid cultivar* Aquilegia *'Crimson Star' has mid-green leaves and upright stems, each one bearing 2 to 3 pendent flowers with ruby red sepals and creamy white petals.*

Top Tip

These plants are fairly easy to grow, and are suited to sunny herbaceous borders. As they hybridise freely, plant different types some distance apart.

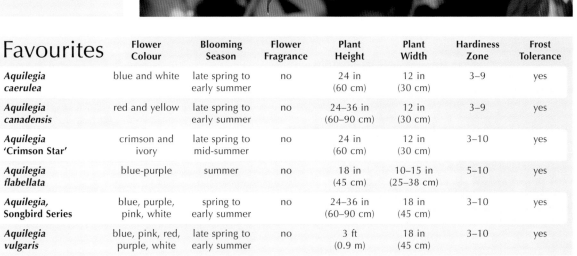

Favourites	Flower Colour	Blooming Season	Flower Fragrance	Plant Height	Plant Width	Hardiness Zone	Frost Tolerance
Aquilegia caerulea	blue and white	late spring to early summer	no	24 in (60 cm)	12 in (30 cm)	3–9	yes
Aquilegia canadensis	red and yellow	late spring to early summer	no	24–36 in (60–90 cm)	12 in (30 cm)	3–9	yes
Aquilegia 'Crimson Star'	crimson and ivory	late spring to mid-summer	no	24 in (60 cm)	12 in (30 cm)	3–10	yes
Aquilegia flabellata	blue-purple	summer	no	18 in (45 cm)	10–15 in (25–38 cm)	5–10	yes
Aquilegia, Songbird Series	blue, purple, pink, white	spring to early summer	no	24–36 in (60–90 cm)	18 in (45 cm)	3–10	yes
Aquilegia vulgaris	blue, pink, red, purple, white	late spring to early summer	no	3 ft (0.9 m)	18 in (45 cm)	3–10	yes

ARCTOTIS

Known as the African daisy, this genus is naturally occurring from the southern tip of Africa northwards to Angola. It consists of around 50 species of low-spreading annuals and perennials that often produce masses of large and brightly coloured flowerheads. The leaves are simple, usually lance-shaped and frequently have felted undersides. For much of the year in mild climates the daisy-like flowers top the foliage, appearing in a wide range of colours. Modern strains now cover most of the colour spectrum except blue. The name *Arctotis* comes from the Greek and means bear's ear, which is what the individual petals on the flower are thought to resemble.

CULTIVATION

African daisies thrive in light well-drained soil, and full sun. They are drought tolerant but flower much more heavily if watered well during the growing season. Propagation is by seed, though the perennial species grow readily from cuttings of the non-flowering stems.

Favourites	Flower Colour	Blooming Season	Flower Fragrance
Arctotis acaulis	yellow-orange to red	mid-summer to autumn	no
Arctotis fastuosa	orange	mid-summer to autumn	no
Arctotis, **Harlequin Hybrids**	yellow, orange, pink, red, white	summer to autumn	no
Arctotis, **Harlequin Hybrids 'Flame'**	orange-red	summer to autumn	no
Arctotis, **Harlequin Hybrids 'Red Devil'**	bright red	summer to autumn	no
Arctotis venusta	yellow, orange, pink, white	mid-summer to autumn	no

BELOW Arctotis acaulis *is a spreading perennial that flowers late in the season. The blooms range in colour from yellow to red, and have a blackish purple centre.*

ABOVE Arctotis, *Harlequin Hybrids 'Flame' is one of the most popular plants in this group, as it has striking orange-red flowers. These hybrids generally produce their best flowers in the first year.*

LEFT Arctotis venusta *is commonly known as the blue-eyed African daisy because of its deep bluish grey eye, which is surrounded by a bright yellow ring.*

Plant Height	Plant Width	Hardiness Zone	Frost Tolerance
12 in (30 cm)	24 in (60 cm)	9–11	no
12–24 in (30–60 cm)	12 in (30 cm)	9–11	no
18–20 in (45–50 cm)	12 in (30 cm)	9–11	no
18–20 in (45–50 cm)	12 in (30 cm)	9–11	no
18–20 in (45–50 cm)	12 in (30 cm)	9–11	no
24 in (60 cm)	15 in (38 cm)	9–11	no

ARMERIA

This genus comprises around 80 species of herbaceous and shrubby perennials found in Eurasia, North Africa and the American Pacific coast. They form dense cushion-like clumps of simple linear leaves above which in spring and summer rounded heads of tiny flowers are borne on slender stems. Flowers may be white, pink or nearly red. The genus was named *Armeria,* the Roman word for *Dianthus* (or carnation), because of a supposed resemblance between the 2 genera, though in fact they are not from the same family. The common name of *Armeria* is thrift—that is, to thrive—which refers to the plant's ability to grow well even under harsh conditions.

CULTIVATION

Known as coastal plants, the species actually occur in a wide range of environments and are easily cultivated, being especially at home in rockeries. Most are quite hardy and prefer moist well-drained soil and a position in full or half sun. Propagate by seed, cuttings or the careful division of well-established clumps.

ABOVE LEFT *Though compact in size,* Armeria maritima *'Bloodstone' is certainly eye-catching. Throughout spring and summer it produces many deep pink to red flowers.*
ABOVE Armeria alliacea *is a robust perennial that bears white, occasionally red-purple, flowers on tall stems that may grow up to 50 cm (20 in) in height.*

Favourites	Flower Colour	Blooming Season	Flower Fragrance	Plant Height	Plant Width	Hardiness Zone	Frost Tolerance
Armeria alliacea	white to red-purple	summer	no	20 in (50 cm)	20 in (50 cm)	5–9	yes
Armeria 'Bee's Ruby'	deep pink	early summer	no	12 in (30 cm)	10 in (25 cm)	5–9	yes
Armeria girardii	lavender-pink	late spring to summer	no	10 in (25 cm)	12 in (30 cm)	6–9	yes
Armeria juniperifolia	light to deep pink	late spring	no	3 in (8 cm)	6 in (15 cm)	5–9	yes
Armeria maritima	white to deep red	spring to summer	no	4 in (10 cm)	8 in (20 cm)	4–9	yes
Armeria 'Westacre Beauty'	pink	spring to summer	no	6 in (15 cm)	12 in (30 cm)	4–9	yes

RIGHT *A mass of pink flowerheads is borne above the grey-green foliage of* Armeria juniperifolia. *Place this hummock-forming plant at the front of a border.*
BELOW Armeria maritima *is ideally suited to this rock garden. In this example, a mass of narrow sea green leaves appears as a cushion to a profusion of red flowers.*

Top Tip

A favourite of the cottage garden, *Armeria* flowers can also be used fresh or dried in floral arrangements. Try tall-stemmed brightly coloured cultivars such as 'Bee's Ruby'.

ASCLEPIAS

This American and African genus consists of over 100 species and includes annuals, perennials, subshrubs and shrubs among its number. The shrubs are generally upright many-branched plants with simple, narrow, elliptical to lance-shaped leaves. They produce heads of small 5-petalled flowers that are followed by inflated seed pods, sometimes oddly shaped and variable in length. Upon ripening, the seed pods open to reveal rows of tightly packed small seeds, each with a small parachute of silky down, hence the common name of silkweed. All parts of the plants exude a milky sap if cut, which may irritate the skin. This sap is the origin of the genus's other common name, milkweed.

CULTIVATION

Asclepias plants are easily grown in any light well-drained soil with full sun. They will, however, bear more luxuriant foliage and a greater profusion of flowers if well-fed and watered. The shrubby species are generally rather frost tender but grow so readily and quickly from seed that they can be treated as annuals or short-lived perennials.

ABOVE *A native of South America, the cultivar* Asclepias curassavica *'Silky Gold' produces yellow-gold flowers and has attractive lance-shaped leaves.*
RIGHT Asclepias incarnata *is a herbaceous perennial from eastern USA. It bears delightful clusters of pinkish purple flowers.*

LEFT *Native to southwestern USA,* Asclepias linaria *is a sun-loving shrubby perennial with needle-like leaves and clusters of white flowers.*

Top Tip

Asclepias plants, particularly the shrubby species, can be trimmed to shape if necessary, but do not cut back to bare wood as the plants can be slow to recover if pruned to excess.

ABOVE *Bold strappy leaves and bright orange-red flowers are features of* Asclepias curassavica, *a plant that is considered invasive in warmer climates.*
RIGHT *Butterflies flock to the hot-coloured flowers of* Asclepias tuberosa, *which is why this plant is commonly known as butterfly weed. It needs lots of sun and well-drained soil.*

Favourites	Flower Colour	Blooming Season	Flower Fragrance	Plant Height	Plant Width	Hardiness Zone	Frost Tolerance
Asclepias curassavica	orange-red	summer to autumn	no	36 in (90 cm)	24–36 in (60–90 cm)	9–12	no
Asclepias incarnata	pinkish purple	mid-summer to early autumn	no	4 ft (1.2 m)	24 in (60 cm)	3–8	yes
Asclepias linaria	white	spring and summer	no	36 in (90 cm)	36 in (90 cm)	9–11	no
Asclepias speciosa	pinkish purple	summer	no	36 in (90 cm)	24 in (60 cm)	2–9	yes
Asclepias subulata	yellowish white	spring to autumn	no	3–5 ft (0.9–1.5 m)	36 in (90 cm)	9–11	no
Asclepias tuberosa	orange-red, orange, yellow	summer	no	24–36 in (60–90 cm)	12 in (30 cm)	3–9	yes

ABOVE Aster × frikartii *'Mönch' is an award-winning cultivar of this garden hybrid. Only 38 cm (15 in) tall, 'Mönch' bears lavender-blue flowers.*

BELOW Aster sedifolius *subsp.* ageratoides *is more compact than the species, with narrower leaves and its darker purple flowers appear later in the season.*

ASTER

This large genus, the type form for the daisy (Asteraceae) family, is made up of over 250 species found mainly in the northern temperate zones, with a toehold in South America. They are mainly herbaceous perennials but also include annuals, biennials and a few rather shrubby species. While some, usually the alpines, form low clumps, most have erect stems topped with massed compound flowerheads. The leaves are simple, linear, lance- or spatula-shaped, sometimes with toothed edges. Summer to mid-autumn is the main flowering season, with pink, mauve and purple the predominant colours. Asters are also known as Michaelmas daisies. In recognition of the flowerhead's shape, the name *Aster* is taken from the Latin word for star.

CULTIVATION
Asters are mostly very frost hardy and prefer a position in full sun with moist well-drained soil. Good air circulation is important to prevent mildew developing. Deadhead routinely to encourage continued flowering. Propagate by division when dormant or from spring basal cuttings.

Favourites	Flower Colour	Blooming Season	Flower Fragrance	Plant Height	Plant Width	Hardiness Zone	Frost Tolerance
Aster ericoides	white, blue, pink	summer to autumn	no	30–40 in (75–100 cm)	20–30 in (50–75 cm)	3–9	yes
Aster × frikartii	violet-blue	late summer to early autumn	no	20–30 in (50–75 cm)	15–24 in (38–60 cm)	5–9	yes
Aster novae-angliae	violet to purple	late summer to early autumn	no	4–5 ft (1.2–1.5 m)	2–4 ft (0.6–1.2 m)	4–9	yes
Aster novae-angliae 'Andenken an Alma Pötschke'	cerise-pink	late summer to early autumn	no	4 ft (1.2 m)	2 ft (0.6 m)	4–9	yes
Aster novi-belgii	violet to purple	late summer to early autumn	no	4 ft (1.2 m)	3 ft (0.9 m)	4–9	yes
Aster sedifolius	white to pale blue	summer	no	36 in (90 cm)	20 in (50 cm)	7–9	yes

BELOW Aster novae-angliae *'Andenken an Alma Pötschke' is one of this species' most popular culti-vars. It is also known by the synonym 'Alma Pötschke'.*

LEFT *This* Aster novi-belgii *cultivar is one of over 400 cultivars belonging to this North American species. Many bloom prolifically, displaying masses of daisy flowers in shades of white, blue, purple and pink.*

ASTILBE

Found mainly in temperate East Asia, this perennial genus of the saxifrage family (Saxifragaceae) includes just 12 species but has been extensively selected and hybridised to produce many garden plants. The shiny toothed leaves sprout directly from the plant's fleshy stem and soon form a generous foliage clump. Striking long-stemmed plumes of tiny flowers appear during spring and summer in colours ranging from white to shades of pink, mauve and red. Surprisingly, given their showy nature, the genus name *Astilbe* actually means without brilliance, coming from the Greek *a* (without) and *stilbe* (brilliance). That is because, although the flowerheads are bright, each flower on its own is tiny and rather dull.

CULTIVATION

Astilbe plants are not drought tolerant nor do they thrive in the hot summer sun; instead they prefer light, moist, humus-rich woodland soil and dappled sunlight. They often thrive around pond margins as they tolerate being waterlogged, especially in winter. To propagate, divide clumps in winter when dormant, then replant immediately.

BELOW LEFT Astilbe japonica *'Deutschland' is grown for its springtime profusion of tiny white flowers borne on plume-like panicles. Foliage is dark to bright green.*
BELOW Astilbe × arendsii *refers to a group of hybrids derived from 4 East Asian species. They are valued for their pretty feathery spikes. 'Gloria', below, has deep pink flowers; lilac, white, crimson and coral pink forms are also available.*

Top Tip

Astilbe flowers can be cut and used in fresh flower arrangements, but they do not last long. For more satisfying results, bring some indoors as pot plants when the flowers are at their best.

ABOVE *Another hybrid from the* Astilbe × arendsii *group, 'Fanal' grows up to 60 cm (24 in). Like many hybrids in this group, it is a striking plant. It has dark leaves and long-lasting, star-shaped, crimson-red flowers.*

RIGHT Astilbe chinensis *'Visions' is an attractive clump-forming plant with toothed, hairy, dark green leaves and dense fluffy spikes of pink-red flowers.*

Favourites	Flower Colour	Blooming Season	Flower Fragrance	Plant Height	Plant Width	Hardiness Zone	Frost Tolerance
Astilbe × arendsii	white to purple-pink	summer	no	24–48 in (60–120 cm)	24 in (60 cm)	6–10	yes
Astilbe chinensis	white flushed with pink or red	summer	no	24 in (60 cm)	24 in (60 cm)	6–10	yes
Astilbe japonica	white	summer	no	36 in (90 cm)	24–36 in (60–90 cm)	5–10	yes
Astilbe koreana	ivory	summer	no	24 in (60 cm)	24 in (60 cm)	6–10	yes
Astilbe simplicifolia	white	summer	no	12 in (30 cm)	18 in (45 cm)	7–10	yes
Astilbe thunbergii	white, turning pink with age	early summer	no	24 in (60 cm)	24–36 in (60–90 cm)	7–10	yes

LEFT Astrantia carniolica *is a native of the southern Alps. It has white flowers with pinkish tints.*

ASTRANTIA

This genus of about 10 species of perennials is mainly European, though it also occurs westwards to Asia, favouring alpine meadows or woodlands. Its most distinguishing feature is its sprays of flowers, which appear above the clump-forming hand-shaped foliage. The small pastel-toned flowers are borne on neat dome-shaped flowerheads and are surrounded by a ring of papery bracts, which are often more showy than the true flowers inside. This genus is variously referred to as masterwort or pin-cushion flower. The name *Astrantia* probably comes from the Latin *aster,* meaning star, referring to the star-shaped flowerheads. These plants are best grown in informal garden situations. They also make excellent dried flowers.

CULTIVATION

Apart from an intolerance of prolonged dry conditions, *Astrantia* plants grow freely in any cool-temperate garden with moderately fertile free-draining soil. The foliage may be more lush in the shade, which is of particular consideration with the variegated cultivars, but they usually flower best with at least half-sun. Propagate by division when dormant or from seed, which needs stratification.

Top Tip

Astrantia plants can be grown in cottage gardens, woodland gardens or herbaceous borders. They make great cut flowers because of their straight wiry stems.

BELOW Astrantia major *bears clusters of delicate white or pink flowerheads that resemble daisies. This species originates from Central and eastern Europe.*

BELOW Astrantia major *has a number of cultivars available in a wide variety of colours.* A. major *subsp.* involucrata *'Moira Reid' (pictured) flowers earlier in the season than the species, and has large green-tipped flowers.*

ABOVE *A favourite in cottage gardens, Astrantia major 'Ruby Wedding' bears ruby red flowers on distinctive maroon stems throughout the summer months.*

Favourites	Flower Colour	Blooming Season	Flower Fragrance	Plant Height	Plant Width	Hardiness Zone	Frost Tolerance
Astrantia carniolica	white tinged pink	summer	no	18–24 in (45–60 cm)	24 in (60 cm)	4–9	yes
Astrantia carniolica 'Rubra'	deep pink with silvery tints	summer	no	18–24 in (45–60 cm)	24 in (60 cm)	4–9	yes
Astrantia major	pink, white, purple, green	summer	no	12–36 in (30–90 cm)	18 in (45 cm)	6–9	yes
Astrantia major 'Ruby Wedding'	deep red	summer	no	12–36 in (30–90 cm)	18 in (45 cm)	6–9	yes
Astrantia major subsp. involucrata 'Moira Reid'	white	summer	no	12–36 in (30–90 cm)	18 in (45 cm)	6–9	yes
Astrantia maxima	pale pink	summer	no	36 in (90 cm)	12 in (30 cm)	5–9	yes

Favourites	Flower Colour	Blooming Season	Flower Fragrance
Begonia boliviensis	orange-red	summer	no
Begonia bowerae	white	winter to early spring	no
Begonia, **Cane-stemmed**	white, pink orange, red	early spring to autumn	no
Begonia, **Rex-cultorum Group**	white, pink	early spring	no
Begonia, **Semperflorens-cultorum Group**	white, pink, red	summer or all year	no
Begonia, **Tuberhybrida Group**	orange, red, pink, yellow, white	summer	no

ABOVE *For a bright and beautiful begonia that will add a touch of warmth to the garden, you can't go past the rose-like blooms of* Begonia, Tuberhybrida Group, 'Apollo'.

Top Tip

The many varieties of begonia offer a range of choices for the keen gardener. Some are suitable for basket planting, others as bedding annuals while some cultivars are suited to terrarium planting.

BEGONIA

This genus belongs to the Begoniaceae family and contains around 900 species of perennials, shrubs and climbers that are found throughout the tropics and subtropics. The most diverse species occur in the Americas. These clump-forming plants have olive green to bright green foliage that may vary greatly in colour, texture and shape but is often lobed and covered in fine hairs. There is usually a single female flower surrounded by 2 or more male flowers, appearing in shades of white, yellow, orange, red and pink. Begonias were named after Michel Bégon, a fifteenth-century Governor of Santo Domingo and later of French Canada, known today as Quebec.

CULTIVATION

Outside of tropical climates, begonias are best grown as indoor container plants. They grow well in a bright but not a sunny position with cool, moist, humus-rich soil and need to be watered and fed well. Begonias are susceptible to fungal diseases so they need to have good air flow around them.

ABOVE *The glossy, heart-shaped leaves of* Begonia *'Merry Christmas'—a member of the Rex-cultorum Group—have a rosy pink central heart, edged in dark green and are sometimes flecked with silver highlights. During autumn and winter, this attractive foliage is complemented by rosy pink flowers.*

Plant Height	Plant Width	Hardiness Zone	Frost Tolerance
36 in (90 cm)	36 in (90 cm)	10–11	no
10 in (25 cm)	12 in (30 cm)	10–12	no
5 ft (1.5 m)	4 ft (1.2 m)	10–11	no
8–12 in (20–30 cm)	18–24 in (45–60 cm)	10–12	no
12 in (30 cm)	12 in (30 cm)	9–11	no
18 in (45 cm)	24 in (60 cm)	9–11	no

ABOVE *The variegated light and dark green leaves of Begonia bowerae 'Tiger' provide a contrast to the small, pure white flowers borne in early summer. It is particularly suited to indoor situations, where it will flower reliably.*

RIGHT *Begonia, Semperflorens-cultorum Group, 'Rose Pink' has delicately pink-flushed white flowers contrasting well with the waxy green leaves.*

LEFT *Contrasting shades of pink, and somewhat crimped petal edges, combine to create the attractive, double, summer-flowering blooms of* Begonia *'Roy Hartley', a member of the Tuberhybrida Group.*

BELOW *A lovely example of the Picotee group of cultivars in the Tuberhybrida Group,* Begonia *'Mardi Gras' bears snow white double blooms, becoming creamier at the centre, with crimson-edged petals.*

BELOW *Featuring pink flowers and prominent whitish green spotting on the large leaves,* Begonia, *Cane-stemmed, 'Flamingo Queen' is a relatively new hybrid cultivar.*

ABOVE *One of the cane-stemmed begonias,* Begonia *'Pinafore' bears small, soft pink flowers on slender stems. Glossy leaves, dark green above and deep red beneath, add interest to this low-growing plant.*

LEFT Begonia, Cane-stemmed, 'Looking Glass' is grown for its stunning foliage. The leaves are silvery green above and red underneath.

ABOVE The glossy dark green leaves of Begonia, Semper-florens-cultorum Group, 'Prelude Bicolor' provide a perfect foil for the coral pink-edged white flowers, which are held above the leaves on long stems.

BERGENIA

Curiously known as pigsqueak, this genus of the saxifrage family (Saxifragaceae) is made up of 8 species of perennials that are found in Asia, extending from Afghanistan to Mongolia. Sprouting from tough woody stems, the large leathery leaves are broad and light green in colour. The 5-petalled flowers grow in clusters on long stems and open in spring. Most species produce flowers in shades of pink but some garden forms occur in white, mauve and red. *Bergenia* is named after an eighteenth-century German botanist, Karl August von Bergen. The common name pigsqueak comes from the sound the wet leaves make when rubbed between the fingers.

CULTIVATION

Bergenia species thrive in sun or shade with humus-rich soil. Planting in partial shade with cool moist conditions will develop lush foliage, whereas full sun will produce flowers at the expense of the leaves. This adaptable genus is extremely suitable as a ground cover or as a rockery plant.

ABOVE *Originating from China,* Bergenia emeiensis *is a relative newcomer to Western gardens. It has proven particularly useful in hybridisation work.*
LEFT *The attractive pink-hued blooms of* Bergenia crassifolia *are carried on long stalks to emerge through the lush foliage.*

Top Tip

Bergenia species will withstand less than ideal soil conditions and some neglect. However, they will benefit from the removal of old flowers and dead leaves.

ABOVE Bergenia ciliata *is popular for both its handsome foliage and attractive flowers. The large, rounded, glossy leaves are around 30 cm (12 in) wide, and are interspersed with pretty clusters of blooms during the flowering season.*
RIGHT *The autumn foliage of* Bergenia cordifolia *'Perfecta' is spectacular, as the glossy heart-shaped leaves take on fiery hues of scarlet and gold. The purple-pink flowers, held on long stems, appear in late winter.*

Favourites	Flower Colour	Blooming Season	Flower Fragrance	Plant Height	Plant Width	Hardiness Zone	Frost Tolerance
Bergenia 'Abendglut'	magenta-red	spring	no	8–12 in (20–30 cm)	18–24 in (45–60 cm)	3–8	yes
Bergenia ciliata	pink, white	early spring	yes	12 in (30 cm)	18 in (45 cm)	5–9	yes
Bergenia cordifolia	purple-pink	late winter to early spring	no	24 in (60 cm)	30 in (75 cm)	3–9	yes
Bergenia crassifolia	rose pink to magenta	early spring	no	18 in (45 cm)	18 in (45 cm)	3–9	yes
Bergenia emeiensis	white flushed pink	early spring	no	8 in (20 cm)	18 in (45 cm)	8–9	yes
Bergenia × *schmidtii*	rose pink	late winter to early spring	no	12 in (30 cm)	24 in (60 cm)	5–10	yes

BILLBERGIA

ABOVE *As the name indicates,* Billbergia venezuelana *is a native of Venezuela. When in flower it grows to about 90 cm (36 in) tall, and has numerous brightly coloured bracts.*

This genus belongs to the large bromeliad family (Bromeliaceae) and consists of around 65 species of evergreen perennials and about 500 cultivars. Most species are epiphytic or rock dwelling and come from Mexico and the warmer regions of Central and South America. The leaves form a tubular rosette and range in colour from dull olive green to grey-green with a variety of attractive markings. Showy stalked flower clusters emerge from the leaf rosettes. The flowers are globular to cylindrical and have side spikes of blue-green to navy blue petals. Bright pink or red banner-like bracts appear underneath the flowerhead. *Billbergia* plants are commonly referred to as vase plants because the central hollow of the plant acts as an important storage area for water between rainfalls.

CULTIVATION

Most plants in this genus are easy to grow and are suitable for both indoor and outdoor planting. If planting outside, keep the plant in a sheltered humid spot in a porous fast-draining soil mix or a mound of stones. Use the shoots that grow from the base of the plant for propagation.

Favourites	Flower Colour	Blooming Season	Flower Fragrance	Plant Height	Plant Width	Hardiness Zone	Frost Tolerance
Billbergia distachia	green-blue	summer	no	20 in (50 cm)	20 in (50 cm)	9–12	no
Billbergia nutans	green-blue	spring	no	20 in (50 cm)	Indefinite	9–12	no
Billbergia pyramidalis	magenta	late summer to mid-winter	no	20 in (50 cm)	10 in (25 cm)	9–12	no
Billbergia sanderiana	lavender-pink and pale green	autumn	no	20–24 in (50–60 cm)	24 in (60 cm)	9–12	no
Billbergia venezuelana	pink-red and yellow-green	autumn to winter	no	36 in (90 cm)	24 in (60 cm)	9–12	no
Billbergia zebrina	pink-red and yellow-green	autumn to winter	no	36 in (90 cm)	24 in (60 cm)	9–12	no

LEFT Billbergia zebrina *is a very hardy plant from South America. Its green leaves are banded in silver or white, and may develop bronze tints in strong light.*

Top Tip

If grown as indoor plants, *Billbergia* species need to be potted in a mixture composed of leaf mould, bark and sand. They do best if placed in a warm sunny position.

RIGHT *The striking features of* Billbergia pyramidalis *are the panicles of magenta-pink flowers tipped in pale blue that appear in summer.* **FAR RIGHT** *Known as the friendship plant,* Billbergia nutans *is valued for its long narrow leaves, and flowers of light green and dark blue, with pink bracts.*

CALCEOLARIA

This genus of around 300 species includes annuals, perennials and even some small shrubs, and is found from Mexico to the southern tip of South America. The leaves tend to be light green and are covered with fine hairs and small glands that make them sticky to the touch. They are known as slipper flower or lady's purse, due to the distinctive pouch-like shape of the flowers, which is common to almost all species. The flowers are 2-lipped, with a small hooded upper lip and a large lower lip that is inflated to form a kind of pouch. Yellow, orange and red shades dominate. *Calceolaria* plants are usually grown as pot plants or in hanging baskets, as the blossoms are rather fragile.

CULTIVATION

While *Calceolaria* plants vary in their frost hardiness and sun tolerance, they all prefer cool, moist soil conditions. Work in plenty of high-humus compost before planting. The shrubby species tend to become rather untidy after a few years, and although pruning can rejuvenate them, replacement with new plants may be more successful. The seed germinates well, but tip cuttings strike so quickly that this is a more successful method of propagation.

ABOVE *'Sunset Red' is one of the many cultivars of the* Calceolaria, Herbeohybrida *Group. It has deep red flowers and is suitable for massed bedding.*

LEFT *A hybrid of uncertain parentage,* Calceolaria *'John Innes' has cheerful yellow and red flowers that bloom throughout summer.*

Top Tip

A liquid fertiliser applied every few weeks to indoor plants will improve the size and colour of the flowers. Make sure not to give them too much water.

Favourites	Flower Colour	Blooming Season	Flower Fragrance	Plant Height	Plant Width	Hardiness Zone	Frost Tolerance
Calceolaria biflora	yellow	summer	no	4–12 in (10–30 cm)	12 in (30 cm)	7–9	yes
Calceolaria, Herbeohybrida Group	various	spring to summer	no	8–18 in (20–45 cm)	6–12 in (15–30 cm)	9–11	no
Calceolaria, Herbeohybrida Group, 'Sunset Red'	red and yellow	spring to summer	no	8 in (20 cm)	10 in (25 cm)	9–11	no
Calceolaria integrifolia	bright yellow	summer	no	2–5 ft (0.6–1.5 m)	2–5 ft (0.6–1.5 m)	8–10	yes
Calceolaria 'John Innes'	yellow with deep red markings	summer	no	6 in (15 cm)	12 in (30 cm)	7–9	yes
Calceolaria uniflora var. darwinii	yellow, white and red	summer	no	4 in (10 cm)	12 in (30 cm)	6–9	yes

LEFT *'Goldbouquet' is one of many named cultivars of Calceolaria integrifolia. These woody-based plants are suitable in pots, borders and hanging baskets, and require lots of sun.*

BELOW *From Patagonia, Calceolaria uniflora var. darwinii has tri-coloured flowers with a large lower lip. If grown indoors, it requires a well-ventilated spot away from strong sun.*

CALENDULA

Now widely naturalised, this genus of about 20 species of annuals and perennials in the daisy (Asteraceae) family originates from the Mediterranean and nearby Atlantic Islands. They often colonise waste ground and thrive in poor soils, which doubtless helped them to establish well away from home. Simple lance- to spatula-shaped leaves, often aromatic, make dense clumps that from mid-winter to late autumn, depending on the species, are covered in cream, yellow or orange flowerheads, often with many ray florets. The genus name *Calendula* reflects this long-flowering habit, as it refers to the first day of the month and indicates that flowers may be found on the plant in almost any month.

CULTIVATION

These undemanding flowers thrive in full sun with light, well-drained soil kept moist through the flowering season. Deadheading frequently will encourage continuous blooming. Mildew can be a problem in autumn. Usually raised from seed, they will self-sow if flowers are left alone.

BELOW Calendula officinalis *'Orange Salad' has petals of a similar colour and flavour to saffron. It can be used as a substitute in rice, soups or garnishes.*

RIGHT *From southern parts of Europe,* Calendula officinalis *is a bushy annual with slightly downy leaves and orange or yellow daisies to 8 cm (3 in) in diameter.*

Favourites	Flower Colour	Blooming Season	Flower Fragrance	Plant Height	Plant Width	Hardiness Zone	Frost Tolerance
Calendula arvensis	yellow, orange	spring to autumn	no	12 in (30 cm)	12 in (30 cm)	6–10	yes
Calendula officinalis	yellow, gold, orange, apricot	spring to autumn	no	12–24 in (30–60 cm)	12–24 in (30–60 cm)	6–10	yes
Calendula officinalis, **Bon Bon Series**	yellow, orange, apricot	spring to autumn	no	8–12 in (20–30 cm)	12 in (30 cm)	6–10	yes
Calendula officinalis, **Fiesta Gitana Group**	cream, yellow, gold, orange	spring to autumn	no	8–12 in (20–30 cm)	15 in (38 cm)	6–10	yes
Calendula officinalis **'Orange Salad'**	orange	spring to autumn	no	8–12 in (20–30 cm)	12 in (30 cm)	6–10	yes
Calendula officinalis, **Pacific Beauty Series**	orange, yellow	spring to autumn	no	18–24 in (45–60 cm)	18 in (45 cm)	6–10	yes

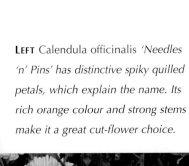

LEFT Calendula officinalis *'Needles 'n' Pins'* has distinctive spiky quilled petals, which explain the name. Its rich orange colour and strong stems make it a great cut-flower choice.

BELOW Calendula officinalis *'Art Shades'* comes in a variety of tones from cream, peach and apricot to yellow and orange. It is a popular strain of a very hardy annual.

CALIBRACHOA

These look like small-flowered, small-leaved petunias and in fact, many in the plant-naming world would still argue that these were indeed just a form of *Petunia*. Nevertheless, they are sold as *Calibrachoa* (or, more likely, by one or another trade name such as 'Million Bells' or 'Superbells').

There are two forms: one grows low and spreads nearly 1 m (3 ft) across; the other is more compact and mounded. Flowering, which begins in spring, continues pretty much right through summer and different named forms flower in purple, red, orange and yellow shades sometimes with bi-coloured flowers.

The spreading types look terrific as a massed summer groundcover while the compact forms are excellent in pots or hanging baskets. They're in the family Solanaceae.

CULTIVATION

Place in full sun in average garden soil or better. They are quite dryness tolerant once they're established but that doesn't mean you should plant and forget them. For the most flowers and the best appearance, keep them lightly moist and apply controlled-release fertiliser around them at planting time and again 3 months later. In frost-free areas they'll often live 2 years.

Top Tip

Try these as a foreground planting to similarly long-blooming dwarf zinnias, especially *Z. angustifolia* in orange, cream or hot pink. Give each plant the room it needs to spread.

LEFT *Teaming this strong cherry red with a purple-flowered form makes a bold combination that doesn't fade in summer's light.*
BELOW *Calibrachoas don't seem to attract pests or diseases. With their long season and ability to withstand heat and some dryness they're a low maintenance choice for summer colour.*

LEFT *The coin-sized flowers of calibrachoas are rain-resistant and shed cleanly when finished. Contrasting speckles are produced on some named varieties broadening the range of other flower colours you can use with them.*

Favourites	Flower Colour	Blooming Season	Flower Fragrance	Plant Height	Plant Width	Hardiness Zone	Frost Tolerance
Calibrachoa 'Superbells'	purple, red, blue white, pink, peach	spring to autumn	no	8–12 in (20–30 cm)	8–12 in (20–30 cm)	7–11	no
Calibrachoa 'Million Bells' Chimes Series	white, violet, cherry yellow, pink	spring to autumn	no	10–12 in (25–30 cm)	20–24 in (50–60 cm)	7–11	no
Calibrachoa 'Million Bells' Trailing Collection	blue, pink, plum, cherry	spring to autumn	no	4–6 in (10–15 cm)	3 ft (0.9 m)	7–11	no

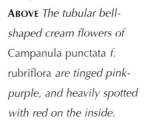

CAMPANULA

A genus of annuals, biennials and perennials, *Campanula* is the type form for the bellflower (Campanulaceae) family. Some of the 300 or so species can be found in Asia and North America but most occur in the Balkans, Caucasus or Mediterranean region. They range from minute crevice dwellers with tiny thimble-like flowers to upright plants with large cup-shaped blooms. The foliage tends to be lance-shaped or rounded, usually toothed or shallowly lobed. The flowers, typically mauve-pink to purple or white, are clustered in heads and can be very abundant. They most often appear from spring to mid-summer. The name *Campanula* comes from the Latin word for bells, *campana*, hence the common name bellflower, and the word campanology (bell-ringing).

CULTIVATION

Requirements vary, with some species needing rockery or alpine-house conditions. Most of the larger types, however, thrive with little care if they are given full sun and fertile, moist, well-drained soil. Propagate by division or from small basal cuttings. The species may be raised from seed.

ABOVE *The tubular bell-shaped cream flowers of* Campanula punctata *f.* rubriflora *are tinged pink-purple, and heavily spotted with red on the inside.*

Top Tip

The amazing variety of bellflowers means there is a species suitable for any rock garden, border, woodland or "wild" garden situation.

RIGHT *A delicate clump-forming perennial from Armenia,* Campanula betulifolia *is an excellent rock-garden plant. It needs protection from winter wet.*

LEFT *A vigorous alpine perennial from southern Europe with small heart-shaped leaves,* Campanula portenschlagiana *blooms profusely in summer.*
BELOW Campanula chamissonis *'Superba' is a low-growing fleshy-stemmed perennial with larger flowers than the species. The flowers are carried on individual stems.*

Favourites	Flower Colour	Blooming Season	Flower Fragrance	Plant Height	Plant Width	Hardiness Zone	Frost Tolerance
Campanula betulifolia	white, pale pink	summer	no	4–12 in (10–30 cm)	12–15 in (30–38 cm)	4–9	yes
Campanula chamissonis	blue and white	summer	no	2–6 in (5–15 cm)	8–12 in (20–30 cm)	3–9	yes
Campanula portenschlagiana	lavender-blue	summer	no	6 in (15 cm)	18–24 in (45–60 cm)	4–9	yes
Campanula poscharskyana	lavender to violet	summer to autumn	no	6–8 in (15–20 cm)	18–24 in (45–60 cm)	6–9	yes
Campanula poscharskyana 'Multiplicity'	lavender-blue	summer to autumn	no	6–8 in (15–20 cm)	18–24 in (45–60 cm)	6–9	yes
Campanula punctata	creamy white to pale pink	early summer	no	12 in (30 cm)	15–18 in (38–45 cm)	4–8	yes

CANNA

Found throughout the tropics and subtropics of the Americas, and widely naturalised elsewhere, there are just 9 species in this genus. Cannas are vigorous perennial plants with strong, upright, reed-like stalks that sprout from rhizomes and bear long lance-shaped leaves. Heads of lily-like flowers—generally in shades of yellow, tangerine and red, either as solid colours or in patterns—appear through the growing season. They make excellent pot plants and are effective in mass plantings. The common name Indian shot comes from the story that the hard, round, black seeds were some-times substituted for buckshot; the seeds are certainly hard enough, but they are so light that their range would have been very limited.

ABOVE *The bright volup-tuous canna is an asset to any tropical garden. Canna iridiflora has gorgeous pink flowers and interesting bluish green leaves.*

LEFT *The flowers of Canna 'Erebus' are salmon pink, and similar in shape to the gladiolus. Cannas are easy to grow, especially in areas with warm climates.*

CULTIVATION

Although often tropical in origin, most species can withstand light frosts when dormant if their roots are well insulated with mulch. Plant in full sun in moist, humus-rich, well-drained soil, and feed well. Propagation of selected forms is by division in early spring. Seeds will often self-sow but rarely result in superior plants.

Favourites	Flower Colour	Blooming Season	Flower Fragranc
Canna 'Erebus'	dark red	summer to autumn	no
Canna 'Intrigue'	orange-red	summer to autumn	no
Canna iridiflora	pink to orange	summer to autumn	no
Canna 'Phasion'	orange	summer to autumn	no
Canna 'Pretoria'	orange	summer to autumn	no
Canna 'Wyoming'	orange	summer to autumn	no

LEFT Canna *'Phasion' is a hot-coloured flamboyant cultivar. As well as its orange flowers, the plant has large leaves dramatically striped in red, green and yellow.*
BELOW *The flowers of many cannas, such as 'Pretoria', have intense colours, but cultivars are also available in more subtle shades of cream, salmon and pink.*

Top Tip

Cannas are not restricted to the tropics—they will happily grow in cold climates in a container or greenhouse. Divide the clumps for easy propagation.

Plant Height	Plant Width	Hardiness Zone	Frost Tolerance
6 ft (1.8 m)	20 in (50 cm)	8–12	no
7 ft (2 m)	20 in (50 cm)	8–12	no
10 ft (3 m)	20 in (50 cm)	9–12	no
6 ft (1.8 m)	20 in (50 cm)	8–12	no
6 ft (1.8 m)	20 in (50 cm)	8–12	no
8 ft (2.4 m)	20 in (50 cm)	8–12	no

CATHARANTHUS

Although related to the common periwinkle *(Vinca)*, the 8 annuals and perennials of this genus are far less hardy and will not tolerate frost. All species are native to Madagascar, and they are bushy plants with simple elliptical leaves on semi-succulent stems. Flat 5-petalled flowers, mainly in pink and mauve shades, appear at the stem tip and leaf axils. Though considered a weed in the tropics and subtropics, the widely cultivated species *Catharanthus roseus* is a perennial often grown as a greenhouse plant or as a summer bedder in temperate gardens. Although highly toxic in its natural form, this species is the source of the drugs known as vinca alkaloids that are used to treat Hodgkin's disease and lymphocytic leukaemia.

CULTIVATION

These plants are very easily grown in part-shade, and can withstand strong sunlight. They are drought tolerant, but flower more heavily with summer moisture. Water moderately in the growing season. Gently pinch back to encourage bushiness. In cool climates with winter frost, bring indoors or discard and replace in spring. Propagate from seed or half-hardened summer cuttings.

RIGHT Catharanthus roseus *'Cooler Blush' is one of the Cooler Series cultivars. It has delicate pale pink flowers with a conspicuous dark pink eye. The petals are broad and overlapping.*

LEFT *The cultivars in the Pacifica Series of* Catharanthus roseus *come in a wide range of beautiful colours. 'Pacifica Punch' has magenta-pink flowers that are darker in the centre.*

Top Tip

Tip prune *Catha-ranthus* species to maintain their full-ness, but don't get too enthusiastic—over-pruning can discourage flower-ing. A bit of liquid fertiliser once a month is also recommended.

ABOVE Catharanthus roseus *is also referred to as "old maid" or the "Madagascar periwinkle". As seen here, the cultivar 'Albus' has dainty white flowers with a yellow eye. A sunny to partly sunny spot is ideal for this plant.*

LEFT *'Stardust Orchid' is one of the most striking cultivars of* Catharanthus roseus. *With its bright magenta flowers featuring a white centre and yellow eye, this plant is ideally used as a colourful border for a garden path.*

Favourites	Flower Colour	Blooming Season	Flower Fragrance	Plant Height	Plant Width	Hardiness Zone	Frost Tolerance
Catharanthus roseus	white, pink, red	spring to autumn	no	24 in (60 cm)	24 in (60 cm)	9–12	no
***Catharanthus roseus* 'Albus'**	white	spring to autumn	no	24 in (60 cm)	24 in (60 cm)	9–12	no
***Catharanthus roseus* 'Blue Pearl'**	lilac-blue	spring to autumn	no	12–18 in (30–45 cm)	18 in (45 cm)	9–12	no
***Catharanthus roseus* 'Cooler Blush'**	white to pink	spring to autumn	no	15–18 in (38–45 cm)	18 in (45 cm)	9–12	no
***Catharanthus roseus,* Pacifica Series**	lilac, pink, white, red	spring to autumn	no	12–15 in (30–38 cm)	18 in (45 cm)	9–12	no
***Catharanthus roseus,* Victory Series**	red, white, rose, carmine	spring to autumn	no	12–15 in (30–38 cm)	18 in (45 cm)	9–12	no

CELOSIA

Found in the tropics of Asia, Africa and the Americas, this genus of around 50 species of annuals and perennials is a member of the amaranth family (Amaranthaceae). The annual *Celosia argentea* is the only widely cultivated species, and it has been developed into many variably flowered and coloured seedling strains. They are upright plants, some growing up to 1.8 m (6 ft) tall, though most are far smaller. Most have simple lance-shaped leaves and tiny vivid yellow, orange or red flowers massed in upright plumes or combs. Commonly known as cockscomb or woolflower, the genus name *Celosia* comes from the Greek word *keleos* (burning), which is an apt description of the flame-like colour and shape of the flowerhead.

CULTIVATION

Although as annuals they can be grown far outside their natural tropical range, *Celosia* plants do need ample warmth to perform well. Plant in fertile well-drained soil in full sun and water well. Raise from seed.

BELOW Celosia spicata *begins blooming from the base of the flower spike. Opening to reveal purplish pink flowers, they gradually fade to silvery pink.*

Favourites	Flower Colour	Blooming Season	Flower Fragrance	Plant Height	Plant Width	Hardiness Zone	Frost Tolerance
Celosia argentea, Plumosa Group	yellow to red, purple	summer to autumn	no	24 in (60 cm)	18 in (45 cm)	10–12	no
Celosia argentea, Plumosa Gp, 'Castle Mix'	gold, pink, red, cream	summer to autumn	no	18 in (45 cm)	12 in (30 cm)	10–12	no
Celosia argentea, Plumosa Gp, 'Forest Fire'	bright scarlet	summer to autumn	no	30 in (75 cm)	18 in (45 cm)	10–12	no
Celosia spicata	purplish pink	summer to autumn	no	24–36 in (60–90 cm)	12 in (30 cm)	10–12	no
Celosia 'Startrek Lilac'	deep rose	summer to autumn	no	4 ft (1.2 m)	24 in (60 cm)	10–12	no
Celosia 'Venezuela'	yellow, red, cerise	summer to autumn	no	24 in (60 cm)	18 in (45 cm)	10–12	no

LEFT *Members of the* Celosia argentea, *Plumosa Group—so named for their plume-like blooms—come in a range of fiery colours, including vibrant reds, hot oranges and golden yellows.*
RIGHT *The feathery flowers of* Celosia argentea, *Plumosa Group, 'Castle Mix' are popular for their colourful mix of hot shades.*
BELOW Celosia argentea, *Plumosa Group, 'Forest Fire' has magnificent plumes of bright red flowers, and rich purple-brown leaves.*

Top Tip

Cut *Celosia* blooms and hang in a dry and well-ventilated location. The dried flowers are ideal for indoor arrangements, with their excellent colour retention properties.

CENTAUREA

Widespread in the temperate zones, this daisy family (Asteraceae) genus, commonly known as cornflower or knapweed, encompasses around 450 species of annuals, perennials and subshrubs. They are a variable lot, though most are readily identifiable by their thistle-like flowerheads, which emerge from an egg-shaped whorl of bracts. The flowerheads often have distinctly different inner and outer florets, with those on the outer having 5 narrow petals. Flower colours include white, yellow, pink, mauve and blue. Plant size varies greatly, but common features are feather-like foliage, often silver-grey, and an upright habit. *Centaurea* was named after Chiron the Centaur, the Greek mythological figure famed for his healing powers, because some species have been used to treat wounds.

LEFT Centaurea dealbata 'Steenbergii' has an erect habit, reaching a height of 90 cm (36 in), and produces lovely large flowerheads in bright cerise.
RIGHT An early-flowering species, Centaurea montana has a wispy outer floret of violet-blue and an inner floret of rosy pink-red.

CULTIVATION

Plant in light well-drained soil in full sun. Good ventilation will lessen any mildew problems. Annuals such as the common cornflower (*Centaurea cyanus*) are raised from seed; perennials may be propagated by division or from softwood cuttings of non-flowering stems.

ABOVE Thistle-like in appearance, Centaurea macrocephala, the globe cornflower, has overlapping brown bracts around the base of the golden yellow flowerheads.

Favourites	Flower Colour	Blooming Season	Flower Fragrance	Plant Height	Plant Width	Hardiness Zone	Frost Tolerance
Centaurea cyanus	purplish blue	spring to summer	no	24–36 in (60–90 cm)	6 in (15 cm)	5–10	yes
Centaurea dealbata	pink	late spring to summer	no	36 in (90 cm)	24 in (60 cm)	4–9	yes
Centaurea macrocephala	yellow	summer	no	36 in (90 cm)	24 in (60 cm)	4–9	yes
Centaurea montana	violet-blue	early summer	no	30 in (75 cm)	24 in (60 cm)	3–9	yes
Centaurea rothrockii	pale purple, cream centre	mid-summer to early autumn	no	4–5 ft (1.2–1.5 m)	24 in (60 cm)	6–10	yes
Centaurea simplicicaulis	rose pink	late spring to early summer	no	10 in (25 cm)	24 in (60 cm)	3–9	yes

Top Tip

Cornflowers will bloom reliably over a long season. Deadheading will often encourage a further show of flowers and increased flower production.

LEFT *The dainty white outer floret surrounding the rose-tinged inner floret gives Centaurea montana 'Alba' a delicate lacy appearance.*

CHRYSANTHEMUM

Numerous species in this once-large genus have been moved to other genera, leaving just 5 European and North African annual species plus a number of hybrids known as florists' chrysanthemums, which are sorted into groups based on flower form. Perennials originally from China, where they have been cultivated for over 2,500 years, chrysanthemums were used medicinally and for flavouring as well as for ornamental purposes. The Japanese adopted chrysanthemums and frequently use them in their art as a symbol of longevity and happiness. The annual species are small plants that closely resemble their daisy family (Asteraceae) relatives and are mainly used for summer bedding or in borders.

ABOVE Chrysanthemum, *Single, 'Megatime' bears pink daisy-like flowers with a greenish yellow central disc. This plant prefers slightly acidic well-drained soil.*

CULTIVATION

The annuals thrive in a sunny position with light well-drained soil. Florists' chrysanthemums prefer a heavier richer soil and will tolerate some shade. They also need pinching back when young and disbudding to ensure the best show of flowers. Annuals are raised from seed; the florists' forms are propagated by division when dormant or from half-hardened summer cuttings.

RIGHT Chrysanthemum, *Spoon-shaped, 'Energy Time' has semi-double rich red blooms with golden yellow centres.*

ABOVE *Chrysanthemum, Incurved, 'Creamest' and 'Gold Creamest' are popular exhibition flowers.*
LEFT *The daisy-like blooms of Chrysanthemum, Single, 'Tiger' look wonderful in mass plantings. The flowers are orange-yellow with a flat central disc.*

Favourites	Flower Colour	Blooming Season	Flower Fragrance	Plant Height	Plant Width	Hardiness Zone	Frost Tolerance
Chrysanthemum, **Anemone-centred**	white, pink, red, yellow, orange	late summer to autumn	no	2–4 ft (0.6–1.2 m)	18–30 in (45–75 cm)	5–10	yes
Chrysanthemum, **Incurved**	white, pink, red yellow, orange	late summer to autumn	no	2–4 ft (0.6–1.2 m)	18–30 in (45–75 cm)	5–10	yes
Chrysanthemum, **Pompon**	white, pink, red yellow, orange	late summer to autumn	no	2–4 ft (0.6–1.2 m)	18–30 in (45–75 cm)	5–10	yes
Chrysanthemum, **Quill-shaped**	white, pink, red yellow, orange	late summer to autumn	no	2–4 ft (0.6–1.2 m)	18–30 in (45–75 cm)	5–10	yes
Chrysanthemum, **Reflexed**	white, pink, red, yellow, orange	late summer to autumn	no	2–4 ft (0.6–1.2 m)	18–30 in (45–75 cm)	5–10	yes
Chrysanthemum, **Single**	white, pink, red yellow, orange	late summer to autumn	no	1–4 ft (0.3–1.2 m)	18–30 in (45–75 cm)	5–10	yes
Chrysanthemum, **Spider-form**	white, pink, red yellow, orange	late summer to autumn	no	2–4 ft (0.6–1.2 m)	18–30 in (45–75 cm)	5–10	yes
Chrysanthemum, **Spoon-shaped**	white, pink, red yellow, orange	late summer to autumn	no	2–4 ft (0.6–1.2 m)	18–30 in (45–75 cm)	5–10	yes
Chrysanthemum, **Spray**	white, pink, red yellow, orange	late summer to autumn	no	2–4 ft (0.6–1.2 m)	18–30 in (45–75 cm)	5–10	yes
Chrysanthemum **weyrichii**	white to pink	summer to autumn	no	6–12 in (15–30 cm)	12–24 in (30–60 cm)	5–9	yes
Chrysanthemum **yezoense**	white	autumn to early winter	no	12–18 in (30–45 cm)	18–30 in (45–75 cm)	6–9	yes
Chrysanthemum **zawadskii**	white, pink	late summer to mid-autumn	no	12–24 in (30–60 cm)	12–24 in (30–60 cm)	5–9	yes

LEFT Chrysanthemum, *Spider-form, 'Mixed Spider'* bears double blooms with long narrow florets that are often coiled at the ends. It comes in an array of colours.

ABOVE Chrysanthemum, *Pompon, 'Furore'* has small, green, spherical flowerheads that are white at the edges. Because the plant is bushy, it is very suitable for use in a border.

LEFT *Rich dark green leaves are the perfect foil for the pale pink flowerheads of* Chrysanthemum weyrichii. *It is a small mat-forming* Chrysanthemum *species.*

Top Tip

Chrysanthemums grow best when they receive full sun all day long, so avoid planting in sites where they have to compete with trees for light and water.

RIGHT *Deep pink blooms fading to pale pink at the petal tips are the hallmark of* Chrysanthemum, *Single, 'Harlekjin', an extremely attractive cultivar.*

BELOW Chrysanthemum, *Spoon-shaped, 'Yellow Biarritz' is another excellent exhibition flower. The tips are yellow and the inside of the bloom is orange-brown.*

BELOW Chrysanthemum, *Anemone-centred, 'Score' has flowers that appear in sprays. The flowers are pink with raised pincushion centres that are deeper pink.*

CLARKIA

A fuchsia family (Onagraceae) genus of 33 species of annuals, commonly known as godetia, *Clarkia* species are found mainly in western North America. They develop quickly from spring to be in flower by the summer solstice. The leaves are small, linear to lance-shaped and sometimes toothed, but the foliage is of little consequence as it soon disappears under an abundance of large, brightly coloured, dark-blotched, 4-petalled flowers, usually in pink, red and mauve shades. Borne on leafy slender stems, they make splendid cut flowers. The genus was named by the Scottish botanist David Douglas after the North American explorer Captain William Clark (1770–1838).

CULTIVATION

An easily cultivated temperate-climate genus, it requires only a bright sunny position with moderately fertile well-drained soil. Deadhead frequently to encourage continued flowering. Propagate from seed, which can be sown in autumn in areas with mild winters.

ABOVE RIGHT Clarkia pul-chella *is a hardy annual that is excellent in a border or in a cottage garden. Because it is pretty and sturdy, children find it fun and satisfying to grow.*
RIGHT *The common names of* Clarkia amoena *are farewell to spring and satin flower. The plant's flowering season is the first 3 weeks in summer.*

Top Tip

When growing clarkias, make sure that the soil is slightly acid. If the soil is too fertile, clarkias do not flower well. They also dislike heat and humidity.

RIGHT Clarkia unguiculata *naturally occurs in California. It produces small flowers, 25 mm (1 in) in diameter, in a range of colours.*
BELOW *Many cultivars have been developed from* Clarkia amoena. *Grace and Satin Series cultivar flowers have contrasting centres, and Satin Series plants are smaller and shrubbier than the species.*

Favourites	Flower Colour	Blooming Season	Flower Fragrance	Plant Height	Plant Width	Hardiness Zone	Frost Tolerance
Clarkia amoena	pink	summer	no	30 in (75 cm)	12 in (30 cm)	7–11	yes
Clarkia amoena, Grace Series	lavender-pink, pink to red	summer	no	24–30 in (60–75 cm)	12 in (30 cm)	7–11	yes
Clarkia amoena, Satin Series	various	summer	no	8 in (20 cm)	8 in (20 cm)	7–11	yes
Clarkia concinna	red	spring to early summer	no	15 in (38 cm)	18 in (45 cm)	8–11	yes
Clarkia pulchella	pink to lavender	spring to summer	no	8–20 in (20–50 cm)	12 in (30 cm)	9–11	no
Clarkia unguiculata	pink, salmon, red, purple	summer	no	12–36 in (30–90 cm)	8 in (20 cm)	7–11	yes

LEFT *There are many cultivars of* Clivia miniata. *'Vico Yellow' is one of several cream and yellow forms available—it has creamy white flowers with a yellow throat.*

BELOW *The flowers of* Clivia caulescens *are narrow, funnel shaped and pendent, and come in a range of warm colours. The plant's leaves can be up to 1.8 m (6 ft) in length.*

CLIVIA

Named not for Robert Clive of India (general and colonial administrator) but instead for his granddaughter, Lady Charlotte Clive, Duchess of Northumberland, this amaryllis family (Amaryllidaceae) genus is made up of just 4 species of perennials from southern Africa. They are commonly known as Kaffir lilies. Clump-forming with stocky rhizomes, they have long, bright green, strappy leaves and at various times, depending on the species, produce strong flower stems topped with heads of large funnel-shaped flowers in yellow, orange and red shades.

CULTIVATION
Tolerating only light frost but otherwise easily grown, *Clivia* plants are superb as greenhouse container specimens. Outdoors they are best grown in dappled shade. Water well during the warmer months and allow to dry off for winter. They are usually propagated by division.

Favourites	Flower Colour	Blooming Season	Flower Fragrance	Plant Height	Plant Width	Hardiness Zone	Frost Tolerance
Clivia caulescens	orange, red, pinkish red	spring to summer	no	24 in (60 cm)	18 in (45 cm)	10–11	no
Clivia × cyrtanthiflora	salmon pink	summer to autumn	no	18–24 in (45–60 cm)	18 in (45 cm)	9–11	no
Clivia miniata	orange to scarlet; yellow throat	spring	no	18 in (45 cm)	18 in (45 cm)	9–11	no
Clivia miniata 'Flame'	red-orange	spring	no	18 in (45 cm)	18 in (45 cm)	9–11	no
Clivia miniata 'Kirstenbosch Yellow'	creamy white; golden mid-stripe	spring	no	18 in (45 cm)	18 in (45 cm)	9–11	no
Clivia miniata 'Striata'	red-orange	spring	no	18 in (45 cm)	18 in (45 cm)	9–11	no

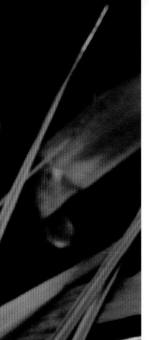

Top Tip

Dark red berry-like fruit often follows the colourful flowers of *Clivia* species. This showy fruit can make an unusual yet highly attractive addition to fresh flower arrangements.

ABOVE Clivia miniata *is commonly known as the bush lily or fire lily. The cultivar 'Striata' has salmon red flowers with a yellow throat, as well as striped cream and green leaves.*
RIGHT *Originally from South Africa,* Clivia miniata *is extremely popular in its native country. C. miniata var. citrina has pretty, yellow, funnel-shaped flowers.*

COLUMNEA

Named by Linnaeus in honour of Italian botanist Fabius Columna (1567–1640), this mainly epiphytic genus from the African violet family (Gesneriaceae) consists of around 160 shrubby species native to the New World tropics. They have slightly arching pendulous stems that form a crown of foliage. The leaves are small, oval to lance-shaped, in opposite pairs and usually downy, as are the stems and outer whorls of the tubular flowers. Orange and red are the common flower colours, but white, yellow, pink and maroon also occur.

CULTIVATION

Intolerant of frost, *Columnea* plants do best as house or greenhouse plants outside of the subtropics. They are nearly always grown in hanging baskets so their trailing flower stems may be best appreciated. They prefer steady temperatures, not necessarily hot, but not widely varying; they need dappled light and shelter from cold draughts. Allow to dry in winter. Propagate from half-hardened tip cuttings.

ABOVE *With a prolonged flowering season, the attractively coloured blooms of Columnea 'Early Bird' are always a welcome addition to the garden.*
LEFT *Native to Costa Rica, Columnea microphylla bears red flowers. Reddish hairs dot the surface of the dark green leaves.*

Top Tip

Most *Columnea* species prefer high humidity. For best results grow them in an open compost mix containing sphagnum moss, peat or charcoal, and mist regularly.

RIGHT *The dark green leaves of* Columnea gloriosa *have a covering of soft hairs. This appealing plant produces hooded scarlet flowers, with striking yellow markings.*

LEFT *The reddish orange flowers of* Columnea scandens *are followed by small globular fruit. This plant has given rise to a number of hybrids, often planted in hanging baskets.*

Favourites	Flower Colour	Blooming Season	Flower Fragrance	Plant Height	Plant Width	Hardiness Zone	Frost Tolerance
Columnea arguta	red	autumn to winter	no	6 ft (1.8 m)	18 in (45 cm)	11–12	no
Columnea 'Early Bird'	orange with yellow throat	most of the year	no	10 in (25 cm)	15 in (38 cm)	10–12	no
Columnea gloriosa	scarlet with yellow throat	autumn to spring	no	6 ft (1.8 m)	18 in (45 cm)	11–12	no
Columnea microphylla	red with yellow markings	autumn to spring	no	6 ft (1.8 m)	24 in (60 cm)	11–12	no
Columnea scandens	red with yellow markings	spring to summer	no	12 in (30 cm)	24 in (60 cm)	11–12	no
Columnea schiedeana	lemon yellow, mottled dull red	spring to autumn	no	18 in (45 cm)	36 in (90 cm)	11–12	no

CONSOLIDA

A Eurasian buttercup family (Ranunculaceae) genus of around 40 species, consolidas are the annual cousins of the delphiniums, with which they were once grouped. Commonly known as larkspurs, most grow to 45–90 cm (18–36 in) tall with fine feathery foliage; about half their height is taken up with upright sometimes branching heads of 5-petalled flowers. Pretty in the garden, they also make excellent cut flowers. Their name comes from the Latin *consolida*, meaning to make whole, referring to the medicinal use of the plant to heal wounds. The juice of the leaves has also been used in herbal preparations, but parts of the plant, especially the seeds, are poisonous.

CULTIVATION

Plant in fertile well-drained soil in full sun. The plants thrive under most conditions and will often self-sow, though the flowers of wild seedlings rarely amount to much. They may need staking. Raise from seed.

RIGHT Consolida, *Giant Imperial Series*, 'Blue Spire' has several vertical stalks that are 1.2 m (4 ft) high. Its double flowers are a lovely shade of rich violet-blue.
BELOW Consolida, *Giant Imperial Series*, 'White King' looks superb in a cottage garden or border. Thin the plants to create space, and flower size will increase.

ABOVE Consolida, *Giant Imperial Series, 'Pink Perfection' produces soft pink double flowers on straight tall stems. They are superb as cut flowers.*

Favourites	Flower Colour	Blooming Season	Flower Fragrance	Plant Height	Plant Width	Hardiness Zone	Frost Tolerance
Consolida ajacis	pink, white, purple	summer	no	4 ft (1.2 m)	10–12 in (25–30 cm)	7–10	yes
Consolida **'Frosted Skies'**	pale blue, darker edges	spring to summer	no	18–24 in (45–60 cm)	12 in (30 cm)	7–10	yes
Consolida, **Giant Imperial Series**	white, pink, red, mauve, blue	spring to summer	no	2–4 ft (0.6–1.2 m)	12 in (30 cm)	7–10	yes
Consolida, **Giant Imperial Series, 'Miss California'**	salmon pink	spring to summer	no	24–36 in (60–90 cm)	12 in (30 cm)	7–10	yes
Consolida, **Giant Imperial Series, 'Rosalie'**	deep pink	spring to summer	no	24–36 in (60–90 cm)	12 in (30 cm)	7–10	yes
Consolida regalis **'Blue Cloud'**	deep blue	summer to early autumn	no	15–30 in (38–75 cm)	15–30 in (38–75 cm)	7–10	yes

CONVOLVULUS

This genus comprises around 200 species of twining climbers, soft-stemmed shrubs and herbaceous perennials from many temperate regions. The leaves are mostly narrow and textured, and shrubby species should be trimmed regularly to encourage density of growth. The flared funnel-shaped flowers appear in succession over a long period from summer to autumn. Blooms appear in a wide range of colours, from white and pink to crimson. The genus name comes from the Latin *convolvo* (to intertwine), which describes the twisting nature of the plants.

CULTIVATION
Most are hardy plants adaptable to a range of soils and situations, and all prefer full sun. They are easily propagated from cuttings.

ABOVE Convolvulus tricolor *is a bushy spreading plant, ideal for a hanging basket or as a ground cover. Flowers are strikingly patterned with bands of purple-blue and white surrounding a vivid yellow centre.*
LEFT *A fast-growing ever-green perennial,* Convolvulus sabatius *bears pretty pale mauve flowers. It does best in sunny rocky situations with some protection from the elements.*

Top Tip

Most *Convolvulus* plants are easy to grow in full sun with dry to moist well-drained soil. Take care to manage plants properly as some can become invasive, such as *C. althaeoides*.

BELOW *The rosy pink flowers of* Convolvulus althaeoides *are highly beguiling, but this species can be difficult to manage. Grow in a pot to contain its root system.*

LEFT *Known as silverbush,* Convolvulus cneorum *has silky silvery foliage and white flowers. A compact plant, it is excellent in mass plantings or rocky crevices.*

Favourites	Flower Colour	Blooming Season	Flower Fragrance	Plant Height	Plant Width	Hardiness Zone	Frost Tolerance
Convolvulus althaeoides	pink to purple	mid- to late summer	no	6 in (15 cm)	24 in (60 cm)	8–10	yes
Convolvulus boissieri	pink-flushed white	early summer	no	3 in (8 cm)	15 in (38 cm)	7–10	yes
Convolvulus cneorum	white; yellow at base	spring to summer	no	24 in (60 cm)	36 in (90 cm)	8–10	yes
Convolvulus lineatus	pink	summer	no	6 in (15 cm)	24 in (60 cm)	7–10	yes
Convolvulus sabatius	pale to deep lilac-blue	summer to early autumn	no	6–8 in (15–20 cm)	36 in (90 cm)	8–11	yes
Convolvulus tricolour	dark purple-blue, white, yellow	summer	no	8–12 in (20–30 cm)	12–24 in (30–60 cm)	8–11	yes

COREOPSIS

This 80-species genus from Mexico and the USA is in the daisy (Asteraceae) family, and includes both annuals and perennials. Species may be sprawling and mounding or upright and shrubby and tend to have fairly simple, often shallowly lobed or linear leaves. Through summer and into autumn they are smothered in bright yellow and/or red, rarely pink flower-heads with ray florets that are often toothed at the tips as if cut by pinking shears. The leaves and flowers of many species were widely used by native North Americans to yield orange to red dyes. The common name tickseed, along with the Greek word *coreopsis* (bug-like), refers to the small black seeds that adhere to clothing and resemble ticks.

Top Tip

Coreopsis blooms are not only great for borders and as cut flowers, but are ideal for attracting butterflies. Dead-heading ensures a longer period of attractive blooms.

CULTIVATION

These flowers are quite drought tolerant and are very easily cultivated in any bright sunny position with light well-drained soil. They will flower better with summer moisture, and for longer if deadheaded frequently. Propagate from seed, which may be sown in situ, from cuttings of non-flowering shoots or by division.

ABOVE RIGHT *Coreopsis lanceolata 'Baby Sun' (syn. 'Sonnenkind') is a small cultivar, to 30 cm (12 in) tall, that rewards with masses of all-golden flowers in summer.*
RIGHT *Coreopsis verticillata 'Grandiflora' (syn. 'Golden Shower') has large bright yellow flowers. Trimming in mid-summer encourages further blooms in autumn.*

ABOVE *Found across much of North America, Coreopsis tinctoria has yellow ray florets, reddening at the base, and red-brown disc florets.*

LEFT *Coreopsis lanceolata 'Sterntaler' is a 40 cm (16 in) tall cultivar, with golden ray florets that have a bronze-red blotch next to the yellow central disc.*

Favourites	Flower Colour	Blooming Season	Flower Fragrance	Plant Height	Plant Width	Hardiness Zone	Frost Tolerance
Coreopsis gigantea	yellow	spring to summer	no	7–10 ft (2–3 m)	32–48 in (80–120 cm)	8–10	yes
Coreopsis grandiflora	golden yellow	late spring to summer	no	12–24 in (30–60 cm)	12–20 in (30–50 cm)	6–10	yes
Coreopsis lanceolata	golden yellow	late spring to summer	no	24 in (60 cm)	12–16 in (30–40 cm)	3–11	yes
Coreopsis 'Sunray'	deep yellow	spring to summer	no	20 in (50 cm)	12–24 in (30–60 cm)	6–10	yes
Coreopsis tinctoria	yellow with maroon centre	summer to autumn	no	36–48 in (90–120 cm)	16–24 in (40–60 cm)	4–10	yes
Coreopsis verticillata	yellow	summer to early autumn	no	36 in (90 cm)	16 in (40 cm)	6–10	yes

COSMOS

A genus of annuals and perennials found from southern USA to northern South America, it belongs to the daisy (Asteraceae) family. Of the 26 species, only 1 perennial and 2 annuals are commonly cultivated. The annuals have fine ferny leaves and produce their large showy flowerheads throughout the warmer months, which in frost-free areas may continue into early winter. The perennials have broader leaflets and smaller, sometimes scented flowers that hint at the relationship between *Cosmos* and *Dahlia*. Appropriately for such a showy and colourful genus, the name is derived from the Greek *kosmos*, meaning "beautiful".

Top Tip

Cosmos love bad conditions. For best results, don't give them any shade, don't over-fertilise the soil and don't water them unless they are wilting.

RIGHT Cosmos bipinnatus, *Sonata Series, a popular dwarf type, ranges in colour from reds and pinks through to the award-winning white.*

CULTIVATION

Cosmos plants thrive in a warm sunny position with light, moist, well-drained soil. The larger annuals produce an abundance of growth, can become top heavy, especially if overfed and are easily damaged by the wind. They may need to be staked, and should certainly be frequently deadheaded. Annuals are raised from seed, and perennials are usually propagated from small basal cuttings.

RIGHT Cosmos bipinnatus 'Picotee Double' *is, as the name suggests, a double form that has light- to medium-pink petals outlined with a contrasting darker pink.*

ABOVE RIGHT *The striking Cosmos bipinnatus 'Picotee' has petals that are white to pale pink flushed and edged with a deep pinkish red, around a yellow disc floret.*

RIGHT *Cosmos bipinnatus is an annual, native to Mexico and southern USA, and has large long-stemmed flower-heads that are coloured pink to lavender in the wild.*

Favourites	Flower Colour	Blooming Season	Flower Fragrance	Plant Height	Plant Width	Hardiness Zone	Frost Tolerance
Cosmos atrosanguineus	dark maroon	mid-summer to autumn	yes	12–24 in (30–60 cm)	18–40 in (45–100 cm)	8–10	yes
Cosmos bipinnatus	pink, red, purple, white	summer to autumn	no	4–7 ft (1.2–2 m)	2–4 ft (0.6–1.2 m)	8–11	no
Cosmos bipinnatus 'Picotee'	white to pale pink	summer to autumn	no	30 in (75 cm)	18 in (45 cm)	8–11	no
Cosmos bipinnatus, Sensation Series	pink, white	summer to autumn	no	36 in (90 cm)	18 in (45 cm)	8–11	no
Cosmos bipinnatus, Sonata Series	crimson, pink, white	summer to autumn	no	18–36 in (45–90 cm)	12–18 in (30–45 cm)	8–11	no
Cosmos sulphureus	yellow to red	summer	no	4–7 ft (1.2–2 m)	2–4 ft (0.6–1.2 m)	8–11	no

CURCUMA

A member of the ginger family (Zingiberaceae), *Curcuma* is a genus of tropical perennials that comes from seasonally dry regions. They occur in India, South-East Asia and far northern Australia, which is home to the lovely Cape York lily (*Curcuma australasica*). All arise from thick rhizomes, producing a short, fleshy stem, big, paddle-like leaves and curious spikes of flowers that consist of overlapping bracts, often beautifully coloured. In their homelands the plants die down as the winter dry season takes hold, emerging into growth again with the first heavy rains of the summer monsoon. As with other members of this important family such as ginger and galangal, the rhizomes of several species are commercially important as spices or foodstuffs. Turmeric, for example is *Curcuma longa* and arrowroot is produced from *Curcuma angustifolia*.

CULTIVATION

These are best in tropical or subtropical areas but can be successful in warm, frost-free areas. *Curcuma* needs good quality, free-draining soil and at least a few hours of sun during the day. The more temperate your climate, the more sun the plants require. All species can be raised in pots and all need plenty of water while leafy.

TOP *Growing 60–90 cm (2–3 ft) tall,* Curcuma petiolata *is from Thailand. It grows in moist ground in steamy, tropical woodlands that dry out in winter. It likes morning sun.*
ABOVE *Though it is commonly called the Siam tulip,* Curcuma alismatifolia *is not even closely related to the tulip. It's a tropical perennial producing showy, usually pink flowers through the summer. Grow in sun or part-shade.*

Favourites	Flower Colour	Blooming Season	Flower Fragrance	Plant Height	Plant Width	Hardiness Zone	Frost Tolerance
Curcuma alismatifolia	pink or white	late summer or autumn	no	12–20 in (30–50 cm)	12–20 in (30–50 cm)	9–11	no
Curcuma australasica	pink	late summer or autumn	no	3–5 ft (0.9–1.5 m)	20–36 in (50–90 cm)	9–11	no
Curcuma petiolata (syn. *C. cordata*)	pink	summer and autumn	no	3–4 ft (0.9–1.2 m)	2–3 ft (0.6–0.9 m)	9–11	no
Curcuma roscoeana	orange	summer and autumn	no	4 ft (1.2 m)	3 ft (0.9m)	9–11	no

ABOVE *Australia's Cape York lily (*Curcuma australasica*) likes a sunny or mostly sunny spot and a dry winter that causes it to die back to its underground rhizome.*

Top Tip

When the clump grows too big for its allotted space, dig up when dormant in winter, divide the rhizomes into smaller sections and replant what you want into renovated soil.

ABOVE Curcuma roscoeana *produces tall spikes of flowers that may be yellow-orange or deep orange. It takes sun or part-shade but needs shelter from strong winds.*

Favourites	Flower Colour	Blooming Season	Flower Fragrance
Delphinium, **Belladonna Group**	blue, white	early to late summer	no
Delphinium, **Elatum Group**	blue, white	summer to autumn	no
Delphinium grandiflorum	blue, white, violet	summer	no
Delphinium **'Michael Ayres'**	dark violet	summer	no
Delphinium nudicaule	red and yellow	late spring to mid-summer	no
Delphinium, **Pacific Hybrids**	blue, white, purple	early to mid-summer	no

ABOVE *Commonly known as butterfly delphinium, D. grandiflorum is a tufted short-lived perennial, often grown as an annual. Large flowers in shades of white, bright blue or violet, such as the cultivar 'Tom Pouce' above, bloom throughout the summer months.*

DELPHINIUM

This genus contains around 250 species of annuals and perennials native to mainly temperate zones in the Northern Hemisphere, and belongs to the widely cultivated buttercup family (Ranunculaceae). The light to bright green leaves are usually hand-shaped and slightly hairy. Delphiniums are generally thought to have tall erect flower stems but many species have short branching ones. All species, however, grow striking 5-petalled flowers along much of the length of the stem. Characteristic flower colours include blue and deep purple, though some species have white, red or pale green flowers. Delphinium comes from the Greek *delphin* (dolphin) and describes the shape of the nectar-containing spurs found at the base of the flower.

CULTIVATION

Plant in full sun with moist, fertile, well-drained soil. Any withered foliage must be cut back to maintain the vigorous growth of the plant. Annuals and species can be propagated from seed, whereas hybrids and cultivars can be propagated by division or from cuttings.

Top Tip

There cannot be many plants more suited to a border or feature bed than delphiniums and, in particular, *D. elatum* is a perfect choice. Stake, if necessary, for extra support.

Plant Height	Plant Width	Hardiness Zone	Frost Tolerance
4 ft (1.2 m)	24 in (60 cm)	3–9	yes
3–6 ft (0.9–1.8 m)	24 in (60 cm)	3–9	yes
18 in (45 cm)	12 in (30 cm)	3–9	yes
5 ft (1.5 m)	18 in (45 cm)	3–9	yes
24 in (60 cm)	8 in (20 cm)	5–7	yes
5 ft (1.5 m)	30 in (75 cm)	7–9	yes

ABOVE AND FAR LEFT
Delphinium elatum *and its hybrids have given rise to many popular garden forms. Plants produce tall spikes tightly packed with flowers, which are ideal for cutting. 'Sungleam', above, bears cream-coloured flowers and 'Albert Shepherd', far left, has soft purple-blue blooms lightly flushed with pink. The flowers of both have pale yellow centres.*

CENTRE LEFT *A favourite with gardeners, Delphinium 'Michael Ayres' is an award-winning plant. Tall spikes grow up to 1.8 m (6 ft) and produce a profusion of flowers along its length in deep violet shades with distinct black eyes.*

DIANTHUS

Often just simply referred to as pinks, this large genus belongs to the carnation family (Caryophyllaceae). It consists of around 300 species of perennials and a few annuals occurring throughout Europe, Asia and southern Africa. Their foliage is fairly unremarkable—consisting of mostly small, blue-grey, tufted mounds—but this is more than compensated for by the flowers, which are borne singly or in clusters on wiry flower stems. Hugely popular as cut flowers and garden plants, there are thousands of cultivars whose flowers vary greatly in size, colour and pattern. This centuries-old flower gets its common name of pink from the petal edges, which appear to be cut with pinking shears.

LEFT *Exuding a clove-scented fragrance, Dianthus 'Monica Wyatt' is a Pink type. With fluffy double blooms featuring soft pink petals that have a rose red base, its delicate colouring and texture belie its hardiness.*

CULTIVATION

This genus varies in hardiness and size; most of the species are ideal for rockeries or small perennial borders, others are suitable for alpine troughs. They are best planted in full sun with gritty well-drained soil. Propagate perennials by layering or from cuttings in summer and annuals from seed in autumn.

LEFT Dianthus gratianopolitanus 'Baker's Variety' has grassy foliage and pink single flowers with a wonderful spicy fragrance.
BELOW A member of the Perpetual-flowering Carnations, Dianthus 'Crimson Tempo' produces gorgeous rich red double flowers throughout the year.

RIGHT *The tall-stemmed, yellow flowers of the Perpetual-flowering Carnation* Dianthus *'Tundra' have petals edged in red. It blooms for most of the year in favourable climates.*

Top Tip

Taller carnations will need to be staked or tied to a support in order to keep the slender stems upright under the weight of the often fully double blooms.

Favourites	Flower Colour	Blooming Season	Flower Fragrance	Plant Height	Plant Width	Hardiness Zone	Frost Tolerance
Dianthus alpinus	deep pink to crimson	summer	no	6 in (15 cm)	4 in (10 cm)	4–9	yes
Dianthus, **Annual Pinks**	white to pink or red, bicoloured	late spring to early autumn	no	8–12 in (20–30 cm)	8–12 in (20–30 cm)	7–10	yes
Dianthus barbatus	pink to red, purple, white	late spring to early summer	yes	18–24 in (45–60 cm)	12 in (30 cm)	4–10	yes
Dianthus, **Border Carnations**	white, pink, lemon, purple, bicoloured	spring to early summer	yes	18–24 in (45–60 cm)	12 in (30 cm)	6–9	yes
Dianthus carthusianorum	deep pink to purple, white	summer	no	8 in (20 cm)	8 in (20 cm)	3–9	yes
Dianthus caryophyllus	pink, purple, white, bicoloured	summer	yes	12–30 in (30–75 cm)	12–15 in (30–38 cm)	8–10	yes
Dianthus deltoides	white, light pink to red	summer	no	6–8 in (15–20 cm)	12 in (30 cm)	3–10	yes
Dianthus gratianopolitanus	dark pink	summer	yes	6–8 in (15–20 cm)	15 in (38 cm)	5–9	yes
Dianthus, **Malmaison Carnations**	white, pink, red	most of year	yes	18–30 in (45–75 cm)	12–18 in (30–45 cm)	9–11	yes
Dianthus pavonius	pale pink to crimson	summer	no	4 in (10 cm)	6–10 in (15–25 cm)	4–9	yes
Dianthus, **Perpetual-flowering Carnations**	white, pink, red, yellow, bicoloured	all year	yes	3 ft (0.9 m)	12 in (30 cm)	8–11	yes
Dianthus, **Pinks**	white, pink to crimson	late spring to early autumn	yes	6–18 in (15–45 cm)	18 in (45 cm)	5–10	yes

LEFT Dianthus *'Lemsii'*, with its fragrant pink flowers, is a dwarf Pink. With a spreading habit, this plant forms large carpets of foliage and flowers in summer.

RIGHT *The deep pink buds of* Dianthus *'Valda Wyatt' open to reveal double pink flowers that are somewhat darker at the centre. These stunning Pink-type flowers are clove scented.*

BELOW Dianthus *'Delphi' is a Perpetual-flowering Carnation producing full, double, snow white blooms.*

RIGHT *The sweetly fragrant flowers of* Dianthus barbatus *'Auricula-eyed Mixed' come in a wide range of colours and have a well-defined eye.*
BELOW RIGHT *For areas that need an infusion of colour,* Dianthus deltoides *will produce rapid results. Flowers in shades of pink, red and white, often red-eyed, are borne throughout summer.*

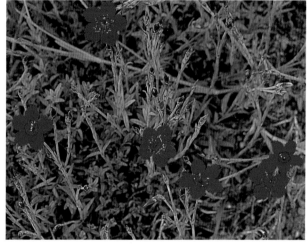

ABOVE *A Perpetual-flowering Carnation,* Dianthus *'Mambo' is very hardy. Providing year-round colour, it bears double apricot flowers with subtle tinges of salmon pink.*

Favourites	Flower Colour	Blooming Season	Flower Fragrance
Diascia barberae	bright pink	summer	no
Diascia barberae 'Blackthorn Apricot'	apricot-pink to soft orange	summer	no
Diascia Coral Belle/'Hecbel'	coral red	summer	no
Diascia fetcaniensis	pink	summer to early autumn	no
Diascia Redstart/'Hecstart'	coral pink to red	summer	no
Diascia vigilis	pink	summer to early winter	no

DIASCIA

In the 30-odd years since this South African genus of around 50 species of annuals and perennials in the foxglove (Scrophulariaceae) family first became better known it has become tremendously popular, primarily because of its heavy flowering and easy cultivation. Consequently, there are now many hybrids and cultivars and they fill an important niche in rockeries, containers and perennial borders. Commonly known as twinspurs, they are generally low compact plants with small, simple, dark green leaves, and are so-named because of the two short spurs behind the flower. The principal flower colours are apricot, pink and mauve. *Diascia* means "two sacs" and refers to the nectar sacs at the base of the spurs.

CULTIVATION

Easily grown in a sunny position with light well-drained soil, the perennials require a climate with a fairly mild winter, but the annuals thrive almost anywhere. Routine deadheading will extend the flowering season. The perennials sometimes self-layer or they can be propagated from cuttings. Raise the annual forms from seed.

ABOVE LEFT Diascia *Coral Belle/'Hecbel' has glossy leaves and coral red flowers. It has a semi-trailing habit that makes it an ideal subject for basket culture.* **BELOW** *With bright green leaves and rose to salmon pink flowers,* Diascia fetcaniensis *adds a welcome splash of colour when used for rockery planting.*

Top Tip

Twinspurs are prolific bloomers, but production can slow if conditions become too hot. To kick-start blooming, keep well watered and pinch back spent flowers.

Plant Height	Plant Width	Hardiness Zone	Frost Tolerance
12 in (30 cm)	12–16 in (30–40 cm)	8–10	yes
10 in (25 cm)	20 in (50 cm)	8–10	yes
8–18 in (20–45 cm)	12–24 in (30–60 cm)	8–10	yes
12 in (30 cm)	20 in (50 cm)	8–10	yes
8–18 in (20–45 cm)	12–24 in (30–60 cm)	8–10	yes
20 in (50 cm)	24 in (60 cm)	8–10	yes

ABOVE Diascia vigilis 'Jack Elliott' is a reliable fleshy-leafed plant that produces racemes of very large, showy, mid-pink flowers.

TOP Diascia vigilis enjoys a longer flowering season than many of its relatives, producing its soft pink flowers, spotted with darker pink at the throat, from summer through to early winter.

DICENTRA

This genus of 19 species of annuals and perennials is a member of the poppy family (Papaveraceae). Naturally occurring across temperate Asian and North American habitats, it is commonly referred to as bleeding heart—a reference to the shape and colour of its pendulous flowers. Apart from red and purple, flowers occur in shades of white, pink and yellow, hanging gracefully from upright or slightly arching stems. This clump-forming genus has grey-green to blue-green fern-like foliage. Many species have unusually shaped flowers that lend themselves to a wide variety of common names such as lady's locket and Dutchman's breeches. The slightly ominous name, stagger weed, refers to the effect the foliage has on animals that graze on the plant.

CULTIVATION

Dicentra species thrive in a climate with clearly defined seasons and are happiest in cool, moist, humus-rich soil and dappled sunlight. Propagate from seed in autumn or by division in late winter.

ABOVE *The finely arching stems of* Dicentra formosa *'Aurora' bear creamy yellow flowers above attractive blue-green foliage.*
LEFT Dicentra *'Bacchanal' makes a glorious bushy addition to a perennial border. Pendulous burgundy flowers hang above ferny bright green foliage.*

Top Tip

Dicentra plants usually flower throughout spring and early summer. Ample watering will encourage a longer-lasting display of the attractive lacy foliage.

ABOVE Dicentra spectabilis *'Alba' produces pure white flowers and softly shaded green leaves.*

BELOW *Clearly demonstrating why this genus is called bleeding heart, the flowers of* Dicentra spectabilis *hang gracefully in a row. The outer petals are a rich pink, and the inner petals are white.*

Favourites	Flower Colour	Blooming Season	Flower Fragrance	Plant Height	Plant Width	Hardiness Zone	Frost Tolerance
Dicentra 'Bacchanal'	burgundy	mid- to late spring	no	18 in (45 cm)	24 in (60 cm)	3–9	yes
Dicentra eximia	light to dark pink, white	summer to early autumn	no	18–24 in (45–60 cm)	18 in (45 cm)	4–8	yes
Dicentra formosa	pink to red	spring and summer	no	18 in (45 cm)	36 in (90 cm)	3–9	yes
Dicentra 'Langtrees'	white tinged with pink	mid-spring to mid-summer	no	12 in (30 cm)	18 in (45 cm)	3–9	yes
Dicentra scandens	yellow, white	summer	no	12 ft (3.5 m)	24 in (60 cm)	4–9	yes
Dicentra spectabilis	rose pink and white	late spring to summer	no	24–36 in (60–90 cm)	18–24 in (45–60 cm)	2–9	yes

DICHORISANDRA

One of the best perennials for intense flower colour in shade, the *Dichorisandra*, or blue ginger, we see is just one of about 25 species, all from tropical South America. Despite its common name, it's not in the ginger family but rather the Commelinaceae and it grows on a thick, fleshy stem that branches into a candelabra shape. Leaves are big and spear shaped. From mid-summer until late autumn it produces clusters of intense violet flowers that are extremely showy. In the tropics, the flowering season is even longer and the plants can grow up to 3 m (10 ft) tall. It's a great plant for a border or massed in clumps, and it's very easy to propagate from cuttings rooted in a bucket of water.

CULTIVATION

Average garden soil seems to suit and the plant is most effective in bright full shade or dappled shade. It will take some sun but too much heat bleaches the flowers.

Once established, it tolerates some dryness but this is a plant of high summer rainfall areas and it likes to be kept moist while in growth. Feed once in spring.

ABOVE *Lush and long-blooming, rooted cuttings of blue ginger will form a clump like this within two years.*
ABOVE RIGHT *The individual blooms clustered on the flower head open in succession. Each lasts many days, producing display that lasts for months even out of the tropics.*

Top Tip

Cut stems to ground anytime from mid- to late winter. Apply controlled-release fertiliser at the end of winter. New stems will shoot in mid-spring, growing to chest height by flowering time.

Species	Flower Colour	Blooming Season	Flower Fragrance	Plant Height	Plant Width	Hardiness Zone	Frost Tolerance
Dichorisandra thyrsiflora	violet	summer and autumn	no	5–10 ft (1.5–3 m)	3–8 ft (1–2.5 m)	9–11	no

DIGITALIS

Foxgloves, members of the foxglove (Scrophulariaceae) family, occur naturally only in Europe and North Africa, but have naturalised in many temperate climates. The genus comprises some 20 species of biennials and perennials and there are also many hybrids and cultivars. Most form a basal foliage clump of large, heavily veined, sometimes downy leaves. From late spring, tall, strongly erect flower spikes develop. The flowers, which occur mostly in shades of pink to purple-red, less commonly white or yellow, are bell-shaped and usually downward-facing. *Digitalis* species contain potent glycosides that were once used in cardiac medicine, and in fact extracts are still used in some herbal remedies.

CULTIVATION

While hardiness varies with the species, most are easily cultivated in temperate areas. They prefer deep, humus-rich, moist, well-drained soil and a position in sun or part-shade. The taller species may need staking. Propagate the perennials by division or from basal offsets; raise annuals from seed.

Top Tip

Foxgloves make excellent border plantings. However, it is best to wear gloves when handling these plants, as contact with the leaves can cause skin irritation.

LEFT *Rich dark green leaves form a dramatic backdrop for the pretty, bell-shaped, primrose yellow flowers of* Digitalis grandiflora *'Carillon'.*

RIGHT Digitalis × fulva *is a natural hybrid from southern Europe. It features somewhat downy leaves and spires of white to pale yellow-green flowers.*

Favourites	Flower Colour	Blooming Season	Flower Fragrance	Plant Height	Plant Width	Hardiness Zone	Frost Tolerance
Digitalis × *fulva*	white to pale yellow-green	late spring to summer	no	40 in (100 cm)	20–24 in (50–60 cm)	7–9	yes
Digitalis grandiflora	lemon yellow	early to mid-summer	no	36 in (90 cm)	18 in (45 cm)	4–9	yes
Digitalis lanata	dull white to buff	late spring to summer	no	40 in (100 cm)	20–24 in (50–60 cm)	6–9	yes
Digitalis × *mertonensis*	pinkish-red to purple-pink	late spring to summer	no	20–30 in (50–75 cm)	16–20 in (40–50 cm)	4–9	yes
Digitalis parviflora	red-brown	early summer	no	24 in (60 cm)	12 in (30 cm)	4–9	yes
Digitalis purpurea	purple, pink, white, yellow	summer	no	3–6 ft (0.9–1.8 m)	2 ft (0.6 m)	5–10	yes

BELOW *The tall spires of downward-facing flowers of* Digitalis purpurea, *Excelsior Group, cultivars make an impressive sight as the blooms open progressively up to the apex.*

ABOVE *Producing a stunning display when in bloom, the rich red-brown flowers of* Digitalis parviflora *have earned it the common name of chocolate foxglove.*

DOROTHEANTHUS

RIGHT *If you want mass colour in winter, these little daisies are for you. They're easy to grow and the show lasts more than a month.*

Top Tip

After bloom, let the seed pods swell and ripen and you can collect seeds for next year. Store them in a paper bag in a dry, dark place.

Commonly called Livingstone daisies, *Dorotheanthus* are among the most cheery and spectacular of the late winter-blooming annual flowers. They're ankle-high succulents in the family Aizoaceae and although there are 6 species in their native South Africa, this delightful little annual is the only one commonly available. It's easily raised from scattered seed or you can buy them from the nursery as seedlings in punnets. Seeds are sown in late autumn, which is also when you should plant seedlings. Flowers start appearing in mid-winter but they don't really get going until late winter and early spring. The flowers come in many bright, sparkling

ABOVE RIGHT *Each bloom is about 5 cm (2 in) across and the petals are not only colourful, they sparkle in the light.*

colours and are incredibly densely produced. In full bloom, a mass of Livingstones looks like a carpet of colour.

CULTIVATION
In late autumn sow seed thinly over bare soil that has been dug over and raked smooth. You don't have to cover them, just water in with a fine mist. Keep lightly moist until seedlings appear. If your winters are rainy no watering is needed. If dry, water once a week. Full sun is essential but fertiliser isn't.

Species	Flower Colour	Blooming Season	Flower Fragrance	Plant Height	Plant Width	Hardiness Zone	Frost Tolerance
Dorotheanthus bellidiformis	purple, pink, orange yellow, white, lavender	late winter to early spring	no	6 in (15 cm)	10 in (25 cm)	7–11	yes

ECHINACEA

Naturally occurring in the eastern USA and closely allied to *Rudbeckia*, this genus of 9 species belongs to the daisy family (Asteraceae). Commonly known as coneflowers, these strongly upright shrubby perennials develop quickly in spring to be in full flower by summer. Their simple leaves are a typical pointed lance shape, but their flowers are distinctive, having a dome-like central cone and large drooping ray florets that are usually purple-pink. Among the earliest American genera to enter European cultivation, arriving in 1640, *Echinacea* is extensively used in herbal medicines, probably more so than any other genus. It is thought to boost the immune system and is a popular cold preventive.

CULTIVATION

Very hardy and adaptable plants, they do best in full sun in well-drained soil that remains moist during the growing season. *Echinacea* plants can grow quite tall and may need staking in exposed positions. Propagate from seed, from root cuttings or by division.

Top Tip

Echinaceas do not take well to disruption. If you must divide to increase your stock, do so very carefully, retaining the shoots. Fertile soil and mulching are also recommended.

ABOVE Echinacea purpurea *'Magnus' is an especially pretty cultivar, with large pinkish purple flowers that have bold orange-red centres. The blooms are well suited for use in a vase on their own or in a mixed flower arrangement.*

RIGHT Echinacea angustifolia *has narrow pale pink or purple ray florets surrounding a high brown cone. Its leaves are hairy and linear. The plant is considered to be an aphrodisiac.*

ABOVE Echinacea purpurea *is the most popular of all the* Echinacea *species, and is commonly known as the purple coneflower. It has lance-shaped leaves, and its pink-purple blooms make good cut flowers.*

RIGHT *'White Swan' is one of several* Echinacea purpurea *cultivars. It looks lovely in a border, a field or as a cut flower, as its fragrant, white, daisy-like blooms have a contrasting green to coppery orange centre*

Favourites	Flower Colour	Blooming Season	Flower Fragrance	Plant Height	Plant Width	Hardiness Zone	Frost Tolerance
Echinacea angustifolia	purple or pink	summer	no	5 ft (1.5 m)	18 in (45 cm)	4–9	yes
Echinacea pallida	purple	summer	no	4 ft (1.2 m)	24 in (60 cm)	5–9	yes
Echinacea purpurea	pinkish purple	summer	no	2–4 ft (0.6–1.2 m)	24 in (60 cm)	3–10	yes
Echinacea purpurea 'Magnus'	deep pink-purple	summer	no	24–36 in (60–90 m)	24 in (60 cm)	3–10	yes
Echinacea purpurea 'White Lustre'	white	summer	no	18–30 in (45–75 cm)	24 in (60 cm)	3–10	yes
Echinacea purpurea 'White Swan'	white	summer	yes	18–24 in (45–60 cm)	18 in (45 cm)	3–10	yes

ECHINOPS

Commonly known as globe thistle, this mainly Eurasian genus of 120-odd annuals and perennials belongs to the daisy family (Asteraceae). The popular *Echinops ritro* has been in cultivation for over 400 years and was a favourite with the Victorians both as a garden plant and for its dried flowers. *Echinops* species grow strongly from early spring, producing a basal clump of silver-grey to almost steel blue leaves that may be simple or feather-like, and are usually spine-tipped at the lobes. The round flowerheads are usually metallic purple-blue; they are without ray florets, but are enclosed in similarly coloured bracts. *Echinops* is from the Greek meaning "like a hedgehog", which is an apt description for the spiky flowerheads.

CULTIVATION

Hardiness varies, but most species are frost tolerant. They will withstand summer heat but prefer not to dry out. Moist, humus-rich, well-drained soil is best. Deadhead the flowers frequently to prolong flowering. Cut plants back to ground level in autumn or early winter. Propagate by division when dormant, or raise from seed.

Top Tip

Echinops plants will thrive on neglect, and can be used in herbaceous borders or field gardens. They are also suitable for cutting and in dried flower arrangements.

ABOVE RIGHT Echinops ritro *'Blue Glow' is a sturdy cultivar with light blue flowers. If you plan to dry out the flowers, cut them before the pollen appears.*
RIGHT Echinops sphaero-cephalus *is a tall plant with large silvery grey flower-heads. Its grey-green leaves are long and jagged, with hairy undersides.*

ABOVE RIGHT *The globose flowerheads of* Echinops ritro *start off as metallic blue, then age to purple-blue. The plant's leaves are stiff and spiny.*

RIGHT Echinops bannaticus *'Taplow Blue' has bright blue-purple flowers, whereas the flowers of the species are pale blue-grey. The stems are grey and woolly.*

Favourites	Flower Colour	Blooming Season	Flower Fragrance	Plant Height	Plant Width	Hardiness Zone	Frost Tolerance
Echinops bannaticus	blue-grey to blue	mid- to late summer	no	4 ft (1.2 m)	24 in (60 cm)	3–9	yes
Echinops bannaticus 'Taplow Blue'	blue-purple	mid- to late summer	no	4 ft (1.2 m)	24 in (60 cm)	3–9	yes
Echinops ritro	blue to purplish blue	summer	no	36 in (90 cm)	36 in (90 cm)	3–9	yes
Echinops ritro 'Blue Glow'	light blue	summer	no	36 in (90 cm)	18 in (45 cm)	3–9	yes
Echinops sphaerocephalus	grey	mid- to late summer	no	6 ft (1.8 m)	3 ft (0.9 m)	3–9	yes
Echinops sphaerocephalus 'Arctic Glow'	white	mid- to late summer	no	30 in (75 cm)	18 in (45 cm)	3–9	yes

ECHIUM

Spread throughout the Mediterranean and nearby Atlantic islands, this borage family (Boraginaceae) genus of 40 species of biennials, perennials and shrubs includes several spectacular flowering plants. All have hairy leaves, usually a simple elongated lance shape and often in basal rosettes. Some plants are small and bushy, some form clumps of rosettes with tall flower stems and others are woody shrubs with conical flower spikes. The flowers are small, 5-petalled, usually purple-blue and heavily massed to produce an intense burst of colour. Several *Echium* species have been used medicinally, and viper's bugloss *(Echium vulgare)* was once considered a cure for snakebite, though it is now better known for the honey made from its nectar.

ABOVE *Native to the Canary Islands,* Echium pininana *flowers during its second year, producing tiny blue-toned flowers on tall spikes up to 3.5 m (12 ft) high.*

CULTIVATION

Of variable hardiness, most species require a bright sunny position with light, gritty, well-drained soil that remains moist during the flowering season. Propagation is by division, from basal cuttings or from seed, depending on the growth form. Some species self-sow readily in milder climates, so pruning of the old flower spikes is recommended.

Favourites	Flower Colour	Blooming Season	Flower Fragrance	Plant Height	Plant Width	Hardiness Zone	Frost Tolerance
Echium amoenum	purple-red	spring to summer	no	6 in (15 cm)	6 in (15 cm)	7–9	yes
Echium candicans	purplish blue	spring to summer	no	4–7 ft (1.2–2 m)	6–10 ft (1.8–3 m)	9–10	no
Echium pininana	blue to lavender blue	mid- to late summer	no	8–12 ft (2.4–3.5 m)	3 ft (0.9 m)	9–10	yes
Echium plantagineum	red to blue-purple	late spring to summer	no	24 in (60 cm)	12 in (30 cm)	9–10	yes
Echium vulgare	blue, white, pink, purple	summer	no	24–36 in (60–90 cm)	12 in (30 cm)	7–10	yes
Echium wildpretii	red to purple	spring to summer	no	6 ft (1.8 m)	12 in (30 cm)	9–10	no

ABOVE Echium vulgare *'Blue Bedder' is an excellent choice for the beach-side garden or border planting.*
LEFT *Native to Madeira,* Echium candicans *bears tall spikes covered with masses of tiny blue-purple flowers.*

Top Tip

Ideally suited to use in the garden border setting, *Echium* species flower reliably, tolerate a range of soil types and require minimal pruning to keep in good order.

LEFT *Initially forming a rosette of narrow leaves,* Echium wildpretii *flowers during its second year. Tall spikes bear masses of rose to coral red flowers, earning this species its common name—tower of jewels.*

EPIMEDIUM

Variously known as barrenwort or bishop's hat, this genus of 25 species of rhizome-rooted herbaceous perennials is found from southern Europe to Japan. The leaves, which are roughly heart shaped with shallowly lobed or toothed edges, are sometimes evergreen in mild climates but are usually deciduous and may colour well in autumn. Sprays of small, dainty, 4-petalled flowers appear in spring as the new leaves expand. The flowers may be white, yellow, pink or red, depending on the species, and may continue into early summer. *Epimedium* extracts, sometimes known as "Yang tonics", are used extensively in traditional Chinese medicines and are also found in commercially available herbal pick-me-ups.

CULTIVATION
Very hardy and suitable as ground covers for woodland situations, in rockeries or perennial borders, these tough little plants are easily grown in partial shade in fertile, moist, humus-rich, well-drained soil. Propagate by division in late winter just as the new growth appears, or raise from seed.

TOP *Easy-to-grow* Epimedium × versicolor *is perfect for adding colour to shady spots in the garden.*
ABOVE *The dainty flowers of* Epimedium acuminatum *are held on stems above the heart-shaped leaflets.*

Top Tip

Though relatively slow-growing, *Epimedium* species do well in shady spots, and are ideal for planting under trees. They are equally happy in containers, and are a versatile addition to the small garden.

RIGHT *Similar to the species but producing larger flowers, slow-growing* Epimedium pinnatum *subsp.* colchicum *spreads to create a mat of colour. Bright yellow blooms appear among the dark green leaves during the spring flowering season.*

Favourites	Flower Colour	Blooming Season	Flower Fragrance	Plant Height	Plant Width	Hardiness Zone	Frost Tolerance
Epimedium acuminatum	purple and pale pink	mid-spring to early summer	no	12 in (30 cm)	18 in (45 cm)	7–9	yes
Epimedium grandiflorum	white, pink, violet, yellow	spring	no	8–12 in (20–30 cm)	12 in (30 cm)	4–9	yes
Epimedium × *perralchicum*	bright yellow	spring	no	15 in (38 cm)	24 in (60 cm)	6–9	yes
Epimedium pinnatum	yellow; purple-brown spurs	late spring to early summer	no	8–12 in (20–30 cm)	8–12 in (20–30 cm)	6–9	yes
Epimedium platypetalum	yellow	spring	no	6 in (15 cm)	8 in (20 cm)	6–9	yes
Epimedium × *versicolor*	yellow and pink with red spurs	spring	no	12 in (30 cm)	12 in (30 cm)	5–9	yes

LEFT *Delicate yellow flowers are held above the heart-shaped leaves of* Epimedium platypetalum *in spring. During autumn, the leaves take on purplish tones, ensuring that the plant adds colour and interest to the garden throughout the year.*

ERYNGIUM

T his genus derives its name from a Greek
word meaning thistle, and indeed many of
its 230-odd species of annuals, biennials and
perennials are thistle-like, though they belong
in the carrot family (Umbelliferae), not among
the composites. While they are widely distributed, most of the cultivated species—which
are commonly known as sea holly—come from
Eurasia and North and South America. The
leaves are often lance shaped or feather-like,
and edged with spine-tipped teeth. Strong
flower stems, usually branching at the top, carry
hemispherical heads of minute flowers backed
by spiny bracts that give the head much of its
colour, often a metallic silver-blue. The roots
have long been used medicinally and appear
to have anti-inflammatory properties.

Top Tip

The long flowering
season of sea
hollies ensures an
enduring and inter-
esting floral display
in the garden. They
can also be dried
successfully for
use in dried flower
arrangements.

RIGHT *The blue-mauve
flowerheads of* Eryngium
*'Jos Eijking' are surrounded
by narrow silvery green
bracts tinged at the base
with purple tones.*

CULTIVATION

Hardiness varies with the species. Plant in a
sunny position in light very well-drained soil,
otherwise roots will
rot during the winter
months. Water well
when growing, but
otherwise allow to
dry off. Propagate
species from seed and
selected forms from
root cuttings or by
division in spring.

RIGHT *Commonly known
as Miss Willmott's ghost,*
Eryngium giganteum *has
green or blue cone-shaped
flowerheads surrounded by
large, silvery, snowflake-
shaped bracts.*

ABOVE *Silvery blue stems hold the blue-mauve flowers of* Eryngium variifolium *above the oval, dark green, white-veined, rather fleshy leaves.*

RIGHT *As its name indicates, the flowerheads of* Eryngium amethystinum *are indeed a lovely amethyst colour. Delicate silvery green bracts form a collar around the flowerheads.*

Favourites	Flower Colour	Blooming Season	Flower Fragrance	Plant Height	Plant Width	Hardiness Zone	Frost Tolerance
Eryngium alpinum	grey-blue to white	mid-summer to early autumn	no	30 in (75 cm)	18 in (45 cm)	3–9	yes
Eryngium amethystinum	grey-blue to amethyst	mid- to late summer	no	30 in (75 cm)	30 in (75 cm)	7–10	yes
Eryngium giganteum	pale green to blue	summer	no	3–4 ft (0.9–1.2 m)	30 in (75 cm)	6–9	yes
Eryngium 'Jos Eijking'	mauve-blue	summer	no	24 in (60 cm)	18 in (45 cm)	5–9	yes
Eryngium planum	blue	summer	no	36 in (90 cm)	18 in (45 cm)	5–9	yes
Eryngium variifolium	blue-grey to mauve	summer	no	18 in (45 cm)	10 in (25 cm)	7–10	yes

Favourites	Flower Colour	Blooming Season	Flower Fragrance
Erysimum bonannianum	lemon yellow	late spring to early winter	yes
Erysimum 'Bowles' Mauve'	bright mauve	late winter to summer	no
Erysimum 'Gold Shot'	golden yellow	late spring	yes
Erysimum kotschyanum	yellow to orange-yellow	summer	yes
Erysimum 'Sunlight'	bright yellow	early summer	no
Erysimum 'Wenlock Beauty'	mauve and yellow	early to late spring	no

ERYSIMUM

Formerly listed under *Cheiranthus*, this genus consists of 80 or so annuals, perennials and subshrubs. *Erysimum* species are found mainly in Europe, western Asia and western North America, and are popularly known as wallflowers. They have simple narrow leaves, are mainly evergreen and range from rockery dwarfs to medium-sized shrubs. Flower stems, tall in the larger species, appear mainly over spring and summer, and also in winter in mild climates. The heads carry dense clusters of small 4-petalled blooms that are often richly fragrant. The petals are usually yellow but may also be orange, red or mauve. The old genus name, *Cheiranthus*, meaning "hand-flower", refers to the custom dating to the Middle Ages when the sweetly scented flowers were often carried in the hand at festivals and events.

CULTIVATION

Wallflowers like cool summers and mild winters. Plant in a sunny open position in moist well-drained soil. If perennials become woody they should be cut back hard. Annuals are raised from seed; perennials are propagated from cuttings of non-flowering stems.

ABOVE LEFT *Low-growing* Erysimum kotschyanum *is native to Turkey. Throughout the flowering season, bright golden yellow flowers appear among the densely clustered dull green leaves.*

ABOVE Erysimum *'Bowles' Mauve' can flower year-round in favourable climates. Appearing among the grey-green leaves, the dark purple-black buds open to reveal bright mauve flowers.*

Plant Height	Plant Width	Hardiness Zone	Frost Tolerance
6–12 in (15–30 cm)	12 in (30 cm)	8–10	yes
30 in (75 cm)	4 ft (1.2 m)	6–11	yes
18 in (45 cm)	12 in (30 cm)	5–8	no
4 in (10 cm)	10 in (25 cm)	6–9	yes
3–4 in (8–10 cm)	18 in (45 cm)	6–9	yes
18 in (45 cm)	18 in (45 cm)	5–8	yes

RIGHT Erysimum *'Gold Shot'* has clusters of fragrant golden yellow flowers and mid-green leaves. This charming sun-loving plant is an ideal choice for rockery, border or container planting.

Top Tip

Choose evergreen long-flowering wallflowers for container planting. The container can be moved around wherever colour and/or fragrance is needed.

RIGHT *Endemic to Sicily and its surrounding islands, Erysimum bonannianum prefers rocky terrain. This species bears clusters of lemon yellow flowers that carry a mild fragrance.*

Favourites	Flower Colour	Blooming Season	Flower Fragrance
Eschscholzia caespitosa	bright yellow	summer	yes
Eschscholzia caespitosa 'Sundew'	light yellow	summer	yes
Eschscholzia californica	yellow to orange-red	spring to autumn	no
Eschscholzia californica 'Purple Gleam'	violet-purple	spring to autumn	no
Eschscholzia lobbii	yellow	spring	no
Eschscholzia mexicana	yellow with orange centre	late winter to spring	no

ABOVE *The lovely clear yellow flowers of* Eschscholzia lobbii *are followed by fruit with rough seeds. These charming flowers close up in overcast weather.*
RIGHT *A brilliant scarlet when they first bloom, the open single flowers of* Eschscholzia californica *'Single Red' gradually turn a vibrant orange-red.*

Top Tip

Undemanding annuals, these plants are ideal for filling large areas of ground with colour. They require little care and reward with colourful blooms.

ESCHSCHOLZIA

Native to western North America and now widely naturalised, this poppy family (Papaveraceae) genus is made up of around 8 annuals and short-lived perennials. Commonly known as California poppies, they have fine feathery foliage, which is often a rather greyish green, and in summer produce masses of bright, golden yellow, 4- to 8-petalled blooms that open only on sunny days. Modern seed strains flower in a wide colour range. Long seed capsules follow. The genus was named in 1820 after Johann Friedrich Eschscholz (1793–1831), leader of the Russian expedition on which it was first collected in 1816. The seeds were among the many taken to England by the Scottish botanist David Douglas.

CULTIVATION

Very easily grown in any sunny position in light, gritty, well-drained soil, *Eschscholzia* species often self-sow and naturalise, especially in gravel riverbeds. Most are very frost hardy and tolerate poor soil. Deadhead regularly to prolong flowering. Raise from seed in spring, which is best sown directly where the plants are to grow as they do not transplant well.

Plant Height	Plant Width	Hardiness Zone	Frost Tolerance
6 in (15 cm)	6 in (15 cm)	7–10	yes
6 in (15 cm)	6 in (15 cm)	7–10	yes
8–12 in (20–30 cm)	12 in (30 cm)	6–11	yes
8–12 in (20–30 cm)	12 in (30 cm)	6–11	yes
4–8 in (10–20 cm)	8 in (20 cm)	7–10	yes
8 in (20 cm)	8 in (20 cm)	7–11	yes

BELOW Eschscholzia californica *produces lovely cup-shaped flowers in bright shades of orange and yellow over a long flowering season.*

EUPHORBIA

This large genus of around 2,000 species of annuals, perennials, shrubs and trees, both evergreen and deciduous, is distributed throughout the world. It covers a diverse range of forms and natural habitats, from the spiny and succulent cactus-like species of hot dry areas to leafy perennials from cooler temperate climates. The true flowers, borne singly or in clusters, are very small and insignificant, but are often accompanied by long-lasting, colourful petal-like bracts. All species contain a poisonous milky sap that can cause severe skin irritation and, sometimes, temporary blindness on contact with the eyes. The purgative qualities of the sap are acknowledged in the common name spurge, from the Latin word *expurgare*, meaning to purge.

CULTIVATION

The diversity of form makes it difficult to generalise cultivation requirements. Consider the plant's natural habitat, and provide similar growing conditions. Because of the toxicity of the sap, care should always be taken when handling these plants. Some species are propagated from seed or by division, while others grow from stem-tip cuttings.

Favourites	Flower Colour	Blooming Season	Flower Fragrance	Plant Height	Plant Width	Hardiness Zone	Frost Tolerance
Euphorbia amygdaloides	greenish yellow	mid-spring to early summer	no	30–36 in (75–90 cm)	12 in (30 cm)	7–9	yes
Euphorbia characias	greenish yellow	spring	no	4 ft (1.2 m)	4 ft (1.2 m)	8–10	yes
Euphorbia cyparissias	yellow-green	late spring to early summer	no	8–15 in (20–38 cm)	8–12 in (20–30 cm)	4–9	yes
Euphorbia griffithii	orange to red	summer	no	36 in (90 cm)	36 in (90 cm)	5–10	yes
Euphorbia keithii	yellow to green	spring to summer	no	6–20 ft (1.8–6 m)	5–8 ft (1.5–2.4 m)	9–11	no
Euphorbia marginata	green and white	late summer to autumn	no	12–36 in (30–90 cm)	24 in (60 cm)	7–11	yes
Euphorbia × *martinii*	yellow-green; dark red centre	spring to mid-summer	no	36 in (90 cm)	36 in (90 cm)	7–10	yes
Euphorbia milii	scarlet, crimson, yellow	most of the year	no	12–24 in (30–60 cm)	36 in (90 cm)	10–11	no
Euphorbia myrsinites	yellow-green	spring to summer	no	4–8 in (10–20 cm)	12 in (30 cm)	5–9	yes
Euphorbia myrsinites subsp. *pontica*	yellow-green tinged with red	spring	no	4–8 in (10–20 cm)	12 in (30 cm)	5–9	yes
Euphorbia nicaeensis	yellow to greenish yellow	late spring to mid-summer	no	30 in (75 cm)	18 in (45 cm)	5–8	yes
Euphorbia pulcherrima	bright red bracts, yellowish flowers	winter to early spring	no	10 ft (3 m)	10 ft (3 m)	10–11	no

LEFT Euphorbia myrsinites *subsp.* pontica *is a good rock-garden plant requiring light well-drained soil.*
RIGHT *Oval-shaped, blue-green, succulent leaves are one of the best features of* Euphorbia myrsinites, *along with its whorls of bracts.*

Top Tip

One of the most popular *Euphorbia* species is the poinsettia from Mexico (*E. pulcherrima),* which needs fertile soil and plenty of sunshine to grow successfully.

ABOVE Euphorbia × martinii, *which bears distinctive chartreuse flowerheads, is best planted in a sheltered spot.*
RIGHT *Bright orange bracts and small yellow flowers give the cultivar* Euphorbia griffithii *'Fireglow' its name.*

ABOVE Euphorbia characias *will readily self seed if it is planted in a well-drained site where it receives plenty of sunshine. It is native to the Mediterranean region.*

BELOW *Commonly known as ghostweed,* Euphorbia marginata *has eye-catching white and green bracts. This fast-growing plant prefers well-drained soil.*

ABOVE Euphorbia characias *'Portuguese Velvet', with its long, bluish green, feather-shaped leaves, is very suitable for a rock garden or a mixed border.*
RIGHT *Valued for its bright red bracts that resemble a large flower, the poinsettia (*Euphorbia pulcherrima*) has long been popular as a Christmas decoration in many parts of the world.*

ABOVE *A semi-succulent shrub,* Euphorbia milii *is an ideal plant for courtyards or in rock gardens. The orange-yellow flowers are surrounded by red bracts.*

RIGHT Euphorbia keithii *is a tall cactus-like plant with grey-blue spines and tiny yellow flowers that appear in spring and continue well into the summer months.*

Favourites	Flower Colour	Blooming Season	Flower Fragrance
Eustoma grandiflorum	white, blue, pink, purple	mid-spring to summer	no
Eustoma grandiflorum 'Echo Blue'	violet-blue	mid-spring to summer	no
Eustoma grandiflorum 'Echo White'	white	mid-spring to summer	no
Eustoma grandiflorum 'Echo Yellow'	pale yellow	mid-spring to summer	no
Eustoma grandiflorum 'Forever Blue'	violet-blue	mid-spring to summer	no
Eustoma grandiflorum 'Lilac Rose'	lilac-pink	mid-spring to summer	no

ABOVE Eustoma grandiflorum *'Echo Blue' is one of the Echo Series cultivars. Its double flowers are somewhat rose-like in appearance and are an appealing shade of violet-blue.*

EUSTOMA

Formerly classified as *Lisianthus*, these long-stemmed gentian relatives (family Gentianaceae) are widely cultivated as cut flowers. Also commonly known as prairie gentians or Texas bluebells, there are 3 annual or short-lived perennial species in this genus, which are found from southern USA to northern South America. They form clumps of succulent oval to narrowly elliptical leaves, and from spring to summer produce showy 5- to 6-petalled, funnel- to bell-shaped flowers. Species sometimes carry their flowers singly, but the cultivated plants have long stems that produce a profusion of eye-catching blooms in a wide range of colour. *Lisianthus* means "bitter flower"; this refers to the taste of the flowers, which were traditionally used in herbal medicine by Native Americans.

CULTIVATION

Eustoma plants are usually cultivated as annuals. Slow growing, they need lengthy warm conditions to flower well. Plant in full or half sun in fertile, moist, well-drained soil. The flower stems are best staked. Propagation can be from cuttings, but it is better to raise plants from seed. Sow in early autumn for spring flowers.

Plant Height	Plant Width	Hardiness Zone	Frost Tolerance
18–30 in (45–75 cm)	12 in (30 cm)	9–11	no
18–24 in (45–60 cm)	12 in (30 cm)	9–11	no
18–24 in (45–60 cm)	12 in (30 cm)	9–11	no
18–24 in (45–60 cm)	12 in (30 cm)	9–11	no
8 in (20 cm)	12 in (30 cm)	9–11	no
12–18 in (30–45 cm)	12 in (30 cm)	9–11	no

ABOVE 'Lilac Rose' is an especially pretty cultivar of Eustoma grandiflorum, *with delicate lilac-pink flowers.* **LEFT** Eustoma grandiflorum 'Forever Blue' has violet-blue flowers, and is much smaller than the species.

Top Tip

Although *Eustoma* species are classified as perennials, they do not perform very well beyond their first season. It is advised to replace the plants after flowering with fresh stock.

LEFT A white-flowered variety, Eustoma grandiflorum 'Forever White' makes an excellent container plant. The cut flowers will last for up to 3 weeks.

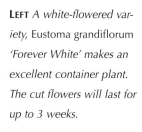

LEFT *The creamy green leaves of* Felicia amelloides *'Variegata' are interspersed with lovely sky blue daisy-like flowers from spring through to early summer.* BELOW LEFT *Sky blue daisy-like flowers smother* Felicia amelloides *over a long flowering season. The bright green leaves are aromatic.*

FELICIA

Commonly known as the kingfisher daisy due to its brilliant blue flowers, this genus includes around 80 species of annuals, perennials and subshrubs naturally occurring from southern Africa to the Arabian Peninsula. Mainly low-growing plants, they have simple oblong leaves that are often covered with fine bristly hairs. The daisy-like flowers are made up of a central yellow disc floret surrounded by a brightly coloured flowerhead, which is often sky blue, although it may be pink or white. *Felicia* species bloom throughout much of spring and summer, and are suitable for rock gardens, containers and beds. The genus was named after Herr Felix, a nineteenth-century mayor of Regensburg, a town on the Danube.

CULTIVATION
These plants are reasonably hardy but will withstand only light frost. The perennials and subshrubs are best suited to a mild climate with warm summers and dry winters. Plant in full sun with light, gritty, well-drained soil. Propagate from cuttings taken in late summer or autumn, or from seed in spring.

Top Tip

These plants need a little attention to keep them tidy. Regular deadheading and pruning of straggly stems will control spread and extend the flowering season.

Favourites	Flower Colour	Blooming Season	Flower Fragrance	Plant Height	Plant Width	Hardiness Zone	Frost Tolerance
Felicia amelloides	sky blue	spring to early summer	no	12–18 in (30–45 cm)	30 in (75 cm)	9–11	no
Felicia amelloides 'Variegata'	sky blue	spring to early summer	no	12–18 in (30–45 cm)	30 in (75 cm)	9–11	no
Felicia bergeriana	blue	late winter to early spring	no	8 in (20 cm)	8 in (20 cm)	9–11	no
Felicia filifolia	mauve to white	spring	no	36 in (90 cm)	36 in (90 cm)	9–11	no
Felicia fruticosa	mauve, white, purple	spring	no	2–4 ft (0.6–1.2 m)	3 ft (0.9 m)	9–11	no
Felicia 'Spring Melchen'	blue, pink, white	spring	no	12 in (30 cm)	18 in (45 cm)	9–11	no

LEFT *Among the mid-green needle-like leaves, tiny mauve or white flowers cover the stems of* Felicia filifolia.
BELOW *A small evergreen shrub,* Felicia fruticosa *bears an abundance of flowers, in shades of pink, purple and white, throughout the spring months.*

GAILLARDIA

Discovered in the Rocky Mountains around 1825, this genus of about 30 species of annual, biennial and perennial daisies (family Asteraceae) occurs mainly in the southern USA and Mexico. The common name of blanket flower comes from a Native American legend of a blanket maker who the spirits rewarded with an ever-blooming blanket of flowers on his grave. Appropriately, these small mounding plants are covered in summer and autumn with vivid flowerheads. The ray florets are typically red at the centre with a yellow outer half. Cultivated garden forms occur in warm tones and have long flowering periods.

ABOVE *One of the taller cultivars available, reaching up to 60 cm (24 in) high,* Gaillardia *'Burgunder' produces flowerheads of burgundy red petals around a red to yellow disc floret.*
RIGHT Gaillardia × grandiflora *'Indian Yellow' bears a profusion of sunny yellow blooms during summer. Regular removal of any spent flowers will prolong the flowering season well into autumn.*

CULTIVATION

Hardiness varies, though they are so easily cultivated that replacing any winter casualties is no problem. Plant in full sun in well-drained soil that remains moist during the growing season. Propagate from seed or basal cuttings.

Favourites	Flower Colour	Blooming Season	Flower Fragrance	Plant Height	Plant Width	Hardiness Zone	Frost Tolerance
Gaillardia 'Burgunder'	dark red	summer to autumn	no	20–24 in (50–60 cm)	18 in (45 cm)	5–10	yes
Gaillardia 'Dazzler'	orange-yellow; dark red centre	summer to autumn	no	24–36 in (60–90 cm)	18–24 in (45–60 cm)	5–10	yes
Gaillardia × *grandiflora*	orange, yellow, red and maroon	early summer to early autumn	no	36 in (90 cm)	18 in (45 cm)	5–10	yes
Gaillardia 'Kobold'	dark red, tipped with yellow	late spring to early autumn	no	12 in (30 cm)	30 in (75 cm)	5–10	yes
Gaillardia pulchella	red, yellow; red and yellow	summer to autumn	no	18–24 in (45–60 cm)	18 in (45 cm)	8–10	yes
Gaillardia pulchella, **Plume Series**	red, yellow	summer to autumn	no	10–18 in (25–45 cm)	24–36 in (60–90 cm)	8–10	yes

ABOVE *Sunflower-like in appearance, Gaillardia 'Kobold' brings dazzling colour to the garden, with its red disc florets and yellow-tipped red petals.*
RIGHT *Pictured here in the wild, Gaillardia pulchella has plump cone-shaped disc florets in rich maroon, surrounded by deep red petals with yellow tips.*

GAZANIA

Commonly known as treasure flowers, the
16 species of annuals and perennials in
this daisy family (Asteraceae) genus are found
mainly in South Africa, with a few species
extending the range to the tropics. They are
low-growing, near-evergreen, clump-forming
plants with simple, narrow, lance-shaped,
sometimes downy leaves with pale undersides.
Their flowers, which appear throughout the
warmer months, are the main attraction as
they are large, brightly coloured, often interestingly marked and showy. While the species
usually have yellow or orange flowers, garden
forms are available in a huge colour range.
The genus was named after Theodore of Gaza
(1398–1478), who translated the botanical
texts of Theophrastus from Greek into Latin.

CULTIVATION

Apart from being somewhat frost tender and
resenting wet winters, they are easily grown in
any sunny position in gritty free-draining soil.
Propagate by division or from basal cuttings in
autumn, or raise from seed in late winter.

Favourites	Flower Colour	Blooming Season	Flower Fragrance
Gazania 'Blackberry Ripple'	burgundy and white	late spring to summer	no
Gazania, Chansonette Series	orange, pink, red, yellow	summer	no
Gazania 'Christopher Lloyd'	bright pink and green	late spring to summer	no
Gazania linearis	orange-yellow	summer to autumn	no
Gazania rigens	orange-yellow	spring to summer	no
Gazania rigens 'Variegata'	orange-yellow	spring to summer	no

ABOVE *Gazanias open in full sun and close up during overcast weather and at dusk. Sun-loving* Gazania rigens *opens to reveal bright yellow daisy-like flowers.*
ABOVE LEFT *With bright pink petals marked emerald green at the base,* Gazania 'Christopher Lloyd' *is an ideal choice when a colourful ground cover is required.*

Plant Height	Plant Width	Hardiness Zone	Frost Tolerance
6 in (15 cm)	24 in (60 cm)	9–11	no
8 in (20 cm)	10 in (25 cm)	8–10	no
6 in (15 cm)	18 in (45 cm)	9–11	no
8–12 in (20–30 cm)	12–18 in (30–45 cm)	9–11	no
6 in (15 cm)	24–36 in (60–90 cm)	9–11	no
6 in (15 cm)	24–36 in (60–90 cm)	9–11	no

RIGHT *Attractive green and cream variegated leaves distinguish Gazania rigens 'Variegata' from the species. The large, open, yellow-orange flowers are distinctly marked black with a white eye towards the petal base.*
BELOW *Creamy white petals streaked with dark purple-pink and highlighted in yellow towards the base are the trademarks of Gazania 'Blackberry Ripple'. These features are accented by the silvery grey leaves.*

Top Tip

Gazanias can add colour to the beach-side garden, as they are very tolerant of coastal conditions. Most species are able to withstand poor dry soils, but appreciate additional humus under these conditions.

LEFT *Ideal for small rock gardens, the leaves of Gentiana acaulis 'Rannoch' form clumps of wonderful bright green foliage from which emerge the stems of large, dark-centred, deep blue flowers.*

BELOW *From western and central Asia, Gentiana septemfida is an easy-to-grow plant that will reward with arching stems of blue bell-shaped flowers and rich green foliage.*

GENTIANA

BELOW *A native of Japan, Gentiana makinoi features mid-green basal leaves. The leafy flower stems produce pretty bell-shaped blue flowers—often spotted on the interior—at the apex and at the leaf axils.*

Around 400 species of annuals, biennials and perennials make up this genus, the type for the family Gentianaceae. They are widely distributed in temperate zones and many are alpine plants. Gentians typically form a small clump or tuft of simple basal leaves or a cluster of wiry stems with opposite pairs of leaves. The genus is renowned for producing intense blue flowers, but not all gentians are blue, many are white, yellow or mauve-blue. The flowering season is mainly spring or autumn. Gentians have several herbal uses and the European yellow gentian *(Gentiana lutea)* was once regarded as a virtual "miracle cure".

CULTIVATION

The usual preference is for a climate with clearly defined seasons, soil that is gritty and free draining yet moisture retentive and a position in sun or half-shade. Many are superb rockery plants. The species are best raised from seed, while the selected forms may be divided and sometimes strike from layers.

Favourites	Flower Colour	Blooming Season	Flower Fragrance	Plant Height	Plant Width	Hardiness Zone	Frost Tolerance
Gentiana acaulis	deep blue, green-spotted interior	spring to early summer	no	4 in (10 cm)	12 in (30 cm)	3–9	yes
Gentiana asclepiadea	violet-blue	late summer to early autumn	no	24 in (60 cm)	18 in (45 cm)	6–9	yes
Gentiana × *macaulayi*	deep blue	summer to autumn	no	4 in (10 cm)	16 in (40 cm)	4–9	yes
Gentiana makinoi	pale blue to violet-blue	summer	no	24 in (60 cm)	16 in (40 cm)	6–9	yes
Gentiana septemfida	dark blue to blue-purple	late summer	no	6–12 in (15–30 cm)	12–16 in (30–40 cm)	3–9	yes
Gentiana sino-ornata	blue	autumn	no	6 in (15 cm)	12 in (30 cm)	6–9	yes

RIGHT *A native of southern Europe, found from Spain to the Balkans,* Gentiana acaulis *features a basal rosette of glossy leaves and green-spotted, dark blue, bell-shaped flowers.*

GERANIUM

The plants often called "geraniums" in fact belong in the genus *Pelargonium*. While both genera are members of the geranium family (Geraniaceae), the true geraniums are a very different group of over 300 species of perennials and subshrubs that are at times evergreen, and are widespread in the temperate zones. Their often finely hairy leaves are usually hand-shaped, with toothed lobes. They bloom in spring and summer and have simple, flat, 5-petalled flowers in pink or purple-blue shades, less often white or darker purple-black. The plant's common name, cranesbill, is attributed to the shape of its long narrow fruit, which somewhat resembles a crane's long beak. The genus name *Geranium* is derived from the Greek word *geranos* (crane).

CULTIVATION

Most species are hardy and will grow in a wide range of conditions, preferring sun or semi-shade and moist humus-rich soil. The roots can be invasive. Geraniums are appealing as ground covers, in rockeries and as part of flower borders. Propagate by division or from cuttings or seed; these plants may self-sow.

Top Tip

Easily divided, geraniums can be used to fill any bare patches in the garden. They can quickly fill an area, and may need to be thinned out and pruned to maintain a tidy appearance.

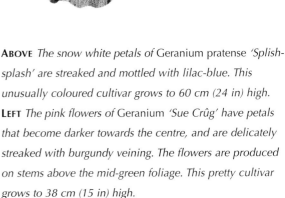

ABOVE *The snow white petals of* Geranium pratense *'Splishsplash' are streaked and mottled with lilac-blue. This unusually coloured cultivar grows to 60 cm (24 in) high.*

LEFT *The pink flowers of* Geranium *'Sue Crûg' have petals that become darker towards the centre, and are delicately streaked with burgundy veining. The flowers are produced on stems above the mid-green foliage. This pretty cultivar grows to 38 cm (15 in) high.*

ABOVE *Grey-green leaves complement the strongly red-veined pink flowers of* Geranium cinereum *'Ballerina'.*
LEFT *From spring to summer, white-centred violet-pink flowers are featured among the mid-green lobed leaves of* Geranium sylvaticum *'Mayflower'.*

Favourites	Flower Colour	Blooming Season	Flower Fragrance	Plant Height	Plant Width	Hardiness Zone	Frost Tolerance
Geranium 'Ann Folkard'	magenta with black centre	mid-summer to mid-autumn	no	24 in (60 cm)	36 in (90 cm)	6–9	yes
Geranium cinereum	white, pale pink	late spring to early summer	no	6 in (15 cm)	12 in (30 cm)	5–9	yes
Geranium maderense	magenta-pink	late winter to late summer	no	5 ft (1.5 m)	4–5 ft (1.2–1.5 m)	9–10	no
Geranium 'Patricia'	magenta	late spring to early summer	no	12–18 in (30–45 cm)	24 in (60 cm)	5–9	yes
Geranium phaeum	purple-black, maroon, mauve	late spring to early summer	no	30 in (75 cm)	18 in (45 cm)	5–10	yes
Geranium pratense	white, violet, blue	summer	no	24–36 in (60–90 cm)	24 in (60 cm)	5–9	yes
Geranium renardii	white with purple veins	early summer	no	12 in (30 cm)	12 in (30 cm)	6–9	yes
Geranium sanguineum	magenta to crimson	summer	no	8 in (20 cm)	12 in (30 cm)	5–9	yes
Geranium sessiliflorum	white	summer	no	6 in (15 cm)	12 in (30 cm)	7–9	yes
Geranium 'Sue Crûg'	mauve-pink with darker veins	late spring to early summer	no	8 in (20 cm)	12 in (30 cm)	4–9	yes
Geranium sylvaticum	white, pink, purple	late spring to summer	no	30 in (75 cm)	24 in (60 cm)	4–9	yes
Geranium tuberosum	purple-pink	spring to early summer	no	8–10 in (20–25 cm)	12 in (30 cm)	7–10	yes

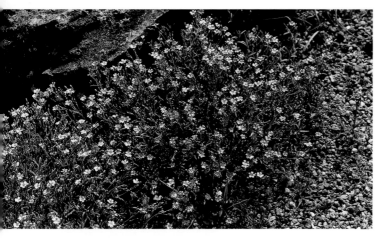

LEFT Gypsophila repens *'Rosa Schönheit'* forms a carpet of tiny, star-shaped, pink flowers amid narrow blue-green leaves.
BELOW LEFT *Perfect for a range of situations including rockeries and hanging baskets, Gypsophila muralis 'Gypsy' bears masses of tiny, double, pink flowers.*

ABOVE *The starry flowers and dainty foliage of* Gypsophila muralis *'Garden Bride' form an airy cloud of pale pink when used in rockeries, borders and window boxes.*

Top Tip

Not fussy about soil type, summer-flowering baby's breath will quickly fill bare areas of the garden where a burst of colour and speedy coverage are needed.

GYPSOPHILA

Related to the carnations (family Caryophyllaceae), the 100-odd annuals and perennials in this genus occur naturally throughout Eurasia. They range from spreading mat-forming plants studded with pink or white blooms to upright shrubby species with billowing heads of tiny flowers. Their simple linear to lance-shaped leaves are sometimes rather fleshy and often blue-green. The flowering season is only short lived, but it can be prolonged by resowing every 3 weeks to give continuous blooms. *Gypsophila paniculata* and its cultivars are popular cut flowers that are often used by florists to add to bunches of brighter bolder blooms as backing foliage. They can also be used successfully in dried flower arrangements.

CULTIVATION

Gypsophila means chalk-loving, but most species are happy in any neutral to slightly alkaline soil that is fertile, moist and well drained. Mat-forming species are excellent rockery plants. Plant in full sun. Larger types will often rebloom if cut back after their first flush. Propagate from basal cuttings or seed.

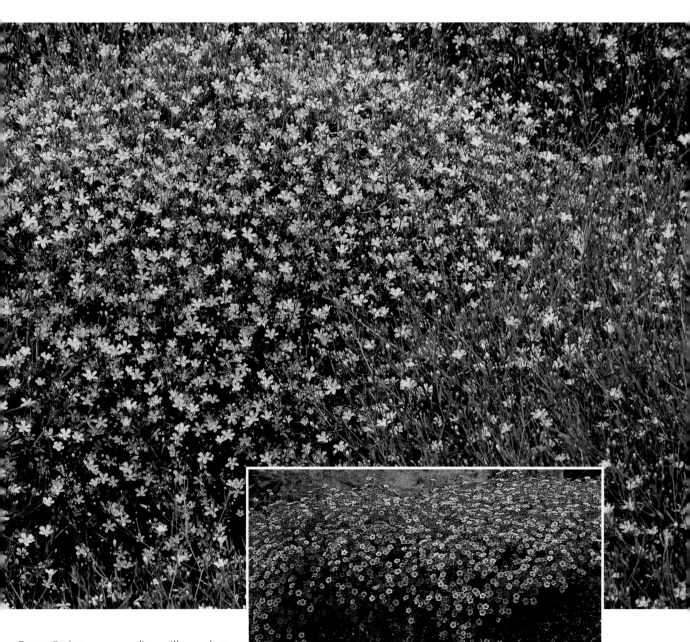

RIGHT *Perfect as a cascading spillover plant, Gypsophila repens has clusters of tiny pink or white flowers and blue-green leaves.*

Favourites	Flower Colour	Blooming Season	Flower Fragrance	Plant Height	Plant Width	Hardiness Zone	Frost Tolerance
Gypsophila cerastoides	white with pink veins	late spring to summer	no	3 in (8 cm)	6 in (15 cm)	5–10	yes
Gypsophila elegans	white, pink	summer	no	24 in (60 cm)	12 in (30 cm)	6–10	yes
Gypsophila muralis	pale pink to white	mid-summer to early autumn	no	6–12 in (15–30 cm)	12–18 in (30–45 cm)	7–10	yes
Gypsophila paniculata	white, pink	spring to summer	no	2–4 ft (0.6–1.2 m)	4 ft (1.2 m)	4–10	yes
Gypsophila paniculata 'Bristol Fairy'	white	summer	no	2–4 ft (0.6–1.2 m)	4 ft (1.2 m)	4–10	yes
Gypsophila repens	white, pink, lilac	summer	no	8 in (20 cm)	12–20 in (30–50 cm)	4–9	yes

HEDYCHIUM

This genus, commonly known as ginger lily or garland lily, is a member of the ginger family and includes some 40 species of perennials native to tropical Asia, the Himalayan region and Madagascar. Strong cane-like stems with large deep green leaves, similar to the canna lily, emerge from heavy fleshy rhizomes. Ginger lilies are grown for their colourful and highly fragrant flower-heads, which are made up of a number of slender mostly tubular-shaped flowers that have protruding anthers. The flowers appear in summer and are mainly yellow or pink in colour, although in some species they can be bright red. The fragrant roots of several *Hedychium* species are used in Indian Ayurvedic medicine.

ABOVE *Dense spikes of bright red flowers and long, pointy, mid-green leaves make* Hedychium greenei *one of the more spectacular ginger lilies. It does best in moist soil.*
LEFT Hedychium gardnerianum, *or Kahili ginger, bears bright orange seed pods containing shiny red seeds in late autumn.*

CULTIVATION

These plants are mostly tolerant of light frosts and are capable of reshooting from the rootstock. They are best planted in sun or shade with moist, humus-rich, well-drained soil. Cut back the stems of spent flowers and any old unproductive canes to encourage new growth. Water liberally during the growing season and add liquid fertiliser once a month. Propagate by division or from seed.

Favourites	Flower Colour	Blooming Season	Flower Fragrance	Plant Height	Plant Width	Hardiness Zone	Frost Tolerance
Hedychium coccineum	orange, pink, red, white	late summer to autumn	yes	3–7 ft (0.9–2 m)	4–8 ft (1.2–2.4 m)	8–11	yes
Hedychium coronarium	white with yellow markings	summer to autumn	yes	6–8 ft (1.8–2.4 m)	6–10 ft (1.8–3 m)	9–12	no
Hedychium densiflorum	orange, yellow	summer to early autumn	yes	3–8 ft (0.9–2.4 m)	6 ft (1.8 m)	8–11	yes
Hedychium gardnerianum	yellow and red	late summer to autumn	yes	4–6 ft (1.2–1.8 m)	4–6 ft (1.2–1.8 m)	8–11	yes
Hedychium greenei	orange-scarlet	late summer to autumn	no	3–5 ft (0.9–1.5 m)	3–5 ft (0.9–1.5 m)	9–12	no
Hedychium spicatum	white and orange	summer to early autumn	no	3–5 ft (0.9–1.5 m)	5 ft (1.5 m)	8–11	yes

Top Tip

When the foliage of *Hedychium* species dies down, the fleshy stems can be lifted and overwintered, to be replaced in spring.

ABOVE *Ginger lilies such as* Hedychium spicatum *benefit from an application of a balanced liquid fertiliser when spring growth begins.*
RIGHT Hedychium coccineum *produces beautiful blooms varying in colour from coral to orange and red, with pink stamens.*

HELENIUM

This mainly North American genus belongs to the daisy family and contains about 40 species of annuals, biennials and perennials. Most species form an upright foliage clump and have simple, lance-shaped, light green leaves, usually covered with fine hairs. From mid-summer until well into autumn they produce large daisy-like flowerheads, consisting of a central cone or disc floret surrounded by large and often slightly drooping ray florets. The central disc is usually yellow as may be the surrounding ray florets, although more often these are in contrasting shades of orange or red. *Helenium* species are commonly known as sneezeweed because Native Americans traditionally used the powdered flowers from certain species to make snuff.

CULTIVATION

Hardiness varies but most species are very frost tolerant. Plant them in a sunny open position in moist well-drained soil. Deadhead regularly to prolong the flowering period. Propagate by division, from cuttings taken from shoots at the base of the plant or from seed.

Favourites	Flower Colour	Blooming Season	Flower Fragrance
Helenium autumnale	yellow	late summer to mid-autumn	no
Helenium bigelovii	yellow and reddish brown	summer	no
Helenium 'Blopip'	yellow and green-brown	summer to early autumn	no
Helenium hoopesii	yellow-orange and brown	summer	no
Helenium 'Waldtraut'	yellow-orange and brown	late summer to early autumn	no
Helenium 'Wyndley'	yellow and brown	mid-summer to early autumn	no

Top Tip

Helenium species are easy to grow and do not require much attention. The taller varieties may need staking and can be planted along fences.

ABOVE *The yellow-brown central disc of* Helenium *'Wyndley' is surrounded by petals of rich butter yellow. It flowers for a long period.*
LEFT Helenium *'Blopip' has large heads of sunflower-like blooms in a rich shade of yellow, and with a lovely greenish brown centre. It is suitable for border plantings.*

Plant Height	Plant Width	Hardiness Zone	Frost Tolerance
5 ft (1.5 m)	18 in (45 cm)	3–9	yes
3 ft (0.9 m)	12 in (30 cm)	7–9	yes
18 in (45 cm)	12 in (30 cm)	4–9	yes
3 ft (0.9 m)	18 in (45 cm)	3–9	yes
3 ft (0.9 m)	24 in (60 cm)	4–9	yes
30 in (75 cm)	24 in (60 cm)	4–9	yes

BELOW Helenium autumnale *is a perennial with daisy-like bright yellow flowers that have a lighter central disc. It benefits from a layer of mulch around the base of the plant.*

BELOW *The cheerful blooms of* Helenium *'Waldtraut' are coppery red to brown and, like all* Helenium *species, make excellent long-lasting cut flowers for indoor decoration.*

HELIANTHUS

It is not hard to see why this genus has the common name sunflower: it not only accurately describes the shape of the blooms but also refers to the way the flowerhead turns to follow the sun during the day. This genus contains about 70 annuals and perennials, mostly from the Americas, and is probably best known for the common or giant sunflower, *Helianthus annuus*, which is widely grown as a garden plant as well as commercially for its seeds and the oil extracted from them. Plants are usually tall, with hairy and often sticky leaves and tall bristly stems. The flowerheads grow above the foliage and are large, daisy-like and nearly always yellow.

CULTIVATION

Plant sunflowers in a sunny open position that has fertile, moist and well-drained soil. Propagate the annuals from seed and the perennials either by division or from cuttings taken from the base of the plant.

ABOVE Helianthus annuus *'Ring of Fire' will indeed bring fiery colours to the garden, with its large flowerheads of bright red and golden yellow.*

RIGHT *The double golden yellow flowerheads of* Helianthus × multiflorus *'Loddon Gold' look more like dahlias than the traditional sunflower.*

ABOVE *A compact grower reaching 90 cm (36 in) high, Helianthus annuus 'Teddy Bear' has attractive, fluffy, double flowerheads of bright golden yellow.*

LEFT *Helianthus annuus 'Sunrich Orange' is great for allergy sufferers, as it produces no pollen. Large yellowish orange flowers bloom from mid-summer on this 1.5 m (5 ft) tall plant.*

RIGHT *Native to central USA, the dark-centred, sunny yellow, 5 cm (2 in) wide flowers of Helianthus salicifolius are daisy-like in appearance.*

Favourites	Flower Colour	Blooming Season	Flower Fragrance	Plant Height	Plant Width	Hardiness Zone	Frost Tolerance
Helianthus annuus	yellow	summer to early autumn	no	8–15 ft (2.4–4.5 m)	24 in (60 cm)	4–11	yes
Helianthus annuus 'Ring of Fire'	yellow and brick red	summer to early autumn	no	3–5 ft (0.9–1.5 m)	18 in (45 cm)	4–11	yes
Helianthus annuus 'Ruby Eclipse'	ruby red	summer to early autumn	no	6 ft (1.8 m)	18 in (45 cm)	4–11	yes
Helianthus maximiliani	golden yellow	summer and autumn	no	5–10 ft (1.5–3 m)	30 in (75 cm)	6–11	yes
Helianthus × multiflorus	golden yellow	late summer to mid-autumn	no	3–6 ft (0.9–1.8 m)	3 ft (0.9 m)	5–9	yes
Helianthus salicifolius	golden yellow	late summer to autumn	no	6–8 ft (1.8–2.4 m)	3 ft (0.9 m)	4–9	yes

ABOVE Helleborus niger, *or Christmas rose, can be difficult to cultivate and often requires protection from winter weather. The stunning white flowers are well worth the effort.*

BELOW *Although it is a pretty plant with pale green flowers, the long dark green leaves of* Helleborus foetidus *emit an unpleasant smell when crushed. Once established, the plant will self-seed quite quickly.*

HELLEBORUS

This genus comprising 15 species belongs to the buttercup family (Ranunculaceae) and is found in temperate zones from Europe to western China. They are mostly low-growing plants with hand-shaped, often toothed, short-stemmed, deep green leaves that emerge from a fleshy rootstock. The simple, 5-petalled, bowl-shaped flowers appear from mid-winter through to spring and occur in unusual shades of green, dusky pink and maroon, as well as white. At the centre of the flower are prominent, green, nectar-containing sacs and a number of yellow stamens. Commonly known as the lenten rose or winter rose, the perennials of this species were favourites of Gertrude Jekyll, a passionate English expert gardener and designer.

CULTIVATION

Helleborus species prefer cooler climates and woodland conditions with deep, fertile, humus-rich, well-drained soil and dappled shade. Some of the smaller types of plants are suitable for rockeries. Many species benefit from having old foliage removed when the plants are dormant. Propagate by division or from seed.

Favourites	Flower Colour	Blooming Season	Flower Fragrance
Helleborus argutifolius	pale green	late winter to early spring	no
Helleborus foetidus	green with red margins	mid-winter to mid-spring	no
Helleborus 'Halliwell Purple'	pinkish purple	mid-winter to early spring	no
Helleborus lividus	greenish with pink-purple tint	mid-winter to early spring	no
Helleborus niger	white, pink; greenish centre	early winter to early spring	no
Helleborus orientalis	white, cream, green, purple	mid-winter to mid-spring	no

Top Tip

All *Helleborus* species are toxic and the sap can cause skin irritation, so exercise caution when handling the plants and keep away from children.

RIGHT Helleborus 'Halliwell Purple' bears slightly drooping, saucer-shaped, dusky rose-coloured flowers and has mid-green leaves.

LEFT Helleborus lividus *has deep green or bluish green glossy leaves and attractive light green flowers. Its compact habit makes it suitable as a border plant.*
BELOW Helleborus orientalis, *or lenten rose, is valued for its large saucer-shaped blooms that come in a range of colours.*

Plant Height	Plant Width	Hardiness Zone	Frost Tolerance
4 ft (1.2 m)	24 in (60 cm)	6–9	yes
30 in (75 cm)	18 in (45 cm)	6–10	yes
18 in (45 cm)	18–24 in (45–60 cm)	6–10	yes
18 in (45 cm)	12 in (30 cm)	7–9	yes
12 in (30 cm)	12–18 in (30–45 cm)	3–9	yes
12–24 in (30–60 cm)	18–24 in (45–60 cm)	6–10	yes

HEMEROCALLIS

Once grouped with the true lilies, this small genus of 15 species of fleshy-root perennials from temperate East Asia is now the type genus for its own family, the Hemerocallidaceae. The plants form clumps of grassy or iris-like leaves with 6-petalled funnel- to bell-shaped flowers held aloft on sturdy stems. Flowers come in a variety of forms and in shades of warm yellow, apricot and red. Individual flowers last only a day—hence the common name of daylily—although the plants do produce a succession of blooms lasting from late spring until autumn. All parts, especially the buds and flowers, are edible and may be added to salads or used as a colourful garnish. Stamens can be used as a saffron colour substitute.

CULTIVATION

Hemerocallis plants are hardy and are easily grown in a sunny or partly shaded position with fertile, moist, well-drained soil. The flowers turn to face the sun, which is an important consideration when positioning the plants in the garden. Propagation is usually by division.

ABOVE Hemerocallis fulva, *a clump-forming perennial, is popular for its tall, orange, trumpet-shaped flowers, which last well when cut.* **BELOW** *Lavender-blue flowers with a bright yellow centre make* Hemerocallis *'Prairie Blue Eyes' a valuable addition to the garden, particularly among shrubs and on the edges of paths.*

Top Tip

Every few years it is a good idea to lift and divide clumps of daylilies as this will help to maintain vigour. Evergreen daylilies should be divided in spring.

Favourites	Flower Colour	Blooming Season	Flower Fragrance	Plant Height	Plant Width	Hardiness Zone	Frost Tolerance
Hemerocallis **'Buzz Bomb'**	orange-red and yellow	summer to early autumn	no	24 in (60 cm)	18–24 in (45–60 cm)	5–11	yes
Hemerocallis **fulva**	orange-brown	summer to early autumn	no	3 ft (0.9 m)	24 in (60 cm)	4–11	yes
Hemerocallis **'Green Flutter'**	yellow with green tints	summer to early autumn	no	20 in (50 cm)	3 ft (0.9 m)	5–11	yes
Hemerocallis **lilioasphodelus**	lemon yellow	early summer	yes	3 ft (0.9 m)	3 ft (0.9 m)	4–9	yes
Hemerocallis **'Prairie Blue Eyes'**	mauve-blue	summer to early autumn	no	27 in (70 cm)	30 in (75 cm)	5–11	yes
Hemerocallis **'Stella de Oro'**	bright yellow	summer	no	12 in (30 cm)	18 in (45 cm)	5–11	yes

ABOVE *Hemerocallis 'Buzz Bomb' displays its showy orange-red blooms in summer. It looks particularly effective in mass plantings.*
RIGHT *The lemon yellow blooms of* Hemerocallis lilioasphodelus *have a pleasing fragrance, which makes them an ideal choice for bouquets.*

372

RIGHT *Heart-shaped leaves and dainty bell-shaped flowers in reds, pinks or whites are the trademark features of the Bressingham Hybrids, popular forms of* Heuchera × brizoides.

HEUCHERA

A North American genus of about 55 species of perennials in the saxifrage (Saxifragaceae) family, it is commonly known as alum root or coral bells. Many are near-evergreen and are grown as much for their foliage as for the flowers. The basic leaf shape is rounded, but the small pointed lobes create a maple-leaf effect. Modern hybrids often have unusually marked foliage. From late spring to autumn they bear erect wiry stems with sprays of sometimes petal-less tiny flowers, usually in shades of white, cream or pink. The genus name honours Johann Heinrich von Heucher (1677–1747), who was professor of medicine at Wittenburg University, and perhaps refers to the plant's use in herbal medicines, as Heucher specialised in medicinal plants.

CULTIVATION

Suitable for rockeries, perennial borders and containers, as well as being hardy and adaptable, *Heuchera* plants should be placed in full or part-sun with fertile, moist, humus-rich, well-drained soil. Deadhead regularly to keep tidy and to encourage continued blooming. Propagate by division or from fresh seed.

Favourites	Flower Colour	Blooming Season	Flower Fragrance
Heuchera × *brizoides*	pink, red, white	late spring to autumn	no
Heuchera 'Chocolate Ruffles'	white	late spring to autumn	no
Heuchera 'Fireglow'	red	late spring to autumn	no
Heuchera 'Mint Frost'	cream	late spring to autumn	no
Heuchera 'Petite Marble Burgundy'	pink	late spring to autumn	no
Heuchera 'Wendy'	pink	late spring to autumn	no

LEFT *Held on elegant tall stems, the fiery red bell-flowers of Heuchera 'Fireglow' tower high above the dense clumps of heart-shaped leaves.*

Top Tip

Although generally rugged and reliable plants, *Heuchera* species will appreciate a regular watering regime during dry periods to keep the foliage looking at its best.

ABOVE *A shimmering silver sheen on the rich green leaves gives a frosted appearance to this aptly named cultivar—Heuchera 'Mint Frost'.*

BELOW *Heuchera 'Petite Marble Burgundy' is grown as much for its impressive foliage of silver-dusted leaves as it is for its attractive, pink, bell-shaped flowers.*

Plant Height	Plant Width	Hardiness Zone	Frost Tolerance
12–30 in (30–75 cm)	12–18 in (30–45 cm)	4–10	yes
12–24 in (30–60 cm)	12–24 in (30–60 cm)	5–10	yes
24 in (60 cm)	12–18 in (30–45 cm)	5–10	yes
24 in (60 cm)	12–18 in (30–45 cm)	5–10	yes
8–10 in (20–25 cm)	12–18 in (30–45 cm)	5–10	yes
24 in (60 cm)	36–48 in (90–120 cm)	5–10	yes

HOSTA

Made up of around 40 species of temperate East Asian herbaceous perennials, commonly known as plantain lilies, *Hosta* is a member of the agave (Aga- vaceae) family. They are grown mainly for their bold heart-shaped foliage, which forms a dense basal clump, though their small, funnel- shaped, lily-like flowers are also attractive. Modern hosta cultivars come in a vast array of foliage colours, sizes and textures, and are indispensable plants for shade. The flowers, usually in mauve and purple shades or white, appear from mid-summer. Although it may be difficult for Western gardeners to imagine, hostas were a staple leaf vegetable in their homelands and are still widely used as such.

CULTIVATION

Hostas prefer deep, cool, moist, humus-rich, well-drained soil and light shade. Although hybridisers have tried hard to produce sun- tolerant forms, hostas are woodlanders at heart. Water and feed well to produce lush foliage and use baits and a dry surface mulch to lessen slug and snail damage. Propagation is most often by division in late winter.

LEFT *The green to blue-green leaves of* Hosta *'Shade Fanfare' are edged in a rich creamy white. Pretty pale mauve flowers are borne from mid-summer.*

Top Tip

Hostas are ideal plants for begin- ners. Adaptable and reliable, they do particularly well in shady spots, flourishing where other plants falter.

RIGHT *Adding textural inter- est to the garden, the large blue-green leaves of* Hosta sieboldiana *'Blue Angel' are etched with veins and have a distinctly puckered surface.*

LEFT Hosta plantaginea, *commonly known as august lily or maruba, has lush bright green leaves that are a perfect foil for the crisp white fragrant flowers.*

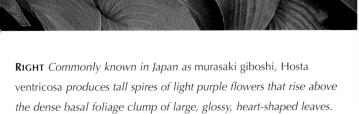

RIGHT *Commonly known in Japan as* murasaki giboshi, *Hosta* ventricosa *produces tall spires of light purple flowers that rise above the dense basal foliage clump of large, glossy, heart-shaped leaves.*

Favourites	Flower Colour	Blooming Season	Flower Fragrance	Plant Height	Plant Width	Hardiness Zone	Frost Tolerance
Hosta 'Frances Williams'	lavender	mid-summer	no	24 in (60 cm)	36 in (90 cm)	6–10	yes
Hosta 'Krossa Regal'	white to pale mauve	mid-summer	no	30–60 in (75–150 cm)	30 in (75 cm)	6–10	yes
Hosta plantaginea	white	mid-summer to autumn	yes	26 in (65 cm)	32 in (80 cm)	8–10	yes
Hosta 'Shade Fanfare'	pale mauve	mid-summer	no	24 in (60 cm)	24 in (60 cm)	6–10	yes
Hosta sieboldiana	white to mauve	mid-summer to early autumn	no	20–24 in (50–60 cm)	36–60 in (90–150 cm)	6–10	yes
Hosta ventricosa	light purple	mid-summer to autumn	no	40 in (100 cm)	24–32 in (60–80 cm)	6–10	yes

IBERIS

Popular for the bold effect of their massed heads of white, pink, mauve or purple flowers, the 30-odd annuals, perennials and subshrubs in this cabbage family (Brassicaceae) genus occur naturally in western and southern Europe and western Asia. They generally have simple, small, narrow leaves, and when not in flower form a rounded bush. The flowerheads open in spring or summer and are borne on short stems that hold them clear of the foliage. Both the genus and common name refer to the home of these plants: *Iberis* is derived from *Iberia*, the Roman name for Spain, while candytuft refers to "the tufted plant from Candia", the former name for Crete.

CULTIVATION

Plant in a sunny position in light, moist, well-drained soil. Deadhead regularly to encourage continuous blooming. *Iberis* plants appreciate a light dressing of dolomite lime. They are useful as ground covers, in rock gardens and in massed displays. Propagate annuals from seed, and the perennials and subshrubs from seed or small cuttings.

Favourites	Flower Colour	Blooming Season	Flower Fragrance	Plant Height	Plant Width	Hardiness Zone	Frost Tolerance
Iberis amara	white, purplish white	summer	yes	12 in (30 cm)	6 in (15 cm)	7–11	yes
Iberis gibraltarica	pink, white with red tinges	summer	no	12 in (30 cm)	12 in (30 cm)	7–11	yes
Iberis saxatalis	white with purple tinges	summer	no	6 in (15 cm)	12 in (30 cm)	7–9	yes
Iberis sempervirens	white	spring to early summer	no	6–12 in (15–30 cm)	18 in (45 cm)	4–11	yes
Iberis sempervirens 'Weisser Zwerg'	white	spring to early summer	no	6 in (15 cm)	18 in (45 cm)	4–11	yes
Iberis umbellata	white, pink, lilac, red, purple	spring to early summer	yes	6–12 in (15–30 cm)	8 in (20 cm)	7–11	yes

RIGHT *The flattened lilac-pink flowers of* Iberis gibraltarica *are tinged white and appear in summer. This is a suitable plant for borders and rock gardens.*

Top Tip

Iberis species make great cut flowers, and because the flowerheads are showy and sometimes fragrant, they are also a popular choice for floral arrangements.

IMPATIENS

Variously known as balsam, busy lizzie or water fuchsia, this genus of around 850 species of annuals, perennials and sub-shrubs is widely distributed throughout the subtropics and tropics of Asia and Africa. They are generally soft-stemmed plants with simple, pointed, lance-shaped leaves that often have toothed edges. The flowers occur in many different colours, appear throughout the year in mild areas, and have 5 petals—an upper standard and the lower 4 fused into 2 pairs. The sepals are also partly fused to form a spur. The flowers are followed by seed pods that, when ripe, explosively eject their contents at the slightest touch. This memorable feature has given rise to the genus name *Impatiens*, which is Latin for impatient.

ABOVE Impatiens, *New Guinea Group, 'Tagula' has deep green pointed leaves, and flowers that are pale pink with a darker centre. This cultivar makes an excellent cut flower.*

CULTIVATION

The annuals are grown as summer plants in cooler climates; the perennials are fairly tender and need mild winters. Shade from hot sun and plant in deep, cool, moist, humus-rich soil. Water and feed well. Propagate annuals from seed and perennials from cuttings. Some species self-sow and may be invasive.

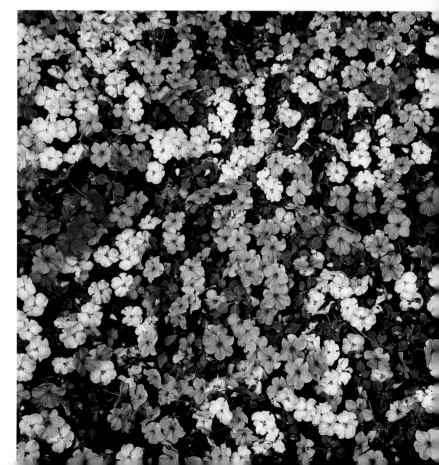

RIGHT Impatiens walleriana *'Super Elfin Blush' is a bushy fast-growing perennial that benefits from a light trim after flowering.*

Top Tip

Most *Impatiens* species make great indoor specimens, either in pots or hanging baskets. Keep the soil moist and tip prune to encourage more compact growth.

ABOVE *The pale lilac single flowers of* Impatiens sodenii *are borne on long stalks, and the lance-shaped leaves have toothed edges. It is best grown in frost-free areas.*

RIGHT Impatiens, *New Guinea Group, 'Fiesta Salmon Sunshine' bears pinkish orange rose-like flowers for a long period in summer. In good conditions it will self-seed readily.*

Favourites	Flower Colour	Blooming Season	Flower Fragrance	Plant Height	Plant Width	Hardiness Zone	Frost Tolerance
Impatiens balsamina	pink, red, purple, white	summer to early autumn	no	12–30 in (30–75 cm)	18 in (45 cm)	9–12	no
Impatiens, New Guinea Group	pink, cerise, red, orange, white	summer	no	8–24 in (20–60 cm)	24–36 in (60–90 cm)	10–12	no
Impatiens niamniamensis	purple, pink, red, yellow	most of the year	no	24–36 in (60–90 cm)	24–36 in (60–90 cm)	10–12	no
Impatiens omeiana	yellow	early autumn	no	12 in (30 cm)	36 in (90 cm)	8–10	no
Impatiens sodenii	lilac, pink, white	summer	no	4–8 ft (1.2–2.4 m)	4 ft (1.2 m)	10–12	no
Impatiens walleriana	red, pink, white, orange, purple	most of the year	no	8–24 in (20–60 cm)	24 in (60 cm)	9–12	no

IRIS

There are 300-odd species of irises scattered over the northern temperate zones, occurring in rhizomatous- and bulbous-rooted forms. Those with very fine stolon-like rhizomes are sometimes called fibrous rooted. *Iris*, the type genus for the family Iridaceae, is named after the Greek goddess of the rainbow. Extremely popular, irises have been cultivated since the time of the Egyptian pharaoh Thutmosis I, around 1500 BC. The leaves, often arranged in fans, are sword shaped and sometimes variegated. The flowers come in all colours and have 6 petals, usually in the typical fleur-de-lis pattern of 3 upright standards and 3 downward-curving falls.

CULTIVATION

There are 4 categories: bog irises need a sunny position near pond margins or in damp soil; woodland irises thrive in dappled sunlight in moist well-drained soil; bearded irises should be dried off after flowering and rockery irises require moist, well-drained, gritty soil. Propagation is usually by division when dormant, less commonly from seed.

ABOVE Iris sibirica 'Tropic Night' bears flowers with velvety petals of deep blue-violet. The falls have contrasting yellowish white markings at the petal base.

LEFT Blooming from late spring to early summer, Iris 'Echo de France' is a Tall Bearded iris with creamy white standards and clear yellow falls. This cultivar can reach a height of 90 cm (36 in).

BELOW Sky blue flowers, coloured yellow at the petal base, are the drawcard of Iris sibirica 'Perry's Blue'. Summer-flowering, this is an old plant that is still popular with gardeners today.

Favourites	Flower Colour	Blooming Season	Flower Fragrance	Plant Height	Plant Width	Hardiness Zone	Frost Tolerance
Iris, Arilbred Hybrids	white, blue, red, yellow, brown	mid-spring to early summer	no	12–30 in (30–75 cm)	8–18 in (20–45 cm)	5–9	yes
Iris, Dutch Hybrids	blue to violet, yellow, orange	spring to early summer	no	10–36 in (25–90 cm)	6 in (15 cm)	7–9	yes
Iris, Dwarf Bearded	various	late spring	no	8–15 in (20–38 cm)	12–24 in (30–60 cm)	5–10	yes
Iris ensata	white, purple, lavender	late spring to early summer	no	36 in (90 cm)	12 in (30 cm)	4–10	yes
Iris germanica	blue-purple	spring	no	2–4 ft (0.6–1.2 m)	12–24 in (30–60 cm)	4–10	yes
Iris, Intermediate Bearded	various	late spring	no	15–24 in (38–60 cm)	12–24 in (30–60 cm)	5–10	yes
Iris, Louisiana Hybrids	various	mid-spring to early summer	no	36 in (90 cm)	36 in (90 cm)	7–11	yes
Iris, Pacific Coast Hybrids	various	mid- to late spring	no	12–24 in (30–60 cm)	12–24 in (30–60 cm)	8–10	yes
Iris sibirica	blue, purple, white	late spring to early summer	no	2–4 ft (0.6–1.2 m)	12–18 in (30–45 cm)	5–10	yes
Iris, Spuria Hybrids	various	late spring to early summer	no	2–4 ft (0.6–1.2 m)	18–24 in (45–60 cm)	4–9	yes
Iris, Tall Bearded	various	late spring	no	30–36 in (75–90 cm)	12–24 in (30–60 cm)	5–10	yes
Iris unguicularis	light to dark violet	autumn to spring	no	12 in (30 cm)	24 in (60 cm)	7–10	yes

ABOVE *Reaching up to 75 cm (30 in) high,* Iris, Tall Bearded, *'Pink Taffeta' has lovely, ruffled, pink petals.*

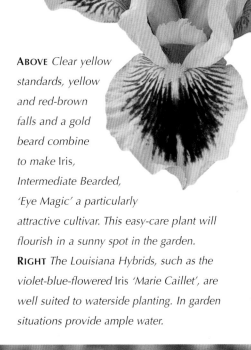

ABOVE *Clear yellow standards, yellow and red-brown falls and a gold beard combine to make Iris, Intermediate Bearded, 'Eye Magic' a particularly attractive cultivar. This easy-care plant will flourish in a sunny spot in the garden.*
RIGHT *The Louisiana Hybrids, such as the violet-blue-flowered Iris 'Marie Caillet', are well suited to waterside planting. In garden situations provide ample water.*

LEFT *One of the Tall Bearded irises, Iris 'Thornbird' has creamy ecru standards and golden brown falls, which are highlighted with purplish veining.*

ABOVE *Extensive violet veining marks the lighter coloured petals of* Iris ensata *'Flying Tiger'. This beautiful award-winning cultivar is ideal for container planting.*
RIGHT *A delicate picotee edging of silver adds a glamorous touch to the ruffled rich mid-blue petals of the aptly named* Iris sibirica *'Silver Edge'.*

KNIPHOFIA

RIGHT *The elegant spikes of Kniphofia 'Primrose Beauty' bear pale yellow tubular flowers above clumps of sword-like leaves.*

BELOW *Truly dazzling from top to bottom, Kniphofia caulescens produces large rosettes of evergreen leaves and copper stems bearing flowers in rainbow shades of coral red to yellow.*

Most of the nearly 70 species in this aloe family (Aloeaceae) genus are native to South Africa. They are clump-forming perennials with grassy to sword-shaped, often evergreen foliage that emerges from vigorous rhizomes. From summer to autumn, bold spikes of intensely coloured flowers are borne in bottlebrush heads at the top of strong, tall, upright stems, giving rise to the common names of red-hot poker and torch lily. Many hybrids and cultivars have been raised in a variety of sizes and flower colours; apart from the original yellows and oranges, white and red flowers are now also available. *Kniphofia* plants, named after the German professor Johann Hieronymus Kniphof (1704–1763), make excellent cut flowers.

CULTIVATION

Hardiness varies, though none will tolerate repeated heavy frosts. They are best planted in an open sunny position with moist, humus-rich, well-drained soil. Water and feed well when in active growth. The bulk will tolerate salt winds and thrive near the coast. Propagation is usually by division after flowering, or from seed.

Favourites	Flower Colour	Blooming Season	Flower Fragrance
Kniphofia **caulescens**	coral red, fading to yellow	late summer to mid-autumn	no
Kniphofia **citrina**	pale greenish yellow	summer to autumn	no
Kniphofia **ensifolia**	greenish yellow, dull pink buds	late summer to mid-autumn	no
Kniphofia **northiae**	pale yellow	summer	no
Kniphofia **'Primrose Beauty'**	light yellow	summer	no
Kniphofia **rooperi**	orange-red to orange-yellow	late summer to autumn	no

LEFT Kniphofia northiae *is of interest for its foliage as well as its flowers. Leaves are arching, broad and blue-green. Orange buds open to pale yellow flowers.*

RIGHT *The robust* Kniphofia rooperi *is a magnificent late-flowerer, with orange-red blooms turning yellow. The spike is rounded rather than typically poker-like.*

Plant Height	Plant Width	Hardiness Zone	Frost Tolerance
4 ft (1.2 m)	24 in (60 cm)	7–10	yes
3 ft (0.9 m)	2–4 ft (0.6–1.2 m)	7–10	yes
2–4 ft (0.6–1.2 m)	24 in (60 cm)	8–10	yes
4–6 ft (1.2–1.8 m)	36 in (90 cm)	6–10	yes
3 ft (0.9 m)	3 ft (0.9 m)	7–10	yes
4 ft (1.2 m)	24 in (60 cm)	8–10	yes

LATHYRUS

A member of the pea family (Fabaceae), this genus has far more than just the old-fashioned sweet pea to offer from among its 110 species of annuals and perennials. Found in Eurasia, North America, temperate South America and the mountains of eastern Africa, many are climbers, others are low spreading plants and some are shrubby. The climbers support themselves with tendrils found at the tips of the pinnate leaves, where the terminal leaflet would normally be. The eye-catching flowers occur in many colours, can be scented and may be solitary or borne in clusters. The genus has long been popular with gardeners, including Thomas Jefferson, who planted *Lathyrus latifolius* at both his birthplace, Shadwell and at his Virginia home, Monticello.

CULTIVATION

Non-climbing perennials require part-shade but otherwise keep the conditions sunny and well ventilated to lessen the risk of mildew and botrytis. Plant in moist well-drained soil and provide stakes or wires for climbers. Propagation is from seed for the annuals and by division when dormant for the perennials.

ABOVE RIGHT Lathyrus vernus *forms clumps of mid-green foliage sprinkled with heads of tiny purple flowers. This is a good border plant as blooms appear early in winter and continue right through spring.*

ABOVE Lathyrus grandiflorus *is a charming old garden perennial climber. It has mid-green leaves and bears deep magenta-pink flowers. As its common name, everlasting pea, suggests, it does not die easily once established.*

Top Tip

Many of these plants are excellent for cut flowers. Regular cutting for indoor use will encourage the further development of flowers, as will deadheading.

Favourites	Flower Colour	Blooming Season	Flower Fragrance	Plant Height	Plant Width	Hardiness Zone	Frost Tolerance
Lathyrus grandiflorus	purple-pink	summer	no	6 ft (1.8 m)	6 ft (1.8 m)	6–9	yes
Lathyrus latifolius	red-purple, pink, white	summer	no	6 ft (1.8 m)	6–12 ft (1.8–3.5 m)	5–10	yes
Lathyrus nervosus	purple-blue	summer	yes	5 ft (1.5 m)	5 ft (1.5 m)	8–10	yes
Lathyrus odoratus	various	late winter to early summer	yes	6 ft (1.8 m)	24–36 in (60–90 cm)	4–10	yes
Lathyrus splendens	pink to purple-red	spring	no	6–10 ft (1.8–3 m)	6 ft (1.8 m)	8–10	yes
Lathyrus vernus	purple-blue	winter to spring	no	24 in (60 cm)	18 in (45 cm)	5–9	yes

RIGHT *The flowers of* Lathyrus odoratus *'Wiltshire Ripple' are a superb bicoloured mix of white flushed with claret. This is a prolific flowerer with a rich scent.*

LEFT Lathyrus odoratus *'Our Harry' bears magnificent deep purple-blue flowers, with frilled petal edges. It makes a stunning garden specimen on its own, or can be planted in beds with* L. odoratus *cultivars of contrasting hues for a breathtaking display of colour.*

LEUCANTHEMUM

Rather pragmatically named from the Greek *leukos* (white) and *anthemon* (flower), most of the 25 species of annual and perennial daisies in this Eurasian genus do indeed have flowers with white ray florets, usually around a central golden disc floret. Species often form quite large clumps of foliage with simple, bright to deep green, linear to spatula-shaped leaves. Stalks bearing their cheerful flowers appear among the foliage from summer to autumn, depending on the species. Hybridisation has produced a wider range of flower form and colour, including pompon-centred flowers, and of much interest to gardeners are the *Leucanthemum × superbum* hybrids. These robust clump-forming plants are commonly known as Shasta daisies, and are excellent in mixed borders and as cut flowers.

CULTIVATION

Leucanthemum plants are very easily grown in any sunny position with moist well-drained soil. Feeding and watering will result in more luxuriant plants but not necessarily more flowers. Tall varieties may need staking. The species are usually propagated from seed, while the cultivars and hybrids are propagated by division or from basal cuttings.

LEFT *The splendid* Leucanthemum × superbum *hybrid cultivars were first developed by Luther Burbank in 1890 at his garden near Mt Shasta in northern California. Flowers are typically crisp white blooms with yellow centres borne on sturdy stems above glossy green foliage. 'T E Killin', left, is a large, flat, double-flowered example.*

BELOW LEFT Leucanthemum × superbum *'Snowcap' is a dwarf form that bears masses of long-lasting flowers, which are quite large for its size.*

Top Tip

Place these trouble-free plants at the front of borders or in containers for maximum effect. They also make great ground covers in a sunny part of the garden.

Favourites	Flower Colour	Blooming Season	Flower Fragrance	Plant Height	Plant Width	Hardiness Zone	Frost Tolerance
Leucanthemum × *superbum*	white	summer to early autumn	no	24–36 in (60–90 cm)	24–36 in (60–90 cm)	5–10	yes
Leucanthemum × *superbum* 'Aglaia'	white	summer to early autumn	no	24 in (60 cm)	24–36 in (60–90 cm)	5–10	yes
Leucanthemum × *superbum* 'Esther Read'	white	summer to early autumn	no	18–24 in (45–60 cm)	24 in (60 cm)	5–10	yes
Leucanthemum × *superbum* 'Snowcap'	white	summer to early autumn	no	18 in (45 cm)	18 in (45 cm)	5–10	yes
Leucanthemum × *superbum* 'T. E. Killin'	white	summer to early autumn	no	30 in (75 cm)	24–36 in (60–90 cm)	5–10	yes
Leucanthemum vulgare	white	summer	no	12–30 in (30–75 cm)	12–24 in (30–60 cm)	3–10	yes

ABOVE *Naturally occurring in Europe and areas of Asia,* Leucanthemum vulgare *can be highly invasive in parts of the USA. It produces solitary white flowers.*
RIGHT *The distinctive fringed semi-double flowers of* Leucanthemum × superbum *'Aglaia' last throughout summer. Deadheading will prolong flowering.*

ABOVE Lewisia longipetala 'Little Plum' is an attractive easy-growing plant. Short stems bear intense rosy purple flowers tinged with orange above fleshy leaves.

BELOW Delicately veined pale pink flowers are held above the dark green leaves of Lewisia columbiana. This compact evergreen is from the Columbia River region.

LEWISIA

This genus consists of around 19 species of exquisite, semi-succulent, evergreen and deciduous, alpine and subalpine perennials of the portulaca family (Portulacaceae). They are found in the Rocky Mountains from New Mexico to southern Canada and usually form rosettes or tufts of fleshy, linear, lance- or spatula-shaped leaves. Their starry, many-petalled flowers may be solitary or clustered and are borne at the end of short wiry stems. Yellow, apricot and pink shades predominate. Hardy plants, they provide interest in rock gardens or even against a wall. The genus is named after North American explorer Captain Meriwether Lewis (1774–1809) of the famed Lewis and Clark expedition of 1804–1807.

CULTIVATION

Most species have deep taproots and prefer a gritty, humus-rich, free-draining soil that remains moist in the growing season but is otherwise dry. Plant in full or half sun and use gravel mulch around the crown to prevent rotting. The deciduous species generally reproduce only from seed, but the evergreen plants can be propagated from seed or offsets.

Favourites	Flower Colour	Blooming Season	Flower Fragrance
Lewisia columbiana	white to pale pink	spring to summer	no
Lewisia cotyledon	white to pale pink	spring to summer	no
Lewisia, **Cotyledon Hybrids**	various	late spring to summer	no
Lewisia longipetala	white, sometimes flushed pink	late spring to early summer	no
Lewisia rediviva	white, pink	spring to summer	no
Lewisia tweedyi	white to peach-pink	spring to summer	no

Plant Height	Plant Width	Hardiness Zone	Frost Tolerance
6 in (15 cm)	8 in (20 cm)	5–9	yes
12 in (30 cm)	10 in (25 cm)	6–10	yes
6–12 in (15–30 cm)	8–15 in (20–38 cm)	6–8	yes
4 in (10 cm)	4 in (10 cm)	4–7	yes
2 in (5 cm)	4 in (10 cm)	4–10	yes
8 in (20 cm)	12 in (30 cm)	5–9	yes

TOP Lewisia cotyledon *has produced a number of hybrids, each exhibiting funnel-shaped flowers and rosettes of thick, toothed, dark green leaves. 'White Splendour', seen here, has pure white flowers, but shades of pink, orange and yellow are also possible.*

ABOVE *From spring through to summer, Lewisia tweedyi produces these attractive, open funnel-shaped, many-petalled flowers in shades of creamy white with a soft flush of pink.*

BELOW *Shorter than the species, the* Liatris spicata *'Floristan' strain comes in 2 colours—purple-flowered 'Floristan Violett' and white-flowered 'Floristan Weiss'.*

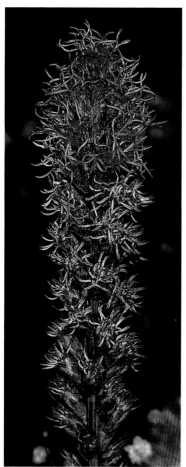

LIATRIS

This genus of 35 perennials from the daisy family (Asteraceae) is native to eastern North America. It makes a bold splash of colour in summer and couldn't be easier to grow. Developing from corms or modified flattened roots, the plants form foliage clumps with simple linear to lance-shaped leaves that are sometimes finely hairy. Tall stems emerge from the clump, developing at their top numerous long, quite un-daisy-like, bottlebrush spikes of filamentous purple-pink flowers. Bees and butterflies are attracted to the fluffy flower spikes. As well as being suitable for borders, *Liatris* plants are ideal as cut flowers. Native Americans used the roots medicinally, and early settlers found that the dried roots were effective for repelling moths. Common names include blazing star and gayfeather.

CULTIVATION

Most are very frost resistant. Wild plants are usually found along watercourses; cultivated plants are easily grown in any sunny position with moist, humus-rich, well-drained soil. Locate at the back of borders to disguise the foliage clump and make use of the flower stem's height. Propagate by division or from seed.

Favourites	Flower Colour	Blooming Season	Flower Fragrance	Plant Height	Plant Width	Hardiness Zone	Frost Tolerance
Liatris ligulistylis	purple	autumn	no	24 in (60 cm)	12 in (30 cm)	3–10	yes
Liatris pycnostachya	red-purple to purple	mid-summer to early autumn	no	5 ft (1.5 m)	18 in (45 cm)	4–9	yes
Liatris spicata	pink-purple	summer to early autumn	no	2–4 ft (0.6–1.2 m)	18 in (45 cm)	3–10	yes
Liatris spicata **'Callilepsis Purple'**	purple-pink	summer to early autumn	no	24–36 in (60–90 cm)	18 in (45 cm)	3–10	yes
Liatris spicata **'Kobold'**	pink-purple	summer to early autumn	no	15 in (38 cm)	12 in (30 cm)	3–10	yes
Liatris tenuifolia	purple-pink	summer to early autumn	no	36 in (90 cm)	12 in (30 cm)	7–10	yes

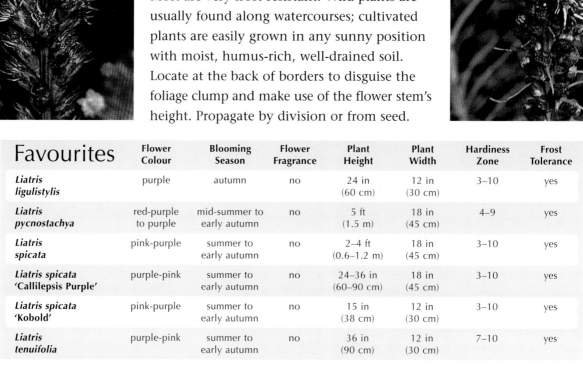

LEFT *A native of southeastern USA, and known as the Kansas gayfeather, the natural habitat of* Liatris pycnostachya *is open woodland and prairie.*

BELOW LEFT Liatris spicata *has given rise to a host of cultivars. Pictured here is 'Callilepsis Purple', with elegant tall spires of rich purple flowers, which can be used to good effect in border situations or wildflower gardens.*

BELOW *Reaching just 38 cm (15 in) high,* Liatris spicata *'Kobold' is a dwarf cultivar which bears bright purple flowers from summer to early autumn.*

Top Tip

Liatris species will perform best in well-drained soil. This will also reduce the possibility of tubers becoming over-wet in winter.

LIGULARIA

While some of the popular species in this temperate Eurasian daisy family genus have been reclassified, including the one which has given the genus its common name of leopard plant, there are still some 180-odd species of perennials in *Ligularia*. They are vigorous plants that soon develop in spring into clumps of large broad leaves, usually kidney- to heart-shaped, with toothed edges. In summer and autumn, upright flower stems appear and may grow to some height, depending on the species. The stems bear eye-catching, large, golden yellow, daisy-like flowers for around half their length. The plants have long been used in herbal cough remedies, and today extracts of the roots are being investigated for their cancer-fighting properties.

CULTIVATION

Ligularia species are mainly very hardy and easily grown in full or half sun. The soil needs to be fertile, humus-rich and deep. Also, it should remain moist throughout the year. Cut back when the flowers and foliage fade. Propagate by division when dormant or raise from seed.

LEFT *Tall spires of yellow flowers appear on purplish stems above the large, up to 30 cm (12 in) wide, dark green leaves of* Ligularia przewalskii.

Favourites	Flower Colour	Blooming Season	Flower Fragranc
Ligularia dentata	orange-yellow	mid-summer to early autumn	no
Ligularia przewalskii	yellow	mid- to late summer	no
Ligularia stenocephala	yellow	summer	no
Ligularia 'The Rocket'	yellow	summer	no
Ligularia veitchiana	yellow	mid- to late summer	no
Ligularia wilsoniana	yellow	summer	no

Top Tip

With ornamental foliage and flowers, *Ligularia* species are well suited to border planting. The taller varieties will add height, depth and interest when in flower.

BELOW *Dark flower stems hold golden yellow flowers up to 1.8 m (6 ft) above the large toothed leaves of Ligularia 'The Rocket', an award-winning cultivar.*

ABOVE *The sunny, orange-yellow, daisy-like blooms of Ligularia dentata are held on tall stems above the large heart-shaped leaves.*
LEFT *Hailing from China and Japan, Ligularia stenocephala bears tall spikes of bright yellow flowers above its long triangular leaves.*

Plant Height	Plant Width	Hardiness Zone	Frost Tolerance
4 ft (1.2 m)	3 ft (0.9 m)	4–9	yes
6 ft (1.8 m)	3 ft (0.9 m)	4–9	yes
5 ft (1.5 m)	3 ft (0.9 m)	5–10	yes
6 ft (1.8 m)	5 ft (1.5 m)	5–10	yes
6 ft (1.8 m)	4 ft (1.2 m)	4–9	yes
6 ft (1.8 m)	4 ft (1.2 m)	5–9	yes

LIMONIUM

This genus of around 150 species of mainly summer-flowering annuals, perennials and small shrubs of the leadwort family (Plumbaginaceae) is widely distributed in the warm-temperate and subtropical zones. Most species form low-growing mounds of foliage rosettes. The leaves vary in size and tend to be lance-shaped or spatula-shaped. The individual flowers are minute but make a great display because they are borne in billowing sprays held well clear of the foliage on branching wiry stems. White, cream and purple shades are common. *Limonium*, which comes from a Greek word meaning meadow, is still widely sold as *Statice*, the name under which it was formerly classified.

CULTIVATION

Many species are rather frost tender, thriving in coastal conditions, with a preference for sheltered sunny locations with light, well-drained, yet moist soil. Propagate from seed, root cuttings or by division, depending on the plant type.

BELOW LEFT Limonium sinuatum, *with its small, papery, white and purple flowers, is often grown as an annual. There are several strains in a range of colours.*
BELOW *Summer-flowering* Limonium perezii, *with its shrubby habit, is suitable for a mixed border. It will tolerate coastal conditions and prefers full sun.*

Top Tip

Limonium species make good dried flowers. As soon as the flowers open, they should be cut and hung upside down to dry in a cool spot with good ventilation.

ABOVE Limonium bourgaei *is easily grown from seed. The flowering stems and branches are covered in a fine growth of hairs, and the flowers are violet and white.*

RIGHT *The flowers of Limonium brassicifolium are tubular, rising from thick woody stems. A light fertiliser should be applied in spring to encourage growth.*

Favourites	Flower Colour	Blooming Season	Flower Fragrance	Plant Height	Plant Width	Hardiness Zone	Frost Tolerance
Limonium bourgaei	purple; white corolla	spring to summer	no	15 in (38 cm)	18 in (45 cm)	9–11	no
Limonium brassicifolium	purple; white corolla	summer to autumn	no	8–15 in (20–38 cm)	18 in (45 cm)	9–11	no
Limonium gmelinii	lilac	summer	no	24 in (60 cm)	24 in (60 cm)	4–10	yes
Limonium latifolium	white, bluish lavender	summer	no	24 in (60 cm)	18 in (45 cm)	5–10	yes
Limonium perezii	blue-mauve; white corolla	summer	no	24 in (60 cm)	24 in (60 cm)	9–11	no
Limonium sinuatum	pink, purple-blue; white corolla	summer to early autumn	no	18 in (45 cm)	12 in (30 cm)	8–10	yes

LOBELIA

A member of the bellflower (Campanulaceae) family, *Lobelia* is an incredibly diverse and widespread genus of some 350 species annuals, perennials and shrubs. Perhaps best known for the small mounding bedding annuals, with their masses of blue, purple or white flowers, *Lobelia* also contributes to the perennial border with a large range of upright clump-forming plants that have a basal clump of simple leaves and showy terminal flower spikes—these perennial lobelias offer a wider colour range than the annuals. *Lobelia* flowers have 5 lobes, the lower 3 of which are enlarged to create a lip. Often, dark-flowered forms have purple- or red-tinted foliage. Found throughout the Americas, lobelias were used extensively by Native Americans in herbal medicines and are now found in homeopathic remedies.

LEFT Lobelia erinus *is commonly known as bedding or edging lobelia. The cultivar pictured here displays the typical mounding habit and dark green foliage.*

CULTIVATION

Lobelias generally prefer a sunny position. The hardy North American perennials will grow in fairly heavy soil; a light free-draining soil is preferable for the annuals. Tall types may need staking. Propagate annuals from seed and perennials by division or from basal cuttings.

RIGHT *Shrubby in habit,* Lobelia laxiflora *is a variable species, commonly known as torch lobelia for the flame-like appearance of its yellow-tipped red flowers.*

Top Tip

As soon as the flowering spikes of lobelias have finished blooming, they should be cut back to the base— this will encourage further flowering.

BELOW *The glossy leaves of* Lobelia aberdarica *cluster around a central point from which the tall flowering panicle emerges, bearing blue to white flowers.*

RIGHT *A Chilean native,* Lobelia tupa *features grey-green leaves with a lightly felted surface. Red flowers are borne on tall flowering spikes to 1.8 m (6 ft) high.*

Favourites	Flower Colour	Blooming Season	Flower Fragrance	Plant Height	Plant Width	Hardiness Zone	Frost Tolerance
Lobelia aberdarica	blue to white	summer	no	8 ft (2.4 m)	10 ft (3 m)	9–11	yes
Lobelia erinus	blue, purple, red, pink, white	spring to early autumn	no	3–8 in (8–20 cm)	12–18 in (30–45 cm)	7–11	no
Lobelia × gerardii	pink or violet to purple	summer	no	60 in (150 cm)	20–24 in (50–60 cm)	7–10	yes
Lobelia laxiflora	red and yellow	summer	no	3 ft (0.9 m)	3–6 ft (0.9–1.8 m)	9–11	yes
Lobelia × speciosa	scarlet to purple	summer to autumn	no	60 in (150 cm)	12 in (30 cm)	4–10	yes
Lobelia tupa	scarlet to red-purple	late summer to autumn	no	3–8 ft (0.9–2.4 m)	3 ft (0.9 m)	8–10	yes

LOBULARIA

Still widely and confusingly known as alyssum, after the genus in which it was originally included, this group of 5 species of annuals and perennials in the cabbage family (Brassicaceae) occurs naturally in the northern temperate zone and especially around the Mediterranean and Canary Islands. They are small mounding plants with simple linear to lance-shaped leaves, sometimes with fine silvery hairs. Their flowers, which appear over the warmer months, are tiny, often sweetly scented and are borne in rounded heads. Garden forms occur in white and shades of primrose, apricot, mauve and purple, and make pretty additions to a bedding scheme. The genus name comes from the Latin *lobulus* (a pod) and refers to the small seed capsules.

CULTIVATION

These plants are hardy and very easily grown in any sunny position with light free-draining soil. Watering will encourage heavier flowering but the plants are often more compact and less inclined to fall apart from the centre if kept rather dry. Propagate from seed, which may be carefully sown or simply broadcast. *Lobularia* plants often self-sow.

BELOW LEFT *A popular, fast-growing, compact annual,* Lobularia maritima *has dull green leaves enlivened by masses of tiny, scented, white blooms.*

BELOW *The* Lobularia maritima *Easter Bonnet Series features a range of colours, including white, pink and the rich purple of 'Easter Bonnet Lavender', below.*

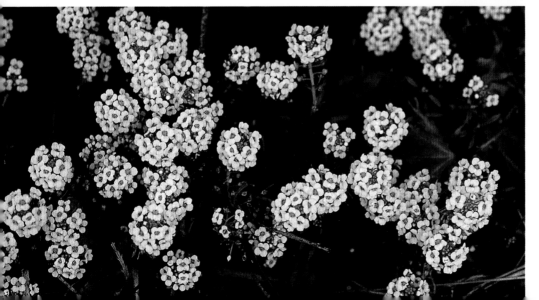

Top Tip

These uniform and compact plants with their heavy blooming and sweet scent are great as fillers in summer beds, as well as along walls and paths.

LEFT Lobularia maritima *'Easter Bonnet Deep Rose'* is enjoyed for its rosy red blooms and lush foliage. **BELOW** Lobularia maritima *'Snow Crystals'* is a half-hardy, mound-forming, compact plant. White flowers smother the plant through spring and summer.

Favourites	Flower Colour	Blooming Season	Flower Fragrance	Plant Height	Plant Width	Hardiness Zone	Frost Tolerance
Lobularia maritima	white	spring to early autumn	yes	3–12 in (8–30 cm)	8–12 in (20–30 cm)	7–10	yes
Lobularia maritima 'Carpet of Snow'	white	spring to early autumn	yes	4 in (10 cm)	8–12 in (20–30 cm)	7–10	yes
Lobularia maritima 'Easter Bonnet Deep Rose'	deep red	spring to early autumn	yes	3–4 in (8–10 cm)	8–12 in (20–30 cm)	7–10	yes
Lobularia maritima 'Easter Bonnet Lavender'	purple-pink	spring to early autumn	yes	3–4 in (8–10 cm)	8–12 in (20–30 cm)	7–10	yes
Lobularia maritima 'Rosie O'Day'	lavender-pink	spring to early autumn	yes	2–4 in (5–10 cm)	8–12 in (20–30 cm)	7–10	yes
Lobularia maritima 'Snow Crystals'	white	spring to early autumn	yes	10 in (25 cm)	8–12 in (20–30 cm)	7–10	yes

LUPINUS

There are about 200 species of annuals, perennials and evergreen shrubs in this genus, which belongs to the legume family. They are found in North and South America, southern Europe and northern Africa, usually in dry habitats. The leaves are palmate with lance-shaped leaflets, and the stems are often covered in fine soft down. Many have highly ornamental flowers borne in showy terminal racemes or spikes. The pea-like flowers appear mainly throughout summer in many colours, including bicolours. A number of species are grown for horticultural purposes such as nitrogen fixing and stock fodder, and the seeds of some are processed in various ways for human consumption.

CULTIVATION

Lupinus species are best grown in full sun in moderately fertile well-drained soil. Shrubby species can be used in shrubberies or mixed borders, and *Lupinus arboreus* can be used for naturalising rough areas. Deadhead spent spikes to ensure strong plants. Propagation is from seed or cuttings. The seedlings should be planted out when small, as these plants dislike root disturbance.

Favourites	Flower Colour	Blooming Season	Flower Fragrance	Plant Height	Plant Width	Hardiness Zone	Frost Tolerance
Lupinus arboreus	yellow	spring to summer	yes	8 ft (2.4 m)	5–8 ft (1.5–2.4 m)	8–10	yes
Lupinus 'Bishop's Tipple'	purple-pink, white flecks	late spring to early summer	no	36 in (90 cm)	24 in (60 cm)	7–10	yes
Lupinus nanus	blue, white-spotted purple	spring to summer	no	20 in (50 cm)	8–12 in (20–30 cm)	7–11	yes
Lupinus 'Pagoda Prince'	magenta and white	spring to early summer	no	36 in (90 cm)	24 in (60 cm)	7–10	yes
Lupinus polyphyllus	blue, purple, red, white	summer	no	5 ft (1.5 m)	24–30 in (60–75 cm)	3–9	yes
Lupinus, Russell Hybrids	various	late spring to summer	yes	3 ft (0.9 m)	2–4 ft (0.6–1.2 m)	3–9	yes

FAR LEFT Lupinus *'Pagoda Prince' is a stunning, tall-stemmed, bicoloured hybrid. Mid-green leaves grow in a dense clump at its base.*

ABOVE *Known as the Russell Hybrids, this famous group of* Lupinus *hybrids was developed by gardener George Russell in the early 1930s. They are strong-growing with long spikes of flowers appearing in many vibrant shades.*
LEFT Lupinus *'Bishop's Tipple' is a tall hybrid with rich mauve blooms flecked with white. Leaflets are arranged in an attractive palmate pattern.*

RIGHT *Naturally occurring in California, the evergreen* Lupinus arboreus *bears hairy grey-green leaves and yellow, sometimes blue, fragrant flowers.*

Top Tip

Lupinus arboreus is an aggressive seeder and should be planted where it can be controlled; *Lupinus*, Russell Hybrids may self-sow, resulting in a variety of colours.

LYCHNIS

Found in the northern temperate and arctic zones, the 20-odd species of biennials and perennials in this genus belong to the carnation family (Caryophyllaceae). They are quite a variable lot and include erect or spreading forms, large clump-forming plants—sometimes with silver-grey leaves—and small alpine species. The flowers are simple 5-petalled structures, but are very brightly coloured and showy, occurring in heads that are usually held well clear of the foliage to maximise the colour effect. *Lychnis* or *lukhnis* is a Greek word meaning lamp; the name was given to the genus by Theophrastus in the third century BC, presumably in reference to its vivid flowerheads. This genus is allied to the *Silene* group of plants.

CULTIVATION

Lychnis species are mostly very hardy and easily grown in any sunny position with moist well-drained soil. The silvery *Lychnis coronaria* prefers fairly dry conditions but most others can be given routine watering. Deadhead frequently to encourage continuous flowering. Propagate from seed, from basal cuttings or by division, depending on the growth form.

Favourites	Flower Colour	Blooming Season	Flower Fragrance	Plant Height	Plant Width	Hardiness Zone	Frost Tolerance
Lychnis alpina	purple-pink	summer	no	6 in (15 cm)	6 in (15 cm)	2–8	yes
Lychnis × arkwrightii	orange-red	summer	no	10–18 in (25–45 cm)	12 in (30 cm)	6–9	yes
Lychnis chalcedonica	scarlet	early summer	no	4 ft (1.2 m)	12 in (30 cm)	4–10	yes
Lychnis coronaria	purple to purple-red	summer	no	30 in (75 cm)	18 in (45 cm)	4–10	yes
Lychnis flos-jovis	pink, scarlet, white	summer	no	24 in (60 cm)	18 in (45 cm)	5–9	yes
Lychnis viscaria	purple-pink	summer	no	18 in (45 cm)	18 in (45 cm)	4–9	yes

RIGHT *An alpine carpet-forming plant,* Lychnis viscaria *is commonly known as sticky catchfly due to its bronze sticky stems. Purple-pink flowers are borne in clusters of 5 to 6.*
BELOW *These twinkling orange-red flowers of* Lychnis × arkwrightii *'Vesuvius' grow to 35 mm (1½ in) across. Foliage is a mix of purple and green, especially on younger plants.*

Top Tip

Plant smaller alpine species like *Lychnis viscaria* in shaded rock gardens, and taller perennials such as *L. coronaria* in borders or informal massed clumps.

LYSIMACHIA

The name *Lysimachia* has a long history: it was given by Dioscorides, a physician in Nero's army of the first century AD for King Lysimachus of Thrace. Today's genus, part of the primrose family (Primulaceae) with around 150 species of perennials and subshrubs, is found not only in Thrace (northern Greece) but also over much of Europe and Asia as well as North America and South Africa. A few species are low spreading plants but most are clump-forming perennials with narrow, lance-shaped, often hairy leaves and upright spikes of small 5-petalled flowers, often in yellow shades, very rarely white or purple-pink. The flowers appear from early summer to autumn: when they appear en masse, they can create quite a dramatic feature in a garden.

CULTIVATION

Some species prefer the damp soil of pond margins or stream banks, others thrive in rockeries but most are perfectly happy in full or half sun with moist well-drained garden soil. Propagate by division, from basal cuttings, or from layers, depending on the growth type.

Top Tip

In colder climates, plants that are not fully hardy will benefit from being overwintered in a greenhouse. Mulch can also be applied around the roots as extra protection.

ABOVE RIGHT *A spreading perennial,* Lysimachia clethroides *has pointed leaves and tapering flowering spikes that are pendent at first, becoming erect as the white blooms mature.*
RIGHT *Yellow-green leaves are almost lost among the dense profusion of deep yellow flowers of* Lysimachia nummularia *'Aurea'.*

Favourites	Flower Colour	Blooming Season	Flower Fragrance	Plant Height	Plant Width	Hardiness Zone	Frost Tolerance
Lysimachia 'Aztec Sunset'	golden yellow	summer	no	36 in (90 cm)	24 in (60 cm)	5–10	yes
Lysimachia ciliata	yellow	summer	no	4 ft (1.2 m)	24 in (60 cm)	4–10	yes
Lysimachia clethroides	white	summer	no	36 in (90 cm)	24 in (60 cm)	4–10	yes
Lysimachia ephemerum	white	summer	no	36 in (90 cm)	12 in (30 cm)	6–10	yes
Lysimachia nummularia	yellow	summer	no	4–8 in (10–20 cm)	24 in (60 cm)	4–10	yes
Lysimachia punctata	yellow	summer	no	36 in (90 cm)	24 in (60 cm)	5–10	yes

RIGHT *Cup-shaped yellow flowers grow among the broad green leaves of* Lysimachia punctata, *an erect perennial known as golden loosestrife.*

BELOW *The outstanding slow-growing* Lysimachia punctata *'Alexander' bears variegated sage green and cream leaves with masses of cup-shaped yellow blooms.*

MATTHIOLA

Famous for its sweet scent, this genus of 55 species of bushy erect annuals, perennials and subshrubs is a member of the cabbage family (Brassicaceae). The species are native to Europe, Central and southwestern Asia and North Africa. The leaves are simple, often grey-green and are sometimes toothed. The flowers, appearing from spring through to summer, are 4-petalled and grow on upright, often branching stems. They range in colour from pink to mauve and purple, and some species can make lovely cut flowers as well as being suitable for garden bedding. Also known as stock or gillyflower, these plants get their genus name from the Italian botanist Pierandrea Mattioli (1501–1577), who grew these plants for "matters of love and lust".

CULTIVATION

Plant in full sun with moist well-drained soil and a light dressing of lime. Taller species need staking and shelter from wind. Propagated from seed, *Matthiola* plants can provide continuous flowering over spring and summer.

ABOVE AND LEFT Matthiola incana *is a woody-based upright perennial or subshrub with very fragrant brightly coloured flowers. Many cultivars have been developed, and it is these that are most often used for garden purposes. 'Vintage Burgundy', above, and 'Vintage Lavender', left, are two examples of the pretty colour range available.*

Top Tip

Cultivars of *Matthiola incana* are well-loved as bedding plants and as cut flowers. Plant in 8 cm (3 in) pots for a pretty window display.

BELOW Matthiola incana *'Cinderella Rose'* bears many double purple-pink flowers; forms with dark purple, pink and softer shades of lavender-blue blooms are also available.

ABOVE *'Cinderella White'* belongs to the Cinderella Series of Matthiola incana *cultivars, and bears double snow white flowers in tall racemes.*

Favourites	Flower Colour	Blooming Season	Flower Fragrance	Plant Height	Plant Width	Hardiness Zone	Frost Tolerance
Matthiola incana	various	spring to summer	yes	24 in (60 cm)	12 in (30 cm)	6–10	yes
Matthiola incana **'Cinderella Rose'**	rose pink	late spring to summer	yes	10 in (25 cm)	12 in (30 cm)	6–10	yes
Matthiola incana **'Cinderella White'**	pure white	late spring to summer	yes	10 in (25 cm)	12 in (30 cm)	6–10	yes
Matthiola incana **'Vintage Burgundy'**	burgundy	late spring to summer	yes	12–18 in (30–45 cm)	18 in (45 cm)	6–10	yes
Matthiola incana **'Vintage Lavender'**	purple-pink	late spring to summer	yes	12–18 in (30–45 cm)	18 in (45 cm)	6–10	yes
Matthiola longipetala	green, yellow, pink	spring	yes	10–20 in (25–50 cm)	12 in (30 cm)	8–10	yes

MECONOPSIS

Found mainly in the Himalayan region, this genus of more than 40 species is a member of the Papaveraceae family and includes annuals, biennials and short-lived perennials. Compact mounding plants, they have coarse hairy leaves that are simple, round or lobed and deeply toothed. The attractive saucer- to cup-shaped flowers usually grow singly on short or tall stems, open in spring or summer and have papery petals with a central cluster of stamens. *Meconopsis* is well known for its blue-flowered plants, but other more easily grown species bloom in the traditional poppy shades of yellow, pink or red. The name comes from the Greek *mecon* (poppy) and *opsis* (to see or looks like), a reference to their resemblance to the poppy.

CULTIVATION

Most species grow best in woodland conditions in a cool-temperate climate with reliable rainfall. Plant in a sheltered and partly shaded position with moist, deep, humus-rich, well-drained soil, and water well in spring and early summer. Propagate from seed.

FAR LEFT *Its likeness to the true poppy and its striking, blue, crinkled, papery petals have earned* Meconopsis betonicifolia *the common name of the blue poppy.*

Favourites	Flower Colour	Blooming Season	Flower Fragrance	Plant Height	Plant Width	Hardiness Zone	Frost Tolerance
Meconopsis betonicifolia	sky blue	late spring to early summer	no	5 ft (1.5 m)	18 in (45 cm)	7–9	yes
Meconopsis cambrica	yellow to orange	mid-spring to mid-autumn	no	18 in (45 cm)	12 in (30 cm)	6–10	yes
Meconopsis grandis	rich blue	early summer	no	4 ft (1.2 m)	24 in (60 cm)	5–9	yes
Meconopsis horridula	light to dark blue	early to mid-summer	no	36 in (90 cm)	18 in (45 cm)	6–9	yes
Meconopsis napaulensis	pink, red, purple to blue	late spring to mid-summer	no	8 ft (2.4 m)	36 in (90 cm)	8–9	yes
Meconopsis × *sheldonii*	blue	late spring to early summer	no	5 ft (1.5 m)	24 in (60 cm)	6–9	yes

Top Tip

Allow time to establish *Meconopsis* species as they can take 3–4 years to flower. Though they usually die off after flowering, they are self-seeding, ensuring further displays.

RIGHT *Flowering just once before dying (monocarpic), Meconopsis horridula was named for the many "horrid" spines found on the leaves, stems and buds.*

MIMULUS

While it is best known for its annuals and perennials, this mostly North and South American genus of some 180 species also includes a few shrubs and fast-growing upright plants. The leaves are generally deep to light green, sharply toothed, hairy and slightly sticky. The stems are also covered in fine hairs and have sticky glands. The tubular flowers have flared mouths and come in a wide range of colours, including brown, orange, yellow, red, pink and crimson. The spotting and mottling on the flowers has been likened to grinning monkey faces, which has resulted in the common name of monkey flower. The genus is also known as musk.

CULTIVATION

In mild climates, shrubby *Mimulus* plants are easy to grow provided they are given full sun and a well-drained soil that remains moist through summer. They are quick growing and become untidy unless routinely pinched back. They tend to be short-lived but are readily raised from seed or half-hardened cuttings.

Top Tip

To add colour in a hurry, plant *Mimulus* species in a border, window box or container. Many of these cute plants also adapt well to wet or damp conditions.

Favourites	Flower Colour	Blooming Season	Flower Fragrance	Plant Height	Plant Width	Hardiness Zone	Frost Tolerance
Mimulus aurantiacus	yellow, orange, crimson	spring to summer	no	36 in (90 cm)	36 in (90 cm)	8–10	yes
Mimulus bifidus	pale orange-yellow to white	spring to summer	no	15–30 in (38–75 cm)	18–36 in (45–90 cm)	8–11	yes
Mimulus cardinalis	scarlet with yellow throat	summer	no	18–36 in (45–90 cm)	18 in (45 cm)	7–11	yes
Mimulus guttatus	yellow with red-marked throat	summer	no	1–4 ft (0.3–1.2 m)	6–18 in (15–45 cm)	6–10	yes
Mimulus 'Highland Red'	deep scarlet	summer	no	8 in (20 cm)	12 in (30 cm)	7–10	yes
Mimulus 'Malibu'	scarlet, orange, yellow, cream	summer	no	6–10 in (15–25 cm)	6–10 in (15–25 cm)	9–11	no

RIGHT Mimulus cardinalis *is happiest when situated near the water's edge. This pretty scarlet-flowered plant is often found on the banks of streams and ponds.*
BELOW *Though short-lived, the award-winning hybrid cultivar* Mimulus *'Highland Red' provides a colourful summer display of large deep red flowers coupled with mid-green leaves.*

MONARDA

This genus of 16 species of perennials and annuals from North America is a member of the mint family (Lamiaceae). These plants form large clumps, dying away completely in winter but recovering quickly in spring to form thickets of angled stems with lance-shaped aromatic leaves that are often red-tinted and hairy, with serrated edges. In summer the top of each stem carries several whorls of tubular flowers backed by leafy bracts. These plants are much loved by bees, which is reflected in the common name of bee balm. Other common names for *Monarda* are bergamot and horsemint. The genus name *Monarda* honours Nicholas Monardes, a fourteenth-century Spanish botanist.

CULTIVATION

Monarda species are very hardy and easily grown in any open sunny position with moist well-drained soil. Mildew is often a problem in late summer, so good ventilation is important. Propagation is by division when dormant or from cuttings taken from the base of the plant.

RIGHT *Sturdy stems hold the feathery flowers of* Monarda *'Ruby Glow' above the red-tinged mid-green leaves. This attractive plant grows to 75 cm (30 in) high.*

ABOVE *In its native habitat,* Monarda didyma *will send out fleshy stems underground to quickly populate an area. In the garden, these stems should be kept under control to minimise spread.*

Top Tip

With aromatic leaves and nectar-rich flowers, not only will the air be deliciously scented, but bees and hummingbirds will be regular visitors to the garden where *Monarda* plants are featured.

Favourites	Flower Colour	Blooming Season	Flower Fragrance	Plant Height	Plant Width	Hardiness Zone	Frost Tolerance
Monarda 'Cambridge Scarlet'	scarlet	mid-summer to early autumn	no	36 in (90 cm)	18 in (45 cm)	4–9	yes
Monarda didyma	white, pink, red	mid- to late summer	no	36 in (90 cm)	18 in (45 cm)	4–10	yes
Monarda didyma 'Violet Queen'	lavender	mid- to late summer	no	36 in (90 cm)	18 in (45 cm)	4–10	yes
Monarda fistulosa	lavender to pale pink	late summer to early autumn	no	4 ft (1.2 m)	18 in (45 cm)	4–10	yes
Monarda 'Ruby Glow'	pinkish red	summer to early autumn	no	24–30 in (60–75 cm)	12–18 in (30–45 cm)	4–9	yes
Monarda 'Vintage Wine'	red-purple	mid-summer to early autumn	no	36 in (90 cm)	18 in (45 cm)	4–9	yes

BELOW *Flowering from mid-summer to early autumn, Monarda 'Vintage Wine' has aromatic leaves and impressive, 2-lipped, purple-red flowers encircled by brown-green bracts.*

RIGHT *Known as wild bergamot, the purple-tinged whitish bracts of Monarda fistulosa carry flowers of lavender to pink. This plant is well suited to a wildflower or cottage garden.*

ABOVE *Myosotis alpestris, known as alpine forget-me-not, bears minute, dainty, blue flowers with a yellow eye.*

MYOSOTIS

This is a genus of around 50 species of annuals, biennials and perennials of the borage family (Boraginaceae), with the centres of distribution in Europe, Asia, the Americas and New Zealand. Most are small tufted plants with simple, blunt, lance-shaped leaves that are sometimes greyish and often covered in fine hairs. Their 5-petalled flowers are tiny but quite showy as they are usually borne in sprays on short branching stems. Most bloom in spring and early summer, and flowers are usually white, cream, pink or various shades of blue and mauve. A German legend attributes the common name of forget-me-not to a lover who, while gathering the flowers, fell into a river and cried "forget-me-not" as he drowned.

Top Tip

Relatively trouble-free, *Myosotis* species thrive in a cool, damp environment, and are especially suitable for woodland gardens or water-side planting.

CULTIVATION

These plants are very easily grown in any position, sunny or shady, as long as it remains moist during summer. Alpine species benefit from a gritty free-draining soil but the others aren't fussy. The perennials may be propagated from seed or by careful division in late winter, the annuals from seed sown in spring.

RIGHT *Throughout spring,* Myosotis sylvatica, *known as the garden forget-me-not, is covered in tiny, yellow-eyed, blue flowers. This European native has given rise to a large number of popular cultivars.*

ABOVE *Ideal as a ground cover,* Myosotis sylvatica *'Music' is smothered in clusters of deep blue, yellow-eyed flowers from spring to early summer.*
LEFT *Low-growing,* Myosotis alpestris *'Alba' is well suited to rockery planting, producing a carpet of dainty white flowers in the spring and summer months.*

Favourites	Flower Colour	Blooming Season	Flower Fragrance	Plant Height	Plant Width	Hardiness Zone	Frost Tolerance
Myosotis alpestris	bright blue with yellow eyes	spring to early summer	no	4–6 in (10–15 cm)	4–6 in (10–15 cm)	4–10	yes
Myosotis explanata	white	early summer	no	8 in (20 cm)	6 in (15 cm)	8–9	yes
Myosotis scorpioides	blue with yellow, white or pink eye	summer	no	12 in (30 cm)	12 in (30 cm)	5–10	yes
Myosotis sylvatica	lavender-blue with yellow eyes	spring to early summer	no	10–18 in (25–45 cm)	12 in (30 cm)	5–10	yes
Myosotis sylvatica 'Blue Ball'	bright blue	spring to early summer	no	4–8 in (10–20 cm)	8 in (20 cm)	5–10	yes
Myosotis sylvatica 'Music'	deep blue with yellow eye	spring to early summer	no	10 in (25 cm)	12 in (30 cm)	5–10	yes

NEMESIA

Confined to South Africa, this figwort family (Scrophulariaceae) genus includes around 65 species of annuals, perennials and subshrubs. They form small mounds of foliage with toothed, linear or lance-shaped leaves. Their flowers, which grow in clusters on short stems, are trumpet-shaped and 2-lipped; the upper lip is 4-lobed, the lower lip 1- or 2-lobed, often in a contrasting colour. The annuals are popular short-lived bedding plants occurring in a wide range of bright colours. While less vividly coloured, the perennials live longer, are sometimes mildly scented and are useful plants for borders, rockeries or pots. The genus is named for Nemesis, the goddess of retribution, though the reason why these inoffensive little plants should bear such a name is intriguingly unclear.

CULTIVATION

Plant in a sunny position with light free-draining soil that can be kept moist. Pinch back leaf tips when plants are young to keep the compact shape. Annuals should be sown in succession for continuous bloom. The perennials tolerate light frosts and grow from the cuttings of non-flowering stems.

Top Tip

Nemesia species flower for only a short time but it is possible to prolong the flowering period by cutting plants back hard when the blooms have finished.

RIGHT *Due to its often bicoloured flowers,* Nemesia strumosa *is a favourite in the garden. It is a small fast-growing plant that is ideal for beds or in pots.*

BELOW *An evergreen plant,* Nemesia caerulea *'Innocence' bears an abundance of tiny clear white flowers with yellow centres from summer to autumn.*

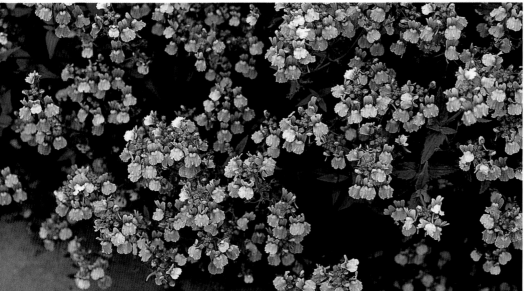

LEFT Nemesia denticulata *is the sort of plant every gardener cherishes. Its only requirement is a sunny spot to produce masses of soft lilac blooms. As an added extra, its perfume permeates the air on a warm day.*

RIGHT Nemesia caerulea
'Hubbird', formerly called
N. fruticosa 'Blue Bird',
makes a bright splash of
purple-blue colour in
containers and baskets,
which are ideally suited
to its semi-trailing habit.

Favourites	Flower Colour	Blooming Season	Flower Fragrance	Plant Height	Plant Width	Hardiness Zone	Frost Tolerance
Nemesia caerulea	pink, lavender, blue	summer to autumn	no	15–24 in (38–60 cm)	12 in (30 cm)	8–10	yes
Nemesia caerulea 'Hubbird'	violet-blue	summer to autumn	no	15 in (38 cm)	18 in (45 cm)	8–10	yes
Nemesia caerulea 'Innocence'	white, yellow centred	summer to autumn	no	15 in (38 cm)	18 in (45 cm)	8–10	yes
Nemesia denticulata	lilac-mauve	late spring to early autumn	yes	15 in (38 cm)	24–36 in (60–90 cm)	7–10	yes
Nemesia strumosa	various	summer to autumn	no	8–12 in (20–30 cm)	12 in (30 cm)	9–11	no
Nemesia versicolor	various	summer to autumn	no	10–18 in (25–45 cm)	8–12 in (20–30 cm)	9–11	no

ABOVE *Nepeta racemosa 'Walker's Low' has finely hairy grey-green leaves and long-blooming violet-blue flowers.* **BELOW** *Dense spikes of purple-blue (occasionally yellow) flowers are borne on the sturdy stems of Nepeta nervosa. The deeply veined leaves grow to a length of 10 cm (4 in).*

NEPETA

A member of the mint family (Lamiaceae), this genus of around 250 mainly aromatic perennials is native to a wide area of Eurasia, North Africa and the mountains of tropical Africa. They are mainly low-growing plants, rather sprawling in habit, with small, toothed, often aromatic leaves. In summer the grey-green foliage disappears under upright spikes bearing many tiny flowers along their length. The 2-lipped flowers range in colour from white to mauve-blue to deep purple. *Nepeta* hybrids make exceptional garden plants and are ideal for herbaceous borders, for edgings or as ground covers. The common names of catnip and catmint refer to the fondness that cats have for playing and lying in this plant.

CULTIVATION

Best grown in full sun, *Nepeta* species prefer light free-draining soil. Pinch back in spring to encourage compact growth and water well. Cutting back the plants each year will maintain their shape and keep them tidy. Propagation is by division, from cuttings taken during late spring or summer or from seed.

LEFT *A vigorous grower,* Nepeta racemosa *is suitable for growing in a herbaceous border. Cutting the short-blooming flowers back will usually result in rebloom.* **BELOW** Nepeta × faassenii *'Six Hills Giant' is wonderful as an edging plant. It tolerates damp conditions better than other cultivars.*

Top Tip

Nepeta species self-seed very freely and can become invasive. To prevent this, give the plants a light trim in the growing season and cut back the old growth in spring.

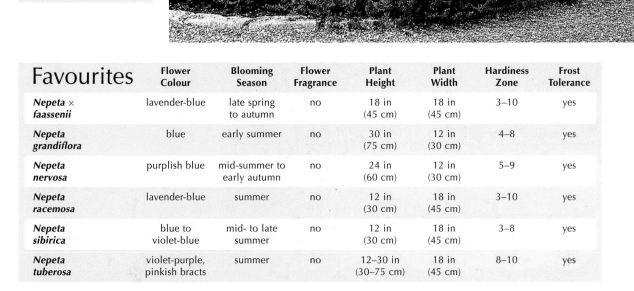

Favourites	Flower Colour	Blooming Season	Flower Fragrance	Plant Height	Plant Width	Hardiness Zone	Frost Tolerance
Nepeta × faassenii	lavender-blue	late spring to autumn	no	18 in (45 cm)	18 in (45 cm)	3–10	yes
Nepeta grandiflora	blue	early summer	no	30 in (75 cm)	12 in (30 cm)	4–8	yes
Nepeta nervosa	purplish blue	mid-summer to early autumn	no	24 in (60 cm)	12 in (30 cm)	5–9	yes
Nepeta racemosa	lavender-blue	summer	no	12 in (30 cm)	18 in (45 cm)	3–10	yes
Nepeta sibirica	blue to violet-blue	mid- to late summer	no	12 in (30 cm)	18 in (45 cm)	3–8	yes
Nepeta tuberosa	violet-purple, pinkish bracts	summer	no	12–30 in (30–75 cm)	18 in (45 cm)	8–10	yes

NICOTIANA

As the genus name indicates, this is the well-known source of tobacco leaf. There are over 65 species in this genus, the bulk of which are annuals and perennials native to tropical and subtropical America, as well as Australia. Most species are tall and tree-like but a few species grow as shrubs, though they tend to be softwooded and short-lived. Their leaves are usually deep green, very large and covered with fine hairs. They are sticky to the touch, and may exude a fragrance when crushed. The attractive flowers are tubular or bell-shaped; mostly white or in pastel shades of green, pale yellow, pink or soft red and usually open only in the early evening or at night. If the blooms are fragrant, the scent is also often released at night.

CULTIVATION

Most tobacco species are marginally frost hardy to frost tender. They grow best in warm humid climates with ample summer rainfall in full sun or partial shade. They require soil that is moist, well-drained and reasonably fertile. Most *Nicotiana* species are propagated from seed sown in the spring, though some will grow from cuttings.

ABOVE *The leaves of* Nicotiana tabacum *have long been used to make tobacco products, but this plant also produces pretty little pink flowers.*
RIGHT Nicotiana alata *'Nicky' is often grown as an annual and produces clusters of scented crimson flowers. It is a good choice for borders.*

Favourites	Flower Colour	Blooming Season	Flower Fragrance	Plant Height	Plant Width	Hardiness Zone	Frost Tolerance
Nicotiana alata	greenish white and white	summer to early autumn	yes	2–4 ft (0.6–1.2 m)	18 in (45 cm)	7–11	no
Nicotiana 'Avalon Bright Pink'	pink	summer to autumn	no	8–12 in (20–30 cm)	8–12 in (20–30 cm)	8–11	no
Nicotiana langsdorffii	green	summer	no	2–5 ft (0.6–1.5 m)	18–30 in (45–75 cm)	9–11	no
Nicotiana 'Saratoga Mixed'	white, greenish white, pink, red	summer to autumn	no	10–12 in (25–30 cm)	10–12 in (25–30 cm)	8–11	no
Nicotiana sylvestris	white	summer	yes	5 ft (1.5 m)	24 in (60 cm)	8–11	no
Nicotiana tabacum	greenish white to dull pink	summer	yes	4–6 ft (1.2–1.8 m)	3 ft (0.9 m)	9–11	no

ABOVE Nicotiana sylvestris *bears long tubular to trumpet-shaped white flowers and is often planted near doors and windows in order to enjoy the evening scent.*

BELOW *If planted in full sun, the white, pale pink, cerise and ruby red flowers of* Nicotiana *'Saratoga Mixed' will open for some time during the day.*

Top Tip

Many *Nicotiana* species are happy in large containers. Use multi-purpose compost and add a slow-release fertiliser to the soil before planting.

OENOTHERA

Commonly referred to as evening primrose, this genus contains over 120 species of annuals, biennials and perennials of the willow herb family (Onagraceae). Species are found in the temperate zones of the Americas and may vary considerably: some have taproots and tend to grow upright; others have fibrous roots and certain species have a sprawling growth habit. The foliage varies from clump-forming with soft, hairy, toothed- or lance-shaped leaves to large rough leaves growing on erect stems. The cup-shaped 4-petalled flowers make a lovely display over summer in bright shades of yellow, or less commonly, pink, red or white. Evening primrose oil is extracted from the plant's tiny seeds and is used in a range of homeopathic remedies.

ABOVE *A clump-forming perennial, Oenothera 'Crown Imperial' produces a breathtaking display of large bright yellow blooms in summer. It has rich green leaves, and the flowers age to orange-red.* **LEFT** *Oenothera 'Lemon Sunset', as its name suggests, bears large lemon yellow blooms that fade to pink as they age.*

CULTIVATION

Mostly very hardy, these tough adaptable plants prefer full sun and light, gritty, free-draining soil. Summer watering produces stronger growth but they will also tolerate drought conditions. Fibrous-rooted species can be divided when dormant, otherwise propagate from seed or from cuttings taken from the base of the plant.

Favourites	Flower Colour	Blooming Season	Flower Fragrance	Plant Height	Plant Width	Hardiness Zone	Frost Tolerance
Oenothera caespitosa	white, ageing to pink	summer	yes	6 in (15 cm)	8 in (20 cm)	5–9	yes
Oenothera 'Crown Imperial'	yellow	early summer	no	18 in (45 cm)	24 in (60 cm)	5–9	yes
Oenothera fruticosa	deep yellow	late spring to summer	no	18–36 in (45–90 cm)	12 in (30 cm)	4–10	yes
Oenothera 'Lemon Sunset'	cream, yellow centre ageing to pink	summer to early autumn	no	24–36 in (60–90 cm)	12 in (30 cm)	5–9	yes
Oenothera macrocarpa	yellow	late spring to early autumn	yes	6–12 in (15–30 cm)	24 in (60 cm)	5–9	yes
Oenothera speciosa	white, ageing to pink	spring to early autumn	yes	18–24 in (45–60 cm)	24 in (60 cm)	5–10	yes

LEFT *Although potentially invasive,* Oenothera speciosa *'Siskiyou' is valued for the delicate pink shade of its shallow saucer-shaped flowers, as well as its long blooming season.*
BELOW Oenothera speciosa *'Alba' bears yellow-centred, pure white, fragrant flowers that open during the day. Its simple charm makes it a cottage garden favourite.*

Top Tip

These plants have both culinary and medicinal uses. Evening primrose oil from the seeds is said to be highly therapeutic, and the leaves can be eaten in salads or used to make tea.

OSTEOSPERMUM

Found mainly in southern Africa, this genus consists of some 70 species of annuals, perennials and subshrubs of the daisy family (Asteraceae). The plants are generally low, spreading or mounding in growth habit with simple, broadly toothed, elliptical to spatula-shaped leaves. *Osteospermum* plants are valued for the cheerful carpet of flowers they provide through the warmer months. The flowers are daisy-like: a large outer ring of petal-like ray florets, mainly pink, purple or white, surrounds a central disc, often an unusual purple-blue colour and sporting golden pollen-bearing anthers, which add to the plant's beauty. The genus name comes from the Greek words *osteon* (bone) and *sperma* (seed) and refers to the hard seeds.

ABOVE Osteospermum jucundum *produces striking solitary, mauve-pink, daisy-like blooms with a purple-blue centre that fades to a yellow colour as it ages. The flowers tend to close on overcast days.*

CULTIVATION
Most species will tolerate only light frosts and prefer a sunny position in light well-drained soil. Avoid over-watering as this can lead to straggly growth. Pinching back and deadheading keeps the plants compact. Propagate annuals from seed and perennials from tip cuttings.

Top Tip
Very hardy plants, *Osteospermum* species suit a range of garden situations including along paths, in borders, over embankments or in rock gardens.

ABOVE Osteospermum 'Orange Symphony' bears light orange blooms with dark blue centres. It has a mounding habit so is often used for container growing. **LEFT** Grow Osteospermum 'Nasinga Purple' en masse in order to fully appreciate the startling quality of the blue-centred purple flowers above clear green leaves. **FAR LEFT** Lovely white petals surround the blue and yellow centre of Osteospermum 'Sunny Gustav'. It has a prostrate habit and benefits from a trim when flowering has finished.

Favourites	Flower Colour	Blooming Season	Flower Fragrance	Plant Height	Plant Width	Hardiness Zone	Frost Tolerance
Osteospermum jucundum	purple-pink	autumn to spring	no	8–12 in (20–30 cm)	36 in (90 cm)	8–10	yes
Osteospermum, Nasinga Series	white, cream, pink, purple	spring to summer	no	12–18 in (30–45 cm)	24 in (60 cm)	8–10	yes
Osteospermum, Side Series	white, mauve-pink, purple-red	spring to summer	no	10–12 in (25–30 cm)	18 in (45 cm)	8–10	yes
Osteospermum 'Sunny Gustav'	white	spring to summer	no	12 in (30 cm)	18 in (45 cm)	8–10	yes
Osteospermum, Symphony Series	cream, yellow, orange, salmon	summer to autumn	no	10–15 in (25–38 cm)	18–24 in (45–60 cm)	8–10	yes
Osteospermum 'Whirligig'	white with grey-blue underside	late spring to autumn	no	18–24 in (45–60 cm)	24 in (60 cm)	8–10	yes

PAPAVER

Instantly recognised as the poppy, this wide-spread group of about 50 species of annuals and perennials belongs to the Papaveraceae family. Leaves grow from the base of the plant to form rosettes and are usually dark to light green, lobed and covered in fine hairs. Upright flower stems covered in bristles grow out of the leaf rosettes and hold aloft the nodding bud that develops into the distinctive flower. These are usually 4-petalled, paper-textured, cup-shaped and occur in shades of white, yellow, orange, pink or red. The poppy is often associated with war remembrance days, a link attributed to Homer, the eighth-century BC Greek poet, who first associated the drooping poppy bud with the form of a dying soldier.

CULTIVATION

Poppies are frost hardy and prefer a sunny position with light, moist and well-drained soil. Most species are propagated from seed although perennial poppy cultivars are propagated from root cuttings.

LEFT *Rich red petals with dramatic black spots make Papaver commutatum a spectacular poppy. The single flowers make their appearance in summer, held on furry grey stems above downy mid-green leaves.*

Favourites	Flower Colour	Blooming Season	Flower Fragrance	Plant Height	Plant Width	Hardiness Zone	Frost Tolerance
Papaver commutatum	bright red; black spot at petal base	summer	no	18–20 in (45–50 cm)	6 in (15 cm)	8–10	yes
Papaver miyabeanum	pale yellow	late spring to early summer	no	6 in (15 cm)	6 in (15 cm)	5–9	yes
Papaver nudicaule	white, yellow, orange, pink	winter to spring	yes	12–24 in (30–60 cm)	6–12 in (15–30 cm)	2–10	yes
Papaver orientale	pink to red; black spot at petal base	summer	no	18–36 in (45–90 cm)	24–36 in (60–90 cm)	3–9	yes
Papaver rupifragum	pale orange to scarlet	summer	no	18–24 in (45–60 cm)	12 in (30 cm)	6–9	yes
Papaver somniferum	white, pink, red, purple	summer	no	2–4 ft (0.6–1.2 m)	12 in (30 cm)	7–10	yes

LEFT Papaver nudicaule 'Meadhome's Strain' has bright orange and yellow flowers that add a uniquely cheerful atmosphere to any style of garden.

BELOW Oriental poppies, such as Papaver orientale 'Marcus Perry', are equally at home in a formal border or a wild garden. These coral blooms suit most situations.

Top Tip

Papaver nudicaule, the Iceland poppy, is the best species for cut flowers. Pick just as the buds are beginning to open, and singe the ends before placing in water.

BELOW As with all Oriental poppies, Papaver orientale, Goliath Group, 'Beauty of Livermere' self-seeds freely. It has the characteristic black spot on each petal.

PELARGONIUM

Most of the 250 species of annuals, perennials and subshrubs in this geranium family (Geraniaceae) genus come from South Africa, with a few from Australia, the Middle East and other parts of Africa. The foliage is quite varied but is often light green, rounded or hand-shaped, with conspicuous lobes, fine hairs and dark blotches. Some species have semi-succulent leaves. The flowers are simple and 5-petalled, often brightly coloured and sometimes grown in a mass of blooms, ranging in colour from white and pink to mauve and purple. The genus name comes from the Greek word *pelargos* (a stork), referring to the shape of the seed pod, as does the genus's common name of storksbill.

CULTIVATION

These mostly frost-tender plants grow well in a mild climate and are suitable for garden beds and pots. Plant in full sun with fertile, light, well-drained soil. Once established, *Pelargonium* plants are drought tolerant. Propagate the annuals and species from seed and the perennials and shrubs from cuttings.

Favourites	Flower Colour	Blooming Season	Flower Fragrance	Plant Height	Plant Width	Hardiness Zone	Frost Tolerance
Pelargonium, Angel	pink, purple, red, white	spring to summer	no	10–18 in (25–45 cm)	12–18 in (30–45 cm)	9–11	no
Pelargonium crispum	pink	spring to summer	no	3 ft (0.9 m)	24 in (60 cm)	9–11	no
Pelargonium, Dwarf	white, pink, orange, red	spring to summer	no	8 in (20 cm)	8 in (20 cm)	9–11	no
Pelargonium echinatum	white, pink to purple-pink	spring to early summer	no	18 in (45 cm)	12 in (30 cm)	9–11	no
Pelargonium, Ivy-leafed	white, pink, red, purple	spring to autumn	no	8–36 in (20–90 cm)	12–36 in (30–90 cm)	9–11	no
Pelargonium, Miniature	white, pink, orange, red	spring to autumn	no	6 in (15 cm)	6 in (15 cm)	9–11	no
Pelargonium, Regal	white, purple, pink to red	late spring to summer	no	24 in (60 cm)	3–5 ft (0.9–1.5 m)	9–11	no
Pelargonium, Scented-leafed	white, pink, purple	spring to early summer	no	12–36 in (30–90 cm)	12–36 in (30–90 cm)	8–11	no
Pelargonium, Stellar	white, pink, orange, red	spring to summer	no	12–30 in (30–75 cm)	12–24 in (30–60 cm)	9–11	no
Pelargonium triste	yellow, green, pink	spring to summer	yes	8–12 in (20–30 cm)	12–18 in (30–45 cm)	9–11	no
Pelargonium, Unique	white, pink, red, purple, orange	spring to early summer	no	18 in (45 cm)	18 in (45 cm)	9–11	no
Pelargonium, Zonal	red, pink, white, orange, cream	spring to autumn	no	2–4 ft (0.6–1.2 m)	18–36 in (45–90 cm)	9–11	no

TOP LEFT *'Gemstone'* is a Scented-leafed Pelargonium. These perennials are grown as much for their foliage, which releases a pleasant fragrance when crushed, as for their attractive flowers.

LEFT Pelargonium, *Zonal*, 'Sassa', with its compact habit, distinctively marked leaves and abundance of mauve-pink flowers, makes an ideal bedding plant.

RIGHT Pelargoniums of the Angel type are recognised by their bushy habit, mid-green leaves and masses of single flowers. 'Suffolk Garnet' bears rich crimson blooms with a white centre.

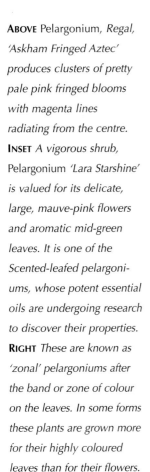

ABOVE Pelargonium, *Regal, 'Askham Fringed Aztec'* produces clusters of pretty pale pink fringed blooms with magenta lines radiating from the centre.
INSET A vigorous shrub, Pelargonium *'Lara Starshine'* is valued for its delicate, large, mauve-pink flowers and aromatic mid-green leaves. It is one of the Scented-leafed pelargoniums, whose potent essential oils are undergoing research to discover their properties.
RIGHT These are known as 'zonal' pelargoniums after the band or zone of colour on the leaves. In some forms these plants are grown more for their highly coloured leaves than for their flowers.

LEFT Pelargonium, *Regal,* '*Kyoto' is awash with lilac-pink and white flowers. Regals are also known as Martha Washington Hybrids.*

RIGHT Pelargonium crispum '*Variegated Prince Rupert'* is often referred to as the lemon geranium, due to the fragrance released when the leaves are crushed.

BELOW Pelargonium, *Angel,* '*Captain Starlight'* is a favourite with gardeners because of its bicoloured blooms—the upper petals are purple-red, while the lower petals are pink-flushed white.

LEFT *Prized as much for its aromatic foliage as it is for its superb pink flowers with dramatic dark markings, Pelargonium 'Orsett' is a Scented-leafed hybrid.*
BELOW RIGHT *With large single flowers of vivid pink, intensifying in colour towards the petal base, and rich green fragrant foliage, Pelargonium 'Bolero' is one of the Unique hybrids.*

RIGHT *Called ivy-leafed geraniums because of the shape of the leaves, this class can be induced to climb if given the support of a trellis.*
BELOW *Pelargonium, Scented-leafed, 'Bodey's Peppermint' has a minty aroma. White flowers are marked dark reddish purple.*

ABOVE *Pelargonium fruticosum, a low-spreading South African perennial, produces dainty starry flowers of white to pink, often with red basal markings.*

LEFT *One of the Scented-leafed hybrids,* Pelargonium *'Sweet Mimosa' not only bears aromatic foliage, but also features dainty flowers of soft pink.*

RIGHT *Native to South Africa's Cape region,* Pelargonium triste *was the first species to enter cultivation. The purple-brown marked yellow flowers appear in spring.*

PENSTEMON

Found mainly in the Americas from Alaska to Guatemala, the 250 species of perennials and subshrubs in this genus—a member of the foxglove (Scrophulariaceae) family—range from tiny carpeting plants to rapid growers that can exceed 1.2 m (4 ft) tall. Most develop into a mounding clump of erect stems with simple linear to lance-shaped leaves. Spikes of 5-lobed, foxglove-like flowers open at the stem tips in summer. In recent years many new garden varieties have become available, generally with increased hardiness. Several species were used by Native Americans, primarily for their analgesic and styptic properties but also to control stomach disorders.

CULTIVATION

Penstemons are best grown in full or half-sun with moist well-drained soil. Alpine species and those from south-western USA often prefer gritty soil. Gardeners in cold areas should try the new hardy types. While the species may be raised from seed, garden penstemons are usually propagated by division or from cuttings of non-flowering stems.

ABOVE *A Californian native,* Penstemon heterophyllus *is known as foothills penstemon. It features slender leaves and lavender-pink to bright blue flowers.*

BELOW *Growing up to 0.9 m (3 ft) tall, compact in habit and bearing large, white-throated, purple-red flowers,* Penstemon *'Maurice Gibbs' is an ideal plant for the perennial border.*

Top Tip

Penstemon culti-vars are mostly good all-round performers, but are particularly suited to border planting, rock gardens or "wild" gardens.

LEFT *A perennial from Arizona and New Mexico in the USA, and neighbouring parts of Mexico, Penstemon pinifolius produces orange-red flowers.*
BELOW *With pretty purple-red flowers during summer, Penstemon 'Rich Ruby' was bred for hardiness—like many hybrid cultivars, it is frost tolerant.*

Favourites	Flower Colour	Blooming Season	Flower Fragrance	Plant Height	Plant Width	Hardiness Zone	Frost Tolerance
Penstemon 'Blackbird'	dark purple	summer	no	36 in (90 cm)	36 in (90 cm)	6–10	yes
Penstemon eatonii	scarlet	spring to summer	no	12–36 in (30–90 cm)	8–24 in (20–60 cm)	4–9	yes
Penstemon heterophyllus	lavender-pink to bright blue	summer	no	12–20 in (30–50 cm)	8–12 in (20–30 cm)	8–10	yes
Penstemon 'Maurice Gibbs'	purple-red	spring to autumn	no	36 in (90 cm)	8–16 in (20–40 cm)	6–10	yes
Penstemon pinifolius	orange-red	late spring to mid-summer	no	6–16 in (15–40 cm)	18 in (45 cm)	8–10	yes
Penstemon 'Rich Ruby'	purple-red	summer	no	36 in (90 cm)	8–16 in (20–40 cm)	6–10	yes

BELOW *The world's favourite summer flower, petunias reliably produce their simple trumpet-shaped flowers over a very long season. This deep violet is one of the most enduringly popular colours.*

ABOVE *The Storm Series cultivars of* Petunia × hybrida, *such as the pink-flowered 'Storm Pink Morn', have been bred for improved weather resistance.*

PETUNIA

Think of the fancy garden petunias and it may be difficult to imagine them as members of the nightshade (Solanaceae) family, but they are, though more closely allied to tobacco *(Nicotiana)*. There are some 35 species in this tropical South American genus, and most are low spreading plants with simple, rounded, downy leaves and large 5-lobed flowers. The wild species are often aromatic, with scented flowers, but as is often the case the fancy garden forms have lost these charms. However, they compensate with an abundance of blooms and a wealth of colour. Modern petunias are remarkably tough plants—their flowers are weather resistant and in mild climates many will flower year-round.

CULTIVATION

Plant in full sun with moist well-drained soil and deadhead frequently to keep the plants flowering. The very fancy double- and large-flowered forms are seed-raised, but the perennial forms will grow from cuttings.

Favourites	Flower Colour	Blooming Season	Flower Fragrance	Plant Height	Plant Width	Hardiness Zone	Frost Tolerance
Petunia × *hybrida*	various	summer	no	4–16 in (10–40 cm)	8–40 in (20–100 cm)	9–11	no
Petunia × *hybrida,* **Fantasy Series**	various	spring to summer	no	10–12 in (25–30 cm)	10–12 in (25–30 cm)	9–11	no
Petunia × *hybrida,* **Mirage Series**	various	summer	no	4–16 in (10–40 cm)	8–40 cm (20–100 cm)	9–11	no
Petunia × *hybrida,* **Storm Series**	purple, pink	summer	no	12 in (30 cm)	12–15 in (30–38 cm)	9–11	no
Petunia × *hybrida,* **Surfinia Series**	purple, pink, mauve, blue	summer	no	4–6 in (10–15 cm)	8–48 in (20–120 cm)	9–11	no
Petunia integrifolia	violet; purple-pink interior	late spring to late autumn	no	12–24 in (30–60 cm)	24 in (60 cm)	9–11	no

RIGHT *Petunias start blooming from about mid-spring and continue right into autumn. As subsequent flowers are produced on lengthening stems, the plants can become leggy. Restore by cutting back by one third, then feed and water.*
BELOW *Throughout the flowering season,* Petunia × hybrida, *Surfinia Series, Surfinia Blue Vein/'Sunsolos' produces abundant mauve flowers, attractively marked with darker veins.*

PHLOX

This North American genus containing 67 species of annuals and perennials belongs to the phlox (Polemoniaceae) family. They are a variable group, ranging from carpeting rockery ground covers through wiry-stemmed trailers to large bushy perennials with strongly erect stems. Their foliage differs markedly too: from tiny linear leaves to lance-shaped dark green foliage over 10 cm (4 in) long. All, however, produce showy heads of small long-tubed flowers with 5 widely flared lobes. Pink to purple and white are the predominant flower colours, and the blooming season ranges from spring to autumn depending on the species.

CULTIVATION

Plant *Phlox* species in full sun or half-shade. Rockery phloxes and those grown in hanging baskets prefer a fairly light soil. Border phloxes need a heavier, more humus-rich soil and may need staking. They also need good ventilation to prevent late-season mildew. Depending on the growth form, *Phlox* species are propagated from seed or cuttings, or by division.

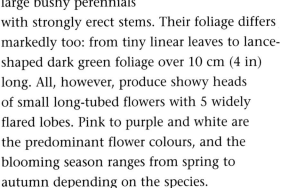

TOP *With a mat-forming growth habit, colourful pink flowers and downy leaves,* Phlox douglasii *'Crackerjack' will add colour and texture to the rock garden.*

ABOVE RIGHT Phlox subulata, *commonly known as moss phlox or mountain phlox, has given rise to many cultivars. 'Bonita', seen here, is a splendid example, with small glossy leaves and abundant pale lavender flowers.*

Top Tip

After flowering, phlox plants should be trimmed back to remove all spent flowers. Thin out overcrowded plants at the same time to encourage healthy vigorous growth next season.

Favourites	Flower Colour	Blooming Season	Flower Fragrance
Phlox carolina	pink, purple	spring to early summer	no
Phlox divaricata	blue, lavender, white	spring	yes
Phlox douglasii	pink, red, mauve, purple	spring to early summer	yes
Phlox drummondii	pink, red, purple, cream	summer to autumn	yes
Phlox paniculata	pink to red, purple, white	summer to autumn	yes
Phlox subulata	pink, lavender-blue, white	late spring to early summer	no

ABOVE Phlox carolina *'Bill Baker' reaches a height of 45 cm (18 in). This compact plant features glossy leathery leaves and attractive, large, pink to mauve flowers.*

Plant Height	Plant Width	Hardiness Zone	Frost Tolerance
48 in (120 cm)	16–24 in (40–60 cm)	5–10	yes
15 in (38 cm)	20–40 in (50–100 cm)	4–9	yes
2–6 in (5–15 cm)	12–20 in (30–50 cm)	5–10	yes
6–15 in (15–38 cm)	8–16 in (20–40 cm)	6–10	yes
24–48 in (60–120 cm)	16–36 in (40–90 cm)	4–9	yes
2–4 in (5–10 cm)	12–30 in (30–75 cm)	3–9	yes

ABOVE *A perennial from eastern USA,* Phlox paniculata *is known as annual or summer phlox. 'Tenor', with its eye-catching reddish pink flowers, is just one of many cultivars.*

PHYGELIUS

BELOW *Slender sturdy stems, often towering up to 0.9 m (3 ft) in height, carry the soft green leaves and pendent pale yellow flowers of* Phygelius aequalis *'Yellow Trumpet'.*

RIGHT Phygelius × rectus *is a cross of garden origin. 'Moonraker', with dark green foliage, displays clusters of tubular, creamy yellow flowers in late summer.*

This South African genus of evergreen perennials or subshrubs is a member of the foxglove (Scrophulariaceae) family. Although there are just 2 species, they have been hybridised and extensively developed to produce a range of garden forms. They are upright to slightly sprawling plants with serrated, lance-shaped to pointed oval leaves. Throughout the warmer months they bear open heads of pendent tubular flowers in shades of yellow, pink, orange or red. The name *Phygelius* is derived from Greek and means "to flee the sun", which is not very appropriate for plants such as these that often need extra warmth in cool climates.

RIGHT *With flowers that resemble those of fuchsias,* Phygelius aequalis *sends up tall stems of dusky pink blooms, accompanied by soft bright green leaves.*

Top Tip

In favourable conditions, *Phygelius* plants are ideal for border planting, adding height and colour to the landscape. Trim after flowering to maintain appearance.

CULTIVATION

These plants are tolerant of occasional moderate frosts but likely to suffer in cool wet winters, though they can re-shoot if cut to the ground by frost. Plant in half-sun with humus-rich, fertile, well-drained soil. Water and feed well when in active growth and during flowering. They are propagated from cuttings of non-flowering stems.

ABOVE *The clusters of pendent, tubular, flesh pink flowers of* Phygelius aequalis *'Trewidden Pink' top the 0.9 m (3 ft) tall leafy stems during late summer.*

Favourites	Flower Colour	Blooming Season	Flower Fragrance	Plant Height	Plant Width	Hardiness Zone	Frost Tolerance
Phygelius aequalis	dusky pink	late summer	no	3 ft (0.9 m)	3 ft (0.9 m)	8–10	yes
Phygelius aequalis 'Yellow Trumpet'	pale yellow	late summer	no	3 ft (0.9 m)	3 ft (0.9 m)	8–11	yes
Phygelius capensis	orange	summer to autumn	no	6 ft (1.8 m)	2 ft (0.6 m)	8–10	yes
Phygelius × rectus	red, orange, yellow	late summer	no	4 ft (1.2 m)	4 ft (1.2 m)	8–10	yes
Phygelius × rectus 'African Queen'	orange	late summer	no	4 ft (1.2 m)	4 ft (1.2 m)	8–10	yes
Phygelius × rectus 'Devil's Tears'	red	late summer	no	4 ft (1.2 m)	4 ft (1.2 m)	8–10	yes

PHYSOSTEGIA

This North American genus is a member of the mint family (Lamiaceae), and is made up of 2 species of perennials. Most form a clump of unbranched upright stems covered with dark green, toothed, narrow elliptical to lance-shaped leaves. From late summer to early autumn, flowerheads develop at the stem tips and are made up of clusters of 5-lobed, tubular to bell-shaped blooms, mainly in pink and purple shades. Though sometimes called false dragonhead, *Physostegia* species are more commonly known as the obedient plant, a reference to the way in which the flowers remain in place when twisted or moved.

CULTIVATION
These easy-growing hardy plants do best in any full or half sun position with moist well-drained soil. They spread by their fleshy roots and can become invasive. Propagate by division.

ABOVE *A graceful easy-growing plant,* Physostegia virginiana *'Alba' produces dense spikes of pure white tubular blooms in summer.*
RIGHT *The flowering spikes of* Physostegia virginiana *'Rose Queen' grow to 70 cm (27 in), and are covered in large rose pink blooms.*

LEFT *A constant favourite with gardeners,* Physostegia virginiana *'Rosea' produces spikes of large pale lilac-pink flowers in summer. This deciduous perennial has a spreading habit, and grows to little more than 0.9 m (3 ft) in height.*

Favourites	Flower Colour	Blooming Season	Flower Fragrance
Physostegia virginiana	blue-pink to magenta, white	late summer to early autumn	no
Physostegia virginiana 'Alba'	white	late summer to early autumn	no
Physostegia virginiana 'Crown of Snow'	white	late summer to early autumn	no
Physostegia virginiana 'Summer Snow'	white	late summer to early autumn	no
Physostegia virginiana 'Variegata'	purple-pink	late summer to early autumn	no
Physostegia virginiana 'Vivid'	rose pink	late summer to early autumn	no

Top Tip

Physostegia plants make excellent choices for the back of borders, as they offer height and colour with their tall flowering spikes, and coverage with the foliage clumps.

BELOW *Position* Physostegia virginiana *'Variegata' where both the soft purple-pink flowers and the interesting grey-green leaves, edged in cream, can be appreciated.*

Plant Height	Plant Width	Hardiness Zone	Frost Tolerance
2–4 ft (0.6–1.2 m)	3 ft (0.9 m)	3–10	yes
2–4 ft (0.6–1.2 m)	3 ft (0.9 m)	3–10	yes
2–4 ft (0.6–1.2 m)	3 ft (0.9 m)	3–10	yes
24–30 in (60–75 cm)	24 in (60 cm)	3–10	yes
24–30 in (60–75 cm)	24 in (60 cm)	3–10	yes
24 in (60 cm)	24 in (60 cm)	3–10	yes

PLATYCODON

The sole species in this bellflower genus (Campanulaceae) is a perennial found in Japan and nearby parts of China. Also known as the Chinese bellflower, it is a fast-growing clump-forming plant with bold, lance-shaped, blue-green leaves with toothed edges. The flowers open from enlarged balloon-like buds, giving the plant the common name of balloon flower. Once opened, the flowers are cup- to bell-shaped, with 5 broad lobes; they are white, pink or blue and, depending on the cultivar, come in double-flowered and dwarf forms. *Platycodon* root has long been used in traditional Chinese medicine and is now being studied for its gene-mutating effects on tumours.

CULTIVATION

This perennial is best in distinctly seasonal temperate climates. Plant in sun or part-shade with moist, humus-rich, well-drained soil. While it may be slow to become established, it is long-lived and very hardy. Propagate from seed or by occasional division.

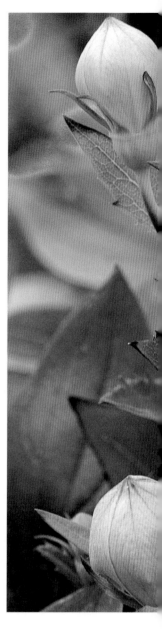

ABOVE *The blue flowers of* Platycodon grandiflorus *emerge from large balloon-shaped buds, which are a feature in themselves.*
ABOVE LEFT Platycodon grandiflorus *'Fuji Blue' stands out in the crowd. It reaches up to 75 cm (30 in) in height, and has large deep blue flowers.*

LEFT Platycodon grandiflorus *'Apoyama' has pretty violet-blue flowers, which are complemented by the attractive, blue-green, lance-shaped leaves.*

ABOVE *Cultivars in the Fuji Series are available in white, blue and pink. Platycodon grandiflorus 'Fuji White' is a tall plant with pure white flowers.*

Top Tip

The hardy versatile *Platycodon* plant is a good specimen for herbaceous borders or rock gardens. It also works as a cut flower.

Favourites	Flower Colour	Blooming Season	Flower Fragrance	Plant Height	Plant Width	Hardiness Zone	Frost Tolerance
Platycodon grandiflorus	blue to purple-blue, white, pink	summer	no	24 in (60 cm)	12 in (30 cm)	4–10	yes
Platycodon grandiflorus 'Apoyama'	deep violet-blue	summer	no	10–12 in (25–30 cm)	8 in (20 cm)	4–10	yes
Platycodon grandiflorus 'Fuji Blue'	blue	summer	no	24–30 in (60–75 cm)	12 in (30 cm)	4–10	yes
Platycodon grandiflorus 'Fuji White'	white	summer	no	24–30 in (60–75 cm)	12 in (30 cm)	4–10	yes
Platycodon grandiflorus 'Mariesii'	deep blue	summer	no	12–18 in (30–45 cm)	12 in (30 cm)	4–10	yes
Platycodon grandiflorus 'Sentimental Blue'	blue	summer	no	8–10 in (20–25 cm)	8 in (20 cm)	4–10	yes

POTENTILLA

This is a large genus of some 500 species belonging to the rose family. While most are herbaceous perennials, the shrubby species can be extremely useful as small ornamental plants. They are indigenous to the Northern Hemisphere, occurring from temperate to arctic regions. The grey-green to dark green leaves are mostly made up of 5 small leaflets and can have the appearance of feathers. The pretty flowers resemble small single roses; they appear from spring to summer and sometimes autumn, in small colourful clusters of yellow, orange, pink and blood red. Some species are used medicinally—the root bark of *Potentilla reptans* is said to stop nosebleeds and even internal bleeding.

CULTIVATION

These are hardy plants that grow in full sun or part-shade, preferring a fertile well-drained soil. Cultivars with orange, red or pink flowers need to be carefully placed where they will receive some shade during the hottest part of the day. Propagation is from cuttings in summer or seed in autumn.

Favourites	Flower Colour	Blooming Season	Flower Fragrance
Potentilla alba	white	spring to summer	no
Potentilla 'Flamenco'	scarlet	late spring to mid-summer	no
Potentilla fruticosa	white to yellow, orange, red	early summer to autumn	no
Potentilla megalantha	bright yellow	summer	no
Potentilla nepalensis	pink to light orange	summer	no
Potentilla recta	yellow	summer	no

ABOVE LEFT *A low-growing shrub,* Potentilla fruticosa *'Red Ace' bears vibrant orange-red flowers. Plant with other potentillas for a pretty hedge.*

BELOW *The fiery Spanish dance was obviously the inspiration behind* Potentilla *'Flamenco'. With its rich red blooms it evokes the passion of the dance.*

Plant Height	Plant Width	Hardiness Zone	Frost Tolerance
4 in (10 cm)	12 in (30 cm)	5–9	yes
18 in (45 cm)	24 in (60 cm)	5–8	yes
3 ft (0.9 m)	4 ft (1.2 m)	3–9	yes
6–12 in (15–30 cm)	12 in (30 cm)	5–9	yes
12–24 in (30–60 cm)	24 in (60 cm)	5–9	yes
18 in (45 cm)	18 in (45 cm)	4–9	yes

ABOVE RIGHT *The beautiful cerise-pink blooms with a darker pink centre of 'Miss Willmott' make it one of the best-loved cultivars of Potentilla nepalensis.*

Top Tip

To make room for new growth, the oldest stems of *Potentilla* plants should be cut out every few years. This should be done only when flowering is over.

ABOVE *The dazzling white blooms of Potentilla alba attract gardeners to this clump-forming perennial, as does its undemanding easy-to-grow nature. Feed the plant in spring.*

PRIMULA

This well-known genus of perennials is native to the Northern Hemisphere. The heavily veined, toothed or scalloped-edged leaves are pale to dark green and form basal rosettes. Single blooms may be tucked in among the leaves or borne in clusters throughout spring. The tubular flowers open out into a funnel shape or flat disc. They are made up of 5 or more petals, which are notched at their tips and come in a variety of colours ranging from white, yellow and pink to lilac and purple. Primulas are known variously as primrose, polyanthus and cowslip, and some have been used medicinally for their astringent and mildly sedative properties.

CULTIVATION
Most species prefer the dappled shade of a woodland garden and like moist, humus-rich, well-drained soil. The so-called bog primroses prefer damper conditions and often naturalise along watersides. Propagate from seed or by dividing established clumps when dormant.

ABOVE *English primrose,* Primula vulgaris, *is an old garden favourite that looks best in massed plantings. It forms tufts of green leaves with pale yellow flowers each held on its own stem above the foliage.*
ABOVE LEFT *The unusual and striking* Primula vialii, *known as Chinese pagoda primrose, bears violet-blue blooms on stout rocket-like flowering spikes.*
LEFT Primula japonica *is a classic candelabra-style of primula. Its deep rich pink flowers open in tiers on tall stems some way above the foliage. Grow in shady or waterside situations.*

ABOVE *Like other primroses,* Primula verticillata *grows in clumps that should be divided when they become crowded or are looking a little tired. Do this after flowering.*

Favourites	Flower Colour	Blooming Season	Flower Fragrance	Plant Height	Plant Width	Hardiness Zone	Frost Tolerance
Primula auricula	various	spring to mid-summer	yes	3–8 in (8–20 cm)	8–12 in (20–30 cm)	3–9	yes
Primula bulleyana	bright yellow, fading to orange	summer	no	24 in (60 cm)	24 in (60 cm)	6–9	yes
Primula denticulata	pink to purple	early to mid-spring	no	12 in (30 cm)	12 in (30 cm)	6–9	yes
Primula florindae	bright yellow	late spring to summer	yes	36 in (90 cm)	24–36 in (60–90 cm)	6–9	yes
Primula forrestii	bright yellow	spring	no	24 in (60 cm)	18 in (45 cm)	6–9	yes
Primula japonica	pink to red-purple, white	late spring to early summer	no	18–24 in (45–60 cm)	18 in (45 cm)	5–10	yes
Primula, Juliana	various	early spring	no	4–6 in (10–15 cm)	8–12 in (20–30 cm)	5–9	yes
Primula pulverulenta	pale pink to red-purple	late spring to summer	no	36 in (90 cm)	24 in (60 cm)	6–9	yes
Primula sieboldii	white, pink, purple	spring to early summer	no	12 in (30 cm)	12 in (30 cm)	5–9	yes
Primula verticillata	yellow	spring	yes	8 in (20 cm)	8 in (20 cm)	8–10	yes
Primula vialii	purple	late spring to summer	yes	24 in (60 cm)	12 in (30 cm)	7–9	yes
Primula vulgaris	pale yellow	early to late spring	yes	8 in (20 cm)	12 in (30 cm)	6–9	yes

ABOVE Primula auricula *'Alicia' needs regular water to produce its glorious ruby red and creamy yellow blooms. It is often grown in pots for indoor decoration.*

BELOW Primula bulleyana is *a rosette-forming perennial that dies down over winter. Dark crimson buds open to yellow flowers, held in tiers on stout stems.*

LEFT *The drumstick primrose,* Primula denticulata, *gets its common name from the rounded head of flowers that come in colours from pink to purple. Plant in a cool shady spot.*
BELOW *The attractive toothed leaves of* Primula sieboldii *'Mikado' usually die back not long after the plant has flowered. Like all primroses, it needs plenty of water.*

LEFT Primula, *Juliana,* 'Iris Mainwaring' bears an abundance of yellow-centred soft pink flowers above neat rosettes of light green leaves.

Top Tip

The polyanthus primulas bring a burst of life to the garden. Easy to grow and readily available, they come in almost any colour imaginable.

PULSATILLA

This genus of about 30 Eurasian and North American deciduous perennials (family Ranunculaceae) forms clumps of ferny leaves, which in most species are made silver by a dense covering of fine hairs. Long-stemmed cup- or bell-shaped flowers are carried singly with 5 to 8 petals and a prominent golden cluster of stamens. The flowers are graceful and occur in shades of white and yellow to violet-blue. The common name of pasque flower is from the old French word *Pasque,* meaning Easter, which is around the time when the plants flower in the Northern Hemisphere.

ABOVE Pulsatilla vulgaris *'Rubra' bears purple-red blooms with a golden centre above dainty foliage. The good-sized flowers make this cultivar a great choice for mass planting.*

CULTIVATION

Pulsatilla plants' flowers are hardy and need a seasonal temperate climate. They grow well in woodland conditions but are at their best with sun or part-shade and gritty, humus-rich, well-drained yet moist soil, such as that found in rocky crevices. Propagate by division when dormant or from seed.

Top Tip

Gardeners with sensitive skin should wear gloves when handling *Pulsatilla* plants, as both the leaves and the flowers may irritate the skin.

LEFT *The violet flowers of* Pulsatilla vulgaris *'Papageno' are followed by attractive seed heads. When these fall, it is time to cut back the plant and tidy the foliage.*

ABOVE Pulsatilla vulgaris *has long been a popular garden plant due to its stunning silky purple flowers, finely dissected leaves and attractive spherical seed heads.*

RIGHT *The low-growing* Pulsatilla montana *makes a good rock-garden plant. Its bell-shaped purple-blue flowers nod gracefully from the top of 15 cm (6 in) stems.*

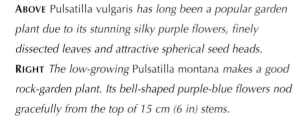

Favourites	Flower Colour	Blooming Season	Flower Fragrance	Plant Height	Plant Width	Hardiness Zone	Frost Tolerance
Pulsatilla albana	yellow, blue-violet	early summer	no	2–8 in (5–20 cm)	8 in (20 cm)	5–9	yes
Pulsatilla hirsutissima	lavender	spring	no	4–6 in (10–15 cm)	8 in (20 cm)	4–9	yes
Pulsatilla montana	deep blue to purple	spring	no	4–8 in (10–20 cm)	8 in (20 cm)	6–9	yes
Pulsatilla patens	purple, yellow	late spring	no	4–6 in (10–15 cm)	4–8 in (10–20 cm)	4–9	yes
Pulsatilla pratensis	light to dark purple	spring to early summer	no	6–12 in (15–30 cm)	8 in (20 cm)	5–9	yes
Pulsatilla vulgaris	white, pink to red, purple	spring to early summer	no	4–10 in (10–25 cm)	10 in (25 cm)	5–9	yes

RHODANTHE

An outstanding Australian genus of relatively low-growing annual and perennial daisies, *Rhodanthe* are found in every state, though with the greatest concentration of species occurring in Western Australia's winter rainfall south-west region. Being daisies, they belong to the big plant family, Asteraceae. All species have long-lasting flowers in white, yellow or pink made up of stiff, papery petals that last almost indefinitely when dried. In some species flowers have just two rows of petals, whereas others have several rows, or so many that the flowerhead appears almost spherical. Flowering occurs from about mid-winter to late spring, depending on the species, and is especially abundant when rainfall or watering has been regular during the previous late autumn and winter.

CULTIVATION

Rhodanthe are easily raised from seed with sowing best done in mid- to late autumn directly where the plants are to grow onto cleared soil. Any free-draining garden soil will do as long as it receives sun for most or all of the day. Scatter the seed thinly, then water in. If rain falls regularly after sowing, no further watering is needed. Plants will tolerate moderate frosts.

Top Tip

Rhodanthe are wildflowers and look terrific when grown as a single mass planting or with one or two other wildflower species such as the golden everlasting, *Schoenia* and native iris *Patersonia*.

RIGHT *The pink sunray (*Rhodanthe manglesii*) is native to the southwest corner of Western Australia. It does best when grown on free-draining, sand-based soils.*

LEFT *Found in all four of Australia's eastern states, a wide distribution that has allowed the chamomile sunray (*Rhodanthe anthemoides*) to mutate into several localised forms. One of the most striking is red in bud yet opens white. Others are all white.*

RIGHT *The typical form of the western sunray has white flowers but the pink-flowered variety* Rhodanthe chlorocephala *subsp.* roseum *is far more popular with gardeners. It produces its papery flowers anytime from mid-winter to mid-spring.*

Favourites	Flower Colour	Blooming Season	Flower Fragrance	Plant Height	Plant Width	Hardiness Zone	Frost Tolerance
Rhodanthe anthemoides	white	winter to spring	no	12 in (30 cm)	24 in (60 cm)	8–9	yes
Rhodanthe chlorocephala	white or pink	winter to spring	no	12–16 in (30–40 cm)	12 in (30 cm)	8–9	yes
Rhodanthe floribunda	white	winter to spring	no	20 in (50 cm)	20 in (50 cm)	8–9	yes
Rhodanthe manglesii	white	winter to spring	no	20 in (50 cm)	20 in (30 cm)	8–9	yes

RUDBECKIA

This North American genus belonging to the daisy family (Asteraceae) consists of 15 species of perennials. It is very popular in gardens because of the plants' great hardiness, ease of cultivation and valuable late season flowering. Most are fairly bulky plants, with branched or unbranched stems, and often have lance-shaped deeply veined leaves. From late summer they carry masses of large golden yellow daisies, usually with dark brown to black disc florets. Dwarf, double-flowered and variously coloured forms are available. They flower until cut back by frost. *Rudbeckia* was named by Linnaeus after a professor at the University of Uppsala, Olaus Rudbeck (1660–1740), who employed the young Linnaeus as a tutor for his children, of which he had 24!

CULTIVATION

Plant in a sunny open position with moist well-drained soil. Deadhead or use as a cut flower to encourage continued blooming. Mildew can occur but usually only late in the season. Propagate by division, from basal cuttings or from seed.

ABOVE *Informal yellow blooms with drooping petals make* Rudbeckia laciniata *an interesting long-lasting cut flower.*
BELOW Rudbeckia fulgida *var.* sullivantii *'Goldsturm' is an old garden favourite with large cheerful flowerheads.*

Top Tip

Because *Rudbeckia* plants bloom late in summer, they bring welcome colour to borders and beds when the blooms of other plants have faded.

BELOW *Black-eyed Susan,* Rudbeckia fulgida, *is a vigorous grower in the garden, but may need an application of liquid fertiliser when cultivated in pots.*

LEFT Rudbeckia hirta *is highly valued for its bright yellow daisy-like flowers featuring a dark brown-purple central disc.*

Favourites	Flower Colour	Blooming Season	Flower Fragrance	Plant Height	Plant Width	Hardiness Zone	Frost Tolerance
Rudbeckia fulgida	orange-yellow; brown centre	late summer to mid-autumn	no	36 in (90 cm)	24 in (60 cm)	3–10	yes
Rudbeckia fulgida var. *sullivantii* 'Goldsturm'	orange-yellow; brown centre	late summer to mid-autumn	no	24 in (60 cm)	24 in (60 cm)	3–10	yes
Rudbeckia hirta	yellow; brown-purple centre	summer to early autumn	no	12–36 in (30–90 cm)	12–24 in (30–60 cm)	3–10	yes
Rudbeckia hirta 'Irish Eyes'	yellow; green centre	summer to early autumn	no	24–30 in (60–75 cm)	24 in (60 cm)	3–10	yes
Rudbeckia laciniata	yellow; greenish centre	mid-summer to mid-autumn	no	4–6 ft (1.2–1.8 m)	3–5 ft (0.9–1.5 m)	3–10	yes
Rudbeckia nitida	yellow; green centre	late summer to early autumn	no	4–6 ft (1.2–1.8 m)	3 ft (0.9 m)	3–10	yes

SALVIA

Containing about 900 species of annuals, perennials and softwooded evergreen shrubs, this genus is the largest in the mint family. They are found in temperate and sub-tropical regions throughout the world, with the exception of Australasia, and grow in a wide range of habitats, from coastal to alpine. A number of *Salvia* species are used for culinary and medicinal purposes, and the genus name is derived from the Latin *salvare*, meaning to heal or save. Most species are hairy to some extent and many have foliage that is aromatic when crushed or rubbed. The flowers are tubular with the petals split into 2 lips, which may be straight or flaring. The flowers vary greatly in size, and the colour range moves through shades of blue to purple, and pink to red, as well as white and some yellows.

CULTIVATION

Most are best grown in full sun and all require a well-drained situation; generally, the shrubby plants dislike heavy wet soils. Propagation of most shrubby species is very easy from soft-wood cuttings taken throughout the growing season. Seed of all species is sown in spring.

ABOVE LEFT *A native of central Mexico, summer-flowering* Salvia patens *has bright green foliage and clear blue flowers.* **BELOW** Salvia officinalis, *or common sage, is the traditional herb used in cooking and for its medicinal properties.*

ABOVE *Emerging from felty purple buds, the purple and white flowers of* Salvia leucantha *are produced on long spikes over a lengthy flowering period.*
LEFT *Persistent reddish purple bracts hold the violet flowers of* Salvia nemorosa *'Lubecca'. Rosettes of grey-green leaves encircle the base of the flowering stems.*

Favourites	Flower Colour	Blooming Season	Flower Fragrance	Plant Height	Plant Width	Hardiness Zone	Frost Tolerance
Salvia coccinea	scarlet	early summer to late autumn	no	24–30 in (60–75 cm)	12–24 in (30–60 cm)	9–11	no
Salvia elegans	bright red	late summer to autumn	no	4–6 ft (1.2–1.8 m)	4–6 ft (1.2–1.8 m)	9–11	no
Salvia farinacea	violet-blue	summer to autumn	no	24 in (60 cm)	12 in (30 cm)	9–11	no
Salvia × jamensis	red, orange, pink, creamy yellow	summer to autumn	no	20–36 in (50–90 cm)	20–36 in (50–90 cm)	8–11	yes
Salvia leucantha	purple and white	winter to spring	no	24–36 in (60–90 cm)	2–5 ft (0.6–1.5 m)	9–11	no
Salvia nemorosa	purple, violet, white to pink	mid-summer to mid-autumn	no	3 ft (0.9 m)	24 in (60 cm)	5–10	yes
Salvia officinalis	lilac-blue	summer	no	18–30 in (45–75 cm)	24–36 in (60–90 cm)	5–10	yes
Salvia patens	blue	mid-summer to mid-autumn	no	18–24 in (45–60 cm)	18 in (45 cm)	8–10	yes
Salvia splendens	bright red	summer to autumn	no	15 in–8 ft (38 cm–2.4 m)	12 in–8 ft (30 cm–2.4 m)	9–12	no
Salvia × superba	violet, purple	mid-summer to early autumn	no	24–36 in (60–90 cm)	18–24 in (45–60 cm)	5–10	yes
Salvia uliginosa	sky blue	late summer to mid-autumn	no	3–6 ft (0.9–1.8 m)	3 ft (0.9 m)	8–10	yes
Salvia verticillata	lilac-blue, violet, rarely white	summer	no	3 ft (0.9 m)	18 in (45 cm)	6–10	yes

LEFT *Reaching 45–50 cm (18–20 in) high,* Salvia farinacea *'Victoria' is an award-winning cultivar with deep violet-blue flowers.*

RIGHT *Known as the bog sage,* Salvia uliginosa *can quickly spread in its favoured conditions of moist soil and full sun.*
BELOW *Hailing from Mexico,* Salvia × jamensis *is a drought-tolerant evergreen species with a bushy habit.*

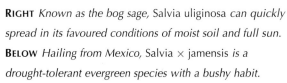

RIGHT Salvia elegans *is usually grown for its lovely pineapple-scented leaves, popular for flavouring drinks or used as a garnish for fruit salads and desserts.*

ABOVE *The spectacular scarlet flowers of* Salvia splendens *are held on tall stems above the light to dark green leaves.*
LEFT Salvia nemorosa *will provide a display of purple, pink or white flowers from summer through to autumn.*

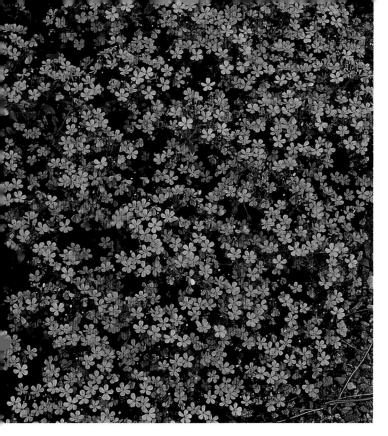

Favourites	Flower Colour	Blooming Season	Flower Fragrance
Saponaria 'Bressingham'	deep pink	summer	no
Saponaria lutea	pale yellow	early summer	no
Saponaria ocymoides	pink to red	summer	no
Saponaria officinalis	white, pink, red	summer to autumn	no
Saponaria × *olivana*	pale pink	summer	no
Saponaria pumilio	purple-pink, rarely white	summer	no

LEFT *When in bloom, the hairy dark green leaves of* Saponaria ocymoides *are almost entirely hidden by the masses of small, pink, starry flowers.*

TOP RIGHT *Long stamens protrude from the pale yellow flowers of* Saponaria lutea. *This perennial species has linear mid-green leaves.*

Top Tip

Making a soft carpet of starry flowers, *Saponaria* species are most at home spilling over banks, in rockeries or placed in sunny perennial borders.

SAPONARIA

This genus belongs to the carnation family (Caryophyllaceae), and features around 20 species of Eurasian annuals and perennials containing saponin, a glucoside that forms a soapy solution when mixed with water. The roots in particular were once used as soap, and the extract is present in detergents and foaming agents—hence the common name of soapwort. That use aside, these are pretty little plants that are well worth growing for their beauty alone. They are mainly low growing and range from tufted mounds to quite wide-spreading ground covers. They have blue-green linear to spatula-shaped leaves, sometimes toothed, and in summer are smothered in heads of small, starry, 5-petalled flowers.

CULTIVATION

Mainly very hardy and easily grown, they do best in gritty, moist, humus-rich, free-draining soil. They will also take slightly alkaline soil. Propagate by cuttings, from layers or from seed.

ABOVE *Carried above the foliage on tall stems, the flowers of* Saponaria officinalis *occur in shades of red, pink or white.*
RIGHT *With its double pink flowers and dark green foliage,* Saponaria officinalis *'Rosea Plena' is a favourite in gardens.*

Plant Height	Plant Width	Hardiness Zone	Frost Tolerance
3 in (8 cm)	12 in (30 cm)	5–10	yes
2–4 in (5–10 cm)	12–18 in (30–45 cm)	5–8	yes
6–10 in (15–25 cm)	18 in (45 cm)	4–9	yes
24 in (60 cm)	20 in (50 cm)	5–10	yes
2 in (5 cm)	6 in (15 cm)	5–9	yes
2 in (5 cm)	12 in (30 cm)	4–8	yes

SCABIOSA

An unpleasant sounding name, *Scabiosa* is derived from *scabies*, a Latin word for scurf or mange, the itchiness of which was said to be relieved by rubbing the affected area with the leaves of these plants. The genus, a member of the teasel family (Dipsacaceae), is composed of around 80 species of annuals and perennials found from Europe and North Africa to Japan. Most species form a spreading basal clump of light green to grey-green, rounded to lance-shaped leaves, with deeply incised notches or lobes. A few species have an erect or branching habit. The flowers are individually tiny but occur in rounded to flattened composite heads on stems that hold them clear of the foliage. White, pale yellow, soft pink, blue and mauve are the usual colours.

ABOVE Scabiosa atropurpurea 'Chile Black' has a gorgeous chocolate brown flowerhead that resembles a pincushion. Regular deadheading will prolong the flowering season into the autumn months.

CULTIVATION

The plants are hardy and easily grown in any sunny position with moderately fertile, moist, free-draining, slightly alkaline soil. Deadhead to prolong flowering. The annuals are raised from seed, and the perennials can be propagated from seed, from basal cuttings or by division.

RIGHT Scabiosa columbaria *var.* ochroleuca *bears lemon yellow blooms on long stalks. Cuttings can be taken in summer, or the plant can be divided in early spring.*

Favourites	Flower Colour	Blooming Season	Flower Fragrance	Plant Height	Plant Width	Hardiness Zone	Frost Tolerance
Scabiosa atropurpurea	purple, pink, rose, white	summer	no	24–36 in (60–90 cm)	10 in (25 cm)	7–11	yes
Scabiosa caucasica	lavender, pale blue	summer	no	24 in (60 cm)	24 in (60 cm)	4–10	yes
Scabiosa caucasica 'Alba'	white	summer	no	24 in (60 cm)	24 in (60 cm)	4–10	yes
Scabiosa caucasica 'Fama'	blue, lavender	summer	no	24–36 in (60–90 cm)	24 in (60 cm)	4–10	yes
Scabiosa columbaria	lilac-blue to reddish purple	summer to early autumn	no	20–27 in (50–70 cm)	3 ft (0.9 m)	6–10	yes
Scabiosa farinosa	mauve	spring to summer	no	12–18 in (30–45 cm)	12–24 in (30–60 cm)	6–10	yes

BELOW Scabiosa caucasica 'Fama' is a clump-forming perennial that produces blue flowerheads in summer. This picture shows the flowerhead in the budding stage.

RIGHT Scabiosa caucasica 'Alba' has a dense centre that resembles a pincushion, from which the pure white flowers radiate. It also makes a very good cut flower.

Top Tip

To attract butterflies and bees to the garden, *Scabiosa* species can be planted in borders and rock gardens. The long-flowering species make good container plants.

SCHOENIA

There are 5 species of these annual daisies found only in Australia, mostly only in Western Australia where they're a significant part of that state's magnificent spring wildflower displays. One species, the thread-leaved everlasting (*Schoenia filifolia*) is available as seed in packs from a well-known seed supplier and another, *Schoenia cassiniana* is sometimes seen in seed packs sold by specialist native nurseries. *Schoenia* deserves to be more widely grown as it makes a charming display if sown in a mass or mixed with other spring flowers. The blooms themselves are about 3 cm (1¼ in) across and have stiff petals seemingly made from glossy paper. They can be hung and dried for long-lasting indoor arrangements. Like all daisies, *Schoenia* is a member of the Asteraceae.

CULTIVATION

In mid- to late autumn sow seed thinly directly where you want it to grow onto cleared, dug-over soil that has been raked smooth. Rake lightly to cover and water in. The plants require plenty of sun to bloom well. If your winters are rainy, no further watering is usually needed. If dry, keep lightly moist over winter. No feeding is necessary.

RIGHT *As everlastings such as* Schoenia cassiniana *all grow through the winter to flower in spring, they are successful when grown in subtropical areas as long as they are watered every week or so from May to September.*

LEFT *Cassini's everlasting (Schoenia cassiniana) is a pretty and easy to grow Australian flower. In South and Western Australia this daisy, seen in vast sheets, is one of the wildflowers tourists flock to see.*
BELOW *The wider the area you can sow with* Schoenia filifolia *the more you'll be impressed. The brilliant yellow daisies bloom in early spring and sometimes return the next year from self-sown seeds.*

Top Tip

These look particularly lovely if sown with another Australian wildflower, the pink paper daisy, *Rhodanthe chlorocephalum*. They both require the same sowing and growing conditions and bloom together.

Favourites	Flower Colour	Blooming Season	Flower Fragrance	Plant Height	Plant Width	Hardiness Zone	Frost Tolerance
Schoenia cassiniana	pink	winter to spring	no	20–30 in (50–75 cm)	15–20 in (38–50 cm)	8–9	yes
Schoenia filifolia	yellow	winter to spring	no	8–24 in (20–60 cm)	4–12 in (10–30 cm)	8–9	yes

SCHIZANTHUS

This Chilean genus of 12 species of annuals and biennials is in the potato family (Solanaceae), though that relationship is not obvious. The cultivated species are small upright plants with soft green ferny foliage, often with a covering of fine hairs. Their flowers, which appear from spring to autumn, are borne in branching panicles held above the foliage. They are beautifully marked and shaped, with a prominent lower lip, hence the common name of poor man's orchid. Modern strains are available in a wide range of colours and sizes. The genus name comes from the Greek *schizo* (divide) and *anthos* (a flower), referring to the deeply divided corolla.

ABOVE Many garden strains originate from Schizanthus × wisetonensis. *This cheerful hybrid comes in an array of colours, all with speckled yellow throats.*

CULTIVATION

Schizanthus plants are tender, but easily grown as annuals where the summer temperatures are warm and even. Elsewhere treat as greenhouse pot plants. Plant in a bright position with fertile, moist, well-drained soil. Raise from seed, with several sowings to ensure continued flowering. Pinch out the growing tips when young to encourage bushiness.

LEFT This dramatic form of Schizanthus × wisetonensis *has deep pink flowers with a black centre and speckled yellow throat.*

Top Tip

Schizanthus plants are a bit fragile, but are worth the time spent providing care and protection. They don't like heavy rain or temperature extremes.

ABOVE Schizanthus *is also known as butterfly flower. This* S. × wisetonensis *variety has rich red flowers, which are nicely complemented by ferny foliage.* **LEFT** *The plants in the Dwarf Bouquet Mix come in lively shades of amber, pink and red. There are also pretty bicoloured forms, such as that seen here.*

Favourites	Flower Colour	Blooming Season	Flower Fragrance	Plant Height	Plant Width	Hardiness Zone	Frost Tolerance
Schizanthus, Angel Wings Mix	pink, red, purple	spring to autumn	no	12–18 in (30–45 cm)	8–12 in (20–30 cm)	9–11	no
Schizanthus, Disco Mix	crimson, pink	spring to autumn	no	8–10 in (20–25 cm)	8–10 in (20–25 cm)	9–11	no
Schizanthus, Dwarf Bouquet Mix	amber, red, pink	spring to autumn	no	12–15 in (30–38 cm)	8–10 in (20–25 cm)	9–11	no
Schizanthus, Star Parade Mix	various	spring to autumn	no	8 in (20 cm)	8 in (20 cm)	9–11	no
Schizanthus 'Sweet Lips'	pink and red, red and white	spring to autumn	no	12–15 in (30–38 cm)	10–12 in (25–30 cm)	9–11	no
Schizanthus × *wisetonensis*	white, blue, pink red-brown	spring to summer	no	8–18 in (20–45 cm)	8–12 in (20–30 cm)	9–11	no

SINNINGIA

Named after Wilhelm Sinning (1792–1874), a horticulturalist and botanist at the University of Bonn, this African violet family (Gesneriaceae) genus is made up of about 40 species of tuberous perennials and small shrubs distributed from Mexico to Argentina. The commonly cultivated species are perennials with large lance- to heart-shaped leaves made velvety by a dense covering of fine hairs. The well-known florist's gloxinia *(Sinningia speciosa)* has large, upward-facing, bell-shaped flowers, although other species have tubular flowers and are sometimes scented. Their vivid showy flowers make the plants ideal for the house or greenhouse, as well as being lovely summer annuals or year-round plants in subtropical to tropical areas.

ABOVE *A native of Brazil,* Sinningia cardinalis *is also known as the cardinal flower. It has large ovate leaves and bears clusters of bright red tubular flowers.*

Top Tip

As indoor pot plants, *Sinningia* species will benefit from half-strength high-potash fertiliser applied every few weeks during the growing season.

CULTIVATION

They prefer warm humid conditions with a bright but not overly sunny exposure. The soil should be well-drained, moist and humus-rich. Propagate by lifting and dividing after the foliage has died back, from seed or by leaf-petiole cuttings. The tubers may be stored dry.

RIGHT Sinningia aggregata *is an interesting-looking plant with red or orange tube-shaped flowers that are solitary or arranged in pairs.*
ABOVE RIGHT Sinningia speciosa, *Lawn Hybrid, 'Sunset' has velvety flowers of rich red that are delicately edged with white.*

Favourites	Flower Colour	Blooming Season	Flower Fragrance	Plant Height	Plant Width	Hardiness Zone	Frost Tolerance
Sinningia aggregata	red, orange	summer	no	15–30 in (38–75 cm)	12–24 in (30–60 cm)	10–12	no
Sinningia canescens	red, pink, orange	late spring to early summer	no	12 in (30 cm)	8–12 in (20–30 cm)	10–12	no
Sinningia cardinalis	purple, pink, red, white	late summer to autumn	no	12 in (30 cm)	12 in (30 cm)	10–12	no
Sinningia pusilla	lilac	summer	no	2 in (5 cm)	2 in (5 cm)	11–12	no
Sinningia speciosa	white, red, purple, blue	summer	no	12 in (30 cm)	12 in (30 cm)	11–12	no
Sinningia tubiflora	white	summer	yes	24 in (60 cm)	18 in (45 cm)	10–12	no

SOLENOSTEMON

This genus of around 60 species of shrubby, sometimes succulent perennials from the tropics of Asia and Africa is known in cultivation through just a few of its members, of which only the coleus or painted nettle (*Solenostemon scutellarioides*) is common. A member of the mint (Lamiaceae) family, *Solenostemon* includes several other species with interestingly coloured foliage, although they have never become popular with gardeners. The flowers are usually small and white, cream or blue in colour, and would be easily overlooked except that they are borne in short spikes.

CULTIVATION

Solenostemon species are generally tender and need winter protection outside the subtropics. They are grown outdoors in cooler climates, but only as summer annuals. Plant in sun or half-shade with moist well-drained soil. To keep the foliage lush, pinch out flower spikes as they develop. The plants may be propagated from seed, though cuttings strike so easily that this is not usually necessary.

ABOVE Solenostemon scutellarioides *'Display' is just one of the many cultivars developed from this tropical species, which was formerly known as* Coleus scutellarioides.

BELOW *The ornamental foliage of* Solenostemon scutellarioides *has been popular since Victorian times. 'Winsley Tapestry' looks at its best when grown en masse.*

Favourites	Flower Colour	Blooming Season	Flower Fragrance	Plant Height	Plant Width	Hardiness Zone	Frost Tolerance
Solenostemon scutellarioides	white, blue	summer to autumn	no	12–36 in (30–90 cm)	12–24 in (30–60 cm)	10–12	no
Solenostemon scutellarioides **'Black Dragon'**	white, blue	late spring to early autumn	no	12–18 in (30–45 cm)	6–8 in (15–20 cm)	10–12	no
Solenostemon scutellarioides **'Crimson Ruffles'**	white, blue	summer to autumn	no (30–90 cm)	12–36 in (30–60 cm)	12–24 in	10–12	no
Solenostemon scutellarioides **'Display'**	white, blue	summer to autumn	no	12–36 in (30–90 cm)	12–24 in (30–60 cm)	10–12	no
Solenostemon scutellarioides **'Walter Turner'**	white, blue	summer to autumn	no	12–36 in (30–90 cm)	12–24 in (30–60 cm)	10–12	no
Solenostemon scutellarioides **'Winsley Tapestry'**	white, blue	summer to autumn	no (30–90 cm)	12–36 in (30–60 cm)	12–24 in	10–12	no

LEFT *A lower-growing cultivar,* Solenostemon scutellarioides *'Black Dragon' has very striking markings, and does best in partial shade.*

ABOVE *A number of cultivars of* Solenostemon scutellarioides *have ruffled leaves. 'Crimson Ruffles' has bright markings along the main leaf veins.*

STOKESIA

Although there is just 1 species in this daisy family (Asteraceae) genus, it has been extensively developed in cultivation and is now available in a wide range of plant sizes, flower colours and forms. A summer- to autumn-flowering perennial from the south-eastern USA, *Stokesia*—or Stokes' aster—was named after Dr Jonathan Stokes, an English doctor and botanist. It arrived in England in 1766 and was in vogue in Victorian times, especially as a cut flower. It later languished but is now popular again. *Stokesia* is an upright plant with simple evergreen leaves borne in basal rosettes and large cornflower-like heads of white, yellow or mauve to deep purple-blue flowers. *Stokesia* plants are well suited to herbaceous borders.

CULTIVATION

Plant in full or half sun in light free-draining soil. Water and feed well. Watch for mildew in late summer. Propagate by division near the end of the dormant period, or raise from seed.

Favourites	Flower Colour	Blooming Season	Flower Fragrance	Plant Height	Plant Width	Hardiness Zone	Frost Tolerance
Stokesia laevis	lilac-blue, pink, white	mid-summer to early autumn	no	12–24 in (30–60 cm)	18 in (45 cm)	6–10	yes
Stokesia laevis 'Blue Danube'	dark blue	mid-summer to early autumn	no	15 in (38 cm)	18 in (45 cm)	6–10	yes
Stokesia laevis 'Bluestone'	blue	mid-summer to early autumn	no	10–12 in (25–30 cm)	15 in (38 cm)	6–10	yes
Stokesia laevis 'Mary Gregory'	lemon yellow	mid-summer to early autumn	no	15–18 in (38–45 cm)	18 in (45 cm)	6–10	yes
Stokesia laevis 'Silver Moon'	whitish silver	mid-summer to early autumn	no	18 in (45 cm)	18 in (45 cm)	6–10	yes
Stokesia laevis 'Wyoming'	dark blue	mid-summer to early autumn	no	18–24 in (45–60 cm)	18 in (45 cm)	6–10	yes

Top Tip

To prolong the *Stokesia* flowering season, remove the spent flower stems immediately. This cornflower look-alike is ideal for cutting and drying.

BELOW *As well as the pretty flowers, the leaves are also a feature of* Stokesia laevis. *They are lance-shaped with a paler midrib, and persist throughout winter.*

STREPTOCARPUS

Although widespread in the African and Asian tropics and subtropics, most of the cultivated plants in this African violet family (Gesneriaceae) genus of around 130 species of annuals and perennials are natives of southern Africa. They are a very diverse group, ranging from tiny rosette-forming plants to others that produce just a single huge leaf. But despite this variation of form they share some features, especially among their flowers. The leaves are velvety, heavily veined and slightly crinkled. The flowers are long-tubed, primrose-like and usually have 5 petals; they occur in heads on short upright stems. The genus name is of Greek origin, derived from *streptos* (twisted) and *karpos* (a fruit), referring to the unusual form of the spirally twisted fruit.

ABOVE Streptocarpus *'Tina' is one of several hybrids widely available. It forms rosettes of duo-toned pink flowers.*

CULTIVATION

Cold tolerance varies, though none withstand more than the lightest frost. Plant in a bright but not sunny position that is warm and draught-free. The soil should be fertile, moist, humus-rich and well drained. Propagate by division, from leaf-petiole cuttings or from seed.

Favourites	Flower Colour	Blooming Season	Flower Fragrance	Plant Height	Plant Width	Hardiness Zone	Frost Tolerance
Streptocarpus baudertii	white to mauve; yellow throat	summer	no	12 in (30 cm)	18 in (45 cm)	9–12	no
Streptocarpus candidus	white with violet and yellow	summer	yes	12 in (30 cm)	24 in (60 cm)	9–12	no
Streptocarpus 'Chorus Line'	white, veined mauve	spring to autumn	no	12 in (30 cm)	18 in (45 cm)	10–12	no
Streptocarpus 'Crystal Ice'	white and lilac	most of the year	no	12 in (30 cm)	18 in (45 cm)	10–12	no
Streptocarpus cyaneus	white, pink, lilac; yellow markings	spring to summer	no	10 in (25 cm)	15 in (38 cm)	9–12	no
Streptocarpus 'Heidi'	lilac-blue; purple centre	spring to autumn	no	10 in (25 cm)	18 in (45 cm)	10–12	no
Streptocarpus johannis	white to mauve	spring	no	12 in (30 cm)	18 in (45 cm)	9–12	no
Streptocarpus 'Kim'	purple	spring to summer	no	8 in (20 cm)	15 in (38 cm)	10–12	no
Streptocarpus primulifolius	mauve and violet	spring to summer	no	10 in (25 cm)	18 in (45 cm)	9–12	no
Streptocarpus 'Ruby'	rose red	spring to autumn	no	12 in (30 cm)	15 in (38 cm)	10–12	no
Streptocarpus saxorum	lilac and white	most of the year	no	6 in (15 cm)	24 in (60 cm)	10–12	no
Streptocarpus 'Tina'	pink and magenta	spring to autumn	no	12 in (30 cm)	15 in (38 cm)	10–12	no

Top Tip

Treat *Streptocarpus* plants similarly to *Saintpaulia* when grown indoors. Use an African violet potting mix and place in a bright but not too sunny spot.

LEFT *White flowers with purple blotches make Streptocarpus 'Crystal Ice' an eye-catching pot plant. It needs a warm position.* **BELOW** Streptocarpus *'Chorus Line' has white trumpet-shaped blooms blotched mauve all over.*

LEFT Streptocarpus cyaneus *subsp.* polackii *has deep green semi-upright leaves and funnel-shaped purple-blue flowers. In cool areas it needs the protection of a greenhouse.*

ABOVE Streptocarpus *'Ruby' bears rich red flowers perfectly complemented by the deep green leaves.*
LEFT Streptocarpus *'Kim' is prized for its production of abundant dark purple flowers and contrasting mid-green leaves.*

ABOVE *The prostrate leaves of* Streptocarpus baudertii *are arranged in a pretty rosette, from which the pale mauve flowers with yellow centres appear. This species needs to be given fertiliser monthly during the growing season, and like all* Streptocarpus *plants it should be repotted each spring.*

SWAINSONA

There are over 80 species of *Swainsona*, all found only in Australia and all members of the big pea family (Fabaceae). *Swainsona* are annual or perennial flowers, sometimes almost shrubby, found in every Australian state usually well away from the coast in the drier inland regions. Some occur in Central Australia where rainfall is low and erratic and may not happen at all for years. In those areas, *Swainsona* tend to be ephemeral annuals that quickly germinate after rain, live their lives while the soil remains moist then flower, set seed and die. The seeds remain dormant until the next good rainfall. One of the most spectacular, indeed one of Australia's most remarkable flowers, Sturt's desert pea (*Swainsona formosa*), is such a plant.

CULTIVATION

Fast drainage is essential with almost all species along with full sun. In higher rainfall areas, desert species such as Sturt's desert pea are grown in tall pots of sandy/gravelly potting mix that allow the roots to go down deep and excess water to escape quickly. They are sometimes successful in fast-draining rockeries or on sunny slopes. Be extra sparing with the fertiliser.

ABOVE *A showy, unusual bushy shrub ideal for inland gardens is* Swainsona gale-gifolia. *Prune after bloom.*
ABOVE RIGHT *Sturt's desert pea (*Swainsona formosa*) is a showy ground cover for drier areas.*

Top Tip

Soak seeds in hot (not boiling) water for 24 hours prior to sowing directly where you want them to grow. Water in but be sparing after that. Too much water causes root rot.

Favourites	Flower Colour	Blooming Season	Flower Fragrance	Plant Height	Plant Width	Hardiness Zone	Frost Tolerance
Swainsona formosa	red, pink or white	winter to spring	no	3 in (8 cm)	3–10 ft (0.9–3 m)	8–9	yes
Swainsona galegifolia	red, white, pink yellow or orange	winter to summer	no	2–3 ft (0.6–0.9 m)	2–5 ft (0.6–1.5 m)	8–9	yes

482

LEFT Tagetes, *Safari Series,* *'Safari Scarlet'* has 8 cm (3 in) wide anemone-type flowers. This series of French marigolds is mainly derived from Tagetes patula. **BELOW** The Little Hero Series of Tagetes, such as 'Little Hero Yellow', are small-growing types. The flowers are 5 cm (2 in) wide and come in a variety of colours.

TAGETES

A genus of some 50 species of annuals and perennials, it belongs to the daisy (Asteraceae) family. Almost all are found naturally in the American tropics and subtropics, which may seem a little strange when the garden forms are commonly known as African or French marigolds, but such are the mysteries of common names. Marigolds have aromatic, dark green, pinnate leaves and, apart from the very compact single-flowered forms, they tend to be upright plants with sturdy stems. Although the flowers may be typically daisy-like, they are often so fully double that the disc florets are hidden. Yellow, orange and brownish red are the usual colours. Marigolds are edible and the flowers yield a yellow dye that is sometimes used as a saffron substitute.

CULTIVATION
Plant in a sunny position with light well-drained soil. Water and feed well for lush foliage and abundant flowers. Also, deadhead frequently to keep the plants blooming. Propagate from seed, either sown in situ in warm soil or started indoors in cooler climates.

Favourites	Flower Colour	Blooming Season	Flower Fragrance
Tagetes 'Jolly Jester'	red and yellow	late spring to autumn	no
Tagetes 'Naughty Marietta'	yellow and red	summer to autumn	no
Tagetes tenuifolia	yellow	summer to autumn	no
Tagetes, Antigua Series	yellow, gold, orange	late spring to autumn	no
Tagetes, Little Hero Series	yellow, red, orange	late spring to autumn	no
Tagetes, Safari Series	yellow, red, orange	late spring to early autumn	no

Top Tip

Planting marigolds is thought to repel both aboveground insects and nematodes attacking plant roots. This has not yet been verified, but may be worth a try.

ABOVE *The pompon-like flowers of Tagetes, Antigua Series, 'Antigua Gold' are 8 cm (3 in) wide, and are carried above the leaves in a spectacular display.*

Plant Height	Plant Width	Hardiness Zone	Frost Tolerance
24 in (60 cm)	24 in (60 cm)	9–12	no
10 in (25 cm)	8 in (20 cm)	9–12	no
12–24 in (30–60 cm)	8–12 in (20–30 cm)	9–12	no
10–12 in (25–30 cm)	12–18 in (30–45 cm)	9–12	no
6–8 in (15–20 cm)	6 in (15 cm)	9–12	no
8–12 in (20–30 cm)	8 in (20 cm)	9–12	no

ABOVE *The harlequin-like yellow stripes on red petals give Tagetes 'Jolly Jester' its name. The bushy plants bear an abundance of flowers which last well in the vase.*

THALICTRUM

A buttercup family (Ranunculaceae) genus of around 130 species of tuberous or rhizome-rooted perennials, *Thalictrum* is found mainly in the northern temperate zone, with a few species straying south of the equator into the tropics. They are upright plants with lacy, pinnate, blue-green leaves reminiscent of aquilegia or maidenhair fern foliage. Tall elegant flower stems grow well above the foliage, and from late spring to autumn, depending on the species, the stems bear clusters of small fluffy flowers. Occurring mainly in pink and mauve, but also in white and yellow, the petal-less flowers may gain colour from the 4 to 5 petal-like sepals. Also known as meadow rue, *Thalictrum* plants were significant in the herbal lore and medicine of ancient Rome.

CULTIVATION

These plants are mostly hardy and easily grown in a temperate climate in full or half sun. The soil should be fertile, humus-rich and well drained. It is usually propagated by division, as cultivated plants are mainly selected forms.

Favourites	Flower Colour	Blooming Season	Flower Fragrance
Thalictrum aquilegifolium	pink, lilac, white	summer	no
Thalictrum delavayi	lilac with yellow stamens	mid-summer to late autumn	no
Thalictrum flavum	yellow	summer	no
Thalictrum kiusianum	mauve-purple	summer	no
Thalictrum orientale	white, pink, lilac	late spring to early summer	no
Thalictrum rochebrunianum	pale lilac	summer	no

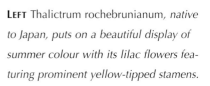

LEFT Thalictrum rochebrunianum, *native to Japan, puts on a beautiful display of summer colour with its lilac flowers featuring prominent yellow-tipped stamens.*

Plant Height	Plant Width	Hardiness Zone	Frost Tolerance
3 ft (0.9 m)	18 in (45 cm)	6–10	yes
4 ft (1.2 m)	24 in (60 cm)	7–10	yes
3 ft (0.9 m)	18 in (45 cm)	6–9	yes
4 in (10 cm)	12 in (30 cm)	8–10	yes
12 in (30 cm)	12 in (30 cm)	5–9	yes
36 in (90 cm)	12 in (30 cm)	8–10	yes

ABOVE Thalictrum orientale *is slow growing, but will reward the patient gardener with attractive deep green leaves and delicate flowers.*
LEFT Thalictrum delavayi *from China takes its name from French botanist and priest Jean Marie Delavay, who introduced many Asian plants to the Western world.*

Top Tip

Thalictrum species are useful plants in woodland gardens, borders or rock gardens. The ferny foliage is an effective backdrop in floral arrangements.

RIGHT Thalictrum delavayi *'Hewitt's Double' needs to be replanted every few years to maintain its vitality. It is a sterile cultivar, propagated only by division.*

TRADESCANTIA

ABOVE Tradescantia 'Little Doll', from the Andersoniana Group, is an easy-going long-blooming perennial. It bears mauve flowers with contrasting bright yellow stamens.
BELOW The flowers of Tradescantia, Andersoniana Group, 'Bilberry Ice' have 3 white petals each with a lilac streak. This plant can be cut back quite severely in late autumn.

Introduced to cultivation in 1637 by John Tradescant the Younger and named after him by Linnaeus, this dayflower family (Commelinaceae) genus of around 70 species of annuals and perennials from the Americas includes a few that, while attractive as garden plants, have become serious pests in some areas. Tuberous or fibrous rooted and often evergreen, they have rather succulent stems and fleshy, pointed elliptical, lance-shaped or narrow leaves. Attractive variegated and coloured foliage forms are common. Clusters of small 3-petalled flowers subtended by bracts appear over the warmer months and are sometimes very bright magenta, though white, soft pink and blue to mauve colours predominate.

CULTIVATION
Most species are tolerant of light to moderate frosts. Some prefer a sunny aspect and are drought tolerant, but most are happier with part-shade and moist well-drained soil. Propagate by division, from tip cuttings, or from seed, depending on the growth form.

LEFT Tradescantia *Andersoniana Group, 'Blue and Gold' is suitable for a range of garden uses—from mixed borders and ground covers to hanging baskets.*

BELOW Tradescantia virginiana *bears 3-petalled purple flowers that last for just a day, but as the plant is rarely out of bloom, summer colour is assured. It self-sows quickly.*

Top Tip

Very hardy in mild climates, *Trade-scantia,* or spider-wort, plants may need to be grown in a greenhouse in cooler areas. A general fertiliser can be of benefit in early spring.

Favourites	Flower Colour	Blooming Season	Flower Fragrance	Plant Height	Plant Width	Hardiness Zone	Frost Tolerance
Tradescantia, Andersoniana Group	white, pink, rose, blue, purple	summer to autumn	no	15–24 in (38–60 cm)	18–24 in (45–60 cm)	7–10	yes
Tradescantia fluminensis	white	throughout the year	no	6 in (15 cm)	24–36 in (60–90 cm)	9–12	no
Tradescantia pallida	pink	summer	no	8 in (20 cm)	15 in (38 cm)	8–11	no
Tradescantia sillamontana	purple-pink	summer	no	12 in (30 cm)	18 in (45 cm)	9–11	no
Tradescantia spathacea	white	throughout the year	no	12 in (30 cm)	12 in (30 cm)	9–12	no
Tradescantia virginiana	violet	summer	no	18 in (45 cm)	18 in (45 cm)	7–10	yes

TRICYRTIS

Found from the eastern Himalayas to Japan, Taiwan and the Philippine Islands, the 16 species of herbaceous perennials in this genus belong in the lily-of-the-valley (Convallariaceae) family. They are mainly woodland perennials but may also be sometimes found in mountainous areas and on cliffsides. They form clumps of arching stems clothed with often glossy, pointed lance-shaped leaves. The waxy, widely flared bell- or trumpet-shaped flowers are often attractively marked, despite the common name of toad lily. They appear from late summer to late autumn, depending on the species. In Japan, the young leaves and shoots of the native species were cooked and eaten.

CULTIVATION

These hardy plants are usually best grown in woodland conditions with cool, moist, well-drained, humus-rich soil and dappled shade. Plants may be divided when dormant, though rather than disturb well-established clumps it is often best just to remove a few offsets from the side. They may also be raised from seed.

BELOW *The orchid-like flowers of* Tricyrtis formosana *open from maroon or brown buds and are borne in terminal clusters. This species is native to Taiwan.*

RIGHT *Easy to grow and fast growing,* Tricyrtis affinis *has large, broadly oval leaves and unusually coloured flowers. It does best in full to part-shade.*

BELOW Tricyrtis macropoda *has small flowers (seen here in bud), but its elegant clumps of erect stems and slightly heart-shaped leaves are very attractive.*

Top Tip

Tricyrtis species are useful plants for a shady border where their flowers are very welcome late in the growing season. Some cultivars have variegated foliage.

Favourites	Flower Colour	Blooming Season	Flower Fragrance	Plant Height	Plant Width	Hardiness Zone	Frost Tolerance
Tricyrtis affinis	white and purple-pink	mid-summer to autumn	no	36 in (90 cm)	24 in (60 cm)	5–9	yes
Tricyrtis formosana	white, pale lilac, and purple-pink	mid-summer to autumn	no	36 in (90 cm)	18 in (45 cm)	5–9	yes
Tricyrtis hirta	white and dark purple	autumn	no	36 in (90 cm)	24 in (60 cm)	4–9	yes
Tricyrtis macropoda	lavender and purple	summer	no	30 in (75 cm)	24 in (60 cm)	5–9	yes
Tricyrtis ohsumiensis	yellow	early autumn	no	20 in (50 cm)	10 in (25 cm)	5–9	yes
***Tricyrtis* 'Tojen'**	white and pale lilac to pink	autumn	no	36 in (90 cm)	20 in (50 cm)	5–9	yes

RIGHT *The striking appearance of* Tricyrtis hirta *makes it one of the most popular* Tricyrtis *species. It spreads slowly, and is known as the hairy toad lily because the stems are slightly hairy.*

TRIFOLIUM

*T*rifolium, or clover, is so well-known that the leaf shape is not just a description in itself, but a symbol, too. Associated with Ireland ever since St Patrick used it to describe the Christian Trinity, the cloverleaf and the 4-leafed shamrock are today primarily associated with good luck and have been adopted by countries, football teams and casinos. Clover is also a vitally important component in the world's pastures while at the same time being far less welcome in its lawns. Found naturally throughout the temperate and subtropical zones except Australasia, *Trifolium* is a genus of around 230 species of annuals, biennials and perennials of the pea family (Fabaceae). Leaves are typically trifoliate and bright green, and are sometimes darkly marked. Examined closely, the individual flowers are very much like pea-flowers. The flowers are borne in rounded heads or terminal racemes.

CULTIVATION
Trifolium species are usually hardy and easily grown. Plant in full or half sun with moist well-drained soil. The plants may be divided, but they usually self-sow.

Top Tip

When growing clover in pots, use a potting mix that contains equal proportions of loam, sand and leafmould. While growing, keep moist during the winter months.

ABOVE *A bushy, vigorous, upright perennial,* Trifolium pannonicum *produces creamy white to yellow flowers that last well when cut for indoor decoration.*
BELOW RIGHT Trifolium repens *is invasive and not normally grown in gardens. Some cultivars are more suitable, however, such as* 'Pentaphyllum' *(pictured).*

Favourites	Flower Colour	Blooming Season	Flower Fragrance	Plant Height	Plant Width	Hardiness Zone	Frost Tolerance
Trifolium pannonicum	cream, ageing to rusty red	spring to early summer	no	12–18 in (30–45 cm)	12–24 in (30–60 cm)	5–9	yes
Trifolium repens	white	spring to autumn	no	3–12 in (8–30 cm)	24–36 in (60–90 cm)	4–10	yes
Trifolium repens 'Green Ice'	white	spring to autumn	no	3–8 in (8–20 cm)	24–36 in (60–90 cm)	4–10	yes
Trifolium repens 'Pentaphyllum'	white	spring to autumn	no	6–12 in (15–30 cm)	18–24 in (45–60 cm)	4–10	yes
Trifolium rubens	reddish purple	spring to early summer	no	12–18 in (30–45 cm)	18 in (45 cm)	7–9	yes
Trifolium uniflorum	creamy white to purple-pink	spring to autumn	no	1–2 in (2.5–5 cm)	12–18 in (30–45 cm)	6–9	yes

ABOVE RIGHT *Suitable for a large rock garden,* Trifolium uniflorum *is grown for its abundance of yellow-white trumpet-shaped flowers. It can quickly cover a bank or tumble over a wall.*

RIGHT *It's not hard to see why* Trifolium rubens *is the most popular garden clover. Allow it sufficient space to display its superb blooms.*

TROPAEOLUM

Found from southern Mexico to Tierra del Fuego in South America's far south, this genus has over 80 species of annuals and perennials. Known as canary bird vine, flame creeper and nasturtium, it belongs to the nasturtium (Tropaeolaceae) family. Some climb using their twining leaf stalks, others, especially the small cultivars of *Tropaeolum majus*, are used as bedding plants. Their foliage, which is often blue-green, is variable and may be many-lobed, trifoliate or shield-shaped. The long-spurred flowers occur mainly in shades of yellow, orange and red and have 5 petals. Many of the species with large tubers were cultivated like potatoes in South America, and nasturtium flowers are widely used as a colourful garnish.

CULTIVATION
While hardiness varies, most species are easily cultivated—sometimes too easily, as they may become invasive. Plant in full or half-sun with moist well-drained soil and trim occasionally. Propagate by division when dormant, from basal cuttings, or from seed.

LEFT Tropaeolum majus *'Whirlibird Cherry Rose' is a very free-flowering dwarf cultivar. The vividly coloured semi-double flowers contrast well with the green foliage.* **BELOW** *The edible bright lemon yellow flowers and the leaves of* Tropaeolum majus *'Gleaming Lemons' can add colour and peppery flavour to a summer salad.*

Top Tip

Nasturtiums are excellent plants for young gardeners. The large seeds are easy to handle, and the plants develop rapidly after sowing, producing big bright flowers.

ABOVE LEFT Tropaeolum majus *'Peach Schnapps' has pinkish orange flowers with dark orange veining, and delightfully marbled leaves. It can be used as a ground cover and in containers.* **LEFT** Tropaeolum tricolor *is a colourful trailer or climber from Bolivia and Chile. The flowers have short yellow or cream petals and long, upturned, black-tipped spurs.*

Favourites	Flower Colour	Blooming Season	Flower Fragrance	Plant Height	Plant Width	Hardiness Zone	Frost Tolerance
Tropaeolum ciliatum	golden yellow	summer	no	20 ft (6 m)	20 ft (6 m)	8–10	yes
Tropaeolum majus	yellow, orange, red	summer to autumn	no	8–24 in (20–60 cm)	36 in (90 cm)	8–11	no
***Tropaeolum majus*, Alaska Series**	cream, red, orange yellow	summer to autumn	no	12 in (30 cm)	18 in (45 cm)	8–11	no
***Tropaeolum majus*, Jewel Series**	red and yellow	spring to autumn	no	12 in (30 cm)	18 in (45 cm)	8–11	no
Tropaeolum polyphyllum	yellow to orange	summer	no	2–3 in (5–8 cm)	36 in (90 cm)	8–11	yes
Tropaeolum tricolor	cream to yellow and red and black	spring to autumn	no	7 ft (2 m)	7 ft (2 m)	8–11	no

VERBASCUM

BELOW Verbascum chaixii *'Mont Blanc' is a tall sturdy plant clothed in downy grey-green leaves. Slender unbranched stems bear tightly packed pure white flowers with yellow centres.*

This figwort family (Scrophulariaceae) genus of some 300 species of annuals, biennials, perennials and subshrubs includes cultivated plants and many that have become weeds outside their natural Eurasian and North African range. The commonly cultivated species usually form basal rosettes of large elliptical leaves, often quite heavily veined and sometimes felted. Tall upright flower spikes emerge from the rosettes carrying massed, small, 5-petalled flowers, usually in white, yellow or pink to lavender shades. The Roman Pliny described *Verbascum,* noting that they attracted moths and thus called them moth mulleins, and in Greek legends the plant featured as a protection against evil and was used as an everyday medicinal plant to treat a variety of illnesses.

CULTIVATION

Hardiness varies with the species. Most prefer a sunny position with light, gritty, free-draining soil. They can tolerate summer drought but need moisture until flowering has ended. Propagate by division or from seed, depending on the growth form.

Top Tip

You can encourage the production of fresh flowering spikes by cutting off the spikes with spent flowers just below the bottommost flower.

ABOVE Verbascum acaule *is
a rosette-forming perennial
with toothed veined leaves.
Bright yellow flowers are
lifted above the foliage on
slender stems.*

LEFT *The attractive copper
pink purple-centred flowers
of* Verbascum chaixii
*'Cotswold Beauty' emerge
from big rosettes of crinkly
grey-green leaves.*

RIGHT *The award-winning*
Verbascum *'Helen Johnson'
is a robust hardy perennial
that performs well in a
variety of conditions,
including seaside gardens.*

Favourites	Flower Colour	Blooming Season	Flower Fragrance	Plant Height	Plant Width	Hardiness Zone	Frost Tolerance
Verbascum acaule	yellow	mid-summer	no	2 in (5 cm)	6 in (15 cm)	6–9	yes
Verbascum bombyciferum	yellow	summer	no	6 ft (1.8 m)	24 in (60 cm)	6–10	yes
Verbascum chaixii	yellow, copper pink	summer	no	36 in (90 cm)	24 in (60 cm)	5–10	yes
Verbascum dumulosum	bright yellow	late spring to early summer	no	6–12 in (15–30 cm)	18 in (45 cm)	8–10	yes
Verbascum 'Helen Johnson'	deep apricot	late spring to early autumn	no	36 in (90 cm)	12 in (30 cm)	7–10	yes
Verbascum 'Jackie'	pinkish yellow	late spring to early autumn	no	18–24 in (45–60 cm)	18 in (45 cm)	7–10	yes

VERBENA

T his genus in the vervain (Verbenaceae) family contains 250 species of annuals, perennials and subshrubs native to tropical and subtropical America. Bringing a welcome splash of colour to the garden, these plants feature clusters of sometimes fragrant, tubular, lobed flowers in vibrant shades of purple, pink, red and white. With a sprawling to erect habit, they make ideal candidates for hanging baskets, ground covers or for use in borders. The small bright green to dark green leaves are variously divided. The genus is commonly known as vervain, derived from the Celtic *ferfaen* meaning "to drive away a stone"—a reference to the use of *Verbena officinalis* as a cure for bladder infections. It was also a supposed aphrodisiac and cure-all for problems ranging from snakebites to heart disease.

CULTIVATION

These colourful additions to the garden do best in full sun in moderately fertile, moist, but well-drained soil. Annuals can be propagated from seed, while perennials can be propagated either from seed, cuttings or by division.

Favourites	Flower Colour	Blooming Season	Flower Fragrance
Verbena bonariensis	purple	mid-summer to autumn	no
Verbena 'Homestead Purple'	purple	summer to autumn	no
Verbena rigida	purple to magenta	spring to autumn	no
Verbena 'Sissinghurst'	magenta-pink	spring to autumn	no
Verbena 'Temari Bright Pink'	bright pink	summer to autumn	no
Verbena tenuisecta	lilac, mauve, purple, blue, white	spring	no

ABOVE LEFT Verbena 'Temari Bright Pink' produces large, brightly coloured flower-heads over a long period, as well as dense mats of dark green, fern-like foliage.

BELOW The tiny flowers of Verbena bonariensis appear in flat-topped clusters above sparse, lance-shaped, serrated leaves. This plant is native to South America.

Plant Height	Plant Width	Hardiness Zone	Frost Tolerance
3–5 ft (0.9–1.5 m)	2 ft (0.6 m)	7–10	yes
8 in (20 cm)	36 in (90 cm)	7–10	yes
24–36 in (60–90 cm)	12 in (30 cm)	8–10	yes
8 in (20 cm)	36 in (90 cm)	7–10	yes
8 in (20 cm)	36 in (90 cm)	7–10	yes
12 in (30 cm)	12–20 in (30–50 cm)	9–11	no

ABOVE RIGHT *Sprawling Verbena tenuisecta is also known as moss verbena. Its stems are aromatic, and the flower spikes can be white, mauve, purple or blue.*

RIGHT *Verbena 'Homestead Purple' is a very vigorous grower and flowers prolifically over a long season. This hybrid is thought to have occurred by chance.*

Top Tip

Most prostrate *Verbena* species are fast growing, so they are an excellent choice as a colourful ground cover for an unsightly bare patch in the garden.

LEFT *An excellent ground cover, Veronica peduncularis 'Georgia Blue' bears wonderfully hued blooms against dark green foliage.* RIGHT *The delicate airy spires of Veronica 'Pink Damask' carry soft pink flowers above clumps of deep green foliage.*

FAR RIGHT *Veronica spicata 'Heidekind' is a mat-forming plant with silver-grey foliage and raspberry pink blooms.* BELOW *Though the blooms of Veronica austriaca subsp. teucrium are small, their abundance and strong clear blue colour make a fabulous display in the garden.*

VERONICA

A figwort family (Scrophulariaceae) genus of 250 species of annuals and perennials, it is widespread in the northern temperate zones. Most species are creeping mat-forming plants that sometimes strike root as they spread. Their leaves tend to be small, oval to lance-shaped, often shallowly toothed and rarely pinnately lobed. A few species have solitary flowers but more often upright spikes bearing many flowers develop in spring and summer. The colour range is mainly in the white and pink to rich purple-blue shades, including some striking deep blue flowers. The genus is probably named in honour of St Veronica, perhaps because the floral markings of some species are said to resemble the marks left on Veronica's sacred veil, with which she wiped Christ's face as he carried the cross.

CULTIVATION

Mostly hardy and easily grown in full or half sun with moist well-drained soil, some are great rockery plants, while others are suited to borders. Propagate from cuttings, self-rooted layers, division or seed.

Favourites	Flower Colour	Blooming Season	Flower Fragrance	Plant Height	Plant Width	Hardiness Zone	Frost Tolerance
Veronica alpina	blue, white	late spring to early autumn	no	4–8 in (10–20 cm)	12 in (30 cm)	5–9	yes
Veronica austriaca	blue	late spring to early summer	no	8–18 in (20–45 cm)	12 in (30 cm)	5–10	yes
Veronica gentianoides	pale blue, sometimes white	late spring	no	12–24 in (30–60 cm)	12–24 in (30–60 cm)	4–9	yes
Veronica peduncularis	blue, white, pink; with pink veining	late spring to early summer	no	4 in (10 cm)	24 in (60 cm)	6–9	yes
Veronica 'Pink Damask'	soft pink	summer to autumn	no	36 in (90 cm)	18 in (45 cm)	5–9	yes
Veronica spicata	blue	summer	no	24 in (60 cm)	36 in (90 cm)	3–9	yes

VIOLA

The type genus for the family Violaceae, *Viola* includes some 500 species of annuals, perennials and subshrubs found in the world's temperate zones, ranging from the subarctic to the mountains of New Zealand. The majority are small clump-forming plants with lobed, kidney-shaped or heart-shaped leaves. All violas have similarly shaped 5-petalled flowers, with the lower petal often carrying dark markings. White, yellow and purple predominate but the flowers occur in every colour, at least among the garden forms—often referred to as violets or pansies. The genus was named after a lover of the god Zeus, and *Viola tricolor* was used as a symbol of Athens.

ABOVE Viola × wittrockiana *'Crystal Bowl Orange' is a member of the Crystal Bowl Series, which is appreciated for both compact form and abundant brightly coloured flowers that are produced throughout summer.*

CULTIVATION

These plants are mostly very hardy and easily grown in sun or shade. The woodland species prefer humus-rich soil, while the rockery types require something grittier, but most are fine in any moist well-drained soil. Propagate by division, or from seed or basal cuttings.

ABOVE *The long-lasting* Viola × wittrockiana *'Molly Sanderson', a Viola cultivar, is notable for its gold centre in an otherwise black flower.*

ABOVE *As its name attests, the small white flowers of the remarkable* Viola sororia *'Freckles' are decorated with violet dots.*
LEFT *An evergreen short-lived perennial,* Viola × wittrockiana *'Irish Molly' is a favourite old* Viola *cultivar. Its smooth-textured flowers are orange-gold.*

Top Tip

Plant garden pansies, violas and violettas in window boxes, containers and borders, or beneath taller shrubs for a splash of bold colour.

Favourites	Flower Colour	Blooming Season	Flower Fragrance	Plant Height	Plant Width	Hardiness Zone	Frost Tolerance
Viola adunca	lavender-blue, violet	spring	yes	2–4 in (5–10 cm)	4 in (10 cm)	4–9	yes
Viola, **Cornuta Hybrids**	white, purple, blue mauve, yellow	summer	no	6–12 in (15–30 cm)	3–6 in (8–15 cm)	4–10	yes
Viola obliqua	violet, white	spring to summer	no	3 in (8 cm)	10 in (25 cm)	8–9	yes
Viola odorata	violet, pink, white	late winter to spring	yes	3–12 in (8–30 cm)	2–4 ft (0.6–1.2 m)	4–10	yes
Viola pedata	violet	early spring to early summer	no	2 in (5 cm)	4 in (10 cm)	4–9	yes
Viola riviniana	pale purple	spring	no	2–4 in (5–10 cm)	8–15 in (20–38 cm)	5–10	yes
Viola sororia	white with violet-blue markings	spring to early summer	no	4–6 in (10–15 cm)	8 in (20 cm)	4–10	yes
Viola tricolor	purple, blue, yellow, white	spring to early autumn	no	6 in (15 cm)	6 in (15 cm)	4–10	yes
Viola, **Violettas**	blue, violet, mauve, yellow, white	spring to summer	yes	4–6 in (10–15 cm)	6–8 in (15–20 cm)	4–10	yes
Viola × *wittrockiana*	various	early spring to summer	no	8 in (20 cm)	8 in (20 cm)	5–10	yes
Viola × *wittrockiana,* **Fancy Pansies**	various	late autumn to early summer	no	4–8 in (10–20 cm)	6–10 in (15–25 cm)	7–10	yes
Viola × *wittrockiana,* **Violas**	white, black, blue, purple, yellow	winter to early summer	yes	3–8 in (8–20 cm)	6–12 in (15–30 cm)	7–10	yes

ZINNIA

BELOW Zinnia angustifolia 'Coral Beauty' bears its vivid flowers on a 0.9 cm (3 ft) tall plant. The profusion of blooms looks stunning in a massed planting.

Centred around Mexico but native to the area from South-Central USA to Argentina, the genus *Zinnia* includes some 20 species of annuals, perennials and small shrubs belonging to the daisy (Asteraceae) family. Most species have soft, downy, light green leaves and simple daisy-like flowers, often in yellow, orange, red or pink shades. Modern garden zinnias are an example of the plant breeder's art, extending the colour range of the species enormously and turning those simple daisies into very fancy flowers. The genus name honours Johann Gottfried Zinn (1727–1759), who first described the genus. He was also a physician, and the "ligament of Zinn" was first noted in his 1755 monograph on the eye.

CULTIVATION

Zinnias prefer full sun, long warm summers and freedom from cold draughts and sudden weather changes. In suitable conditions few other flowers can make such a prolonged display. The soil should be light and well drained. Deadhead frequently and use liquid fertilisers to ensure continued blooming and steady growth.

BELOW Zinnia angustifolia 'Coral Beauty' bears its vivid flowers on a 0.9 cm (3 ft) tall plant. The profusion of blooms looks stunning in a massed planting.

ABOVE *Excellent for cutting, the flowers of* Zinnia elegans, *Oklahoma Series, 'Oklahoma Pink' are semi-double, 35 mm (1½ in) wide and are borne on sturdy stems.*

LEFT Zinnia peruviana *'Yellow Peruvian' (syn. 'Bonita Yellow') grows to about 0.6 m (2 ft) tall, and bears single, 25 mm (1 in) wide flowers that fade to a soft gold colour.*

Top Tip

Cutting zinnias regularly will not only prolong the blooming time and encourage branching, but also supply brightly coloured cut flowers that last well in the vase.

RIGHT *The award-winning Zinnia elegans 'Profusion Orange' is very easy to grow, and bears abundant 5–8 cm (2–3 in) wide flowers.*

Favourites	Flower Colour	Blooming Season	Flower Fragrance	Plant Height	Plant Width	Hardiness Zone	Frost Tolerance
Zinnia angustifolia	orange	summer	no	8–16 in (20–40 cm)	12–20 in (30–50 cm)	9–11	no
Zinnia elegans	various	summer to autumn	no	10–30 in (25–75 cm)	12–18 in (30–45 cm)	8–11	no
Zinnia elegans, Ruffles Series	various	summer to autumn	no	24–36 in (60–90 cm)	12–24 in (30–60 cm)	8–11	no
Zinnia grandiflora	yellow	summer	no	12 in (30 cm)	24–32 in (60–80 cm)	9–11	no
Zinnia haageana	orange, yellow, bronze	summer to early autumn	no	24 in (60 cm)	8–12 in (20–30 cm)	8–11	no
Zinnia peruviana	yellow, red, tangerine	summer to early autumn	no	24–36 in (60–90 cm)	12–16 in (30–40 cm)	8–11	no

GRASSES, SEDGES AND BAMBOOS

Comprising some of the most adaptable and widespread plants on Earth, grasses, sedges and bamboos can be found in virtually every part of the planet from the Arctic to the Antarctic. They are of tremendous economic importance: all of our cereals and grains have been derived from grasses, including barley, maize, oats, rice, rye and wheat—all foodstuffs upon which civilisations and trade have been built. For many years, the use of grass for lawns and sports fields around the world has overshadowed the ornamental use of grasses, sedges and bamboos in the garden. But their adaptability, beauty, subtlety and unique qualities of movement are now attracting well-deserved attention.

RIGHT *Bamboos are giant grasses, though their size and woody hollow stems distinguish them from most grasses. The* Bambusa *genus features many decorative cultivars.*

LEFT *The distinctively coloured blue-green foliage of* Festuca glauca *adds interest to any garden. 'Elijah Blue', seen here, is one of several popular cultivars of this species.*

MORE THAN JUST LAWNS

LEFT *When the delicate soft reddish purple flower plumes of Pennisetum setaceum 'Atrosanguineum' move in the breeze, their pollen is spread far and wide. The foliage is burgundy coloured.*
BELOW *Miscanthus sinensis 'Yaku jima' produces masses of tall flowerheads in late summer through autumn. These often remain on the plant for several months, giving winter appeal.*

Grasses actually consist of some 635 genera and 9,000 species, including the bamboos. There are also a number of grass-like plants often lumped together with the grasses—these include sedges, rushes and a number of lily relatives.

True grasses are herbs that have solid or hollow stems and clumping, tussock-forming or rhizomatous root systems. Their long narrow leaves grow in 2 rows within a sheath, and flowers are produced in spikelets on stalks that can be hefty or delicate, depending on the species.

There is a surprising degree of variety among grasses. Some, such as blue fescue *(Festuca glauca),* are small and form neat tufts. Others, such as giant silver grass *(Miscanthus* 'Giganteus'), form large clumps and can reach over 4.5 m (15 ft) tall. Grasses can be thin- or thick-leafed, stiff and upright or wispy and graceful. Some are dense and suitable for screening; others have an airy see-through quality.

Herbaceous grasses, which put up fresh growth each spring (as opposed to evergreens), often retain their dried leaves through winter, providing warm tawny colour and structure. A number of grasses

are prized for their winter colour and stature, including silver grass (*Miscanthus* species) and feather reed grass (*Calamagrostis* species). But evergreen grasses also have their virtues: not only do they provide structure, warm living colour and texture in winter, but their maintenance needs are few, requiring only a quick springtime trim of any winter-burned foliage. A particularly attractive evergreen grass is pink muhly *(Muhlenbergia capillaris)* from the USA.

Foliage colour is generally subtle and includes silvery and steely blue, purple-blue, blue-green, yellow-green, yellow, rust, reddish brown, copper and blood red. Grasses, with their rich tones and variable shapes, work beautifully with other plants in the garden, both as foil and as feature.

Bamboos are members of the grass family, and the diversity among them is amazing. Encompassing some 100 genera and 1,500 species, along with a multitude of cultivated varieties, bamboos range from hip-high ground covers to timber bamboos reaching over 21 m (70 ft) in height. There are also lesser-known climbing bamboos and even herbaceous species. Bamboo roots can be clumping or running. Clumping types gradually increase in size, while running types are sometimes feared for their vigorous spreading root systems. However, they can be contained by various planting techniques, including the use of bamboo barriers and annual pruning or by planting in containers, to which they are well suited.

There are a number of exceptionally cold-hardy bamboos, including *Phyllostachys bissettii*, one of only a small handful of bamboos hardy to –29°C (–20°F). Numerous tropical and subtropical bamboos make elegant garden subjects, including members of the beautiful and diverse genus *Bambusa*. In between the cold-hardy and tropical types is a world of options, including bamboos used for hedges and borders, screens, bonsai, house plants, edible shoots and wood for building. Others tolerate deep shade, waterlogged soil, alkaline soil and salt air.

And then there are grass look-alikes that are actually not members of the grass family, including sedges (*Carex* species), a genus of grass-like clumping plants found worldwide and grown for their long, often evergreen leaves and unusual colours and markings. Examples include *Carex testacea* from New Zealand, with narrow arching leaves varying from green to yellow-brown with orange tips, or *Carex morrowii* 'Variegata', a cultivar of a Japanese sedge, with crisp white-striped leaves. Another attractive sedge is the bright yellow Bowles golden grass (*Carex elata* 'Aurea'), a plant that thrives in standing water. For warm climates, the umbrella plant *(Cyperus alternifolius)* is an attractive sedge for damp to wet areas, while its close relative, the historic papyrus of paper-making fame *(C. papyrus)* is suited to tropical regions. Both plants make excellent additions to ponds and outdoor water features and thrive in bright conditions indoors, particularly when their roots are partially submerged in water.

Grasses, sedges and bamboos are especially good at lending a natural relaxed air to landscapes. Even though some possess substantial architectural presence, strong lines and even imposing height, they still somehow suggest something appealingly casual. Whether true grasses or look-alikes, the ornamentals we call "grasses" are coming into their own. Planted in containers, integrated into perennial beds or used in swathes, grasses, sedges and bamboos bring welcome life and movement into the landscape.

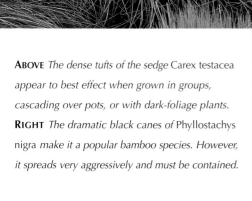

ABOVE *The dense tufts of the sedge* Carex testacea *appear to best effect when grown in groups, cascading over pots, or with dark-foliage plants.*
RIGHT *The dramatic black canes of* Phyllostachys nigra *make it a popular bamboo species. However, it spreads very aggressively and must be contained.*

BAMBUSA

Found in most of the tropics and extending into the subtropics of Asia, this is a genus of about 120 species of giant grasses—commonly known as bamboo—belonging to the family Poaceae. Non-suckering, they form clumps of smooth, strongly erect stems called culms that can be over 24 m (80 ft) tall. Feathery flowerheads appear sporadically, and some species die after flowering. The stems are hollow, except at the nodes where small branching sprays of narrow leaves appear, and are remarkably strong yet flexible. In the West we think of bamboo as being used for small ornamental objects and garden furniture, but until one visits East Asia, it is difficult to appreciate bamboo's importance as a construction material. Even today, it is used not only in country areas as it always has been, but in scaffolding and screening in cities.

Favourites	Plant Height	Plant Width	Hardiness Zone	Frost Tolerance
Bambusa multiplex	35 ft (10 m)	10 ft (3 m)	9–12	no
Bambusa multiplex 'Alphonse Karr'	25–35 ft (8–10 m)	10 ft (3 m)	9–12	no
Bambusa multiplex 'Fernleaf'	20 ft (6 m)	5–10 ft (1.5–3 m)	9–12	no
Bambusa oldhamii	60 ft (18 m)	20–40 ft (6–12 m)	9–12	no
Bambusa vulgaris	50 ft (15 m)	15–30 ft (4.5–9 m)	9–12	no
Bambusa vulgaris 'Striata'	5–6 ft (1.5–1.8 m)	2–3 ft (0.6–0.9 m)	9–12	no

CULTIVATION

Hardiness varies, though few species can tolerate repeated frosts and most prefer to grow in warm humid conditions with humus-rich well-drained soil and a steady supply of moisture. Plant in a sheltered but sunny position. Bamboo is most often propagated by division.

BELOW Bambusa vulgaris *'Striata' (syn. 'Vittata') is distinguished from the species by its golden yellow culms that are randomly striped with dark green.*

Top Tip

Bambusa species are generally less invasive than many other bamboos, so they can be put to use in the garden for screening, informal hedges or windbreaks.

CALAMAGROSTIS

BELOW *When young, the leaves of* Calamagrostis foliosa *'Zebrina' are light green with horizontal bands of green and yellow. In summer, plumes of light green flowers are produced.*

The 250 species of grasses that make up this genus in the family Poaceae are widespread in the northern temperate zones. Commonly known as reed grass, many are too large or invasive for domestic gardens but a few species and their cultivars are grown for the foliage, which is often variegated, and for their fluffy flower spikes that are usually held clear of the foliage. The flowerheads remain attractive as they dry and set seed. Reed grasses are known for the wave-like movement of the flowerheads and foliage when touched by the slightest breeze.

CULTIVATION

Reed grasses are very hardy and easily grown in full or half-sun with moist well-drained soil. Some species are moderately drought tolerant once established. Cut back the dried foliage in early winter. As most of the cultivated plants are selected forms, propagation is usually by division in late winter. A few species are considered local weeds.

BELOW *Growing slightly taller than the species,* Calamagrostis × acutiflora *'Stricta' produces fluffy, pinkish bronze-tinged, summer flowerheads that age to a buff colour.*

Favourites	Plant Height	Plant Width	Hardiness Zone	Frost Tolerance
Calamagrostis × acutiflora	5–7 ft (1.5–2 m)	3–4 ft (0.9–1.2 m)	4–10	yes
Calamagrostis × acutiflora **'Karl Foerster'**	5–6 ft (1.5–1.8 m)	2–3 ft (0.6–0.9 m)	4–10	yes
Calamagrostis × acutiflora **'Overdam'**	2–3 ft (0.6–0.9 m)	2–3 ft (0.6–0.9 m)	4–10	yes
Calamagrostis brachytricha	40 in (100 cm)	20–40 in (50–100 cm)	7–9	yes
Calamagrostis foliosa	6–16 in (15–40 cm)	8–20 in (20–50 cm)	7–9	yes
Calamagrostis foliosa **'Zebrina'**	6–16 in (15–40 cm)	8–20 in (20–50 cm)	7–9	yes

CAREX

This worldwide genus of grass-like sedges belonging to the family Cyperaceae is usually found growing in permanently moist or seasonally boggy conditions. Their leaves may be green, red or brown and range from fine and hair-like, sometimes with curled tips, to quite broad with a noticeable midrib and sometimes razor-sharp edges. Short flowerheads develop in the warmer months, and although these are held clear of the foliage, they are seldom much of a feature, the plants being grown for their form and colour of the foliage. In New Zealand, *Carex* sedges or tussocks are among the dominant plants in grassland areas, and have produced several popular cultivars.

CULTIVATION

Plant *Carex* species in full sun with moist well-drained soil. Despite their natural preference for damp conditions, some species will tolerate drought and can be extremely effective at binding thin soils. Sedges are easy-care plants, though some species can be invasive. New plants can be raised from seed but as most species quickly reach divisible size, it is seldom necessary.

BELOW Carex pendula *is a native of Europe. Throughout the flowering season, arching stems hold catkin-like spikes of flowers above the bright green foliage.*

TOP RIGHT Carex comans *'Frosted Curls' is so-named for the curling light-coloured tips of the pale green- to buff-coloured grassy leaves.*
RIGHT Carex elata *is a European species, known as the tufted sedge. 'Aurea', pictured here, has golden leaves edged in green and is usually seen in cultivation more often than the true species.*

Favourites	Plant Height	Plant Width	Hardiness Zone	Frost Tolerance
Carex *buchananii*	24–30 in (60–75 cm)	18–24 in (45–60 cm)	7–10	yes
Carex *comans*	12–16 in (30–40 cm)	24–30 in (60–75 cm)	7–10	yes
Carex *elata*	3 ft (0.9 m)	3 ft (0.9 m)	7–10	yes
Carex *grayi*	30 in (75 cm)	30 in (75 cm)	7–10	yes
Carex *oshimensis*	12 in (30 cm)	18 in (45 cm)	5–10	yes
Carex *pendula*	3 ft (0.9 m)	3–6 ft (0.9–1.8 m)	5–10	yes

BELOW *The dried seed heads of* Carex *species are popular for use in floral arrangements. In particular, the spiky seed heads of* Carex grayi *are valued for their unusual structure.*

CYPERUS

Widespread throughout tropical and warm-temperate regions, *Cyperus* is the type genus for the sedge (Cyperaceae) family and includes some 600-odd annual and perennial species. Some species, such as nut grass (*Cyperus rotundus*), are extremely serious weeds. Others, however, are ornamental and sometimes useful. Many are marginal plants found around lakes and streams or in boggy areas. They have strongly upright grassy stems and very prominent, umbrella-like, green to brown flowerheads on thickened stalks up to 1.5 m (5 ft) high or more. The earliest form of paper, the papyrus of the Egyptians, was made from the pith of the stems of *Cyperus papyrus*.

CULTIVATION

Most *Cyperus* species prefer a bright sunny position and will grow in ordinary well-drained garden soil, though many species can tolerate up to 5 cm (2 in) of water over the roots. Hardiness varies greatly, and some of the best ornamentals need mild winters and hot summers. Propagate from seed or by division.

ABOVE RIGHT Cyperus longus *is commonly known as galingale. Quite at home growing in shallow water, the erect bright green stems bear spoke-like bracts around tiny brownish flowers.*
RIGHT *Long bright green bracts radiate out around the cluster of tiny flowers of* Cyperus involucratus. *Regarded as a weed in some areas, this species hails from Africa.*

Favourites	Plant Height	Plant Width	Hardiness Zone	Frost Tolerance
Cyperus albostriatus	24 in (60 cm)	12 in (30 cm)	9–12	no
Cyperus involucratus	3–7 ft (0.9–2 m)	2–3 ft (0.6–0.9 m)	9–12	no
Cyperus involucratus 'Variegatus'	3–7 ft (0.9–2 m)	2–3 ft (0.6–0.9 m)	9–12	no
Cyperus longus	3–5 ft (0.9–1.5 m)	1–3 ft (0.3–0.9 m)	6–9	yes
Cyperus papyrus	7–17 ft (2–5 m)	5–10 ft (1.5–3 m)	9–12	no
Cyperus papyrus 'Nanus'	4–6 ft (1.2–1.8 m)	2–3 ft (0.6–0.9 m)	9–12	no

Top Tip

Despite their natural affinity with watery locations, *Cyperus* species make attractive indoor plants, and can overwinter safely indoors in cooler climates.

DESCHAMPSIA

A charming genus of about 50 species in the grass (Poaceae) family, *Deschampsia* are clump-forming perennial plants that can be evergreen or herbaceous. They are widely distributed throughout temperate to cold regions, preferring habitats such as woodlands, moors and mountainous areas. Commonly known as hair grass, they are grown for their thin graceful foliage and airy flowerheads, which are popular in floral arrangements. Many interesting clones have been selected by growers, especially in Germany.

CULTIVATION

Deschampsia plants will grow in any good garden soil in sun or light shade, but prefer moist humus-rich soil and part-shade. Remove spent flower stems in early spring to allow for new growth. Propagate the species from seed, but named clones must be divided in spring.

Favourites	Plant Height	Plant Width	Hardiness Zone	Frost Tolerance
Deschampsia cespitosa	5–7 ft (1.5–2 m)	4–5 ft (1.2–1.5 m)	5–10	yes
Deschampsia cespitosa Golden Dew/'Goldtau'	24–36 in (60–90 cm)	20 in (50 cm)	5–10	yes
Deschampsia flexuosa	27–36 in (70–90 cm)	6–8 in (15–20 cm)	5–9	yes

ABOVE *Commonly known as tufted hair grass or tussock grass,* Deschampsia cespitosa *forms a clump of wispy leaves. Tall plumes carry abundant small flowers in summer.*

LEFT *In summer, the flowers of* Deschampsia cespitosa *Golden Dew/'Goldtau' create a billowy golden green haze high above the clump of fine narrow leaf blades.*

Top Tip

Using ornamental grasses adds interest to the landscape. Hair grass can be a useful accent plant, but provision should be made for the tall summer flower spikes.

FESTUCA

A genus of some 300 species belonging to the grass (Poaceae) family, it has a global distribution. Often better known by their common name of fescue, the plants in this genus are mostly small and unassuming, though they have tremendous ornamental value, and are also considered some of the finest lawn grasses available, especially for high-quality low-traffic lawns. The leaves, often distinctively coloured, are usually folded around the midrib, making the foliage very fine and hair-like in some species. Usually standing taller than the foliage, the showy flower plumes are feathery and open.

CULTIVATION

While hardiness varies, most fescues are at home in temperate zones and thrive in most soils with minimal attention, though few will tolerate prolonged poor drainage. Plant in full sun or partial shade. As lawn grasses, they appreciate annual dethatching and aeration. In favourable conditions they will remain green year-round. Propagate by dividing established clumps, or raise from seed.

Favourites	Plant Height	Plant Width	Hardiness Zone	Frost Tolerance
Festuca californica	24–36 in (60–90 cm)	24 in (60 cm)	5–9	yes
Festuca californica 'Serpentine Blue'	24–36 in (60–90 cm)	24 in (60 cm)	5–9	yes
Festuca glauca	12 in (30 cm)	10 in (25 cm)	4–10	yes
Festuca glauca 'Blaufuchs'	6–10 in (15–25 cm)	10 in (25 cm)	4–10	yes
Festuca valesiaca	6 in (15 cm)	6 in (15 cm)	5–9	yes
Festuca varia	22 in (55 cm)	15 in (38 cm)	5–9	yes

Top Tip

Fescues are able to withstand many extremes of nature, such as dry, frosty or salty conditions. Their salt tolerance makes them ideal subjects for gardens near the sea.

LEFT *The fine, grassy, silvery blue-toned foliage of* Festuca glauca *'Blauglut' (syn. 'Blue Glow') makes a dramatic contrast when situated near green-leafed plants.*

RIGHT *Found in mountain areas of southern Europe,* Festuca varia subsp. scoparia *forms a clump of wispy blue-tipped leaves.*

GLYCERIA

A genus of 16 species of perennial marsh grasses, *Glyceria* is a member of the family Poaceae. Commonly known as manna grass, meadow grass or sweet grass, they are widely distributed throughout the northern temperate zones and temperate regions of South America, Australia and New Zealand. They spread by rhizomes, from which develop reed-like stems bearing long, strappy, succulent leaves. Large flower plumes, often purple-tinted, develop in summer, followed by edible small seeds. *Glyceria* plants will grow in shallow water, and are useful as pond plants.

CULTIVATION

Glyceria plants are mostly frost hardy and easily grown in any temperate climate. Plant in full sun with moist humus-rich soil. Although naturally adapted to damp conditions, they will grow well enough in regular garden soils if they are kept moist. Propagate from seed or by division.

ABOVE *A North American species found growing in moist woodland and swampy areas,* Glyceria striata *is commonly known as fowl manna grass. The narrow leaves are pale to bright green.*

Favourites	Plant Height	Plant Width	Hardiness Zone	Frost Tolerance
Glyceria maxima	3–8 ft (0.9–2.4 m)	5–10 ft (1.5–3 m)	3–9	yes
Glyceria maxima var. variegata	3–5 ft (0.9–1.5 m)	5–10 ft (1.5–3 m)	3–9	yes
Glyceria striata	12–36 in (30–90 cm)	12–36 in (30–90 cm)	3–9	yes

Top Tip

Glyceria species are useful for waterside planting, however, they have the potential to become invasive and their spread should be closely monitored and controlled.

LEFT *The cream-edged green leaves of* Glyceria maxima *var.* variegata *(striped manna grass) form a mound of arching foliage. Tall plumes of ivory flowers are borne in summer.*

LOMANDRA

This largely Australian genus is made up of around 50 species of clump-forming perennials, belonging to the grass-tree (Xanthorrhoeaceae) family. Rush- or sedge-like, they have rather coarse grassy foliage and their flower panicles are largely hidden among the foliage. While not among the most attractive plants, mat-rushes are very drought tolerant and useful for binding together light soils that would otherwise easily erode. In its native Australia, the genus was once despised by farmers as a destroyer of pastures but is now recognised as important in maintaining a habitat for ground-nesting birds, lizards and other easily threatened species.

Favourites	Plant Height	Plant Width	Hardiness Zone	Frost Tolerance
Lomandra banksii	3–5 ft (0.9–1.5 m)	2–4 ft (0.6–1.2 m)	10–12	no
Lomandra glauca	8 in (20 cm)	15 in (38 cm)	10–11	no
Lomandra longifolia	20–40 in (50–100 cm)	30–36 in (75–90 cm)	8–12	no

CULTIVATION

Hardiness varies, though none of the grass-trees will tolerate repeated hard frosts or prolonged wet winters. Plant in full sun with light well-drained soil. A thatch of dead foliage tends to build up around the base of the plants, and can be removed by cutting back hard or raking the clump, though burning off the tops encourages a lush thicket of new growth. They are easily propagated from seed or by division.

ABOVE *Often used in gardens for its ornamental qualities,* Lomandra longifolia *is a tussock-forming evergreen perennial from eastern Australia.*

LEFT *Commonly known as clumping mat-rush or May rush,* Lomandra banksii *features above-ground stems with strap-like bright green leaves.*

Top Tip

Lomandra species are easily cultivated and can serve as background foliage in border plantings. They appreciate regular watering throughout the growing season.

MISCANTHUS

This genus, belonging to the grass (Poaceae) family, contains about 20 deciduous or evergreen species, used widely in ornamental gardens as a feature and for screening. Their natural distribution ranges from Africa to East Asia. Tufted spreading plants, they have showy, green, silver, white and mottled foliage. Commonly referred to as reeds, they have clumps of leaves that cascade from rounded upright stems. They bear masses of tall flowerheads in late summer to autumn, sometimes taking on autumnal colours of orange, yellow, red or purple, and often remaining on plants right through winter. Fresh or dried, the flowerheads are ideal subjects for floral arrangements.

Top Tip

The unique ornamental qualities of *Miscanthus* species can add a touch of simple elegance to borders. They are also well suited to waterside planting.

CULTIVATION

Miscanthus species do best in moist open soils with a sunny aspect. Propagate by dividing into small clumps in autumn. They can also be propagated from seed, though it is often slow to germinate. Seed should be sown in containers in spring after the risk of frost has passed.

ABOVE *Appearing in autumn and often remaining well into winter, the tall flower plumes of* Miscanthus sinensis *'Variegatus' are held above the green-and-white striped leaves.*

BELOW Miscanthus sinensis *var.* condensatus *is a clump-forming grass that grows taller than the species. A fine ornamental grass, it features wide leaves accented by a central cream stripe.*

Favourites	Plant Height	Plant Width	Hardiness Zone	Frost Tolerance
Miscanthus oligostachyus	40 in (100 cm)	32 in (80 cm)	5–9	yes
Miscanthus sacchariflorus	5 ft (1.5 m)	5 ft (1.5 m)	5–9	yes
Miscanthus sinensis	15 ft (4.5 m)	4 ft (1.2 m)	5–9	yes
Miscanthus sinensis 'Gracillimus'	4–6 ft (1.2–1.8 m)	6–8 ft (1.8–2.4 m)	5–9	yes
Miscanthus sinensis 'Morning Light'	5–6 ft (1.5–1.8 m)	3–4 ft (0.9–1.2 m)	5–9	yes
Miscanthus transmorrisonensis	40 in (100 cm)	36 in (90 cm)	7–10	yes

MUHLENBERGIA

Commonly known as muhly grass, this genus of 125 species of often spectacular grasses in the family Poaceae is native to the Americas and temperate East Asia. They form large clumps of fine foliage and during the summer months produce billowing plumes of flowers, often in soft pink to purple-red shades. Some species are grown for their foliage, which can be blue-grey, others for their flowerheads and a few for both. Strangely, for such showy plants, these grasses have only recently become appreciated as garden plants. Some species are useful for sand dune stabilisation.

CULTIVATION

Hardiness varies considerably, but the tougher muhly grasses are easily grown in any sunny position with moist well-drained soil. The tender species are often worth cultivating as annuals in colder areas, or they may be potted and moved under cover for winter. They may be raised from seed but the best forms must be propagated by division, usually in late winter.

Favourites	Plant Height	Plant Width	Hardiness Zone	Frost Tolerance
Muhlenbergia capillaris	3 ft (0.9 m)	6 ft (1.8 m)	9–11	yes
Muhlenbergia emersleyi	18 in (45 cm)	3–4 ft (0.9–1.2 m)	9–11	yes
Muhlenbergia japonica	12–20 in (30–50 cm)	24 in (60 cm)	9–11	yes
Muhlenbergia japonica 'Cream Delight'	12–20 in (30–50 cm)	24 in (60 cm)	9–11	yes
Muhlenbergia lindheimeri	5 ft (1.5 m)	5 ft (1.5 m)	9–11	yes
Muhlenbergia rigens	5 ft (1.5 m)	4 ft (1.2 m)	9–11	yes

BELOW LEFT *An ideal accent plant,* Muhlenbergia capillaris *(syn. M. filipes) forms a neat mound of foliage. In summer, towering plumes of flowers are produced.*
BELOW RIGHT *Native to southern North America and Mexico,* Muhlenbergia rigens *is a clump-forming species that is commonly known as deer grass.*

Top Tip

Drought tolerant, muhly grasses are able to survive on minimal water. However, they will perform to their full potential if extra water is provided in dry times.

LEFT *Commonly known as fountain grass for its cascading form,* Pennisetum setaceum *bears pink to purple summer flowerheads that often last into autumn.*

ABOVE *The fine bristles that cover the flowerheads of* Pennisetum villosum *give a feathery effect, earning this perennial grass the common name of feathertop.*

PENNISETUM

A genus of about 80 species of grasses in the family Poaceae, it includes some very ornamental species and others that are among the worst weeds. Widespread in warm-temperate to tropical areas, they spread by rhizomes or stolons to form clumps of over-arching, short-stemmed, narrow to quite broad leaves that often have a prominent midrib. The flower stems usually extend above the foliage clump and carry plume-like heads of flowers that are often strongly pink-tinted. Many gardeners have been put off this genus by kikuyu grass *(Pennisetum flaccidum)*, which can be extremely difficult to control. Pearl millet *(Pennisetum americanum)* is a minor pasture, fodder and grain crop.

Top Tip

Trim off the fluffy flower plumes of *Pennisetum* species before the seeds mature to prevent seed dispersal. The dried plumes can be used in floral arrangements.

CULTIVATION

The commonly cultivated species will tolerate light to moderate frosts but prefer mild winters. They are otherwise easily grown in any sunny or lightly shaded position with moist well-drained soil. The species may be raised from seed, the cultivars by division in late winter.

Favourites	Plant Height	Plant Width	Hardiness Zone	Frost Tolerance
Pennisetum alopecuroides	48–60 in (120–150 cm)	18–24 in (45–60 cm)	5–9	yes
Pennisetum alopecuroides 'Little Bunny'	12–18 in (30–45 cm)	18–24 in (45–60 cm)	5–9	yes
Pennisetum orientale	5–6 ft (1.5–1.8 m)	3–4 ft (0.9–1.2 m)	8–10	yes
Pennisetum setaceum	3–5 ft (0.9–1.5 m)	2–3 ft (0.6–0.9 m)	9–10	no
Pennisetum setaceum 'Atrosanguineum'	3–5 ft (0.9–1.5 m)	2–3 ft (0.6–0.9 m)	9–10	no
Pennisetum villosum	24–48 in (60–120 cm)	18–24 in (45–60 cm)	8–10	no

PHYLLOSTACHYS

Found from the Himalayas to Japan, with most native to China, the 50-odd species of bamboos in this genus belong to the family Poaceae. Their vigorous spreading rhizomes sprout widely spaced culms that usually have a flattened side, sometimes with a shallow longitudinal groove. Other distinguishing features are the branching lower nodes and the waxy powder that sometimes appears below the nodes. The leaves are simple and usually relatively short. Even the giant *Phyllostachys bambusoides*, which can reach 30 m (100 ft) tall, has leaves only 20 cm (8 in) long. Several species are cultivated for their edible young shoots. Others are grown for medicinal use, canes and even for structural timber.

ABOVE *A native of China,* Phyllostachys flexuosa *is commonly known as zig-zag bamboo. This fast-growing bamboo develops an elegant arching form.*

BELOW Phyllostachys aureo-sulcata, *a vigorous spreading bamboo, hails from northeastern China. The culms are etched with a distinctive yellow groove.*

CULTIVATION

Most *Phyllostachys* species are surprisingly frost hardy, though they do need warm humid summers to grow well. Smaller species are suitable for planting in tubs or planter boxes, but need to be kept well watered. These bamboos are easily propagated by division.

Favourites	Plant Height	Plant Width	Hardiness Zone	Frost Tolerance
Phyllostachys aurea	25 ft (8 m)	20–40 ft (6–12 m)	7–11	yes
Phyllostachys aureosulcata	25 ft (8 m)	25–50 ft (8–15 m)	6–11	yes
Phyllostachys bambusoides	40–100 ft (12–30 m)	20–60 ft (6–18 m)	7–11	yes
Phyllostachys edulis	40–75 ft (12–23 m)	30–100 ft (9–30 m)	6–10	yes
Phyllostachys flexuosa	8–15 ft (2.4–4.5 m)	10–20 ft (3–6 m)	6–10	yes
Phyllostachys nigra	25–50 ft (8–15 m)	20–50 ft (6–15 m)	7–10	yes

PLEIOBLASTUS

A genus of some 20 species of mostly low-growing bamboos that have running rhizomes, they are largely confined to Japan and China, and are in the grass (Poaceae) family. They form clumps of fine canes with variably sized dark green leaves, sometimes with narrow longitudinal stripes of lighter coloration. Japanese gardeners have produced many variegated cultivars but due to difficulties in classification some are listed as species when they are most likely to be of garden origin. Several species produce edible shoots or canes that can be used as plant stakes or tool handles.

CULTIVATION

Though mostly very hardy and not too tall, in mild areas they will quickly fill a fairly large area. Their running habit means that they should be contained with solid underground barriers. The foliage can be kept lush by cutting the clumps back to the ground in late winter. Propagation is by division.

Favourites	Plant Height	Plant Width	Hardiness Zone	Frost Tolerance
Pleioblastus auricomus	3–6 ft (0.9–1.8 m)	3–5 ft (0.9–1.5 m)	6–10	yes
Pleioblastus chino	6–12 ft (1.8–3.5 m)	6 ft (1.8 m)	7–11	yes
Pleioblastus gramineus	6–15 ft (1.8–4.5 m)	6 ft (1.8 m)	7–11	yes
Pleioblastus humilis	4 ft (1.2 m)	5 ft (1.5 m)	7–11	yes
Pleioblastus pygmaeus	16 in (40 cm)	5 ft (1.5 m)	6–10	yes
Pleioblastus variegatus	27–40 in (70–100 cm)	3–5 ft (0.9–1.5 m)	5–10	yes

LEFT *Pleioblastus variegatus, an upright form from Japan also known as dwarf white-striped bamboo, has leaves to 15 cm (6 in) long, boldly striped with white.*

BELOW *With distinct nodes that divide stem segments, Pleioblastus auricomus has attractive green and gold variegated leaves to 25 cm (10 in) long.*

Top Tip

Division is best in early spring, before new shoots appear. The larger the transplant, the better the chance of success. Lightly fertilise, and water heavily for 2 weeks afterwards.

SASA

A grass (Poaceae) family genus, it has 60 species of bamboos found in temperate East Asia from southeastern Russia to southern China, Korea and Japan. They have running rhizomes and quickly form dense thickets of fairly fine, arching canes that are seldom over 2 m (7 ft) tall. Foliage is often dense and the leaves can be broad. The leaves of some species tend to dry off along the edges, but rather than appearing damaged or dying, they can benefit from an interesting variegated effect. *Sasa* or *Zasa* is the Japanese name for bamboo and is used in the common names of several types, not just those found in this genus, for example *Pleioblastus auricomus* is known as kamuro-zasa.

BELOW *A Japanese cultivar, Sasa palmata 'Nebulosa' has stems with distinctive brown to black markings and large oblong palm-like leaves, as the species name indicates.*

ABOVE *Sasa veitchii has 25 cm (10 in) long leaves that turn white at the edges. Its purple stems branch from each node, with a whitish powder beneath each node.*

CULTIVATION

Mostly very hardy with a greater preference for cooler summer conditions than other bamboos, plant them in half-sun or dappled sunlight with moist, humus-rich, well-drained soil. They have strong running rhizomes that need to be contained. Propagation is by division.

Favourites	Plant Height	Plant Width	Hardiness Zone	Frost Tolerance
Sasa kurilensis	3–10 ft (0.9–3 m)	10–20 ft (3–6 m)	7–11	yes
Sasa palmata	7 ft (2 m)	10–20 ft (3–6 m)	7–11	yes
Sasa palmata 'Nebulosa'	6–8 ft (1.8–2.4 m)	10–20 ft (3–6 m)	7–11	yes
Sasa tsuboiana	4–6 ft (1.2–1.8 m)	10–20 ft (3–6 m)	8–10	yes
Sasa veitchii	3–5 ft (0.9–1.5 m)	10–20 ft (3–6 m)	6–11	yes
Sasa veitchii f. minor	2 ft (0.6 m)	5–10 ft (1.5–3 m)	8–10	yes

TYPHA

The type genus for the bul-rush (Typhaceae) family, *Typha* contains up to 12 species of marginal aquatic perennials with a near-worldwide distribution outside the polar regions. Most have tall, strongly erect stems that are very light and have pithy centres. Conspicuous sheaths cover the young stems, peeling away and dying as the stems mature. The leaves are long, flat, narrow and deep green to blue green when young. Dense cylindrical flower spikes appear near the top of pointed spear-like flower stems and eventually disintegrate, dispersing their seeds on the wind. The small species tend to be more grass-like. Bulrush clumps aid in their own demise, as their roots and debris help fill and drain the ponds in which they grow.

Top Tip

Outdoors, bul-rushes usually demand plenty of space. To enjoy them on a smaller scale, plant them in pots where they can be a focal point when in flower.

CULTIVATION

Bulrushes will grow in up to 30 cm (12 in) of water and should be planted in full sun. They are too large for small ponds, but where they can run wild they need little or no maintenance. Propagate from seed or by division.

BELOW LEFT *The striking foliage of* Typha latifolia *'Variegata' makes it popular for aquatic and waterside plantings. The slender blades are striped with cream.*

ABOVE Typha shuttleworthii *is a bulrush from southern Europe. Throughout summer it produces brown to silvery grey flowers that are followed by tiny fruit.*

Favourites	Plant Height	Plant Width	Hardiness Zone	Frost Tolerance
Typha angustifolia	7 ft (2 m)	3–5 ft (0.9–1.5 m)	3–9	yes
Typha latifolia	3–10 ft (0.9–3 m)	3–5 ft (0.9–1.5 m)	3–10	yes
Typha latifolia 'Variegata'	3–5 ft (0.9–1.5 m)	3–5 ft (0.9–1.5 m)	3–10	yes
Typha minima	2½–3 in (6–8 cm)	1¼–2 in (3–5 cm)	3–11	yes
Typha orientalis	3–8 ft (0.9–2.4 m)	1–2 ft (0.3–0.6 m)	9–11	yes
Typha shuttleworthii	3–5 ft (0.9–1.5 m)	1–3 ft (0.3–0.9 m)	5–8	yes

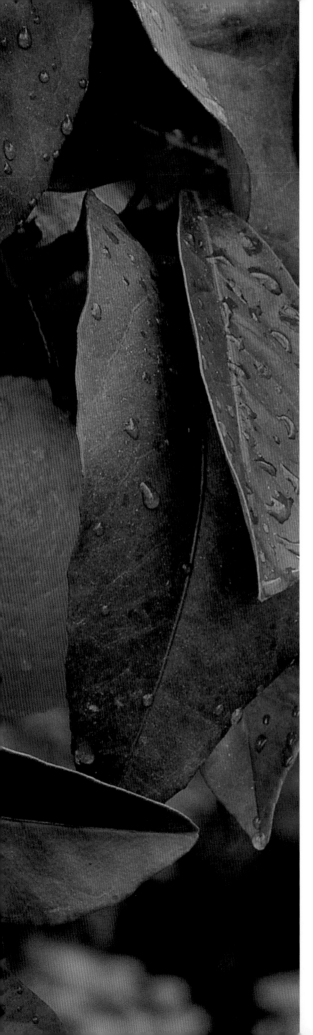

FRUIT TREES, NUT TREES AND OTHER FRUITS

Harvesting food from the garden is one of the most rewarding aspects of gardening. In addition to the satisfaction of polishing the bloom off a sun-warmed apple and crunching into it or tasting the difference between store-bought and fresh walnuts, there are many practical reasons for growing fruits and nuts. Home-grown fruits and nuts can be raised with minimal to no pesticides, particularly if attention is paid at the outset to choosing suitable varieties for the region. Home-grown fruits are less expensive and more accessible than store-bought fruits. And garden varieties may be chosen for flavour rather than for the qualities commercial growers seek.

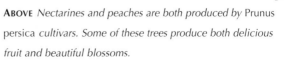

ABOVE *Nectarines and peaches are both produced by* Prunus persica *cultivars. Some of these trees produce both delicious fruit and beautiful blossoms.*

LEFT *Their dark glossy leaves, fragrant white flowers and edible fruits make citrus trees very attractive. The Valencia orange* (Citrus × aurantium *'Valencia') is a good example.*

A Fruitful Garden Harvest

Fruit, whether on a tree, bush or vine, is essentially a mature ovary enclosing and protecting a plant's seed. In order to guard the seed, most fruit is distinctly bitter and unpalatable until the seed is ripe and ready for dispersal—at which point the fruit becomes sweet and delicious, attracting potential foragers. Nuts, while internally organised somewhat differently (the ovary becomes a hard shell protecting the nut), essentially function the same way: foraging creatures are kept at bay by the unpalatable flavour and impossibly hard shell until the seed is developed sufficiently and ready for dispersal.

Over the centuries, humans have manipulated the flavour of various wild fruits and nuts to satisfy our tastes and preferences. As well as selecting for flavour, we have selected for qualities such as size, colour, skin or rind thickness, seedlessness, storage quality and ripening time. In terms of the plants themselves, we have sought larger or smaller trees, heavier cropping, disease and insect resistance and other qualities that improve crops.

Only since the rise of mass production in the past century has the flavour of fruits been so sacrificed for the sake of storage and shipping convenience.

Perhaps for no reason other than this, backyard fruit production is tremendously gratifying, for it allows the gardener to seek out the most delicious varieties, old and new, without having to take into account commercial concerns. If the varieties chosen are appropriate to the climate and are planted and cultivated with some attention, it is not difficult to enjoy some of the finest fresh food the earth has to offer.

The first matter to consider is climate. Many temperate-climate fruits such as apples (*Malus* species) require a certain number of hours of cool weather (chill time) between 0° and 7°C (32° and 45°F). Raspberries (*Rubus* species) also require some winter chill to produce well. Tropical fruits such as mangoes (*Mangifera* species), on the other hand, grow and fruit best where winter temperatures remain above 7°C (45°F). *Prunus* species such as peaches, apricots and almonds tolerate considerable cold in winter, but flower early in the season and can lose their buds—and consequently the entire season's fruit—in areas prone to late frosts. In addition, many fruits require warmth to ripen. These include *Citrus* species and mangoes. Within the *Citrus* genus, lemons, limes and other sour types generally need less heat to ripen than oranges and other sweet forms.

Above left Prunus persica 'Jerseyglo' is a freestone peach with sweet firm flesh that ripens late in the season. The tree is spreading and strong growing.

Left The wineberry or wine raspberry (Rubus phoenicolasius) bears juicy fruit in summer on arching canes. Like blackberries, these can become invasive.

ABOVE *Although blueberries* (Vaccinium corymbosum) *are best known for their flavoursome fruit, these attractive plants also make interesting informal hedges.*
RIGHT *Colourful cowberries* (Vaccinium vitis-idaea) *appear on a low-growing ever-green bush. They have a slightly sour taste.*

Most fruits and nuts require full sun in all but the hottest climates. Moist but well-drained and reasonably fertile soil that is slightly acidic is best. Exceptions include blueberries and other *Vaccinium* species, which prefer very acidic soil with lower fertility and plenty of humus.

Many, but not all, fruits require a pollinator. Cane fruits such as raspberries and blackberries (*Rubus* species) do not need pollination, but Chinese gooseberries, or kiwifruit (*Actinidia* species) will not produce fruit without a pollinator. For apples and pears (*Pyrus* species), good pollinators are often, but not always, varieties whose flowering times overlap. Blueberries do not require cross-pollination, but their production is much improved by it. When planting a new fruit, it is important to find out whether more than one plant is needed to produce fruit and, if so, which kind is needed for pollination.

Most fruiting plants need annual pruning to balance the amount of new and old wood, prevent disease and improve photosynthesis. Some are best pruned directly after harvest, such as cane fruits;

others, like pears and apples, are pruned in early spring, before buds break their winter dormancy.

Although most fruits are produced on trees and shrubs, there are a number of desirable fruiting vines such as grapes (*Vitis* species) and kiwifruit or Chinese gooseberry (*Actinidia* species). Both of these are highly ornamental and can produce large quantities of delicious fruit.

Fruiting plants encompass a tremendously varied group of many genera, and span climates from the frigid to the tropical. Most regions of the world are known for their local fruits, and in many cases there are locally adapted and commonly grown varieties that have proven their suitability over many years. While it is always good to try new varieties and test boundaries, it is also worth knowing which varieties have a track record in an area and making use of local expertise when choosing which varieties to grow.

ACTINIDIA

A genus of around 60 species of vigorous evergreen and deciduous twining East Asian vines, it is part of the Actinidiaceae family. Some species are grown just for their ornamental foliage but the 2 best known species, *Actinidia deliciosa* and *Actinidia arguta*, are cultivated for their fruit. Most parts of the plant are bristly, except the cream flowers, which open from late spring and can pose pollination difficulties. The fruit develops during summer to be ripe by early winter. That kiwifruit is synonymous with New Zealand shows the power of marketing; it is really a Chinese native.

ABOVE *The fruit of* Actinidia chinensis *is almost hairless when ripe and has bright yellow to reddish flesh of a rich, aromatic, sweet flavour.*

CULTIVATION

Both male and female vines are required for fruit production. Plant where the roots will be cool and the tops will receive plenty of sunlight. The soil should be deep, fertile, humusrich, and well drained. Strong supports are necessary for these heavy vines. Water well when in flower and as the fruit ripens. Prune after harvesting. So that their sex is known, vines are usually propagated vegetatively from cuttings, or by layering or grafting.

Top Tip

Actinidia kolomikta is a good choice for those in cooler climates. It survives freezing conditions and also produces grape-sized fruit that tastes similar to regular kiwifruit.

Favourites	Flower Colour	Blooming Season	Produce Season	Plant Height	Plant Width	Hardiness Zone	Frost Tolerance
Actinidia arguta	white, tinged green	mid- to late summer	late summer to autumn	20–30 ft (6–9 m)	20–30 ft (6–9 m)	4–9	yes
Actinidia arguta 'Issai'	white, tinged green	mid- to late summer	late summer to autumn	20–30 ft (6–9 m)	20–30 ft (6–9 m)	4–9	yes
Actinidia chinensis	cream	spring	late summer to autumn	10–20 ft (3–6 m)	15–30 ft (4.5–9 m)	7–10	yes
Actinidia deliciosa	cream	spring	late autumn to winter	35 ft (10 m)	35 ft (10 m)	7–10	yes
Actinidia deliciosa Zespri Green/'Hayward'	cream	spring	late autumn to winter	35 ft (10 m)	35 ft (10 m)	7–10	yes
Actinidia kolomikta	white	late spring to summer	late autumn to winter	20–35 ft (6–10 m)	17–20 ft (5–6 m)	4–9	yes

ABOVE *Zespri Green is the trade-marked name of* Actinidia deliciosa *'Hayward', the commercial form most commonly seen on shelves, and best known as kiwifruit.*

LEFT *A climber native to East Asia,* Actinidia kolomikta *has handsome leaves, tipped white or pink and variegated after 1 or 2 years. It is not produced commercially.*

ABOVE LEFT Actinidia arguta *is a vigorous twining vine of variable habit that comes from Japan, Korea and northeastern China. It has oval serrated leaves to 15 cm (6 in) long.*

CITRUS

The genus *Citrus* is part of the rue (Rutaceae) family and is made up of around 20 species of evergreen aromatic trees and shrubs found naturally in South-East Asia and the Pacific Islands. They are usually neat rounded plants with lustrous mid- to deep green leaves and fragrant, waxy, white flowers. The fruits that follow, such as oranges, lemons, limes, grapefruit and mandarins, vary in size and flavour but share a similar segmented structure and slow-ripening habit. The first recorded use of the word "orange" is in a poem dated around AD 1044, but the fruit did not arrive in Europe until at least AD 1200. The word "orange" was derived from the Sanskrit *na rangi*.

CULTIVATION

Citrus need sunlight, warmth, water and feeding to develop. Plant in a sheltered sunny position with moist, humus-rich, well-drained, slightly acidic soil. Trim lightly at harvesting time. *Citrus* tolerate only light frost and can make attractive pot plants in colder areas. Fruiting varieties are propagated from cuttings or grafts.

Top Tip

During the growing season, citrus trees need plenty of water and regular feeding of nitrogen-based fertiliser to promote fruit size and growth.

BELOW LEFT Citrus × aurantium *'Washington Navel'* *(syn. C. sinensis 'Washington Navel') belongs to the Sweet Orange Group. This group's fruit is delicious.*
BELOW *The fruit of* Citrus japonica, *the cumquat tree, has a unique flavour and the peel is eaten with the flesh.*

LEFT Citrus × meyeri 'Meyer' is a lemon/orange hybrid. It is usually treated as a lemon, due perhaps to its shape, but it is not as acidic as a true lemon.

ABOVE Citrus × microcarpa is a popular ornamental shrub that is a hybrid of the cumquat and the mandarin. It can be successfully grown in pots, indoors and out.

Favourites	Flower Colour	Blooming Season	Produce Season	Plant Height	Plant Width	Hardiness Zone	Frost Tolerance
Citrus aurantiifolia	white	spring to summer	summer to winter	8–15 ft (2.4–4.5 m)	10 ft (3 m)	11–12	no
Citrus aurantium	white	spring to summer	autumn to spring	15–35 ft (4.5–10 m)	10–20 ft (3–6 m)	9–11	no
Citrus japonica	white	spring to summer	autumn to spring	6 ft (1.8 m)	3 ft (0.9 m)	9–10	no
Citrus maxima	white	spring to summer	autumn to spring	20–40 ft (6–12 m)	10 ft (3 m)	10–12	no
Citrus meyeri 'Meyer'	cream	most of year	most of year	7–10 ft (2–3 m)	5–8 ft (1.5–2.4 m)	9–11	no
Citrus microcarpa	white	most of year	most of year	8 ft (2.4 m)	4 ft (1.2 m)	9–11	no

ABOVE *It's the leaves and rind of the knobbly fruit of the unusual kaffir or makrut lime (Citrus hystrix) that are the most highly prized for use in Asian dishes.*

BELOW Citrus glauca *or desert lime is an Australian species thought to have high potential for commercial production in dry areas. Fruit is small, sour and juicy.*

ABOVE *The grapefruit 'Ruby' originated in Texas and was the first reliably pink variety. Today, it remains the most popular and widely grown of the coloured grapefruit. It needs a long hot summer to colour well.*

RIGHT *The finger lime* (Citrus australasica) *is another Australian species in the early stages of commercialisation. It's a spiny, rainforest shrub that produces elongated fruit full of sour juice inside tiny, globular sacs.*

ABOVE *The mandarin 'Imperial' is the most widely sold variety in Australia but little known elsewhere. Both its rind and flesh have the strong smell and taste associated with mandarins. It crops in autumn.*

RIGHT *Blood oranges are a winter crop that develop the best colour and flavour in inland areas where there is at least a 10°C (50°F) difference between day and night temperatures. Mild nights result in poor colour.*

CORYLUS

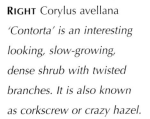

*C*orylus is a genus in the birch (Betulaceae) family that has about 15 species of deciduous shrubs and trees native to the northern temperate zones. They have heavily veined, mid-green, rounded leaves, and from mid- to late winter they bear yellowish male flower catkins that persist until the new leaves form in the spring. The female flowers are inconspicuous but develop into the nuts, which are ripe when they fall in late summer or early autumn.

CULTIVATION

Hazels are very hardy and grow well in a sunny position with fertile well-drained soil. Although flowers of both sexes occur on the same plant, if grown for their fruit, pollinators are required to ensure a good yield. Special varieties, such as 'Daviana', can pollinate at least 20 trees in the near vicinity. Removing suckers is the simplest propagation method, or use half-hardened summer cuttings, treated with hormone powder. The seed germinates if layered but the nuts will be of variable quality.

ABOVE *The nuts produced by* Corylus cornuta *are enclosed in a long, tubular, leafy, beak-like husk. The nut itself is round, smooth and very hard.*

RIGHT *Corylus avellana 'Contorta' is an interesting looking, slow-growing, dense shrub with twisted branches. It is also known as corkscrew or crazy hazel.*

Favourites	Flower Colour	Blooming Season	Produce Season	Plant Height	Plant Width	Hardiness Zone	Frost Tolerance
Corylus americana	light brown and red	autumn to spring	late summer to autumn	10 ft (3 m)	10 ft (3 m)	4–8	yes
Corylus avellana	yellow and red	winter to early spring	late summer	15 ft (4.5 m)	15 ft (4.5 m)	4–8	yes
Corylus colurna	yellow and red	winter to early spring	early autumn	80 ft (24 m)	25 ft (8 m)	4–8	yes
Corylus cornuta	light brown and red	autumn to spring	late summer	10 ft (3 m)	10 ft (3 m)	4–8	yes
Corylus maxima	reddish purple and red	late winter to spring	mid- to late autumn	15–30 ft (4.5–9 m)	15 ft (4.5 m)	5–9	yes
Corylus maxima 'Purpurea'	reddish purple and red	late winter to spring	mid- to late autumn	15–30 ft (4.5–9 m)	15 ft (4.5 m)	5–9	yes

ABOVE *Purple-leaf hazelnut, Corylus maxima, is widely grown in gardens for the coppery purple tint in its young leaves. This cultivar is 'Purpurea'.*

BELOW *Corylus colurna thrives in continental climates—hot summers and cold winters. It is unusual to the genus, growing with one straight trunk.*

Top Tip

Corylus species can be used as hedging plants. Leave untrimmed or trimmed only very lightly if you wish the shrubs to bear a crop of nuts.

FRAGARIA

*F*ragaria is a genus of 12 species of perennials in the rose (Rosaceae) family. Found in the northern temperate zones and Chile, they are tough adaptable plants that spread by runners. Commonly known as strawberries, their foliage is usually trifoliate, with broad toothed leaflets. From spring, clusters of small white flowers appear, which are followed by the luscious fruit. Strawberries bear their seeds on the outside and strictly speaking, this means that they are not really a fruit.

CULTIVATION

Strawberries are very hardy and grow well in full sun on broad mounds of moist well-drained soil, or with a surrounding of dry mulch, such as straw, to prevent the fruit rotting before it ripens. Cultivars vary in their fruiting period, the earliest flower in winter and their fruit may need frost protection. Often the entire crop will need to be covered with netting to prevent bird damage. Propagate by layering the stolons or by using them as cuttings.

TOP RIGHT *Fragaria × ananassa 'Eros' is a very hardy cultivar that has been bred to be resistant to the disease red stele. It bears large, glossy, red fruit.*
RIGHT *Fragaria × ananassa 'Tribute' is one of the most successful varieties of strawberries for commerical plantings. It produces medium to large, flavoursome fruit.*

Favourites	Flower Colour	Blooming Season	Produce Season	Plant Height	Plant Width	Hardiness Zone	Frost Tolerance
Fragaria × *ananassa*	white	late spring to autumn	summer to autumn	6 in (15 cm)	40 in (100 cm)	3–10	yes
Fragaria × *ananassa* 'Benton'	white	late spring to autumn	summer to autumn	6 in (15 cm)	40 in (100 cm)	3–10	yes
Fragaria × *ananassa* 'Fort Laramie'	white	late spring to autumn	summer to autumn	6 in (15 cm)	40 in (100 cm)	3–10	yes
Fragaria × *ananassa* 'Rainier'	white	late spring to autumn	summer to autumn	6 in (15 cm)	40 in (100 cm)	3–10	yes
Fragaria chiloensis	white	spring to summer	autumn	6 in (15 cm)	20 in (50 cm)	4–10	yes
Fragaria 'Rosie'	red	spring to autumn	summer to autumn	2–6 in (5–15 cm)	8–60 in (20–150 cm)	5–9	yes

Top Tip

During the first growing season of a strawberry plant, remove the flowers for the first month. The plant will grow stronger, producing a larger fruit crop the following year.

ABOVE *As well as producing a good yield of fruit, the hybrid cultivar 'Rosie' has red blooms instead of white. This plant makes a pretty and practical ground cover.*

RIGHT *When selecting a strawberry variety, consider season of ripening and disease resistance. Fragaria × ananassa 'Symphony' produces late-season fruit.*

JUGLANS

The type genus for the walnut (Juglandaceae) family, *Juglans* is composed of some 20 species of deciduous trees found in southern Europe and the temperate regions of the Americas and East Asia. They have large pinnate leaves and grow very quickly when young. The flowers, small and often well hidden among the foliage, develop into large fruit that matures from late summer around hard cases that contain the nuts. In addition to the fruit, walnuts have wonderfully grained timber that is prized for the finest furniture, ornamental items and veneers. Some species produce juglose, which can poison apple trees.

ABOVE *Commonly known as the butternut,* Juglans cinerea *is found from New Brunswick, Canada to Georgia, USA. It is particularly cultivated in New England where its nuts are used to make maple-butternut candy.*
RIGHT Juglans regia, *the English or Persian walnut, produces the largest and most easily cracked nuts. Cultivars of the Carpathian Group are cold hardy and popular throughout USA, particularly as commercial crops.*

CULTIVATION

Mature trees are very hardy but the soft spring growth is easily damaged by late frosts and strong winds. Grow in a bright position with moist, deep, well-drained soil, and water well as the fruit matures. The nuts may be subject to fungal problems in areas with high summer humidity. Sow ripe seeds in early spring from cool storage. Prune to shape when young.

Top Tip

Prune walnut trees when the plant is either fully dormant or fully in leaf. Otherwise any cuts will bleed profusely and severely weaken the tree.

RIGHT *Be sure to plant this species,* Juglans cathayensis, *in its permanent position. This tree produces a deep tap root and does not tolerate root disturbance. It will bear nuts after 4 or 5 years.*

RIGHT *The leaves of* Juglans regia *are aromatic, have 7 leaflets up to 12 cm (5 in) long, and are smooth. The leaflets of this cultivar, 'Laciniata', are more deeply cut.*

Favourites	Flower Colour	Blooming Season	Produce Season	Plant Height	Plant Width	Hardiness Zone	Frost Tolerance
Juglans ailanthifolia	brown and red	summer	autumn	50 ft (15 m)	40 ft (12 m)	4–9	yes
Juglans cathayensis	brown and greenish	spring to summer	autumn	50–70 ft (15–21 m)	50 ft (15 m)	5–10	yes
Juglans cinerea	yellowish green	spring to summer	autumn	60 ft (18 m)	50 ft (15 m)	4–9	yes
Juglans major	yellowish green	late spring to early summer	autumn to winter	50 ft (15 m)	30 ft (9 m)	9–11	yes
Juglans nigra	yellowish green	late spring to early summer	autumn	100 ft (30 m)	70 ft (21 m)	4–10	yes
Juglans regia	yellowish green	summer	autumn	40–60 ft (12–18 m)	35 ft (10 m)	4–10	yes

MACADAMIA

The 2 species of macadamia that bear the famous nuts are both natives of the forests of subtropical eastern Australia. Another 8 or so species are found in eastern Australia and nearby tropical islands but these don't bear edible nuts and are rarely grown. All macadamias are in the plant family Proteaceae. The nut-bearing macadamias are moderately slow-growing, long-lived, evergreen trees with stiff, spiny-edged leaves and tiny, insignificant flowers carried on pendulous racemes. In nature, they are found growing beneath taller trees, which means they can be grown in part-shade and still bear nuts. They can also be grown to fruiting size in tubs and kept at a manageable size by pruning. Best in warm climates but able to take odd frosts.

Top Tip

For maximum yield of best quality nuts buy a grafted, named hybrid rather than starting a plant from seed. Seed-raised trees may or may not produce nuts of the same quality as the parent plant.

RIGHT Macadamia integrifolia *is found only in south-east Queensland. It and M.* tetraphylla *form the basis of the macadamia nut industry in both Australia and Hawaii.*

CULTIVATION

In the subtropics or tropics plant in part-shade. In cooler areas full sun produces better crops. Free-draining soil that retains moisture thanks to its high organic matter content is most suitable. Plants are dryness tolerant once established but will not bear nuts during droughts unless watered well in summer. Do not feed excessively. Apply controlled-release fertiliser formulated for native plants once in the spring.

RIGHT Macadamia tetraphylla *is a rainforest tree. Its native range straddles the border of New South Wales and Queensland. The main difference between it and the other species shown is the prickly edges to the leaves.*

ABOVE RIGHT *The nuts form in tight clusters and ripen from late summer. Macadamias are renowned for the hardness of their outer shells.*

RIGHT *The white flowers, which are produced on long racemes, appear from about mid-winter. Each blossom is small and strongly resembles other members of the family.*

Favourites	Flower Colour	Blooming Season	Produce Season	Plant Height	Plant Width	Hardiness Zone	Frost Tolerance
Macadamia integrifolia	whitish	spring	summer to winter	26–33 ft (8–10 m)	26–33 ft (8–10 m)	8–10	yes
Macadamia tetraphylla	pinkish	spring	summer to winter	26–33 ft (8–10 m)	26–33 ft (8–10 m)	8–10	yes

MALUS

The *Malus* genus of about 35 species in the family Rosaceae, can be divided into two classes, the crab apples, which are grown for their flowers and the apples, which are grown for their fruit. Eating apples have been important to humans almost since there were humans and, like their cousins the quinces and pears, they originated in western Asia and the Caucasus region. Since they are so valuable to people, apples have long been crossed and re-crossed in order to produce fruit that is bigger, better tasting, longer lasting, earlier ripening, later ripening, good for cider—in fact, for virtually any reason you'd want an apple. Now there are thousands of different forms but most are grown only by enthusiasts or in distinct locations.

CULTIVATION

Apples are deciduous trees that require a considerable period of cold in order to flower and set fruit. They are not well suited to frost-free areas. It's not necessary to have two varieties to achieve pollination although having a second variety will result in much heavier crops. Apples need full sun, fertile, free-draining soil and shelter from strong winds.

ABOVE AND RIGHT *With a relatively low chilling requirement, 'Fuji' can be grown in areas usually considered too mild for apples, making it one of the most popular varieties for home gardeners. The high quality fruit, one of the best for eating, ripens in autumn and keeps well in a dark, cool cellar. You'll get the most fruit with a pollinator such as 'Jonathon' but you'll still get a satisfactory crop without one.*

Top Tip

'Jonathon' and 'Delicious' are able to pollinate a very wide range of other apple varieties. An alternative to two trees is to graft 'Jonathon' onto the other variety you want to grow.

ABOVE *Crisp and tart-sweet, a good 'Jonathon' is still one of the best apples of all. It is an ideal choice for a pollinator as it is compatible with most other varieties.*

TOP *Liking a colder climate, 'Delicious' grows quickly into a quite large tree. Fruit ripens mid-season and is best eaten under-ripe when it is crisp, sweet and delicious.*

Favourites	Flower Colour	Blooming Season	Produce Season	Plant Height	Plant Width	Hardiness Zone	Frost Tolerance
Malus domestica 'Fuji'	white, often tinged pink	spring	autumn	20–30 ft (6–9 m)	15–25 ft (4.5–8 m)	7–9	yes
'Jonathon'	white	spring	summer	20–25 ft (6–8 m)	15–25 ft (4.5–8 m)	7–9	yes
'Delicious'	white	spring	late summer	30–40 ft (9–12 m)	25–35 ft (4.5–7.5 m)	7–8	yes

RIGHT Mangifera indica *is from South-East Asia, especially Myanmar and eastern India. It has leaves that are red when young, but which age to a shiny dark green over time.*
FAR RIGHT *There are many cultivars of the mango species* Mangifera indica. *'Campeche' is a cultivar that has bright green leaves and deep yellow fruit with a reddish pink tinge.*

Top Tip

Give plenty of water through late spring and summer, less in autumn and none from winter to early spring. Fertilise trees 2 or 3 times each summer, once established.

MANGIFERA

Although this cashew (Anacardiaceae) family genus contains around 50 species of evergreen shrubs and trees found from India to the Solomon Islands, only one, *Mangifera indica,* is widely cultivated. Commonly known as the mango, it is an Indian native that develops quickly to form a large, many-branched, spreading tree. Panicles of small yellow to red flowers develop into clusters of oval greenish yellow fruit with a red blush. The fruit has quite a distinctive odour and flavour and contains 1 large seed. The timber is hard and durable but needs careful handling as the sap and sawdust can cause dermatitis and eye irritations.

CULTIVATION

Mangoes prefer a warm frost-free climate to crop well. Plant them in full or half-sun in a well-drained humus-rich soil. Mangoes occur naturally in areas with seasonal rainfall and so they prefer dry conditions at flowering and fruit set but need more moisture thereafter. They may be raised from seed but superior cultivars are grafted.

RIGHT Mangifera indica *has fruit that is fleshy and irregularly egg-shaped. It may be "alternate-bearing", fruiting heavily only every 2 to 4 years.*

ABOVE Mangifera caesia *can grow up to 36 m (120 ft) in the wild. Also known as jack or binjai, its fruit flavour is said to resemble a mix of mango and pineapple.*

Favourites	Flower Colour	Blooming Season	Produce Season	Plant Height	Plant Width	Hardiness Zone	Frost Tolerance
Mangifera caesia	lavender-blue	spring	mid-spring to summer	120 ft (36 m)	30 ft (9 m)	11–12	no
Mangifera indica	yellowish or reddish	spring	mid-spring to summer	80 ft (24 m)	25 ft (8 m)	11–12	no
Mangifera indica 'Campeche'	yellowish or reddish	spring	mid-spring to summer	50 ft (15 m)	20 ft (6 m)	11–12	no
Mangifera indica 'Edward'	yellowish or reddish	spring	mid-spring to summer	50 ft (15 m)	20 ft (6 m)	11–12	no
Mangifera indica 'Kensington Pride'	yellowish or reddish	spring	mid-spring to summer	50 ft (15 m)	20 ft (6 m)	11–12	no
Mangifera indica 'Kent'	yellowish or reddish	spring	mid-spring to summer	50 ft (15 m)	20 ft (6 m)	11–12	no

Olea

Without olives the ancient societies of the Mediterranean region would not have had lighting, cooking oil or a major item of their diet. It can be truly said of this tree that it nourished the rise of western civilisation. The olive is the plant that gave the family, Oleaceae, its name, and the genus *Olea* contains about 20 species, none as important as *Olea europaea*, the fruiting olive. This is a tree of dry areas where almost all the year's rain falls between mid-autumn and early spring. It can live for hundreds of years, old specimens developing stout, gnarled trunks. Leaves are leathery, grey-green on top, whitish underneath. Pale spring flowers are insignificant but lead to late summer fruit.

Cultivation

Full sun is the main requirement as these trees are not demanding about soil, able to grow in almost anything that drains well. They tolerate coastal or inland conditions, can withstand long, dry spells and can be kept in big pots. Ideal is weekly rain or water from late autumn to early spring with much less rain over summer. They don't love high humidity.

> ## Top Tip
>
> If you love the look of olive trees but don't want masses of fruit each year, seek out the non-fruiting hybrid 'Swan Hill'. It grows more slowly than regular varieties and remains a smaller, more compact tree.

Right *All olives ripen from green to black and can be picked when either fully grown but under-ripe (green) or when fully ripe and black. These are the variety 'Manzanilla'.*

Favourites	Flower Colour	Blooming Season	Produce Season	Plant Height	Plant Width	Hardiness Zone	Frost Tolerance
Olive 'Kalamata'	cream	mid-spring	autumn	26–60 ft (8–18 m)	20–50 ft (6–15 m)	7–9	yes
Olive 'Manzanilla'	cream	early spring	late summer	20–40 ft (6–12 m)	30–50 ft (9–15 m)	7–9	yes
Olive 'Nab Tamri'	cream	spring	early autumn	20–30 ft (6–9 m)	30–45 ft (9–13.5 m)	8–9	yes

ABOVE *The tiny white flowers come in mid-spring. They are wind pollinated and if you want the heaviest crop you'll need two trees near each other. With just one tree you'll still get a good crop.*

RIGHT *'Kalamata' is the famous Greek olive grown mainly as a table olive although it can also be processed into oil. 'Kalamata' is a late ripening variety that is always picked black.*

PASSIFLORA

This is a big genus of tropical vines with over 500 species. Only about 50 species produce edible fruit. In Australia, the most important by far is the black passionfruit, *Passiflora edulis*, but the banana passionfruit and the granadilla also have their adherents. All passionfruit vines are vigorous evergreens, requiring a warm climate with a long, hot summer in order to flower and fruit well. In the cooler limit of their range, it's usual for spring and early summer flowers not to set fruit as the plants require warm soil to bring their fruit to ripeness. In warmer areas, fruiting begins in early summer and continues right through until winter. The plants have ornamental lobed leaves and very attractive flowers. They are in the Passifloraceae family.

Top Tip

Passionfruit are susceptible to stem rots. Though mulching is desirable, keep it 15 cm (6 in) away from the trunk and don't dig within 3 m (10 ft) of the trunk.

ABOVE *An equatorial variety, the red banana passionfruit* (Passiflora antioquiensis) *produces highly ornamental flowers followed by juicy, sweet fruit similar to a banana passionfruit. It needs a tropical climate.*

ABOVE RIGHT *The black passionfruit* (Passiflora edulis) *is the most widely grown and best known form.*

LEFT *Passionfruit ripens from green to black when both soil and air temperatures are consistently warm. The seedy, tart-sweet fruit can be an acquired taste for those unused to these plants.*

RIGHT *The banana passion-fruit (Passiflora mollissima) takes a much cooler climate than the black. It is a very vigorous vine, inclined to sucker. The sweet fruit is mild in flavour.*

CULTIVATION

Grow in humus-rich, fertile, free-draining soil against wire mesh or other supporting structure. Passionfruit must have full sun both for warmth and maximum flowering and fruiting. Out of the tropics or subtropics, plant in the warmest sunny spot available. From mid-spring, keep moist and mulch periodically with manure and apply a fertiliser formulated for flower and fruit.

Favourites	Flower Colour	Blooming Season	Produce Season	Plant Height	Plant Width	Hardiness Zone	Frost Tolerance
Passiflora antioquiensis	pink and red	summer and autumn	late summer to winter	to 25 ft (to 8 m)	to 25 ft (to 8 m)	10–11	no
Passiflora edulis	white and purple	spring to early winter	summer to winter	to 25 ft (to 8 m)	to 25 ft (to 8 m)	9–11	yes
Passiflora mollissima	pink and red	summer and autumn	late summer to winter	50 ft or more (15 m or more)	50 ft or more (15 m or more)	8–9	yes

PISTACIA

A major food source for early peoples in the Mediterranean and Central Asian regions, pistachio nuts grow wild on the rocky slopes of hills and mountains from the eastern shores of the Mediterranean to Afghanistan.

They must experience a hot, dry summer or fruit won't set but they also need a cold, rainy winter to initiate flowering. In Australia, the area around the Murray River in South Australia seems most promising for commercial production as it has the climate these trees need. Trees are either male or female and you will need one of each. However, one male tree can pollinate up to 10 females planted around it. The tree itself is fairly small with an open habit and irregular branches. *Pistacia* is in the cashew family, Anacardiaceae.

CULTIVATION

Grow in full sun in good-quality free-draining soil. Winters must be cold with repeated frosts and reasonably rainy, too. As spring progresses, rain should decline with summers being hot and dry. If your garden is subjected to occasional heavy rain, plant on a slope or in a mound of fast-draining soil. Some irrigation in summer, with water being applied to the soil only, helps with nut production.

RIGHT *Pistachio nuts start to form when trees are about 5 years old with production increasing as the tree ages. When ripe, the outer hull splits from the hard, inner shell.*

Species	Flower Colour	Blooming Season	Produce Season	Plant Height	Plant Width	Hardiness Zone	Frost Tolerance
Pistacia vera 'Kerman'	reddish brown	spring	late summer	23–33 ft (7–10 m)	25–40 ft (8–12 m)	8	yes

LEFT *Pistachio trees will crop extra heavily one year with few or no nuts the following season. Overcome this by thinning the tiny nutlets by at least a third in heavy bearing years.*

BELOW *High humidity causes fungus diseases that destroy pistachio nuts on the tree. They are rarely successful anywhere other than in dry, inland areas where summers are hot.*

Top Tip

As well as a hot, dry summer, pistachios need to experience considerable cold in winter. The minimum chilling requirement is a total of 600 hours below 7°C (45°F). The plants can tolerate –15°C (5°F).

PRUNUS

Among the most beloved of flowering trees and also extremely useful for the wide range of fruits they produce, the 430 species of the genus *Prunus* are members of the rose (Rosaceae) family. Those grown for their fruit are medium-sized deciduous trees with simple, serrated, elliptical leaves. Their brilliant spring show of white, pink, crimson or soft orange flowers soon gives way to a heavy crop of fleshy fruit with a hard pit or stone at the centre. The fruit matures quite quickly and may be ripe by mid-summer. The foliage often develops fiery autumn tones. Cherry wood is dark and beautifully grained, and is often used for inlays and small objects.

CULTIVATION

Mostly very hardy, but prone to flower damage through late frosts, *Prunus* are reliable trees that, with the exceptions of apricots, peaches and nectarines, will fruit well even in areas with cool summers. Plant in a bright position with moist, humus-rich, well-drained soil. Keep the trees evenly moist but do not use overhead irrigation or the fruit may split. Superior fruiting forms are grafted.

Top Tip

Most *Prunus* cultivars need to be grown with another different cultivar for cross-pollination and fruit production to occur. Not all cultivars are compatible.

RIGHT *A form of the common plum,* Prunus × domestica *'Hauszwetsch' has purple-skinned edible fruit. The fruiting forms of* Prunus *must be propagated by grafting, and must be pruned correctly.*

LEFT *There are many cultivars of* Prunus persica *available, both ornamental and fruiting.*

ABOVE *The fragrant white flowers of* Prunus tomentosa *are followed by downy red fruit. This species is also known as the Manchu, or Nanking, cherry.*

Favourites	Flower Colour	Blooming Season	Produce Season	Plant Height	Plant Width	Hardiness Zone	Frost Tolerance
Prunus domestica	white	spring	summer to autumn	30 ft (9 m)	15 ft (4.5 m)	5–9	yes
Prunus maackii	creamy white	mid-spring	summer	30–50 ft (9–15 m)	25 ft (8 m)	2–9	yes
Prunus mume	rose pink	mid-winter to early spring	early summer	20–30 ft (6–9 m)	25 ft (8 m)	6–10	yes
Prunus persica	white, pink	late winter to early spring	summer to early autumn	8–20 ft (2.4–6 m)	6–20 ft (1.8–6 m)	5–10	yes
Prunus salicina	white	spring	summer to early autumn	30 ft (9 m)	25 ft (8 m)	6–10	yes
Prunus salicina 'Satsuma'	white	spring	summer	25 ft (8 m)	25 ft (8 m)	6–10	yes
Prunus serrula	white	mid-spring	summer	30 ft (9 m)	30 ft (9 m)	6–8	yes
Prunus subhirtella	white, pink	autumn, spring	summer	50 ft (15 m)	25 ft (8 m)	5–9	yes
Prunus subhirtella 'Autumnalis'	pink and white	late autumn, spring	summer	25 ft (8 m)	25 ft (8 m)	5–9	yes
Prunus tomentosa	white to pale pink	early spring	summer	8 ft (2.4 m)	8 ft (2.4 m)	2–8	yes
Prunus triloba	pink	spring	summer	6–12 ft (1.8–3.5 m)	8–12 ft (2.4–3.5 m)	5–9	yes
Prunus, Sato-zakura Group	white, pink	spring	no fruit	30 ft (9 m)	30 ft (9 m)	5–9	yes

RIGHT *The fruit of* Prunus mume *are known as umeboshi plums, a Japanese delicacy. This cultivar, 'Geisha', is grown for its fragrant, pink, semi-double flowers.*

BELOW *Produced early to mid-season,* Prunus persica *'Texstar' peaches have yellow flesh. The best quality fruit is fully ripened on the tree.*

ABOVE Prunus × domestica *'Mount Royal' can be trained into an attractive shape by using wires and clever pruning.*

LEFT Prunus × domestica, the European plum, usually has yellow- or red-skinned fruit. 'Beühlerfrühwetsch' is a purple-skinned cultivar from Germany.
BELOW Prunus persica 'Cresthaven' produces late-season, yellow-fleshed, freestone peaches.

ABOVE Pyrus communis *'Doyenné du Comice' (syn. 'Comice') is regarded as one of the best cultivars. The fruit has sweet, creamy, juicy flesh.*

RIGHT *The thorny branches of* Pyrus communis *are covered with blossoms in spring. This species has been cultivated for centuries for its large sweet-tasting fruit.*

PYRUS

A genus in the rose (Rosaceae) family, *Pyrus* is closely related to the apples *(Malus)*. There are around 20 species of pears, but the cultivated fruiting forms are all cultivars of the common pear *(Pyrus communis)* of Eurasia or the China pear *(Pyrus pyrifolia)* from Japan and China. They have leathery deep green leaves with shallowly serrated edges and in spring are smothered in white flowers. These soon fall and the fruit develops. It ripens slowly and may not become really sweet until it has been in storage for a while. Pear wood is heavy, fine-grained and durable. It is used mainly in musical instruments.

CULTIVATION

Pyrus plants tolerate a wide range of soil types and climatic conditions but can be difficult to grow in very mild areas or those with late frosts. Plant in a sunny position with moist well-drained soil and shelter from strong winds. Prune to shape when young and trim annually. Dwarf varieties are grafted onto quince stocks and can be espaliered. The best forms are propagated by grafting.

Top Tip

Thin out the developing fruit if necessary. Leave only one pear in each cluster, with about 15 cm (6 in) between pears. This will increase the size of the remaining fruit.

BELOW *The fruit of* Pyrus pyrifolia *is known as Asian pear or nashi, and is sweet, crisp and juicy. 'Hosui' is a popular cultivar with particularly good flavour.*

LEFT Pyrus pyrifolia *'Nijisseiki' is a Japanese cultivar first bred in 1898, and its name means "twentieth century" in Japanese. It bears green-yellow fruits.*

Favourites	Flower Colour	Blooming Season	Produce Season	Plant Height	Plant Width	Hardiness Zone	Frost Tolerance
Pyrus calleryana	white	spring	autumn	40 ft (12 m)	40 ft (12 m)	5–9	yes
Pyrus communis	white	spring	summer to autumn	50 ft (15 m)	20 ft (6 m)	2–9	yes
Pyrus communis **'Doyenné du Comice'**	white	spring	summer to autumn	12–20 ft (3.5–6 m)	7–15 ft (2–4.5 m)	2–9	yes
Pyrus pyrifolia	white	spring	summer to autumn	50 ft (15 m)	30 ft (9 m)	4–9	yes
Pyrus pyrifolia **'Nijisseiki'**	white	spring	summer to autumn	12–20 ft (3.5–6 m)	7–15 ft (2–4.5 m)	4–9	yes
Pyrus salicifolia	white	spring	summer to autumn	25 ft (8 m)	15 ft (4.5 m)	4–9	yes

RIGHT Ribes aureum *is known as the golden currant and is mainly grown as an ornamental. The flowers are strongly scented. The berries ripen to blue-black.*

RIBES

A genus of the gooseberry (Grossulariaceae) family, this has over 150 species of deciduous and evergreen shrubs from the northern temperate zones with a few in South America. Those grown for fruit are deciduous bushes with lobed, often bristly leaves and sometimes thorny stems. Sprays of small cream, yellow, green or pink flowers open in spring and may be inconspicuous. Berries (generally known as currants) in varying colours follow and are a rich source of vitamin C. The name *Ribes* is derived from the Persian, *ribas*, meaning "acid-tasting", which describes the unripe fruit.

CULTIVATION

Currant bushes do not require much winter chilling but often crop better with cold winters. They will grow in most soils but they must be well drained. Prune to shape when young and thin out old wood annually. Fruit forms on short lateral branches. The main branches should be cut back to allow lateral fruiting spurs to develop. Feed annually with a balanced general fertiliser. Propagate good fruiting forms from cuttings or layers.

RIGHT Ribes nigrum *'Ben Connan' is a very high-yielding cultivar with a compact growth habit. It produces a delicious fresh fruit that can also be used for jam-making.*

Favourites	Flower Colour	Blooming Season	Produce Season	Plant Height	Plant Width	Hardiness Zone	Frost Tolerance
Ribes aureum	yellow	spring	summer	6 ft (1.8 m)	6 ft (1.8 m)	2–9	yes
Ribes malvaceum	pink	mid-winter to spring	late spring to summer	6 ft (1.8 m)	6 ft (1.8 m)	7–10	yes
Ribes nigrum	yellow-green	spring	summer	7 ft (2 m)	6 ft (1.8 m)	5–9	yes
Ribes rubrum	red and green	late spring to early summer	summer	3–5 ft (0.9–1.5 m)	5–7 ft (1.5–2 m)	3–9	yes
Ribes uva-crispa	green	late winter to early spring	late spring to summer	3 ft (0.9 m)	3 ft (0.9 m)	5–9	yes
Ribes uva-crispa 'Leveller'	green	spring	summer	3 ft (0.9 m)	3 ft (0.9 m)	5–9	yes

LEFT *Commonly known as the gooseberry, the fruit of* Ribes uva-crispa *is cooked to make excellent tarts, pies and jams. The taste ranges from sweet to acid.*

Top Tip

The newer cultivars of currants and gooseberries have larger fruit and better resistance to a range of diseases than the selections available earlier.

RIGHT *The red currant,* Ribes rubrum, *is a deciduous shrub that produces translucent red berries. It makes a good garden ornamental, and the berries taste good too.*

Rubus

A near-worldwide genus belonging to the rose (Rosaceae) family, *Rubus* has 250 species of often thorny deciduous and evergreen shrubs, scramblers and vines. Those grown for their fruit are deciduous shrubs that form clumps of erect or arching canes that are fiercely thorny. The foliage is lobed and usually bristly. Simple 4- or 5-petalled white or pale pink flowers open in spring and are soon followed by soft multi-celled fruit, usually red or purple-black. Native Americans used the roots medicinally and made dyes from the fruit.

Cultivation

While the canes need training and support for maximum production, *Rubus* plants are easily cultivated. Add plenty of compost to the soil before planting, grow in full sun and water well as the fruit ripens. The canes fruit in their second year and are best trained along wires or against a fence. Remove any spent canes after harvest. Bird damage and fungal diseases are the main risks. Propagate from cuttings or layers, or by division.

Above *A late-bearing cultivar, Rubus idaeus 'Heritage' produces heavily into early autumn and requires fewer hours of winter chilling than other raspberries.*

Left *Rubus 'Tayberry' is the result of a cross between a raspberry and a blackberry. The freely produced berries ripen to purple, and have a delightful sweet flavour.*

Favourites	Flower Colour	Blooming Season	Produce Season	Plant Height	Plant Width	Hardiness Zone	Frost Tolerance
Rubus idaeus	white	late spring to early summer	summer	5 ft (1.5 m)	4 ft (1.2 m)	3–9	yes
Rubus idaeus 'Autumn Bliss'	white	summer	autumn	5 ft (1.5 m)	18 in (45 cm)	3–9	yes
Rubus idaeus 'Tulameen'	white	spring to summer	summer	5 ft (1.5 m)	18 in (45 cm)	3–9	yes
Rubus parviflorus	white	summer	summer	15 ft (4.5 m)	10 ft (3 m)	3–9	yes
Rubus spectabilis	pink-purple	spring	summer to autumn	6 ft (1.8 m)	5 ft (1.5 m)	5–9	yes
Rubus 'Tayberry'	white	summer	late summer to autumn	6 ft (1.8 m)	6 ft (1.8 m)	5–9	yes

BELOW *Although the flowers of* Rubus parviflorus *are small, they are still quite attractive. They are followed by even smaller fruit, hence the common name of thimbleberry.*

Top Tip

Trellising *Rubus* plants makes access to the fruit easier, and allows more sunlight to reach the leaves and branches. This will increase the amount of fruit produced.

ABOVE *The pink to purple flowers of* Rubus spectabilis *are carried on thorny stems. Native to western North America, these plants often form dense thickets.*

VACCINIUM

This primarily northern temperate to sub-arctic genus in the heath (Ericaceae) family contains around 450 species of evergreen and deciduous shrubs, small trees and vines, and includes several species cultivated for their edible fruit and many others from which the fruit is gathered in the wild. The cultivated species are deciduous bushes with dark green lance-shaped leaves and wiry stems. Clusters of cream to pale pink, downward-facing, urn-shaped flowers open in spring and are followed by red, purple-blue or black berries, sometimes with a powdery bloom. In recent years the anti-oxidant properties of blueberries have seen them promoted as something of a wonder drug, but regardless of how true that proves to be, they taste very good.

CULTIVATION

These hardy deciduous bushes prefer moist, well-drained, humus-rich, acid soil and may take a few years before producing regular crops. The fruit develops on one-year-old wood and once cropping well the bushes should be pruned and thinned annually. Propagate from half-hardened cuttings or layers.

ABOVE *A northern highbush blueberry (the most widely planted group),* Vaccinium corymbosum *'Earliblue' bears medium-sized sweet fruit on an erect bush.*
LEFT Vaccinium vitis-idaea *is a creeping evergreen shrub. The tiny oval leaves develop bronze tones in winter, and bright red edible but tart berries known as cowberries follow the flower clusters.*
RIGHT *In mild areas* Vaccinium *'Sharpeblue' (syn. 'Sharpblue') will flower and fruit for most of the year. Plants are fast growing and high yielding.*

Favourites	Flower Colour	Blooming Season	Produce Season	Plant Height	Plant Width	Hardiness Zone	Frost Tolerance
Vaccinium corymbosum	white, white and red	spring	summer	3–6 ft (0.9–1.8 m)	5 ft (1.5 m)	2–9	yes
Vaccinium corymbosum 'Bluecrop'	white	spring	summer	6–8 ft (1.8–2.4 m)	6–8 ft (1.8–2.4 m)	3–9	yes
Vaccinium corymbosum 'Patriot'	white	early spring	early to mid-summer	6–8 ft (1.8–2.4 m)	6–8 ft (1.8–2.4 m)	2–9	yes
Vaccinium nummularia	pink	late spring	summer	12–15 in (30–38 cm)	12–15 in (30–38 cm)	7–10	yes
Vaccinium 'Sharpeblue'	white	early spring	late spring to summer	6 ft (1.8 m)	6 ft (1.8 m)	7–10	yes
Vaccinium vitis-idaea	white to pink	late spring	autumn	6 in (15 cm)	24–48 in (60–120 cm)	2–8	yes

BELOW *An attractive ground cover or rock-garden plant,* Vaccinium nummularia *makes a small evergreen shrub. Edible blue-black berries follow the flowers.*

Top Tip

A thick layer of mulch will reduce the risk of damage to the very shallow roots of blueberries. Mulching will also help keep the soil cool and moist, especially in pots.

VITIS

As befits one of the longest cultivated plants, *Vitis* is the type genus for the grape (Vitaceae) family, and is composed of around 60 species of woody deciduous vines from the temperate Northern Hemisphere. Most of the cultivated grape varieties are derived from one species, *Vitis vinifera*, though others, such as the North American native *Vitis labrusca*, are grown in small quantities. Grapes have large, lobed or occasionally toothed leaves, and in spring produce small clusters of green flowers that soon start to develop into the familiar bunches of round berries. No plant has a more colourful history than the grape, which probably features in more legends than all other plants combined.

CULTIVATION

Grape varieties differ most obviously in fruit colour: white, red or black. Some are table grapes, others wine grapes and a few are dual purpose. Plant in full sun with light well-drained soil. Table grapes will benefit from additional humus and summer moisture for producing the plumpest fruit. In winter, prune back to within two buds of the main stem to encourage the strong new growth on which the flowers and fruit will form. Grapes are best trained along wires or against fences. Propagate from cuttings, or by layering or grafting.

ABOVE Vitis vinifera *'Merlot'* grapes ripen to medium-sized blue-black fruit that is used to produce smooth red wines. These plants need some protection from wind.

LEFT *An Austrian cultivar,* Vitis vinifera *'Gelber Muskateller' is grown for white wine-making. It has aromatic qualities, and is a member of the muscat group of grapes.*

Top Tip

Grapes change colour well before reaching their best size and sweetness, so taste-test before picking. Flavour does not improve after harvesting.

LEFT *The small round fruit of* Vitis vinifera *'Chardonnay' is used to make white wine. This vigorous vine usually produces a reliable crop of grapes.*

ABOVE *Another wine-making cultivar,* Vitis vinifera *'Pinot Noir' produces small to medium-sized grapes. These vines can be slow to establish, but are reliable producers.*

Favourites	Flower Colour	Blooming Season	Produce Season	Plant Height	Plant Width	Hardiness Zone	Frost Tolerance
Vitis 'Concord'	green	spring	summer to autumn	15–20 ft (4.5–6 m)	15–20 ft (4.5–6 m)	5–8	yes
Vitis vinifera	green	late spring to early summer	late summer to autumn	35 ft (10 m)	15–30 ft (4.5–9 m)	6–9	yes
Vitis vinifera 'Cabernet Sauvignon'	green	late spring to early summer	late summer to autumn	35 ft (10 m)	15–30 ft (4.5–9 m)	6–9	yes
Vitis vinifera 'Chardonnay'	green	late spring to early summer	late summer to autumn	35 ft (10 m)	15–30 ft (4.5–9 m)	6–9	yes
Vitis vinifera 'Pinot Gris'	green	late spring to early summer	late summer to autumn	35 ft (10 m)	15–30 ft (4.5–9 m)	6–9	yes
Vitis vinifera 'Thompson Seedless'	green	spring	summer to autumn	35 ft (10 m)	15–30 ft (4.5–9 m)	6–9	yes

BULBS, CORMS AND TUBERS

Bulbs, corms and tubers produce some of the most exciting plants in the garden. Half the thrill comes from the speed at which they can grow from embryonic bud to voluptuous flower. The other half comes from the many ways they contribute to our garden. They offer paintbox-colourful blossoms, as with Persian ranunculus; distinctive shapes such as the curiously backward-curving blossoms of cyclamen; huge architectural flowers like the larger flowering onions (*Allium* species) and calla lilies (*Zantedeschia* species) and flowers from the earliest inkling of spring (*Crocus* species) to its end (*Schizostylis* species).

ABOVE *Whether used as potted specimen plants or in massed plantings, tulips add beauty and colour. Tulipa 'Jacqueline' belongs to the Lily-flowered Group.*

LEFT *Hyacinthus cultivars are grown in an amazing variety of colours. The fragrance of these showy blooms is another attractive feature, and they are popular cut flowers.*

SURPRISE PACKETS OF THE GARDEN

Plants possessing underground storage systems of different types, including bulbs, corms and tubers, are known scientifically as geophytes, but are generally all called bulbs. The seasonal dormancy they employ is a strategy to survive periods of adverse weather: usually cold winter temperatures or summer droughts.

True bulbs are perhaps the best known of these types of plants. A true bulb is a modified bud comprised of compressed leaf scales that emerge from a basal plate. Some bulbs consist of fleshy scaly leaves surrounding an embryonic central stem, such as lilies (*Lilium* species). Others, such as daffodils (*Narcissus* species), tulips (*Tulipa* species) and onions (*Allium* species), are covered with a thin papery tunic.

ABOVE *The white calla lily is better known, but* Zantedeschia *'Flame' is a more compact and colourful hybrid cultivar of this rhizomatous genus.*
RIGHT Lilium *'Royal Sunset' is a recent LA Hybrid. Lilies have been cultivated for over 5,000 years.*

Corms consist of a swollen underground stem, replaced annually, that does not contain leaves packed inside. Corms include colchicums, crocuses and dogtooth violets (*Erythronium* species). Although some corms such as colchicums are covered with a papery tunic, most—such as crocuses and gladioli (*Gladiolus* species)—have a more fibrous tunic.

Tubers are specialised underground stems with a fleshy non-scaly structure. The potato is perhaps the most renowned tuber; other examples include dahlias, cyclamen and many anemones. Some plants, such as *Schizostylis coccinea* and its cultivars, have a slightly different underground stem called a rhizome. Many iris family plants are rhizomatous.

Most bulbous plants from regions with a pronounced wet–dry period evolved in response to seasonal drought. Some require a dry baking rest period in summer and can rot if they receive excessive water at this time. These include many tulip species, daffodils, crocus species and fritillaries (*Fritillaria* species). Some bulbs, such as certain dogtooth violets and wake robins (*Trillium* species), come from moister environments. They grow well in shady woodland garden conditions. Still others, such as the common calla lily (*Zantedeschia aethiopica*), thrive in very moist soil.

Many types of bulbous plants, such as crocosmia, lilies and schizostylis, behave as regular perennial border plants that arise in spring and are cut back in winter. But many others completely disappear into the ground after flowering, either in late spring for early spring bloomers (crocus, muscari, tulips, fritillaries, hyacinths and daffodils) or in late summer or autumn for plants blooming in summer (summer-flowering onions). While it can be hard to remember where bulbs are when they disappear below ground, making it easy to accidentally plant on top of them, many gardeners make an art of combining bulbs with perennials and shrubs by planting successive waves of colour and timing them to take maximum advantage of space.

For that reason, bulbs make a wonderful addition to the border. Bulbs that are integrated into a border should be smaller, such as the more diminutive daffodils and flowering onions. Larger daffodils, with their vigorous spreading habit, can occupy too much space, both in the soil and with their coarse leaves that take a month or more to die back. Larger daffodils and tulips are some of the best bulbs for solo mass plantings, creating wonderful seasonal displays—and then being removed so that something new may be planted. Other good border mixers include *Crocosmia* species, *Gladiolus* species and lilies.

Bulbs from the Mediterranean and the steppes of Central Asia are well suited to sunny dry areas with well-drained soil. These include fritillaries, crocus, smaller daffodils, and tulip species. They look good planted in gravel with lavender

(*Lavandula* species), *Agave* species, *Yucca* species and *Penstemon* species, as well as other drought-adapted plants. Taller daffodils make fine naturalised wild-meadow plants, flowering in spring, then dying back in time for the first mowing of the season.

Bulbs are some of the most dramatic container plants, either by themselves or in combination with herbs and other perennials. A pot thickly planted with the simplest red tulips or packed with spidery pink nerines makes a gorgeous display, inside or out. Perhaps the most famous indoor flowering bulbs are amaryllis (*Hippeastrum* plants), which brighten cold-climate winters with their huge colourful blossoms. In warm climates, mass plantings of amaryllis make a spectacular display.

Containers may also be layered with crocus, early daffodils and later-blooming flowering onions for a long-lasting display. Crocus and other smaller bulbs are lovely peeking through ground covers, or with perennials such as euphorbias, whose growing leaves obscure the bulbs' foliage as it dries. With so many different bulbs hailing from such diverse climates worldwide, the possibilities are limitless.

ABOVE *One of the grape hyacinths,* Muscari aucheri *is a summer-flowering bulb. It makes a good bedding display.*
RIGHT *Tulips are perhaps the best known bulbs.* Tulipa 'Golden Parade' *is a stunning Darwin Hybrid Group tulip.*

Top Tip

The ornamental species of *Allium* make excellent long-lasting cut flowers. Alternatively they can be cut and dried for use in floral arrangements.

BELOW *Slender yet strong upright stems hold aloft the rich purple flowers of* Allium rosenbachianum *'Purple King'. The contrasting foliage is blue-green.*

ALLIUM

Unlike the ornamental onions, the edible species among the 700 members of this genus are not grown for their flowers but for their bulbs or foliage. The type genus for the onion (Alliaceae) family, they typically have blue-green foliage that may be grassy, as with chives, strappy like that of leeks or broad-based and hollow, as with onion leaves. With the exception of chives, which are perennial, the edible alliums tend to be biennial and if the flowers appear they are said to have "run to seed" and the bulbs will be of poor quality or useless. The genus features widely in myths and legends, of which the use of garlic to ward off vampires is probably the best known.

CULTIVATION

Onions fall into two basic categories: those to be used immediately and those that will keep for several months. They are either raised from seed sown in situ or from transplants. Shallots and garlic are grown from offsets (cloves) planted in well-drained soil in full sun, usually around mid-winter. They are ready when the tops die back, which is usually in mid-summer. Leeks demand a rich soil with plenty of organic matter. The seed may be sown from spring to early autumn. Bought seedlings are a common method of establishing a crop and can be planted out from spring until early winter. Modern varieties are largely self-blanching but better results are still obtained by mounding soil around the stems as they mature.

ABOVE *Exquisitely dainty, the heads of pure white nodding flowers of* Allium paradoxum *var.* normale *can each contain up to 10 blooms. Unlike the species, it does not produce bulbils (small bulb-like shoots that develop from the base of the parent bulb).*

BELOW Allium howellii *is a Californian native. In late spring it bears rounded heads of starry white, sometimes cream, flowers with prominent stamens.*

RIGHT *Best known for its aromatic grass-like leaves,* Allium schoenoprasum, *or chives, can make a wonderful addition to the herb garden. The pretty pink summer flowers are an added bonus.*

Favourites	Flower Colour	Blooming Season	Flower Fragrance	Plant Height	Plant Width	Hardiness Zone	Frost Tolerance
Allium howellii	white to cream	late spring	no	12–20 in (30–50 cm)	6–8 in (15–20 cm)	8–10	yes
Allium moly	golden yellow	late spring	no	8–15 in (20–38 cm)	8–12 in (20–30 cm)	4–9	yes
Allium paradoxum	white	spring	no	6–12 in (15–30 cm)	4–8 in (10–20 cm)	5–9	yes
Allium rosenbachianum	purple, white	spring	no	24–40 in (60–100 cm)	12–20 in (30–50 cm)	7–10	yes
Allium schoenoprasum	pink	summer	no	6–20 in (15–50 cm)	4–12 in (10–30 cm)	5–10	yes
Allium tuberosum	white	late summer	yes	20 in (50 cm)	8–12 in (20–30 cm)	7–10	yes

ANEMONE

This genus of about 120 species of perennials is part of the buttercup (Ranunculaceae) family. Widespread in the temperate zones, they are a variable lot, ranging from tiny alpines through small woodland natives to large, spreading, clump-forming species, some with fibrous roots, others forming rhizomes or tubers. In addition to the many species, there are countless hybrids and cultivars. Most form a basal clump of finely divided, sometimes ferny foliage. Flowers appear throughout the warmer months, varying in time, size and colour with the species. *Anemos* was an ancient Greek word for wind (hence the common name, windflower) and is also the origin of the name for the anemometer, the wind-measuring instrument.

ABOVE Anemone blanda *is found from southeastern Europe to the Caucasus region. It features tuberous roots, strong fleshy stems and ferny base leaves.*

RIGHT *Also known as the anemone of Greece,* Anemone pavonina *is a clump-forming tuberous species. Its foliage is bright green and fern-like.*

CULTIVATION

Anemones vary in their requirements. Alpine species prefer gritty but moisture-retentive soil and full sun; woodland species like humus-rich soil and cool partial shade; and the bedding forms are best grown in a sunny border and should be kept moist when in flower. Propagate by division or from seed.

Favourites	Flower Colour	Blooming Season	Flower Fragrance	Plant Height	Plant Width	Hardiness Zone	Frost Tolerance
Anemone blanda	white, blue, pink	spring	no	4–8 in (10–20 cm)	6–12 in (15–30 cm)	6–9	yes
Anemone coronaria	various	spring	no	15–24 in (38–60 cm)	8–15 in (20–38 cm)	8–10	yes
Anemone × hybrida	white to pink	late summer to autumn	no	4–5 ft (1.2–1.5 m)	7 ft (2 m)	6–10	yes
Anemone nemorosa	white-cream	early spring	no	3–6 in (8–15 cm)	12 in (30 cm)	5–9	yes
Anemone pavonina	various	spring	no	12 in (30 cm)	12–15 in (30–38 cm)	8–10	yes
Anemone sylvestris	white	spring and early summer	yes	12 in (30 cm)	12 in (30 cm)	4–9	yes

ABOVE *The white, slightly drooping flowers of the fleshy-stemmed* Anemone sylvestris *are the reason for its common names of snowdrop anemone and snowdrop windflower.*

Top Tip

Their variety means that an anemone can be found for almost any outdoor spot, and some (especially the tuberous ones) make good container plants.

ABOVE Anemone coronaria *bears large flowers in most shades apart from yellow. Also known as the florists' anemone and the wind poppy, it has tuberous roots.*

ARISAEMA

This genus of about 150 tuberous perennials is a member of the Araceae (arum) family. Species are found in Africa, North America and Asia, usually growing in moist woodland. Their ornamental leaves and stems and bizarre flowers make them interesting garden subjects. Leaves may be compound or divided and the stems are often mottled in pink to purplish shades. The large hooded flower spathes may be yellow, green, brown, red or pink, striped or mottled. They surround the spadix, a central column of small true flowers, which varies from short and club-like to long and drooping. Dense clusters of orange-red berries form on the spadix following the flowers.

CULTIVATION

Grow frost-tolerant species in a sheltered, semi-shaded or woodland position in a moist, cool, peaty soil. Cover with protective mulch over winter and guard from slugs. Tropical species grown in the greenhouse require a deep pot in an equal mix of leaf mould, grit and slightly acid loam. Propagate from seed or division of the tubers.

ABOVE *The new tubular spathe emerges from the basal leaf-like bracts of this* Arisaema concinnum *plant.*
TOP RIGHT *The hooded spathe of* Arisaema amurense *grows up to 12 cm (5 in) long, striped with dark purple or green.*

Favourites	Flower Colour	Blooming Season	Flower Fragrance	Plant Height	Plant Width	Hardiness Zone	Frost Tolerance
Arisaema amurense	purple and white	spring	no	18 in (45 cm)	6 in (15 cm)	5–9	yes
Arisaema concinnum	green and white	early summer	no	20 in (50 cm)	12 in (30 cm)	8–10	yes
Arisaema kishidae	green and white	early summer	no	18 in (45 cm)	12 in (30 cm)	5–9	yes
Arisaema limbatum	deep purple and white	early summer	no	15 in (38 cm)	10 in (25 cm)	6–9	yes
Arisaema ringens	purple and green	early summer	no	12 in (30 cm)	4 in (10 cm)	6–9	yes
Arisaema sikokianum	deep purple	spring to early summer	no	12–20 in (30–50 cm)	6 in (15 cm)	7–9	yes

BELOW *This Japanese species,* Arisaema kishidae, *is a stocky plant whose flowers are nonetheless striking: the brown-green spathe, mottled white, surrounds a slender spadix.*

RIGHT *Most* Arisaema *plants bear a single flower spike in spring or early summer, held aloft on flowering spikes that may vary considerably in height.* Arisaema limbatum *has a deep purple spathe, striped with white, and a pale green spadix.*

Top Tip

These plants are generally fairly hardy and can be planted outdoors in light or dappled shade. Provide ample water during the growing season. Protect from slugs.

LEFT Calochortus albus *is also known as the fairy lantern or white globe lily. It has pretty globe-shaped flowers and is native to southern California.*
BELOW Calochortus tolmiei *can survive in poor soil like that of its native habitat on the west coast of the USA. Its white to lilac flowers are bearded on the inside with violet hairs.*

CALOCHORTUS

This group of around 60 species of bulbs is found in the Americas, especially the western regions of the USA. Variously known as mariposa tulip, sego lily or fairy lantern, most species form a clump of narrow grassy leaves, and in spring and summer wiry stems carry flowers with 3 petals and 3 petal-like sepals. The flowers, which cover a wide colour range and are often beautifully marked, may be upright or nodding, and when upward facing they can be rather tulip-like. The genus name *Calochortus* comes from the Greek *kallos* (beautiful) and *chortos* (grass). In the past, Native Americans ate the bulbs of certain species.

CULTIVATION
Although mainly very hardy, mariposa tulips require a climate that is warm and dry in summer. Plant them in full sun in gritty free-draining soil—a rockery or raised bed is ideal. Water well from late winter on but allow them to dry off after flowering. Propagate by division in autumn or raise from seed.

Favourites	Flower Colour	Blooming Season	Flower Fragrance
Calochortus albus	white early	spring to summer	no
Calochortus luteus	yellow	spring	no (20–50 cm
Calochortus monophyllus	yellow	spring	no (15–25 cm
Calochortus nuttallii	white to yellow	late spring to summer	no
Calochortus splendens	pale pinkish lilac	late spring to early summer	no
Calochortus tolmiei	white, cream or pale mauve	spring to early summer	no

Top Tip

Calochortus species are thought to be difficult to grow, but given plenty of summer sun, a good location and enough water when growing, they will reward gardeners with lovely blooms.

ABOVE Calochortus monophyllus *is one of the upward-facing tulip-like species. The flowers are a clear yellow.*
LEFT *The flowers of* Calochortus splendens *are white to pale lilac. The plant needs good soil and part-shade.*
BELOW *The spring flowers of* Calochortus luteus *are extremely interesting. They are bell-shaped and yellow, with reddish brown spots and markings. There are also fine hairs inside.*

Plant Height	Plant Width	Hardiness Zone	Frost Tolerance
8–20 in (20–50 cm)	4 in (10 cm)	5–9	yes
8–20 in (8 cm)	3 in	5–10	yes
6–10 in (10 cm)	4 in	5–9	yes
6–15 in (15–38 cm)	4 in (10 cm)	5–9	yes
12–24 in (30–60 cm)	4 in (10 cm)	5–10	yes
6–15 in (15–38 cm)	4 in (10 cm)	5–10	yes

RIGHT Camassia cusickii is native to northeastern Oregon, and produces starry pale blue flowers on tall slender spikes.

CAMASSIA

This genus of 5 species of bulbs belongs to the hyacinth family (Hyacinthaceae) and occurs mainly in western North America. The Latin name *Camassia* comes from the Native American name, which is usually transliterated as *Quamash*. The meaning of the name is unclear, but what is known is that the edible bulbs were an important element in the diet of the native peoples. As garden plants they are tough and very adaptable, and 1 species, *Camassia leichtlinii,* has been extensively developed into garden forms. *Camassia* species have long narrow leaves, and in late spring and early summer they produce heads of 6-petalled flowers atop strong stems, rather reminiscent of some of the *Agapanthus* species.

CULTIVATION

The plants are mostly frost hardy and easily grown in fertile well-drained soil that does not dry out. Plant in full or half sun. Species may be raised from seed, but these take up to 5 years to bloom. Most garden plants are cultivars and may be propagated by division during winter.

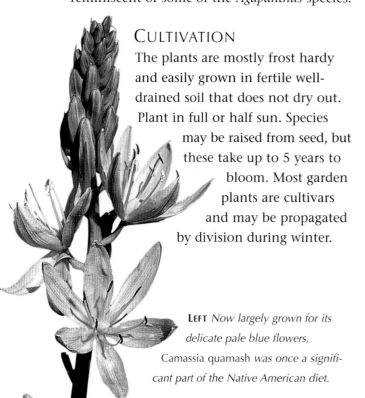

LEFT Now largely grown for its delicate pale blue flowers, Camassia quamash was once a significant part of the Native American diet.

RIGHT Camassia leichtlinii is particularly attractive for its gentle colours. Its slender flower stems are pale green, complemented by a covering of soft white flowers.

Top Tip

These bulbous perennials are ideal for borders in temperate climates. The dead flowers tend to persist on the plant, so they need to be trimmed off periodically.

Favourites	Flower Colour	Blooming Season	Flower Fragrance	Plant Height	Plant Width	Hardiness Zone	Frost Tolerance
Camassia cusickii	blue	late spring to early summer	no	24–36 in (60–90 cm)	6 in (15 cm)	5–9	yes
Camassia leichtlinii	creamy white	late spring	no	2–4 ft (0.6–1.2 m)	6 in (15 cm)	4–9	yes
Camassia leichtlinii 'Semiplena'	creamy white	late spring	no	2–4 ft (0.6–1.2 m)	6 in (15 cm)	4–9	yes
Camassia leichtlinii subsp. *suksdorfii*	blue to violet	late spring	no	24–36 in (60–90 cm)	6 in (15 cm)	4–9	yes
Camassia quamash	blue	spring and early summer	no	8–30 in (20–75 cm)	6 in (15 cm)	4–9	yes
Camassia scilloides	blue, violet, white	late summer	no	8–30 in (20–75 cm)	4 in (10 cm)	4–9	yes

RIGHT Camassia leichtlinii *subsp.* leichtlinii *is also known as* C. leichtlinii 'Alba'. *It bears racemes of creamy white flowers in late spring.*

COLCHICUM

ABOVE *An easily grown cultivar, Colchium speciosum 'Album' displays its goblet-shaped, weather-resistant, white flowers in autumn.*

ABOVE *Colchium speciosum 'The Giant' is a robust perennial producing violet-pink flowers with white bases. The flowers are larger than those of other species.*

This genus of around 45 species of corms is found from eastern Europe to northern Africa and eastwards to China. Although not related to the true crocuses, the common name of autumn crocus is an apt description of the habit and appearance of many of the species. The plants are dormant and leafless in summer. Their flowers have 6 petals, usually in 2 whorls, and start to appear from early autumn before the foliage develops. Double-flowered forms are available. This genus is famous as the source of the cancer treatment drug colchicine, a mutagen that affects cell division and is sometimes used by plant breeders to produce new cultivars.

CULTIVATION

Hardy and adaptable plants that are great favourites with enthusiasts of rockery gardens, *Colchicum* species thrive in zones that have 4 distinct seasons. Some species require a hot dry summer to flower well, but most plants are happy in any fertile well-drained soil in either full or half sun. They also do well in containers.

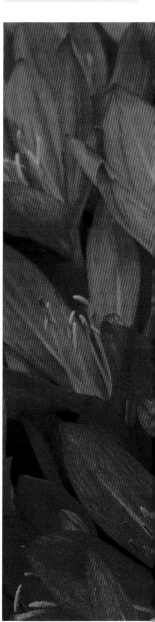

Favourites	Flower Colour	Blooming Season	Flower Fragrance	Plant Height	Plant Width	Hardiness Zone	Frost Tolerance
Colchicum agrippinum	lilac-pink	early autumn	no	3–4 in (8–10 cm)	2 in (5 cm)	5–9	yes
Colchicum autumnale	lilac-pink	late summer to mid-autumn	no	4–6 in (10–15 cm)	3 in (8 cm)	5–9	yes
Colchicum cilicicum	pinkish purple	autumn	no	4 in (10 cm)	3 in (8 cm)	4–9	yes
Colchicum parnassicum	lilac-pink	autumn	no	4–6 in (10–15 cm)	3 in (8 cm)	5–9	yes
Colchicum speciosum	lilac-pink; white throat	autumn	no	7 in (18 cm)	4–6 in (10–15 cm)	6–9	yes
Colchicum speciosum 'Album'	white	autumn	no	7 in (18 cm)	4–6 in (10–15 cm)	6–9	yes

LEFT Colchium cilicicum *needs deep soil and full sun to produce its purplish pink funnel-shaped flowers. Lance-shaped leaves grow to 38 cm (15 in) long.*
BELOW *When the lilac-pink flowers of* Colchicum parnassicum *appear, it is said to be an early sign of autumn. They grow in clusters and are quite large.*

CONVALLARIA

Better known as lily-of-the-valley, this plant has been cultivated since at least 1000 BC, which is not surprising considering its unique and intense fragrance and the ease with which it grows. The sole species in the genus is a low-spreading perennial found over much of the northern temperate zone. Its vigorous rhizomes can colonise a large area, and in spring it produces bright green lance-shaped leaves and short-stemmed flower-heads with their white bell-shaped blooms. A pale pink-flowered form is available. These are followed by red berries. When seventeenth-century herbalists prescribed lily-of-the-valley to strengthen the heartbeat they were correct, because it contains glycoside compounds that have been used in modern-day heart medications.

ABOVE *'Hardwick Hall',* a cultivar of Convallaria majalis, is *characterised by very wide green leaves edged with pale green.*

Top Tip

Lily-of-the-valley can be grown indoors in a container, then planted outside after flowering. A top dressing of leaf mould is recommended in autumn.

CULTIVATION

Plant in dappled shade with deep, moist, well-drained soil. A cool winter is required for proper dormancy. The rhizomes, known as pips, are somewhat invasive in loose soil. Propagate by division.

RIGHT Convallaria majalis *'Prolificans' bears inflorescences of fragrant white flowers. The flowers do not have the distinctive bell shape of the species— some people have described them as malformed.*

LEFT *The pink-flowered varieties of* Convallaria majalis *are referred to as* C. majalis *var.* rosea. *Like the species, they are valued for their beautiful sweet perfume.*

BELOW *Although lily-of-the-valley (*Convallaria majalis*) is now one of the most popular flowers in the world, it was once considered bad luck to cultivate this plant.*

Favourites	Flower Colour	Blooming Season	Flower Fragrance	Plant Height	Plant Width	Hardiness Zone	Frost Tolerance
Convallaria majalis	white	late spring to early summer	yes	8–12 in (20–30 cm)	12 in (30 cm)	3–9	yes
Convallaria majalis 'Aureomarginata'	white	late spring to early summer	yes	8–12 in (20–30 cm)	12 in (30 cm)	3–9	yes
Convallaria majalis 'Hardwick Hall'	white	late spring to early summer	yes	8–12 in (20–30 cm)	12 in (30 cm)	3–9	yes
Convallaria majalis 'Prolificans'	white	late spring to early summer	yes	8–12 in (20–30 cm)	12 in (30 cm)	3–9	yes
Convallaria majalis var. *rosea*	pink	late spring to early summer	yes	8–12 in (20–30 cm)	12 in (30 cm)	3–9	yes
Convallaria majalis 'Variegata'	white	late spring to early summer	yes	8–12 in (20–30 cm)	12 in (30 cm)	3–9	yes

CRINUM

Found throughout the tropics and subtropics, this is a genus of around 130 species of bulbs belonging to the amaryllis family (Amaryllidaceae). Leaves are usually long and strappy, may be evergreen or deciduous and range from no more than about 5 cm (2 in) long in the smallest species to well over 0.9 m (3 ft) in the largest. Strong flower stems develop in the centre of the foliage clump and carry heads of large, often fragrant, 6-lobed, trumpet-shaped flowers in shades of white or pink. Round seed pods follow. The genus name comes from the Greek *krinon* (a lily), and though poisonous, extracts of the bulbs have been used medicinally, mainly in poultices for wounds.

CULTIVATION

Few species will tolerate any but the lightest frosts, and all prefer a warm climate. Although often found in damp ground, they grow just as well in moist well-drained soil. Plant in full or half sun with the bulb neck above the surface. Propagation is mainly from seed.

BELOW Crinum × powellii *'Album' is the white form of this popular hybrid. It is usually easily cultivated, but may need staking.*
BELOW LEFT Crinum × powellii *has light to mid-green strap-like foliage and bears umbels of fragrant deep pink blooms from late summer to autumn.*

Top Tip

Crinum species are best planted in spring and should be kept well watered during the growing season. Keep moist after flowering.

ABOVE Crinum moorei *is quite a cold-hardy species and will grow well in light to deep shade. The soft pink flowers are borne on stems that are up to 90 cm (36 in) high.*
RIGHT Crinum americanum, *the southern swamp lily, bears up to 6 pure white flowers, growing up to 12 cm (5 in) long.*

Favourites	Flower Colour	Blooming Season	Flower Fragrance	Plant Height	Plant Width	Hardiness Zone	Frost Tolerance
Crinum americanum	white	spring to autumn	yes	20 in (50 cm)	18 in (45 cm)	9–11	no
Crinum bulbispermum	white to pink; red mid-stripe	late spring	yes	24 in (60 cm)	18 in (45 cm)	6–10	yes
Crinum 'Ellen Bosanquet'	deep reddish pink	summer	no	18–24 in (45–60 m)	18 in (45 cm)	8–11	yes
Crinum erubescens	white	summer to autumn	yes	36 in (90 cm)	4 ft (1.2 m)	9–12	no
Crinum moorei	white to pink	late summer to early autumn	yes	36 in (90 cm)	24 in (60 cm)	8–11	yes
Crinum × powellii	pink	late summer to autumn	yes	3–5 ft (0.9–1.5 m)	24 in (60 cm)	7–10	yes

CROCUS

Known as a harbinger of spring, *Crocus* is a member of the iris (Iridaceae) family. This Eurasian genus includes a few autumn-flowering species, though it should not be confused with autumn crocus (*Colchicum* species). *Crocus* is made up of around 80 species of corms that usually have fine grassy foliage and short-stemmed, long-tubed, 6-petalled flowers with a conspicuous divided style at the centre. The flowers may be white, yellow or any shade from lavender to purple. The brightly coloured styles of *Crocus sativus* are the source of saffron, the high cost of which is understandable since it takes 4,000 hand-picked crocuses to produce 28 g (1 oz) of saffron.

CULTIVATION

Mostly very hardy and easily grown in any sunny or partly shaded position, crocuses do well in rockeries or may be naturalised in lawns or deciduous woodlands. While their seeds germinate freely, established clumps multiply naturally and can be broken up every few years.

Top Tip

Crocus bulbs can be left undisturbed in the garden for years if winters are not too wet. Established bulbs will bloom earlier in the season than newly planted ones.

Favourites	Flower Colour	Blooming Season	Flower Fragrance	Plant Height	Plant Width	Hardiness Zone	Frost Tolerance
Crocus chrysanthus	pale yellow to orange-yellow	spring	yes	3–4 in (8–10 cm)	4 in (10 cm)	4–9	yes
Crocus 'Jeanne d'Arc'	white	spring	no	4 in (10 cm)	4 in (10 cm)	4–9	yes
Crocus sativus	lilac-purple, white	autumn	yes	2–4 in (5–10 cm)	4 in (10 cm)	6–8	yes
Crocus serotinus	white to mauve	autumn	yes	2–4 in (5–10 cm)	4 in (10 cm)	5–9	yes
Crocus sieberi	white, lilac-blue; yellow throat	spring to summer	yes	3–4 in (8–10 cm)	3 in (8 cm)	7–9	yes
Crocus tommasinianus	lavender-blue; silver highlights	late winter to spring	no	6 in (15 cm)	3 in (8 cm)	5–9	yes

LEFT *The grass-like leaves of* Crocus serotinus *may emerge with the flowers in autumn. The flowers of strong-growing C. s. subsp. salzmannii, seen here, are larger than the species.*
BELOW *The source of saffron,* Crocus sativus *is a low-growing plant with decorative flowers. The red style is harvested by hand, then dried before being used as a flavouring.*

ABOVE *One of the very large Dutch hybrids,* Crocus 'Jeanne d'Arc' *has pure white flowers that can be used as a contrast with other colours or massed together.*
ABOVE LEFT *A particularly beautiful cultivar,* Crocus tommasinianus 'Bobbo' *has been a favourite since it was first bred in 1924.*

RIGHT *Cyclamen cilicium 'Album' bears masses of snow white flowers displaying the slightly twisted petals of the species. This vigorous plant has rounded heart-shaped leaves.*

BELOW *The dainty flowers of* Cyclamen hederifolium *(syn. C. neapolitanum) make an attractive display, especially when grouped in large numbers.*

CYCLAMEN

Instantly recognisable because of the popularity of the potted florists' cyclamen (cultivars of *Cyclamen persicum*), this genus in the primrose (Primulaceae) family has 19 species of tuberous perennials that in their wild forms are far daintier than those usually seen. They occur naturally around the Mediterranean and in western Asia, and most species have heart-shaped leaves, often with marbled patterning. The foliage may be evergreen or briefly deciduous. At varying times depending on the species, long-stemmed, nodding, white, pink, red or purple flowers develop from the centre of the tuber. *Cyclamen* is known as sow-bread, as pigs relish the tubers. Don't be tempted to try them though, as they apparently have drastic purgative effects on people.

CULTIVATION

Cyclamen vary in hardiness but few will tolerate prolonged cold wet conditions. They need perfect drainage, preferably with the tuber planted on or near the soil surface. Dappled shade is best and a cool rockery is ideal. Some do well in deciduous woodlands. Propagate from seed or by division.

Top Tip

Whether growing florists' cyclamens indoors or wild species in the garden, the right amount of water is the key to success. Never over-water.

Favourites	Flower Colour	Blooming Season	Flower Fragrance
Cyclamen africanum	pale to deep pink	autumn	no
Cyclamen cilicium	soft pink, darker at petal base	autumn to early spring	yes
Cyclamen coum	white, pink, purple-pink	winter to early spring	no
Cyclamen hederifolium	pink, darker at petal base	autumn	yes
Cyclamen persicum	white, mauve, pink	winter	yes
Cyclamen purpurascens	pale to dark purple-red	summer	yes

RIGHT *The large silver-marked leaves of* Cyclamen purpurascens *appear with the vibrantly coloured strongly scented flowers during summer.*

BELOW Cyclamen persicum *flowers occur naturally in shades of white, pink and mauve, with darker centres. The leaves, too, are variably coloured and marked.*

Plant Height	Plant Width	Hardiness Zone	Frost Tolerance
6 in (15 cm)	8–12 in (20–30 cm)	9–10	no
3–5 in (8–12 cm)	4–6 in (10–15 cm)	7–10	yes
2–4 in (5–10 cm)	6–12 in (15–30 cm)	6–10	yes
4–6 in (10–15 cm)	6–12 in (15–30 cm)	6–9	yes
8–12 in (20–30 cm)	6–12 in (15–30 cm)	9–10	no
4–6 in (10–15 cm)	6–12 in (15–30 cm)	5–9	yes

CYRTANTHUS

*C*yrtanthus is a southern African genus of about 50 species, a few of which are grown. In their homelands, they come from a variety of climates so there's a *Cyrtanthus* suitable for areas where winter is the rainiest time (flowers in spring), where summer is the rainiest time (flowers in autumn and winter) and where rain is evenly spread through the year (either spring or autumn flowers). The only thing they don't like is repeated sharp frosts though the autumn blooming types, which are dormant in the winter dry season, will tolerate light frosts. Flowers are mainly in the orange and red range though pink, yellow or cream forms are also available. *Cyrtanthus* is in the Amaryllidaceae or hippeastrum family.

CULTIVATION

Plant bulbs in spring or autumn, mostly a few centimetres underground although the impressive Scarborough lily (*Cyrtanthus elatus*) is planted with its neck and shoulders above ground. Good soil drainage is essential and these bulbs do best in fertile soil that contains rotted organic matter. Full sun gives the best flowering performance but they will take a few hours shade each day.

ABOVE *The South African bulb* Cyrtanthus obliquus *flowers in early summer. It takes sun or part shade but not repeated heavy frosts.* **LEFT** *Once known as* Vallota *but now included in* Cyrtanthus, C. elatus *or Scarborough lily is the showiest of the genus. The scarlet flowers appear in early summer.*

LEFT *Dying back over the winter, the not very frost-tolerant fire lily (Cyrtanthus falcatus) produces attractive clusters of pendulous flowers in early spring. Plant with a third of the bulb above ground.*

BELOW *After the Vallota (opposite, left) the red ifafa lily (Cyrtanthus obrienii) is probably the most widely grown member of the genus. Early spring flowers are produced straight from the bare ground, before the leaves.*

Top Tip

Evergreen types like moisture throughout the year but those that die back to the ground for a period need dryness at that time. All can be grown in pots kept dry as needed.

Favourites	Flower Colour	Blooming Season	Flower Fragrance	Plant Height	Plant Width	Hardiness Zone	Frost Tolerance
Cyrtanthus elatus	scarlet, pink	spring	no	20–24 in (50–60 cm)	12–18 in (30–45 cm)	8–9	no
Cyrtanthus obrienii	bright red	spring	no	12–15 in (30–38 cm)	12–15 in (30–38 cm)	8–9	yes
Cyrtanthus 'Red Prince'	bright red	spring	no	20–24 in (50–60 cm)	12–18 in (30–45 cm)	8–9	no

DAHLIA

Beloved by gardeners everywhere, this daisy family genus consists of around 30 species of tuberous rooted perennials and subshrubs. They have attractive foliage, with deep to bright green lobed leaves, hollow stems and bold flowerheads that, due to much cultivation, may vary greatly. Dahlias can be broadly divided into tall border plants and low-growing bedding dahlias, though a more detailed classification sorts them into 10 groups based on the size and type of flowerhead; this ranges from tiny pompon to large giant-flowered cactus types. Colours include shades of white and cream to bright yellow and deep red. Mostly native to Mexico, these flamboyant plants were originally cultivated by the Aztecs for their large edible roots.

ABOVE *One of the Decorative cultivars,* Dahlia *'Ted's Choice' bears beautiful full purple-pink blooms, spanning 10–15 cm (4–6 in) across, complemented by rich green foliage.*

CULTIVATION

Plant dahlias in a sunny open position with fertile, free-draining, humus-rich soil. In cold climates, where frozen or waterlogged soil is likely to occur, the tubers should be lifted and stored near-dry in a frost-free place. Most species can be propagated by dividing the tubers or by taking cuttings off young shoots.

ABOVE *Fast-growing* Dahlia *'Alfred Grille' can reach a height of 1.2–1.8 m (4–6 ft). This lovely Cactus dahlia has wispy blooms in shades of yellow and pink.*

LEFT *Recently introduced,* Dahlia *'Lilac Taratahi' is a Cactus dahlia. Bursting open on elegant tall stems, the ray florets of lilac-pink quill-like petals give the lovely full blooms a delicate appearance.*

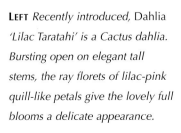

Top Tip

When planting dahlias, select a site that is sheltered from strong winds. Even in a protected spot, dahlias will often need staking to prevent them falling over.

ABOVE *The snow white flowers of Dahlia 'My Love' are a stunning addition to any garden. This Semi-cactus dahlia is popular for floral arrangements, particularly bridal bouquets.*

Favourites	Flower Colour	Blooming Season	Flower Fragrance	Plant Height	Plant Width	Hardiness Zone	Frost Tolerance
Dahlia, Anemone-flowered	white to pink, red, yellow, orange	summer to autumn	no	2–6 ft (0.6–1.8 m)	12–24 in (30–60 cm)	8–11	yes
Dahlia, Ball	white to pink, red, yellow, orange	summer to autumn	no	1–6 ft (0.3–1.8 m)	12–24 in (30–60 cm)	8–11	yes
Dahlia, Cactus	white to pink, red, yellow, orange	summer to autumn	no	4–6 ft (1.2–1.8 m)	18–30 in (45–75 cm)	8–11	yes
Dahlia coccinea	yellow, orange to dark red	summer to autumn	no	10 ft (3 m)	4 ft (1.2 m)	8–11	yes
Dahlia, Collarette	white to pink, red, yellow, orange	summer to autumn	no	4 ft (1.2 m)	18 in (45 cm)	9–11	yes
Dahlia, Decorative	white to pink, red, yellow, orange	summer to autumn	no	3–6 ft (0.9–1.8 m)	18–30 in (45–75 cm)	8–11	yes
Dahlia imperialis	lavender, pink, white	late autumn to winter	no	12–20 ft (3.5–6 m)	5–10 ft (1.5–3 m)	9–11	yes
Dahlia merckii	white to pink or purple	summer to autumn	no	2–5 ft (0.6–1.5 m)	36 in (90 cm)	8–11	yes
Dahlia, Pompon	white to pink, red, yellow, orange	summer to autumn	no	12–36 in (30–90 cm)	12–24 in (30–60 cm)	8–11	yes
Dahlia, Semi-cactus	white to pink, red, yellow, orange	summer to autumn	no	4–6 ft (1.2–1.8 m)	18–30 in (45–75 cm)	8–11	yes
Dahlia, Single	white to pink, red, yellow, orange	summer to autumn	no	1–5 ft (0.3–1.5 m)	12–24 in (30–60 cm)	8–11	yes
Dahlia, Waterlily	white to pink, red, yellow, orange	summer to autumn	no	3–5 ft (0.9–1.5 m)	18–30 in (45–75 cm)	8–11	yes

LEFT *With large leaves and single large flowers in pink, lavender or white,* Dahlia imperialis *is a native of Central America. This species can reach a height of up to 6 m (20 ft).*
BELOW *While* Dahlia 'Explosion' *is classed as a Semi-cactus type of dahlia, it is often called a "dinner-plate dahlia", as its huge red-striped yellow flowerheads are as large as the name suggests.*

LEFT Dahlia 'Aurwen's Violet' *is a Pompon dahlia. With mid-green leaves and a hemispherical head of purple-red petals held on tall thin stems, this elegant plant reaches a height of up to 90 cm (36 in).*
RIGHT *Flowering from early summer to early autumn,* Dahlia 'Gay Princess' *is a Waterlily dahlia with rich green foliage and 10–15 cm (4–6 in) wide flowers in shades of pink or white.*

LEFT Dahlia *'Golden Charmer'* is a Semi-cactus dahlia with broad florets of yellow-bronze petals. The large flowerheads are 10–15 cm (4–6 in) across.

Top Tip

How dahlia tubers are stored prior to planting is crucial. They should be kept in a dark spot with high humidity, and then regularly checked for signs of rotting or mould.

ABOVE Dahlia *'Rot'* is a member of the Single-flowered group of dahlias, which means it has the simple wide-open single flowerhead that is typical of this form.

BELOW *Creamy white petals, deepening to rich yellow towards the base, and leaves mottled with brown are the signature characteristics of Erythronium helenae.*

ERYTHRONIUM

Belonging to the lily (Liliaceae) family, this genus of spring-flowering bulbs contains around 20 species. Commonly known as trout lily or dogtooth violet, many species are North American, while a few are found from Europe to temperate East Asia. The leaves may be matt to quite glossy and in some cases are marbled, mottled or spotted with silver, brown, maroon or bronze. The white, cream, soft yellow or pink flowers often face downwards and are starry, with 6 reflexed petals. The seed pods and bulbs were popular foods with Native Americans, though as some are known to be emetic it seems unlikely that they were eaten in large quantities.

CULTIVATION

Natural woodlanders, *Erythronium* species are most at home under deciduous trees or in shaded rockeries. They prefer dappled shade with gritty yet humus-rich well-drained soil. They do not tolerate humid heat. Most prefer cool climates. Most species multiply quickly, sometimes by stolons, and may be divided after a few years. Otherwise, raise from seed, which should be sown as soon as it ripens.

RIGHT *As the pink buds of Erythronium revolutum open, the petals gradually recurve to display a beautiful colouring of cyclamen pink, centred with yellow.*

ABOVE *A Californian native,* Erythronium tuolumnense *bears yellow lily-like flowers on tall stems. Otherwise unadorned, the leaves are slightly wavy at the edges.* **LEFT** *With mottled leaves and nodding creamy white flowers marked with yellow and maroon,* Erythronium californicum *'White Beauty' is a popular cultivar.*

Top Tip

Once established, *Erythronium* species resent disturbance to their roots. Plant them where they are to remain, and divide them only when they become too crowded.

Favourites	Flower Colour	Blooming Season	Flower Fragrance	Plant Height	Plant Width	Hardiness Zone	Frost Tolerance
Erythronium californicum	creamy white, yellow centre	spring	no	10 in (25 cm)	6 in (15 cm)	4–9	yes
Erythronium dens-canis	white, pink, lilac	spring to early summer	no	6–8 in (15–20 cm)	6 in (15 cm)	3–9	yes
Erythronium helenae	white to cream, yellow centre	spring	no	6–15 in (15–38 cm)	4 in (10 cm)	4–9	yes
Erythronium 'Pagoda'	sulfur yellow	spring	no	6–12 in (15–30 cm)	8 in (20 cm)	4–9	yes
Erythronium revolutum	cyclamen pink, yellow centre	spring	no	6–8 in (15–20 cm)	6 in (15 cm)	4–9	yes
Erythronium tuolumnense	bright yellow	spring	no	8–15 in (20–38 cm)	8 in (20 cm)	4–9	yes

EUCOMIS

This mainly South African genus, which is made up of 15 species of bulbs, is classified in the hyacinth family (Hyacinthaceae). The species have glossy, light green, strappy leaves and form large clumps of basal foliage rosettes. In summer they produce long stems bearing simple, star-shaped, mostly green to white flowers with an interesting tuft of foliage at the top, rather like that atop a pineapple—hence they are commonly known as pineapple lilies. (As well, the genus name comes from the Greek *eukomos,* which means lovely haired.) The flower stems are often arching and may fall over under their own weight. They make attractive cut decorations and last for weeks in water. The bulbs are edible and were used as a food source by tribespeople in Africa.

CULTIVATION

Of variable hardiness, the most commonly cultivated species in this genus are reasonably tough. In frosty areas they can be safely stored for winter indoors as dormant bulbs in moist soil. Plant out in full sun in moist, humus-rich, well-drained soil. Propagation is usually by division, but *Eucomis* species can be raised from seed and may self-sow.

ABOVE *The summer display of purple-edged greenish flowers of* Eucomis bicolor *is followed by bright green fruit. A crown of light green bracts tops the flower stem.*

Top Tip

Use *Eucomis* species indoors as a potted plant to create an interesting focal point. If repotted each year, they will thrive and flower for years.

ABOVE *Beneath the tuft of mid-green bracts, this* Eucomis comosa *hybrid bears creamy white flowers on tall purple-spotted stems.* **LEFT** *Emerging from rosettes of strappy leaves, the stems of* Eucomis zambesiaca *are covered with masses of white flowers and topped by bright green bracts.*

Above *Greenish white flowers add tonal and textural contrast to the fresh bright green of the strappy leaves, thick stems and rosette of stem-top bracts of* Eucomis autumnalis.

Favourites	Flower Colour	Blooming Season	Flower Fragrance	Plant Height	Plant Width	Hardiness Zone	Frost Tolerance
Eucomis *autumnalis*	greenish white to green	summer to autumn	no	18–30 in (45–75 cm)	24 in (60 cm)	7–10	yes
Eucomis *bicolor*	green, edged with purple	summer	no	15–24 in (38–60 cm)	18 in (45 cm)	8–10	yes
Eucomis *comosa*	greenish white; purple markings	late summer to autumn	no	30–36 in (75–90 cm)	30 in (75 cm)	8–11	yes
Eucomis *'Sparkling Burgundy'*	pale green to pale purple	mid- to late summer	no	18–24 in (45–60 cm)	18 in (45 cm)	7–10	yes
Eucomis *pallidiflora*	greenish white	summer	no	18–30 in (45–75 cm)	30 in (75 cm)	8–10	yes
Eucomis *zambesiaca*	white	late summer	no	12–18 in (30–45 cm)	15 in (38 cm)	8–10	yes

LEFT *Native to northwestern USA and northeastern Asia,* Fritillaria camschatcensis *has pendent bell-shaped flowers in shades of dark purple, maroon-brown and sometimes green-purple.*

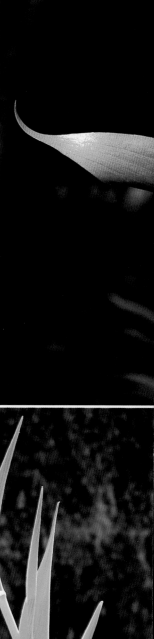

Top Tip

Not every *Fritillaria* species is easy to grow; good species to start with are *F. imperialis,* *F. meleagris* and *F. michailovskyi.* Use in herbaceous borders or pots.

FRITILLARIA

A member of the lily family, this genus of about 100 species includes some rare species that are coveted by many plant collectors. Most are native to the Balkans and the Mediterranean, though species also occur in much of the temperate areas of the Northern Hemisphere. The leaves are narrow and simple with tubular or bell-shaped pendulous flowers borne on erect stems. Petals may be alternately coloured, striped or speckled, often in rather unusual colours, such as chocolate, lime green, sulfur yellow, dusky rose and even grey. Both the genus and common name (fritillary) derive from the Latin word *fritillus*, meaning chequered dice box, an image suggested by the alternately coloured flower petals.

CULTIVATION

These generally frost-hardy plants prefer a climate with distinct seasons. Most species grow well in rockeries or woodland conditions in part-shade with moist, humus-rich, very well-drained soil. Propagation is by seed.

BELOW *Commonly known as the snake's head fritillary,* Fritillaria meleagris *is highly appreciated for its maroon, green or purple flowers, which are strikingly etched or chequered with purple.*

ABOVE *This unusual-looking species,* Fritillaria imperialis, *bears up to 8 red to yellow flowers in a tight pendent cluster, which is crowned with a tuft of upright leaf-like bracts.*
LEFT *The small and graceful* Fritillaria michailovskyi *has lance-shaped clear green leaves and bell-shaped flowers. These are a rich purple-brown colour, with yellow tips.*

Favourites	Flower Colour	Blooming Season	Flower Fragrance	Plant Height	Plant Width	Hardiness Zone	Frost Tolerance
Fritillaria camschatcensis	purple-black, maroon, green	summer	no	10–18 in (25–45 cm)	3–4 in (8–10 cm)	4–9	yes
Fritillaria imperialis	yellow, orange, red	late spring to early summer	no	5 ft (1.5 m)	10–12 in (25–30 cm)	4–9	yes
Fritillaria meleagris	white, green, pink to purple	spring	no	12 in (30 cm)	6 in (15 cm)	4–9	yes
Fritillaria michailovskyi	purple-brown edged in yellow	summer	no	8 in (20 cm)	3 in (8 cm)	7–9	yes
Fritillaria pallidiflora	pale yellow	late spring to early summer	no	15 in (38 m)	6 in (15 cm)	3–9	yes
Fritillaria persica	dark purple	spring	no	3 ft (0.9 m)	12 in (30 cm)	5–9	yes

GALANTHUS

Probably the most welcome harbinger of spring, this normally late winter-flowering Eurasian genus of 15 bulbs in the amaryllis family (Amaryllidaceae) also includes a few species that bloom in autumn. The narrow grassy leaves usually break through shortly after mid-winter, followed by short flower stems that each carry 1 pendulous, white, mildly scented, 6-petalled flower. The inner 3 petals are short and green-tipped. Double-flowered forms are also available. Familiarly known as snowdrop, the genus name *Galanthus* comes from the Greek *gala* (milk) and *anthos* (a flower), referring to the colour of the flower. According to Christian legend, the snowdrop first bloomed to coincide with the Feast of Purification held on 2 February, known as Candlemas Day.

CULTIVATION

Galanthus plants perform best in cool-temperate climates and thrive in woodland or rockery conditions. They prefer dappled shade; moist humus-rich soil and, while very hardy, do need watering during dry times. They may be propagated from seed but usually multiply quickly enough so that division after the foliage dies back is more practical.

Top Tip

Do not allow divided snowdrop bulbs to dry out. Plant promptly, at a depth of 8 cm (3 in), and a similar distance apart.

ABOVE Galanthus plicatus, the Crimean snowdrop, hails from Turkey and Eastern Europe. The inner petals of the snow white flowers are marked with green.

RIGHT As the graceful, nodding, white flowers of Galanthus 'S. Arnott' burst open, they fill the winter garden with a delicious honey fragrance.

Favourites	Flower Colour	Blooming Season	Flower Fragrance	Plant Height	Plant Width	Hardiness Zone	Frost Tolerance
Galanthus elwesii	white with green markings	late winter to spring	yes	10 in (25 cm)	6 in (15 cm)	6–9	yes
Galanthus ikarae	white with green markings	winter	no	6 in (15 cm)	4 in (10 cm)	6–9	yes
Galanthus nivalis	white with green markings	late winter	yes	6 in (15 cm)	8 in (20 cm)	4–9	yes
Galanthus nivalis 'Flore Pleno'	white	late winter	no	6 in (15 cm)	8 in (20 cm)	4–9	yes
Galanthus plicatus	white with green markings	late winter to early spring	no	8 in (20 cm)	6 in (15 cm)	6–9	yes
Galanthus 'S. Arnott'	white	late winter to spring	yes	8 in (20 cm)	6 in (15 cm)	4–9	yes

BELOW *Slender 15–20 cm (6–8 in) high stems carry the dainty, nodding, white flowers of* Galanthus nivalis, *the common snowdrop.*

RIGHT *Blue-green foliage offsets the large, white, scented flowers of* Galanthus elwesii. *Each of the inner petals has delicate green markings.*

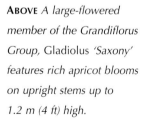

GLADIOLUS

Amember of the iris (Iridaceae) family, this genus comprises some 180 species of cormous perennials found from Europe to western Asia and southern Africa. The leaves range from grassy to sword-like, and the flowers, which are funnel-shaped and borne in a spike, usually open in summer. The large-flowered garden hybrids are mainly derived from South African species, and while their showy flowers will always make them the most popular plants, the less flamboyant species have their own charms, such as the evening scent of *Gladiolus tristis*. A *gladius*—also the origin of the word gladiator—was a Roman sword and the name reflects the sword-shaped foliage.

CULTIVATION

Plant *Gladiolus* species in a sunny position with moist well-drained soil. The corms are best planted fairly deeply as this ensures that the stems are well anchored, sturdy and less susceptible to wind damage. Keep well watered while flowering then allow to dry. In cold areas the corms may be lifted and stored dry. Propagate from natural offsets.

ABOVE *A large-flowered member of the Grandiflorus Group,* Gladiolus *'Saxony' features rich apricot blooms on upright stems up to 1.2 m (4 ft) high.*

RIGHT *Available in a wide range of colours, the small flowers of* Gladiolus, *Primulinus Group hybrid cultivars have a hooded upper petal, as seen in this deep pink-flowered form.*

ABOVE *Commonly known as the Abyssinian sword lily, each stem of* Gladiolus callianthus *carries up to 10 fragrant white flowers, marked with red or purple.*

Top Tip

Use the height of taller *Gladiolus* species to advantage in border plantings. Smaller-growing types make excellent container plants.

RIGHT *Magnificent 15 cm (6 in) wide flowers are the signature of* Gladiolus, Grandiflorus Group. 'Blue Bird' *is a fine example with large purple-blue flowers.*

Favourites	Flower Colour	Blooming Season	Flower Fragrance	Plant Height	Plant Width	Hardiness Zone	Frost Tolerance
Gladiolus callianthus	white with purple or red markings	late summer to early autumn	yes	36–40 in (90–100 cm)	2–12 in (5–30 cm)	9–11	no
Gladiolus communis	pink with red or white markings	spring to summer	no	36–40 in (90–100 cm)	10–12 in (25–30 cm)	6–10	yes
Gladiolus tristis	creamy yellow	spring	yes	24–60 in (60–150 cm)	8–12 in (20–30 cm)	7–10	no
Gladiolus viridiflorus	yellow-green and dull pink	late autumn to winter	no	6–12 in (15–30 cm)	6 in (15 cm)	7–10	yes
***Gladiolus,* Grandiflorus Group**	various	late spring to summer	no	24–60 in (60–150 cm)	12 in (30 cm)	9–11	yes
***Gladiolus,* Primulinus Group**	various	summer	no	24 in (60 cm)	12 in (30 cm)	9–11	yes

HIPPEASTRUM

Also known as amaryllis and knight's star lily, this genus of around 80 species belongs to the bulb family and is indigenous to the Americas. They produce long, strap-like, rather fleshy leaves and magnificent, large, funnel-shaped flowers borne on strong flower stems. The flowers are made up of 6 petals occurring in 2 whorls of 3 petals. There are many common cultivars, and the flowers, opening in late winter, are white, pink or red with widely varying patterns; different species show an even wider colour range. The name *Hippeastrum* comes from the Greek *hippos* (horse) and *astrum* (of the flower), and refers to the resemblance between the shape of the flowerhead and a horse's head.

CULTIVATION
Grow outdoors in frost-free areas or as greenhouse plants in cooler climates. Plant with the tip of the bulb exposed, in moist humus-rich soil. Plenty of water and feeding during the growing period will encourage large flowers. Allow the bulb to dry off after the foliage dies down and flowering finishes. These plants can be grown only from bulbs.

Top Tip

All *Hippeastrum* cultivars make suitable potted house plants and flower well indoors. They grow best in a good-quality loam-based potting mix.

BELOW LEFT Hippeastrum *'Pamela' is valued because it is a profuse bloomer, bearing glorious scarlet flowers that measure up to 25 cm (10 in) in length.*

BELOW Hippeastrum 'Picotee' has beautiful white flowers, each petal edged with a fine red line. It needs warmth and light to produce its best blooms.

ABOVE Hippeastrum 'Christmas Star', with its red, white and green flowers, makes a festive decoration.
LEFT The large, single, deep red flowers of Hippeastrum 'Royal Velvet' lend a tropical warmth to the home when they appear on a potted indoor plant in winter.

Favourites	Flower Colour	Blooming Season	Flower Fragrance	Plant Height	Plant Width	Hardiness Zone	Frost Tolerance
Hippeastrum 'Christmas Star'	red and white; greenish throat	late winter to mid-summer	no	18–24 in (45–60 cm)	12 in (30 cm)	9–12	no
Hippeastrum × johnsonii	red with white streaks	late winter to spring	no	18–24 in (45–60 cm)	12 in (30 cm)	7–11	no
Hippeastrum 'Pamela'	scarlet	late winter to mid-summer	no	18–24 in (45–60 cm)	12 in (30 cm)	9–12	no
Hippeastrum papilio	greenish white; red markings	spring to early summer	no	18–30 in (45–75 cm)	12 in (30 cm)	9–12	no
Hippeastrum 'Picotee'	white, edged with red	late winter to mid-summer	no	12–18 in (30–45 cm)	12 in (30 cm)	9–12	no
Hippeastrum 'Royal Velvet'	deep red	late winter to mid-summer	no	18–24 in (45–60 cm)	12 in (30 cm)	9–12	no

HYACINTHUS

The type genus for its family, the Hyacinth-aceae, *Hyacinthus* contains just 3 species of spring-flowering bulbs found throughout western and Central Asia. The glossy green leaves are narrow and strap-like, rolling slightly inward towards the centre of the plant. The flowers, a widely flared tubular bell-shape, are crowded in clusters on sturdy flower spikes. The garden cultivars come in a range of colours, from white to creamy yellow and shades of pink, red and purple. Although famed for its scent, only 1 species, the common *Hyacinthus orientalis*, is especially fragrant. According to Greek mythology, this flower grew from the bleeding wound of Hyacinth, a boy loved by the god Apollo.

RIGHT *From the middle of spring,* Hyacinthus orientalis *'City of Haarlem' produces tall flower spikes smothered with fragrant creamy yellow blooms. Plant this popular cultivar alongside contrasting single-coloured daffodils (*Narcissus *species) and tulips (*Tulipa *species) for a stunning floral display.*

Top Tip

Flowering potted hyacinths make a lovely gift. Because they are available in colours ranging from blue and pink to purple and white, there's a hyacinth to suit everyone.

CULTIVATION

For spring flowers plant the bulbs in autumn, positioned in half sun with deep, cool, moist, well-drained soil. Plant bulbs at a depth of about 10 cm (4 in), and after initially watering in, water during winter only if conditions are exceptionally dry. Although the bulbs multiply by themselves, showy modern strains tend to weaken with age, bearing fewer flowers, and will need to be replaced annually.

ABOVE Hyacinthus orientalis *'Queen of the Pinks' lives up to its name by bearing a host of pink flowers in spring. Spent flower stems should be removed.*

RIGHT *The sweet scent of* Hyacinthus orientalis *'Jan Bos' makes this a garden favourite. The waxy deep pink blooms look wonderful in mass plantings.*

ABOVE Hyacinthus orientalis 'Blue Jacket' bears long spikes covered with purple-blue blooms and long, erect, bright green leaves. The bulbs flower best in their first year.

RIGHT Hyacinthus orientalis 'Amethyst' makes an excellent container plant. Make sure the soil is well drained and keep moist during the growing season.

Favourites	Flower Colour	Blooming Season	Flower Fragrance	Plant Height	Plant Width	Hardiness Zone	Frost Tolerance
Hyacinthus orientalis	white, pink, blue to purple	early to mid-spring	yes	8–12 in (20–30 cm)	3 in (8 cm)	5–9	yes
Hyacinthus orientalis 'Blue Jacket'	blue with purple stripes	mid-spring	yes	8–12 in (20–30 cm)	3 in (8 cm)	5–9	yes
Hyacinthus orientalis 'Carnegie'	white	mid-spring	yes	8–12 in (20–30 cm)	3 in (8 cm)	5–9	yes
Hyacinthus orientalis 'City of Haarlem'	creamy yellow	mid-spring	yes	8–12 in (20–30 cm)	3 in (8 cm)	5–9	yes
Hyacinthus orientalis 'Jan Bos'	deep pink	mid-spring	yes	8–12 in (20–30 cm)	3 in (8 cm)	5–9	yes
Hyacinthus orientalis 'Pink Pearl'	dark pink, lighter edges	mid-spring	yes	8–12 in (20–30 cm)	3 in (8 cm)	5–9	yes

Ixia

Commonly known as corn lilies or wand flowers, this South African iris family (Iridaceae) genus contains some 50 species of corms with fine grassy foliage that is usually quite short in comparison to the tall, wiry, often arching flower stems. The flowers are simple 5- or 6-petalled structures, often star-shaped, and are borne massed in spikes at the stem tips. There are many cultivars, which are often brightly coloured or may be pale with brighter markings. They also occur in some unusual shades, such as pale blue-green. It is a pity that the name of such beautiful flowers has rather an unpleasant origin: *ixia* is a Greek word for bird droppings, apparently a reference to the sticky sap.

Cultivation

Easily grown in a sunny position, *Ixia* species prefer a light well-drained soil. In hot areas the flowers will last longer in shade. Water well in spring but allow to dry off after flowering. Propagation is usually from offsets or by division of the corms, less commonly from seed. Plant bulbs 5–8 cm (2–3 in) apart.

Right Ixia maculata *has orange to yellow starry flowers, marked brown at the centre, often with reddish undersides. The clusters of flowers appear on thin 45 cm (18 in) high stems.*

Top Tip

In a sunny spot, *Ixia* plants will flatten out their cup-shaped flowers to soak up the sun. In cooler climates they do best in a green-house environment.

LEFT *Ivory or pale lemon flowers, often with nuances of pink, top the slender stems of* Ixia paniculata *from spring to summer.* **BELOW** Ixia curta *bears its lovely flowers in spring. The orange petals have darker markings at the base, and are often deeper coloured on the undersides.*

Favourites	Flower Colour	Blooming Season	Flower Fragrance	Plant Height	Plant Width	Hardiness Zone	Frost Tolerance
Ixia curta	orange with brownish blotch	spring	no	12–18 in (30–45 cm)	6 in (15 cm)	9–10	no
Ixia dubia	orange, yellow; brown centre	spring to summer	no	8–18 in (20–45 cm)	6 in (15 cm)	9–10	no
Ixia maculata	orange, yellow; brown centre	spring to early summer	no	15 in (38 cm)	6 in (15 cm)	9–10	no
Ixia monadelpha	white, pink, blue, mauve, purple	spring to early summer	no	12–18 in (30–45 cm)	6 in (15 cm)	10–11	no
Ixia paniculata	cream, yellow; tinged pink	late spring to early summer	no	12–24 in (30–60 cm)	10 in (25 cm)	9–10	no
Ixia viridiflora	pale green with purple centre	spring to early summer	no	24–36 in (60–90 cm)	8 in (20 cm)	9–10	no

LILIUM

The type genus for the lily (Liliaceae) family, *Lilium* is a group of 100 species of mainly summer-flowering scaly bulbs found through most of the northern temperate zones, especially in East Asia. They are narrow erect plants, usually with one leafy stem per bulb. Large, sometimes fragrant, trumpet-shaped flowers with widely flared or recurved petals form at the top of the stems. The flowers occur in all colours except blue and are often beautifully marked with contrasting colours. Ernest Wilson (1876–1930), who introduced *Lilium regale*, broke his leg during the expedition in which he discovered this plant and thereafter walked with what he referred to as his "lily limp".

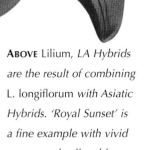

RIGHT *The flowers of* Lilium nepalense *are striking for their darker colour palette. Funnel-shaped pale green flowers curve back to reveal a maroon-red centre.*

CULTIVATION

Lilies will grow in sun or part-shade and prefer a deep, cool, humus-rich soil, preferably made fertile with well-rotted manure. They need good drainage but must not be allowed to dry out. Lilies are easily propagated from natural offsets, bulb scales, seeds and sometimes from bulbils that form in the leaf axils.

ABOVE Lilium, *LA Hybrids are the result of combining* L. longiflorum *with Asiatic Hybrids. 'Royal Sunset' is a fine example with vivid orange and yellow blooms.*

Top Tip

Apply mulch around lily plants. This will provide an insulating layer and will also minimise weeding, thus preventing damage to the roots caused by garden tools.

RIGHT *One of the Asiatic Hybrids, with trumpet flowers characteristic of the group,* Lilium *'Her Grace' has gorgeous golden yellow blooms that face outwards.*

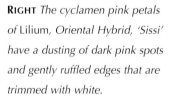

RIGHT *The cyclamen pink petals of* Lilium, *Oriental Hybrid, 'Sissi' have a dusting of dark pink spots and gently ruffled edges that are trimmed with white.*

Favourites	Flower Colour	Blooming Season	Flower Fragrance	Plant Height	Plant Width	Hardiness Zone	Frost Tolerance
Lilium candidum	white	summer to early autumn	yes	3–7 ft (0.9–2 m)	12–18 in (30–45 cm)	6–9	yes
Lilium martagon	dull pink	early summer to early autumn	no	3–8 ft (0.9–2.4 m)	12–18 in (30–45 cm)	4–9	yes
Lilium nepalense	yellow-green; maroon markings	summer	no	24–40 in (60–100 cm)	12–18 in (30–45 cm)	5–9	yes
Lilium pumilum	bright scarlet	summer to early autumn	yes	15–18 in (38–45 cm)	12–18 in (30–45 cm)	5–9	yes
Lilium, American Hybrids	pink, yellow, red, darker spotted	summer	no	4–6 ft (1.2–1.8 m)	12 in (30 cm)	5–10	yes
Lilium, Asiatic Hybrids	various	summer	no	18–48 in (45–120 cm)	12–18 in (30–45 cm)	5–10	yes
Lilium, Candidum Hybrids	white, pink to orange-red	summer	no	24–48 in (60–120 cm)	12–18 in (30–45 cm)	6–9	yes
Lilium, LA Hybrids	various	early to mid-summer	yes	18–36 in (45–90 cm)	12–24 in (30–60 cm)	5–9	yes
Lilium, Longiflorum Hybrids	white	late spring to summer	yes	36 in (90 cm)	24 in (60 cm)	5–10	yes
Lilium, Martagon Hybrids	cream, pink, gold, dull red	mid-summer	yes	5–6 ft (1.5–1.8 m)	12–18 in (30–45 cm)	5–9	yes
Lilium, Oriental Hybrids	white, pink, red, yellow stripe	summer to ealry autumn	yes	4–7 ft (1.2–2 m)	15–24 in (38–60 cm)	6–9	yes
Lilium, Trumpet and Aurelian Hybrids	white, gold, pink, deep red, greenish	summer	no	3–6 ft (0.9–1.8 m)	12–18 in (30–45 cm)	5–9	yes

LEFT *One of the Oriental Hybrids,* Lilium *'Expression' features large glowing white blooms with recurved petals, centred with prominent stamens.*

BELOW Lilium *'Salmon Classic' is a member of the LA Hybrids. Beautifully scented, the attractive apricot flowers feature light spotting at the petal base and a slightly deeper coloured midrib.*

ABOVE Lilium *'Montreaux' is from the large group of Asiatic Hybrids; it has unscented, upward-facing, pale pink flowers dotted brown at the centre.*

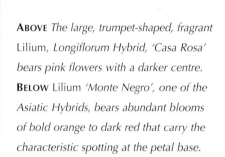

ABOVE *The large, trumpet-shaped, fragrant Lilium,* Longiflorum Hybrid, 'Casa Rosa' *bears pink flowers with a darker centre.*
BELOW *Lilium* 'Monte Negro', *one of the Asiatic Hybrids, bears abundant blooms of bold orange to dark red that carry the characteristic spotting at the petal base.*

ABOVE Lilium, *Oriental Hybrid, 'Acapulco' has large dark pink blooms enhanced with crimson spotting at the throat and ruffled edges. Leaves are a glossy green.*
LEFT *The strawberries-and-cream colouring of* Lilium, *Oriental Hybrid, 'Sorbonne' has made it popular for both garden cultivation and as a cut flower.*

ABOVE *Borne on sturdy stems, the dark purplish buds of* Muscari macrocarpum *open to reveal delicately scented greenish yellow flowers.*

MUSCARI

This Mediterranean and western Asian genus of 30 species of spring-flowering bulbs in the hyacinth (Hyacinthaceae) family is commonly known as grape hyacinth. The grassy to strap-like foliage may be evergreen or deciduous, depending on species and climate. Spikes of tiny, downward-facing, bell-shaped flowers open from late winter and range in colour from white and soft yellow through blue shades to deepest purple. Small seed pods follow. The closely related genus *Bellevalia* is often mistaken for *Muscari*. The genus name is derived from the Turkish name for these bulbs.

CULTIVATION

Grape hyacinths are very easily cultivated, often far too easily, though there are much worse weeds than these pretty bulbs. Plant in sun or part-shade with moist well-drained soil. Clumps can be divided every few years. The seed germinates freely and often self-sows.

Top Tip

Grape hyacinths are versatile plants that are suitable for woodland gardens, for planting beneath trees, using in rockeries or as pot plants.

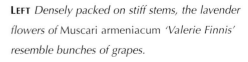

LEFT *Densely packed on stiff stems, the lavender flowers of* Muscari armeniacum *'Valerie Finnis' resemble bunches of grapes.*

Favourites	Flower Colour	Blooming Season	Flower Fragrance	Plant Height	Plant Width	Hardiness Zone	Frost Tolerance
Muscari armeniacum	bright blue	summer	yes	8 in (20 cm)	2 in (5 cm)	6–9	yes
Muscari aucheri	bright blue	early summer	no	4–6 in (10–15 cm)	2 in (5 cm)	6–9	yes
Muscari azureum	bright blue	early summer	yes	4–6 in (10–15 cm)	2 in (5 cm)	6–9	yes
Muscari botryoides	bright blue	early summer	yes	4–6 in (10–15 cm)	2 in (5 cm)	6–9	yes
Muscari latifolium	violet-black	early summer	no	8 in (20 cm)	2 in (5 cm)	6–9	yes
Muscari macrocarpum	greenish yellow	spring	yes	4–6 in (10–15 cm)	4 in (10 cm)	8–9	yes

LEFT *Held above the single mid-green leaves, the flower spikes of* Muscari latifolium *have a two-tone appearance, with violet-black fertile flowers topped by violet-blue sterile flowers.*

RIGHT *The crowded spikes of* Muscari armeniacum *'Blue Spike' are laden with dainty, double, urn-shaped flowers of soft blue, finely rimmed with white.*

RIGHT *With its head gracefully bowed,
Narcissus 'W. P. Milner', a Trumpet daffodil,
bears lemon yellow flowers that age to white.*

NARCISSUS

Is any spring-flowering bulb better known
than the daffodil? However, there is not
just one daffodil but over 50 species and
countless hybrids and cultivars. They are
members of the amaryllis (Amaryllidaceae)
family and occur naturally from southern
Europe to North Africa and Japan. Many have
the typical strappy blue-green leaves but some
have fine grassy foliage. The flowers have a
cup- or trumpet-shaped corona backed by
6 petals that are sometimes very much reduced
in size. Daffodils, including the species, are
divided into 10 groups based on their flower
shape and form. All parts are poisonous and
can cause a form of hyperactive seizure that
leads to depression and possibly coma.

CULTIVATION

Daffodils have varying soil preferences.
The traditional large-cupped forms do
best in a fairly heavy loam, while the
southern Mediterranean and North African
species like a drier grittier soil—but they
all need good drainage. Leave the foliage to
die off naturally before lifting. While seed
can be sown, propagation is normally from
natural offsets.

Top Tip

Daffodils make
excellent cut
flowers and are
best picked when
the buds are almost
ready to open.
Change the water
daily or use a good
cut flower additive.

ABOVE *A Large-cupped daffodil, Narcissus 'Salomé' is
an attractive hybrid cultivar
that features a prominent
golden corona surrounded
by 6 white petals.*

RIGHT *The Small-cupped daffodils have outer petals three
times as long as the corona. Narcissus 'Verger' has white
petals and a yellow corona edged in orange.*

RIGHT *Native to France, Spain and Portugal, the yellow petals of* Narcissus bulbocodium *look like narrow rays behind the matching coloured flaring trumpet.*

Favourites	Flower Colour	Blooming Season	Flower Fragrance	Plant Height	Plant Width	Hardiness Zone	Frost Tolerance
Narcissus bulbocodium	soft lemon to bright yellow	early spring	no	4–6 in (10–15 cm)	12 in (30 cm)	6–10	yes
Narcissus pseudonarcissus	yellow	early spring	yes	8–15 in (20–38 cm)	12 in (30 cm)	4–10	yes
Narcissus, Cyclamineus	pale to deep yellow, orange	early to mid-spring	no	6–12 in (15–30 cm)	3–8 in (8–20 cm)	5–10	yes
Narcissus, Double-flowered	white to deep yellow	mid-spring	no	10–18 in (25–45 cm)	6–12 in (15–30 cm)	4–10	yes
Narcissus, Jonquilla	pale to deep yellow	mid- to late spring	yes	8–18 in (20–45 cm)	6–12 in (15–30 cm)	4–10	yes
Narcissus, Large-cupped	white, yellow, orange, pink	mid-spring	no	12–18 in (30–45 cm)	6–12 in (15–30 cm)	4–10	yes
Narcissus, Poeticus	white with orange-scarlet centre	late spring to early summer	yes	6–18 in (15–45 cm)	6–10 in (15–25 cm)	4–10	yes
Narcissus, Small-cupped	white, yellow, orange, pink	early to mid-spring	no	12–18 in (30–45 cm)	6–12 in (15–30 cm)	4–10	yes
Narcissus, Split-corona	white, yellow, orange, pink	spring	no	12–18 in (30–45 cm)	6–12 in (15–30 cm)	4–10	yes
Narcissus, Tazetta	white to yellow, orange centre	autumn to spring	yes	12–18 in (30–45 cm)	8–18 in (20–45 cm)	5–10	yes
Narcissus, Triandrus	white to deep yellow	mid- to late spring	no	6–12 in (15–30 cm)	4–8 in (10–20 cm)	4–10	yes
Narcissus, Trumpet	white, yellow, orange, pink	spring	no	12–18 in (30–45 cm)	6–12 in (15–30 cm)	4–10	yes

RIGHT *Petals of softest yellow frame the clear yellow cup of* Narcissus, Tazetta, *'Minnow'. Tazetta daffodils are small-flowered, with up to 20 flowers per stem.*
BELOW *Double-flowered* Narcissus *plants have twice as many petals or cups—or both—than other cultivar groups. 'Cheerfulness' has an old-fashioned charm with its ruffled creamy petals.*

Top Tip

The delicate beauty of daffodils belies their robust nature. Although almost maintenance-free, they will appreciate supplemental water during dry periods.

LEFT *The yellow and orange corona of this Double daffodil,* Narcissus *'Tahiti', is comprised of many parts rather than the single unit of other daffodil groups.*
RIGHT *'Actaea' is an award-winning* Narcissus *from the Poeticus group. As is typical with flowers from that group, it bears a single pure white flower per stem with a small yellow cup, edged in scarlet.*

LEFT Narcissus, *Jonquilla and Apodanthus*, *'Trevithian'* usually bears 2 or more blooms per stem, typically with small, shallow, wide orange cups and lemon yellow petals. They are enjoyed for their fragrance.

BELOW *A brilliant orange cup that appears almost flat surrounded by pale yellow petals are the signature of Narcissus 'Charles Sturt', a Large-cupped daffodil.*

RIGHT *The large pink flowers of* Nerine bowdenii *are held aloft on tall, 60 cm (24 in) high, leafless stems.*

NERINE

Commonly known as the spider lily or Guernsey lily, this genus is an autumn-flowering member of the amaryllis family and includes around 30 species of bulbs that often resemble smaller versions of *Amaryllis*. Native to southern Africa, these plants may be evergreen or die down in summer. The deep to bright green leaves vary from grassy to strap-like and surround upright flower stems carrying many-flowered heads of long-tubed funnel-shaped blooms each with 6 widely flared, narrow petals. Flower colour ranges from pink and red to scarlet and white. A story, probably apocryphal, says the Guernsey lily was so-named because *Nerine* was introduced to Europe when a bulb washed up on the island of Guernsey.

CULTIVATION

Plant, with the neck of the bulb exposed, in half or full sun in well-drained, humus-rich, sandy soil. Grow in pots in areas of severe frosts. Water well during the growth period but keep dry when dormant; the watering program should be maintained for evergreen species. Propagate by division, from shoots growing at the base of the plant or from seed.

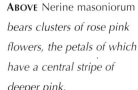

ABOVE *Nerine masoniorum bears clusters of rose pink flowers, the petals of which have a central stripe of deeper pink.*

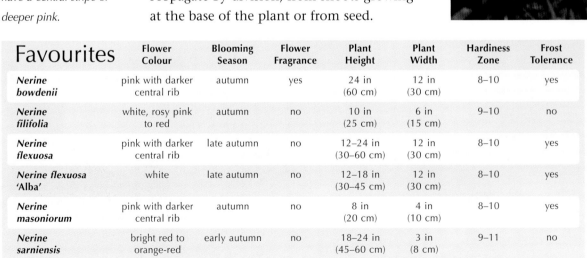

Favourites	Flower Colour	Blooming Season	Flower Fragrance	Plant Height	Plant Width	Hardiness Zone	Frost Tolerance
Nerine bowdenii	pink with darker central rib	autumn	yes	24 in (60 cm)	12 in (30 cm)	8–10	yes
Nerine filifolia	white, rosy pink to red	autumn	no	10 in (25 cm)	6 in (15 cm)	9–10	no
Nerine flexuosa	pink with darker central rib	late autumn	no	12–24 in (30–60 cm)	12 in (30 cm)	8–10	yes
Nerine flexuosa 'Alba'	white	late autumn	no	12–18 in (30–45 cm)	12 in (30 cm)	8–10	yes
Nerine masoniorum	pink with darker central rib	autumn	no	8 in (20 cm)	4 in (10 cm)	8–10	yes
Nerine sarniensis	bright red to orange-red	early autumn	no	18–24 in (45–60 cm)	3 in (8 cm)	9–11	no

ABOVE *Spectacular in both colour and form, the brilliant red flowers of* Nerine sarniensis *are enhanced by long red stamens with golden yellow tips.*
BELOW Nerine sarniensis *var.* curvifolia *f.* fothergillii *'Major' is an early-flowering variety, which bears clusters of vivid red flowers with prominent stamens.*

Top Tip

In cooler climates, containers of *Nerine* species can be brought indoors, where the long-lasting statuesque flowers will create a dramatic effect.

ORNITHOGALUM

Top Tip

Although popular in rock gardens, *Ornithogalum* species also do well in containers. Use a loam-based potting mix and water sufficiently for moist but not damp soil.

This large genus belongs to the hyacinth family (Hyacinthaceae) and contains around 80 species of bulbs native to South Africa and the Mediterranean region. They quickly form large clumps of grassy to strap-like leaves, sometimes with a rib down the middle of them. In spring or summer, depending on the species, upright conical spikes of white to cream flowers appear. Often called chincherinchee or the star-of-Bethlehem, the flowers are sometimes mildly scented. They are usually starry or cup-shaped and have 6 petals in 2 whorls of 3. The botanical name comes from the Greek *ornis* (a bird) and *gala* (milk), as the flowers resemble a white bird when they are spread out. They are striking additions to a rock garden or border.

BELOW *Standing well clear of the strappy foliage below, the funnel-shaped white flowers of* Ornithogalum reverchonii *make excellent border or cut flowers.*

CULTIVATION

Most of the European species tolerate moderate frosts whereas the South African species are frost tender and may need to be lifted for winter. Plant in a sunny open position with light well-drained soil. Water well when flowering, then dry off when the plants are dormant. Propagate by division.

LEFT Ornithogalum nutans *has distinctive star-like flowers with recurved white and green petals and a cluster of yellow-tipped stamens in the centre.*

Favourites	Flower Colour	Blooming Season	Flower Fragrance	Plant Height	Plant Width	Hardiness Zone	Frost Tolerance
Ornithogalum arabicum	white with black eye	early summer	yes	12–24 in (30–60 cm)	8 in (20 cm)	9–11	no
Ornithogalum dubium	orange, yellow, red, with black eye	winter to spring	yes	6–12 in (15–30 cm)	4 in (10 cm)	7–10	yes
Ornithogalum narbonense	white with black eye	late spring to early summer	no	12–36 in (30–90 cm)	8 in (20 cm)	7–10	yes
Ornithogalum nutans	white with green stripes	late spring to early summer	no	12–24 in (30–60 cm)	10 in (25 cm)	6–10	yes
Ornithogalum reverchonii	white	late spring to early summer	no	24 in (60 cm)	8 in (20 cm)	5–9	yes
Ornithogalum umbellatum	white with green stripes	early summer	no	12 in (30 cm)	4 in (10 cm)	5–10	yes

RIGHT *Bold yellow-orange blooms with a black eye attract gardeners to* Ornithogalum dubium. *When the leaves have finished, do not water until the foliage reappears.*
BELOW Ornithogalum arabicum *bears 6-petalled white flowers with a large shiny centre. They do best in a warm sunny spot in the garden and require little water.*

RANUNCULUS

This large cosmopolitan genus of the buttercup (Ranunculaceae) family includes among its 400 members several species with thickened rhizomes that were once considered a type of corm. The foliage is usually pinnate and often deeply cut and divided. The wild species usually have simple, 5-petalled, yellow or red flowers, but garden forms often have fully double flowers in a wide colour range. Spring is the main flowering season, but the blooming may be extended with staggered planting. A seed head tightly packed with feathered seeds, technically an achene, follows but is best removed to prolong flowering. The commonly grown turban buttercup *(Ranunculus asiaticus)* is sometimes known as the Persian crowsfoot because of the shape of the "corms".

CULTIVATION

Plant *Ranunculus* species in a sunny or partly shaded position with moist well-drained soil. They are hardy where the soil does not freeze, but in colder climates the "corms" should be lifted and stored dry. They can be propagated either from seed or by division.

ABOVE Ranunculus asiaticus, *Bloomingdale Series, 'Pure Yellow' has fully double flowers with flounced petals of rich buttercup yellow.*

Top Tip

Once the leaves appear, *Ranunculus asiaticus* and its many attractive hybrids and culti-vars appreciate extra water during the growing and blooming season.

LEFT *The Tecolote Hybrids of* Ranunculus asiaticus *have a compact growth habit and large double blooms. They are sold in single colours or mixed colour strains.*

LEFT *The pure white flowers of* Ranunculus asiaticus, *Bloomingdale Series, 'White' bring a touch of stylish elegance to the garden in spring and summer.*

RIGHT *Lower growing than the species,* Ranunculus asiaticus, *Bloomingdale Series offers large, fully double, ruffled blooms in a wide range of colours.*

Favourites	Flower Colour	Blooming Season	Flower Fragrance	Plant Height	Plant Width	Hardiness Zone	Frost Tolerance
Ranunculus asiaticus	white, pink, red, yellow, orange	spring to summer	no	8–18 in (20–45 cm)	8–12 in (20–30 cm)	8–10	yes
Ranunculus asiaticus, Bloomingdale Series	various	spring to summer	no	8–10 in (20–25 cm)	8–16 in (20–40 cm)	8–10	yes
Ranunculus asiaticus 'Cappucino'	white; pink edges	spring to summer	no	10–15 in (25–38 cm)	8–12 in (20–30 cm)	8–10	yes
Ranunculus asiaticus 'Double Mixed'	various	spring to summer	no	8–18 in (20–45 cm)	8–12 in (20–30 cm)	8–10	yes
Ranunculus asiaticus, Tecolote Hybrids	various	spring to summer	no	12–16 in (30–40 cm)	12–16 in (30–40 cm)	8–10	yes
Ranunculus asiaticus, Victoria Series	various	spring to summer	no	8–18 in (20–45 cm)	8–12 in (20–30 cm)	8–10	yes

Scadoxus

A small, entirely African genus of bulb-like perennials, *Scadoxus* is in the hippeastrum family (Amaryllidaceae).

Two of the South African species are reasonably well known in warm-climate regions, both having big orange scarlet flowers atop thick, leafless stems. In *Scadoxus puniceus* these shoot straight from the ground in late winter, before the leaves, whereas in *S. multiflorus* flowers occur in late spring, also before the leaves. The variant *S. multiflorus* subsp. *katharinae* is evergreen and flowers later in summer. *Scadoxus* was once included in the genus *Haemanthus* and many gardeners still refer to it by that name. The difference lies in the texture and number of leaves; in *Scadoxus* they're thin and numerous whereas *Haemanthus* produces only two thick leaves.

Cultivation

All species prefer bright dappled shade and will even grow and flower in full shade. Free-draining but moisture-retentive soil is ideal, or raise the plants in pots where they are happy to remain for several years.

Scadoxus are not particularly frost hardy but will accept the odd, light freeze. Propagate from seed sown when ripe and expect flowers from seedlings in three years.

Right *A spectacular choice for summer-rainfall areas where few other bulbs thrive, the Natal paintbrush blooms in late winter in either bright full shade or part-shade.*

Top Tip

Plants slowly form clumps that can be lifted and divided when dormant in winter or spring. Don't do this more than once every five years as these plants resent disturbance.

BELOW Scadoxus multiflorus *subsp.* katharinae *blooms in summer, often after Christmas. Its flowerheads are more open than those of* S. multiflorus *and usually a richer orange, too. It is dormant in winter.*

ABOVE Scadoxus multiflorus *comes from northern South Africa and Zimbabwe. Its late-spring flowers arise straight from the ground before the leaves, the leafless stalks supporting a tight sphere of pinkish-orange, staminate flowers. Best in dappled shade.*

Favourites	Flower Colour	Blooming Season	Flower Fragrance	Plant Height	Plant Width	Hardiness Zone	Frost Tolerance
Scadoxus multiflorus	pinky-orange	late spring	no	20–24 in (50–60 cm)	18–20 in (45–50 cm)	8–11	no
Scadoxus multiflorus subsp. *katharinae*	orange to scarlet	summer	no	22–26 in (55–65 cm)	18–20 in (45–50 cm)	8–11	no
Scadoxus puniceus	bright orange	late winter to spring	no	20–24 in (50–60 cm)	18–20 in (45–50 cm)	8–11	no

SCHIZOSTYLIS

The sole species in this genus in the iris (Iridaceae) family is a variable bulbous-rooted perennial from South Africa, though in the future it may be reclassified into the genus *Hesperantha*. It has grassy near-evergreen foliage and its flowers, which appear from mid-autumn, are clustered in heads at the top of wiry stems that often well exceed the foliage height. The simple, starry, 6-petalled flowers are usually red, but garden forms are just as likely to be pink or white. *Schizostylis* multiplies freely and is considered a minor weed in some areas.

CULTIVATION

In the wild, this genus is usually found along watercourses and seasonally damp areas, but it is equally well at home in normal well-drained garden soil, provided it never becomes completely dry. It combines well with late-flowering perennials, such as golden-rod, Michaelmas daisies and *Rudbeckia*. Plant in full sun or morning shade and propagate from seed or natural offsets.

Favourites	Flower Colour	Blooming Season	Flower Fragrance
Schizostylis coccinea	red to pink or white	autumn	no
Schizostylis coccinea 'Alba'	white	autumn	no
Schizostylis coccinea 'Jennifer'	pale pink	autumn	no
Schizostylis coccinea 'Major'	red	autumn	no
Schizostylis coccinea 'Sunrise'	salmon pink	autumn	no
Schizostylis coccinea 'Viscountess Byng'	pale pink	autumn	no

ABOVE *The spectacular scarlet red flowers of* Schizostylis coccinea *'Major' add great autumn colour to a sunny border or a bed along a concrete path.*

Top Tip

Schizostylis plants provide excellent cut flowers. They can be grown in containers and should be divided regularly to maintain vigour. Divide the plants in spring.

LEFT Schizostylis coccinea *blooms steadily from autumn until temperatures fall. In mild climates, it has the potential to be in flower all winter.*

Plant Height	Plant Width	Hardiness Zone	Frost Tolerance
12–24 in (30–60 cm)	12–24 in (30–60 cm)	6–9	yes
12–24 in (30–60 cm)	12–24 in (30–60 cm)	6–9	yes
12–24 in (30–60 cm)	12–24 in (30–60 cm)	6–9	yes
12–24 in (30–60 cm)	12–24 in (30–60 cm)	6–9	yes
12–24 in (30–60 cm)	12–24 in (30–60 cm)	6–9	yes
12–24 in (30–60 cm)	12–24 in (30–60 cm)	6–9	yes

ABOVE Schizostylis coccinea hybrids are commonly known as kaffir lilies, river lilies or crimson flag. Each flower spike contains 5 to 20 flowers.

LEFT Schizostylis coccinea 'Sunrise' bears large salmon pink flowers 5 cm (2 in) across, larger than most other hybrids. It also has a longer blooming period. In bad weather, pick the buds and bring them inside to flower away from the frost.

SCILLA

A genus of around 90 species of bulbs in the hyacinth (Hyacinthaceae) family, *Scilla* species are found from Europe to South Africa and temperate Asia. The foliage is strap-like or grassy, may be near-evergreen in mild climates, and can be long and lax, making for a rather untidy foliage clump. Commonly known as squills or bluebells, the species vary in flowering time, though most bloom in spring or early summer. While some have open hyacinth-like flowerheads, many have densely packed rounded heads on strong stems. Purple or blue are the predominant flower colours; white, pink and lavender are less common. *Scilla* extracts are used in herbal medicines but the "squill" often referred to in the literature is a different plant, *Urginea maritima*.

CULTIVATION

Scilla species are mostly hardy and easily grown in sun or part-shade with moist, humus-rich, well-drained soil. Propagation is usually by division in winter when dormant or from seed, which sometimes self-sows.

ABOVE Scilla hyacinthoides *is found throughout the Mediterranean region. From mid-spring its tall stems are filled with numerous starry violet-blue flowers.*

BELOW *Native to France and Spain, and known as the Pyrenean squill,* Scilla liliohyacinthus *has glossy strap-like leaves. The pale violet flowers are borne on sturdy stems.*

BELOW Scilla peruviana *is a wondrous sight when in bloom, as its tall stems rise above the glossy leaves bearing their clusters of starry blue flowers.*

RIGHT *With grassy leaves and violet-blue flowers,* Scilla ramburei *is a lovely subject for borders and bedding and is well suited to coastal environments.*

Top Tip

Scilla flower spikes are naturals for cut flowers. Those left on the plant should be trimmed back to near ground level once the flowers are spent.

Favourites	Flower Colour	Blooming Season	Flower Fragrance	Plant Height	Plant Width	Hardiness Zone	Frost Tolerance
Scilla hyacinthoides	violet-blue	mid-spring	no	36 in (90 cm)	12 in (30 cm)	8–11	yes
Scilla liliohyacinthus	pale violet	mid- to late spring	no	4 in (10 cm)	4 in (10 cm)	6–8	yes
Scilla peruviana	indigo blue	mid-spring to early summer	no	12 in (30 cm)	18 in (45 cm)	8–11	yes
Scilla ramburei	violet-blue	spring	no	6 in (15 cm)	4 in (10 cm)	7–10	yes
Scilla siberica	bright blue	early spring	no	6 in (15 cm)	3 in (8 cm)	2–8	yes
Scilla tubergeniana	white, pale blue	early spring	no	5 in (12 cm)	4 in (10 cm)	5–7	yes

Top Tip

Sparaxis species are suitable for the front of borders or in raised beds. In cold areas they may need to be placed in a greenhouse, or planted against a sunny wall, protected from wind.

RIGHT *Sparaxis grandiflora usually has flowers that are purple-red, but there is also a delightful white-flowered form. Each bloom has a stunning yellow throat.*

BELOW *The summer garden will certainly be enlivened by the presence of* Sparaxis tricolor *flowers, as their hot-coloured petals are accentuated by a yellow centre lined with black.*

SPARAXIS

A South African genus of 6 species of corms of the iris family (Iridaceae), *Sparaxis* plants will naturalise and form large drifts of brightly coloured flowers under suitable conditions. The leaves are grassy to sword-shaped with prominent ribbing, and develop quickly from late winter. They are soon followed by wiry spikes carrying anywhere from just a few blooms to fan-like sprays of funnel-shaped 6-petalled flowers. The flowers may be white, yellow or shades of pink to orange and red, usually with a yellow centre and contrasting dark colours in the throat. The genus name comes from the Greek word *sparasso* (to tear), referring to the lacerated bracts at the base of the flowers.

CULTIVATION

These plants are not hardy where the soil freezes but are otherwise easily grown in full sun with fertile, moist, well-drained soil. In cold areas they can be lifted in autumn and replanted in early spring for a later flower show. Propagate from seed or by division.

Favourites	Flower Colour	Blooming Season	Flower Fragrance	Plant Height	Plant Width	Hardiness Zone	Frost Tolerance
Sparaxis elegans	various	spring to summer	no	4–12 in (10–30 cm)	4 in (10 cm)	9–10	no
Sparaxis fragrans	various	spring	yes	4–10 in (10–25 cm)	4 in (10 cm)	9–10	no
Sparaxis grandiflora	purple-red; yellow tubes	spring	no	4–15 in (10–38 cm)	6 in (15 cm)	9–10	no
Sparaxis pillansii	rose pink, red; yellow centre	spring	no	12–24 in (30–60 cm)	6 in (15 cm)	9–10	no
Sparaxis tricolor	pink to orange; yellow and black	spring to summer	no	4–15 in (10–38 cm)	4 in (10 cm)	9–10	no
Sparaxis variegata	purple	spring	no	6–12 in (15–30 cm)	4 in (10 cm)	9–10	no

BELOW Sparaxis fragrans *subsp.* acutiloba *is taller than the species, growing to 45 cm (18 in). The flowers are purple or yellow, occasionally with black markings.*

TRILLIUM

Primarily North American, with a few temperate Asian representatives, this group of 30 species of perennials forms the type genus for the wake-robin (Trilliaceae) family. The most visible parts of the plants are grouped in threes: each stem has 3 leaves and the flowers have 3 petals and 3 sepals. While completely dormant in winter, with the arrival of spring the plants develop quickly, first producing their often mottled foliage and then the flowers, which form at the intersection of the 3 leaves. The petals may be white, soft yellow, pink or maroon-red; the sepals are often green but can be the same colour as the petals. Native North Americans used the roots medicinally.

CULTIVATION

While some of the smaller species thrive in rockeries, most trilliums are woodland plants that prefer deep, fertile, humus-rich, moist soil and dappled shade, ideally beneath an airy canopy of deciduous trees. Propagation is usually by division or from seed.

Favourites	Flower Colour	Blooming Season	Flower Fragrance
Trillium chloropetalum	white, yellow, pink, maroon	spring	yes
Trillium cuneatum	burgundy to yellow-green	early spring	yes
Trillium erectum	red-and-green	spring	no
Trillium grandiflorum	white, fading to pink	late spring to early summer	no
Trillium luteum	yellow to yellow-green	early spring	yes
Trillium rivale	white	early spring	no

Top Tip

Trillium species will do best in shady spots. If sited in a favourable position, there is little maintenance required other than to remove dead foliage in autumn.

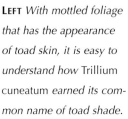

LEFT *With mottled foliage that has the appearance of toad skin, it is easy to understand how* Trillium cuneatum *earned its common name of toad shade.*

Plant Height	Plant Width	Hardiness Zone	Frost Tolerance
8–20 in (20–50 cm)	8–20 in (20–50 cm)	6–9	yes
24 in (60 cm)	16 in (40 cm)	6–9	yes
8–20 in (20–50 cm)	12–20 in (30–50 cm)	4–9	yes
10–18 in (25–45 cm)	12–20 in (30–50 cm)	3–9	yes
18 in (45 cm)	18 in (45 cm)	5–9	yes
4 in (10 cm)	6 in (15 cm)	5–9	yes

ABOVE *The yellow wake robin—Trillium luteum—bursts into bloom in early spring. The yellow to yellow-green petals are held erect above the mottled foliage.*

ABOVE *A charming woodland species from California, Trillium chloropetalum features large, often mottled leaves and fragrant, white, yellow or maroon flowers.*

RIGHT *Visually beautiful, Trillium erectum has bright green leaves coupled with red-and-green flowers. The plant, however, carries an unpleasant scent.*

TULIPA

Widespread in the northern temperate zones but based around Central Asia, this spring-flowering genus belonging to the lily (Liliaceae) family includes around 100 species of bulbs, some of which have been cultivated for centuries. Most tulips have just a few stemless, broad, blue-green leaves and most often just one 6-petalled flower, though some have up to 6 flowers per bulb. The flowers occur in all colours except true blue. The genus is divided into 15 groups based on flower type and parentage. When the Dutch "tulipomania" of the 1630s subsided, some of those who lost fortunes found out through necessity what tribespeople of Central Asia had long known: tulip bulbs are edible.

Top Tip

Give potted tulips for a lasting gift. When they have finished flowering indoors the bulbs can be transferred to the garden at the appropriate time.

CULTIVATION

Tulips do best in temperate areas with distinct seasons and relatively cool summers. Cold weather is necessary for proper dormancy and hot weather can split the bulbs. Plant bulbs in autumn at a depth of about 15 cm (6 in) in a sunny position with fertile well-drained soil. Propagation is usually from natural offsets, though of course they may also be raised from seed.

ABOVE *The Single Early Group, such as* Tulipa *'Apricot Beauty' seen here, are among the first tulips to bloom, bringing a flush of colour to the spring garden.*
RIGHT Tulipa *'African Queen' is a splendid example of the Triumph Group tulips, with tall blooms of deep purple-red, each petal featuring a fine feathered edge of white.*

ABOVE Tulipa 'Primavera', one of the
Single Late Group, features fiery orange-
red petals that shade to yellow at the
base and to almost white at the edges.
LEFT An impressive edging of gold adorns
the brilliant orange-red petals of Tulipa
'Ad Rem', one of the Darwin Hybrid
Group, sometimes called cottage tulips.

Favourites	Flower Colour	Blooming Season	Flower Fragrance	Plant Height	Plant Width	Hardiness Zone	Frost Tolerance
Tulipa clusiana	red; white interior	mid- to late spring	no	8–12 in (20–30 cm)	2–4 in (5–10 cm)	3–8	yes
Tulipa tarda	cream to yellow	spring	yes	4–6 in (10–15 cm)	6–8 in (15–20 cm)	5–9	yes
Tulipa, **Darwin Hybrid Group**	yellow, orange, red, pink	spring	no	20–27 in (50–70 cm)	6 in (15 cm)	5–9	yes
Tulipa, **Double Early Group**	yellow, pink, red, purple	spring	no	12–16 in (30–40 cm)	4–12 in (10–30 cm)	5–9	yes
Tulipa, **Fringed Group**	white, yellow, pink to purple	late spring	no	18–26 in (45–65 cm)	4–12 in (10–30 cm)	5–9	yes
Tulipa, **Greigii Group**	yellow to red	early to mid-spring	no	6–12 in (15–30 cm)	8 in (20 cm)	5–9	yes
Tulipa, **Lily-flowered Group**	various	late spring	no	15–26 in (38–65 cm)	6 in (15 cm)	5–9	yes
Tulipa, **Parrot Group**	various	late spring	no	18–26 in (45–65 cm)	6 in (15 cm)	5–9	yes
Tulipa, **Single Early Group**	white to deep purple	early to mid-spring	no	6–18 in (15–45 cm)	6 in (15 cm)	5–9	yes
Tulipa, **Single Late Group**	various	late spring	no	18–30 in (45–75 cm)	6 in (15 cm)	5–9	yes
Tulipa, **Triumph Group**	various	mid- to late spring	no	15–24 in (38–60 cm)	6 in (15 cm)	5–9	yes
Tulipa, **Viridiflora Group**	various	late spring	no	12–22 in (30–55 cm)	6 in (15 cm)	5–9	yes

RIGHT *Lifting their heads skywards, the fragrant starry flowers of* Tulipa tarda *have green to maroon shading on the petal reverse, and a cream to yellow interior.*

ABOVE *The Greigii Group tulips, such as the magnificently coloured* Tulipa *'Plaisir' seen here, are small in stature and are sometimes known as rock or rockery tulips.*
RIGHT *Crystalline fringed edges identify the Fringed Group of tulips.* Tulipa *'Maja' features goblet-shaped blooms of bright yellow, with the signature edging.*

RIGHT *Pink and red colours predominate on the ruffled petals of* Tulipa *'Salmon Parrot', a Parrot Group tulip, highlighted with shades of yellow and cream.*

LEFT *The Double Early tulips resemble peonies and flower in early spring.* Tulipa *'Peach Blossom' has large deep pink blooms flecked with white and shading to golden yellow at the centre.*

ABOVE The colours and patterning of Tulipa 'Colour Spectacle' are sure to gain attention, with scarlet stripes emblazoned on the golden yellow petals.

RIGHT The stunning Tulipa, Lily-flowered Group, 'Ballerina' almost glows in the sunlight. It has pointed arching petals that are sunset orange.

Top Tip

ZANTEDESCHIA

Related to but not of the same genus as the true arums (*Arum* species) and callas (*Calla* species), this genus of 6 species, commonly known as arum lilies or calla lilies, occurs naturally from South Africa to Malawi. Members of the arum (Araceae) family, they form clumps of sturdy stems with large arrowhead- to heart-shaped leaves that are often mottled with small translucent spots. The long-stemmed flower-heads open through the warmer months. They have a cup-like spathe that encircles a fairly short spadix. While the species have white, pale pink or yellow spathes, garden hybrids and cultivars are available in many colours. The genus name honours Giovanni Zantedeschi (1773–1846), who was an Italian botanist.

CULTIVATION

While *Zantedeschia aethiopica* will grow in fairly wet conditions and is often planted around pond margins, other species and the cut-flower hybrids prefer normal garden conditions and thrive in sun or part-shade with moist, humus-rich, well-drained soil. Watch for snail and slug damage, particularly on young leaves. Propagate the species from seed or by division, the hybrids by division only.

ABOVE *With flowers arising like orange beacons above the large, spotted, dark green leaves,* Zantedeschia *'Flame' adds a tropical element to the garden.* **LEFT** *The stately bright red spathes of* Zantedeschia *'Scarlet Pimpernel' are borne among the white-speckled dark green leaves.*

RIGHT *As though crafted from a pliable medium, the pristine white flowers of Zantedeschia aethiopica 'Crowborough' are popular for floral arrangements.*

BELOW *While the bright green spathes of Zantedeschia aethiopica 'Green Goddess' are appealing, this plant has the potential to become invasive.*

Favourites	Flower Colour	Blooming Season	Flower Fragrance	Plant Height	Plant Width	Hardiness Zone	Frost Tolerance
Zantedeschia aethiopica	white	spring to autumn	no	3–6 ft (0.9–1.8 m)	2–5 ft (0.6–1.5 m)	8–11	yes
Zantedeschia aethiopica '**Childsiana**'	white; pink tinted	spring to autumn	no	12 in (30 cm)	2–5 ft (0.6–1.5 m)	8–11	yes
Zantedeschia elliottiana	deep yellow	summer	no	12–18 in (30–45 cm)	12–18 in (30–45 cm)	9–11	yes
Zantedeschia '**Flame**'	yellow-orange, flecked red	summer	no	18–24 in (45–60 cm)	12 in (30 cm)	9–11	yes
Zantedeschia pentlandii	golden yellow	summer	no	12–36 in (30–90 cm)	8–16 in (20–40 cm)	9–11	yes
Zantedeschia '**Scarlet Pimpernel**'	red-orange	spring to summer	no	18–36 in (45–90 cm)	12–24 in (30–60 cm)	9–11	yes

CACTI AND SUCCULENTS

Ranging from tiny cliff-hugging ground covers to immense tree-like specimens, succulents—which include cacti—feature a vast array of forms and occupy habitats from frosty plains to seashores to the canopy of tropical rainforests. By growing slowly, evading competition and using a variety of physiological adaptations, succulents are able to make maximum use of limited available water. Succulents have been used since ancient times for purposes including medicine, religious ceremonies, shelter and fabric construction, food and drink. *Aloe vera* is perhaps the best-known succulent of all; mentioned on Sumerian clay tablets nearly 4,000 years ago, it is still used today for medicinal purposes.

ABOVE *The succulent leaves of* Crassula pseudohemisphaerica *are arranged in tightly spiralled rosettes that bear spikes of tubular flowers in spring.*

LEFT Kalanchoe tomentosa *has unusual heavily felted leaves with brown markings. Like many succulents, it makes an ornamental indoor plant in cooler climates.*

THE CAMELS OF THE GARDEN

The term "succulent" describes a plant that stores water in its leaves, stems or roots for use during periods when water is unavailable. Most succulents employ a variety of methods to prevent water loss. The characteristic round or barrel shape of most cacti and many other succulents is designed to minimise the surface area exposed to the drying sun. Ribs, thorns and furry hairs allow any available nightly dew to condense, run down the side of the plant and be collected by the roots.

In the species classified as leaf succulents, virtually the whole leaf is devoted to water storage tissue. Leaf succulents have very short stems, and different species have evolved various methods to reduce water loss. Crassulas, for example, have a waxy skin to prevent water loss, while aloes have compacted leaves providing protection from the sun. Those species that store water in their leaves include some of the most common and readily available succulents, such as the popular jade plant *(Crassula ovata)*, as well as agaves and aloes, with their fleshy pointed leaves.

Succulents that store water in their stems have few or no leaves. The stems are responsible for water collection and transpiration. Stem succulents have varied forms and can range from small mounds to elongated plants with multiple stems. Cacti, a group of New World plants, are a type of stem succulent and possess a number of distinctive features including a modified axillary bud from which spines, branches and flowers arise. Containing some 2,500 species (about a quarter of all succulent plants), all members of the cactus (Cactaceae) family are succulents—but not all succulents are cacti. Examples include the genera *Echinocereus*, *Mammillaria*, *Opuntia* and *Rebutia*.

Root succulents survive dry conditions by storing water and nutrients in tuberous or swollen roots. Belowground storage prevents moisture loss and protects the roots from both fire and grazing animals. Many such root succulents are deciduous, losing their leaves during dormancy. Some of the strangest and most interesting root succulents are caudiciforms, named after the swollen aboveground root or stem base called a caudex. These plants can have small, globular, aboveground caudexes or massive ones such as the famous African baobab tree *(Adansonia digitata)*, capable of developing a trunk

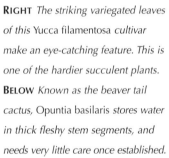

RIGHT *The striking variegated leaves of this* Yucca filamentosa *cultivar make an eye-catching feature. This is one of the hardier succulent plants.*
BELOW *Known as the beaver tail cactus,* Opuntia basilaris *stores water in thick fleshy stem segments, and needs very little care once established.*

that is 10 m (35 ft) in diameter. Many other genera more suitable to garden cultivation, such as *Crassula* and *Sedum,* have caudiciform members.

Being adapted to periodic drought, most succulents are best grown in gritty well-drained or sandy soil. In most cases, full sun is preferred. But as the habitats from which they come vary, so too do their requirements for light, warmth, water and nutrients.

Succulents look gorgeous planted in gravel and near stone, materials that often surround them in their native habitats. They make fine container plants and often thrive in the excellent drainage afforded by terracotta pots. Particularly fine in pots or massed in warm-climate borders are *Echeveria* species, with exquisitely ruffled, tinted and hued leaves in smoky blue-greens, lavenders and pinks. Planted in dry gardens, succulents of all sorts are complemented by other drought-tolerant plants such as rock roses (*Cistus* species), beardtongues (*Penstemon* species), sages (*Salvia* species) and treasure flowers (*Gazania* species). Ground-cover succulents such as *Delosperma* species, with their brilliantly coloured starry blossoms, look wonderful planted on rock walls and hot dry banks. Taller spiky types such as aloes and yuccas can be grown as specimens or used to lend architectural presence and stature to perennial beds.

In cool climates, many succulents take well to indoor culture, enjoying a bright spot inside during the winter and a summer holiday on a porch or patio when possible. During the winter, growth generally slows and watering should be likewise minimised. In the summer, succulents in containers appreciate plenty of water, but they need to dry out between waterings. If kept indoors for the summer, they need bright but indirect sun to avoid burning.

Many succulents are surprisingly hardy: Adam's needle (*Yucca filamentosa*), banana yucca (*Y. baccata*) and soapweed (*Y. glauca*) tolerate freezing temperatures. Frost-tolerant cacti include claret cup cactus (*Echinocereus triglochidiatus*) and *E. reichenbachii.* The genus *Opuntia* also contains some cold-hardy species. And sedums are among the most popular of perennials and are grown in temperate climates around the world. For their diversity, adaptability and sheer beauty, there is a place for succulents in every garden.

Favourites	Flower Colour	Blooming Season	Flower Fragrance
Agave americana	yellow	spring	no
Agave attenuata	pale yellow	spring	no
Agave colorata	bright yellow to orange	spring	no
Agave filifera	greenish with purple tinge	spring	no
Agave parryi	yellow, tinged red	spring	no
Agave victoriae-reginae	green to cream	varies	no

ABOVE Agave americana *is a highly variable species from northeastern Mexico. The variegated 'Mediopicta Alba' has a white mid-stripe distinguishing its leaves.*

BELOW Agave colorata *is an attractive small plant from Sonora, Mexico. Grey-blue wavy-edged leaves grow to 60 cm (24 in) long, and flower spikes can reach 2–3 m (7–10 ft) in length.*

AGAVE

The type genus for the agave (Agavaceae) family is a group of some 225 species of fleshy-leafed perennials found from southern USA through the Caribbean and Central America to Venezuela and Colombia. Forming rosettes of large leaves, they often have fiercely toothed edges and long spines at the tips. The cream to chrome yellow flowers are borne in clusters on tall branching stems. While flower stems can be spectacular both in size and colour, agave rosettes are often monocarpic (dying after flowering), and those species with only a few very large rosettes, such as *Agave americana*, are grown mainly for their foliage and form. The alcoholic drink tequila is made from the pith of the foliage of *Agave tequilana*.

CULTIVATION

Hardiness varies and some species are very tender. Plant in full sun with very free-draining, rather gritty soil. While agaves appreciate reliable moisture during the growing season, they can survive without it and may suffer in prolonged wet conditions, especially in winter.

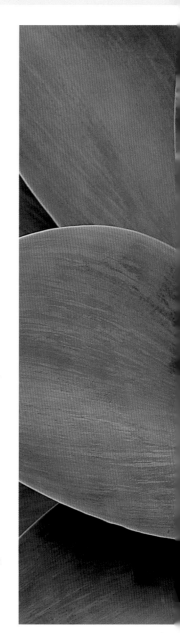

Plant Height	Plant Width	Hardiness Zone	Frost Tolerance
17–50 ft (5–15 m)	7–15 ft (2–4.5 m)	8–11	yes
3–7 ft (0.9–2 m)	2–5 ft (0.6–1.5 m)	9–11	no
7–10 ft (2–3 m)	4–6 ft (1.2–1.8 m)	9–11	no
7–8 ft (2–2.4 m)	27 in (70 cm)	8–11	yes
12–20 ft (3.5–6 m)	20–27 in (50–70 cm)	8–11	yes
10–15 ft (3–4.5 m)	20–27 in (50–70 cm)	9–11	no

ABOVE *The distinctive* Agave victoriae-reginae *'Variegata' has recently been renamed as 'Golden Princess'. Its creamy yellow leaf margins stand out best in part-shade.*
LEFT Agave attenuata *has brittle, almost flat, rounded, lime green to bluish green leaves, lacking teeth and a terminal spike, and is from just a few Mexican habitats.*

Top Tip

The common name for the agave is the century plant, and the right conditions will see them out-live their owners. Remember to allow enough room for them to expand.

Top Tip

Aloes should not be grown outside if there is any risk at all of freezing, but they will make very good house plants with enough light, doing even better if summered outside.

BELOW *Forming rosettes of light-spotted, narrow, fleshy, green leaves, and valued for the medicinal properties of its sap,* Aloe vera *is perhaps the best known of all aloes.*

ALOE

Formerly listed in the lily (Liliaceae) family but now considered the type genus for the aloe (Aloaceae) family, this group of over 300 species of fleshy-leafed, rosette-forming, sometimes tree-like succulents is found from the Arabian Peninsula and down through Africa to Madagascar. Their long leaves taper to a fine point and are often edged with sharp teeth. Flowers are tubular, usually in warm shades such as yellow, orange or red, and are borne in spikes at the tips of long, sometimes branching inflorescences. The pithy jelly from the leaves of one species, *Aloe vera*, is so widely used around the world medicinally, as well as cosmetically, that it is often known as the "medicine plant".

CULTIVATION

A few species will tolerate light frosts but many are tender and all prefer warm dry conditions. Plant in full sun with light, very free-draining soil. Water when actively growing and flowering, but otherwise keep dry. Numerous species adapt to greenhouse or container conditions quite well. Propagation is from offsets, stem cuttings or seed.

Favourites	Flower Colour	Blooming Season	Flower Fragrance	Plant Height	Plant Width	Hardiness Zone	Frost Tolerance
Aloe arborescens	orange to red	winter	no	10 ft (3 m)	6 ft (1.8 m)	9–11	no
Aloe brevifolia	red with green tips	early summer	no	20 in (50 cm)	20–32 in (50–80 cm)	9–11	no
Aloe chabaudii	red-brown	winter	no	2–5 ft (0.6–1.5 m)	3–5 ft (0.9–1.5 m)	9–11	no
Aloe claviflora	pinkish red to orange	spring to summer	no	5 ft (1.5 m)	3–7 ft (0.9–2 m)	9–11	no
Aloe dorotheae	yellow to red with green tips	winter	no	20–32 in (50–80 cm)	3–7 ft (0.9–2 m)	10–11	no
Aloe ferox	orange-red and golden yellow	late winter	no	7–17 ft (2–5 m)	5–10 ft (1.5–3 m)	9–11	no
Aloe plicatilis	red	winter	no	15 ft (4.5 m)	7 ft (2 m)	9–11	no
Aloe polyphylla	red to orange-pink	spring	no	30 in (75 cm)	16–32 in (40–80 cm)	8–10	yes
Aloe × spinosissima	orange-red	winter	no	40 in (100 cm)	24–48 in (60–120 cm)	9–11	no
Aloe striata	dull to bright red	winter	no	3 ft (0.9 m)	4–7 ft (1.2–2 m)	9–11	no
Aloe vera	yellow	summer	no	32 in (80 cm)	24–48 in (60–120 cm)	9–12	no
Aloe virens	red	spring to summer	no	20 in (50 cm)	20–32 in (50–80 cm)	10–11	no

LEFT *An* Aloe petricola *hybrid, 'Saturn' forms large rosettes of succulent, toothed leaves from which emerge candelabras of long-lasting flowers. Most aloes bloom in mid- to late winter.*
BELOW *Yellow, orange and red are the colours in aloe blooms but there are many combinations of these colours in the various hybrids. Shown is the* Aloe ferox *hybrid, 'Capricorn'.*

Top Tip

When growing in pots use a cactus compost, and in areas of frost grow under glass. Liquid fertiliser, applied each month from spring to autumn, can improve results.

CRASSULA

*C*rassula contains some 300 species, many of them spreading perennials or bushy, woody-stemmed succulents. The type genus for the stonecrop (Crassulaceae) family, species of it occur naturally from Asia to South Africa. The leaves are usually short and stemless, and are often closely spaced, opposite and spiralled around the stems. Many species have a grey powdery bloom on their foliage, and heads of small, sometimes vividly coloured, flowers open generally in spring or after rain. The name *Crassula* comes from the Latin *crassus* meaning "thick", and refers to the thickened leaves.

RIGHT Crassula *'Buddha's Temple' has thin, upward-curved, grey-green leaves tiered like a pagoda roof, and pale cream flowers.*

CULTIVATION

Often cultivated as house plants, these are equally at home out-doors in mild, near frost-free areas in full or half-sun. Plant in light, gritty, well-drained soil, watering them when actively growing and flowering, but otherwise keeping dry. Deadhead to keep compact and encourage new growth. Propagation is usually from leaf cuttings or small stem cuttings; seeds germinate freely, but seedlings are slow to develop.

Favourites	Flower Colour	Blooming Season	Flower Fragrance	Plant Height	Plant Width	Hardiness Zone	Frost Tolerance
Crassula anomala	cream to pale pink	spring	no	12 in (30 cm)	12 in (30 cm)	9–11	no
Crassula 'Buddha's Temple'	pale cream	spring	no	2–8 in (5–20 cm)	2–10 in (5–25 cm)	9–11	no
Crassula 'Morgan's Beauty'	soft pink ageing to red	spring	no	2–8 in (5–20 cm)	2–10 in (5–25 cm)	9–11	no
Crassula ovata	pink-tinted white	autumn to spring	no	18 in (45 cm)	24–48 in (60–120 cm)	10–11	no
Crassula perfoliata	white through pink to red	summer	no	60 in (150 cm)	24–40 in (60–100 cm)	9–11	no
Crassula rupestris	red-tinted white	summer	no	8–20 in (20–50 cm)	6–12 in (15–30 cm)	9–11	no

LEFT *Native to South Africa,* Crassula ovata *is an upright branching shrub with fleshy rounded leaves, usually a shiny green with red or paler green edges.*

BELOW Crassula perfoliata *has thickened grey-green leaves, which can be almost flat. Leafy thick-stemmed flowerheads bear blooms of white through pink to red.*

ABOVE Crassula *'Morgan's Beauty' has mounding rosettes of fleshy, flat, grey-green leaves to 5 cm (2 in) long, and showy soft pink flowers that open from pink buds and age red.*

DELOSPERMA

This genus is one of several genera known
as ice plants. It contains about 150 species
of annuals, perennials and subshrubs found
throughout southern and eastern Africa.
Species are generally drought tolerant and are
excellent for desert gardens. They have dense
yellow-green foliage that is made up of small,
fleshy and usually cylindrical leaves growing
in opposite pairs on the stem. During spring
and summer, the daisy-like flowers are borne
in vivid shades of white, yellow, orange-red
and bright magenta, with the result that the
spreading species form boldly-coloured carpets
of blooms. Several species have been used in
herbal and traditional medicines, and recent
studies show that they contain fairly high
concentrations of a mildly hallucinogenic
drug (dimethyltryptamine).

CULTIVATION

Delosperma species prefer full sun in a sheltered
spot with light, gritty, well-drained soil. They
are ideally suited for coastal areas and rockeries.
A few species will tolerate light frosts. Propagate
from seed or cuttings.

BELOW *The flowers of*
Delosperma nubigenum *are
only small but compensate
for this with their brightness;
flowers are mostly vibrant
yellow or orange-red.*

LEFT *A prostrate succulent
perennial,* Delosperma
cooperi *has cylindrical light
green leaves that provide
excellent ground coverage.
Its bright magenta flowers
have contrasting white
anthers and can grow up
to 5 cm (2 in) in diameter.*

Top Tip

These hardy south-ern African species will perform best if water is withheld during autumn, allowing the plants to harden off for winter. During the growing period, water regularly, applying fertiliser every 3 weeks.

ABOVE Delosperma sutherlandii *occurs naturally in the grasslands and rocky areas of Transvaal and Natal in South Africa. Its purple-pink blooms are among the largest flowers of the ice plants, growing up to 6 cm (2½ in) wide.*
RIGHT *The trailing succulent* Delosperma lehmannii *is an ideal choice for any sunny dry rock crevice or corner. It bears triangular-shaped grey-green leaves and pale yellow flowers that usually open in the afternoon.*

Favourites	Flower Colour	Blooming Season	Flower Fragrance	Plant Height	Plant Width	Hardiness Zone	Frost Tolerance
Delosperma congestum	bright yellow	summer to early autumn	no	2 in (5 cm)	10 in (25 cm)	8–10	yes
Delosperma cooperi	magenta	mid- to late summer	no	2–3 in (5–8 cm)	18–24 in (45–60 cm)	9–11	no
Delosperma lehmannii	lemon yellow	summer	no	6 in (15 cm)	24 in (60 cm)	9–11	no
Delosperma nubigenum	bright yellow to orange-red	late spring to summer	no	1 in (25 mm)	36 in (90 cm)	7–11	yes
Delosperma sphalmanthoides	pink-purple	spring to summer	no	2 in (5 cm)	12 in (30 cm)	9–11	no
Delosperma sutherlandii	magenta	summer	no	2 in (5 cm)	6 in (15 cm)	8–11	yes

ECHEVERIA

T his genus of 150 species of mainly small, rosette-forming succulents of the stonecrop (Crassulaceae) family is found principally in Mexico, but a few species range down to Central America. Often the rosettes are densely clustered and may form a small mound. Short-stemmed, small, yellow, orange, pink or red blooms develop from late spring, but the plants are grown more often for the unusual blue-green foliage, sometimes with a powdery coating, which may develop red tints at the tips and edges. *Echeveria* is named after Atanasio Echeverria Codoy, an eighteenth-century Spanish botanical artist who illustrated a monograph on the genus.

ABOVE Echeveria gigantea *is a winter-flowering species that has loose open rosettes. This cultivar, 'Dee', has broad blue-green leaves that age red in the sun.*

Top Tip

Indoor pot plants will enjoy summers spent outdoors. Water plants from below; avoid water on the leaves as it will pool into the rosette centre and can lead to rotting.

BELOW Echeveria pallida *has broad, spoon-shaped, light-textured, pale green leaves, which form loose, open rosettes, and has pink flowers during winter.*

CULTIVATION

BELOW Echeveria 'Dondo', *a hybrid of* E. dehrenbergii *and* E. setosa, *has rosettes of grey-blue leaves with scalloped and pointed tips, and pretty golden yellow flowers.*

Hardiness varies but few will tolerate cold wet winters and repeated frosts. Plant in full or half-sun with light, gritty, very free-draining soil. Water occasionally when in active growth, otherwise keep dry, especially in winter. Propagate from stem or leaf cuttings or from seed, which germinates freely but can be prone to damping off.

Favourites	Flower Colour	Blooming Season	Flower Fragrance	Plant Height	Plant Width	Hardiness Zone	Frost Tolerance
Echeveria agavoides	orange-pink, yellow inside	spring to early summer	no	6–8 in (15–20 cm)	8–12 in (20–30 cm)	9–11	no
Echeveria 'Dondo'	golden yellow	spring to early summer	no	6–24 in (15–60 cm)	4–18 in (10–45 cm)	9–11	no
Echeveria elegans	deep pink, gold centre	spring to early summer	no	6–8 in (15–20 cm)	12–16 in (30–40 cm)	9–11	no
Echeveria 'Fire Light'	orange-yellow to pink-red	spring to early summer	no	6–24 in (15–60 cm)	4–18 in (10–45 cm)	9–11	no
Echeveria gigantea	deep pink-red	winter	no	5–7 ft (1.5–2 m)	20 in (50 cm)	10–12	no
Echeveria leucotricha	orange with red edges	spring to early summer	no	24 in (60 cm)	20–40 in (50–100 cm)	9–11	no
Echeveria 'Morning Light'	bright pink	spring to early summer	no	6–24 in (15–60 cm)	4–18 in (10–45 cm)	9–11	no
Echeveria pallida	pink	winter	no	24–40 in (60–100 cm)	16–24 in (40–60 cm)	9–11	no
Echeveria peacockii	soft orange to pinkish red	spring to early summer	no	12 in (30 cm)	12–24 in (30–60 cm)	9–11	no
Echeveria 'Princess Lace'	orange-yellow to pink-red	spring to early summer	no	6–24 in (15–60 cm)	4–18 in (10–45 cm)	9–11	no
Echeveria 'Violet Queen'	orange-yellow to pink-red	spring to early summer	no	6–24 in (15–60 cm)	4–18 in (10–45 cm)	9–11	no
Echeveria, Galaxy Series	orange-red, yellow petal tips	spring to early summer	no	6–24 in (15–60 cm)	4–18 in (10–45 cm)	9–11	no

ABOVE Echeveria *'Violet Queen' is an award-winning hybrid cultivar with clusters of 15 cm (6 in) wide, pink-edged, pale blue-green rosettes. It is hardy, with a clumping habit.*

LEFT *Echinocereus viereckii is a low alpine species from Mexico with clusters of deep green branching stems that are upright then spreading and have tiny tubercles.*
RIGHT *Native to the western USA–Mexico border region, Echinocereus triglochidiatus var.* melanacanthus *has red flowers and the descriptive common name claret cup.*

ECHINOCEREUS

A small globose or cylindrically stemmed genus, it belongs to the cacti (Cactaceae) family and is native to Mexico and southern USA. Including about 120 species, the genus now incorporates many of the species previously in *Lobivia* and *Trichocereus*. The stems are usually many-ribbed and have conspicuous areoles on tubercles or on the ribs themselves. Spines, often large in comparison to the plant size, may be curved or hooked, and flowers, in shades of cream, pink, orange and red, appear from spring to mid-summer. These blooms are tubular, long and often spectacular. *Echinocereus* means "hedgehog cactus", and as much care should be exercised when tending this cactus as if handling its spiny namesake.

CULTIVATION
Plant in full sun with light, gritty, very well-drained soil. Water occasionally when young or in periods of extreme drought, but otherwise leave to survive on natural rainfall. The seed germinates well but seedlings are slow to develop and inclined to rot at the base. Offsets are easier to establish and are often numerous.

BELOW *From Mexico, the solitary or few stems of* Echinocereus subinermis *have up to 11 well-defined ribs bearing starry clusters of usually short stout spines.*

Top Tip

Grow *Echinocereus* plants in a shallow soil—without organic matter—that is fast draining and in full sun. The soil should be allowed to dry out between summer waterings.

ABOVE *From the western USA–Mexico border region,* Echinocereus stramineus *forms dense colonies of up to several hundred narrow cylindrical stems in the wild.*

Favourites	Flower Colour	Blooming Season	Flower Fragrance	Plant Height	Plant Width	Hardiness Zone	Frost Tolerance
Echinocereus coccineus	scarlet, yellow at centre	spring to summer	no	3 in (8 cm)	4 in (10 cm)	6–11	yes
Echinocereus engelmannii	lavender to purple-red	summer	no	10–20 in (25–50 cm)	10–24 in (25–60 cm)	8–11	yes
Echinocereus stramineus	bright magenta	mid-summer	no	12–18 in (30–45 cm)	16–84 in (40–200 cm)	8–11	yes
Echinocereus subinermis	yellow	summer	no	8–10 in (20–25 cm)	6–12 in (15–30 cm)	9–11	no
Echinocereus triglochidiatus	scarlet	spring to summer	no	6–16 in (15–40 cm)	8–36 in (20–90 cm)	8–11	yes
Echinocereus viereckii	purple, mauve	spring to autumn	no	12 in (30 cm)	12–24 in (30–60 cm)	9–11	no

KALANCHOE

A member of the stonecrop (Crassulaceae) family, this genus has around 125 species of mostly bushy succulents found mainly in eastern and southern Africa, with a few species in Asia. They are a variable group, often with rather large, powder-coated or felted, silver-grey leaves that have notched edges. Some species produce tiny plantlets along the leaf margins. The small, starry, 4-petalled flowers are clustered in heads. They open at varying times depending on the species and may be very brightly coloured, often in yellow, orange or red shades. *Kalanchoe beharensis* is among the largest-leafed succulents, with foliage to 30 cm (12 in) long.

CULTIVATION

Smaller species and cultivars are often grown as house plants. Outdoors, most require frost-free conditions; full sun for those with silver leaves; light, gritty, free-draining soil; and some water during the growing season. Propagate from stem cuttings, leaf cuttings or seed, or by removing plantlets.

ABOVE *An upright spreading succulent,* Kalanchoe fedtschenkoi *makes an attractive ground cover. The flowers can vary in colour.*

LEFT *A mature* Kalanchoe beharensis *'Oak Leaf' plant has many small, tubular, yellowish flowers and large, felted, oak-shaped leaves.*

Top Tip

Whether grown for their ornamental foliage or tightly packed long-lasting flower clusters, *Kalanchoe* make low-maintenance indoor plants for a bright position.

ABOVE RIGHT *The colourful flowers of* Kalanchoe pumila *contrast strongly with the white-frosted leaves. These plants need full sun for the foliage to be at its best.*

RIGHT *Hybrids of* Kalanchoe blossfeldiana *are grown for their showy display of bright orange, yellow, pink, red, white or purple flowers and interesting fleshy leaves.*

Favourites	Flower Colour	Blooming Season	Flower Fragrance	Plant Height	Plant Width	Hardiness Zone	Frost Tolerance
Kalanchoe beharensis	yellow	late winter	no	10 ft (3 m)	3 ft (0.9 m)	10–11	no
Kalanchoe blossfeldiana	deep red	early spring	no	15 in (38 cm)	15 in (38 cm)	10–12	no
Kalanchoe fedtschenkoi	orange to red	spring	no	20 in (50 cm)	12 in (30 cm)	11–12	no
Kalanchoe pumila	pink with purple markings	spring	no	8 in (20 cm)	18 in (45 cm)	11–12	no
Kalanchoe thyrsiflora	yellow	spring	yes	24 in (60 cm)	12 in (30 cm)	11–12	no
Kalanchoe tomentosa	purple-tinged yellow-green	early spring	no	15–36 in (38–90 cm)	8 in (20 cm)	10–12	no

LAMPRANTHUS

This genus of 225-odd species from South Africa and Namibia contains many popular succulent garden plants, justifiably loved for their masses of colourful flowers, which are produced year-round, and especially in spring and summer. Most forms are low-growing mats or short shrubs, with pairs of short, waxy, cylindrical to triangular, yellow-green to blue-green leaves. The lustrous flowers open in the morning and close in the late afternoon, and are produced in such profusion that they usually obscure the entire plant body. Colours include pure white, red, yellow, orange, pink and intermediate shades including bicoloured forms. Curiously called pig face in Australia, the genus name is more complimentary; it comes from the Greek words *lampros* (bright) and *anthos* (flower).

ABOVE *Known as the midday flower,* Lampranthus amoenus *is a shrubby succulent perennial that needs full sun and good drainage.* **BELOW** Lampranthus auriantiacus *'Gold Nugget' has yellow-centred bright orange flowers. In summer, the foliage is hidden by a spectacular blanket of colour.*

CULTIVATION

Lampranthus species and their cultivars are reasonably easy to grow, though gardeners must remember not to over-water them. They are somewhat frost tender plants; however, they can withstand periods of drought. Grow either from cuttings or from seed.

ABOVE Lampranthus glaucus *is particularly recommended for the garden. It is characterised by its canary yellow daisy-like flowers and rough-spotted leaves.*
RIGHT Lampranthus aurantiacus *has a spreading shrubby habit, and bears a profusion of yellow and orange flowers.*

Favourites	Flower Colour	Blooming Season	Flower Fragrance	Plant Height	Plant Width	Hardiness Zone	Frost Tolerance
Lampranthus amoenus	rose purple	spring to summer	no	2–3 ft (0.6–0.9 m)	3–4 ft (0.9–1.2 m)	9–11	no
Lampranthus aurantiacus	orange and yellow	summer	no	18 in (45 cm)	30 in (75 cm)	9–11	no
Lampranthus aurantiacus 'Gold Nugget'	orange	summer	no	18 in (45 cm)	30 in (75 cm)	9–11	no
Lampranthus filicaulis	pale pink	early spring	no	3 in (8 cm)	36 in (90 cm)	9–11	no
Lampranthus glaucus	yellow	late spring	no	12 in (30 cm)	2–4 ft (0.6–1.2 m)	9–11	no
Lampranthus spectabilis	purple, pink, red	spring to summer	no	6–12 in (15–30 cm)	18–36 in (45–90 cm)	9–11	no

MAMMILLARIA

Hailing from southwestern USA, Mexico, Central America and northern South America, this genus, commonly known as pincushion cactus, is a member of the family Cactaceae and contains more than 150 species. These solitary or clustering cacti have round to cylindrical, spiny, green stems. The spines appear from the pimple-like openings (tubercles) of the raised segments (areoles) on the stems. Funnel-shaped flowers, in colours ranging from white to yellow, green, or pink to purple, encircle the crowns of the stems throughout spring and summer. The attractive flowers are followed by round berry-like seed pods.

ABOVE *A clustered mound-forming cactus,* Mammillaria geminispina *usually has short cylindrical stems. This mutated "crest" form has an interesting twisted growth habit.*

CULTIVATION

These plants do well in well-drained soils in an open sunny position. Reduce watering in winter. Propagate most species by division of offsets, or from seed in spring and summer.

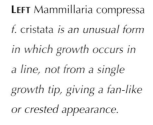

LEFT Mammillaria compressa *f.* cristata *is an unusual form in which growth occurs in a line, not from a single growth tip, giving a fan-like or crested appearance.*

ABOVE *The bright pink flowers of* Mammillaria melanocentra *are carried at the top of its single undivided stem. They are followed by pinkish red fruit.*

LEFT Mammillaria canelensis *begins as a single-stemmed plant but later develops more stems. The flowers add a touch of colour when they open during the day.*

Top Tip

Mammillaria species are often grown for their flowers. Water and fertilise regularly throughout the growing season to encourage flower production.

Favourites	Flower Colour	Blooming Season	Flower Fragrance	Plant Height	Plant Width	Hardiness Zone	Frost Tolerance
Mammillaria bocasana	creamy white, rose pink	spring to summer	no	4–8 in (10–20 cm)	12–24 in (30–60 cm)	9–11	no
Mammillaria canelensis	pink to red, yellow	summer	no	6–8 in (15–20 cm)	3–4 in (8–10 cm)	9–11	no
Mammillaria carmenae	pink- or cream-tinged white	spring	no	2–3 in (5–8 cm)	2–3 in (5–8 cm)	9–11	no
Mammillaria compressa	purplish pink	spring	no	1½–2½ in (3.5–6 cm)	6 in (15 cm)	9–11	no
Mammillaria geminispina	deep pink to red	spring to autumn	no	6–10 in (15–25 cm)	6–20 in (15–50 cm)	9–11	no
Mammillaria klissingiana	pink, ageing to red	summer	no	4–6 in (10–15 cm)	2½–4 in (6–10 cm)	9–11	no
Mammillaria laui	purplish pink	spring	no	1–1½ in (2.5–3.5 cm)	1½–2 in (3.5–5 cm)	9–11	no
Mammillaria longimamma	bright yellow	summer	no	3–5 in (8–12 cm)	3–5 in (8–12 cm)	9–11	no
Mammillaria melanocentra	pink	spring	no	3–5 in (8–12 cm)	4–6 in (10–15 cm)	9–11	no
Mammillaria parkinsonii	brown- or pink-tinged yellow	spring	no	4–6 in (10–15 cm)	3–6 in (8–15 cm)	9–11	no
Mammillaria tayloriorum	reddish pink	spring	no	3–6 in (8–15 cm)	2½–3 in (6–8 cm)	9–11	no
Mammillaria winterae	yellow and white	summer	no	8–12 in (20–30 cm)	8–12 in (20–30 cm)	9–11	no

OPUNTIA

This genus in the cactus (Cactaceae) family is made up of around 180 species, some of them tree-like, that are widespread in the Americas and include some of the hardiest cacti, found as far north as southern Canada. The best-known forms have flat, paddle-shaped, areole-studded stem segments, that develop yellow, orange or red flowers along the margins. The flowers are followed by soft, rounded, red or yellow fruit called prickly pears. Not all species follow this pattern; some have cylindrical stems, a few are ground covers, and some have insignificant fruit. *Opuntia stricta* was introduced to Australia in the 1830s to provide hedging material in arid regions. It quickly covered vast areas, but in an early example of natural management was brought under control by introduced insects.

CULTIVATION

These cacti are very adaptable and well able to survive outside what would be considered "normal" cactus conditions. Plant in full or half-sun with gritty, very free-draining soil and water only when absolutely necessary. Propagate from stem cuttings or by division.

Favourites	Flower Colour	Blooming Season	Flower Fragrance
Opuntia aciculata	yellow, red	spring to summer	no
Opuntia aoracantha	white to yellow, pinkish	spring to summer	no
Opuntia basilaris	purplish red	summer	no
Opuntia macrocentra	bright yellow, orange-red at base	spring	no
Opuntia microdasys	red-tinged yellow	spring to summer	no
Opuntia strigil	creamy white	spring to summer	no

ABOVE Opuntia strigil *has fleshy red fruit that follows the creamy white flowers. This prickly pear species can grow as an upright or sprawling shrub.*

LEFT *The bright flowers of* Opuntia macrocentra *are about 6 cm (2½ in) wide. They will last only 1 day out in the sun, but will last for 2–3 days if taken inside.*

Top Tip

Most *Opuntia* species are easy to grow and make excellent house plants. They do best in full sun, and flower production will fall if conditions are too dark.

Plant Height	Plant Width	Hardiness Zone	Frost Tolerance
3–5 ft (0.9–1.5 m)	3–5 ft (0.9–1.5 m)	9–11	no
12–24 in (30–60 cm)	12–24 in (30–60 cm)	9–11	no
2–3 ft (0.6–0.9 m)	4 ft (1.2 m)	9–11	no
4 ft (1.2 m)	4 ft (1.2 m)	9–11	no
18–24 in (45–60 cm)	18–24 in (45–60 cm)	8–11	no
2–3 ft (0.6–0.9 m)	4–7 ft (1.2–2 m)	9–11	no

BELOW Opuntia aciculata *has flattened stem segments dotted with tufts of spines and bristles. Protuberant flowers appear on the stem segment edge.*

ABOVE *The colourful flowers of* Opuntia aoracantha *have thick stems called pericarpels. This is a small species, often branching at ground level.*

REBUTIA

Found in the Bolivian Andes and neighbouring parts of Argentina, *Rebutia* is a genus in the cactus (Cactaceae) family of around 40 small, almost spherical- or cylindrical-stemmed species. Their clustered stems are densely studded with spine-bearing tubercles, and the spines are often very fine and bristle-like, though still sharp. Brightly coloured funnel-shaped flowers develop around the tops of the stems and can be abundant. The flowers close at night. The botanist Karl Schumann classified the genus in 1895, naming it after a French cactus grower and vigneron with whom he corresponded, Monsieur P Rebut.

Top Tip

It is good to re-pot rebutias regularly, particularly when they are young. This will increase the number and size of the stems and the number of flowers produced.

CULTIVATION

Although tolerant of occasional very light frosts, *Rebutia* species usually perform best with mild winter conditions. Plant in full or half-sun with gritty, very free-draining soil. Water during the growing season but otherwise keep dry. These cacti are very easily propagated from the numerous offsets.

ABOVE *The pretty funnel-shaped flowers of* Rebutia neocumingii *bloom during the day. They are yellow to orange in colour and grow to 25 mm (1 in) long.*
LEFT Rebutia marsoneri *typically flowers a bright and vibrant yellow. However, there are varieties that have red flowers.*

LEFT Rebutia fiebrigii, *native to the mountainous regions of Bolivia and north-western Argentina, is a hardy specimen with bristly but soft white spines.*

BELOW *Usually a spherical solitary species,* Rebutia flavistyla *can be grown from seed. It bears long-tubed, vivid orange flowers from spring.*

Favourites	Flower Colour	Blooming Season	Flower Fragrance	Plant Height	Plant Width	Hardiness Zone	Frost Tolerance
Rebutia fiebrigii	orange to red	summer	no	1¼–2 in (3–5 cm)	1¼–3 in (3–8 cm)	9–12	no
Rebutia flavistyla	orange	spring	no	2–4 in (5–10 cm)	2–6 in (5–15 cm)	10–12	no
Rebutia heliosa	dark pink to orange-pink	summer	no	¾–2 in (18–50 mm)	½–4 in (12–100 mm)	9–12	no
Rebutia marsoneri	yellow, red, or orange-yellow	summer	no	1¼–4 in (3–10 cm)	1½–8 in (3.5–20 cm)	9–12	no
Rebutia neocumingii	yellow to orange	summer	no	4–8 in (10–20 cm)	3–4 in (8–10 cm)	9–10	no
Rebutia perplexa	lilac-pink	summer	no	½–1 in (12–25 mm)	1–3 in (25–80 mm)	9–12	no

SEDUM

This genus of 300 species of mainly low spreading succulents is found over much of the Northern Hemisphere. It is part of the stonecrop (Crassulaceae) family. Their leaves are usually short, very fleshy and often develop bright red or bronze tones in the sun. Dense sprays of tiny, light to golden yellow or pink flowers develop at the stem tips, most often during the warmer months. Many of the larger autumn-flowering species are now classified under *Hylotelephium* and *Rhodiola*. The name *Sedum* is from the Latin *sedere*, to sit, referring to the low spreading habit.

CULTIVATION

Of varying hardiness, they are otherwise easily grown in any sunny or partly shaded position with light well-drained soil. The hardier species are often quite at home in everyday garden conditions, but those from arid areas should be kept dry during winter. Remove spent flowerheads as they dry. Propagation is from short stem cuttings, leaf cuttings or seed. Many species will self-layer.

RIGHT *Plant this species,* Sedum kamtschaticum, *in a well-drained border. It will also grow well in cracks and crevices in walls and pavements.*

LEFT *The foliage of* Sedum spathulifolium *'Purpureum' turns purplish red in the sun. The yellow flowers appear in spring and early summer.*
BELOW LEFT *Sedum* spectabile, *known as ice plant and showy sedum, can survive drought conditions but does best with regular watering.*

Top Tip

Sedum species transplant readily from cuttings, often rooting from broken foliage. Clumps may be divided and replanted at any time during the growing season.

Favourites	Flower Colour	Blooming Season	Flower Fragrance	Plant Height	Plant Width	Hardiness Zone	Frost Tolerance
Sedum album	white	summer	no	2–6 in (5–15 cm)	2–24 in (30–60 cm)	6–10	yes
Sedum kamtschaticum	golden yellow	summer	no	4–12 in (10–30 cm)	10–24 in (25–60 cm)	7–10	yes
Sedum rubrotinctum	pale yellow	spring	no	10 in (25 cm)	12–24 in (30–60 cm)	9–11	no
Sedum sieboldii	pale pink	autumn	no	4 in (10 cm)	12–20 in (30–50 cm)	7–10	yes
Sedum spathulifolium	yellow	late spring to early summer	no	4–6 in (10–15 cm)	24 in (60 cm)	7–10	yes
Sedum spectabile	pink to red	late summer to autumn	no	18–27 in (45–70 cm)	16–32 in (40–80 cm)	7–10	yes

SEMPERVIVUM

Though we usually think of succulents as plants from hot arid areas, aridity is not always accompanied by heat and succulents have also evolved on the dry, often frozen slopes of mountain ranges or on rocky headlands of temperate coasts. *Sempervivum* are good examples. Most are European and virtually all can tolerate –15°C/5°F. They really do well only in temperate regions, tending to rot where summers are hot, rainy and humid. *Sempervivum* form tight rosettes of pointy leaves that come in a range of colours. As the plants grow, offsets are produced so that eventually an attractive spreading mat is formed. There are more than 40 species, many popular with gardeners for rockeries or scree gardens. They belong to the family Crassulaceae.

CULTIVATION

Grow in fast-draining sandy or gravelly soil in full sun or with a few hours afternoon shade. In containers, choose a cactus and succulent potting mix. Keep dryish in winter and summer with a little more water being given in autumn and spring. As a clump becomes overcrowded, separate into smaller clumps or individuals and replant. Do this in spring.

Top Tip

The different leaf colours available in *Sempervivum* allow you to create interesting, tapestry-like effects either in the garden or in wide, shallow pots. Leave room for the individual colours to spread.

RIGHT Sempervivum tector- *um quickly forms clumps of wax-textured foliage rosettes. In early summer, each rosette produces at least one spike, which carries pendulous orange and yellow flowers.*

Favourites	Leaf Colour	Flower Colour	Blooming Season	Plant Height	Plant Width	Hardiness Zone	Frost Tolerance
Sempervivum arachnoideum	grey-green	dark pink	summer	2–4 in (5–10 cm)	12–24 in (30–60 cm)	7–9	yes
Sempervivum 'Butterbur'	olive green with reddish brown centre	dull pink and red	summer	4–6 in (10–15 cm)	4–6 in (10–15 cm)	7–9	yes
Sempervivum 'Director Jacobs'	red and green	pink	summer	3–4 in (8–10 cm)	4–5 in (10–13 cm)	7–9	yes
Sempervivum tectorum	pale green with pinkish tips	pink	summer	4–6 in (10–15 cm)	12–24 in (30–60 cm)	7–9	yes

RIGHT *Tight rosettes in rusty red and lime green make* Sempervivum *'Director Jacobs' one of the more unusually coloured forms.*
LEFT *To make a distinctive pattern, use the deeply coloured forms, such as 'Corona', to contrast with the lighter-leafed varieties. Its rich red and green leaves make it highly sought after.*

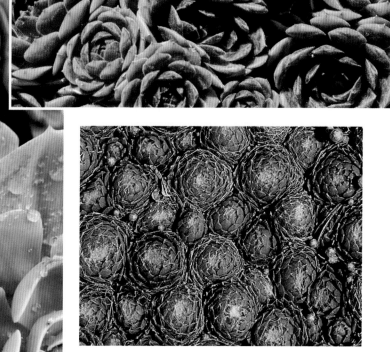

ABOVE Sempervivum arachnoideum *and its cultivars, such as 'Cebanse' shown here, are small plants. Its leaves are covered with a web-like material. It is quick to reproduce itself.*

YUCCA

Native to hot dry regions stretching from North to Central America and the West Indies, there are about 40 species in this genus within the Agavaceae family, including evergreen herbaceous perennials, trees and shrubs. They have a strong bold form with strap- to lance-shaped leaves arranged in rosettes. Bell- to cup-shaped flowers are held on mostly erect panicles. Flowers are usually white or cream, though they may be tinged with purple. *Yucca whipplei* holds the record for the fastest plant growth; its flowering spike emerges and grows to 3.5 m (12 ft) in just 14 days.

CULTIVATION

Yucca species grow best in loamy soil with good drainage, but will tolerate poor sandy soil. They range from frost hardy to frost tender. In colder areas it is advisable to grow the tender species in large pots in loam-based potting compost and overwinter indoors. If grown outdoors they need good light in summer, a monthly feed, and careful watering. Propagation is by sowing seed in spring, although seed may take some time to germinate. Take root cuttings in winter, or remove suckers in spring.

Top Tip

With their dramatic foliage and form, these are not plants for crowded corners. As in their native environment—deserts and sand dunes— a sparse setting suits them best.

Favourites	Flower Colour	Blooming Season	Flower Fragrance
Yucca elata	creamy white	summer	yes
Yucca filamentosa	white	summer	no
Yucca gloriosa	white with pinkish tints	late summer to autumn	no
Yucca recurvifolia	cream	late summer to autumn	no
Yucca rostrata	white	autumn	no
Yucca whipplei	white	summer	no

RIGHT *The flowering stalk of* Yucca elata *grows to 1.8 m (6 ft) tall with creamy white flowers, sometimes tinted pink or green. The new green leaves are edged with fine hairs.*

RIGHT *Found from North Carolina to Florida, USA,* Yucca gloriosa *has stiff, thin, lance-shaped, blue-green leaves that turn dark green with age. Its pendent bell-shaped flowers are white, occasionally tinged pink.*

Plant Height	Plant Width	Hardiness Zone	Frost Tolerance
10–30 ft (3–9 m)	4–8 ft (1.2–2.4 m)	7–11	yes
4–12 ft (1.2–3.5 m)	5–8 ft (1.5–2.4 m)	4–10	yes
6–15 ft (1.8–4.5 m)	6–12 ft (1.8–3.5 m)	7–10	yes
5–8 ft (1.5–2.4 m)	4–8 ft (1.2–2.4 m)	7–11	yes
8–15 ft (2.4–4.5 m)	4–8 ft (1.2–2.4 m)	7–11	yes
6–12 ft (1.8–3.5 m)	3–6 ft (0.9–1.8 m)	7–11	yes

ABOVE *The remarkable* Yucca whipplei *subsp.* parishii *may grow to 2–6 m (7–20 ft) tall, and the purple-tinged flowerhead, consisting of many flowers, averages 1.8 m (6 ft) tall.*
BELOW Yucca filamentosa *'Bright Edge' is a dwarf cultivar that produces multiple, long, yellow-edged leaves, and a number of flower stems bearing pendulous creamy blooms.*

VEGETABLES AND HERBS

Vegetables and herbs are some of the most prized and practical plants in the garden. Even those who claim not to care about plants will often grow (or aspire to grow) a tomato plant and a few herbs. The flavour of home-grown vegetables cannot be compared to store-bought: even the best vegetable stands and farmers' markets cannot offer vegetables that have spent less than an hour between the garden and the plate. Still warm from the sun and at the peak of ripeness, freshly harvested vegetables and herbs seem to distil the essence of all that is good about gardening—and eating.

ABOVE *Tomatoes* (Lycopersicon esculentum) *are among the most common plants in the home vegetable garden, perhaps because freshly picked perfectly ripe tomatoes taste so good.*
LEFT *A herb and vegetable garden can range in size from a small pot to quite a large area. Whatever the size, the rewards will be high, in flavour and sense of achievement.*

GROW YOUR OWN DELICIOUS FOOD

Vegetables and herbs encompass a vast range of mostly herbaceous annual, biennial and perennial plants with many uses in the kitchen, in medicine and in arts and crafts. Edible or useful parts include roots, tubers, stems, leaves, flowers, seeds or fruit.

LEFT *Widely used in salads, lettuce is now available in a variety of forms and colours. Lactuca sativa 'Cosmic' is an award-winning cos-type lettuce.*

Root crops include beets, carrots, garlic, onions, artichokes, parsnips, potatoes and turnips. These plants store water and nutrients in their plump rootstocks. Some, such as potatoes and Jerusalem artichokes, are actually tubers.

Many vegetables are primarily leaf crops. Some are typically cooked; others are eaten raw. Leaf crops include kales and cabbages, spinach, leeks, Asian greens and the many salad crops including lettuce, radicchio (chicory), arugula (rocket) and corn salad (mache). Brussels sprouts are composed of tiny leaf buds produced directly from the plant's main stem.

A number of vegetable plants are grown for their stems. These include the popular celery and asparagus, a perennial plant with spears that are best eaten when young and tender in early spring.

The bulk of garden vegetables are grown for their edible fruit, seeds or flowers. These include the legumes (peas and beans), eggplants (aubergines), capsicums (peppers), cucumbers, melons, sweet corn, pumpkins, squash (marrows) and tomatoes. Broccoli and cauliflower are grown for their immature flower buds.

Many vegetables spring from the same basic plant, and have been cultivated over the centuries to create diverse forms. For example, the brassicas (family Brassicaceae) include the non-heading kales (*Brassica oleracea*, Acephala Group), broccoli and cauliflower (*B. o.,* Botrytis Group), cabbages (*B. o.,* Capitata Group), Brussels sprouts (*B. o.,* Gemmifera Group), kohlrabi (*B. o.,* Gongylodes Group) and sprouting broccoli (*B. o.,* Italica Group). Other edible brassicas include turnip (*B. rapa,*

ABOVE *Capsicum annuum,* Grossum Group, *contains sweet bell peppers in various colours. 'Blushing Beauty' ripens to apricot-flushed yellow.*
LEFT *Broccoli is an easy-to-grow cool-season vegetable. Award-winning 'Shogun' belongs to the Botrytis Group within* Brassica oleracea.

Rapifera Group) and bok choy (*B. rapa*, Chinensis Group). Mustards such as brown mustard, Chinese mustard and mustard greens are all derived from *Brassica juncea*. Rutabagas (swedes) and a number of other important brassicas are derived from *Brassica napus*.

Vegetables can be grown from seed or purchased as young seedlings. Vegetable packets typically indicate how many weeks ahead of the last frost date each type needs to be started. When selecting which plant to grow, consider flavour, colour, fruit or plant size, ripening time, storage quality and resistance to insects or diseases. Heirloom varieties may take up more space, produce later or be more prone to certain diseases—but their flavour is usually better. New varieties are bred as much for compact size and fruit production as for flavour.

ABOVE *The purple-red leaves of* Ocimum basilicum *'Red Rubin' basil are a decorative and flavoursome addition to the herb garden.*
LEFT Mentha suaveolens *is known as apple mint. Mint plants can be invasive and are often grown in pots.*

Additionally, many vegetables are better suited to particular climates than others. A tomato variety that ripens well in Sydney, Australia, might not suit the climate of London, England. Local information about suitable varieties is essential.

Although there are many kinds of vegetables, the best vegetables are produced when plants are grown in full sun in reasonably rich soil and supplied with consistent moisture during the growing season. Since many vegetables are annuals or tender biennials or perennials growing for only one season, it is essential that plants receive everything they need to reach maturity quickly. For instance, mulching warms the soil, conserves moisture and increases the level of organic matter. Crop rotation prevents nutrient depletion and minimises disease.

Broadly defined, herbs are plants that are used to flavour foods and beverages, dye cloth, repel insects, scent toiletries and prevent or treat ailments. Encompassing annuals, biennials and perennials, the plants range in size from prostrate species to large evergreen trees. Herbs are generally ornamental and their flowers are often nectar-rich and sought after by butterflies and bees. Many herbs do well in pots, are suitable as low hedges or can be integrated into perennial beds.

Most herbs are aromatic to some degree. Sunny dry climates increase the taste, fragrance and potency of many of the aromatic Mediterranean herbs such as lavender, oregano, rosemary, thyme and sage, most of which grow in rather dry poor soil in their native habitats. While most Mediterranean herbs thrive in full sun, there are many that tolerate shade, such as mint (*Mentha* species). Herbs such as basil, parsley and dill prefer more moisture and nutrients, as they are prone to bolting (going to seed) when stressed.

Vegetables and herbs are easy to work into almost any garden, requiring only some initial attention to available soil, moisture and light. Whether grown for culinary or ornamental purposes, they are easy to grow and can provide access to fresh organic food that tastes more delicious than almost anything purchased commercially. While the flavour of fresh vegetables and herbs is enough in itself to inspire one to tend a produce garden, the sense of achievement derived is also a great impetus.

ALLIUM

A big genus of bulbous plants in the family Alliaceae, *Allium* includes many important food crops such as onions, garlic, leeks, shallots and chives. They occur naturally only in the Northern Hemisphere but are widespread there. Alliums have been grown and eaten by humans for thousands of years and because they have always been such an important food, they've been selected and hybridised with the aim of producing more and better crops for almost all that time. Plants grow as leafy, cylindrical stems usually from bulbs, although the leek has no bulb and is raised from seed. In most cases both the bulbs and stems can be eaten. Flowers are globose heads made up of many tiny blooms in white, pink, purple, magenta or yellow.

CULTIVATION

Grow in full sun in fertile, free-draining soil. Some of the edible members of the genus, such as garlic, require a cool to cold winter in order to do well. Others, such as onions, are day-length sensitive with particular varieties needing to be planted at certain times of the year. In general, they are winter growing, summer harvesting plants.

ABOVE *Onions come in early, mid-season and late maturing varieties. Choose a variety suitable for your location and day lengths.* **RIGHT** *Raise leeks from seed sown in pots for planting. Or, buy as seedlings. Plant seedlings with only a quarter of their leaf length showing.* **BELOW LEFT** *Grow garlic from cloves planted mid-autumn to early winter. If planting store-bought garlic, the base plate must not have been scooped out.*

Top Tip

Leeks can be harvested any time from pencil thickness but onions and garlic are pulled only when the tops turn yellow and start to die back. Chives are cut anytime and will re-shoot.

ABOVE *Onions sometimes push themselves out of the ground when nearing maturity. You don't need to re-bury them.*

ABOVE AND LEFT *Chives are perennials that form dense clumps of tubular leaves. To harvest, cut the number of leaves you want at ground level. New leaves will form at the cut bases. The rosy-purple flowers are edible and add extra colour to salads.*

Favourites	Common Name	Produce Season	Plant Height	Plant Width	Hardiness Zone	Frost Tolerance
Allium cepa	onion, shallots	all year	24 in (60 cm)	4 in (10 cm)	7–9	yes
Allium porrum	leek	autumn and winter	24 in (60 cm)	12 in (30 cm)	7–8	yes
Allium sativum	garlic	summer and autumn	24–36 in (60–90 cm)	10 in (25 cm)	7–8	yes
Allium schoenoprasum	chives	all year	8–10 in (20–25 cm)	¼ in (1 cm)	7–10	yes
Allium tuberosum	Chinese chives	all year	10–12 in (25–30 cm)	¼ in (1 cm)	7–10	yes

ASPARAGUS

The asparagus family (Asparagaceae) is composed of about 300 species of tuberous or rhizomatous perennial herbs, shrubs and climbers that are widespread outside the Americas. The species most often grown for its succulent young stems is *Asparagus officinalis*, which produces clusters of slender stems from its underground rhizomes. Each stem is topped with feathery foliage with small white flowers and red berries. Plants are not only long lived (they can be expected to produce for up to 25 years), but are also versatile—in herbal medicine *Asparagus* is considered to have a cleansing effect on both the liver and kidneys.

ABOVE *Asparagus officinalis 'Larac' is a French variety noted for its wide adaptability. Like the species, it has rich green feathery foliage, but its spears are white.*

CULTIVATION

The fresh new shoots are the edible part and it takes several seasons for new crowns (roots) to become fully productive. Before planting, work in plenty of compost, enough to raise the bed. If necessary, add coarse sand or fine gravel to improve the drainage. Harvest the young spears by cutting them off under ground level with a sharp knife. Do not harvest any spears until the crowns are at least 2 years old. Propagate by dividing the crowns. Plants can be raised from seed but only male plants produce an edible crop.

LEFT *In the third year after planting, harvest spears for 6 weeks only from the time they appear.*

Top Tip

Growing from seed will mean a 3-year wait for first harvest, so it is best to use crowns (roots) purchased from a nursery when planting out the crop.

RIGHT *Asparagus officinalis is the species people generally mean when referring to asparagus. Widely grown as a food crop, it has erect multi-branched stems.*

Favourites	Common Name	Produce Season	Plant Height	Plant Width	Hardiness Zone	Frost Tolerance
Asparagus officinalis	asparagus	spring	3–5 ft (0.9–1.5 m)	3–5 ft (0.9–1.5 m)	4–8	yes
Asparagus officinalis 'Mary Washington'	Mary Washington asparagus	spring	3–5 ft (0.9–1.5 m)	3–5 ft (0.9–1.5 m)	7–8	yes
Asparagus officinalis 'UC 157'	asparagus	spring	3–5 ft (0.9–1.5 m)	3–5 ft (0.9–1.5 m)	7–8	yes

BETA

The sole species in this genus of the goosefoot (Chenopiaceae) family is a Eurasian biennial that occurs in 2 main forms. One is grown for its edible swollen roots (beets), the other for its iron-rich deep green to purple-red foliage (chards). The leaves of both forms are edible, the leaves of chards being heavily puckered with a thick and often contrastingly coloured mid-rib. With beets, the top of the root often emerges from the soil as it matures. Roots were used as a food source from the sixteenth century. In times past beet juice was considered a virtual cure-all, able to alleviate everything from ringing in the ears to toothache.

CULTIVATION

Although generally raised from seed sown from spring through to mid-summer, in mild areas autumn sowings may also be successful. Beets favour light well-drained soil, provided it is not too rich. Chards prefer rich, moist, well-drained soil. Both need to be planted in full sun. Any nutrient deficiencies, usually of manganese, show up in chards as yellowing leaves and poorly formed roots. Very heavy soil also has a tendency to lead to poorly formed or stunted roots.

ABOVE *The Conditiva Group includes vegetables such as sugar beet and beetroot. Beta vulgaris, Conditiva Group, 'Bull's Blood' has red leaves and striped roots.* **BELOW** *Beta vulgaris, Cicla Group, 'Rhubarb Chard' has crimson stalks and dark green crinkly leaves. Its mid-ribs can be used as a celery or asparagus substitute.*

Top Tip

Beets are slightly tolerant to drought, but keep chards moist. Water both before the soil entirely dries out. Beet roots will crack if moisture varies too much.

BELOW *The Cicla Group includes spinach and silver beet.* Beta vulgaris, *Cicla Group, 'Bright Lights' has stems in shades of orange, red, yellow, pink or white.*

Favourites	Common Name	Produce Season	Plant Height	Plant Width	Hardiness Zone	Frost Tolerance
Beta vulgaris	beet	spring to early summer	27 in (70 cm)	27 in (70 cm)	8–11	yes
Beta vulgaris, Cicla Group	spinach, chard, silver beet	spring to early summer	27 in (70 cm)	27 in (70 cm)	8–11	yes
Beta vulgaris, Cicla Group, 'Bright Lights'	Swiss chard	spring to early summer	24 in (60 cm)	12 in (30 cm)	8–11	yes
Beta vulgaris, Cicla Group, 'Rhubarb Chard'	ruby chard	spring to early summer	27 in (70 cm)	27 in (70 cm)	8–11	yes
Beta vulgaris Conditiva Group	beet	spring to early summer	27 in (70 cm)	27 in (70 cm)	8–11	yes
Beta vulgaris, Conditiva Group, 'Forono'	beetroot	spring to early summer	27 in (70 cm)	27 in (70 cm)	8–11	yes

ABOVE Beta vulgaris, *Cicla Group, 'Bright Yellow' is a Swiss chard whose green crinkly leaves can be used as a spinach substitute. Its golden stalks are a colourful addition to any vegetable garden and can be steamed, or eaten raw when young.*

LEFT Brassica oleracea, *Botrytis Group, 'Perfection' is a mini cauliflower with a cream-coloured head that grows to about 10 cm (4 in) in diameter in 2 months.*

BRASSICA

With a history of use spanning thousands of years, the cabbage and its relatives feature in many of the world's cuisines. There are few species but many subspecies, groups and cultivars, treated as annuals, biennials and perennials, depending on climate. Originally from temperate coastal regions of Europe and North Africa, the versatile brassicas are grown for their leaves (cabbages, kale, Asian greens), their flowering parts (broccoli, cauliflower, Brussels sprouts), their seed (rape/canola) or their roots (turnip, swede). As a rule, the leaves are large and waxy with a whitish bloom, and flowers are usually yellow, but are sometimes white. Flowering times will be dictated by the climatic region and the age of the plant.

CULTIVATION

These easy-to-grow adaptable plants do best in well-drained moist soil that has been enriched with well-rotted manure. Propagate from seed throughout the year, depending on the variety.

ABOVE Brassica rapa, *Rapifera Group, 'Atlantic' is a purple-topped turnip that is harvested when it reaches the size of a golf ball. Its leaves can be used in salads.*

BELOW Brassica oleracea, *Capitata Group, 'Primavoy' is a good storage cabbage cultivar, with compact flattened heads and dark blue-green puckered leaves.*

LEFT Brassica oleracea, *Capitata Group, 'Dynamo'* is a cabbage developed in Germany, which has a small head, a mild flavour, and is not prone to splitting.
RIGHT Brussels sprouts must experience a cold winter to perform well. In mild conditions the sprouts often fail to form solid hearts. Where winters are frosty, set out in early autumn.
BELOW Traditionally white, cauliflower can also be had with purple, green or yellow curds. Not just visually novel, these have their own distinctive taste as well.

Favourites	Common Name	Produce Season	Plant Height	Plant Width	Hardiness Zone	Frost Tolerance
Brassica juncea	mustard	summer	8–40 in (20–100 cm)	8–40 in (20–100 cm)	9–11	no
Brassica napus	swede	summer	8–16 in (20–40 cm)	8–16 in (20–40 cm)	8–11	yes
Brassica oleracea	wild cabbage	summer	16 in (40 cm)	12 in (30 cm)	8–11	yes
Brassica oleracea, **Botrytis Group**	cauliflower and broccoli	early summer	16 in (40 cm)	12 in (30 cm)	8–11	yes
Brassica oleracea, **Capitata Group**	cabbage	summer	16 in (40 cm)	12 in (30 cm)	8–11	yes
Brassica rapa	turnip	spring to autumn	12–20 in (30–50 cm)	12–20 in (30–50 cm)	9–11	no

Top Tip

Rotate *Brassica* plants in vegetable gardens to prevent soil-borne diseases. Use a different site each year for 3 years, starting again in the fourth year.

BELOW *Mustard cabbage or Gai choy is grown for its peppery hot leaves that add zing to salads and can also be used in stir-fries. Younger leaves are the best eating.*

BELOW *Its textured leaves have earned kale a place in the ornamental garden but its foliage can be harvested and steamed like spinach or cabbage. It looks great in the vegie patch.*

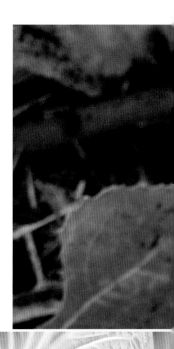

LEFT *Scatter rocket seeds in early spring and be picking for salads 4 weeks later. Sow a new batch every 4 weeks and you'll never be short of these nutty, peppery leaves.*

BELOW *All parts of pak choi (bok choi, Chinese white cabbage) except the root are used in many Asian dishes. The leaves are eaten raw but the stems are cooked.*

ABOVE *Chinese cabbages resemble the cos lettuce in the upright growth habit and do not form the solid heart so typical of European cabbages. They are fast to grow and mature and delicious in stir-fries.*

ABOVE *Swedes or rutabagas are started in late spring or early summer for harvesting in autumn or winter. They are similar to turnips except that most varieties have drier, yellow flesh.*

ABOVE *Collards are a form of kale. Where winters are cold, plant in spring for summer harvest. In warmer areas, plant in late summer for winter picking. They are easy to grow.*

CAPSICUM

A nightshade (Solanaceae) family genus of 10 species of annuals and short-lived perennials, peppers have been cultivated for thousands of years and are derived from several species, mainly *Capsicum annuum*. The 2 primary groups they fall into are sweet or bell peppers, which are mild, and chillies, which can be spicy to extremely hot. Typically small bushes with dark green ovate leaves, they have small white flowers that appear at the leaf axils and develop into variably shaped and coloured fruit. The heat of chillies can be measured on the Scoville dilution scale. The super-hot 'Habanero' pepper is still detectable when diluted to 1/300,000th of its original strength and the molten 'Tezpur' is reputedly stronger still.

LEFT *Capsicum annuum, Longum Group, 'Sweet Banana' grows to 50 cm (20 in) tall, and has pale yellowish fruit that matures to red, crisp, sweet flesh.*

Top Tip

To avoid carryover diseases, don't plant peppers where any other nightshade family members—such as tomatoes, potatoes, eggplants or other peppers—have grown before.

CULTIVATION

Peppers need long warm summers to mature well. Plant in full sun with moist well-drained soil and feed well when young, but reduce feeding as the bulk of the fruit sets. Fruit may be harvested before colour develops, provided it has reached full size. Propagation is from seed.

Favourites	Common Name	Produce Season	Plant Height	Plant Width	Hardiness Zone	Frost Tolerance
Capsicum annuum	bell pepper, chilli pepper	summer	8–60 in (20–150 cm)	8–20 in (20–50 cm)	6–12	yes
Capsicum annuum, **Cerasiforme Group**	bell pepper	summer	8–60 in (20–150 cm)	8–20 in (20–50 cm)	6–12	yes
Capsicum annuum, **Conioides Group**	chilli pepper	summer	8–60 in (20–150 cm)	8–20 in (20–50 cm)	6–12	yes
Capsicum annuum, **Grossum Group**	sweet bell pepper	summer	8–60 in (20–150 cm)	8–20 in (20–50 cm)	6–12	yes
Capsicum annuum, **Longum Group**	chilli pepper	summer	8–60 in (20–150 cm)	8–20 in (20–50 cm)	6–12	yes
Capsicum frutescens	chilli pepper, goat pepper	summer	8–60 in (20–150 cm)	8–20 in (20–50 cm)	6–12	yes

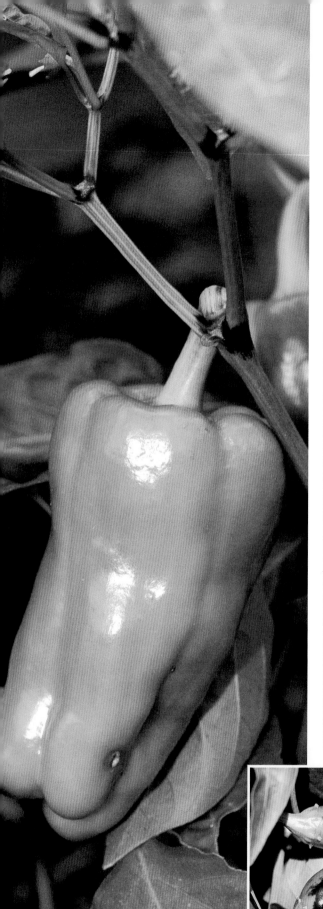

Left Capsicum annuum, *Cerasiforme Group cultivars have spherical, aromatic, small fruit. 'Guantanamo' has smooth green skin and walls of medium thickness.*

Below Capsicum annuum, *Longum Group members have hot fruit. This cultivar, 'Cayenne', has long, thin, slightly curved fruit, dried to make cayenne pepper.*

Left Capsicum annuum, *Conioides Group, 'Jalapeño' is a Mexican variety, known commonly as hot pepper or chilli. Dark green-black fruit ripens to a hot red hue.*

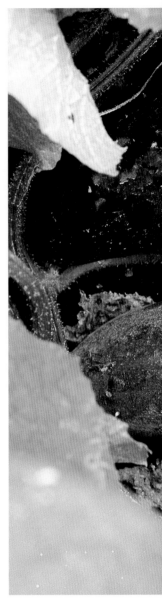

CUCUMIS

This genus of about 25 species of trailing or climbing annuals originating from warm to tropical areas of Africa and Asia belongs to the pumpkin (Cucurbitaceae) family. Probably better known as cucumbers and melons, these plants are now grown worldwide for their fruits, which are generally green and either long and narrow or round, with smooth, bumpy, spiny or ridged skin. Both male and female flowers —usually yellow or orange—are borne on the same plant. Cultivated since 3000 BC, the use of melons was recorded by the Persians, and cucumbers are now thought to have left India by around 1000 BC, spreading to Greece and Italy, where they were a favourite of the Romans, and then on to China.

CULTIVATION

Cucumbers appreciate a rich soil with lots of organic matter and a constant supply of moisture during a lengthy warm growing period. Melons are less demanding. Both are suitable for greenhouse culture where summers are short. Propagate from seed.

ABOVE Cucumis sativus *'Muncher' is a cucumber with thin smooth skin, which is easily digestible. It is tasty both when young and when mature.*

BELOW Cucumis sativus *'Spacemaster' has disease-resistant, compact, dark green fruit that is good for pickling when small and for slicing when mature.*

ABOVE Cucumis sativus 'Bush Champion' is a compact bush-type cucumber, which is good for slicing. Bright green straight fruit grows to around 25 cm (10 in) long, and is produced over a long season.

Favourites	Common Name	Produce Season	Plant Height	Plant Width	Hardiness Zone	Frost Tolerance
Cucumis anguria	cucumber, gherkin	summer	20 in (50 cm)	7–10 ft (2–3 m)	9–12	no
Cucumis melo	cantaloupe, honeydew melon	summer	16–27 in (40–70 cm)	7–10 ft (2–3 m)	9–12	no
Cucumis melo, **Cantalupensis Group**	sweet fragrant melons	summer	16–27 in (40–70 cm)	7–10 ft (2–3 m)	9–12	no
Cucumis melo, **Reticulatus Group**	netted melons	summer	16–27 in (40–70 cm)	7–10 ft (2–3 m)	9–12	no
Cucumis sativus	cucumber, gherkin	summer	8–20 in (20–50 cm)	3–10 ft (0.9–3 m)	9–11	no
Cucumis sativus, **Alpha Group**	Lebanese cucumber	summer	8–20 in (20–50 cm)	3–10 ft (0.9–3 m)	9–11	no

ABOVE Cucumis sativus 'Sunsweet' has fruit that is shaped like a lemon. The cream-coloured young fruit is sweet and can be eaten raw; the yellowy orange mature fruit has a sharper taste and is best cooked.

CUCURBITA

A pumpkin (Cucurbitaceae) family genus, it has 27 species of annual or perennial ground covers and vines found in the Americas. Their stems and large lobed leaves are bristly or prickly, and spiralled clinging tendrils are often present at the leaf axils. Yellow or orange trumpet-shaped flowers develop into variably sized, shaped, marked and coloured fruits. The title of the world's largest fruit is currently held by a 821.2 kg (1,810$\frac{1}{2}$ lb) pumpkin grown in Stillwater, Minnesota, USA in 2010.

RIGHT Cucurbita pepo *'Gold Rush'* has rich golden yellow zucchini- or courgette-type fruit. It is easy to harvest and its colour can add variety and interest to summer meals.

BELOW *Dark green-striped Cucurbita pepo 'Delicata' is a sweet potato squash, with very orange flesh that is excellent for stuffing and baking. It is a good keeper.*

CULTIVATION

Pumpkins and squashes are very rapid-growing plants, which are best grown in a well-drained humus-enriched soil in full sun with a long and warm growing season. A popular method for the raising of pumpkins is to sow the seed in a patch of warm compost, but starting in pots is often more convenient. Only when all danger of frost has passed should they be planted. Feed plants regularly with a liquid fertiliser and make sure that fruit is not sitting on wet soil. Mildew and botrytis can occur in humid areas. Some cultivars are better keepers than others, but this makes no difference to their growth requirements.

Favourites	Common Name	Produce Season	Plant Height	Plant Width	Hardiness Zone	Frost Tolerance
Cucurbita ficifolia	gourd	winter	12–20 in (30–50 cm)	3–10 ft (0.9–3 m)	8–11	yes
Cucurbita maxima	squash	winter	12–20 in (30–50 cm)	3–10 ft (0.9–3 m)	8–11	yes
Cucurbita moschata	pumpkin	winter	12–20 in (30–50 cm)	3–10 ft (0.9–3 m)	8–11	yes
Cucurbita moschata 'Butternut'	pumpkin	winter	12–20 in (30–50 cm)	3–10 ft (0.9–3 m)	8–11	yes
Cucurbita pepo	zucchini	summer	12–20 in (30–50 cm)	3–10 ft (0.9–3 m)	8–11	yes
Cucurbita pepo 'Gold Rush'	zucchini	summer	12–20 in (30–50 cm)	3–10 ft (0.9–3 m)	8–11	yes

Top Tip

Only harvest pumpkins when the shell is completely hardened. Leave the stems on; this helps thwart bacteria entry, and prevents early spoilage. Do not store in the sun.

ABOVE Cucurbita maxima 'Autumn Cup' is a butternut-type hybrid. It produces a dark green squash with fine orange flesh that tastes good steamed, boiled or baked.

RIGHT Cucurbita maxima 'Atlantic Giant' is the largest of the pumpkins and the biggest fruit in the world—fruit over 450 kg (1,000 lb) is not uncommon.

CURCUMA

Natives of the winter-dry regions of tropical Asia and northern Australia, the 40 or so species of *Curcuma* belong to the ginger family (Zingiberaceae). They are all rhizomatous perennials that grow as clumps of short, thick stems from which paddle-shaped leaves emerge at intervals. Some species are valuable food plants, the best known being turmeric (*Curcuma longa*), which gives a warm spiciness and rich yellow colour to curries and is used as a dye. *C. amado* has a ginger-like flavour, *C. angustifolia* is a source of the thickening agent arrowroot and *C. zedoaria* is made into the spice zedoary. The rhizomes are the most valuable but leaves, stems and flowers have uses in the kitchen.

CULTIVATION

Plant store-bought rhizomes horizontally into good-quality, free-draining soil enriched with manure and compost. Mid- to late spring is the best time to plant turmeric, but don't water until growth is visible. It thrives in a warm climate and though it will take some sun, bright dappled shade suits it in hot areas. Let it go dry late autumn to early spring.

Top Tip

Start harvesting in the third year by uncovering the rhizomes and snapping off a few from the outer edges. Re-cover with soil for future growth. Strongest flavour develops in autumn.

TOP *Beneath the thin skin of the turmeric rhizome is a bright orange flesh that adds colour and flavour to curries. Store-bought rhizomes grow into plants.*

ABOVE *The spice zedoary, made from the root of* Curcuma zedoaria, *tastes like bitter ginger. It is added to curries, pickled and eaten raw.*

Favourites	Common Name	Produce Season	Plant Height	Plant Width	Hardiness Zone	Frost Tolerance
Curcuma longa	turmeric	summer to winter	20–36 in (50–100 cm)	forms a spreading clump 3–5 ft (0.9–1.5 m) across	9–11	no
Curcuma zedoaria	zedoary	summer to winter	3–5 ft (0.9–1.5 m)	forms a spreading clump 3–5 ft (0.9–1.5 m) across	9–11	no

CYMBOPOGON

Lemongrass is one of over 50 species in the family Poaceae. It is a true grass growing as a dense clump of pencil-thick stems topped with long, thin leaves that arch out in a fountain shape. All species are from tropical and subtropical regions and, in gardens, do best in areas where frosts are light and rare or unknown. The lemongrass of kitchens is native to southern India and Sri Lanka where it grows in seasonally dry savannahs. The whole plant is lemon scented and the leaves can be used in teas though the sweetest, most strongly lemon flavoured and most tender section is the area of white stem closest to the ground. This is the part most valued by cooks.

CULTIVATION

Grow in full sun or with just a few hours shade each day. Lemongrass needs at least average quality garden soil and plenty of water during the warmest months of the year (all year-round in the tropics). In cooler areas, let the rain do the watering in winter. Feed with cow or pelletised chicken manure in spring and summer.

Top Tip

Renovate a winter-worn clump by cutting to the ground in early spring then feed and water deeply to start regrowth. Plants need division every few years to maintain vigour.

ABOVE AND LEFT
Lemongrass (Cymbopogon citratus) is both ornamental and useful. Cutting a few stems for tea or for use in dishes instead of lemon will not harm a well-grown plant. The succulent, white lower stem has the most flavour.

Species	Common Name	Produce Season	Plant Height	Plant Width	Hardiness Zone	Frost Tolerance
Cymbopogon citratus	lemongrass	year-round	3 ft (0.9 m)	3 ft (0.9 m)	9–11	no

DAUCUS

This widely distributed carrot (Apiaceae) family genus is made up of 22 species of annuals and biennials of which one, *Daucus carota,* is widely cultivated for its long, orange, edible taproot. Carrots have bright green ferny foliage, which is relished by grazing animals, and long flower stems with sprays of small white flowers, though the roots are harvested in the first year, before flowerheads develop. The longest carrot on record was over 5 m (17 ft), the heaviest was over 6.8 kg (15 lb).

CULTIVATION

Carrots require careful cultivation to give their best. Sow the seed in a soil that has been worked to a fine tilth. Heavy soil will result in poor root development. The seed usually germinates well, unless the soil surface becomes caked hard. In many areas carrot fly, the larvae of which tunnels into the root, can be a major problem. Late sowing lessens the problem, or soil insecticides can be applied at sowing time. Carrots take about 80 days to reach full maturity but they can be used from a younger age.

ABOVE *The word carrot is a Celtic one, and means "red of colour". Daucus carota* subsp. *sativus 'Corrie', seen here, typifies the rich hues that gave the plant its name.* **LEFT** Daucus carota *subsp.* sativus *'Vita-Treat'. A case of "green shoulders", where the sun hits the top of the root; this will turn it green and also make it taste bitter.*

Favourites	Common Name	Produce Season	Plant Height	Plant Width	Hardiness Zone	Frost Tolerance
Daucus carota	wild carrot	autumn to spring	40 in (100 cm)	20 in (50 cm)	3–9	yes
Daucus carota subsp. sativus	carrot	autumn to spring	40 in (100 cm)	20 in (50 cm)	3–9	yes
Daucus carota subsp. sativus 'Canada'	carrot	autumn to spring	40 in (100 cm)	20 in (50 cm)	3–9	yes
Daucus carota subsp. sativus 'Red Intermediate'	carrot	autumn to spring	40 in (100 cm)	20 in (50 cm)	3–9	yes
Daucus carota subsp. sativus 'Topweight'	carrot	autumn to spring	40 in (100 cm)	20 in (50 cm)	3–9	yes
Daucus carota subsp. sativus 'Vita-Treat'	carrot	autumn to spring	40 in (100 cm)	20 in (50 cm)	3–9	yes

Top Tip

Carrots prefer an even soil moisture. Mulching can help retain dampness, as well as preventing "green shoulders" where carrot tops are sun-exposed.

LACTUCA

Although this Northern Hemisphere daisy (Asteraceae) family genus contains about 75 species of annuals and perennials, only 1 species, *Lactuca sativa*, is widely cultivated. It is of course grown for its foliage rather than for its flowers, which are small white, yellow or soft blue daisies that are borne on a tall stem. The cultivated varieties show a large range of foliage texture and colour and also vary in flavour. The milky sap of some lettuce leaves is used in herbal medicines.

CULTIVATION

In many areas lettuces may be planted year-round. The two main types are heart-forming (romaine) and non-heart-forming (cos). Heart-forming lettuces are usually cut whole when mature, while non-hearting lettuces can be used as they grow, a few leaves picked as required. Lettuces need well-drained soil and a steady supply of moisture and nutrients. Compost should be added before planting and liquid feed while growing. Slugs and snails often damage the foliage and birds will destroy young plants that are not covered with netting or other protection. Aphids can be another potential problem. Raise from seed.

ABOVE *A winter lettuce for growing in unheated green-houses or outdoors,* Lactuca sativa *'Valdor' is resistant to botrytis. Sow seed in autumn for a spring harvest.*

RIGHT *Bred in the UK, the award-winner* Lactuca sativa *'Bubbles' is a compact green lettuce, which has notably blistered leaves and a fairly firm sweet head.*

Top Tip

With planning, lettuces can be grown all year-round. If aiming at a mid-summer harvest, however, grow in part-shade as the summer sun will trigger bolting.

ABOVE Lactuca sativa 'Cocarde' is a red oak-leaf type with large, tender, arrow-shaped leaves, which are tinged red. Pick lettuces before they go to seed to avoid bitterness.

ABOVE Lactuca sativa 'Red Salad Bowl' is a red-tinged form of 'Oak Leaf', which is a loose-leaf variety with deeply divided leaves like those of an oak, first listed in France in the 1770s.

Favourites	Common Name	Produce Season	Plant Height	Plant Width	Hardiness Zone	Frost Tolerance
Lactuca sativa	lettuce	spring to winter	4–12 in (10–30 cm)	4–12 in (10–30 cm)	6–11	yes
Lactuca sativa 'Bubbles'	lettuce	spring to winter	4–12 in (10–30 cm)	4–12 in (10–30 cm)	6–11	yes
Lactuca sativa 'Cocarde'	lettuce	spring to winter	4–12 in (10–30 cm)	4–12 in (10–30 cm)	6–11	yes
Lactuca sativa 'Iceberg'	lettuce	spring to winter	4–12 in (10–30 cm)	4–12 in (10–30 cm)	6–11	yes
Lactuca sativa 'Little Gem'	lettuce	spring to winter	4–12 in (10–30 cm)	4–12 in (10–30 cm)	6–11	yes
Lactuca sativa 'Valdor'	lettuce	spring to winter	4–12 in (10–30 cm)	4–12 in (10–30 cm)	6–11	yes

LAURUS

This genus of the Mediterranean coast and Canary Islands contains only 2 species, the best known of which is the bay tree (*Laurus nobilis*). It's an evergreen tree in the family *Lauraceae* with dark green leathery leaves that carry an aroma highly valued in many Mediterranean cuisines. The tree itself has ornamental uses, too. Being amenable to clipping and shaping, it's a popular choice for topiary and hedging and it makes an excellent screening or shade tree if allowed to develop naturally. In the Mediterranean region, the bay tree is often seen growing on rocky cliffs or other seemingly barren places but it will always be found that there is some source of moisture seeping around the roots.

CULTIVATION

Grow in full sun in either large pots or free-draining but fertile and moisture-retentive soil. Plants will tolerate light to moderate frosts but don't care for freezing winds and need the shelter of a wall where that is possible. Plants are susceptible to infestation of scale insects and associated sooty mould. Control by spraying non-toxic horticultural oil twice in a month.

Top Tip

Hang bunches of bay leaves in warm shade to dry before using them in recipes. The drying process improves the flavour and removes the bitter aftertaste fresh leaves impart.

ABOVE *In spring, clusters of tiny cream flowers appear at the end of every stem. Though not particularly showy, they are highly attractive to bees, which then pollinate other crops.*

Species	Common Name	Produce Season	Plant Height	Plant Width	Hardiness Zone	Frost Tolerance
Laurus nobilis	bay, sweet bay, bay laurel	year-round	26–40 ft (8–12 m)	26–30 ft (8–9 m)	8–9	yes

Top Tip

Planted in late summer, tomatoes classed as 'indeterminate' will continue to grow and crop through winter if your winter days are sunny and mild and nights frost free.

LYCOPERSICON

ABOVE *'Green Zebra' is a vigorous high-yielding hybrid cultivar. As the tomatoes ripen they become more yellow, but the green stripes are still visible.*

This genus of 7 species of aromatic herbs in the nightshade (Solanaceae) family is best known for *Lycopersicon esculentum*—the tomato. Annuals or short-lived perennials with an erect or sprawling habit, they originate from western South America and the Galapagos Islands, and were reputedly introduced to Western civilisation following the Spanish conquest of South and Central America. They have hair-covered stems and aromatic toothed leaves. The starry yellow flowers feature a 5-lobed calyx, and are followed by fleshy berries that have 2 or more seed-filled chambers. While the fruit of wild species is usually small, the fruit of the cultivars varies considerably in size, from as small as a grape to massive fruit weighing 1.8 kg (4 lb).

CULTIVATION

In areas with a long warm growing season, plant in fertile well-drained soil in an open sunny position. In cooler areas seedlings may need to be protected from late frosts. Propagation is from seed.

ABOVE *A tall-growing, indeterminate variety, 'Yellow Pear' starts producing about 11 weeks after seedlings emerge. Fruit is about the size of a cherry tomato and is sweet and tasty.*

BELOW *With pinkish fruit on a late-maturing plant, 'Brandywine' is a large, meaty tomato ideal for slicing or processing.*

ABOVE *'Sungold' produces an excellent crop of very sweet tangerine-coloured cherry tomatoes. This outstanding hybrid makes a neat bush.*

Favourites	Common Name	Produce Season	Plant Height	Plant Width	Hardiness Zone	Frost Tolerance
Lycopersicon **'Banana Legs'**	plum tomato	summer	5–7 ft (1.5–2 m)	4–5 ft (1.2–1.5 m)	8–11	no
Lycopersicon **'Bandy'**	slicing tomato	late summer to autumn	6–8 ft (1.8–2.4 m)	3–7 ft (0.9–2 m)	8–11	no
Lycopersicon **'Black Russian'**	salad tomato	summer and autumn	6–7 ft (1.8–2 m)	3–5 ft (0.9–1.5 m)	8–11	no
Lycopersicon **'Constoluto'**	slicing tomato	summer to autumn	6–8 ft (1.8–2.4 m)	3–7 ft (0.9–2 m)	8–11	no
Lycopersicon **'Green Zebra'**	tomato	summer to autumn	6–8 ft (1.8–2.4 m)	1–2 ft (0.3–0.6 m)	8–11	no
Lycopersicon **'Moneymaker'**	bush tomato	summer to autumn	3–4 ft (0.9–1.2 m)	3–4 ft (0.9–1.2 m)	8–11	no
Lycopersicon **'Sungold'**	cherry tomato	summer to autumn	4–6 ft (1.2–1.8 m)	1–2 ft (0.3–0.6 m)	8–11	no
Lycopersicon **'Tommy Toe'**	salad tomato	spring to autumn	5–7 ft (1.5–2 m)	4–5 ft (1.2–1.5 m)	8–11	no
Lycopersicon **'Wild Sweetie'**	currant tomato	spring to autumn	6–7 ft (1.8–2 m)	3–5 ft (0.9–1.5 m)	8–11	no
Lycopersicon **'Yellow Pear'**	pear tomato	spring to autumn	6–8 ft (1.8–2.4 m)	3–5 ft (0.9–1.5 m)	8–11	no

LEFT *Tomatoes are produced in heavy clusters on viney stems that are not very strong. It's important to support the lax stems with stakes or to prune out excess branches.*

ABOVE *The sweetest tomato of all, the tiny fruit of 'Wild Sweetie' is twice as sweet as others. The plants are productive for half a year.*
LEFT *A novelty in shape and colour, 'Banana Legs' produces firm fruit of good flavour, well suited to cooking. It is ready to pick about 3 months after seedlings emerge.*

LEFT *'Costoluto' or 'Costoluto Genovese' has been grown in Italy for hundreds of years and is still a favourite today. It's suitable for all uses.*

Top Tip

Use stakes to provide support for taller plants, or grow them against a fence or trellis, securing taller stems as they grow. Keep branches off the ground.

ABOVE *A good choice for cooler areas where summers are short, 'Black Russian' can be started in early spring to ripen in less than 3 months.*
RIGHT *'Tommy Toe' can be ready to pick in as little as 8 weeks. Plum-sized fruit has outstanding flavour.*

MENTHA

The type genus for the mint (Lamiaceae) family, *Mentha* is made up of 25 species of aromatic perennial herbs found from Europe to North Africa and Asia. Commonly known as mint, they have angled upright stems with soft, often heavily veined leaves that may have wavy or scalloped edges. All parts are aromatic, especially when crushed. The species have a variety of flavours (apple, pineapple and spearmint). Corsican mint (*Mentha requienii*) is a small-leafed ground cover with a strong crème de menthe scent. In addition to their culinary uses, mints are widely used as medicinal herbs and for fragrance.

Top Tip

Most mint species reproduce from shallow, creeping, long stems. Stop the plant taking over the garden by burying a large container almost to the top and placing the plant within it.

CULTIVATION

Mint is probably the best-known culinary herb and flavouring, but has a bad reputation for being attacked by a rust disease, though rust-resistant types are available. It is best grown in moist soil in light shade. Propagate from half-hardened cuttings, self-layered stems or suckers. Mint spreads by underground runners and can be invasive. Plant where it can be contained.

ABOVE Mentha suaveolens *(syn. M. rotundifolia) is known as applemint because its aroma is of apples and mint combined. It makes a lovely ground cover where its spread can be contained.*

LEFT *The leaves of* Mentha × piperita, *or peppermint, have an intense minty flavour and aroma. The mauve-pink flowers appear in summer.*

Favourites	Plant Height	Plant Width	Hardiness Zone	Frost Tolerance
Mentha × piperita	2–3 ft (0.6–0.9 m)	3 ft (0.9 m)	3–7	yes
Mentha pulegium	8–12 in (20–30 cm)	20 in (50 cm)	7–9	yes
Mentha requienii	$^3/_4$ in (1.8 cm)	27 in (70 cm)	7–10	yes
Mentha spicata	4 ft (1.2 m)	3–6 ft (0.9–1.8 m)	3–7	yes
Mentha suaveolens	3 ft (0.9 m)	3 ft (0.9 m)	6–9	yes
Mentha × villosa	3 ft (0.9 m)	5 ft (1.5 m)	5–8	yes

LEFT Ocimum basilicum *'Genova'* is a spicy Italian cultivar with a strong scent. It is very productive over a particularly long growing season.

BELOW The curly and frilly leaf edges of Ocimum basilicum *'Green Ruffles'* make this cultivar a decorative as well as flavoursome choice for use in a salad or as a fresh garnish.

OCIMUM

A genus of 35 species of aromatic annuals and perennials of the mint (Lamiaceae) family, the plants occur naturally in the tropics and subtropics of Africa and Asia. They develop quickly into small soft-stemmed bushes with oval to elliptical leaves that often have toothed or lobed edges. Erect spikes of flowers develop at the stem tips but these are usually removed to encourage continued foliage production. The genus is commonly known as basil, and its leaves are used as a flavouring in cooking. Sweet basil *(Ocimum basilicum)* also has a long history of medicinal use, and yields an oil used in fragrances and aromatherapy.

CULTIVATION

Basil is a very popular culinary herb and some species have cultivars in several sizes and with coloured foliaged forms. Basil is very sensitive to cold when young and should be planted in moist well-drained soil in a position sheltered from draughts. When young, pinch out the tips to encourage bushy growth. Raise the annuals from seed, the perennials from seed or cuttings.

Favourites	Plant Height	Plant Width	Hardiness Zone	Frost Tolerance
Ocimum basilicum	12–24 in (30–60 cm)	12 in (30 cm)	10–12	no
Ocimum basilicum var. *minimum*	10–12 in (25–30 cm)	6–10 in (15–25 cm)	10–12	no
Ocimum basilicum **'Genova'**	24 in (60 cm)	18 in (45 cm)	10–12	no
Ocimum basilicum **'Green Ruffles'**	18–24 in (45–60 cm)	18–24 in (45–60 cm)	10–12	no
Ocimum basilicum **'Red Rubin'**	18–24 in (45–60 cm)	12–15 in (30–38 cm)	10–12	no
Ocimum tenuiflorum	12–36 in (30–90 cm)	6–12 in (15–30 cm)	9–10	yes

BELOW Ocimum basilicum *'Purple Ruffles'* is a striking addition to the herb garden. Its large, purple, glossy leaves with serrated edges are very aromatic.

Top Tip

Pinch back the top of basil plants regularly and remove flower spikes to encourage foliage growth and better leaf flavour. The taste is not as good after flowers appear.

BELOW Ocimum basilicum *'Siam Queen'* is a compact bush with fragrant licorice-flavoured leaves and rosy purple flowers. It is very suitable for Thai cooking.

ORIGANUM

A member of the mint (Lamiaceae) family, this genus includes some 20 species of aromatic perennials and subshrubs found from the Mediterranean to East Asia. Most are low spreading bushes with simple, small, rounded leaves in shades from yellow-green to deep green. The ornamental forms often have their flowers enclosed within large colourful bracts, but those grown as herbs usually have simple starry pink flowers, though often in abundance. The various species of *Origanum* are popular pot herbs right around the Mediterranean, especially in Italy, where oregano *(Origanum vulgare)* adds its distinctive flavour to many dishes. Several species yield oils used in perfumery and flavourings.

CULTIVATION

Hardiness varies, though few will tolerate hard frosts or prolonged wet cold winters. Grow in light well-drained soil in a sunny position. Propagate the species from seed, the hybrids from half-hardened cuttings or layers.

ABOVE *With attractively variegated leaves,* Origanum vulgare *'Gold Tip' is a popular cultivar. It looks even better in summer when the pink flowers appear.*

ABOVE LEFT Origanum *'Kent Beauty' is among the best ornamental hybrids. Ideal for the rockery or border, it produces tubular flowers with deep rose pink bracts in summer.*

Top Tip

The flavour of the leaves is directly proportional to the amount of sun they receive. The more intense the light, the stronger the flavour.

Favourites	Plant Height	Plant Width	Hardiness Zone	Frost Tolerance
Origanum amanum	2–4 in (5–10 cm)	6 in (15 cm)	8–10	yes
Origanum 'Kent Beauty'	8–10 in (20–25 cm)	12–18 in (30–45 cm)	6–9	yes
Origanum laevigatum	12–24 in (30–60 cm)	18–24 in (45–60 cm)	8–10	yes
Origanum majorana	24 in (60 cm)	18 in (45 cm)	7–10	yes
Origanum rotundifolium	12 in (30 cm)	12 in (30 cm)	8–10	yes
Origanum vulgare	12–18 in (30–45 cm)	12 in (30 cm)	5–9	yes

LEFT Origanum vulgare *is the best-known species in this genus. It is a popular culinary herb with very aromatic foliage that can be used fresh from the garden or dried for later use.*

BELOW Origanum vulgare *var.* humile *makes a useful flowering ground cover. It is quite drought tolerant, and the tasty leaves can be used in cooking.*

LEFT Petroselinum crispum var. neopolitanum, *known as Italian or Continental parsley, is flat-leafed. It is claimed to be the superior sort for culinary purposes. It is said to have the best flavour.*
BELOW Petroselinum crispum *'Forest Green' is a strongly flavoured variety. Such varieties are good to dry for later use, but parsley retains more flavour if it is frozen fresh.*

PETROSELINUM

Probably best known in its triple-curled form, which is a very popular garnish, this Eurasian genus in the carrot (Apiaceae) family is made up of just 3 species of annuals and biennials but it is cultivated in a wide variety of forms. The finely divided, broadly triangular leaves are a bright or deep green and often rolled and curled at the edges of the leaflets. Parsley is usually spent and bitter once the sprays of tiny white flowers appear. In some forms, such as *Petroselinum crispum* var. *tuberosum*, the taproot is enlarged and can be used like a small parsnip. Parsley also has numerous uses in herbal medicine and provides an oil used as a fragrance fixative in men's toiletries.

CULTIVATION

Parsley prefers to grow in cool moist soil in light shade. Water it well or the foliage may become stringy and bitter. Cutting the foliage promotes fresh growth. Raise from fresh seed sown in spring, or autumn in frost-free areas.

RIGHT *Parsley has a higher vitamin C content than an orange and is a natural breath freshener.* Petroselinum crispum *'Bravour' is a winter-hardy parsley and has a mild flavour.*

ABOVE Petroselinum crispum *'Krausa'* has triple-curled leaves that keep their crisp texture and bright green colour very well in the garden and after harvest.

Favourites

	Plant Height	Plant Width	Hardiness Zone	Frost Tolerance
Petroselinum crispum	12–36 in (30–90 cm)	8–36 in (20–90 cm)	7–9	yes
Petroselinum crispum var. *neopolitanum*	12–36 in (30–90 cm)	8–36 in (20–90 cm)	7–9	yes
Petroselinum crispum var. *tuberosum*	12–36 in (30–90 cm)	8–36 in (20–90 cm)	7–9	yes
Petroselinum crispum 'Bravour'	12–36 in (30–90 cm)	8–36 in (20–90 cm)	7–9	yes
Petroselinum crispum 'Forest Green'	12–36 in (30–90 cm)	8–36 in (20–90 cm)	7–9	yes
Petroselinum crispum 'Krausa'	12–36 in (30–90 cm)	8–36 in (20–90 cm)	7–9	yes

PHASEOLUS

A member of the pea-flower subfamily of the legume (Fabaceae) family, this genus of around 20 species of annuals and perennials, often climbing, is grown for its edible seed pods or for the beans held within. Found from south-western USA to northern South America, most have thin, often downy, heart-shaped leaves and a twining habit. Short racemes of white, pale yellow, mauve or orange-red flowers develop into flat pods that vary in size with the species. Kidney beans yield a reddish dye.

LEFT Phaseolus vulgaris *'Ferrari' is an award-winning dwarf cultivar. It gives a good supply of stringless beans.*
ABOVE Phaseolus vulgaris *is the most popular bean species. Although green beans are the norm, decorative cultivars like 'Purple Speckled' are also available.*
BELOW *One of the large-seeded pole-type of lima beans,* Phaseolus lunatus *'King of the Garden' is easy to grow.*

CULTIVATION

The common types of bean are the bushy dwarf beans or French beans, lima beans and kidney beans, and climbing runner beans. Plant in humus-enriched well-drained soil in full sun and keep the soil moist or the beans will age prematurely. Plants are often raised from fresh seed each year but runner beans will reshoot from the base and can be left in the ground for several years.

Top Tip

When grown for the pods, beans should be picked before the pods become stringy; otherwise, let the beans develop before picking.

Favourites	Common Name	Produce Season	Plant Height	Plant Width	Hardiness Zone	Frost Tolerance
Phaseolus acutifolius	tepary bean	summer to autumn	18–40 in (45–100 cm)	12–24 in (30–60 cm)	8–10	no
Phaseolus coccineus	scarlet runner bean	summer to autumn	6–12 ft (1.8–3.5 m)	2 ft (0.6 m)	8–10	no
Phaseolus coccineus 'Painted Lady'	scarlet runner bean	summer to autumn	6–10 ft (1.8–3 m)	2 ft (0.6 m)	8–10	no
Phaseolus lunatus	lima bean	summer to autumn	24–36 in (60–90 cm)	8–12 in (20–30 cm)	8–10	no
Phaseolus vulgaris	French/string/ snap bean	summer	3–10 ft (0.9–3 m)	6–10 in (15–25 cm)	8–11	no
Phaseolus vulgaris 'Goldmarie'	French/string/ snap bean	summer	8 ft (2.4 m)	1 ft (0.3 m)	8–11	no

BELOW *The attractive and colourful flowers of* Phaseolus coccineus *'Painted Lady' look and taste good in salads. The beans that follow are delicious, too.*

RIGHT Rosmarinus officinalis *'Albiflorus'* bears striking white flowers on an upright bush. The leaves of this unusual white rosemary can be used in cooking like the others.

LEFT *A free-flowering, aromatic, evergreen shrub,* Rosmarinus officinalis *'Tuscan Blue' responds well to pruning and can be shaped into an attractive hedge or screen.*

Top Tip

The upright forms of *Rosmarinus* make good subjects for topiary. The prostrate types look great cascading over pots and in rock gardens.

ROSMARINUS

Just 2 species of evergreen aromatic shrubs from southern Europe and North Africa make up this genus in the mint (Lamiaceae) family. Grown for both ornament and function, rosemary has stiff woody stems that are densely covered with short, narrow, dark green to bronze-green leaves. From winter's end, small mauve-blue to purple flowers appear in the leaf axils and are followed by small seed pods. The foliage is very pungent and distinctively flavoured, and is among the most widely used herbs in Western cooking. Rosemary is also dried and used in potpourri, and the oil can be found in many perfumes and cosmetics.

CULTIVATION

Surprisingly hardy, rosemary grows best in a bright sunny position with moist well-drained soil. It is drought tolerant once established and prefers to stay fairly dry in winter. Most of the plants in gardens are cultivars propagated from half-hardened cuttings or layers; the species may be raised from seed.

Favourites	Flower Colour	Blooming Season	Flower Fragrance	Plant Height	Plant Width	Hardiness Zone	Frost Tolerance
Rosmarinus officinalis	pale blue to purple-blue	spring to autumn	no	3–7 ft (0.9–2 m)	5–6 ft (1.5–1.8 m)	6–11	yes
Rosmarinus officinalis 'Benenden Blue'	blue	spring to autumn	no	5 ft (1.5 m)	3 ft (0.9 m)	6–11	yes
Rosmarinus officinalis 'Joyce DeBaggio'	blue	spring to autumn	no	3 ft (0.9 m)	5 ft (1.5 m)	6–11	yes
Rosmarinus officinalis 'Majorca Pink'	lilac-pink	spring to autumn	no	3 ft (0.9 m)	5 ft (1.5 m)	6–11	yes
Rosmarinus officinalis 'Sissinghurst Blue'	blue	spring to autumn	no	5 ft (1.5 m)	6 ft (1.8 m)	6–11	yes
Rosmarinus officinalis 'Tuscan Blue'	blue	spring to autumn	no	5 ft (1.5 m)	5 ft (1.5 m)	6–11	yes

ABOVE *Award-winning* Rosmarinus officinalis *'Benenden Blue' (syn. 'Balsam') makes a good container plant. Its strongly pine-scented leaves can be used in potpourri.*

LEFT *The lilac-pink flowers of* Rosmarinus officinalis *'Majorca Pink' are borne on long, densely leafed, arching branches. This is one of the best of the pink-flowered cultivars.*

FAR LEFT AND LEFT
Common sage is an attractive plant. As well as the typical grey-green form, common sage comes in coloured leaf varieties such as Salvia officinalis *'Purpurascens' (far left) and* S. officinalis *'Icterina' (left).*

SALVIA

O f the 900 or so species of *Salvia* only a few are grown as culinary herbs, the best known being sage or *Salvia officinalis*. The aromatic, flavoursome leaves of this thigh-high, shrubby perennial from the shores of the Mediterranean are widely used in cooking. The common variety has pebbly–textured grey-green leaves, but there are numerous named forms with differently coloured flowers or with variegated leaves in a range of shades. For cooking, the natural, unadorned species offers the best flavour but the more ornamental forms can be more attractive in the garden and, of course, their leaves still can be used in recipes. Other useful varieties include *S. hispanica*, the source of chia and clary sage, *S. sclarea*. *Salvia* is in the mint family, Lamiaceae.

CULTIVATION
In general full sun and free-draining soil of average quality will do. These are easy plants to grow and are mostly long blooming and quite dryness tolerant. Some but not all tend to run and these need cutting back to keep them to their allotted spaces. All varieties can be cut down at the end of winter to re-shoot afresh.

Top Tip

To control running types, push a sharp spade into the ground right around the base of the plant several times from spring to autumn. Pull up severed runners.

ABOVE Salvia officinalis *'Minor' is a dwarf form of edible sage. It grows to half the size of the regular plant.*

Favourites	Flower Colour	Blooming Season	Produce Season	Plant Height	Plant Width	Hardiness Zone	Frost Tolerance
Salvia officinalis	lavender or purple, pink or white	spring and summer	spring to autumn	24–36 in (60–90 cm)	24–36 in (60–90 cm)	7–9	yes
Salvia officinalis 'Icterina'	lavender or white	spring and summer	spring to autumn	24 in 60 cm	24–36 in (60–90 cm)	8–9	yes
Salvia officinalis 'Purpurascens'	lavender or white	spring and summer	spring to autumn	24–30 in (60–75 cm)	24–30 in (60–75 cm)	8–9	yes

SOLANUM

A member of the nightshade family (Solanaceae), this big genus has about 1,400 species, mostly from Central and South America. The bulk are not important to either gardeners or farmers but the genus does include a handful of important food crops, most notably the potato, one of the most widely grown crops of all. Other productive species are the eggplant (aubergine), the pepino and the little known naranjilla. Tomatoes and capsicums, though not of the genus *Solanum*, are close relatives. Oddly, the leaves of many species, including the food-producing species, are poisonous, and some of the minor species actually produce toxic fruit as well. In potatoes, the toxin solanin is produced in the tubers if they are exposed to light and turn green.

CULTIVATION

Potatoes and eggplants are warm-season plants unable to tolerate frost or even prolonged chilly weather. Tamarillos and pepinos are more cold tolerant, but neither is suited to areas of persistent frosts. All like a warm, sheltered, fully sunny position in enriched soil that drains fast. Potatoes are grown from virus-free, "seed" potatoes but the remainder can be raised from seed in spring.

RIGHT *The tiny, squat, reddish orange fruit of Solanum melongena 'Turkish Orange' resembles tomatoes, but tends to be bitter. It is best eaten when it is still green, but is great for stuffing when ripe.*

ABOVE *An unusual, very fast-growing shrubby perennial, the naranjilla (Solanum quitoense) requires a long hot growing season to produce its tart-sweet, orange fruit. The plant itself has highly ornamental fuzzy, purplish green leaves.*
LEFT *As the name of this unassuming plant suggests, Solanum tuberosum 'All Blue' produces potatoes with blue skin and lavender-blue flesh. The texture of the flesh is moist, and the flavour is somewhat smoky.*

RIGHT *Melon-like in flavour, the juicy fruit of the pepino (Solanum muricatum) takes about 5 months to ripen. Plants are attractive and grow to a little over 1 m (0.9 ft) tall.*
BELOW *Potatoes are an easy crop to raise and you get a good harvest for your efforts. Try growing varieties that are either expensive to buy or hard to find.*

LEFT *Potato cultivars offer tubers of varying textures, flavours, skin colours and maturing times. Solanum tuberosum 'Mimi' produces small reddish-brown-skinned tubers.*

Favourites	Common Name	Produce Season	Plant Height	Plant Width	Hardiness Zone	Frost Tolerance
Solanum melongena	eggplant	summer, early autumn	3 ft (0.9 m)	30 in (75 cm)	8–11	no
Solanum muricatum	pepino	summer, autumn early winter	4 ft (1.2 m)	3 ft (0.9 m)	8–11	no
Solanum quitoense	naranjilla	late spring, summer, autumn	7–14 ft (2–4 m)	8 ft (2–3 m)	9–11	no
Solanum tuberosum	potato	late spring, summer, autumn	18–24 in (45–60 cm)	18 in (45 cm)	7–11	no

ABOVE *The fruit of the Japanese eggplant (aubergine) cultivars is smaller and more elongated in shape than the others. Solanum melongena 'Ping Tung' bears well.*

RIGHT *The pale flowers of Solanum melongena 'Black Beauty' are followed by nearly black oval fruit. This is one of the most popular eggplant (aubergine) cultivars.*

ABOVE *There are many different Solanum melongena cultivars available, with fruit ranging from orange to purple to almost black. The fruit known as eggplants, or aubergines, have become popular vegetables in recent years.*

Top Tip

Potatoes will grow in most areas. They can be grown almost all year in warm climates, but in cold climates must be fully grown before the onset of severe frosts.

RIGHT *An early producing type of eggplant (aubergine), Solanum melongena 'Black Bell' has purple-black round to oval fruit that hangs pendulously from the stems.*

THYMUS

Thyme is a genus of around 350 species of low spreading perennials and subshrubs in the mint (Lamiaceae) family. Although mostly found around the Mediterranean, they are also grown from western Europe to North Africa, and eastward to Japan. They have very fine wiry stems and minute, often hairy leaves that form a dense mat. Heads of tiny flowers in all shades of pink and purple, or white, appear mainly in summer and can be very showy. Commonly grown for ornamental reasons, as a culinary herb and for thyme oil, which is used in fragrances and disinfectants, thyme is also popular with herbalists because the oil contains thymol, a phenol with important pharmacological properties.

CULTIVATION

Thyme prefers to grow in full or half-sun with moist well-drained soil. Shear off the old dry flowerheads to encourage fresh growth. The species may be raised from seed, but selected forms must be propagated vegetatively, usually from small cuttings or self-layered pieces.

ABOVE RIGHT *An ideal plant to sprawl over small rocks or ledges in a rock garden,* Thymus polytrichus *subsp.* britannicus *also looks brilliant on dry slopes.*

LEFT *The leaves of* Thymus serpyllum *'Snow Drift' have a faint scent, and its white flowers form over a spreading mat. This species is known as creeping thyme.*

ABOVE Thymus pulegioides *is a European species. It is popular as a ground cover, bears aromatic leaves, and blooms a colourful pink-purple in spring–summer.*

Top Tip

Thyme grows well in containers. Pot in loose fertile soil. If you are growing thyme indoors, place the plant in a well-lit position, perhaps on the kitchen windowsill.

LEFT *Thymus praecox 'Albiflorus' is a cultivar that produces white flowers on dark green foliage. Most species of* T. praecox *produce mauve-purple blooms.*

Favourites	Flower Colour	Blooming Season	Flower Fragrance	Plant Height	Plant Width	Hardiness Zone	Frost Tolerance
Thymus × citriodorus	lavender-pink	summer	yes	6–12 in (15–30 cm)	24 in (60 cm)	5–10	yes
Thymus polytrichus	pale to deep purple with white blotches	summer	yes	2 in (5 cm)	24 in (60 cm)	5–9	yes
Thymus praecox	mauve, purple or white	summer	yes	2–4 in (5–10 cm)	24 in (60 cm)	4–9	yes
Thymus pulegioides	pink and purple	spring to summer	yes	10 in (25 cm)	12 in (30 cm)	4–9	yes
Thymus serpyllum	lavender-purple	early summer	yes	1–4 in (2.5–10 cm)	36 in (90 cm)	4–9	yes
Thymus vulgaris	white to pinkish purple	summer to autumn	yes	12 in (30 cm)	10 in (25 cm)	7–10	yes

RIGHT *Corn usually requires a long warm season to ripen the cob. Zea mays 'Earlivee' is a sweet corn. It is compact, with an early maturing yellow form.*

ZEA

This is a genus of 4 species of large grasses. Native to Central America, they are grown for their edible seeds which are massed in elongated heads around a core and more commonly known as corn cobs or ears of corn. They have erect cane-like stems and long, broad, drooping leaves. Heads of male flowers appear at the top of the plant and shed pollen on the female flowers in the leaf axils, which then develop into the cobs. Until the 1930s, the British considered maize fit only for animals. This practice was revised after observing American soldiers eating corn during World War II.

CULTIVATION

Sweet corn or maize is the only cereal crop commonly grown in domestic gardens. Plants are raised from seed, which is sown in spring once the soil has warmed to around 15°C (60°F), or germinated indoors and then planted out once all danger of frost has passed. Plant in humus-enriched soil in full sun with very good drainage. To lessen wind damage and enhance pollination it is best to plant corn in blocks or at least double rows. The cobs are ripe once the flower tassels have withered.

Favourites	Common Name	Produce Season	Plant Height	Plant Width	Hardiness Zone	Frost Tolerance
Zea mays	corn, maize, sweet corn	late summer to autumn	7–15 ft (2–4.5 m)	20–40 in (50–100 cm)	8–10	no
Zea mays 'Blue Jade'	corn, maize, sweet corn	late summer to autumn	24 in (60 cm)	20–40 in (50–100 cm)	8–10	no
Zea mays 'Cuties Pops'	corn, maize, sweet corn	late summer to autumn	7–15 ft (2–4.5 m)	20–40 in (50–100 cm)	8–10	no
Zea mays 'Earlivee'	corn, maize, sweet corn	summer to autumn	4 ft (1.2 m)	20–40 in (50–100 cm)	8–10	no
Zea mays 'Indian Summer'	corn, maize, sweet corn	late summer to autumn	7–15 ft (2–4.5 m)	20–40 in (50–100 cm)	8–10	no
Zea mays 'New Excellence'	corn, maize, sweet corn	late summer to autumn	7–15 ft (2–4.5 m)	20–40 in (50–100 cm)	8–10	no

LEFT *The white, yellow, red and purple kernels of Zea mays 'Indian Summer' will develop a stronger colour as the cob matures.*

BELOW *Zea mays 'Cuties Pops' is an ornamental variety. Its foliage is striped with purple and the kernels on the cob are also multi-coloured.*

BELOW *Zea mays 'New Excellence' is a cultivar that produces cobs with sweet yellow kernels. It is grown almost wholly for human consumption.*

Top Tip

Set out corn plants about 30 cm (12 in) apart. If they are too far apart the plants will produce fewer cobs and the stalks will grow weak and spindly.

ZINGIBER

The Zingiberaceae or ginger family includes about 1,300 species, all of which grow from fleshy underground rhizomes. These are aromatic, highly so in some species, and that feature has led some members of the family to be grown for their culinary value. Ginger is the best example and this plant is now grown commercially all around the tropical world. The plants are herbaceous, their stems dying back to the rhizome each year in late autumn, reshooting in late spring or earliest summer. New growth arises from extensions of the rhizome with each extension producing one or more finger-thick stems clothed in narrow, slightly fragrant leaves. Small flowers bloom mid-autumn from curious spherical structures that appear atop their own stems.

CULTIVATION

In late spring, plant 7–10 cm (3–4 in) lengths of rhizome bought from the fruit shop. Plant horizontally into pots or garden beds of humus-rich soil or potting mix through which you have blended cow or other manure. Water in and keep lightly moist. Give plenty of water and feed often during summer but ease off as the weather turns cooler in autumn.

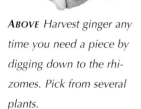

ABOVE Harvest ginger any time you need a piece by digging down to the rhizomes. Pick from several plants.

Top Tip

Don't harvest any rhizomes until the third summer to give plants a chance to establish. Sweet, tender, mild "green ginger" is harvested before plants flower. Mature ginger is harvested after bloom.

BELOW *In autumn, the ginger plant produces tennis-ball-sized structures from which tiny red flowers protrude.*

Species	Common Name	Produce Season	Plant Height	Plant Width	Hardiness Zone	Frost Tolerance
Zingiber officinale	ginger	summer and autumn	24–36 in (60–90 cm)	forms expanding clump	9–11	no

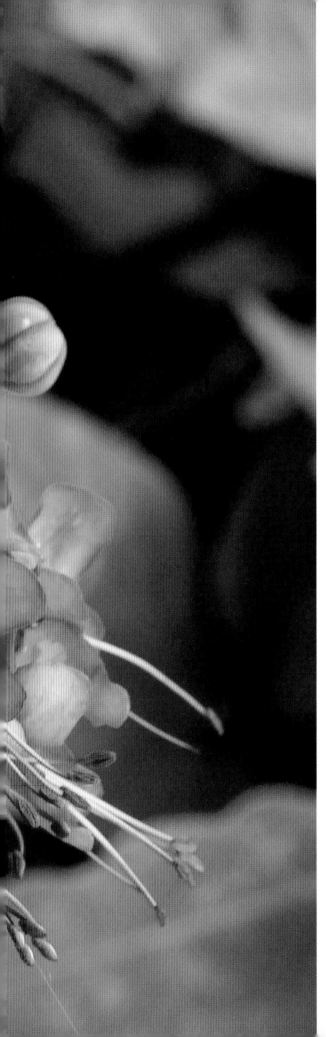

CLIMBERS AND CREEPERS

Featuring some of the garden's most versatile plants, climbers and creepers are equally at home festooning an arbour with bright flowers or modestly cloaking a bare patch on the ground. They offer all sorts of enticing creative possibilities, with their seemingly endless array of leaf and flower colours, sizes and textures. Their upward or spreading growth habit means they are among the easiest plants to weave into any garden, taking advantage as they do of some of the most underutilised outdoor space. These useful plants lend height and dimension to the garden, whether winding up arbours or trellises, clambering up walls, scaling trees or weaving through shrubs.

ABOVE *Like many climbers,* Clematis, Patens Group, *'Doctor Ruppel' produces stunning blooms. Some flowering climbers enliven the garden with a year-round floral display.*

LEFT *Partly deciduous at the coolest limit of its range but fully evergreen in the tropics, the Java glory vine* (Clerodendrum × speciosum) *gives months of colour. Prune at the start of spring.*

DIVINE VINES FOR THE GARDEN

Broadly encompassing any plants that climb, clamber, scramble or otherwise ascend, vines achieve height through various methods including coiling stems, tendrils, hook-like thorns and aerial rootlets. Many, such as *Allamanda, Bougainvillea* and *Thunbergia* species, add a touch of tropical colour to the garden, while others are more famous for their wonderfully scented flowers (*Jasminum* and *Trachelospermum* species).

Twining species that coil or wrap themselves around supports include wisteria, jasmine, mandevilla and wax flower (*Hoya* species). Some form thick tree-like trunks, as in the case of wisteria, and it is best to provide sturdy, relatively permanent supports for these heavier vines. Vines such as poet's jasmine (*Jasminum officinale*) and Chilean jasmine (*Mandevilla laxa*) also coil somewhat, although their smaller size and looser twining habit make them less likely to overwhelm their supports than wisteria.

Other vines use various sorts of tendrils, shoots or leaves to grasp their hosts and ascend. Vines such as clematis use their twisting leaf stalks to clamber, while some such as passionflowers (*Passiflora* species) have tightly curling tendrils that encircle small twigs, wires or other supports.

Using either aerial roots or tiny adhesive grips, self-clinging vines attach themselves to tree trunks, stone, masonry, wood fences or other rough structures. Trumpet vines (*Campsis* species) and English ivy (*Hedera helix*) are examples of aerial-rooting vines. The tender wax flower (*Hoya carnosa*), known for its heavy clusters of chocolate-scented pink to white flowers, employs aerial rootlets, although it also twines. Boston and Virginia creepers (*Parthenocissus* species) are tendril climbers that use adhesive pads to cling. Either way, the result is the same: self-clinging vines do not need assistance to climb, except perhaps during their first season as they establish a firm grip.

Some shrubs employ long supple shoots armed with stiff downward-facing thorns to scale to great heights. Bougainvilleas and rambling roses have such hefty thorns, both for climbing and also as a defence against browsing beasts. Designed to hook and tangle their way up large trees and through brush in order to reach the sun, these shrubs produce frothy swags of blossoms and can reach the tops of trees or completely cover an enormous arbour. Though

ABOVE LEFT *The large bluish purple blooms of* Clematis, *Patens Group, 'Rhapsody' have a slight scent.*

LEFT *Twining climbers, such as* Hoya carnosa, *need a support that offers surfaces to coil around, rather than a solid vertical surface.*

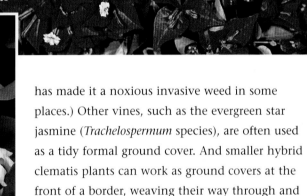

RIGHT *Using thorns to hold fast to their climbing surface, bougainvilleas, such as* Bougainvillea *'Alexandra', will quickly blanket surfaces with vibrant colour.*

BELOW *Many climbers offer the added bonus of intoxicating fragrance. Traditional favourites like* Jasminum sambac *will provide year-round fragrant blooms.*

pruning of climbers can be challenging, annual removal of the oldest wood can keep them in check if they are grown on smaller structures.

There are a number of so-called vines that are actually scandent shrubs. Producing long supple stems that sometimes root at the tips, these plants can be grown as mounded shrubs if left freestanding, or be trained up a wall or through a trellis. Scandent shrubs include winter jasmine *(Jasminum nudiflorum)*, whose bare green stems are clothed in acid yellow flowers in late winter.

Many vines make marvellous ground covers. The most vigorous, such as English ivy, can cover a considerable area, mounding over small plants, walls or other obstacles. (The rampant growth of English ivy has made it a noxious invasive weed in some places.) Other vines, such as the evergreen star jasmine (*Trachelospermum* species), are often used as a tidy formal ground cover. And smaller hybrid clematis plants can work as ground covers at the front of a border, weaving their way through and between other plants.

Evergreen vines such as jasmine, star jasmine (*Trachelospermum* species) and evergreen clematis (*Clematis armandii)*, are ideal where year-round coverage is desired. Alternatively, deciduous vines can shade the sunny side of a house in summer, yet allow winter light to penetrate.

Although some 90 per cent of vines come from only 10 botanical families, they are nevertheless a very diverse group of plants, with correspondingly different cultural needs. Most appreciate sun, but some, such as Dutchman's pipe (*Aristolochia* species), *Cissus* species, *Parthenocissus* species and *Clematis* species, tolerate shade—even requiring some shade in hot climates, particularly at their roots. Some need plenty of water when in growth, while others, such as English ivy, are drought tolerant. Most appreciate well-drained soil that is rich in organic matter, although bougainvilleas prefer lean soil.

Climbers and creepers are marvellous for covering fences and arbours, screening or framing views, creating shade, visually softening bare walls and reducing noise. They work beautifully in virtually any garden and should be used far more often.

ALLAMANDA

Hailing from tropical America, the genus *Allamanda* contains 12 species of evergreen shrubs, including both semi-climbing and upright types. Members of the dogbane (Apocynaceae) family, these luxuriant and exotic plants are the epitome of a tropical shrub. The large, glossy, deep green leaves and usually deep golden yellow flowers strike the perfect partnership. Appearing mainly in summer and autumn, the dramatic trumpet-shaped flowers feature a widely flared throat of 5 large overlapping petals. Popular for ornamental use in climates similar to their native habitat, these plants can also be grown in sheltered areas or conservatories in cooler climates. The genus is named after an eighteenth-century Swiss botanist—Frédéric Allamand.

ABOVE *Allamanda cathartica is a vigorous climber, variously known as the climbing allamanda or the golden trumpet. It has given rise to a number of cultivars.*

Top Tip

Wear gloves when taking cuttings of *Allamanda* species, or when pruning. A milky sap is exuded when they are cut, which can sometimes cause skin irritations.

CULTIVATION

As a rule, allamandas are frost-tender plants, best suited to a moist subtropical to tropical climate. The combination of rich well-drained soil and plenty of summer moisture will promote a prolific flower display over a long flowering season. Allamandas are most often propagated from half-hardened cuttings.

LEFT *The dusky pink flowers of Allamanda blanchetii distinguish it from its fellow species. It bears the typical glossy leaves and is ideal for training on a trellis.*

Favourites	Flower Colour	Blooming Season	Flower Fragrance	Plant Height	Plant Width	Hardiness Zone	Frost Tolerance
Allamanda blanchetii	pink to purple	summer to autumn	no	6–8 ft (1.8–2.4 m)	6–8 ft (1.8–2.4 m)	11–12	no
Allamanda cathartica	bright yellow	summer	no	17 ft (5 m)	10 ft (3 m)	10–12	no
Allamanda schottii	golden yellow	summer to autumn	no	6 ft (1.8 m)	6 ft (1.8 m)	11–12	no

BOUGAINVILLEA

Like the Papua New Guinean island that honours the same man, this genus is named after the famous French explorer Louis Antoine de Bougainville (1729–1811). Members of the four-o-clock (Nyctaginaceae) family, the 14 species in this genus are scrambling shrubs that can become vigorous climbers in favourable conditions resembling the climate of their native habitat—warm-temperate to tropical South America. If unsupported, these plants will remain compact or behave as ground covers, while if given support they will climb vigorously, using their sharp thorns as a means of attachment. While the thin-textured, downy, tapering leaves and small, tubular, ivory to yellow flowers play a role in the overall attractive appearance of these plants, it is the brilliantly coloured petal-like bracts that create its dramatic impact.

BELOW *The tiny, tubular, white flowers of* Bougain-villea *'Elizabeth Doxey' are surrounded by white bracts that sometimes bear tinges of soft green.*

CULTIVATION

For best results, plant bougainvilleas in a light well-drained soil in a sunny spot. They appreciate regular watering during summer. These plants will not tolerate heavy or repeated frosts. Propagate from cuttings taken in summer.

RIGHT *Bougainvilleas—such as the mauve-pink-bracted 'Zakiriana' seen here—can be used as screening plants, providing a curtain of colour when in bloom.*

LEFT *A tall climber reaching up to 4.5 m (15 ft) high, Bougainvillea × buttiana 'Enid Lancaster' features bracts of soft yellow that slowly age to gold.*

BELOW *A Brazilian species, commonly known as paper flower, Bougainvillea glabra bears white or magenta bracts that almost obscure the dark green foliage.*

Favourites	Flower Colour	Blooming Season	Flower Fragrance	Plant Height	Plant Width	Hardiness Zone	Frost Tolerance
Bougainvillea × buttiana	orange-pink to red bracts	spring to autumn	no	17–40 ft (5–12 m)	10–20 ft (3–6 m)	9–12	no
Bougainvillea × buttiana 'Raspberry Ice'	magenta bracts	summer to autumn	no	3–4 ft (0.9–1.2 m)	3–4 ft (0.9–1.2 m)	9–12	no
Bougainvillea 'Elizabeth Doxey'	white bracts	summer to autumn	no	12–15 ft (3.5–4.5 m)	5–20 ft (1.5–6 m)	9–12	no
Bougainvillea glabra	white to magenta bracts	spring to autumn	no	10–30 ft (3–9 m)	10–20 ft (3–6 m)	10–12	no
Bougainvillea spectabilis	pink to purple bracts	spring	no	12 ft (3.5 m)	15 ft (4.5 m)	10–12	no
Bougainvillea 'Zakiriana'	mauve-pink bracts	summer to autumn	no	2–20 ft (0.6–6 m)	5–20 ft (1.5–6 m)	9–12	no

CAMPSIS

Belonging to the bignonia (Bignoniaceae) family, and commonly known as trumpet creeper, this genus contains just 2 species of impressive climbing plants. Their origins vary, one coming from China and Japan, the other being a North American native, where it is considered a weed in some places. Ideal for growing over walls or fences, these vigorous deciduous climbers use their aerial roots to cling to their support. Lance-shaped toothed-edged leaflets are arranged in pairs giving the long leaves a feathery appearance. Throughout summer and autumn widely flared trumpet-shaped flowers can have a dramatic impact in the garden—not only through the gorgeous orange or red hues that add a colourful splash to their setting, but also through the birdlife that is attracted by the nectar-rich blooms.

CULTIVATION

Plant in a well-drained soil in full sun. In cool climates, place them in a warm sheltered spot to encourage greater flowering. Plants that produce few aerial roots need to be attached to their support. To keep plants manageable, prune back hard in late winter/early spring. Propagate from cuttings, layers or seed.

ABOVE Campsis grandiflora *has orange to red trumpet-shaped flowers that are 8–10 cm (3–4 in) wide, borne on 50 cm (20 in) panicles from summer.*
LEFT Campsis × tagliabuana *'Madame Galen' is a robust vine that climbs with aerial roots. It has loose panicles of large flaring flowers in rich salmon orange shades.*

Top Tip

Keep *Campsis* vines well pruned as they mature. Left alone, the top becomes too heavy and the vine can collapse. Once established, cut many of the plant stems back.

Favourites	Flower Colour	Blooming Season	Flower Fragrance	Plant Height	Plant Width	Hardiness Zone	Frost Tolerance
Campsis grandiflora	scarlet to orange	late summer to autumn	no	10–30 ft (3–9 m)	8–15 ft (2.4–4.5 m)	7–11	yes
Campsis radicans	orange to red	late summer to autumn	no	15–35 ft (4.5–10 m)	8–15 ft (2.4–4.5 m)	4–10	yes
Campsis × tagliabuana	orange to red	summer	no	8–20 ft (2.4–6 m)	8–15 ft (2.4–4.5 m)	6–10	yes

CLEMATIS

nown by many as Virgin's bower
or traveller's joy, the 200 species
in this genus belong to the buttercup
family (Ranunculaceae) and encompass
a wide range of plants. Mainly climbing or
scrambling, though sometimes shrubby or
perennial, deciduous or evergreen; flowering
at any time and in any colour; occurring in
both northern and southern temperate
zones and at higher altitudes in the tropics—
there seems to be a clematis for any season
and place. Their leaves may be simple or
pinnate, and their flowers are nearly always
showy, with 4 to 8 petal-like sepals. Numerous
fluffy seed heads follow. The name Virgin's
bower comes from a German legend that Mary
and Jesus sheltered under clematis during
their flight into Egypt.

ABOVE *The Viticella Group includes deciduous vines from southern Europe and western Asia. 'Ville de Lyon' (pictured) has carmine-red flowers with dark margins.*

CULTIVATION

The general rule is that the foliage should be
in the sun while the roots are kept cool and
moist. Incorporate plenty of humus-rich compost before planting, and water well. Clematis
wilt disease is a problem in many areas.
Propagate from cut-
tings or by layering.
Species may be raised
from seed but sex will
be undetermined
before flowering.

LEFT *The violet-blue flowers of* Clematis macropetala *are followed by silvery pink seed heads. The foliage is pale to mid-green, and there are a number of cultivars available.*

ABOVE Clematis, *Patens Group, 'Fireworks' has stunning, large, pink and mauve striped flowers. It requires part-shade to full sun, fairly moist soil and plenty of fertiliser during the growing season.*

Top Tip

Clematis vines can
become tangled;
they need yearly
pruning to
achieve maximum
flowering. Pruning
techniques vary,
depending on the
plant group.

ABOVE *This elegant hybrid in the Texensis Group is known as* Clematis *'Princess Diana'. These plants prefer warm dry areas, and are fast growing.*

Favourites	Flower Colour	Blooming Season	Flower Fragrance	Plant Height	Plant Width	Hardiness Zone	Frost Tolerance
Clematis armandii	white	spring	yes	10–15 ft (3–4.5 m)	6–10 ft (1.8–3 m)	5–9	yes
Clematis cirrhosa	cream	late winter to early spring	no	8–10 ft (2.4–3 m)	5 ft (1.5 m)	7–9	yes
Clematis, Diversifolia Group	blue-violet, rose pink	summer to early autumn	no	3–6 ft (0.9–1.8 m)	3 ft (0.9 m)	5–9	yes
Clematis, Florida Group	white to purple	late spring to summer	no	8 ft (2.4 m)	3 ft (0.9 m)	7–9	yes
Clematis, Forsteri Group	white to greenish yellow	mid-spring to early summer	yes	8–12 ft (2.4–3.5 m)	10 ft (3 m)	8–10	yes
Clematis integrifolia	purple-blue	summer	no	24 in (60 cm)	24 in (60 cm)	3–9	yes
Clematis, Jackmanii Group	pink, red, blue to purple	summer to autumn	no	7–20 ft (2–6 m)	5–10 ft (1.5–3 m)	5–9	yes
Clematis, Lanuginosa Group	white to red to violet	summer to autumn	no	8–12 ft (2.4–3.5 m)	5–8 ft (1.5–2.4 m)	5–9	yes
Clematis macropetala	violet-blue	spring to early summer	no	6–10 ft (1.8–3 m)	5 ft (1.5 m)	3–9	yes
Clematis, Patens Group	white, blue, red, purple	late spring to summer	no	6–12 ft (1.8–3.5 m)	5–8 ft (1.5–2.4 m)	5–9	yes
Clematis, Texensis Group	pink, red	summer to mid-autumn	no	6–12 ft (1.8–3.5 m)	3–6 ft (0.9–1.8 m)	5–9	yes
Clematis, Viticella Group	white to red to purple	summer to early autumn	no	8–12 ft (2.4–3.5 m)	5–8 ft (1.5–2.4 m)	6–9	yes

Top Tip

A layer of mulch around the plant base will keep *Clematis* roots cool. Alternatively, plant ground-cover or low-growing shade plants around the base of the plant.

BELOW Clematis, *Forsteri Group, 'Early Sensation'* produces white flowers in winter and spring. It is a good climbing plant and needs a sunny protected position for best results.

RIGHT Clematis, *Diversifolia Group, 'Arabella'* produces mauve-purple flowers from mid-summer to early autumn. It flowers freely, has a scrambling habit and will climb with support.

BELOW *Impressive fully double blooms of silvery mauve are the trademark characteristic of* Clematis *'Belle of Woking', a Florida Group hybrid.*

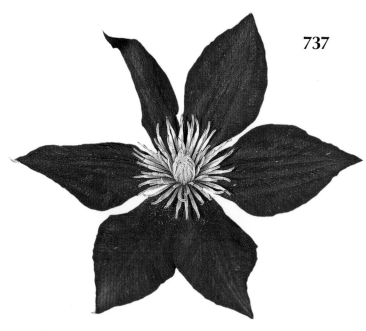

ABOVE *Flowering in summer, Clematis 'Beauty of Worcester', a Lanuginosa Group member, bears stunning large flowers of violet-blue, highlighted with creamy white stamens.*

ABOVE Clematis armandii *needs a sunny spot, and liberal pruning after the flowering season. 'Snowdrift' (pictured) is an attractive white-flowered cultivar.*

LEFT *The single large blooms of Clematis 'Pink Fantasy', a Jackmanii Group hybrid, feature soft pink pointed sepals with a mid-stripe of darker pink.*

CLERODENDRUM

Widespread in the tropics of Asia and Africa, the *Clerodendrum* genus is made up of about 400 species of trees, shrubs and climbers in the verbena family (Verbenaceae). The climbers are particularly lovely—long blooming and, as a rule, not too rampant. None is suitable for areas where winters are cold and damp and none will tolerate much more than a rare light frost. Though naturally evergreen, in an area that is at the limit of these plants' tolerance for cold, they may lose most of their leaves over winter, re-shooting from about mid-spring. Clerodendrums are more scramblers than climbers, their stiff stems needing early training to a support—they're not natural twiners and don't have tendrils.

Top Tip

In late winter or early spring tidy up by cutting away dead stems and the remains of flowered shoots. Shorten other stems as needed and tie in to support.

CULTIVATION

The hotter your summers and the warmer your winters, the more bright shade these plants will accept and still flower. Full sun can be a little too hot for them so middle-day shade is preferred. They don't seem fussy about soil as long as it drains well and is of average fertility. Apply controlled-release fertiliser once in mid-spring.

RIGHT *A spectacular climber that doesn't get out of hand when grown in frost-free areas out of the topics and subtropics. Bleeding heart (Clerodendrum thomsoniae) flowers for many weeks in late spring and summer.*

Favourites	Flower Colour	Blooming Season	Flower Fragrance	Plant Height	Plant Width	Hardiness Zone	Frost Tolerance
Clerodendrum × speciosum (syn. *C. balfouriana*)	pink and red	late spring to autumn	no	13–20 ft (4.2–6 m)	10–16 ft (3–4.9 m)	9–11	no
Clerodendrum splendens	scarlet	summer to winter	no	10–12 ft (3–4 m)	12–20 ft (4–6 m)	9–11	no
Clerodendrum thomsoniae	red and white	spring and summer	no	15–20 ft (4.5–6 m)	10–15 ft (3–4.5 m)	9–11	no

LEFT *Magnificent when in full bloom in summer,* Clerodendrum splendens, *though tropical in origin, will grow against a sheltered, sunny wall, well beyond the tropics.*

RIGHT *The scarlet flowers on rosy-pink calyces of Clerodendrum ×* speciosum *make an eye-catching display. In non-tropical, frost-free areas, it blooms from early summer to late autumn.*

HARDENBERGIA

Found only in Australia and only 3 species in extent, yet one or another of the *Hardenbergia* species is found in every state. They are peas, belonging to important and big family Fabaceae. One species, *H. violacea* is widely grown in gardens and would have to be one of the most popular of all native plants. All species are climbers though *H. violacea* has shrubby forms as well. Leaves are evergreen, dark in colour and somewhat leathery in texture. Flowers, which appear in winter or early spring in great abundance, are normally violet or a mauvey-purple but forms with white or pink flowers are also sold. You can use this plant as a climber or allow it to sprawl as a ground cover.

CULTIVATION

Full sun usually gives the best floral display but these plants will take a considerable amount of shade and still bloom reasonably well. Average garden soil suits them and though they will withstand dry spells they don't cope well with long droughts and heat without supplementary water. Cut back to a framework of stems immediately after flowering has finished.

RIGHT *Once available only in purple, hardenbergias now come in a range of colours including this unusual combination of purple, green and lavender. It's called 'Mystic Marvel'.*

Top Tip

To propagate from seed, the hard seed coat must first be softened. Pour hot (not boiling) water over the seeds and allow to soak for 24 hours before sowing.

ABOVE *From the southwest corner of Western Australia,* Hardenbergia comptoniana *is a vigorous climber flowering from late winter into spring. It likes a little shade.*

RIGHT Hardenbergia violacea *is from eastern Australia and can grow into a fairly large vine. It flowers in July and takes sun or quite a lot of shade.*

Favourites	Flower Colour	Blooming Season	Flower Fragrance	Plant Height	Plant Width	Hardiness Zone	Frost Tolerance
Hardenbergia comptoniana	lavender, purple white, pink	late winter to spring	no	10–16 ft (3–4.9 m)	10–16 ft (3–4.9 m)	8–9	yes
Hardenbergia violacea 'Happy Wanderer'	violet, white pink	mid-winter to spring	no	20–33 ft (6–10 m)	20–33 ft (6–10 m)	8–9	yes

RIGHT Hoya carnosa is a climber native to India and southeastern China widely grown as a house plant. It has white to palest pink flowers with a red centre.

HOYA

Popularly known as wax flowers, the 200 species in this genus, a member of the milk-weed (Asclepiadaceae) family, are mainly climbing, sometimes shrubby or succulent, evergreen plants. Originating in Asia, Polynesia and Australia, they are woody-stemmed plants, which in the wild can reach 6 m (20 ft) tall or more. The glossy dark green foliage provides a backdrop for the exquisite waxy flowers that resemble fine porcelain. The dainty fragrant blooms are arranged in a star-upon-star configuration—a "star" of thick petals, usually white or in pale shades of pink, studded at the centre with a contrasting starry corona.

Top Tip

Hoya plants prefer it if their soil is left to dry out somewhat between waterings. Be careful where the plants are positioned, particularly if hanging, as they drip a sticky nectar.

CULTIVATION

In suitably warm climates grow outdoors in semi-shade in a moist, rich, free-draining soil. Elsewhere wax flowers are popular house plants often grown in hanging baskets. Grow them in bright filtered light in a well-drained potting mix. Feed and water regularly, ensuring a high level of humidity is maintained. Propagate from cuttings.

Favourites	Flower Colour	Blooming Season	Flower Fragrance	Plant Height	Plant Width	Hardiness Zone	Frost Tolerance
Hoya australis	white to pale pink	summer	yes	12–30 ft (3.5–9 m)	10 ft (3 m)	10–12	no
Hoya carnosa	white to pale pink	summer	yes	10–20 ft (3–6 m)	10 ft (3 m)	10–12	no
Hoya carnosa 'Exotica'	white to pale pink	summer	yes	10 ft (3 m)	3 ft (0.9 m)	10–12	no
Hoya carnosa 'Krinkle Kurl'	white to pale pink	summer	yes	10 ft (3 m)	3 ft (0.9 m)	10–12	no
Hoya carnosa 'Rubra'	white to pale pink	summer	yes	10 ft (3 m)	3 ft (0.9 m)	10–12	no
Hoya carnosa 'Variegata'	white to pale pink	summer	yes	10 ft (3 m)	3 ft (0.9 m)	10–12	no

ABOVE Hoya australis *is an Australian climber that has thick, shiny, dark green leaves and umbels of small, starry, scented, white to pale pink flowers, with reddish purple coronas.*
LEFT Hoya carnosa *'Exotica' has flowers that are similar in appearance to the species, but differs in that it has showy variegated leaves, which are yellow and pink with green margins.*

JASMINUM

Jasmine is a traditional favourite with gardeners. Its powerful evocative scent wafts through gardens, often signalling the onset of warmer weather. With a range of natural distribution from Africa to Asia, and a solitary American representative, the genus *Jasminum* contains some 200 or so species of deciduous, semi-deciduous and evergreen shrubs and woody-stemmed climbers that are members of the olive (Oleaceae) family. The variable leaves encompass a range of textures and colours. Appearing in clusters at the branch tips and leaf axils, the usually white, white flushed pink or yellow tubular flowers have 5 widely flared lobes. Though jasmine is synonymous with beautiful fragrance, there are a number of species that have little or no perfume.

CULTIVATION

Growing requirements for *Jasminum* species vary, though most will not tolerate repeated severe frosts or drought. They do best in moist, humus-rich, well-drained soil in full sun or part-shade. Given the right conditions most jasmines grow rapidly and can become invasive. Propagate from seed, cuttings or layers, which with some low-growing species may form naturally.

LEFT Jasminum nudiflorum *is commonly known as winter jasmine. This yellow-flowered species will provide a welcome splash of colour in the often sombre winter garden.*

Favourites	Flower Colour	Blooming Season	Flower Fragrance
Jasminum azoricum	white	late summer	yes
Jasminum humile	bright yellow	spring to autumn	yes
Jasminum nudiflorum	bright yellow	late winter to early spring	no
Jasminum officinale	white or pale pink	summer to early autumn	yes
Jasminum polyanthum	white	spring	yes
Jasminum × stephanense	pale pink	summer to autumn	yes

FAR LEFT *Known as Azores jasmine for its native habitat,* Jasminum azoricum *is an evergreen climber. It has dark green leaves and highly scented white flowers.*

LEFT *The dainty pink buds of* Jasminum polyanthum *begin to appear from late winter. They open in late spring to reveal highly perfumed white flowers.*

Top Tip

Although the climbing jasmines are generally vigorous and adaptable, they may need supplemental water during extended dry periods to perform well.

ABOVE *When in bloom during late spring and into summer, the starry golden flowers of* Jasminum humile *'Revolutum' are a perfect foil for the lush dark green leaves.*

Plant Height	Plant Width	Hardiness Zone	Frost Tolerance
20 ft (6 m)	20 ft (6 m)	10–11	no
8–12 ft (2.4–3.5 m)	10–12 ft (3–3.5 m)	8–10	yes
5–10 ft (1.5–3 m)	10 ft (3 m)	6–9	yes
8–30 ft (2.4–9 m)	8–15 ft (2.4–4.5 m)	6–10	yes
10–17 ft (3–5 m)	25 ft (8 m)	7–9	yes
3–17 ft (0.9–5 m)	5–10 ft (1.5–3 m)	7–11	yes

LEFT *Known as Chilean jasmine, Mandevilla laxa has strongly scented white to creamy white flowers and glossy, deep green, heart-shaped leaves.*
BELOW *The lush mid- to deep green foliage of Mandevilla × amabilis 'Alice du Pont' is adorned with abundant pink flowers throughout summer.*

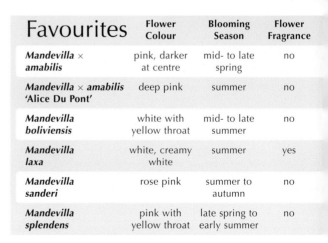

MANDEVILLA

This large genus from Central and South America consists of around 120 species of mainly tuberous-rooted twining vines, and some perennials and subshrubs. Rather beautiful fast-growing climbers, they have large, deep green, elliptical to lance-shaped leaves with prominent drip-tips. They produce large numbers of showy trumpet-shaped flowers throughout the warmer months, which makes them popular plants for the garden trellis or arch. The 5-lobed flowers grow singly on long stems, and are often large, fragrant in some species and occur in white to cream and various shades of pink. The genus *Mandevilla* was named after the nineteenth-century British diplomat and gardener, Henry Mandeville.

CULTIVATION

Only a few species will tolerate frost, the majority generally preferring a mild to warm climate, dappled sunlight and moist, humus-rich, well-drained soil. Occasional feeding will produce lush foliage but will lead to rampant growth. Propagate from seed in spring or from cuttings in spring or summer.

Favourites	Flower Colour	Blooming Season	Flower Fragrance
Mandevilla × amabilis	pink, darker at centre	mid- to late spring	no
Mandevilla × amabilis 'Alice Du Pont'	deep pink	summer	no
Mandevilla boliviensis	white with yellow throat	mid- to late summer	no
Mandevilla laxa	white, creamy white	summer	yes
Mandevilla sanderi	rose pink	summer to autumn	no
Mandevilla splendens	pink with yellow throat	late spring to early summer	no

LEFT *With a prolonged flowering season in warmer climates,* Mandevilla sanderi *'Scarlet Pimpernel' bears gorgeous, yellow-throated, scarlet-pink blooms.*
BELOW *The lustrous, dark green, pointed leaves of* Mandevilla boliviensis *are a perfect foil for the funnel-shaped, golden-throated, white flowers.*

Plant Height	Plant Width	Hardiness Zone	Frost Tolerance
12 ft (3.5 m)	6 ft (1.8 m)	10–12	no
20–30 ft (6–9 m)	6 ft (1.8 m)	10–12	no
12 ft (3.5 m)	4 ft (1.2 m)	10–12	no
15 ft (4.5 m)	15 ft (4.5 m)	9–11	no
3–10 ft (0.9–3 m)	24 in (60 cm)	10–12	no
10–20 ft (3–6 m)	6 ft (1.8 m)	10–12	no

PANDOREA

In the Bignoniaceae, a family of many spectacular climbers and flowering trees, *Pandorea* is a small genus of 8 species, mostly Australian but also found on the islands to the north. Two of the Australian species, *Pandorea jasminoides* and *P. pandorana*, are showy and very popular with gardeners. Both are evergreen, twining climbers with dark, glossy, pinnate leaves and dense clusters of flowers that may be white, cream, pink, lemon, deep red or brownish gold depending on the species or hybrid chosen. They are easy vines to grow and though both can reach quite a large size, both can also be kept within bounds by pruning to any degree necessary to achieve that. Always prune them straight after bloom to allow the plant time to regrow.

CULTIVATION

Pandorea come from the higher rainfall east coast and do best in better quality soils that contain plenty of rotted organic matter. They like to be kept evenly moist during the growing season but can go drier in winter. Fertiliser isn't usually needed for good growth but in poor soils a single dose of controlled-release fertiliser in spring will do.

ABOVE LEFT *The pure white 'Lady Di' is one of the most popular forms of* Pandorea jasminoides. *It will grow and flower in part shade but is most floriferous in full sun.*
LEFT *Commonly called bower of beauty, in full bloom,* Pandorea jasminoides *is one of the showiest climbers you can grow. There are a number of colour varieties to choose from.*

ABOVE *The other popular form is the wonga wonga vine* (Pandorea pandorana). *In spring it produces masses of small, tubular flowers that are usually pink but can be white or yellow. It is widespread in eastern Australia.*

RIGHT *'Golden Showers' is an unusual, bronzy-gold flowered form of* Pandorea pandorana. *It looks good when interplanted with* Hardenbergia comptoniana, *the two flower colours contrasting well.*

Top Tip

Don't plant within 5 m (16 ft) of a sewer or underground drain. These plants will invade already leaky pipes, worsening the crack and blocking the drain by filling it with roots.

Favourites	Flower Colour	Blooming Season	Flower Fragrance	Plant Height	Plant Width	Hardiness Zone	Frost Tolerance
Pandorea jasminoides	soft pink with deep pink throat	spring	no	20–40 ft (6–12 m)	10–20 ft (3–6 m)	8–11	yes
Pandorea jasminoides 'Lady Di'	white with lemon throat	spring	no	20–40 ft (6–12 m)	10–20 ft (3–6 m)	8–11	yes
Pandorea pandorana	white, pink or cream	spring	no	30–60 ft (9–18 m)	10–20 ft (3–6 m)	8–11	yes
Pandorea pandorana 'Golden Showers'	brownish orange	spring	no	20–40 ft (6–12 m)	10–20 ft (3–6 m)	8–11	yes

PARTHENOCISSUS

Perhaps better known by its common names—Virginia creeper or Boston ivy—*Parthenocissus* is a member of the grape (Vitaceae) family. The genus comprises 10 species of deciduous tendril-producing climbers from East Asia and North America. They are grown for their attractive foliage and, in most species, their clinging ability, which makes them ideal to clothe walls and fences. Most species feature adhesive discs on the tendrils, which they use to hold fast to their climbing surface. The leaves are either divided into leaflets or maple-like, and usually take on fiery autumn colouring before they fall. Tiny and green, the flowers arew somewhat insignificant, with little ornamental value. Small black berries follow the flowers.

CULTIVATION
Undemanding plants, Virginia creepers will grow in any moderately fertile soil in sun or part-shade. They can be
propagated from cuttings at almost any time or by removing rooted layers. Alternatively, raise from seed.

ABOVE *Found from eastern USA down to Mexico,* Parthenocissus quinquefolia *has somewhat shiny dark green leaves that turn glowing red in autumn before falling.*
BELOW *Interspersed among the leaves as they develop their spectacular autumn colouring are the small black berries of* Parthenocissus tricuspidata *'Veitchii'.*

Top Tip
Virginia creepers grown over pergolas and similar structures will provide leafy shade in summer and allow in welcome winter sun when the leaves fall.

Favourites	Plant Height	Plant Width	Hardiness Zone	Frost Tolerance
Parthenocissus henryana	30–35 ft (9–10 m)	20 ft (6 m)	7–10	yes
Parthenocissus inserta	30–35 ft (9–10 m)	30 ft (9 m)	3–10	yes
Parthenocissus quinquefolia	40–50 ft (12–15 m)	30 ft (9 m)	3–10	yes
Parthenocissus tricuspidata	50–70 ft (15–21 m)	20 ft (6 m)	4–10	yes
Parthenocissus tricuspidata 'Lowii'	10–20 ft (3–6 m)	10–20 ft (3–6 m)	4–10	yes
Parthenocissus tricuspidata 'Veitchii'	40–60 ft (12–18 m)	20 ft (6 m)	4–10	yes

BELOW *The white veining on the mid-green leaves of* Parthenocissus henryana *becomes more pronounced when the plant is grown in shade.*

ABOVE *Ablaze with a "traffic light" colouring of green, orange and red, the autumn leaves of* Parthenocissus tricuspidata *overlap to form a blanket of colour.*

PETREA

This genus from Central America consists of vines, shrubs and a few trees but it is one of the vines that has captured gardening hearts across the tropical and subtropical world. *Petrea volubilis*, the sandpaper vine or queen's wreath, as it is commonly known, is another of those astonishingly beautiful vines so typical of the tropics. It's a moderately vigorous evergreen that develops thick stems and mid-green elliptic leaves that are rough and sandpapery to the touch. The true flowers, which are purple, are set in starry sky blue calyces

that persist for weeks after the flowers have fallen. Flowering occurs in spring but, in the tropics, it often re-blooms in summer and again in autumn. It's in the plant family Verbenaceae.

CULTIVATION

Out of the tropics, grow in full sun for the best flowering performance. In the tropics it will accept some shade but don't consider it a shade lover. Petrea is sometimes seen in warm temperate areas but needs the protection of a sunny wall there. At least average-quality soil is needed and the vine expects and needs plenty of summer rain or watering and high humidity at that time.

Top Tip

Petrea can be grown as a free-standing shrub by pruning regularly from an early age. The aim is to develop a few stems from which many shortish branches grow.

FAR LEFT AND LEFT *In a suitably warm climate,* Petrea *will literally disappear beneath a cloak of these purple on blue flowers. The purple flowers soon fall but the five-pointed calyces linger, extending the display for weeks. Blackening of foliage, as seen at far left, can occur in winter if temperatures are too low but it does no harm to the vine.*

Species	Flower Colour	Blooming Season	Flower Fragrance	Plant Height	Plant Width	Hardiness Zone	Frost Tolerance
Petrea volubilis	blue and purple	spring, summer autumn	no	10–25 ft (3–8 m)	10–25 ft (3–8 m)	9–11	no

PYROSTEGIA

This is a small genus of twining tendril climbers from South America, one of which is spectacular in bloom and very popular in tropical, subtropical and warm-temperate gardens. That is the flame vine or golden shower, *Pyrostegia venusta*, a member of the Bignoniaceae. It's a vigorous evergreen, easily covering a long run of fence or climbing to the top of the tallest tree. It adores the sunny warmth and winter dryness of tropical regions but also does well in warm temperate areas with winter rain. In full sun this vine will completely cover its own foliage in brilliant orange flowers for many weeks starting in the middle of winter. It will also flower with some shade during the day but not as densely.

CULTIVATION

Grow in fast-draining but moisture-retentive soil that contains rotted organic matter. This plant grows well in sandy soil as long as it does not go dry for long periods. In warm temperate areas, grow against a sunny north-facing wall or somewhere else it can be sheltered from cold winds. Apply controlled-release fertiliser once in spring. It needs summer rain or watering.

LEFT *Flamboyant and warmly coloured in the middle of winter, there's nothing more extravagant than this vine's flowering performance. It can cover a long run of fence.*

Top Tip

Confine this vine to quite a small area by cutting down almost to the base of its stem every year straight after bloom in earliest spring. Less severe pruning results in a bigger plant.

Species	Flower Colour	Blooming Season	Flower Fragrance	Plant Height	Plant Width	Hardiness Zone	Frost Tolerance
Pyrostegia venusta	orange	late autumn to spring	no	30–50 ft (9–15 m)	30–50 ft (9–15 m)	8–11	no

Top Tip

Flowers are waxy, thick textured and very long lasting either on the plant or cut for bouquets or posies. Beware of the allergenic milky sap when cutting or pruning.

ABOVE *The flowers are strongly perfumed and abundantly produced on mature plants. These emit a lot of fragrance which can be cloying on warm, still nights. Be sure you like this plant's perfume before planting it.*

STEPHANOTIS

In the plant family Asclepiadacea, *Stephanotis*, or bridal wreath, is a leathery-leaved, evergreen twining climber from Madagascar. It does not produce dense growth but what there is, is adequate for partial screening and this vine is often grown over a stout arch or garden arbour or under the outer edge of a veranda. Flowers are strongly perfumed, exuding a thick, heavy fragrance especially on warm nights. Blooming begins in mid- to late spring and continues in flushes through the summer. In the tropics, *Stephanotis* will bloom sporadically right through the year. This is a plant for warm climates for although it will tolerate the odd light frost, it prefers not to. It's a heavy vine so ensure its supporting structure is strong.

CULTIVATION

Plant in a warm, sheltered spot that receives morning sun then passes into bright, broken shade. In the tropics it grows well in dappled shade all day. *Stephanotis* likes good-quality soil that contains rotted organic matter and retains moisture but not excess wetness. As stems will hang down, it is a good choice for a structure where that can happen.

Species	Flower Colour	Blooming Season	Flower Fragrance	Plant Height	Plant Width	Hardiness Zone	Frost Tolerance
Stephanotis floribunda	white	spring, summer autumn	yes, strong	20–30 ft (6–9 m)	20–30 ft (6–9 m)	9–11	no

THUNBERGIA

Belonging to the acanthus (Acanthaceae) family, the genus *Thunbergia* contains some 100 species of annuals, perennials and shrubs. Natives of tropical Africa and Asia, and also found in Madagascar and South Africa, there are many twining climbers, as well as some shrubby types in this variable genus. They are admired for their attractive foliage and flowers, and the vigorous climbers are a popular choice when quick coverage is a requirement. The leaves usually range from pointed oval to heart-shaped and can be lobed or smooth-edged. The long-tubed trumpet-flowers occur in many colours, but are most often yellow, orange and purple-blue shades. The genus was named after Carl Peter Thunberg (1743–1828), a Swedish physician and botanist.

CULTIVATION

At best, these plants are tolerant of only the very lightest of frosts. They do best in a warm sheltered position in moist, humus-rich, well-drained soil, benefiting from frequent watering and feeding. Any essential pruning should be carried out in early spring. Propagate from cuttings or seed, rarely by division.

ABOVE *Dangling in long racemes, the maroon buds of* Thunbergia mysorensis *open to reveal the deep red and yellow flowers. They are produced throughout the year, peaking in spring.*
LEFT *Hailing from tropical Africa,* Thunbergia gregorii *is commonly known as orange clock vine. This perennial climber is often grown as an annual in cooler climates.*
FAR RIGHT *The stunning summer blooms of* Thunbergia togoensis *are richly coloured. Glowing yellow at the throat, the large lobes are imperial purple.*
RIGHT *With its long summer display of abundant golden flowers, the black-eyed Susan vine,* Thunbergia alata, *is an ideal candidate for growing in hanging baskets.*

Favourites	Flower Colour	Blooming Season	Flower Fragrance	Plant Height	Plant Width	Hardiness Zone	Frost Tolerance
Thunbergia alata	gold with black centre	summer to autumn	no	5–10 ft (1.5–3 m)	10 ft (3 m)	9–12	no
Thunbergia erecta	creamy yellow; purple lobes	summer	no	4–8 ft (1.2–2.4 m)	2–7 ft (0.6–2 m)	10–12	no
Thunbergia grandiflora	sky blue to dark blue	summer	no	15–30 ft (4.5–9 m)	10–15 ft (3–4.5 m)	10–12	no
Thunbergia gregorii	orange	summer	no	6 ft (1.8 m)	6 ft (1.8 m)	9–12	no
Thunbergia mysorensis	yellow and deep red	spring	no	10–20 ft (3–6 m)	10–20 ft (3–6 m)	10–12	no
Thunbergia togoensis	violet-blue; yellow centre	summer	no	10–20 ft (3–6 m)	6–20 ft (1.8–6 m)	10–12	no

Top Tip

Though they generally require tropical conditions, some *Thunbergia* species can be grown as annuals in cooler climates. Many are quick to establish and bloom.

TRACHELOSPERMUM

Found in woodland areas from Japan to India, the 20 species in this genus are evergreen climbing and twining plants belonging to the dogbane (Apocynaceae) family. Commonly known as confederate jasmine or star jasmine, they feature attractive, glossy, oval leaves that are pointed at both ends, and—as the common names suggest—fragrant, white, starry, jasmine-like flowers, in summer. These versatile plants are very effective when used to cover fences and pergolas or to clamber up tree trunks, as they cling readily to hard surfaces and clamber over supports with ease. They are also useful for softening the appearance of outdoor walls, will absorb heat in urban landscapes and are suitable as ground covers and container plants. Their versatility extends to the indoors, as they make great house plants or greenhouse specimens.

ABOVE *Coloured cream or pink when young, the leaves of* Trachelospermum jasminoides *'Tricolor' age to green, with some mottling. It is a slow-growing cultivar.*

CULTIVATION

While these plants prefer well-drained situations with some organic matter, they are not fussy as to soil type or aspect. They require average amounts of water initially, but are somewhat drought tolerant once established. Propagate from half-hardened cuttings in summer.

RIGHT Trachelospermum jasminoides *'Variegatum' has white-marked green leaves. This award-winning cultivar is one of the most popular of this species.*

Favourites	Flower Colour	Blooming Season	Flower Fragrance	Plant Height	Plant Width	Hardiness Zone	Frost Tolerance
Trachelospermum asiaticum	white	summer	yes	20 ft (6 m)	10–17 ft (3–5 m)	8–10	yes
Trachelospermum jasminoides	white	summer to mid-autumn	yes	30 ft (9 m)	17–25 ft (5–8 m)	9–10	yes
Trachelospermum jasminoides 'Variegatum'	white	summer to mid-autumn	yes	15 ft (4.5 m)	8–12 ft (2.4–3.5 m)	9–10	yes

LEFT Trachelospermum jasminoides *is a fast-growing climber that is covered with masses of very fragrant clusters of white flowers during the warmer months.*
BELOW *The glossy leaves of* Trachelospermum asiaticum *can grow up to 5 cm (2 in) long. 'Bronze Beauty' has bronze new growth which matures to rich green.*

Top Tip

These plants will climb if support is provided, otherwise they make fragrant ground covers or spreading bushes. Prune as required to keep them under control.

WISTERIA

The 10 species of twining vines in this genus are members of the pea-flower subfamily of the legume (Fabaceae) family, and are natives of China, Japan and eastern USA. These hardy, heavy-wooded, vigorous, deciduous vines are invaluable for screening and for draping over verandas and porches, with the dense foliage providing cool shade during the warmer months, then as the weather cools and the leaves fall, the winter sun is allowed to penetrate. Initially soft bronze-green, the young leaves mature to light green. Wisterias are a magnificent sight when in bloom, with abundant, long, pendent racemes of usually mauve flowers that are often highly scented. The limited colour range of the species is extended in the cultivated forms to include white and a range of pink to purple tones.

CULTIVATION

Wisterias like to grow in a sunny spot, but the roots must be kept cool—moist, humus-rich, well-drained soil is the preferred growing medium. Routine trimming is required to contain the spread of these nimble climbers. They can be propagated from cuttings or seed, or by layering or grafting.

Top Tip

While wisterias are best known for their climbing ability, the cascades of flowers can be displayed to full advantage when the plants are espaliered.

LEFT *From late spring, the profuse violet flowers of* Wisteria × formosa, *enhanced by their heady perfume, will become a focal point in the garden.*

LEFT *Cascading among the the foliage, there can be up to 100 white flowers on each of the 60 cm (24 in) long racemes of* Wisteria floribunda *'Alba'.*

LEFT *Drooping gracefully, the racemes of soft, light pink flowers of* Wisteria floribunda *'Kuchi-beni' are decorated with touches of rosy purple and gold.*

ABOVE Wisteria brachybotrys *'Shiro-kapitan' has leaves with a fine covering of silky hairs and highly fragrant white, sometimes pink-tinged, flowers.*

Favourites	Flower Colour	Blooming Season	Flower Fragrance	Plant Height	Plant Width	Hardiness Zone	Frost Tolerance
Wisteria brachybotrys	white	late spring to early summer	yes	30 ft (9 m)	30 ft (9 m)	6–10	yes
Wisteria floribunda	white, pink, violet, magenta-red	late spring to early summer	yes	15–30 ft (4.5–9 m)	10–30 ft (3–9 m)	5–10	yes
Wisteria floribunda 'Rosea'	rose pink	late spring to early summer	yes	15–30 ft (4.5–9 m)	10–30 ft (3–9 m)	5–10	yes
Wisteria × formosa	pale violet	late spring to early summer	yes	15–30 ft (4.5–9 m)	10–30 ft (3–9 m)	5–10	yes
Wisteria sinensis	lavender, purple-blue	mid-spring to early summer	yes	15–35 ft (4.5–10 m)	10–35 ft (3–10 m)	5–10	yes
Wisteria sinensis 'Caroline'	greyish purple	spring	yes	15–35 ft (4.5–10 m)	10–30 ft (3–9 m)	5–10	yes

ORCHIDS

Without a doubt, orchids rank among the most beautiful and coveted plants on Earth. Individual orchid flowers can range from almost microscopic to some 20 cm (8 in) across, while the plants themselves range from less than 5 cm (2 in) high to 21 m (70 ft) tall. Flowers can be flat or nearly tubular, and arranged in racemes, spikes or clusters of one to dozens of blooms that can be deliciously scented, lacking scent or even foetid (to humans). The colour spectrum is amazing: whether single-toned or elaborately patterned, flowers range from brown, green, yellow, blue and nearly black to torrid shades of purple, red and pink.

ABOVE *Though exotic and tropical in appearance, there are orchids suited to a wide variety of climates.* Paphiopedilum insigne *is a cool-growing orchid that bears winter flowers.*
LEFT *Orchids are popular with gardeners around the world, and with glamorous examples such as* Cymbidium *Highland Advent, the attraction and fascination are understandable.*

NATURE'S MOST UNIQUE FLOWERS

LEFT *Cattleyas are among the most popular orchids in cultivation, and have given rise to thousands of beautiful hybrids, such as the striking* Cattleya (Browniae × loddigesii) *seen here.*
BELOW *With long-lived blooms in a vast range of colours, vandas, such as* Vanda *Reverend Masao Yamada, are epiphytic warm-growing orchids that are highly valued as cut flowers.*

Orchids comprise the largest plant family—Orchidaceae—in the world of flowering plants. Containing over 20,000 species within 900 genera, and found on every continent except Antarctica, they are both widespread and diverse. However different they may look, all orchids have several traits in common: 3 sepals (the outer sheath of the bud) and 3 petals, of which one is usually lower than the others and is called the labellum, or lip. The lip is usually larger and more brightly coloured than the other segments and can be marked with speckles or stripes. In some orchids, the labellum is modified to form a pouch, as with slipper orchids such as *Paphiopedilum* plants.

Another distinctive feature in orchids is the column, a fleshy structure integral to the unique pollination strategies of orchids that combines the reproductive organs of stamen, style and stigma. The reproductive techniques of orchids are some of the most fascinating, if not bizarre, in the plant kingdom and have preoccupied botanists for centuries. Orchids attract their pollinators with a variety of tricks such as insect mimicry, tantalising odours and slippery ramps that cause insects to be dunked in nectar then doused with pollen. Some are pollinated by only one species of insect, snail or bat, without which the orchid cannot reproduce.

Once pollinated, orchids produce millions of microscopic seeds that are wind dispersed, sometimes travelling long distances. Lacking food reserves, the seeds depend on specific fungi, without which they will not germinate. While the necessary nutrients can now be supplied in laboratories, permitting the orchid seeds to germinate without the fungi, those plants growing in the wild depend on a complex but fragile ecological web.

Orchid plants vary greatly in their growth forms. Three main types are recognised: saprophytic, terrestrial and epiphytic. Saprophytes mainly grow underground and, lacking chlorophyll, absorb nutrients from decaying matter in the soil.

Temperate terrestrial orchids such as marsh orchids (*Dactylorhiza* plants) are perennial herbs that obtain nutrients from the soil, like other herbaceous plants. Most terrestrial orchids have tubers or fleshy roots for water storage and are dormant for a while, either in winter or summer. *Pleione,* a warm-temperate climate orchid, is almost entirely terrestrial but has a plump pseudobulb, unlike most terrestrial orchids.

Over half of all orchids are epiphytes, including most of the cattleyas, dendrobiums and cymbidiums commonly seen in florists' bouquets and sold in shops. In their native habitats, epiphytic orchids are found suspended from trees, shrubs and sometimes rocks, secured by tenacious roots. Epiphytes gather moisture from rain, fog and dew. Nutrients mainly come from rotting organic matter. Epiphytic orchids that grow on rocks are called lithophytes.

Mostly found in the tropics and subtropics, epiphytic orchids often come from climates that dry out seasonally, with only nighttime dew for moisture. The plump pseudobulbs, or thickened stems, of many orchids are designed to store moisture and nutrients during these dry periods. Although pseudobulbs vary in size and shape, each is adapted to the vagaries of its native environment. The epiphytic moth orchids (*Phalaenopsis* plants), on the other hand, cling to trees or occasionally rocks in damp shady areas of the tropics where temperatures, rainfall and ambient moisture are uniform.

In general, orchids are not difficult to grow, provided their basic needs are met. They require appropriate light, temperature, air circulation, moisture (watering and humidity) and nutrients.

ABOVE *Many orchids are embellished with decorative markings or spots, as seen here in* Phalaenopsis *Night Shine.*
RIGHT *A vital component of the cut flower industry,* Dendrobium *includes such lovely hybrids as Colorado Springs.*

Since temperature is usually the most challenging and expensive variable to control, it is best to begin with species suited to the temperatures at hand.

Vandas generally require a great deal of warmth and light and are best grown in tropical climates. On the other hand, many cymbidiums require cool night temperatures to flower. In cool- to warm-temperate climates, they perform well in bright unheated rooms where minimum winter temperatures stay above 10°C (50°F) at night. Subtropical and warm-temperate climates can support a range of warm- and cool-growing orchids, although few of the lusciously flowered orchids will tolerate any measure of frost.

While there are a few transitional orchids with exotic flowers that are nearly frost tolerant, such as *Epidendrum ibaguense* and *Cymbidium tracyanum,* most cool- to warm-temperate gardeners must rely on the rich and varied hardy terrestrial orchids outdoors and protect the more exotic types indoors in winter. Greenhouses, sunrooms and windowsills where overnight temperatures can be maintained above 10–21°C (50–70°F) can house a variety of exquisite orchids and provide immense satisfaction.

CATTLEYA

A member of the family Orchidaceae, *Cattleya* is a tropical American genus of about 50 species, most of which are epiphytes or lithophytes. Their sprays of large, colourful and often fragrant flowers develop from conspicuous pseudobulbs that have 1 or 2 thick leathery leaves. They occur in a range of flower colours. The sepals and petals are similarly coloured, but the lip (labellum) may be contrasting. As well as being a popular genus in its own right, *Cattleya* has been extensively hybridised with other genera.

CULTIVATION

Spectacular and reasonably tough plants, *Cattleya* are easy for beginners and often represent the next step after *Cymbidium*. They like bright, lightly shaded conditions and those with 2 leaves per pseudobulb will withstand a little winter cold. The large pseudobulbs endow them with reasonable drought tolerance, and they prefer to dry out between waterings. They may be divided when dormant into clusters of 4 or more pseudobulbs.

ABOVE *The large flowers of Cattleya* Earl 'Imperialis' *are pristine white, with a bold shot of gold at the throat. The petals feature attractive ruffling along the edges.*

LEFT *Stunning cyclamen pink flowers, accented with a white labellum that is tinged with pink and gold, are the hallmark characteristics of* Cattleya loddigesii 'Impassionata'.

RIGHT Cattleya intermedia *is a dainty orchid from Brazil. While the flowers can vary in size, shape and colour, they all carry a distinctive heady perfume.*

Favourites	Flower Colour	Blooming Season	Flower Fragrance	Plant Height	Plant Width	Hardiness Zone	Frost Tolerance
Cattleya bicolor	green to greenish brown	autumn	yes	8–48 in (20–120 cm)	8–24 in (20–60 cm)	10–12	no
Cattleya Earl 'Imperialis'	white	autumn to spring	yes	8–32 in (20–80 cm)	8–24 in (20–60 cm)	10–12	no
Cattleya Frasquita	golden brown	autumn to spring	yes	8–32 in (20–80 cm)	8–24 in (20–60 cm)	10–12	no
Cattleya intermedia	white to deep purple	spring	yes	6–16 in (15–40 cm)	4–12 in (10–30 cm)	10–12	no
Cattleya loddigesii	white, pale pink to purple	autumn	yes	6–24 in (15–60 cm)	4–18 in (10–45 cm)	10–12	no
Cattleya Penny Kuroda 'Spots'	pink; darker spotting	autumn to spring	yes	8–32 in (20–80 cm)	8–24 in (20–60 cm)	10–12	no

ABOVE *The striking combination of lustrous blooms of golden brown coupled with a hot pink labellum make Cattleya* Frasquita *an eye-catching orchid.*

Top Tip

Cattleyas grow well in plastic or terra-cotta pots. Plant in a bark-based medium, ensuring both the medium and pot allow for excellent drainage.

CYMBIDIUM

With a long history of cultivation in China and Japan, *Cymbidium* is an enormously popular genus in the family Orchidaceae. It contains around 50 species that are found from subtropical and tropical East Asia to northern Australia. Lowland species tend to be epiphytic, while those from higher altitudes are terrestrial. The pseudobulbs, which can form large clumps, each have many long strappy leaves. Borne on long stems, the flowers occur in an enormous range of colours and patterns, and most often open from winter to late spring. *Cymbidium* is one of the most important orchids for the cut-flower trade.

ABOVE *Long arching stems carry the green flowers of* Cymbidium lowianum. *The contrasting lip is a rich cream colour, and features strong red markings.*

CULTIVATION

Cymbidium is the ideal choice of orchid for the beginner. Adaptable, tough, drought tolerant and able to survive extended periods with overnight temperatures of 4°C (40°F), it is very hard to kill a *Cymbidium* but they do so much better when looked after. In winter, allow the soil to dry out before watering, but keep the plants moist when in active growth and feed regularly. Propagate by dividing the clumps down as far as single pseudobulbs.

ABOVE Cymbidium *Anita 'Pymble' is one of the large-flowered cymbidiums. The greenish cream flowers contrast with the cream lip boldly edged in raspberry red.*

Top Tip

Cymbidiums are the most widely grown orchids around the world. Whether growing them inside or out, they prefer a spot with medium to high light levels.

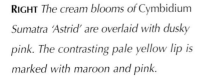

RIGHT *The cream blooms of* Cymbidium Sumatra 'Astrid' *are overlaid with dusky pink. The contrasting pale yellow lip is marked with maroon and pink.*

BELOW *Pure white flowers, pink tinged at the base, and a dusty pink lip spotted with maroon are the eye-catching features of* Cymbidium Baldoyle 'Melbury'.

ABOVE *Simple yet stunning sums up the blooms of* Cymbidium erythrostylum. *The golden lip is marked with red-orange and is surrounded by the pristine white petals.*

Favourites	Flower Colour	Blooming Season	Flower Fragrance	Plant Height	Plant Width	Hardiness Zone	Frost Tolerance
Cymbidium Anita 'Pymble'	greenish cream; lip with red markings	winter to spring	no	12–48 in (30–120 cm)	8–36 in (20–90 cm)	7–11	yes
Cymbidium Astronaut 'Raja'	yellow; lip with dark spotting	winter to spring	no	12–48 in (30–120 cm)	8–36 in (20–90 cm)	7–11	yes
Cymbidium Baldoyle 'Melbury'	white; pink lip spotted maroon	winter to spring	no	12–48 in (30–120 cm)	8–36 in (20–90 cm)	7–11	yes
Cymbidium Bolton Grange	creamy white; lip with maroon markings	winter to spring	no	12–48 in (30–120 cm)	8–36 in (20–90 cm)	7–11	yes
Cymbidium Bulbarrow 'Friar Tuck'	cream; lip with maroon markings	winter to spring	no	12–48 in (30–120 cm)	8–36 in (20–90 cm)	7–11	yes
Cymbidium ensifolium	pale yellow to green	summer	yes	12–27 in (30–70 cm)	12 in (30 cm)	9–12	no
Cymbidium erythrostylum	white; yellow lip with red veining	spring to summer	no	12–27 in (30–70 cm)	8–24 in (20–60 cm)	8–10	yes
Cymbidium Fanfare 'Spring'	green; cream lip with maroon markings	winter to spring	no	12–48 in (30–120 cm)	8–36 in (20–90 cm)	7–11	yes
Cymbidium Little Big Horn 'Prairie'	green; cream lip with maroon spotting	winter to spring	no	12–18 in (30–45 cm)	8–36 in (20–90 cm)	7–11	yes
Cymbidium lowianum	green; cream lip with red markings	spring	no	12–48 in (30–120 cm)	8–36 in (20–90 cm)	7–11	yes
Cymbidium Mavourneen 'Jester'	green with maroon markings	winter to spring	no	12–48 in (30–120 cm)	8–36 in (20–90 cm)	7–11	yes
Cymbidium Sumatra 'Astrid'	dark pink; yellow lip with maroon markings	winter to spring	no	12–48 in (30–120 cm)	8–36 in (20–90 cm)	7–11	yes

DACTYLORHIZA

Commonly known as the marsh orchid, the genus *Dactylorhiza* comprises around 35 species of deciduous, tuberous, spring- to summer-flowering, terrestrial orchids. Belonging to the family Orchidaceae, they are widespread in the northern temperate zones, where they are usually found growing in moist grasslands. They form a clump of broad, often maroon-spotted basal leaves that taper to a point. Upright stems with shorter narrower leaves bear conical spikes with flowers ranging from palest pink to deep purple-red in colour, usually with darker spotting. The 2-pronged tubers are quite edible and yield an extract called salep, which is reputedly very nutritious and also has some medicinal uses.

CULTIVATION

Most marsh orchids are frost hardy and easily grown in moist humus-rich soil with a position in dappled sunlight. Propagate by breaking up established clumps when dormant.

Top Tip

Marsh orchids are popular plants for cool rockeries and also do well in containers. Keep well watered in summer. Plants must be kept drier in winter.

RIGHT Dactylorhiza fuchsii, *the common spotted orchid, has maroon-spotted green leaves and abundant mauve-spotted white flowers.*

BELOW *Known as the early marsh orchid,* Dactylorhiza incarnata *is found through-out Europe. In spring and summer it produces small pink to purple-pink flowers.*

BELOW *The white blooms and bright green leaves of* Dactylorhiza fuchsii *'Rachel' will brighten the garden in summer. It makes an attractive subject for waterside planting.*

BELOW *Commonly known as the Madeiran orchid,* Dactylorhiza foliosa *bears pink to purple flowers. It has unspotted leaves, unlike many of the species in the genus.*

Favourites	Flower Colour	Blooming Season	Flower Fragrance	Plant Height	Plant Width	Hardiness Zone	Frost Tolerance
Dactylorhiza foliosa	pink to purple	spring to summer	no	12–27 in (30–70 cm)	4–10 in (10–25 cm)	6–9	yes
Dactylorhiza fuchsii	pink, white, mauve	summer	no	8–24 in (20–60 cm)	4–10 in (10–25 cm)	6–9	yes
Dactylorhiza incarnata	purple-pink	spring to summer	no	8–24 in (20–60 cm)	4–10 in (10–25 cm)	6–9	yes
Dactylorhiza praetermissa	red-purple	summer	no	8–27 in (20–70 cm)	4–10 in (10–25 cm)	6–9	yes
Dactylorhiza purpurella	purple-red	summer	no	12–16 in (30–40 cm)	4–10 in (10–25 cm)	6–9	yes
Dactylorhiza urvilleana	lilac to purple	spring to summer	no	10–32 in (25–80 cm)	4–10 in (10–25 cm)	6–9	yes

DENDROBIUM

An enormously diverse genus of both hardy and tender orchids, *Dendrobium* contains up to 1,400 mainly epiphytic and lithophytic species. Members of the family Orchidaceae, they are found from China and Japan through Indonesia and the Pacific Islands to Australia and New Zealand. Some have long cane-like stems with leaves along the stems, others develop conspicuous leafy pseudobulbs and most produce their flowers on long canes. The flowers are usually quite small but abundant, varying widely in shape. Some have very narrow sepals and petals, others are broader and more rounded. The lip may be almost absent or enlarged and frilly, and the colour range is huge. Few orchid genera cover as wide a latitude range as *Dendrobium*: from 45°N to 45°S.

ABOVE Dendrobium victoriae-reginae *does best in cool moist conditions. Blooming year-round, up to a dozen cream and purple flowers are carried on each raceme.*

CULTIVATION

The hardy *Dendrobium* species are seldom cultivated outside their natural range. Most interest is in the tropical species and their many hybrids, which require reasonably warm night temperatures preferably not falling below 12°C (54°F) in winter. The stems of species that produce aerial roots may be used as cuttings; those with pseudobulbs may be divided.

Favourites	Flower Colour	Blooming Season	Flower Fragrance	Plant Height	Plant Width	Hardiness Zone	Frost Tolerance
Dendrobium bigibbum	white, mauve to magenta, pink	autumn to winter	no	8–36 in (20–90 cm)	8–24 in (20–60 cm)	11–12	no
Dendrobium bigibbum subsp. *compactum*	pink	autumn to winter	no	5 in (12 cm)	8–24 in (20–60 cm)	11–12	no
Dendrobium cuthbertsonii	various	spring	no	1–3 in (2.5–8 cm)	2–8 in (5–20 cm)	10–11	no
Dendrobium fimbriatum	yellow to orange	late spring	no	1–7 ft (0.3–2 m)	1–4 ft (0.3–1.2 m)	10–12	no
Dendrobium kingianum	pink, red, mauve, purple, white	late winter to spring	yes	2–36 in (5–90 cm)	4–48 in (10–120 cm)	9–11	no
Dendrobium nobile	deep purple to white	spring	yes	8–24 in (20–60 cm)	8–24 in (20–60 cm)	9–12	no
Dendrobium speciosum	white to yellow	late winter to spring	yes	4–48 in (10–120 cm)	1–10 ft (0.3–3 m)	9–11	no
Dendrobium victoriae-reginae	lilac to deep purplish blue	year-round	no	8–24 in (20–60 cm)	8–20 in (20–50 cm)	9–11	no
Dendrobium, **Australian Hybrids**	various	winter to spring	yes	4–24 in (10–60 cm)	8–30 in (20–75 cm)	9–11	no
Dendrobium, **"Hardcane" Hybrids**	various	year-round	no	8–40 in (20–100 cm)	8–32 in (20–80 cm)	11–12	no
Dendrobium, **"Nigrohirsute" Hybrids**	white to cream	spring to summer	no	8–16 in (20–40 cm)	8–16 in (20–40 cm)	10–12	no
Dendrobium, **"Softcane" Hybrids**	various	spring	no	8–24 in (20–60 cm)	6–16 in (15–40 cm)	9–11	no

Top Tip

When choosing *Dendrobium* species for the garden or greenhouse, select those for which the conditions of the native habitat can be most closely matched.

ABOVE LEFT *Mauve-pink tipped blooms of pure white and a lemony yellow centre are the appeal of* Dendrobium *Sailor Boy, a "Softcane" Hybrid.*

ABOVE *The many-flowered racemes of* Dendrobium *White Fairy—a "Hardcane" Hybrid—carry pure white flowers accented with an ivory to lemon-green lip.*

ABOVE *A favourite of orchid lovers,* Dendrobium *Hilda Poxon is an Australian Hybrid. This spectacular orchid bears wispy yellow-green blooms.*

LEFT *Qualities such as compact habit, pleasant fragrance and a colour range from white to purple make* Dendrobium kingianum *a popular orchid.*

EPIDENDRUM

BELOW *An unusual species from Ecuador,* Epidendrum ilense *was thought to be extinct in its native habitat, until the recent discovery of a very small population.*

There are up to 1,000 members of this orchid genus from South and Central America. A member of the family Orchidaceae, the genus contains epiphytes, lithophytes and terrestrial species. The common "crucifix" orchids, such as *Epidendrum ibaguense*, are terrestrial species with reed-like stems and many aerial roots, but others, especially the epiphytes, often have much shorter stems. The flowers range from minute to large and are starry, with the petals and sepals held flat. A few species have very elongated, almost filament-like sepals and petals. The lip is usually long-tubed and projects from the centre of the flower.

CULTIVATION

Some *Epidendrum* species can tolerate very light frosts, but most require at least frost-free conditions, preferably with winter minimums above 10°C (50°F). Plant in a bright position and water and feed well while actively growing and flowering. Some species do not have a dormant period. The reed-stemmed species are propagated by removing pieces with aerial roots and growing them on, while the smaller species are divided.

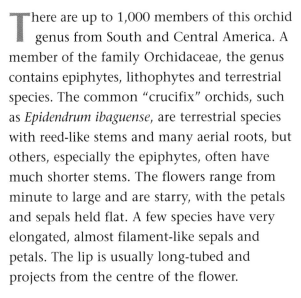

RIGHT *Bright yellow starry blooms and a delicately fringed labellum are the drawcards of* Epidendrum Pele 'Pretty Princess'.

BELOW RIGHT *Whether in a sunny spot in the garden or in a container,* Epidendrum Hokulea 'Santa Barbara' *will provide year-round colour with its scarlet blooms.*

FAR RIGHT Epidendrum parkinsonianum *features fleshy leaves that are tinged with purple, and spidery spring blooms of greenish yellow accented with a crisp white labellum.*

Favourites

	Flower Colour	Blooming Season	Flower Fragrance	Plant Height	Plant Width	Hardiness Zone	Frost Tolerance
Epidendrum ciliare	green; white lip	summer to autumn	yes	8–24 in (20–60 cm)	8–36 in (20–90 cm)	10–12	no
Epidendrum Hokulea 'Santa Barbara'	scarlet	year-round	no	8–24 in (20–60 cm)	8–48 in (20–120 cm)	9–12	no
Epidendrum ibaguense	red to orange	year-round	no	8–48 in (20–120 cm)	8–48 in (20–120 cm)	9–12	no
Epidendrum ilense	pinkish green; white lip	year-round	no	8–48 in (20–120 cm)	8–24 in (20–60 cm)	11–12	no
Epidendrum parkinsonianum	green to yellow-green; white lip	spring	no	1–7 ft (0.3–2 m)	8–24 in (20–60 cm)	10–12	no
Epidendrum Pele 'Pretty Princess'	yellow	year-round	no	8–48 in (20–120 cm)	8–48 in (20–120 cm)	9–12	no

LAELIA

This genus consists of around 50 species of mostly epiphytic orchids, occurring naturally from Central America to Brazil and Argentina. They are a popular group, appreciated for their easily grown, showy and colourful flowers. Most have elongated bulb-like stems, which bear 1, sometimes 2, thick semi-rigid leaves. Rather beautiful flowers are borne from the apex, or tip, of the stem, and they can vary greatly in size and colour. Shades of white, pink, purple and yellow are common, though with the introduction of the *Laeliacattleya* hybrids, which are a result of interbreeding between the *Laelia* and *Cattleya* genera, there are now even more colours to choose from.

CULTIVATION

Most *Laelia* species require bright, warm and moist conditions while the plants are in active growth during the summer months; cool dry conditions are best during winter, when most species are dormant. Cultivated plants must have drainage that is unimpeded, and they can be mounted or grown in pots using a coarse bark-based medium.

ABOVE Laelia purpurata 'Carnea' is popular because of its well-formed, beautifully coloured salmon lip, and its temperature tolerance.
BELOW *A relatively small plant,* Laelia milleri *has become a favourite in the last 20 years due to the intensity of its red to red-orange flowers. It requires warmth and bright light.*

Top Tip

In general, *Laelia* plants do not like being disturbed. They need bright light, and will withstand long periods of drought. Apply a nitrogen fertiliser in summer.

BELOW Laelia *Canariensis is an old hybrid that requires a dry period of dormancy so it can flower at its best.*

ABOVE *The flowers of 'Fort Caroline' are distinguished by their striking purple-blue lip. This plant is a cultivar of* Laelia anceps, *a Mexican species that can be grown indoors.*

Favourites	Flower Colour	Blooming Season	Flower Fragrance	Plant Height	Plant Width	Hardiness Zone	Frost Tolerance
Laelia anceps	lavender-pink; darker lip	winter	yes	18–24 in (45–60 cm)	12 in (30 cm)	10–12	no
Laelia autumnalis	rose pink; darker lip	autumn	yes	12–36 in (30–90 cm)	12 in (30 cm)	10–12	no
Laelia Canariensis	golden yellow	autumn	yes	18–24 in (45–60 cm)	12 in (30 cm)	10–12	no
Laelia crispa	white; purple and yellow lip	summer	yes	18–24 in (45–60 cm)	12 in (30 cm)	10–12	no
Laelia milleri	red to orange-red; yellow at throat	summer	no	12–18 in (30–45 cm)	12 in (30 cm)	10–12	no
Laelia purpurata	white; white and purple lip	spring to summer	yes	18 in (45 cm)	12 in (30 cm)	11–12	no

MILTONIOPSIS

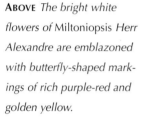

This pretty genus is commonly known as pansy orchid and contains around 5 species, primarily from Colombia and Ecuador. They are low-growing clump-forming plants with pale green strap-like leaves that grow from a bulb-like fleshy stem. The flowers grow in small clusters and generally appear in late spring. The large, flat, almost circular flowers have vivid markings reminiscent of pansies and are extremely colourful, blooming in shades of bright yellow, white, red and pink, often with gold, purple or brown blotches or streaks. A number of decorative hybrids have been cultivated for garden use and can look spectacular when grown in small pots.

CULTIVATION

The plants do best in open compost and light shade. They can grow outdoors in tropical and subtropical climates but need to be kept in a greenhouse if the climate is cooler. Pot-grown *Miltoniopsis* plants will grow well in sphagnum moss. Propagate by division after flowering.

ABOVE *The bright white flowers of* Miltoniopsis *Herr Alexandre are emblazoned with butterfly-shaped markings of rich purple-red and golden yellow.*

BELOW RIGHT *The eye-catching purple-pink flowers of* Miltoniopsis *Jean Carlson are accented with white and bright orange-red markings at the base of the lip.*

Top Tip

These gorgeous plants will reward with flowers in dazzling strong colours, with some flowering twice in a season. They dislike direct sunlight, preferring shady humid conditions.

LEFT Miltoniopsis *Hudson Bay* has white petals boldly coloured with rich purple-red. The markings are strongest on the upper petals, with softer markings delicately etched on the lower lip.
BELOW *Flowering from late spring to autumn, the pretty soft yellow blooms of* Miltoniopsis *Zorro 'Yellow Delight' are highlighted by red and gold markings.*

Favourites	Flower Colour	Blooming Season	Flower Fragrance	Plant Height	Plant Width	Hardiness Zone	Frost Tolerance
Miltoniopsis **Herr Alexandre**	white, deep rose, yellow spots	late spring to summer	no	12 in (30 cm)	12 in (30 cm)	9–11	no
Miltoniopsis **Hudson Bay**	white, maroon blotch and stripes	summer to autumn	no	12 in (30 cm)	12 in (30 cm)	9–11	no
Miltoniopsis **Jean Carlson**	magenta with vermilion centre	late spring to autumn	no	12 in (30 cm)	12 in (30 cm)	9–11	no
Miltoniopsis **Rouge 'California Plum'**	maroon and deep rose, edged white	late spring to autumn	no	12 in (30 cm)	12 in (30 cm)	9–11	no
Miltoniopsis **Saint Helier 'Pink Delight'**	mauve-pink, maroon, and white	late spring to early summer	no	12 in (30 cm)	12 in (30 cm)	9–11	no
Miltoniopsis **Zorro 'Yellow Delight'**	pale lemon with red blotch	late spring to autumn	no	12 in (30 cm)	12 in (30 cm)	9–11	no

ONCIDIUM

ailing from tropical America, the genus *Oncidium* belongs to the family Orchidaceae and is commonly known as the dancing lady orchid. The 650-odd species of epiphytic, litho-phytic and terrestrial multi-stemmed orchids in the genus have clustered pseudobulbs that range from hard-to-find to large and conspicuous, each with one or a few blunt-tipped strappy leaves. Most species have small yellow and brown flowers, some a little remi-niscent of pansies, massed on wiry branching stems. Sometimes the sepals and petals are very much reduced, mak-ing the lip—which usually has large lobes and may be multi-coloured—the main feature.

CULTIVATION

This very complex genus is allied with other genera, such as *Miltonia* and *Brassia,* and inter-generic forms are common. *Oncidium* species and hybrids require bright conditions and winter lows of not less than 10°C (50°F). Plant in a bright but shaded position with coarse, very free-draining mix and allow to dry before watering. Propagation is by division.

Top Tip

In favourable con-ditions, mount *Oncidium* plants on cork slabs to allow the roots freedom to develop. Smaller species often make good candidates for pot culture.

Favourites	Flower Colour	Blooming Season	Flower Fragrance	Plant Height	Plant Width	Hardiness Zone	Frost Tolerance
Oncidium cebolleta	golden yellow and brown	summer	no	8–48 in (20–120 cm)	4–16 in (10–40 cm)	11–12	no
Oncidium croesus	yellow and brown	spring	no	4–8 in (10–20 cm)	4–12 in (10–30 cm)	10–12	no
Oncidium flexuosum	bright yellow	mid-summer	no	8–60 in (20–150 cm)	8–36 in (20–90 cm)	10–12	no
Oncidium Sharry Baby 'Sweet Fragrance'	reddish pink, brown, and white	year-round	yes	8–48 in (20–120 cm)	8–36 in (20–90 cm)	10–12	no
Oncidium sphacelatum	yellow and brown	spring	no	8–60 in (20–150 cm)	8–36 in (20–90 cm)	10–12	no
Oncidium Sweet Sugar	bright yellow; tan markings	year-round	no	8–48 in (20–120 cm)	8–36 in (20–90 cm)	10–12	no

LEFT Oncidium cebolleta *bears summer sprays of yellow and brown flowers. It is often known as a "rat's tail" oncidium—referring to its long cylindrical leaves.*

RIGHT *Oncidiums are known as dancing lady orchids for their resemblance to a full-skirted dancer, as is seen in the bright yellow and tan blooms of* Oncidium *Sweet Sugar.*

BELOW *A miniature species from Brazil,* Oncidium croesus *produces attractive pansy-like blooms of brown and yellow in spring.*

PAPHIOPEDILUM

Commonly known as slipper orchids for the large slipper-shaped lip common to most species, this genus of around 80 species of terrestrial, lithophytic and epiphytic orchids belongs to the family Orchidaceae. Firm favourites with orchid growers, they have long, strappy, often mottled leaves and are found from India to the Philippines and the Solomon Islands. The flowers are very distinctive, with a large erect sepal, 2 lateral petals that sometimes arch downwards and the slipper-like lip. The colour range is huge and the flowers are often intricately marked. *Paphiopedilum* or paphs, as they are known, are popular buttonhole orchids, though perhaps not the near-black forms known as "macabres".

Top Tip

Slipper orchids are well suited to pot culture. Do not use too large a pot—the roots should be comfortably contained, in order to remain moist but not wet.

LEFT *In conjunction with several other species,* Paphiopedilum insigne *has played a role in the development of many of the "complex hybrids".*
RIGHT *With chequered leaves and gleaming single blooms of green and pink,* Paphiopedilum hainanense *is a beautiful species from China's Hainan Island.*

CULTIVATION

Slipper orchids are easily grown, except that meeting their temperature requirements can present difficulties. Most require warm winter nights with temperatures above 15°C (60°F). Daytime temperatures should be below 25°C (77°F) year-round. They prefer low to medium light levels and should be kept moist throughout the year, with routine feeding during the growing season. Propagate by division.

RIGHT *A popular species,* Paphiopedilum villosum *features narrow strap-like leaves and lustrous flowers in shades of green with red to maroon markings.*

LEFT *The green leaves of* Paphiopedilum victoria-regina *are often flushed with purple on the undersides. The exotic blooms, in shades of green, pink and maroon, often appear throughout the year.*

Favourites	Flower Colour	Blooming Season	Flower Fragrance	Plant Height	Plant Width	Hardiness Zone	Frost Tolerance
Paphiopedilum hainanense	green and pink-purple	late winter to spring	no	6–20 in (15–50 cm)	8–12 in (20–30 cm)	10–12	no
Paphiopedilum insigne	yellow-green and reddish brown	autumn to spring	no	4–18 in (10–45 cm)	8–18 in (20–45 cm)	9–11	no
Paphiopedilum rothschildianum	green and maroon	spring to summer	no	8–36 in (20–90 cm)	8–32 in (20–80 cm)	10–12	no
Paphiopedilum spicerianum	olive green and white	autumn	no	4–16 in (10–40 cm)	8–12 in (20–30 cm)	9–11	no
Paphiopedilum victoria-regina	green, maroon, and pink	year-round	no	4–27 in (10–70 cm)	8–24 in (20–60 cm)	10–12	no
Paphiopedilum villosum	green, brown; maroon markings	winter to spring	no	4–16 in (10–40 cm)	8–12 in (20–30 cm)	9–11	no

PHALAENOPSIS

Found from subtropical East Asia to north-eastern Australia, the genus *Phalaenopsis* contains about 60 species of epiphytic orchids in the family Orchidaceae. They form a cluster of short leathery leaves from which emerge stems with flowers that have 2 large, wing-like, horizontal petals; 3 smaller and narrower sepals and a conspicuous, usually lobed lip. The wings are the origin of the common name—the moth orchid—though in the fancier hybrids the sepals are often almost as large, creating a rather round flower. The colour range is enormous, especially in pink and gold shades. Moth orchids are popular buttonhole orchids, as any wedding guest will confirm.

Top Tip

To promote vigorous new growth, cut back stems of *Phalaenopsis* plants. This should be done only after flowering potential is exhausted and the stem has died off.

CULTIVATION

Moth orchids require winter temperatures above 12°C (54°F) and prefer comfortable day-time temperatures. Most prefer low to medium light and moderate humidity, and they need plenty of air at the roots and are consequently best grown in baskets in a very coarse mix. Small pieces with aerial roots can sometimes be taken for growing on, otherwise plants are usually bought from tissue culture specialists.

ABOVE *White petals and sepals with deep pink vein-ing, overlaid with rose pink, frame the pink-red lip of* Phalaenopsis *Taisuco Pixie.* **RIGHT** *The yellow blooms of* Phalaenopsis *Brother Golden Wish are finely spattered with deep red across their lustrous surface.*

LEFT *The classic white* Phalaenopsis *hybrids are enduringly popular. Cottonwood is no exception, with its elegant form and muted colours at the lip.* **BELOW** *Show-stopping blooms of bright magenta-pink, with the merest hint of orange at the lip, are the hallmark of* Phalaenopsis Queen Beer.

Favourites	Flower Colour	Blooming Season	Flower Fragrance	Plant Height	Plant Width	Hardiness Zone	Frost Tolerance
Phalaenopsis amabilis	white	spring to summer	yes	12–36 in (30–90 cm)	8–20 in (20–50 cm)	11–12	no
Phalaenopsis aphrodite subsp. *formosana*	cream to white	spring to summer	yes	12–36 in (30–90 cm)	8–16 in (20–40 cm)	11–12	no
Phalaenopsis Brother Golden Wish	yellow-bronze	year-round	no	8–36 in (20–90 cm)	5–24 in (12–60 cm)	11–12	no
Phalaenopsis City Girl	white; rose red lip	year-round	no	8–36 in (20–90 cm)	5–24 in (12–60 cm)	11–12	no
Phalaenopsis Cottonwood	white	year-round	no	8–36 in (20–90 cm)	5–24 in (12–60 cm)	11–12	no
Phalaenopsis equestris	pink to rose purple	autumn to winter	no	4–12 in (10–30 cm)	5–12 in (12–30 cm)	11–12	no
Phalaenopsis Hsinying Facia	rose pink with magenta markings	year-round	no	8–36 in (20–90 cm)	5–24 in (12–60 cm)	11–12	no
Phalaenopsis Oregon Delight	white	year-round	no	8–36 in (20–90 cm)	5–24 in (12–60 cm)	11–12	no
Phalaenopsis Pumpkin Patch	yellow; red-orange spotted	year-round	no	8–36 in (20–90 cm)	5–24 in (12–60 cm)	11–12	no
Phalaenopsis Queen Beer	magenta	year-round	no	8–36 in (20–90 cm)	5–24 in (12–60 cm)	11–12	no
Phalaenopsis Quilted Beauty	white with magenta markings	year-round	no	8–36 in (20–90 cm)	5–24 in (12–60 cm)	11–12	no
Phalaenopsis Taisuco Pixie	white with rose pink markings	year-round	no	8–36 in (20–90 cm)	5–24 in (12–60 cm)	11–12	no

PLEIONE

Known for the very high prices that superior forms fetch, *Pleione* is a genus of about 20 terrestrial and epiphytic orchids. These natives of Nepal and China are members of the family Orchidaceae. Forming small clumps of narrow leaves, these unassuming crocus-like plants produce a dazzling display of orchids. The flowers are large in comparison to the plant size and have narrow petals and sepals, with a large frilly-edged lip that is often contrastingly coloured. The genus name comes from Greek mythology: Pleione was the wife of Atlas and the mother of Pleiades.

CULTIVATION

Pleione species and hybrids are mostly quite hardy and easily grown with average indoor conditions on a bright but lightly shaded windowsill. They are usually grown in shallow pans and are not fussy about soil type as long as it is gritty and well drained. Water and feed well when in active growth, but keep dry until spring once the foliage has fallen. Propagate by division.

ABOVE *The large starry blooms of* Pleione El Pico *are a vibrant hot purple-pink. The heavily fringed lip is decorated with impressive rich red spotting.*

ABOVE *As elegant as the palace name it bears,* Pleione Versailles *is a stunning hybrid with narrow petals and sepals of rich pink, adorned with a tan-spotted fringed lip.*

Favourites	Flower Colour	Blooming Season	Flower Fragrance	Plant Height	Plant Width	Hardiness Zone	Frost Tolerance
Pleione El Pico	purple-pink	early spring	no	8–16 in (20–40 cm)	8–16 in (20–40 cm)	8–10	yes
Pleione formosana	pink	early spring	no	16 in (40 cm)	16 in (40 cm)	8–10	yes
Pleione Shantung	peach and cream to pink and lilac	early spring	no	8–16 in (20–40 cm)	8–16 in (20–40 cm)	8–10	yes
Pleione Soufrière	pink	early spring	no	8–16 in (20–40 cm)	8–16 in (20–40 cm)	8–10	yes
Pleione Tolima	purple	early spring	no	8–16 in (20–40 cm)	8–16 in (20–40 cm)	8–10	yes
Pleione Versailles	pink to purple	early spring	no	8–16 in (20–40 cm)	8–16 in (20–40 cm)	8–10	yes

BELOW Pleione *Shantung* bears gorgeous blooms that can vary from cream hues to mauve. Pleiones generally bear large flowers relative to overall plant size.

BOTTOM *The delicate pink colouring on the petals and sepals of* Pleione *Soufrière contrasts with the white labellum that is boldly spotted with bronze-red.*

VANDA

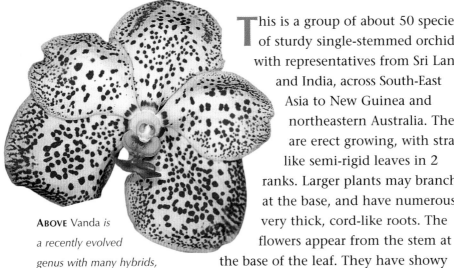

ABOVE Vanda *is a recently evolved genus with many hybrids, which often display the best of the genus's features, such as this superb speckling on the flowers of Pranerm Prai.*

This is a group of about 50 species of sturdy single-stemmed orchids with representatives from Sri Lanka and India, across South-East Asia to New Guinea and northeastern Australia. They are erect growing, with strap-like semi-rigid leaves in 2 ranks. Larger plants may branch at the base, and have numerous, very thick, cord-like roots. The flowers appear from the stem at the base of the leaf. They have showy long-lasting blooms, which come in a range of colours, often with delicate markings. This is one of the most important genera of plants for cut-flower production in Thailand and Singapore. A large export industry has developed using a handful of species in an extensive hybrid-ising program, both within *Vanda* and in combination with related genera.

CULTIVATION

Vanda plants are easy to grow in wooden baskets, with most thriving in bright, humid and warm to intermediate con-ditions. During the warmer months they require liberal water-ing; reduce this over winter. Plants are mostly frost tender.

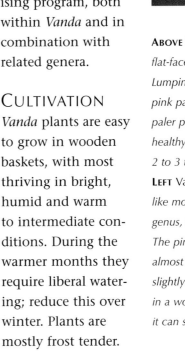

ABOVE *These magnificent flat-faced flowers of* Vanda Lumpini Red 'AM' *have hot pink patterning against a paler pink background. A healthy plant may flower 2 to 3 times a year.*

LEFT Vanda *Marlie Dolera, like most plants in the genus, thrives on sunlight. The pink blooms appear almost inquisitive on their slightly arching stems. Plant in a wooden basket, where it can stay for years.*

Top Tip

Vanda plants need a coarse growing medium, so add charcoal or bark chips to the potting mix. Humidity is also important—regularly spray the leaves with a fine mist of water.

RIGHT Vanda *Tailor Blue has rich violet chequering on a white background. All* Vanda *plants are superb in hanging baskets or attached to the trunk of a water-tolerant plant.*

Favourites	Flower Colour	Blooming Season	Flower Fragrance	Plant Height	Plant Width	Hardiness Zone	Frost Tolerance
Vanda **Lumpini Red 'AM'**	rose pink and cerise	most of the year	no	24–36 in (60–90 cm)	24 in (60 cm)	11–12	no
Vanda **Marlie Dolera**	deep rose and cerise	most of the year	no	3–6 ft (0.9–1.8 m)	18 in (45 cm)	11–12	no
Vanda **Pranerm Prai**	pale yellow with red markings	most of the year	no	24–36 in (60–90 cm)	24 in (60 cm)	11–12	no
Vanda **Rothschildiana**	violet-blue, dark-veined	most of the year	no	24 in (60 cm)	18 in (45 cm)	11–12	no
Vanda sanderiana **var.** *albata*	white and pale yellow-green	autumn	no	18–36 in (45–90 cm)	24 in (60 cm)	11–12	no
Vanda **Tailor Blue**	violet and white	most of the year	no	24–36 in (60–90 cm)	24 in (60 cm)	11–12	no

ZYGOPETALUM

Native to South America, *Zygopetalum* is a genus of 16 terrestrial and epiphytic orchids in the family Orchidaceae. Most species have conspicuous pale green pseudobulbs and long narrow leaves. The flowers are the main attraction, with maroon-mottled green sepals and petals contrasting with the large lip, which is usually white with purple-pink markings or solid pink. The small hood may be a different colour. Interesting tetraploid forms have been created by treating plants with colchicine.

CULTIVATION

Zygopetalum species and hybrids will tolerate brief periods of cool conditions in winter, but prefer minimum temperatures above 12°C (55°F). They should be planted in deep pots with coarse, very free-draining potting mix and kept in a bright position, out of direct sunlight. Plants should be kept moist year-round but fed only during the growing season. Propagation is by division.

LEFT *Glossy strap-like leaves form a clump from which the erect stems emerge carrying the fragrant and eye-catching blooms of* Zygopetalum crinitum.

Favourites	Flower Colour	Blooming Season	Flower Fragrance	Plant Height	Plant Width	Hardiness Zone	Frost Tolerance
Zygopetalum **Alan Greatwood**	maroon-brown and green	autumn to winter	yes	4–16 in (10–40 cm)	4–16 in (10–40 cm)	9–11	no
Zygopetalum **crinitum**	yellow-green with maroon markings	winter to spring	yes	8–24 in (20–60 cm)	4–16 in (10–40 cm)	9–11	no
Zygopetalum **intermedium**	green with maroon-purple markings	autumn to winter	yes	4–16 in (10–40 cm)	4–16 in (10–40 cm)	9–11	no
Zygopetalum **Kiwi Dust**	green with maroon markings	autumn to winter	yes	4–16 in (10–40 cm)	4–16 in (10–40 cm)	9–11	no
Zygopetalum **mackayi**	green with maroon-purple markings	autumn to winter	yes	4–16 in (10–40 cm)	4–16 in (10–40 cm)	9–11	no
Zygopetalum **Titanic**	green with maroon markings	autumn to winter	yes	4–16 in (10–40 cm)	4–16 in (10–40 cm)	9–11	no

BELOW *The maroon-brown blooms of Zygopetalum Alan Greatwood are edged with green. The dark colouring contrasts well with the purple-veined white lip.*

ABOVE Zygopetalum inter-*medium bears striking green blooms that are heavily marked with maroon. The impressive lip is white with extensive purple veining.*

ABOVE *A Brazilian species,* Zygopetalum mackayi *has maroon-spotted green petals and similarly coloured shorter sepals, with a large white lip speckled with purple.*

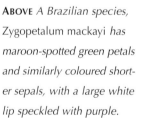

Top Tip

Situate zygopetalums in a well-ventilated spot with high humidity to prevent foliage from becoming disfigured under adverse conditions.

FERNS, PALMS AND CYCADS

Botanically, ferns, palms and cycads are completely different, but they are all used to add lush tropical greenery to the garden. Ferns are an extremely diverse group, but their main contribution is one of charm and grace. Palms and cycads are arguably the landscape plants with the strongest presence and form in the garden. Commanding attention with their solid trunks, stiffly arching leaves and sometimes formidable size, they suggest grandeur and opulence like few other plants do. Cycads, although unrelated to palms, are often mistaken for them, having a central trunk from which rosettes of leaves emerge.

ABOVE Adiantum reniforme *is an unusual maidenhair fern, because each frond has just a single, thick, leathery blade. This is a small creeping fern with short rhizomes.*

LEFT *Palms have leaves varying from less than 30 cm (12 in) to 21 m (70 ft) long. The cliff date palm* (Phoenix rupicola) *has arching fronds that can grow up to 3 m (10 ft) long.*

ANCIENT PLANTS FOR MODERN GARDENS

Ferns belong to a primitive group of plants known as pteridophytes. Rather than flowering and producing seeds or fruit, ferns reproduce by spores—reproductive cells that, once shed by the parent plant, grow directly into a new plant.

While their forms and sizes vary, all ferns consist of a leaf (or frond), a rhizome or stem, and roots. There are terrestrial, epiphytic and even aquatic ferns, and their sizes vary from diminutive creepers to towering tree ferns reaching up to 15 m (50 ft) high. Contrary to popular belief, ferns are widespread in habitat, from the Arctic to the tropics. Not all ferns require moisture: there are desert ferns as well as swamp-dwellers.

While this means that there is a fern for virtually any garden, it also means that care varies greatly. However, most ferns appreciate filtered light; moist, rich, well-drained soil and a reasonable degree of humidity. Ferns make beautiful potted specimens, often growing in lower-light areas of the house or outdoors. The Boston fern (*Nephrolepis exaltata* 'Bostoniensis') was popular during the Victorian era for its tolerance of stuffy, dimly lit parlours, and is still a popular cool-climate house plant. Suitable choices for a temperate garden include Himalayan maidenhair fern (*Adiantum venustum*), with lacy fronds atop wiry black stems, and the Japanese painted fern (*Athyrium niponicum* var. *pictum*), whose new fronds emerge a metallic grey suffused with pink.

Indigenous to every continent except Antarctica, palms occur as far north as southern Europe and as far south as New Zealand's North Island, with the majority occurring in equatorial climates. Their habitats range from dry bluffs and desert oases to coastal mangrove areas and freshwater swamps—even to fully aquatic environments.

Palms are diverse in size and form—not surprising, given that there are around 2,300 species within some 190 genera. There are shrubby, tree-like and even vining forms of palms. They range from 15 cm (6 in) to over 45 m (150 ft) in height. Foliage can be palm-shaped, ferny or bamboo-like. The solitary or clumping trunks can be smooth, textured with the marks of former leaves, or feature rings of spines. Some species develop a "petticoat" of dried leaves. Palms are flowering plants and, while individual blossoms are small, their flower clusters and resulting fruit can be immense, sprouting from various points on the trunk or leaves. Some palms produce edible fruit, such as the date palm (*Phoenix dactylifera*).

Most palms appreciate full sun, steady moisture and neutral to slightly acidic soil, but some accept varying degrees of drought, shade, alkaline soil, salt spray and frost. Perhaps the most cold-tolerant

palm is the Chinese windmill palm *(Trachycarpus fortunei)*, which can tolerate temperatures below –12°C (10°F). Quite a few palms from arid grasslands and deserts can survive a fair amount of drought.

Cycads resemble palms, but are not related. Consisting of some 250 species within 11 genera, they come from warm-temperate to tropical regions and range in size from almost trunkless ground-huggers like *Zamia pygmaea* to the Kwango giant cycad *(Encephalartos laurentianus)*, reaching some 15–18 m (50–60 ft) in height. While both cycads and palms produce similar rosettes of leaves at the top of a woody trunk, cycad leaves are much tougher, stiffer and often shorter.

Cycads are known to have lived over 200 million years ago, and these ancient plants are botanically closer to conifers than to palms. Cycad plants are dioecious (they have male

ABOVE *Cycas revoluta has male and female plants. The female flowerhead looks like an array of feathers. These extremely slow-growing plants are the most widely grown cycads.*

BELOW LEFT *Date palms* (Phoenix dactylifera) *have been grown for thousands of years. They make good landscaping plants.*

and female reproductive structures borne on separate plants). Both male and female cycads produce a rosette of leaves emerging from a central point at the top of a single trunk or several trunks. At the centre emerges a cone that, on female plants, bears red or orange seeds.

Several species of cycad are grown in gardens. Particularly popular is the sago cycad *(Cycas revoluta)*, often cultivated in warm-climate gardens or in pots in cooler climates. The sago cycad is known for its tidy elegant appearance and for its relative cold hardiness to –9°C (15°F). Also seen is guayiga *(Zamia pumila)*. Both species, along with a number of others, make superb and long-lived container specimens as well as distinguished subjects for beds and borders in warm climates. Requiring only good drainage (many species grow in sand or poor soils) and plenty of light, most cycads do best when watered and lightly fertilised, but are nevertheless quite tolerant of drought conditions.

ADIANTUM

Commonly known as maidenhair fern, this cosmopolitan genus of about 200 terrestrial fern species in the brake (Pteridaceae) family includes some popular indoor plants. They feature a wide range of frond colours: new growths are often pink and red, maturing to shades of green, and are sometimes variegated. The black or brown stems are thin and shiny, with oblong or fan-shaped leaflets. Spores are produced around the edge of the leaflets. The genus name comes from the Greek *adiantos*, meaning dry, unmoistened or unwettable, because the leaflets appear to be waterproof.

CULTIVATION

Adiantum species require organically rich loams, which should be kept just moist. Surface mulching should be provided in humid semi-shaded situations. Soil pH requirements vary with the species. These plants need plenty of light, but should be protected from direct sun and wind. They can be propagated from spores or by division.

Favourites	Plant Height	Plant Width	Hardiness Zone	Frost Tolerance
Adiantum excisum	12–20 in (30–50 cm)	12–20 in (30–50 cm)	9–12	no
Adiantum excisum 'Rubrum'	12–20 in (30–50 cm)	12–20 in (30–50 cm)	9–12	no
Adiantum hispidulum	12–20 in (30–50 cm)	12–20 in (30–50 cm)	9–12	no
Adiantum pedatum	12–24 in (30–60 cm)	12–24 in (30–60 cm)	4–9	yes
Adiantum peruvianum	32–40 in (80–100 cm)	32–40 in (80–100 cm)	10–12	no
Adiantum raddianum	18–24 in (45–60 cm)	18–24 in (45–60 cm)	11–12	no

BELOW Adiantum hispidulum is commonly known as rosy maidenhair—a reference to its bronzy pink new growth. The fronds gradually mature to dark green.

ABOVE Adiantum raddianum is a popular fern that features fronds with delicate lacy leaflets. It has given rise to many cultivars, such as 'Waltonii' seen here.

Top Tip

Maidenhair ferns are very popular indoor plants. They need a well-ventilated spot with a humid atmosphere—bathrooms often offer the ideal environment.

ARCHONTOPHOENIX

A n eastern Australian genus, *Archontophoenix* contains 6 species of slender-trunked feather palms in the family Arecaceae. They have rather open foliage heads and the slightly twisted fronds are of moderate length, some-times with rather drooping leaflets. The trunks are prominently ringed and often bulge slightly near the base. Flower stems emerge at the base of the crownshaft, bearing many small mauve-pink flowers that develop into red fruit. The central bud mass or "cabbage" is edible but would be a survival food only.

BELOW LEFT *Commonly known as the bangalow or piccabeen palm,* Archontophoenix cunninghamiana *has a crown of drooping mid-green fronds.*

BELOW RIGHT *Found in a small region of far north Queensland, Australia, the fronds of* Archontophoenix purpurea *emerge from a purplish grey crownshaft.*

CULTIVATION

Most *Archontophoenix* species are able to toler-ate occasional very light frosts but are best grown in mild areas in sun or half-shade with moist, well-drained, humus-rich soil. These palms are very popular because of their predictable growth and tidiness: they don't constantly shed fronds or debris. They are also widely cultivated as container plants. Propagate from fresh seed.

Favourites	Plant Height	Plant Width	Hardiness Zone	Frost Tolerance
Archontophoenix alexandrae	50 ft (15 m)	15 ft (4.5 m)	10–12	no
Archontophoenix cunninghamiana	60 ft (18 m)	15 ft (4.5 m)	10–11	no
Archontophoenix purpurea	80 ft (24 m)	15 ft (4.5 m)	9–12	no

ASPLENIUM

Common throughout the tropics and subtropics and extending into the temperate
zones, *Asplenium* is a grouping of around
600 species of mostly terrestrial evergreen
ferns. It is the type genus for the spleenwort
(Aspleniaceae) family. These ferns spread by
scaly rhizomes and rarely develop a trunk. The
fronds are variable and may be feathery and
finely divided, pinnate or long, leathery and
undivided. Fertile and sterile fronds have the
same shape. Some species are used in modern
herbal medicines, and the genus takes its name
from the Greek *a* (not) and *spleen* (spleen), in
reference to its medicinal properties.

BOTTOM *Slender stems, up to 15 cm (6 in) long, hold the dark green fronds of Asplenium sagittatum, an Australian species often known as mule's fern.*

ABOVE *The lustrous bright green fronds of Asplenium scolopendrium 'Crispum Speciosum' have a pleated appearance, and sometimes feature yellow striping.*

CULTIVATION

Hardiness varies, and many *Asplenium*
species are frost tender. Plant in a cool
shaded position with ample humus,
moisture and humidity. Several of the
species are cultivated as indoor plants
because they can tolerate low light
and cool drafts. Propagate by division,
from spores or by removing and growing on the plantlets that form on the
fronds of some species.

Favourites	Plant Height	Plant Width	Hardiness Zone	Frost Tolerance
Asplenium bulbiferum	24–48 in (60–120 cm)	24–48 in (60–120 cm)	9–11	no
Asplenium nidus	18–60 in (45–150 cm)	18–60 in (45–150 cm)	10–12	no
Asplenium sagittatum	4–6 in (10–15 cm)	4–6 in (10–15 cm)	8–10	yes
Asplenium scolopendrium	8–24 in (20–60 cm)	8–24 in (20–60 cm)	4–10	yes
Asplenium scolopend-rium 'Kaye's Lacerated'	8–24 in (20–60 cm)	8–24 in (20–60 cm)	4–10	yes
Asplenium trichomanes	3–16 in (8–40 cm)	3–16 in (8–40 cm)	2–6	yes

Top Tip

Though diverse in
appearance, all
Asplenium species
will appreciate
occasional feed-
ing—this will
ensure the pro-
duction of lush
dark green foliage.

ATHYRIUM

A thyrium is a genus of about 100 species of evergreen and deciduous terrestrial ferns that are widespread in the temperate and tropical zones. Members of the shield-fern (Dryopteridaceae) family, they have short scaly rhizomes and spread to form small clumps. The sometimes brittle fronds are usually bipinnate and may be very finely divided but are seldom very long. The common lady fern *(Athyrium filix-femina)* often produces interestingly mutated fronds and it was a particular favourite with nineteenth-century collectors—so much so that it was, for a brief time, endangered in the wild.

CULTIVATION

Hardiness of these ferns varies with the native range of the species. Plant in moist humus-rich soil in shade or dappled sunlight. Propagate by division or from spores. Some of the species produce plantlets that can be removed and grown on.

Favourites	Plant Height	Plant Width	Hardiness Zone	Frost Tolerance
Athyrium filix-femina	2–5 ft (0.6–1.5 m)	3–7 ft (0.9–2 m)	3–6	yes
Athyrium filix-femina **'Vernoniae'**	2–5 ft (0.6–1.5 m)	3–7 ft (0.9–2 m)	3–6	yes
Athyrium niponicum	12–15 in (30–38 cm)	20–24 in (50–60 cm)	3–6	yes
Athyrium niponicum var. *pictum*	12–15 in (30–38 cm)	20–24 in (50–60 cm)	3–6	yes
Athyrium otophorum	12–18 in (30–45 cm)	15–24 in (38–60 cm)	4–8	yes
Athyrium otophorum var. *okanum*	12–18 in (30–45 cm)	15–24 in (38–60 cm)	4–8	yes

Top Tip

Athyrium species need to be kept well watered during summer. Mist leaves to provide additional moisture. Protect young fronds from slugs and snails.

ABOVE RIGHT Athyrium filix-femina *has feathery bright green fronds that can be spreading or arching. This species has given rise to hundreds of cultivars.*
RIGHT Athyrium niponicum *var.* pictum *is known as the Japanese painted fern—so-named for the new fronds that are metallic grey tinged with red or blue.*

CHAMAEDOREA

A Central American genus containing around 100 species of feather palms, *Chamaedorea* belongs to the family Arecaceae. Most of the species do not form a single trunk but instead develop into a cluster of cane-like stems, which better suits their natural role as understorey plants. The fronds are not always divided and may remain until maturity in the "fishtail" form often seen in juvenile *Chamaedorea*. The sprays of yellow-green to orange flowers can appear at any time of year. The male and female flowers are borne on separate plants, and female flowers develop into fruit. The unopened inflorescences of some species are eaten by local peoples.

CULTIVATION

Chamaedorea species are very frost tender but surprisingly tolerant of cool conditions, which along with their compact growth has made them popular as indoor plants. Plant in part- or full shade with moist humus-rich soil, preferably in a warm humid area. They are mostly propagated from seed, though it is occasionally possible to remove a rooted sucker.

TOP RIGHT *In stark contrast to the matt green fronds of* Chamaedorea microspadix, *the small single-seeded berries that follow the green female flowers are coloured vivid scarlet.*

RIGHT Chamaedorea elegans, *commonly known as the parlour palm, is an extremely popular indoor plant, beloved for its attractive appearance, slow growth and easy-care nature.*

Top Tip

Limited space can often restrict plant choice. Potted *Chamaedorea* palms can add tropical ambience and can be placed indoors or out.

Favourites	Plant Height	Plant Width	Hardiness Zone	Frost Tolerance
Chamaedorea elegans	6 ft (1.8 m)	3 ft (0.9 m)	10–12	no
Chamaedorea elegans 'Bella'	6 ft (1.8 m)	1 ft (0.3 m)	10–12	no
Chamaedorea geonomiformis	5–7 ft (1.5–2 m)	4 ft (1.2 m)	10–12	no
Chamaedorea microspadix	8 ft (2.4 m)	10 ft (3 m)	10–12	no
Chamaedorea plumosa	10–12 ft (3–3.5 m)	5–8 ft (1.5–2.4 m)	9–12	no
Chamaedorea stolonifera	3–5 ft (0.9–1.5 m)	3–5 ft (0.9–1.5 m)	9–11	no

CYCAS

The 60-odd species in this genus are ancient plants, and have been traced back to prehistoric times. Members of the cycad (Cycadaceae) family, these slow-growing woody-stemmed plants are palm-like in appearance, and are mostly natives of tropical and subtropical habitats. A crown of bright green glossy foliage emerges from the top of the sturdy trunk. The male and female cones develop on separate plants. Several species can be garden grown, though they do best in climates similar to their native environment. In cooler climates, some of the forest dwellers have adapted to indoor conditions.

CULTIVATION

Though they can tolerate periods of drought, *Cycas* species perform best when planted in well-drained soil in full sun. They can be propagated from seed or by removing and rooting dormant buds which can be taken from the mature plants' trunks.

Favourites	Plant Height	Plant Width	Hardiness Zone	Frost Tolerance
Cycas angulata	25–40 ft (8–12 m)	6–12 ft (1.8–3.5 m)	9–11	no
Cycas circinalis	15 ft (4.5 m)	15 ft (4.5 m)	10–12	no
Cycas media	15 ft (4.5 m)	10 ft (3 m)	10–12	no
Cycas revoluta	10 ft (3 m)	6 ft (1.8 m)	9–12	no
Cycas rumphii	20–30 ft (6–9 m)	10–12 ft (3–3.5 m)	9–11	no
Cycas taitungensis	10–15 ft (3–4.5 m)	5–10 ft (1.5–3 m)	8–10	no

Top Tip

Cycas species are stunning plants, but are extremely slow growing. For more immediate results mature plants can be purchased, but these can be costly.

TOP *The sago palm,* Cycas circinalis, *often forms several trunks, with a dense crown of lustrous green arching fronds topping each grey-brown trunk.*

LEFT Cycas media *is native to northern Australia. When its stiff, glossy, dark green fronds eventually fall, they leave a hatched pattern of scars on the stout trunk.*

DICKSONIA

A genus of mostly tree ferns in a plant family named after it, the *Dicksoniaceae*. There are about 25 species in Australia, New Zealand, South-East Asia, the Pacific Islands and the Americas. In habit, they vary from quite fast to very slow growing. Their most notable feature is the stout trunk they form, which is topped with a wide-spreading canopy of narrowly triangular fronds that can each be 2 m (7 ft) or more long. The leaves are hard and stiff to the touch. *Dicksonia* grow in high-rainfall forested areas, often near creeks, sometimes in quite a lot of sun but, more usually, in dappled or broken shade. Those from southern Australia and New Zealand can tolerate at least –5°C (23°F).

Favourites	Plant Height	Plant Width	Hardiness Zone	Frost Tolerance
Dicksonia antarctica	7–33 ft (2–10 m)	10–15 ft (3–4.5 m)	7–10	yes
Dicksonia fibrosa	7–25 ft (2–8 m)	5–13 ft (1.5–4.2 m)	7–9	yes
Dicksonia squarrosa	10–20 ft (3–6 m)	7–10 ft (2–3 m)	7–9	yes

CULTIVATION

Plant in at least average quality garden soil that contains enough organic matter to retain moisture. For young plants especially, a position with shade during the hot middle and afternoon hours is best. As they mature, tree ferns can take more sun as long as they are not deprived of moisture. Apply water to the trunks and into the crowns of the plants.

ABOVE *Called Wheki-ponga in New Zealand,* Dicksonia fibrosa *takes years to reach its full height but is attractive at all stages of growth.*
LEFT *The soft tree fern,* Dicksonia antarctica *is found in rainforest and damp gullies throughout eastern Australia. It is slow growing but reaches the size of a small, spreading tree.*

Top Tip

Tree ferns look good planted as a little grove under tall, high branching or open trees. Space them at least 2.5 m (8 ft) apart to allow room for the spreading fronds.

ENCEPHALARTOS

The big plant group we call cycads are ancient plants that were on Earth well before anything with flowers. The genus *Encephalartos* is one of the biggest in the cycad family, *Zamiaceae*, with over 60 species. All *Encephalartos* come from sub-Saharan Africa in habitats that range from semi-arid through to grassland and open forest. They are not plants of rainforests. In habit they are quite variable. Some have only underground trunks, the plants showing only a crown of leaves above ground. Others do develop a trunk, which can range in ultimate height from 1–2 m (3–7 ft) to a tree-like 15 m (50 ft). In general, they are fairly slow growing for, like many other cycads, they produce only one flush of leaves per year.

CULTIVATION

Plant in full sun in any free-draining, reasonably fertile soil. Regular fertilising is not necessary and a single dose of controlled-release fertiliser applied under the spread of the foliage in spring is plenty of nutrition. Once established, these plants will live on rain providing you are not experiencing an extended drought. Trim off dead fronds as needed.

Favourites	Plant Height	Plant Width	Hardiness Zone	Frost Tolerance
Encephalartos kisambo	5–12 ft (1.5–3.5 m)	10–20 ft (3–6 m)	8–11	yes
Encephalartos longifolius	10–20 ft (3–6 m)	6–14 ft (1.8–4 m)	7–11	yes
Encephalartos villosus	3–5 ft (0.9–1.5 m)	5–10 ft (1.5–3 m)	8–11	yes

ABOVE *From Kenya,* Encephalartos kisambo *is a fast growing and handsome example of the genus. In the wild it is a plant of tropical highland regions of high rainfall and humidity with the odd frost.*
BELOW LEFT *The South African* Encephalartos longifolius *comes from habitats that may be well watered and forested or sparse and semi-arid.*

Top Tip

Grow a trunk-forming species in a widely spaced group of three as a lawn specimen. They do not cast enough shade to damage the lawn and are beautifully displayed that way.

LEPIDOZAMIA

Only two species exist, both native to the high rainfall forests of Australia's tropical and subtropical east coast. *Lepidozamia* is in the cycad family *Zamiaceae* and both species are trunk forming with long, arching fronds made up of many narrow, leathery, dark green and glossy leaflets. *Lepidozamia hopei* from Queensland's wet tropics can grow to nearly 18 m (60 ft) tall whereas *L. peroffskyana*, from the subtropical coast of NSW and southern Queensland usually tops out at no more than 6 m (20 ft). Both make handsome and dramatic garden plants and neither carries any type of spine or prickle. Growth of both species is relatively fast for a cycad, especially if they are given regular water and gentle fertilising.

CULTIVATION

Lepidozamia can be grown in either full sun or bright, broken shade. Position to allow room for the fronds to spread out and speed growth with two doses of controlled-release fertiliser, one in early spring, the other in early summer. It is dryness-tolerant once established but better looking if soil moisture is maintained at least during spring, summer and early autumn.

ABOVE *The world's tallest cycad,* Lepidozamia hopei *is from far north Queensland. It will also grow well in cooler, temperate regions, but much more slowly than in the wet tropics.*

LEFT *The very handsome* Lepidozamia peroffskyana *is a popular landscaping plant in its native Australia. It takes full sun through to dappled shade and is not harmed by light to moderate frosts. It is fast growing in good conditions.*

Top Tip

Lepidozamia make beautiful container plants, especially when young and relatively compact. They grow well in bright rooms or on covered verandas or decks. Feed sparingly to prevent rapid growth.

Favourites	Plant Height	Plant Width	Hardiness Zone	Frost Tolerance
Lepidozamia hopei	to 60 ft (18 m)	13–20 ft (4.2–6 m)	9–11	no
Lepidozamia peroffskyana	to 20 ft (6 m)	13–20 ft (4.2–6 m)	9–11	no

NEPHROLEPIS

Widespread in the tropics, *Nephrolepis* is a genus of around 40 species of terrestrial and epiphytic ferns in the family Oleandraceae. They have short rhizomes and spread by fine wiry runners that can often be seen cascading from plants growing in trees or in pots. The fronds, which are often held erect and can be long, are usually simply divided with opposite pairs of leaflets of similar length. Fertile fronds may differ slightly, having narrower leaflets. The genus as a whole has become known as Boston fern because of the enormous popularity of *Nephrolepis exaltata* 'Bostoniensis', a nineteenth-century cultivar discovered in Boston, Massachusetts, USA.

CULTIVATION

Boston ferns are frost tender but are easily grown in mild areas in full or part-shade with moist humus-rich soil and steady high humidity. Some species are rapid colonisers and are considered serious weeds in several countries. They can be propagated by division or from spores.

BELOW LEFT *The long yellow-green to dark green fronds of* Nephrolepis cordifolia *carry many leathery leaflets. Frost tender, it is otherwise adaptable and easy to grow.*

ABOVE *Impressive in hanging baskets, where the leaflets can flutter in the breeze,* Nephrolepis exaltata *is more commonly seen in the form of its many cultivars.*

Favourites	Plant Height	Plant Width	Hardiness Zone	Frost Tolerance
Nephrolepis cordifolia	1–4 ft (0.3–1.2 m)	1–4 ft (0.3–1.2 m)	11–12	no
Nephrolepis cordifolia 'Duffii'	18–24 in (45–60 cm)	18–24 in (45–60 cm)	11–12	no
Nephrolepis exaltata	3 ft (0.9 m)	3 ft (0.9 m)	11–12	no
Nephrolepis exaltata 'Bostoniensis'	3 ft (0.9 m)	3 ft (0.9 m)	11–12	no
Nephrolepis exaltata 'Childsii'	6–12 in (15–30 cm)	6–12 in (15–30 cm)	11–12	no
Nephrolepis falcata	8 ft (2.4 m)	5 ft (1.5 m)	9–11	no

Top Tip

Boston ferns are widely cultivated as indoor plants. In cooler climates, if they are grown in heated indoor situations, ensure they receive plenty of bright filtered light and ample water.

PHOENIX

This feather palm genus in the family Arecaceae is made up of around 7 species found from the Canary Islands through the Mediterranean and Arabia to East Asia. Most have strong trunks ringed with old leaf bases and long, gracefully arching fronds. Large golden-stemmed sprays of yellow flowers are followed by soft, single-seeded, orange to near-black fruit. *Phoenix* species yield many products, including commercial dates, other fruits, sugar syrup from the sap and an edible central "cabbage". Also, the fronds have been used as temporary thatching material.

CULTIVATION

Hardiness varies, as does the summer heat requirement. The Canary Island date palm *(Phoenix canariensis)* is the least demanding species and will tolerate moderate frosts and cool summers. Others, such as the date palm *(Phoenix dactylifera)*, need hot summers and some need subtropical conditions. Plant in sun or half-shade with light well-drained soil. They are propagated mainly from seed but will grow from suckers.

ABOVE RIGHT *The lush bright green fronds of Phoenix rupicola sprout fountain-like from the crown of the slender trunk.*
TOP RIGHT *Phoenix canariensis features a crown of long arching fronds atop a stout trunk. Cream to yellow flowers are followed by orange fruit.*

Top Tip

Phoenix species are adaptable to a range of soil types, but will do best in fertile soil. Keep the plants well watered, particularly while establishing.

Favourites	Plant Height	Plant Width	Hardiness Zone	Frost Tolerance
Phoenix canariensis	70 ft (21 m)	30 ft (9 m)	9–11	yes
Phoenix dactylifera	70 ft (21 m)	30 ft (9 m)	9–12	no
Phoenix loureiroi	6–15 ft (1.8–4.5 m)	12 ft (3.5 m)	10–12	no
Phoenix reclinata	40 ft (12 m)	25 ft (8 m)	9–11	no
Phoenix roebelenii	10 ft (3 m)	8 ft (2.4 m)	10–12	no
Phoenix rupicola	25 ft (8 m)	15 ft (4.5 m)	10–12	no

POLYSTICHUM

A cosmopolitan genus in the shield-fern (Dryopteridaceae) family, *Polystichum* is composed of around 175 species of evergreen and deciduous terrestrial ferns. They have strong, woody, scaly rhizomes that may be spreading or erect, sometimes developing into a short stocky trunk. The fronds are often stiff and bristly, leathery, very dark green and long, sometimes with scaly undersides. The fronds are usually bipinnate and may be very finely divided. The fertile fronds appear similar. The soft shield fern *(Polystichum setiferum)* often produces crested or otherwise mutated fronds, and unusual forms are popular with collectors.

CULTIVATION

Many *Polystichum* species are very hardy and are among the toughest ferns. They appreciate cool, moist, humus-rich soil in shade or dappled sunlight, but can survive in drier brighter locations. While not overly invasive, the strong rhizomes are difficult to remove and some species are local weeds. Propagate by division in spring or from spores in summer.

ABOVE *An attractive ever-green fern native to two very different regions—eastern North America and the Portuguese island of Madeira—*Polystichum fal-cinellum *has bright green sword-shaped fronds.*

Top Tip

Delicate in appearance but fairly robust in nature, *Polystichum* species are ideal for shady borders and rock gardens, and also make great container plants.

LEFT *Polystichum setiferum, Divisilobum Group, 'Herrenhausen' is an attractive dwarf cultivar that forms a dense clump of arching, dark green, leathery fronds with finely cut leaflets. This easily grown fern is an excellent subject for container planting.*

ABOVE Polystichum andersonii *is a North American fern commonly known as Alaskan holly fern or Anderson's sword fern. Numerous leaflets are packed along each of the sword-shaped fronds.*

ABOVE *Distinguished by the rough dry scales that coat the fronds,* Polystichum polyblepharum var. fibrilloso-paleaceum *otherwise resembles the species.*

Favourites	Plant Height	Plant Width	Hardiness Zone	Frost Tolerance
Polystichum acrostichoides	18–24 in (45–60 cm)	18–24 in (45–60 cm)	3–9	yes
Polystichum aculeatum	18–24 in (45–60 cm)	18–24 in (45–60 cm)	4–8	yes
Polystichum andersonii	24–30 in (60–75 cm)	24–30 in (60–75 cm)	4–8	yes
Polystichum braunii	2–3 ft (0.6–0.9 m)	2–3 ft (0.6–0.9 m)	4–8	yes
Polystichum californicum	20–30 in (50–75 cm)	20–30 in (50–75 cm)	7–9	yes
Polystichum falcinellum	18–24 in (45–60 cm)	18–24 in (45–60 cm)	5–8	yes
Polystichum munitum	3–4 ft (0.9–1.2 m)	3–4 ft (0.9–1.2 m)	4–6	yes
Polystichum polyblepharum	4 ft (1.2 m)	4 ft (1.2 m)	5–9	yes
Polystichum setiferum	18–24 in (45–60 cm)	18–24 in (45–60 cm)	5–7	yes
Polystichum setiferum 'Divisilobum'	18–36 in (45–90 cm)	18–36 in (45–90 cm)	5–7	yes
Polystichum × setigerum	18–24 in (45–60 cm)	18–24 in (45–60 cm)	3–6	yes
Polystichum tussimense	6–18 in (15–45 cm)	12–16 in (30–40 cm)	6–9	yes

SABAL

Commonly known as palmetto, *Sabal* comprises around 16 species found from southern USA to northern South America and the Caribbean. Belonging to the family Arecaceae, some are low and clumping, while others have tall sturdy trunks. The fronds are often blue-tinted, sometimes quite large and the leaflets are usually narrow and sometimes sharp-tipped. Sprays of small cream flowers open from late spring and are followed by small black fruit. The central "cabbage" is edible, though harvesting it destroys the plant. Native Americans used the fronds in basketry and other weaving.

Favourites	Plant Height	Plant Width	Hardiness Zone	Frost Tolerance
Sabal bermudana	40 ft (12 m)	10 ft (3 m)	10–11	no
Sabal causiarum	50 ft (15 m)	20 ft (6 m)	9–12	no
Sabal mexicana	60 ft (18 m)	12 ft (3.5 m)	9–12	no
Sabal minor	10 ft (3 m)	12 ft (3.5 m)	8–11	yes
Sabal palmetto	80 ft (24 m)	15 ft (4.5 m)	8–12	yes
Sabal uresana	25 ft (8 m)	10 ft (3 m)	8–12	yes

CULTIVATION

The hardier *Sabal* species are among some of the tougher palms and will survive reasonably hard winters provided the summers are warm enough and long enough to encourage steady growth. Plant in full sun or half-sun with light well-drained yet moisture-retentive soil. Water well when young and during active growth. Propagation is usually from seed, although rooted suckers can occasionally be removed.

ABOVE Sabal palmetto is *native to southeastern USA. The single stem bears fan-shaped fronds of blue-green.*
LEFT *An elegant palm perfect for tropical gardens,* Sabal bermudana—*commonly known as the Bermuda palmetto—has a single stem with a crown of fan-shaped fronds.*

BELOW *Commonly known as the Puerto Rico hat palm,* Sabal causiarum *is a single-stemmed palm with fan-shaped fronds of bright green to blue-green.*

ABOVE *Found from Texas to Mexico,* Sabal mexicana *is a single-trunked palm that displays a crown of light green to bright green deeply divided fronds.*

Top Tip

When in active growth, palmettos will benefit from routine feeding. A neat and tidy appearance will be maintained if dead fronds are cut back.

TRACHYCARPUS

A member of the family Arecaceae, *Trachycarpus* contains 6 species of palms found in southern China and the Himalayan region. They are tall and have medium-sized bright green fronds with fairly narrow leaflets and sometimes spiny leaf stalks. The most distinguishing feature is the thick thatch of hairy fibres that cover the trunk. The large sprays of soft yellow flowers are followed by small grape-like fruit that ripens to steel blue or black. The unopened inflorescences of some species are eaten raw or cooked by local peoples, and extracts of the roots are used medicinally. The fibre from the trunks has been used to make ropes and coarse cloth.

CULTIVATION

Hardy for palms, *Trachycarpus* species are easily cultivated in temperate to subtropical regions and will grow in sun or light shade. Give them moist, well-drained, humus-rich soil to ensure lush foliage. Propagate these palms from fresh seed in spring.

Favourites	Plant Height	Plant Width	Hardiness Zone	Frost Tolerance
Trachycarpus fortunei	35 ft (10 m)	12 ft (3.5 m)	8–11	yes
Trachycarpus martianus	50 ft (15 m)	10 ft (3 m)	9–11	yes
Trachycarpus wagnerianus	10–20 ft (3–6 m)	8 ft (2.4 m)	9–10	yes

Top Tip

Although they are reasonably hardy, *Trachycarpus* species are easily damaged by wind, and should be planted in a sheltered position.

ABOVE *The single trunk of* Trachycarpus fortunei *bears old leaf bases and a dense covering of fibres. The fan-shaped fronds are deep green.*

LEFT *Many palms are impractical for smaller gardens, but smaller palms such as* Trachycarpus wagnerianus *can provide a tropical element in a limited space.*

WASHINGTONIA

A genus of just 2 species of tall fan palms found in southwestern USA and north-western Mexico, *Washingtonia* is a member of the family Arecaceae. They have strongly erect, very narrow trunks, a feature that has made them popular avenue trees. The fronds make a dense head at the top of the trunk and often form a thick thatch or "skirt" of dead fronds around the crownshaft. Fiercely hooked teeth edge the frond stalks and small fibrous hairs hang from the fronds. The clusters of cream to soft pink flowers develop into small edible fruit. The foliage has been used for weaving and thatching.

CULTIVATION

Both species tolerate moderate frost and are quite adaptable. They prefer to be slightly shaded when young, and although drought tolerant they grow best with moist well-drained soil. They are propagated from seed, which germinates freely and remains viable for a long period of time.

Favourites	Plant Height	Plant Width	Hardiness Zone	Frost Tolerance
Washingtonia filifera	50 ft (15 m)	25 ft (8 m)	9–11	yes
Washingtonia robusta	80 ft (24 m)	25 ft (8 m)	9–11	yes

Top Tip

The characteristic "skirt" of old fronds that is typical of *Washingtonia* species can pose a fire hazard. Where possible, old fronds should be removed to reduce fire risk.

RIGHT *Sometimes known as the petticoat palm for its "petticoat" of persistent old fronds,* Washingtonia filifera *has a stout grey trunk and grey-green fronds.*

RIGHT Washingtonia robusta *is a tall-growing palm with a slender trunk. Reaching a height of up to 24 m (80 ft), this palm is best suited to parks and larger gardens.*

ZAMIA

The type-genus of the family Zamia-ceae, *Zamia* is made up of around 55 species of cycads from the American tropics and subtropics. The tuber-like stem is usually subterranean but may be partly emergent, forming a short trunk. The pinnate fern- or palm-like leaves often emerge directly from the soil and have thick leathery leaflets. Male and female cones are borne on separate plants and some species may drop some of their foliage as the cones mature. The seeds within the cones are often very toxic. The starchy stems, however, were used by local peoples to make a type of bread.

Favourites	Plant Height	Plant Width	Hardiness Zone	Frost Tolerance
Zamia fairchildiana	8 ft (2.4 m)	5 ft (1.5 m)	11–12	no
Zamia furfuracea	3 ft (0.9 m)	7 ft (2 m)	11–12	no
Zamia loddigesii	5 ft (1.5 m)	5–6 ft (1.5–1.8 m)	9–12	no
Zamia pumila	5 ft (1.5 m)	6 ft (1.8 m)	10–12	no
Zamia splendens	5 ft (1.5 m)	4–10 ft (1.2–3 m)	10–12	no
Zamia vazquezii	5 ft (1.5 m)	4–10 ft (1.2–3 m)	9–12	no

CULTIVATION

Most *Zamia* species are intolerant of frost. To thrive they require lightly shaded, warm, humid conditions with moist, humus-rich, well-drained soil. Keep well watered during active growth. Propagate from fresh seed.

ABOVE *Zamia furfuracea, a native of Mexico, is commonly known as the cardboard palm. The spiny stalks carry pairs of stiff olive green leaflets that can be toothed.* **LEFT** *Appearing among the often dense foliage, the cylindrical pink to brown male and female cones of* Zamia furfuracea *are borne on separate plants.*

Top Tip

Though best suited to tropical or sub-tropical climates, *Zamia* species make excellent container plants for cooler regions and may be kept outdoors in summer.

INDEX

Picture Credits

Key:
(t) = top; (b) = bottom; (l) = left; (r) = right; (c) = centre of page

Australian National Botanic Gardens
M. Fagg © Australian National Botanic Gardens.
Alloxylon flammeum (a5193): *130(l)*; Ceratopetalum gummiferum (dig 1295): *44(t)*; Curcuma australasica (dig 3849): *315(r)*; Hardenbergia 'Mystic Marvel' (dig 5877): *740(b)*; Pandorea jasminoides 'Lady Di' (dig 5725): *748(t)*; Schoenia cassiniana (a1751): *468(b)*; Schoenia cassiniana (a20953): *468–469*; Swainsona galegifolia (dig 6958): *481(c)*.

P. Ollerenshaw © Australian National Botanic Gardens.
Pimelea spectabilis (wae 282): *204(c)*.

R. Hotchkiss © Australian National Botanic Gardens.
Pandorea pandorana 'Golden Showers' (x 794): *749(r)*.

Totterdell C © Australian National Botanic Gardens.
Rhodanthe anthemoides (a11078): *456–457(t)*.

Alamy
Curcuma petiolata: *314(tl)*; Curcuma zedoaria: *696(cl)*; Fuji tree: *542–543(b)*; ivy-leafed geranium: *434(c)*; Passiflora antioquiensis (red banana passionfruit): *548(l)*; Petrea: 752–753; Schoenia filifolia: *469 (b)*.

Aloe–Aloe horticulture
Aloe ferox 'Capricorn': *651(br)*; Aloe 'Copper Shower' with Aloe 'Tusker' – photo Kim Woods: *650(t)*; Aloe petricola 'Saturn': *650–651*.

Corbis
Citrus australica (finger lime): *533(tr)*.

Getty
Mandarin 'Imperial': *532–533(tl)*; Scadoxus multiflorus: *628–629*.

Istockphoto
apple 'Delicious': *543(tr)*; asparagus spear: *682(b)*; blood oranges: *533(b)*; bok choi: *688(bl)*; chinese cabbage: *688(c)*;

Dorotheanthus: *329*; garlic cloves: *680 (br)*; grapefruit'Ruby': *532(r)*; kaffir lime: *532(tl)*; lemongrass 1: *697(tr)*; lemongrass 2: *697(c)*; olive 'Kalamata': *547(br)*; pistachio branch: *550–551(t)*; pistachio tree: *550(br)*; pistachio trees: *551(br)*; purple sage: *717 (tl)*; sage: *717 (tr)*; Sempervivum 'Director Jacobs': *673(tr)*; Sempervivum tectorum: *672–673(b)*; Stephanotis: *754*; tomatoes on vine: *704(tl)*; 'zonal ' pelargoniums: *432(br)*.

Jody Haynes, The Cycad Society Inc., www.cycad.org
Encephalartos kisambo: *803(tl)*.

Shutterstock
apple 'Jonathon': *543(cr)*; brandy: *703(cr)*; chive: *681(cr)*; collard: *689(br)*; 'Costoluto': *705(tr)*; Cyrtanthus obliquus: *590(r)*; Curcuma alismatifolia (Slam tulip): *314(cl)*; ginger: *725(tl)*; ginger plant: *725(br)*; Mussaenda philippica: *190(bl)*; Natal paintbrush: *628(b)*; olive 'Manzanilla': *546(r)*.

Starr Images (photographers Forest & Kim Starr)
banana passionfruit (Passiflora mollisima): *549(r)*; black passionfruit (Passifloraedulis): *548–549*; Cassia javanica: *43(bl)*; Clerodendrum speciosum: *727(l)*; Clerodendrum splendens: 739; Clerodendrum thomsoniae (bleeding heart): *738(c)*; macadamias: *541(tr)*; Macadamia integrifolia: *540–541*; Macadamia integrifolia flowers: *541(br)*; mustard cabbage: *687(cr)*; Pandorea jasminoides: *748 (bl)*; passionfruit ripening: *549(tr)*; pepino (Solanum muricatum): *719(tr)*; Petrea: *753(r)*; Plumeria pudica: *85(cr)*; Tabebuia caraiba: *92(tl)*; turmeric rhizome: *696(tl)*.

The African Garden
Cyrtanthus obrienil: *591(tl)*.

The Diggers Club
'banana legs': *704(br)*; brussel sprouts: *687(tl)*; kale: *687(br)*; purple cauliflower: *686–687*; rocket: *688(tl)*; swede: *688–389*; tomato 'Black Russian': *705(cl)*; tomato 'Tommy Toe': *705(br)*; tomato 'Wild Sweetie': *704–705(c)*.

All other photographs from the Global Book Publishing Picture Library